Frommer's®

Chile
& Easter Island

3rd Edition

by Nicholas Gill, Christie Pashby &
Kristina Schreck

WILEY

Wiley Publishing, Inc.

ABOUT THE AUTHORS

Writer and photographer **Nicholas Gill** (chapters 10, 11, and 14) is based in Lima, Peru and Brooklyn, New York. His work regularly appears in publications such as the *New York Times, Conde Nast Traveler, Caribbean Travel & Life,* and *World Hum.* He has also contributed to *Frommer's South America* and *Frommer's Central America* and written *Frommer's Honduras.*

Christie Pashby (chapters 12 and 13) is the author of *Frommer's Banff and Jasper National Parks* and a contributing writer to *Frommer's Argentina* and *Frommer's South America.* She divides her time between the Canadian Rockies and Patagonia, where she runs a small guiding business with her husband.

Kristina Schreck (chapters 1–9) spends an endless amount of time on the road, but is happiest when back in Santiago, Chile, where she lives. She has traveled widely around the globe, and has lived in Argentina and Chile for nearly a decade, working as a freelance writer, an outdoor guide, and the marketing manager of Portillo ski resort. She is the former managing editor of *Adventure Journal magazine.*

Published by:

WILEY PUBLISHING, INC.

111 River St.
Hoboken, NJ 07030-5774

ISBN 978-0-470-95139-2 (paper); ISBN 978-1-118-10187-2 (ebk); ISBN 978-1-118-10188-9 (ebk); ISBN 978-1-118-10189-6 (ebk)

Editor: Jennifer Reilly
Production Editor: Erin Amick
Cartographer: Anton Crane
Photo Editor: Richard Fox
Production by Wiley Indianapolis Composition Services
Front Cover Photo: Torres del Paine/ ©André Viegas / iStock Photo
Back Cover Photo: Stone carvings, Ahu Tahai. Eastern Island, Chile / ©Walter Bibikow / AGE Fotostock, Inc.

For information on our other products and services or to obtain technical support, please contact our Customer Care Department within the U.S. at 877/762-2974, outside the U.S. at 317/572-3993 or fax 317/572-4002.

Wiley also publishes its books in a variety of electronic formats. Some content that appears in print may not be available in electronic formats.

Manufactured in the United States of America

5 4 3 2 1

CONTENTS

FROMMER'S STAR RATINGS, ICONS & ABBREVIATIONS

Every hotel, restaurant, and attraction listing in this guide has been ranked for quality, value, service, amenities, and special features using a **star-rating system.** In country, state, and regional guides, we also rate towns and regions to help you narrow down your choices and budget your time accordingly. Hotels and restaurants are rated on a scale of zero (recommended) to three stars (exceptional). Attractions, shopping, nightlife, towns, and regions are rated according to the following scale: zero stars (recommended), one star (highly recommended), two stars (very highly recommended), and three stars (must-see).

In addition to the star-rating system, we also use **seven feature icons** that point you to the great deals, in-the-know advice, and unique experiences that separate travelers from tourists. Throughout the book, look for:

special finds—those places only insiders know about

fun facts—details that make travelers more informed and their trips more fun

kids—best bets for kids and advice for the whole family

special moments—those experiences that memories are made of

overrated—places or experiences not worth your time or money

insider tips—great ways to save time and money

great values—where to get the best deals

The following abbreviations are used for credit cards:

AE American Express	DISC Discover	V Visa
DC Diners Club	MC MasterCard	

TRAVEL RESOURCES AT FROMMERS.COM

Frommer's travel resources don't end with this guide. Frommer's website, **www.frommers. com,** has travel information on more than 4,000 destinations. We update features regularly, giving you access to the most current trip-planning information and the best airfare, lodging, and car-rental bargains. You can also listen to podcasts, connect with other Frommers. com members through our active-reader forums, share your travel photos, read blogs from guidebook editors and fellow travelers, and much more.

LIST OF MAPS

HOW TO CONTACT US

In researching this book, we discovered many wonderful places—hotels, restaurants, shops, and more. We're sure you'll find others. Please tell us about them, so we can share the information with your fellow travelers in upcoming editions. If you were disappointed with a recommendation, we'd love to know that, too. Please write to:

Frommer's Chile & Easter Island, 3rd Edition
Wiley Publishing, Inc. • 111 River St. • Hoboken, NJ 07030-5774
frommersfeedback@wiley.com

ADVISORY & DISCLAIMER

Travel information can change quickly and unexpectedly, and we strongly advise you to confirm important details locally before traveling, including information on visas, health and safety, traffic and transport, accommodation, shopping and eating out. We also encourage you to stay alert while traveling and to remain aware of your surroundings. Avoid civil disturbances, and keep a close eye on cameras, purses, wallets and other valuables.

While we have endeavored to ensure that the information contained within this guide is accurate and up-to-date at the time of publication, we make no representations or warranties with respect to the accuracy or completeness of the contents of this work and specifically disclaim all warranties, including without limitation warranties of fitness for a particular purpose. We accept no responsibility or liability for any inaccuracy or errors or omissions, or for any inconvenience, loss, damage, costs or expenses of any nature whatsoever incurred or suffered by anyone as a result of any advice or information contained in this guide.

The inclusion of a company, organization or Website in this guide as a service provider and/or potential source of further information does not mean that we endorse them or the information they provide. Be aware that information provided through some Websites may be unreliable and can change without notice. Neither the publisher or author shall be liable for any damages arising herefrom.

THE BEST OF CHILE

Chile's tremendous length covers a hugely diverse array of landscapes, from the desolate moonscape of Chile's Atacama Desert, to the fertile vineyards of the Central Valley, to the lush rainforests of the Lake District, down to the magnificent glaciers and peaks of Patagonia—not to mention more than 4,830km (3,000 miles) of coastline and Easter Island. It's truly mind-boggling to think of how many different experiences a traveler can have in just 2 or 3 weeks in this South American nation. The following is a list of the best Chile has to offer, including hotels, restaurants, and outdoor activities—so read on and start planning!

THE most UNFORGETTABLE TRAVEL EXPERIENCES

o **Wandering the Madcap Streets of Valparaíso:** The ramshackle, colorful, and sinuous streets of Valparaíso offer a walking tour unlike any other. Antique Victorians and tin-walled buildings cling to steep hillsides, roads and walkways wind haphazardly around the slopes like a rabbit's warren, and rickety funiculars lift visitors to the tops of hills. Beyond the fun of exploring this city, Valparaíso boasts gourmet restaurants and boutique hotels, too. Bohemian, chaotic, and enigmatic, Valparaíso embodies the soul of poet Pablo Neruda, whose old home La Sebastiana is now a museum. See chapter 7.

o **Sunset Anywhere in the Atacama Desert:** The barren beauty of the Atacama desert presents a surreal odyssey that plays out the sci-fi fantasies of every youth. As the sun rises and falls upon this rarified, ethereal landscape of timeless volcanoes, serrated mountains, and striated mesas, some of nature's most foreboding glories are reinvented again and again as the palette shifts from beige and golden brown to improbable pinks, blues, and greens, and silhouettes recast the imagination to thoughts of lost civilizations. See chapter 9.

o **From Ocean to the World's Highest Lake:** Only 200km (124 miles) separate the Pacific Ocean from Lake Chungará, one of the world's highest bodies of water. Head up the lush Lluta Valley, dramatically hemmed in by desert walls featuring giant geoglyphs centuries old. Time crunches and space can be dizzying as you ascend high altitude terrain quickly. Take it slow, break the journey into 2 days to acclimatize, and immerse yourself in wondrous sights, from colonial churches to perfect snowcapped volcanoes and the world's highest trees, along with teeming wildlife. See chapter 9.

o **Stargazing in the Southern Hemisphere's Clearest Skies:** Northern Chile's dry skies are some of the clearest in the world, which is why so many international research teams have flocked to this region to erect multimillion-dollar observatories. There are plenty of stargazing opportunities for the amateur, too. The area around La Serena is home to several observatories that are open to visitors. A couple of hotels, including Elqui Domos in the Elqui Valley, and the Alto Atacama Desert Lodge & Spa and Explora at San Pedro de Atacama, have on-site telescopes; or you can book a night tour with a degreed guide who can point out Southern Hemisphere constellations and other celestial wonders. The stunning Elqui Valley also offers new age–like experiences geared to travelers looking to immerse themselves in outdoor pursuits and achieve holistic equanimity. See chapter 8.

o **Sailing the Quiet Fjords of Southern Chile:** Quietly sailing through the lush beauty of Chile's southern fjords is an accessible experience that all can afford. Budget travelers get a kick out of Navimag's 3-day sail between Puerto Montt and Puerto Natales, mid-range travelers enjoy Skorpios's programmed journeys to hot springs and the Chiloé coast, and the luxury market loves the freedom of a deluxe yacht like Nomads of the Seas' *Atmosphere*. These pristine, remote fjords rival the drama and beauty of Norway's coast, and often the camaraderie that grows between passengers, in the end, is what makes for such a fulfilling trip. See chapter 12.

o **Traveling to the End of the World:** It's a tough, crunchy drive along 1,000km (620 miles) of partially gravel road, but that is precisely why Chile's "Southern Highway" has kept the crowds at bay. This natural wonderland, saturated in green and hemmed in by jagged, snowcapped peaks, offers a journey for those seeking to travel through some of Chile's most remote and stunning territory. It can be done in a variety of directions and segments, but you'll need a rental car unless you have a lot of time. There are plenty of great stops along the way, including rainforest walks, the idyllic mountain valley of Futaleufú, the wet primeval forests of Pumalín and Parque Queulat, Puyuhuapi and its thermal spas, and the untouched wilds around Lake General Carrera. Top it off with a stop at Mt. Fitzroy and Torres del Paine near the southern tip of the continent, crossing through Argentina. See chapters 12 and 13.

o **Glimpsing the Cuernos and Torres del Paine:** It's the iconic image of Patagonia, one of the most stunning horizons on the planet. But the weather makes it far from a sure thing; many make the arduous journey to the end of the world without ever actually seeing the majestic horns and towers that make up the Paine Massif. Those who are fortunate enough to be rewarded with even a quick glance through the stormy clouds will never, ever forget the sight. See chapter 13.

o **Exploring Easter Island:** Easter Island, or "Rapa Nui," is famous for its ethereal moai sculptures that defy hyperbole, regardless of how many tourist brochure images of them you've seen. Traveling to the world's most remote island—it's located farther away from land than any other island—will make for an unforgettable odyssey. The entire island is a veritable living museum; it boasts two gorgeous beaches, phenomenal scuba diving in indigo blue water, wild horses, and a rich Polynesian culture that has survived against all odds. See chapter 14.

THE most CHARMING SMALL TOWNS

o **San Pedro de Atacama:** Quaint, unhurried, and built of adobe brick, San Pedro de Atacama has drawn travelers the world over who have come to experience the mellow charm and New Age spirituality that wafts through the dusty roads of this town. Its location in the driest desert in the world makes for starry skies and breathtaking views of the weird and wonderful land formations that are just a stone's throw away. A distinctive collection of adobe hotels, which embody so effortlessly the concept of rustic chic, completes the town's lost pueblo ambience. See chapter 9.

o **Putre:** At a breathtaking 3,500m (11,500 ft.), splendidly backed by the double summits of the 5,775m (19,000-ft.) Tarapacá Volcano, this tranquil Aymara village is a compelling vision of Andean culture. With 17th- to 19th-century stone portals flanking doors at many houses and a charming central square, it's a pretty place, reminiscent of pre-colonial Inca villages. Putre is the gateway to Chile's altiplano, and many tiny colonial villages nearby are still well off the beaten track. See chapter 9.

o **Pucón:** Not only was Pucón bestowed with a stunning location at the skirt of a smoking volcano and the shore of a glittering lake, but it's also Chile's self-proclaimed adventure capital, offering so many outdoor activities that you could keep busy for a week. But Pucón also has plenty of low-key activities if your idea of a vacation is plopping yourself down on a beach. You'll find everything you want and need without forfeiting small-town charm (that is, if you don't come with the Jan and Feb crowds). Rough-hewn wood restaurants, pubs, and crafts stores fill downtown, blending harmoniously with the forested surroundings. See chapter 10.

o **Frutillar & Puerto Varas:** Built by German immigrants who settled here in the early 1900s, these neighboring towns bear the clear stamp of Prussian order and workmanship, from the crisp lines of trees to the picturesque, shingled homes and tidy plazas ringed with roses. If you're lucky, you can still catch a few old-timers chatting in German over coffee and *küchen* (cake). Both towns feature a glorious view of Volcán Osorno and a lakefront address, a picture-postcard location that makes for an excellent boardwalk stroll. If that isn't enough, both towns also offer above-par lodging and a few of the best restaurants in the country. See chapter 10.

o **Futaleufú:** Nestled in a green valley surrounded by an amphitheater of craggy, snow-encrusted peaks, Futaleufú is made of colorful, clapboard homes and unpaved streets, and is, without a doubt, one of the prettiest villages in Chile. The population of 1,200 swells during the summer, when the hordes descend for rafting adventures on the nearby Class V river; but it hasn't changed the town's fabric too dramatically, and locals rarely saunter past a visitor without a tip of the hat and a *"Buenas tardes."* See chapter 12.

o **Caleta Tortel:** This remarkable little logging town near the very end of the Carretera Austral is an unreal, S-shaped place suspended somewhere between the steep slopes of a cypress forest and the pistachio green waters at the mouth of the Baker River. Wood-shingled houses cling precariously to the hillside, and cypress wood walkways and boats are the only way to get around. Cars are banished to a lot at the end of the Carretera Austral—even the fire truck is a boat, just like in

Venice. Hiking trails and fishermen's boats can take you to even more remote spots, including glaciers. See chapter 12.

o **Puerto Natales:** Set on the stunning shores of the Ultima Esperanza fjord, with the rugged steppe to the east and giant mountains to the north and west, this Patagonian outpost is a modern mecca for adventurers. Nestled within the wind-ravaged streets are cozy cafes, lovely inns, funky bistros, and bookstores, and nature-lovers can head into or out of one of the finest pieces of wilderness in the world, nearby Parque Nacional Torres del Paine. You may think it's just a jumping-off point, but you'll find Natales to be friendly, warm, and rich with memory-making moments. See chapter 13.

THE best OUTDOOR ADVENTURES

o **Skiing & Snowboarding the Andes:** Visiting the Andes, the second-highest peaks outside the Himalayas, is an exhilarating experience, since they are one of the world's best places to ski or snowboard—during the "summer," or from June to October. **Portillo** has been around for more than 50 years, and its steep chutes offer formidable challenges for advanced skiers. **Valle Nevado** is the country's most modern and largest resort, with the continent's best heliskiing. **Termas de Chillán** is on a geothermal fault line and adds hot springs to its après-ski scene. A laid-back scene, few people on the slopes, and a convivial atmosphere are the hallmarks of any Chile ski trip. See chapter 7.

o **Follow in Darwin's footsteps and hike to the summit of Parque Nacional La Campana:** Less than an hour's drive from Santiago, the precipitous lookout point of this lush national park was immortalized by Charles Darwin in *Voyage of the Beagle;* Darwin eulogized that never had he enjoyed a day so much than the one spent atop this mountain. It is a challenging but infinitely rewarding 8-hour trek to reach the summit at 1,771m (5,905 ft). There are also several tamer trails which offer the unique opportunity to trek through dense concentrations of palma chilena, the world's southernmost species of palm tree. See chapter 7.

o **Summiting a Volcano:** There's something more thrilling about summiting a volcano than any old mountain, especially when the volcano threatens to blow at any given time. Chile is home to a large share of the world's volcanoes, some of which are perfectly conical and entirely feasible to climb, such as **Volcán Villarrica** in Pucón and **Volcán Osorno** near Puerto Varas. Active Villarrica is a relatively moderate climb to the gaseous crater, followed by a fun slide on your rear down a human toboggan chute. Osorno offers a more technical climb, roping up for a crampon-aided walk past glacier crevasses and caves. In the far north, perfect conical volcanoes include **Parinacota,** east of Arica, and **Licancabur,** near San Pedro, both on the border with Bolivia. And in southern Aysén, ice fields around **San Valentín** beckon adventurous climbers. See chapters 9, 10, and 12.

o **Rafting & Kayaking the Futaleufú River or Pacific Ocean:** With churning river sections that are frightening enough to be dubbed "Hell" and "The Terminator," the Class V Futaleufú River, or the "Fu," as it's known, is solemnly revered by rafting and kayaking enthusiasts around the world as one of the most difficult to descend. A little too much white-knuckle excitement for your nerves? Rafting companies offer short-section rafting trips on the Futaleufú and down the tamer, crystalline waters of the neighboring Espolón River—kayak schools use this stretch, too. The scenery here redefines mountain beauty. An alternative is sea kayaking along the Patagonian channels or around Isla Damas, at the southern fringe of the Atacama Desert, both renowned for their teeming wildlife; see chapters 10 and 12.

o **Casting a Line for Jumbo Trout:** Chile has literally thousands of spots for fly-fishing, from the Lake District all the way down to the sub-Antarctic wilderness of Tierra del Fuego. Above all, the many lodges along the remote Carretera Austral draw fishing aficionados from around the world to rivers and lakes full of trout, weighing in from a pound to the hefty 8- to 10-pounders around Villa O'Higgins at the end of the road. Remember that the farther south you go, the shorter the season gets. See chapters 5 and 12.

o **Trekking in Torres del Paine:** Torres del Paine is one of the most spectacular national parks in the world, with hundreds of kilometers of trails through ever-changing landscapes of jagged peaks and one-of-a-kind granite spires, undulating meadows, milky turquoise lakes and rivers, and mammoth glaciers. The park has a well-organized system of *refugios* and campgrounds, but there are also several hotels, and visitors can access the park's major highlights on a day hike. See chapter 13.

THE best SPLURGE HOTELS

o **Ritz-Carlton,** Santiago (© 2/470-8500; www.ritzcarlton.com): If old-world grandeur, superlative service, and flawless attention to detail are at the top of your list, you'll want to stay at the Ritz. This hotel lives up to its luxurious brand name with such amenities as a heated pool and a serene spa, plus a convenient location close to the Metro and several of the city's finest restaurants. The glass-domed top floor affords beautiful panoramas of the city and the Andes. For the ultimate in decadence, soak in a bath of carmenère wine, prepared by your very own bath butler, then head down to the manly bar, brimming with brass, leather, and mahogany, which offers an unholy alliance of top shelf liquors, cigars, and delectable snacks well into the early hours. See p. 88.

o **Hotel del Mar,** Viña del Mar (© 32/250-0800; www.hoteldelmar.cl.): Viña's new Sheraton pales next to the classic Hotel del Mar, with its central location, regal Greco-Roman decor, and Monte Carlo–style casino. Best of all, everything's within reach, including the beach, just a hop across the street. For families, there's a children's center and proximity to kid-pleasing carriage rides and ice cream stands. See p. 127.

o **Casa Higueras,** Valparaíso (© 2/657-3950; www.hotelcasahigueras.cl): Clinging to a hillside above the emblematic city, this restored mansion is now a sumptuous boutique hotel that defies hyperbole: gorgeous decor, luxurious bathrooms, views, service, gourmet cuisine, and the only hotel swimming pool in town. See p. 142.

o **Casa Lapostolle Residence,** Santa Cruz (© 72/953360; www.lapostolle.com): If money is no object, 2 nights in one of the four deluxe *casitas* at Lapostolle's state-of-the-art Clos Apalta winery are the perfect indulgence for any oenophile. Nestled on a gentle slope high above the expansive Apalta Valley in the Colchagua Valley, this is one of the country's most exclusive lodgings. Each secluded, one-room cottage is pared-down yet sophisticated, and an adjoining deck provides what is certainly the best view from any lodging unit in Chile's wine country. Horseback riding, gourmet meals, wine tastings, tours, and a bottle of Chile's finest wine are included in the package. See p. 177.

- **Alto Atacama Desert Lodge & Spa,** San Pedro de Atacama (✆ 2/957-0300): Of the handful of luxury properties in the San Pedro area, this is the only lodge outside of town, enveloped in the natural surroundings of the beautiful Catarpe Valley. Its dedication to service and commitment to the environment puts it a step ahead of its competitors. The ecolodge was designed to blend into the background, with adobe walls that mimic the terracotta salt hills that rise high above the lodge, and six swimming pools scattered about that resemble an oasis. Many of the staff are indigenous and give a unique perspective to the more than 30 excursions the lodge offers. Healthy gourmet meals, fine wine, and a sybaritic spa round out the offerings. See p. 225.

- **Hotel Antumalal,** Pucón (✆ 45/441011; www.antumalal.cl): This low-slung, Bauhaus-influenced country inn is one of the most special places to lodge in Chile. Located high above the shore of Lake Villarrica and a sloping, terraced garden, the hotel literally sinks into its surroundings, offering a cozy ambience and an excellent view of the evening sunset. A warm welcome and a room with no lock are all part of making you feel at home. The inn has outstanding cuisine and a newly renovated spa, too. See p. 266.

- **Hacienda Tres Lagos** (✆ 2/333-4122 in Santiago; www.haciendatreslagos.com): Nestled near the southwest corner of spectacular Lake General Carrera, this *estancia*-style resort has a lake—and beach—of its own. Accommodations vary from hotel suites in the main lodge to family-oriented, independent *cabañas* to romantic yet very modern luxury apartments, but all share the lakefront view of Lago Negro and the Patagonian Andes beyond, and all are finely decorated with great attention to detail. As befits its location, it offers plenty of outdoor activities on foot, horseback, boats, or farther afield to the Tamango Nature Reserve to try to glimpse the endangered huemul deer. See p. 368.

- **explora Patagonia—Hotel Salto Chico,** Parque Nacional Torres del Paine (✆ 866/750-6699 in the U.S., or 2/206-6060 in Santiago; www.explora.com): This is the hotel that put Torres del Paine on the map and created a new sense of outdoor luxury, where great hiking and divine service go hand in hand. And while $700 per person per night may be tough to swallow, consider that your stay here includes everything from superb bilingual guides, hikes, and horseback rides to fresh-baked cookies, an excellent wine list, and a spa. Plush beds, soaker tubs, and all meals are also included. See chapter 13.

THE best MODERATELY PRICED HOTELS

- **Hotel Orly,** Santiago (✆ 2/231-8947; www.hotelorly.cl): An all-around favorite for reasonable prices; an absolutely ideal location near the Metro, shops, and restaurants; cheerful service; and coziness. Like the Vilafranca (below), this former mansion has rooms of varying sizes, so book accordingly. See p. 87.

- **Vilafranca Petit Hotel,** Santiago (✆ 2/232-1413; www.vilafranca.cl): Santiago's hectic pace slows down when you step into this delightful B&B. Steeped in French Provençal decor, this former home has been converted into a B&B that is economically priced and a cozy place to stay, even if the rooms are rather small. See p. 87.

- **Hotel Harrington,** Valparaíso (✆ 32/212-1338): A reasonably priced B&B located in a lovely old 1920s home on Cerro Concepción in Valparaíso, the Harrington doesn't have a front desk or elevator service but it is decorated with chic, contemporary linens and prints, it's squeaky-clean, and it provides more amenities than most hotels in its price category in Valparaíso. See p. 143.

○ **El Puesto,** Puerto Río Tranquilo (© 2/196-4555; www.elpuesto.cl): One of Patagonia's top places to stay is this three-room boutique hotel in tiny Puerto Río Tranquilo, on Lake General Carrera. While not directly on the lakeshore, family-run El Puesto is the perfect place to relax after a day of wilderness activities, from hiking on glaciers, visits to the beautiful Marble Cathedral and Chapel in the lake, to soaring through forest canopies. The whole place exudes a cozy, light atmosphere. See p. 368.

○ **Altiplánico Sur,** Puerto Natales (© 61/412525): Amidst a sea of stunning (and stunningly expensive) modern hotels, this smaller inn (with just 22 rooms) maintains the area's contemporary style, but has more reasonable prices. With grass-covered roofs and exterior walls made of unpainted adobe, much of the property is hidden underground. Inside, plush sheepskins, bright cushions, and cozy music bring warmth to concrete-heavy rooms and hallways. See p. 391.

THE best DINING EXPERIENCES

○ **Aquí Está Coco,** Santiago (© 2/410-6200): This restaurant is wildly popular with foreign visitors, with good reason: The elegant yet kitschy atmosphere is as fun as the food is mouthwatering. The restaurant is packed with marine memorabilia and has an old Chiloé-style boat as a bar, as well as an underground seating area that once was the cellar of an old home. The restaurant boasts very fresh seafood, well-prepared cocktails, and attentive service. See p. 96.

○ **Coquinaria,** Santiago (© 2/245-1934): Beyond the fact that the food here is hearty, well-proportioned, and outstanding in quality, and the cost is reasonable given the hike in restaurant prices in Santiago lately, the truly enjoyable element of Coquinaria is that it is part of the city's best gourmet market. Organic produce, cheese, charcuterie, fresh bread, and local products from throughout Chile can be purchased here following your meal. Coquinaria serves gourmet cuisine that is not too precious and over-thought, and they have an excellent weekend brunch. See p. 98.

○ **Bar Liguria,** Santiago (© 2/235-7914): The two Bar Ligurias in Providencia are equally lively and loads of fun, often filling up before 10pm and spilling out onto tables on the sidewalk. Everyone loves the Ligurias: actors, artists, businessmen, and locals converge here in a vibrant mélange that always feels celebratory. The Chilean fare is hearty and delicious, and the sharply dressed waiters rushing to and fro provide quick, attentive service. See p. 97.

○ **Montealegre,** Valparaíso (© 32/657-249-7900): Whether day or night, the panoramic views here of the chaotic hills of Valparaíso and the city's main port are stupendous. There is indoor seating within the gorgeous confines of the Hotel Casa Higueras, where the restaurant is located, but the outdoor patio is where you want to be while dining on truly delicious gourmet cuisine. Chic yet unpretentious, Montealegre offers a memorable evening that goes beyond just cuisine. An outstanding wine list and cocktails are on hand, too. See p. 146.

- **Casa Silva,** San Fernando (☎ 72/710180): Casa Silva's new restaurant is nestled in a thick grove of vines and faces a forest fronted by an impossibly emerald-green polo field. It's a dreamy landscape and more often than not diners can watch polo players and horse-jumping exercises while they dine. A crisp, airy decor and outdoor seating really make this place a gem, and the Casa Silva wine is varied and delicious. The grill-based menu is quite straightforward, but the beef here is Angus and Kobe and the quality is top-notch. There are tapas, too, for light snacks. See p. 179.

- **Espejo de Luna,** Aituy, Chiloé (☎ 97/431-3090): Worth the drive to the isolated south of the island, this enchanting restaurant set within dreamlike architecture is one of the most unexpected finds anywhere in Chile. The talented chef sources food direct from local farms and fishermen, and the imaginative dishes may make you want to stick around in one of their cabins for a few days. See p. 334.

- **Afrigonia,** Puerto Natales (☎ 61/412232): The surprise element is in full force at this tiny restaurant in Patagonia—in the superb presentation of their king crab with mangos and *ceviche* appetizer, in the flavorful local lamb, cooked in Carmenère, and perhaps most surprisingly, in the divine work of a brilliant and utterly unpretentious chef, who is an immigrant from Zambia. With his Chilean wife serving tables, it's a friendly and unique dining delight. See p. 393.

THE best MUSEUMS

- **Museo Chileno de Arte Precolombino,** Santiago (☎ 2/688-7348): More than 1,500 objects related to indigenous life and culture throughout the Americas make the Pre-Columbian Museum one of the best in Santiago. Artifacts include textiles, metals, paintings, figurines, and ceramics from Mexico to Chile. All objects are handsomely lit and mounted throughout seven exhibition rooms that are divided into the Mesoamerica, Intermedia, Andina, and Surandina regions of Latin America. The museum is housed in the old Royal Customs House built in 1807. If you need a break, there's a patio with a small cafe and a good bookstore to browse. See p. 103.

- **Iglesia, Convento y Museo de San Francisco,** Santiago (☎ 2/638-3238): One step into this museum and you'll feel like you've been instantly beamed out of downtown Santiago. This is the oldest standing building in Santiago and home to a serene garden patio where the only sounds are a trickling fountain and the cooing of pigeons. The museum boasts 54 paintings depicting the life and death of San Francisco, one of the largest and best-conserved displays of 17th-century art in South America. On the altar of the church, you'll see the famous *Vírgen del Socorro,* the first Virgin Mary icon in Chile. See p. 105.

- **Museo de la Moda,** Santiago (☎ 2/219-3623): You'd never believe that one of the world's best fashion museums lies in the heart of Santiago, Chile. The brainchild of the son of a wealthy textile factory owner, this museum has more than 8,000 pieces from the early 20th century to the present, which it displays in revolving exhibits that are usually themed, such as "War Fashion." The museum is within the retrofitted old home of the owner and is a gem of mid-century architecture; some areas are set as period pieces with the family's original furniture. See p. 109.

- **Casa Pablo Neruda,** Isla Negra (☎ 35/461-2844; www.fundacionneruda.org): This was Nobel Prize–winning poet Pablo Neruda's favorite home, and although his other residences in Valparaíso and Santiago are as eccentric and absorbing, this is the best preserved of the three. The home is stuffed with books by his favorite authors and the whimsical curios, trinkets, and toys he collected during his travels around the world, including African masks, ships in bottles, butterflies, and more. The museum can be found in Isla Negra, south of Valparaíso. See p. 149.

o **Museo de Colchagua,** Santa Cruz (© **72/821050;** www.museocolchagua.cl): In terms of historical range and scope, this is arguably Chile's best museum. You'll find a stunning collection of everything from pre-Hispanic objects throughout the Americas and local Indian artifacts to Spanish conquest–era helmets and artillery and *huaso* ponchos, and more. This museum is a not-to-be-missed stop while visiting the wine country. Unbelievably, the museum is really the private collection of a local man who earned his fortune in bomb manufacturing and arms dealing, and because he cannot leave the country (and risk arrest by the FBI), he has reinvested in projects such as this in his hometown. See p. 176.

o **Museo Arqueológico Padre le Paige,** San Pedro de Atacama (© **55/851002**): This little museum will come as an unexpected surprise for its wealth of indigenous artifacts, such as "Miss Chile," a leathered mummy whose skin, teeth, and hair are mostly intact, as well as a display of skulls that show the creepy ancient custom of cranial deformation practiced by the elite as a status symbol. The Atacama Desert is the driest in the world, and this climate has produced some of the best-preserved artifacts in Latin America, on view here. See p. 221.

o **Museo Arqueológico San Miguel de Azapa,** Arica (© **58/205555;** www.uta.cl/masma): For anyone with even a minimal interest in history and archaeology, this small museum belongs to the top attractions in the Western Hemisphere. Around 5,000 B.C.—long before even the Egyptians began to mummify their dead—the Chinchorro culture developed a technique of its own to preserve bodies for eternity. A brand-new display of the museum's complete collection of mummies is superb, and there are displays that outline the entire history of pre-Columbian cultures in the Arica area through Tiahuanaco and the Inca periods. The museum also has a section devoted to recent and contemporary Aymara culture in the area. See p. 237.

o **Museo Regional de Magallanes,** Punta Arenas (© **61/248840**): The Museo Regional de Magallanes is the former home of one of Patagonia's wealthiest families. Tapestries, furniture from France, Italian marble fireplaces, hand-painted wallpaper—this veritable palace is a testament to the Braun family's insatiable need to match European elite society. Several small salons are devoted to ranching and maritime history, but the grandeur of this museum is really the reason for a visit. See p. 380.

o **Museo Salesiano Maggiorino Borgatello,** Punta Arenas (© **61/221001**): There's so much on display here that you could spend more than an hour wandering and marveling at the hodgepodge collection of archaeological artifacts, photo exhibits, petroleum production interpretative exhibitions, ranch furniture, industrial gadgets, and, best of all, the macabre collection of stuffed and mounted regional wildlife gathered by a Salesian priest. See p. 379.

THE best AFTER-DARK FUN

o **Barrio Bellavista,** Santiago: Santiago's bohemian district is replete with night spots that range from the funky to chic to the homespun. Try **La Casa en el Aire** (© **2/735-6680;** www.lacasaenelaire.cl) for folk and poetry reading; **El Perseguidor** (© **2/777-6763;** www.elperseguidor.cl) for jazz, with nightly performances starting around 11pm and a smooth, romantic candlelit ambience; or **Etniko** (© **2/738-0288**) with a trendy bar scene, open-air dance floor, and Asian food. See p. 107.

o **Catedral,** Santiago (© **2/664-3048**): The chic Catedral is one of the capital's most ebullient bars, and it's where the gilded and glamorous gather to preen and strut. Arrive early in the summer to claim one of the coveted outdoor seats on the rooftop patio. See p. 93.

o **W Hotel,** Santiago (© **2/770-0000**): The place to see and be seen, with an over-the-top lounge wrapped in mirrors, two world-class restaurants, and a rooftop bar that opens at 7pm and offers sparkling views of Santiago's city skyline. See p. 89.

o **La Piedra Feliz,** Valparaíso (© **225-6788**): This Valparaíso institution has something for everyone, including an underground lounge with electronic music, a jazz club, a sophisticated bar, tango dancing, and more. Piedra Feliz is located within the old storehouse of a shipping company. See p. 148.

o **Bravo Cabrera,** Puerto Varas (© **65/233441**): Choose among several dozen Chilean microbrews and munch on wood-fired pizza pies, while this bar's hip DJs provide a fitting soundtrack for the lakeside setting. See p. 303.

o **Termas Los Pozones,** Pucón (no phone): The natural setting, 24-hour schedule, and cheap prices of Los Pozones hot springs in Pucón prove a decadent lure for young Chileans and travelers who are keen to keep in a party spirit after the discos have closed up shop for the night. See p. 273.

o **Mama Rosa Bar at Indigo Hotel,** Puerto Natales (© **61/413609**): After a day out in the blustering weather of Patagonia, slip behind the tall iron door into this converted hostel for a pisco sour (choose from 15 different options), some cool tunes, and warm vibes. Through giant windows, watch the sun set behind the fjords and mountains in the distance and toast the sense of adventure that just oozes through the air here. See p. 391.

o **Topatangi,** Hanga Roa (© **32/255-1554**): From Thursday to Saturday nights in Hanga Roa, the dance floor at Topatangi Pub floods with Rapa Nui 20- and 30-something island girls and guys grooving to the sounds of local bands that jam everything from traditional sounds to '70s American rock. Don't go before 10pm and don't leave before sunrise. See p. 433.

CHILE IN DEPTH

With its desert northern fringes, its toes dipped in the Antarctic, and its slender core spliced by the serrated peaks of the iconic Andes, Chile is a landmass which is at once as absurd to contemplate as it is extreme to experience. Unfathomable in its breathtaking diversity, which ranges from crystal blue lakes to ethereal desert landscapes, rugged mountains to golden coastline, lush vineyards to grassy plains, Chile presents any traveler with an epic, stirring journey.

Unlike some of its more unstable neighbors, Chile also boasts a solid democracy, a low crime rate, little corruption, and a robust economy. The country's modern transportation infrastructure, fine hotels, clean streets, and warm, inviting people encourage camaraderie at every turn and facilitate a smooth travel adventure. Culture fans have a surplus of character-rich and sophisticated venues in such cities as Santiago and Valparaíso. Adrenaline junkies will find an adventurous playground with more active travel opportunities than any other South American nation.

What follows is a historical and cultural introduction to a country where adventure, beauty, and hospitality await the receptive traveler.

CHILE TODAY

The Chilean economy is one of the strongest in Latin America, both admired and scorned by its envious neighbors. Chile is a market-oriented economy that is highly dependent on foreign trade, with the exportation of the country's rich supply of natural resources—including mining, forestry, seafood, agriculture, and wine—representing 40% of its gross domestic product (GDP). Chile is the world's largest producer of copper, an industry that has recently been fueled by China's hungry demand for the raw material. Chile's government relies heavily on taxing profits from the mining industry to support its fiscal expenditures. Tourism is a quickly growing force in the economic development of Chile, representing about 4% of the country's GDP.

Chile has bounced back quickly from the 2008 global financial meltdown and, more recently, the 2010 earthquake, a colossal 8.8-magnitude quake that devastated the Concepcion area and trigged tsunamis along the south-central coast and the Juan Fernandez islands. (For more on the earthquake, see the "After the Earthquake" box in chapter 7.) By the end of 2010, Chile's economy had expanded by 7%, the fastest in 5 years, the peso strengthened against the dollar, and unemployment dropped to 7.6%. Still, this figure does not show a clear picture of the current Chilean working conditions. Many of Chile's service workers are casual laborers,

CHILE MINE rescue

The 2010 mining disaster at the San Jose mine near Copiapó in northern Chile enraptured the world, as an estimated one billion people tuned in to watch one of the most dramatic rescue operations in modern time. On the 5th of August, 33 men were trapped in an underground mine tunnel following a catastrophic cave-in that left them cut off without communication or any escape route. Most believed they wouldn't survive; the men were located the equivalent of two Empire State buildings underground, in a tortuously hot and humid hell, without any idea if they'd be saved or given up for dead.

Following 17 days of isolation, during which the miners survived on two spoonfuls of tuna and a half a cup of milk every 48 hours, workers made contact using a drill to bore a space large enough for a tube, called a *paloma* or dove, to send down supplies, a communications system, and words of encouragement. But it would be 69 days before the miners would finally be hoisted to the surface via a "Phoenix 1" capsule specially designed for the rescue, a stunning event that was only made possible by the government's can-do attitude and the intense pressure by the miners' families to rescue the men, as well as a highly talented team of Chilean and international rescue workers and drillers using cutting-edge technology. It also required a lot of luck.

The mining event thrust Chile into the spotlight and gave the country an enormously positive image, but it also exposed a Chilean mining industry that often hires poor workers who are frequently subjected to precarious and dangerous conditions in exchange for relatively little pay. Following a media blitz, gifts, and invitations for travel around the world, the Chilean miners have come home different men and, as of 2011, all were still seeking psychological help and trying to come to terms with their ordeal.

and a recent survey by Chile's National Statistics Institute showed the bottom 20% of the population earning just US$350 per month; the minimum wage in Chile, in fact, is just over US$300 per month.

In 2009, Chile's governing center-left Concertación coalition was defeated for the first time since the end of General Augusto Pinochet's dictatorship in 1990 (see "Looking Back at Chile" later in this chapter). Countering South America's steady drift to the left, Chileans voted in the center-right opposition candidate Sebastian Piñera, a billionaire businessman representing the Alianza (Alliance) party, a more moderate version of the country's right-wing UDI party. Chileans, weary of the impotent Concertación party, not to mention a truly lackluster presidential campaign against Piñera, have come to view right-leaning political parties in a new light and no longer see the right as the political machine of the Pinochet dictatorship.

More than one-third of Chile's nearly 16 million people live in the Santiago metropolis alone. About 90% of the population is *mestizo*, a mix of indigenous and European blood that includes Spanish, German (in the Lake District), and Croatian (in southern Patagonia). Other nationalities, such as Italian, Russian, and English, have contributed a smaller influence. In general, visitors will find that the average Chilean looks like a southern European. Indigenous groups such as the Aymara in the northern desert and the Mapuche in the Lake District still exist in large numbers, although nothing compared to their size before the Spanish conquest. There are approximately 750,000 Mapuches, many of whom live on poverty-stricken *reduccio-nes* (literally "reductions"), where they continue to use their language and carry on their customs. The Mapuches, considered the fiercest of all indigenous groups in the Americas, continue to fight for the repatriation of their land, sometimes violently— for years Mapuches were subject to anti-terrorism laws until 2009, when hunger strikers were successful in overturning the laws. In southern Chile and Tierra del Fuego, indigenous groups such as the Alacalufe and Yagan have been diminished to only a few people, and some, such as the Patagonian Ona, have been completely extinguished.

Defying the stereotype of the flamboyant and eternally gregarious Latino, Chileans are more conservative in character than their South American counterparts, arguably the result of Chile being hemmed in by the Andes and the Pacific Ocean and there-fore "cut off" from connection with the rest of South America. Though not inherently a racist country (there is little racial diversity here), Chile suffers from an unhealthy amount of classism. The elite are known as *cuicos,* and the poor as *rotos* or *ordinarios.* Chile's economy has produced a burgeoning middle class, evidenced by jam-packed shopping malls and new condominium buildings springing up around Santiago, yet few talented Chileans from middle-class and poor families stand a chance at rising to the top without the right connections, known as *pituto.* It is quite common to see elite Chileans in managerial positions or other high-level positions without having had any direct experience related to their job.

In spite of this, Chileans are united in their enormous sense of patriotism, evidenced by celebrations during the multiday festival surrounding Independence Day, when Chileans festoon streets and vehicles with Chilean flags and decorations in a display of national pride. More recently, Chile's 2010 earthquake and the rescue of 33 miners from a subterranean pit (see the "Chile Mine Rescue" box for more information) pulled

CHILEAN customs

Chilean dress has relaxed greatly over the years, and it is common to see people in shorts and T-shirts on the streets of Santiago. That said, Chileans are still rather formal in their manner of dress, so skip the Hawaiian shirt.

Chileans tend to appreciate formali-ties, so always greet a Chilean with a *"Buenos días"* or *"Buenas tardes."* When two women, or a man and a woman, greet each other in a social setting, they do so with one kiss on the right cheek. Men greet each other with a handshake, or with a quick hug if they are intimate friends or family. The same is true in business, but Chileans understand that some North Americans are uncomfort-able with this and will greet you with a handshake if they know you're a

foreigner. Like most Latin Americans, Chileans require less personal space when talking to another person; it can feel a bit awkward, but try not to step away.

Punctuality is appreciated in business settings, but don't be surprised if your Chilean guest shows up 30 to 45 min-utes late for a dinner party. In contrast to North America, the do-it-yourself spirit is not very esteemed in Chile; rather, your ability to hire help to do it for you is what people value. Live-in or daily maids are very common in Chile, which means that, as a guest staying with a well-to-do family, you are not expected to make your bed or help around the house. When entering a room, you are expected to greet every-one individually or as a group.

the country together in an outpouring of national camaraderie. In rural areas and small towns outside Santiago, Chileans are warmly affectionate and hospitable to strangers.

Given the provinciality of Chileans and the country's former era of dictatorship and censorship, Chileans have created an art form out of gossiping; no topic, it seems, is out of bounds for a good dish, invented or real. Chileans also tend to be indirect and eager to please: When asking for directions, you may find that Chileans use constructive guesswork, often sending you on a false path rather than admitting that they can't help. Even in business situations, overt directness can be considered an affront and even be construed as rude.

Chileans strongly value the family unit, and they love kids. Unless a young adult marries or travels outside his or her hometown to study, most leave home at a late age. It is common to see a young adult who is 25 or 27 still at home and without any pressure to leave. Because kids and young adults are coddled by their mothers and maids (especially males), travelers often remark that Chilean young adults seem more immature than their foreign counterparts. Also, travelers tend to notice heaps of amorous couples kissing and strolling through parks, another result of young Chileans who leave home at a late age and do not have the independence of living on their own. Chileans traditionally marry before 30 and have kids shortly thereafter, yet this trend is on the decline with more young adults waiting until their early 30s to tie the knot. Divorce was only pronounced legal in 2004, and Chile was the last Latin American country to grant dissolution of marriage.

LOOKING BACK AT CHILE

Early History

Archaeologists have reconstructed what they can of Chile's indigenous history from artifacts discovered at burial sites and in ancient villages and defensive forts. Far more is known about the northern cultures of Chile than their southern counterparts because the extreme aridity of the northern region aided in the preservation of artifacts as fragile as 3,000-year-old Chinchorro mummies. Northern tribes, such as the Atacama, developed a culture based around the production of ceramic pottery, textiles, and objects made of gold and silver, but for the most part, early indigenous cultures in Chile were small, scattered tribes that fished and cultivated simple crops. The primitive, nomadic tribes of Patagonia and Tierra del Fuego never developed beyond a society of hunters and gatherers because severe weather and terrain hindered the development of agriculture. Interestingly, it was at the Monte Verde site in southern Chile where archeologists in 1975 discovered the oldest prehistoric settlement in the Americas, dated to 14,800 years, and dispelled the previous belief that settlement in the Americas began 13,500 years ago.

In the middle of the 15th century, the great Inca civilization pushed south in a tremendous period of expansion. Although the Incas were able to subjugate tribes in the north, they never made it past the fierce Mapuche Indians in southern Chile.

The Spanish Invade

In 1535, and several years after Spaniards Diego de Almagro and Francisco Pizarro had successfully conquered the Inca Empire in Peru, the Spanish turned their attention south after hearing tales of riches that lay in what is today Chile. Already flushed with wealth garnered from Incan gold and silver, an inspired Diego de Almagro and more than 400 men set off on what would become a disastrous journey that left many dead from exposure and famine. De Almagro found nothing of the fabled riches, and he retreated to Peru.

Three years later, a distinguished officer of Pizarro's army, Spanish-born Pedro de Valdivia, secured permission to settle the land south of Peru in the name of the Spanish crown. Valdivia left with just 10 soldiers and little ammunition, but his band grew to 150 by the time he reached the Aconcagua Valley, where he founded Santiago de la Nueva Extremadura on February 12, 1541. Fire, Indian attacks, and famine beset the colonists, but the town nonetheless held firm. Valdivia succeeded in founding several other outposts, including Concepción, La Serena, and Valdivia, but like the Incas before him, he was unable to overcome the Mapuche Indians south of the Río Bío-Bío. In a violent Mapuche rebellion, Valdivia was captured and suffered a gruesome death, sending frightened colonists north. As they had with the Incas, the Mapuche tribe effectively defended its territory from colonists for 300 years, essentially splitting Chile in two until the late 1800s.

Early Chile was a colonial backwater of no substantive interest to Spain, although Spain did see to the development of a feudal land-owning system called an *encomienda*. Prominent Spaniards were issued enormous tracts of land and an *encomienda,* or a group of Indian slaves that the landowner was charged with caring for and converting to Christianity. Thus rose Chile's traditional and nearly self-supporting *hacienda,* known as a *latifundo,* as well as a rigid class system that defined the population. At the top were the *peninsulares* (those born in Spain), followed by the *criollos* (Creoles, or Spaniards born in the New World). Next down the ladder were *mestizos* (a mix of Spanish and Indian blood), followed by Indians themselves. As the indigenous population succumbed to disease, the *latifundo* system replaced slaves with rootless *mestizos* who were willing, or forced, to work for a miserable wage. This form of land ownership would define Chile for centuries to come, and traces of this antiquated system hold firm even in modern Chilean businesses today.

Chile Gains Independence

Chile tasted independence for the first time during Napoleon's invasion of Spain in 1808 and the subsequent sacking of King Ferdinand VII, whom Napoleon replaced with his own brother. On September 18, 1810, leaders in Santiago agreed that the country would be self-governed until the king was reinstated as the rightful ruler of Spain. Although the self-rule was intended as a temporary measure, this date is now celebrated as Chile's independence day.

Semi-independence did not satisfy many *criollos,* and soon thereafter Jose Miguel Carrera, the power-hungry son of a wealthy family, appointed himself leader and stated that the government would not answer to Spain or the viceroy of Peru. But Carrera was an ineffective and controversial leader, and it was soon determined that one of his generals, Bernardo O'Higgins, would prove more adept at shaping Chile's future. Loyalist troops from Peru took advantage of the struggle between the two and crushed the fragile independence movement, sending Carrera, O'Higgins, and their troops fleeing to Argentina. This became known as the Spanish "reconquest." Across the border in Mendoza, O'Higgins met José de San Martín, an Argentine general who had already been plotting the liberation of South America. San Martín sought to liberate Chile first and then launch a sea attack on the viceroyalty seat in Peru from Chile's shore. In 1817, O'Higgins and San Martín crossed the Andes with their well-prepared troops and quickly defeated Spanish forces in Chacabuco, securing the capital. In April 1818, San Martín's army triumphed in the bloody battle of Maipú, and full independence from Spain was won. An assembly of prominent leaders elected O'Higgins as Supreme Director of Chile, but discontent within his ranks and with landowners forced him to quit office and spend his remaining years in exile in Peru.

The War of the Pacific

The robust growth of the nation during the mid- to late 1800s saw the development of railways and roads that connected previously remote regions with Santiago. The government began promoting European immigration to populate these regions, and it was primarily Germans who accepted, settling and clearing farms around the Lake District.

Growing international trade boosted Chile's economy, but it was the country's northern mines, specifically nitrate mines, that held the greatest economic promise. Border disputes with Bolivia in this profitable region ensued until a treaty was signed giving Antofagasta to Bolivia in exchange for low taxes on Chilean mines. Bolivia did an about-face and hiked taxes, sparking the War of the Pacific that pitted allies Peru and Bolivia against Chile in the fight for the nitrate fields. The odds were against Chile, but the country's well-trained troops were a force to reckon with. The war's turning point came with the capture of Peru's major warship, the *Huáscar*. Chilean troops invaded Peru and pushed on until they had captured the capital, Lima. With Chile as the final victor, both countries signed treaties that conceded Peru's Tarapacá region and Antofagasta to Chile that, incredibly, increased Chile's size by one-third with nitrate- and silver-rich land, and cut Bolivia off from the coast. More than a century later, Bolivia and Peru are still rallying against the Chilean government for wider access to the coastal waters off northern Chile.

The Military Dictatorship

No political event defines modern Chile better than the country's former military dictatorship. In 1970, Dr. Salvador Allende, Chile's first socialist president, was narrowly voted into office. Allende vowed to improve the lives of Chile's poorer citizens by instituting a series of radical changes that might redistribute the nation's lopsided wealth. Although the first year showed promising signs, Allende's reforms ultimately sent the country spiraling into economic ruin. Large estates were seized by the government and by independent, organized groups of peasants to be divided among rural workers, many of them uneducated and unprepared. Major industries were nationalized, but productivity lagged, and the falling price of copper reduced the government's fiscal intake. With spending outpacing income, the country's deficit soared. Worst of all, uncontrollable inflation and price controls led to shortages, and Chileans were forced to wait in long lines to buy basic goods.

Meanwhile, the United States (led by Richard Nixon and Henry Kissinger) was closely monitoring the situation in Chile. With anti-Communist sentiment running high in the U.S. government, the CIA allocated $8 million to undermine the Allende government by funding right-wing opposition and supporting a governmental takeover.

On September 11, 1973, military forces led by General Augusto Pinochet toppled Allende's government with a dramatic coup d'état. Military tanks rolled through the streets and jets dropped bombs on the presidential palace. Inside, Allende refused to surrender and accept an offer to be exiled. After delivering an emotional radio speech, Allende took his own life.

Wealthy Chileans who had lost much under Allende celebrated the coup as an economic and political salvation. But nobody was prepared for the brutal repression that would haunt Chile for the next 17 years. Pinochet shut down Congress, banned political parties, censored the news media, and imposed a strict curfew, and inexperienced military officers took over previously nationalized industries and universities. Pinochet snuffed out his adversaries by rounding up and killing more than 3,000 citizens and torturing 28,000 political activists, journalists, professors, and any other "subversives." Thousands more fled the country.

Pinochet set out to rebuild the economy using Milton Freeman–inspired free-market policies that included selling off nationalized industries, curtailing government spending, reducing import tariffs, and eliminating price controls. From 1976 to 1981, the economy grew at such a pace that it was hailed as the "Chilean Miracle," but the miracle did nothing to address the country's high unemployment rate, worsening social conditions, and falling wages. More importantly, Chileans were unable to speak out against the government and those who did often "disappeared," taken from their homes by Pinochet's secret police, never to be heard from again. Culture was filtered, and artists, writers, and musicians were censored.

The End of the Military Dictatorship

The worldwide recession of 1982 put an end to Chile's economic run, but the economy bounced back again in the late 1980s. The Catholic Church began voicing opposition to Pinochet's brutal human-rights abuses, and a strong desire for a return to democracy saw the beginning of nationwide protests and international pressure, especially from the United States. In a pivotal 1988 "yes or no" plebiscite, 55% of Chileans voted no to further rule by Pinochet, electing centrist Christian Democrat Patricio Aylwin president of Chile, but not before Pinochet promulgated a constitution that allowed him and a right-wing minority to continue to exert influence over the democratically elected government. It also shielded Pinochet and the military from any future prosecution.

It is difficult for most foreigners to fathom the blind support Pinochet's followers bestowed upon him in spite of the increasing revelation of grotesque human rights abuses during his rule. Supporters justified their views with Chile's thriving economy as testament to the "necessity" of authoritarian rule and the killings of the left-wing opponents. Following Aylwin's election, Pinochet led a cushy life protected by security guards and filled with speaking engagements and other social events. What Pinochet hadn't counted on, however, was the dogged pursuit by international jurists to bring him to trial, and when in London in 1998 to undergo surgery, a Spanish judge leveled murder and torture charges against the former dictator and issued a request for his extradition.

Sixteen months of legal wrangling ended with Pinochet's release and return to Chile, but the ball was set in motion and soon thereafter Chile's Supreme Court stripped Pinochet and his military officers from immunity in order to face prosecution. Pinochet began pointing fingers, and old age and dementia shielded him

---

Neruda's Victory

Never, forever . . . they do not concern me. Victory leaves a vanishing footprint in the sand. I live a bedeviled man, disposed, like any other, to cherish my human affinities. Whoever you are, I love you.
—Pablo Neruda, "Evening" (from *One Hundred Love Sonnets*, 1960)

from prosecution—but not from public humiliation. In 2004, it emerged that Pinochet had stashed $28 million in secret accounts worldwide, quashing his support by even his closest allies given that Pinochet advocated austerity and railed against corruption as proof of his "just" war. Endless international news reports and the publication of torture victims' accounts furthered the humiliation that many believe caused Pinochet more harm than any trial ever could.

The election of Chile's first female president, Michelle Bachelet, in 2006 proved how far Chile had come since the brutal repression of Pinochet. Bachelet, a Socialist who was tortured and exiled during Pinochet's rule, is also a divorcee who worked her way up the political ranks, including a post as the Minister of Defense. Shortly after Bachelet's election, Pinochet died at age 91.

THE LAY OF THE LAND
Chile's Ecosystems

Chile is sandwiched between the Andes and the Pacific Ocean with a width that averages just 180km (112 miles) and a length measuring some 4,830km (3,000 miles). The country encompasses an extraordinarily diverse array of landscapes, temperate zones, and microclimates. It is, in fact, difficult to believe such variation can exist in just one country.

Nearly one-third of Chile's northern region is high-altitude desert, which includes the world's driest desert, the Atacama. This beautiful, eerie "wasteland" is set below a chain of purple and pink volcanoes and encompasses salt flats, geysers, sand dunes, salt mountains, and vast spaces, with an average altitude of 2,000m (6,560 ft.).

The central region of Chile, including Santiago and its environs, enjoys a mild, Mediterranean climate ideal for agricultural production and grape-growing for wine production. The Andes mountain peaks in the central region are their highest and most rugged, and rise high above verdant, patchwork valleys.

As the name clearly indicates, Chile's Lake District is known for hundreds of lakes, yet the lush region is as famous for its conical, snowcapped volcanoes, temperate rainforest, and hot springs. South of Puerto Montt is Chile's "frontier" highway, known as the Carretera Austral, where tiny villages appear from among the thick virgin rainforest and waterfalls descend from rugged peaks. Southwest from Puerto Montt is the peculiar and infinitely beautiful island Chiloé, known for its emerald, rolling hills, crashing sea, and quiet fishing coves. Along the Carretera Austral and farther south, Chile breaks up into thousands of islands, nearly all of which are uninhabited and reachable only by boat. This is where travelers can sail the country's famous fjords, which rival anything found in Norway or elsewhere on the planet.

Patagonia, also known as the Magallanes region, is characterized by vast open *pampa* (steppe), the Northern and Southern Patagonian Ice Fields and their hundreds of mighty glaciers, dramatic granite peaks, and gale-force winds and highly changeable weather. At lower altitudes, valley ecosystems composed of granite rocks have been chafed by glaciations and sedimentary deposits. Vegetation here is characterized by *coiron* grass, low-lying shrubs, and beech trees. There is no dry season, and rainfall can happen any time of the year.

Easter Island is the most remote inhabited island in the world and features a subtropical climate unlike the Chilean mainland climate. The island was formed by volcanic activity, and craters and lava-formed caves can be seen throughout. Mass deforestation led to the extinction of the island's unique palm and other shrubs and trees; however, the Royal, Kew, and Gothenburg botanical gardens preserved samples of Easter Island's extinct *toromiro* tree, and plans are currently afoot to reintroduce the species to the island.

For detailed information on Chile's flora, see chapter 17.

Searching for Wildlife

Many of Chile's forest-dwelling animals are nocturnal, and during the day they are usually elusive and on the watch for predators. Birds are easier to spot in clearings or secondary forests than they are in primary forests. The wide-open spaces of the *altiplano* and immense steppe of Patagonia are especially conducive to wildlife watching. In the Atacama region, many species—flamingos, vicuñas, and guanacos—are easily encountered close to water sources such as lagoons, lakes, and oases.

For detailed information on Chile's fauna, see chapter 17. Here are a few helpful hints for wildlife-watching in Chile:

o **Listen.** Pay attention to rustling in the leaves; whether it's a Magellanic woodpecker or a *pudú* deer in the forest, you're most likely to hear an animal before seeing one.

o **Keep quiet.** Noise will scare off animals and prevent you from hearing their movements and calls.

o **Don't try too hard.** Soften your focus and allow your peripheral vision to take over. This way you can catch glimpses of motion and then focus in on the prey.

o **Bring binoculars.** It's also a good idea to practice a little first to get the hang of them. It would be a shame to be fiddling around and staring into space while everyone else in your group oohs and aahs over a condor.

o **Dress appropriately.** You'll have a hard time focusing your binoculars if you're busy swatting flies. Light, long pants and long-sleeved shirts are your best bet. Comfortable hiking boots are a real boon, except where heavy rubber boots are necessary. Avoid loud colors; the better you blend in with your surroundings, the better your chances are of spotting wildlife.

o **Be patient.** The forest isn't on a schedule. However, your best shots at seeing forest fauna are in the very early morning and late afternoon hours.

o **Read up.** Familiarize yourself with what you're most likely to see—most hotels and lodges have field guides to Chile.

CHILE IN POPULAR CULTURE: BOOKS, FILM & MUSIC

Books

A History of Chile, by John L. Rector, chronicles the political history of Chile during the second half of the 20th century. Sara Wheeler's *Travels in a Thin Country* is the story of an Englishwoman's trip to Chile, but it can be frustratingly superficial. A better read is *Chile: A Traveler's Companion,* translated by Katherine Silver, which provides readers with a well-rounded collection of regionally based memoirs penned by Chile's best contemporary writers, and arranged geographically so that readers may "travel" through the country's diverse landscapes.

Popular titles by Chile's top literary artists Pablo Neruda, Gabriela Mistral, and Isabel Allende have been translated into English. Neruda's masterful *Canto General* and *The Heights of Machu Picchu* will make a poetry lover out of anyone. Mistral's

gabriela MISTRAL

In 1945, Gabriela Mistral became the first Latin American woman to win the Nobel Prize for Literature. While Pablo Neruda was embraced in Chile and throughout Latin America for his charisma, passion, and gregarious nature, Mistral was an enigma to her fellow countrymen, an introverted woman whose still waters ran very deep. Reserved, laconic, and stern, Mistral's tragic life found powerful expression in the wistful, haunting, and yearning sonnets for which she was internationally renowned. The dominant themes in Mistral's poetry are love, death, childhood, justice, motherhood, religion, and the power of nature.

Born Lucila Godoy Alcayaga in Vicuña, in 1889, the second daughter of a Basque mother and an Indian/Jewish father, who was both a poet and school teacher, Gabriela embodied a spirit of feisty, Spanish individualism and of Indian stoicism. Tragedy struck Mistral early in life when her father abandoned the family when she was just 3 years old, establishing a heartbreaking pattern of lost love that would haunt her childhood and early adult years.

Gabriela's schooling was short but profound. She began school at the age of 9 but completed just 3 years. However, it was during this time that she discovered her affinity for poetry and began to compose her own poems under the pen name of Gabriela Mistral. Gabriela's older sister Emelina was a teacher and she continued to school Gabriela at home and stirred her desires to become a teacher. At just 16 years old, Gabriela began to support her mother by working as a teacher's assistant.

In 1906, Gabriela moved to La Cantera, where she met a young railway worker named Romeo Ureta. She fell

extraordinary poetry can be found in *Selected Poems of Gabriela Mistral*, in Spanish and English, translated by Ursula K. Le Guin, and Mistral's story has been brought to life for children in the book *My Name is Gabriela* by Monica Brown and John Parra. See the box on Mistral later for more information. Isabel Allende is Chile's most famous contemporary writer, well known for such works as the love-it-or-hate-it *The House of the Spirits, Eva Luna*, and her memoirs of the country she was forced to leave in exile, *My Invented Country*. Chilean expat and writer Roberto Bolaño is considered the most talented of the recent generation of Latin American writers. Though he died in 2003, Bolaño posthumously won the National Book Critics Circle Award for his much-lauded novel *2666*. Bolaño is also known for *The Savage Detectives*, a novel deemed "infrarealistic"; its philosophical narrative centers around young poets in search of a missing Mexican poet.

While not specifically set in Chile, Chilean writer Ariel Dorfman's lauded play *Death and the Maiden* deals with the aftermath of an era of torture and "disappearings." Other works that debate the Allende years and the Pinochet dictatorship that, depending on whom you talk to, are either accurate or dishonest, are ex-Allende translator Marc Cooper's memoirs in *Pinochet and Me*; Roger Burbach's *The Pinochet Affair: State Terrorism and Global Justice*, a scholarly yet lucid account of Allende and Pinochet, with more sympathies for the former than the latter; and Thomas Hauser's *The Execution of Charles Horman: An American Sacrifice*, which was adapted for the 1982 film *Missing*.

Film

The Pinochet regime placed various limits on artistic liberties, which resulted in a dearth of mainstream cinematic production in the country during much of the late instantly in love with him, drawn to his sensitive and tortured soul. Less than 2 years after their relationship began, Ureta committed suicide, an event that affected Gabriela profoundly and from which she never recovered.

After receiving a teaching diploma in 1912, Gabriela began to teach elementary and secondary school to make ends meet until, in 1914, the publication of *Sonetos de la muerte* made her renowned throughout Latin America and earned her a national prize in poetry. In 1922, she published *Desolación* (Desolation), the first volume of her collected poems, an expression of her feelings toward suffering and death. Tragedy struck again when Gabriela's nephew, whom she treated very much as her own son, committed suicide at the age of 17.

An intensely private individual, Gabriela didn't welcome the fame that accompanied her art but she was, however, able to utilize it to full effect to attain her humanitarian ambitions. In 1922, Gabriela was invited by José Vasconcelos, Mexico's minister of education, to establish educational programs for the disadvantaged. One of her achievements was to allow greater access to literature for low-income people living in rural areas through such initiatives as mobile libraries.

In 1923, the Chilean government awarded Mistral the title "Teacher of the Nation." In 1957, Gabriela died in the U.S. Her body was repatriated, and she was buried in Monte Grande. On her tomb are inscribed her own words:

"What the soul is to the body, so is the artist to his people."

20th century. Movie production increased during the 1990s, but a lack of funding has so far precluded international exposure. At the moment, Chileans are renowned for preferring imported American movies (Hollywood movies that have been filmed or set here include *The Motorcycle Diaries, The Quantum of Solace,* and *Missing*) to home-grown independent productions. However, the success of Sebastian Silva's film *La Nana (The Maid),* which received international recognition at the 2009 Sundance Film Festival, seems to have ushered in a new era of cinematic pride and could be the start of a movie industry renaissance.

The Santiago International Film Festival (SANFIC) takes place every August and features national and international cinema (www.sanfic.cl); the **Valdivia Film Festival** takes place in Valdivia in October and highlights Chilean films and documentaries (www.ficv.cl), as does the **Viña del Mar International Film Festival,** which takes place every November (www.cinevina.cl).

Music

Nueva Canción (New Song) is the most significant musical genre in Chile. These lyrical songs first became popular in the 1960s in both Chile and Argentina via the work of troubadours **Atahualpa Yupanqui** and **Violeta Parra;** their songs were instilled with political messages and soon became known in other Latin American countries and the Caribbean. The art form has been highly influential in terms of its political and social impact, most notably during the Pinochet years when many Nueva Canción artists suffered persecution and even death. Perhaps the most legendary Nueva Canción songwriter and singer, **Victor Jara,** was murdered by the Pinochet regime.

Because Nueva Canción's significance peaked during the analog years, it is rather difficult to find CDs and digital recordings but the most popular ones follow. Jara's album *Manifesto* features the haunting love song *Te recuerdo Amanda* as well as *Estadio Chile,* which was later recorded by Violeta Parra as *Ay Canto,* and is the artist's final composition. *Canto a mi América* is the quintessential collection of Violeta Parra, who remains one of South America's most beloved artists. The group **Quilapayún** recorded the anthem *El Pueblo Unido Jamás Será Vencido,* which was one of the most influential Chilean songs of the 1970s.

Today, the folk group **Illapu,** which excels at Andean instrumentals and salsa-tinged ballads, is perhaps the most popular band in Chile. Other popular bands include the funk rock band **Chancho en Piedra,** as well as indie rockers **Lucybell** and **Los Bunkers,** who enjoy a high profile in both the U.S. and the U.K. The immensely popular, Grammy-award-winning, pop rock band **La Ley** split in 2005, ostensibly to work on solo projects, but are still one of the most frequently played Chilean bands. Latin pop diva and darling of the press, **Myriam Hernández,** now in her 40s, has been topping the charts since she was catapulted into the spotlight at age 11. **Los Tres** blend rock with Latin American music such as bolero and the Chilean *cueca.*

EATING & DRINKING IN CHILE

While classic Chilean country-style dishes are as popular as ever, Chilean haute cuisine came to be about a decade ago. Interest in international cuisine and cooking techniques, and a general eagerness by chefs to update and reinvent traditional dishes, has led to something of a gastronomic revolution in Chile. Still, most Chilean restaurants, especially in rural areas and small towns, continue to serve uninspired cuisine of simply prepared, grilled or fried meats and fish paired with mashed potatoes or rice. The country still has a ways to go before it reaches the culinary level of its neighbors Peru and Argentina. Chile's *cocina de autor* (nouvelle and fusion cuisine) can be found mostly in Santiago, at restaurants in tourist-oriented destinations, and most major hotels with talented chefs who usually have studied and worked abroad.

When ordering lunch, opt for the *menú del día, colación,* or *menú ejecutivo,* which is a fixed-price lunch that costs between C$3,500 and C$7,000, and typically includes an appetizer, main course, beverage, and dessert. The lunch *menú* is a cheaper and fresher alternative to anything listed on the *carta* (menu).

What beef is to Argentina, seafood is to Chile, and Chileans eat it all, from sole to sea urchin to conger eel. Oddly though, many Chileans dine on seafood in restaurants but rarely at home, which is why you'll see a larger selection of seafood at any given restaurant than you will in the local grocery store.

Chilean waiters operate at a languid pace, and foreign diners might have trouble adjusting to this. Waiters for the most part in Chile are not service-oriented, and often you'll find yourself craning your neck trying to catch the attention of a waiter who is busy chatting or hiding out in the kitchen. Also, waiters in Chile do not automatically bring the check—you'll have to request it. It is customary to tip 10%, which you may do in cash or by adding the tip onto the credit card slip *before* the card is run through.

The cost to dine in Chile is on the rise, with main courses ranging between C$4,000 to C$9,000; cocktails cost around C$4,000, but then again barmen here make them doubly strong. In this guide, dining prices are shown as the cost of a main course: Expensive is more than C$9,975, Moderate is C$5,225 to C$9,975, and Inexpensive is less than C$4,750.

DINING CUSTOMS   All hotels in Chile, except, occasionally, dirt-cheap hostels, serve breakfast free of charge, which may be a skimpy continental breakfast with coffee, juice, and a roll, or a full "American" breakfast with eggs. Few restaurants serve breakfast outside of major hotels. In Chile, lunch is served between 1 and 3pm, and it is considered the main meal of the day and taken very seriously. Businesses may close during the lunch hour, and it is difficult to reach anyone by phone during this time.

North Americans might need some adjusting to get used to the country's dinner hours. Most restaurants open at 8pm and close at 11pm or midnight, and on weekends they'll stay open until 1 or 2am. Even in private homes, families eat dinner around 9 or 10pm. This giant hunger gap between lunch and dinner has given rise to the Chilean tradition of *onces*—literally "elevenses," or afternoon tea. At home, a Chilean might have a cup of tea with a roll and jam, but you'll find *salones de té* throughout the country that serve complete *onces* that can include rich, sugary cakes, toasted cheese sandwiches, juice, ice cream, and more. Many Chileans have a light sandwich during this time and call it an early dinner.

Food

APPETIZERS   *Entradas* are appetizers or a first course; bar appetizers are known as *picoteos,* which are platters, usually with meat and cheese and other goodies. Appetizers are often the same price or only slightly less than a main course.

SANDWICHES & SNACKS   Chileans favor the traditional, hearty lunch, but many also lunch or snack on sandwiches or *empanadas,* which are tasty fried or baked turnovers filled with shellfish, cheese, or a beef and onion mixture known as *pino.* Sandwiches are outrageously large and often require a knife and fork. A grilled ham and cheese is known as a *barros jarpa,* and a meat and melted cheese is known as a *barros luco.* Then there's the *completo,* a hot dog topped with mustard, mayonnaise, and sauerkraut; or the *italiano,* a hot dog with globs of mayonnaise, mashed avocado, and chopped tomato, an impossibly messy Chilean favorite. Cheap cafes, known as *fuentes de soda* or *schoperías* (from the word *schop,* or draft beer), serve fast snacks and sandwiches. One of the most common and inexpensive dishes is *cazuela,* a satisfyingly delicious soup made with either chicken or beef, and potato, corn, rice, and green beans—*cazuela* is comfort food when you're sick or have stayed out too late the night before.

MEAT   Although Chilean meat consumption is no match for the carnivores of Argentina, they do consume a lot of it. Chileans in the Patagonia region adore lamb, especially when a whole lamb is butterflied, tied to a spit and slowly roasted over a wood fire. Beef and *costillas de cerdo* (pork ribs) are the focal point for the social Chilean *asado,* or barbecue, that commonly begins with an appetizer of *choripán,* or savory sausage served in a roll. The most tender cuts of steak are the *lomo* and the *filete.* One classic beef dish is *plateada* (stewed beef). Pork ribs served with spicy mashed potatoes is a classic Chilean dish, and the *arrollado* (chopped pork blended with spices, rolled up in pork fat and boiled), isn't very attractive but it is out-of-this-world delicious. Chicken can be found on most menus but it is considered an "inferior" meat here. You'll either love or hate *pastel de choclo,* a casserole of ground beef and chicken, topped with a sugary sweet corn crust baked golden brown.

Sustainable Seafood

Much confusion and controversy surrounds the famed "Chilean sea bass," served less and less frequently in North American restaurants because overfishing has brought the fish to the brink of extinction. Its real name is a lot less glamorous: Patagonian toothfish. Sea bass is really *corvina;* you'll want to avoid Patagonian toothfish if you're trying to eat sustainably.

SEAFOOD Fruits of the sea are this country's specialty, and the Chileans' passion for the variety of weird and wonderful shellfish seems limitless. Popular shellfish include *machas* (razor clams), the occasionally hard-to-find *loco* (a meaty, thick abalone), *choros* or *choritos* (mussels), *ostras* (oysters), *ostiones* (scallops), *erizo* (sea urchin), and the outstanding but expensive *centolla* (king crab). Less familiar are *picorocos* (barnacles) and the exotic *piure* (sometimes referred to in English as a sea squirt), an iodine-rich, alien-looking red blob that attaches itself to rocks. The most common fish you'll see on the menu are salmon, the buttery *congrio* (conger eel), *merluza* (hake), *corvina* (sea bass), *albacora* (swordfish), *reineta,* and increasingly, *mero* (grouper), *lenguado* (sole), and *atún* (yellowfin tuna). Popular Chilean-style seafood dishes are *paila marina* (shellfish stew), ceviche (diced raw fish pickled in lemon juice), *chupes* (a creamy casserole made with crab or abalone), or *caldillo* (a fish stew).

VEGETABLES Chile produces an extraordinary variety of fresh, healthy vegetables. Chile's Central Valley is the country's agricultural belt; in the southern regions that are prone to cold weather and heavy rainfall, vegetables are grown in greenhouses—in fact, it seems that every rural household has one in its backyard. Increased greenhouse production in Patagonia has made fresh produce less difficult to come by than in former times, although many tiny markets in rural areas still lack variety and might sell withered, secondary-quality produce. You can order just about any kind of vegetable in an *ensalada surtida,* or assorted salad, including beets, corn, green beans, hearts of palm, and so on. The avocado, called *palta,* is ubiquitous, well-loved, and cheap, as are the tomato and onion, both of which are combined to form an *ensalada chilena.* Vegetarian meals are gaining a foothold in Chile, especially in Santiago, but in rural restaurants you might need to settle for french fries and a salad.

FRUITS As with vegetables, Chile harvests a flavorful assortment of fruits in its central valley, with citrus grown in desert valleys of the northern region. Much of Chile's fruit is exported to the northern hemisphere, especially the U.S. Apples, oranges, and bananas are common, but you'll want to sample exotic fruits such as the *chirimoya* (custard apple), *tuna* (cactus fruit), *pepino dulce* (a sweet pepper that tastes somewhat like melon), or *membrillo* (quince).

DESSERTS Chileans do not consider a meal a meal without dessert, and they often have it at lunch and at dinner, even if it's just chopped fresh fruit or gelatin. Nothing is more Chilean, really, than *mote con huesillo,* a dessert popular during the summer and in rural areas, which combines dried peaches soaked in light syrup and served over barley grain. *Mil hojas* is a cake layered with a "thousand" flaky dough layers; *lucuma,* a butterscotch-flavored fruit, is surprisingly good in cakes and ice cream. German immigration left its mark on Chile's cuisine with dense cakes called *küchen,* a specialty throughout the Lake District. Other desserts to look out for are the gooey, sugary *suspiro limeño,* which originates from Peru, and the *torta tres leches,* made of three kinds of milk (regular, evaporated, and condensed), and ridiculously sweet and rich.

Beverages

Chileans guzzle *bebidas* (soft drinks) such as Coca-Cola, Sprite, or the country's own fantasy flavors, the nuclear-red Biltz and lemon-yellow Pap—you'll just need to try them because their taste defies description. Fruit juice is very popular, sold either in boxes at the supermarket or served fresh in restaurants, cafes, and roadway stalls. These fresh juices are delightful and are usually made of *frambuesa* (raspberry), *naranja* (orange), or *durazno* (peach).

If you love coffee, you're in for a disappointment. High-end restaurants serve espresso drinks or brewed coffee, but even high-tab eateries occasionally try to get away with serving a packet of Nescafe and a cup of boiling water. Ask if a restaurant serves real *café-café,* or if they have an espresso machine. Chileans do not favor *mate* as widely as their neighbors in Argentina, with the exception of southern Chileans in rural Patagonia

The water in Chile is safe to drink (the one exception is tap water in San Pedro de Atacama), though travelers with very sensitive stomachs and pregnant women might stick to drinking bottled water. You'll find bottled water sold everywhere either as *agua mineral sin gas* (still water), or *agua mineral con gas* (sparkling water).

BEER, WINE & LIQUOR   Start your meal the way Chileans do with a pisco sour, a popular aperitif and the national drink of Chile (much to the chagrin of Peruvians, who invented pisco). The cocktail is made with pisco, a grape brandy, fresh-squeezed lemon juice, sugar, and usually an egg white and a dash of bitters. Stick to a maximum of two—these babies are potent!

Chile has garnered worldwide recognition for its excellent wines, the bulk of which are exported to outside markets. If you're looking to bring a bottle home, search for boutique wines not found outside Chile at a specialty wine shop. Moderate-quality wines are low in price by international standards, but expect to pay premium for reserve and icon wines. See p. 167 for info on shipping wine, and chapter 7 for info on many of the country's wineries.

Chile's lager beers are (listed from lightest to strongest): Cristal, Becker, Austral, Imperial, and Escudo. The Peruvian beer Paceña is catching on, as is the Brazilian beer Brahma. Microbrew beers have launched a cottage industry and now travelers can find a dozen or so versions such as Kross, Kunstmann, and Capital. You'll find Corona, Budweiser, Heineken, and Guinness in most shops and restaurants.

SHOPPING IN CHILE

The **handicraft** industry (called *artesanía*) is burgeoning with nonprofit associations supporting local artisans throughout Chile with seed money and sales channels, and today travelers will find an excellent selection of ceramics, wood carvings and utensils, textiles, artistic figurines, and more. *Ferias artesenales* are large handicrafts markets that are as enjoyable for shopping as they are for local color and people watching. The quality of markets varies and some lower-end markets might also hawk goods that are of poor quality or machine-made, so try to stick to markets mentioned in this guide. Also, markets and shops in Santiago for the most part sell the country's best-made handicrafts.

Look out for items made by the indigenous Aymara and Mapuche tribes; *zampoñes* (flutes), *kultrunes* (ceremonial drums), and *palos de agua* (rain sticks). In the northern desert region, **alpaca sweaters, ponchos, heavy wool throws,** and **scarves** are the more readily available and eye-catching souvenirs (and most practical, given the high altitude chill). Crafts markets in La Serena and Chillan feature **leather** items that are quite striking; you can find everything from saddles and stirrups to belts and boots—if you want to look the part, you can even pick up some idiosyncratic *huaso* (cowboy) items such as a straw hat or poncho.

Jewelry, ranging from copper bangles to stunning **lapis lazuli** and **Mapuche silverware,** is Chile's prize purchase. The semiprecious, indigo-blue *lapis lazuli* stone is typically found only in Chile and Afghanistan and is normally set in silver to form pendants, chokers, rings, earrings, and bracelets. While it is generally less expensive than in the U.S. and Europe, it is still a rather pricey investment—a pair of simple lapis lazuli stud earrings costs around C$20,000. It is always best to buy lapis lazuli from a reputable jewelry store (one exception being the excellent Pueblito de los Dominicos market, just west of Los Condes; p. 112), and always look for the deepest color stones, which are considered to be of superior quality. In Santiago, you will find stores along Avenida Bellavista in the Bellavista neighborhood.

The Lake District is the best place to purchase **Mapuche silver ware.** Still worn by indigenous women, these striking silver designs and extravagant headdresses were originally designed to be a show of wealth; the artful fusion of the practical and the decorous in these pieces is both distinctive and dramatic.

Chilean **wine** is considered to be among the finest and best value of the New World wines. Don't get too carried away however; there are strict customs limitations on how much you can take home. See p. 167 for info. If you plan to tour the **pisco** distilleries of La Serena and Pisco Elquí, you can learn about the nuances of the local pisco grapes and make informed decisions on the best bottle to take home for a cocktail-hour pisco sour. See chapter 8 for options.

PLANNING YOUR TRIP TO CHILE

Chile, a gorgeous string bean of a country, is one of the hottest destinations in South America, given its solid tourism infrastructure, ethereal landscapes, and myriad outdoor activities. The country gives visitors the chance to pack a lot of diversity into a single trip. For a start in narrowing down your choices of where to go, see the "Suggested Chile Itineraries" and "Active Vacation Planner" chapters 4 and 5, as well as the "Best Of" selections in chapter 1.

Compared to much of Latin America, Chile is not a country that requires intense advance planning to visit. No vaccinations are required, and most foreign nationals do not require a visa. Politically, Chile is very stable, with an economy that is strong by regional standards with low inflation, although compared to its continental neighbors to the north, it is expensive. Basic questions, such as when to visit and what kind of hotel suits you best, need to be addressed right from the get-go. This chapter provides answers to many trip-planning questions so that you can be prepared when you arrive in Chile.

For additional help in planning your trip, please turn to the "Fast Facts: Chile" chapter on p. 434.

WHEN TO GO

South Americans vacation during the summer from around December 15 to the end of February, and students have a winter break for 2 weeks in July and during Holy Week (*Semana Santa*), the week preceding Easter Sunday. February is especially languid, as all of Chile seems to leave on holiday for the entire month, and consequently the teeming masses seen in popular destinations such as Pucón or Viña del Mar during this time can be overwhelming. Hotels and businesses in tourist areas jack up prices in anticipation of vacationers who come with money to burn. If you travel to Chile during this time, book a room *well* in advance.

Or you can do as most North Americans and Europeans do and come from late September to early December for the spring bloom, or from March to June, when the trees turn color; both seasons have pleasant weather, and destinations around Chile are less crowded or in some cases completely empty of people. In fact, it's preferable to be in the extreme regions of Chile during these "off-seasons." In northern regions, such as San Pedro de Atacama, the searing heat during the summer is a killer. In Patagonia, the fierce wind blows from October to April but is most consistent from December through February.

The only exception to this high-season rule is in Santiago. Summer is in fact the most pleasant time to visit, as Santiaguinos head out for vacation, easing traffic, reducing smog, and dropping rates in most hotels.

Climate

Chile's thin, drawn-out territory stretches over 38 degrees of latitude, encompassing every climate found in the world except tropical. In many areas there are microclimates, pockets of localized weather that can completely alter the vegetation and landscape of a small area.

The northern region of Chile is so dry that some desert areas have never recorded rain. Summer temperatures from early December to late February in this region can top 100°F (38°C), then drop dramatically at night to 30°F (–1°C). Winter days, from mid-June to late August, are crisp but sunny and pleasant; but, as soon as the sun drops, the temperature turns bitterly cold. Along the coast, the weather is mild and dry, ranging from 60° to 90°F (16°–32°C) during the summer.

The Santiago and Central Valley region features a Mediterranean climate, with rain during the winter only and temperatures that range from 32° to 55°F (0°–13°C) in the winter, and 60° to 95°F (16°–35°C) during the summer. Farther south, the Lake District and the Carretera Austral are home to sopping wet winters, and overcast days and rain are not uncommon during the summer, especially in the regions around Valdivia and Puerto Montt.

The Magellanic Region presents unpredictable weather patterns, especially during the summer, with extraordinary windstorms that can reach upwards of 120kmph (75 mph), and occasional rain. The windiest months are mid-December to late February, but it can blow any time between October and April. Winters are calm, with irregular snowfall and temperatures that can dip to 5°F (–15°C).

Public Holidays

Chile's national holidays are New Year's Day (Jan 1), Good Friday (late Mar or Apr), Labor Day (May 1), Remembrance of the War of the Pacific Victory (May 21), Corpus Christi (late May or early June), St. Peter & St. Paul Day (June 26), Asunción de la Virgen (Aug 15), Independence Day and Armed Forces Day, the major holiday of the year (Sept 18–19), Indigenous Day (Oct 12), All Saints' Day (Nov 1), Feast of the Immaculate Conception (Dec 8), and Christmas (Dec 25).

Virtually every business in Chile shuts on public holidays, as is the case with national and local elections (midnight–midnight). Alcohol is not sold on election days.

Chile Calendar of Events

The following are some of Chile's major events and festivals that take place during the year.

JANUARY

Carnival de Valparaíso. Art, theater, and music take to the streets of this bohemian city with a flurry of events at the end of January. Carnival typically lasts 3 days, and there's plenty to see and participate in: art exhibitions, live music, street performances, and literature readings at cafes.

FEBRUARY

Festival Costumbrista Chilote, Chiloé. The city of Castro hosts a celebration of the culture, history, and mythical folklore that makes the island unique. Part of this celebration is centered around making *chicha* from fermented apples and *curanto,* a slowly cooked combo of shellfish and pork steamed over hot rocks in the ground and covered with *nalca* leaves. Early February.

Semana Valdiviana, Valdivia. This grand weeklong event features a variety of maritime-theme activities, contests, expositions, and more. The highlight takes place on the third Saturday of February, the "Noche Valdiviana," when the Río Valdivia fills with festively decorated boats and candles, and the skies fill with fireworks. This is a very crowded event, and advance hotel reservations are essential. Mid-February.

Festival de la Canción, Viña del Mar. The gala Festival of Song showcases Latin American performers and usually one or two hot international acts during a 5-day festival of concerts held in the city's outdoor amphitheater. The spectacle draws thousands of visitors to an already packed Viña del Mar, so plan your hotel reservations accordingly. Late February.

MARCH/APRIL

Fiesta de Cuasimodo. This event is held mostly in towns in central Chile, in which *huaso* cowboys parade through the streets accompanied by Catholic priests who often pay visits to the infirm and people with disabilities. First Sunday after Easter.

JUNE

Fiesta de San Pedro. Fishermen celebrate in towns along the coast of Chile to bring about good fortune, weather, and bountiful catches. They decorate their boats, light candles, arm themselves with an image of their patron saint, and drift along the coast. A great place to check out this event is Valparaíso. June 29.

JULY

La Tirana. Almost abandoned during most of the year, this tiny Atacama Desert village, east of Iquique, hosts Chile's most important traditional religious festivals, including La Tirana ("The Tyrant"), named after a legendary—and legendarily cruel—Inca princess who converted to Christianity

and was martyred. Close to a quarter million of the faithful, including 207 religious associations in colorful costumes, swarm the town for the Virgen del Carmen commemorations. It's best to stay in Iquique, though the dancing goes on all night. Other major pilgrimages here occur on January 5 and 6 (Three Wise Men or Magi), during Holy Week, and on Independence Day. July 10–19.

Virgen del Carmen. The patron saint of the armed forces is celebrated with military parades throughout the country, especially near Maipú, where Chile's liberators O'Higgins and San Martín defeated Spanish forces in the fight for independence. July 16.

Carnaval de Invierno. Two days' worth of parade floats and fireworks inject some cheer into the dank, dark, sub-Antarctic winter in Punta Arenas. Last week of July.

SEPTEMBER

Independence Day. While serious, stiff official commemorative parades are held in Santiago and Valparaíso, everywhere in Chile around "El Dieciocho" (the 18th) and Armed Forces Day (the 19th), festivities abound in *fondas,* mostly outdoor fairs under *armadas,* tree branches and reeds offering shade or a place to string up multicolored light bulbs. The biggest celebration is La Pampilla, near Coquimbo. Grilled meats and *empanadas* abound, along with rivers of wine and pisco, and live traditional music adds to the merry-making under ubiquitous national flags. September 18–19.

Rodeo season kick-off. Chile's rodeo season starts on Independence Day and culminates with a championship in the city of Rancagua around late March or early April. There are a variety of rodeo dates throughout the Central Valley, but September 18 and the championships are festivals in their own right, with food stalls, lots of *chicha* (a fermented fruit cider) drinking, and traditional *cueca* dancing. Contact the Federación de Rodeos in Santiago at ©/fax **2/420-2553,** or visit www.huasosyrodeo.cl for a schedule of rodeos throughout Chile. September 18.

USEFUL websites

o **ContactChile** (www.contactchile.cl): This Santiago-based agency assists foreigners with room rentals, internships, and Spanish-language courses. It also provides travelers with a beginner's guide to Chilean culture, cuisine, transportation, and other tourism-related topics.

o **Chilean Cultural Heritage Corporation** (www.nuestro.cl): Run by the nonprofit, philanthropic Chilean Cultural Heritage Corporation, this is Chile's most comprehensive guide to music, arts, literature, museums, and archaeological monuments. It's an essential site for information about cultural news and events.

o **Chile Inside** (www.chileinside.cl): This agency places travelers in internships, working holiday programs, and volunteer projects throughout Chile. Chile Inside also organizes Spanish-language programs. The agency is run by a group of expats who have been living in Chile for years.

o **South American Explorers** (www.saexplorers.org): The South American Explorers website includes up-to-date information about health and political crises, as well as frequently asked questions, travelogues, discounts, advice, and a quarterly journal. However, information is for members only, and it costs $60 (single) or $90 (couple) to join.

o **Wines of Chile** (www.winesofchile.org): This Santiago- and U.K.-based promotional association for export wines offers information about its 85 member wineries, plus links to the five established wine routes. Or try **www.vinasdechile.cl** for wine-tasting reservation info for Chile's more traditional wineries and wine-related news.

o **AndesWeb** (www.andesweb.com): A blanket guide to ski resorts small and large in Chile and Argentina, with transportation information, snow conditions, and, best of all, a travel forum for swapping information and opinions.

o **Andes Handbook** (www.andeshandbook.cl): The definitive site for mountaineering in Chile, with guides to more than 150 peaks, including location, height, routes, and difficulty ratings. Climbers may also download topographical maps here.

DECEMBER

Fiesta Grande. The remote mining village of Andacollo, south of La Serena, proudly boasts a purportedly miracle-working wooden statue of the Virgin Mary. In her honor, an astounding 400,000 pilgrims congregate here on December 26, following a tradition begun in 1584, with dancers drawing on pre-colonial traditions. A smaller commemoration takes place on the first Sunday in October. December 26.

ENTRY REQUIREMENTS
Passports & Visas

For information on how to get a passport, go to "Passports" in the "Fast Facts, Toll Free Numbers & Websites" chapter—the websites listed provide downloadable passport applications as well as the current fees for processing passport applications. For an up-to-date, country-by-country listing of passport requirements around the world, go to the "Foreign Entry Requirement" Web page of the U.S. Department of State at **http://travel.state.gov**.

Citizens of the United States, Canada, the United Kingdom, Australia, and New Zealand need only a valid passport to enter Chile. Chile charges a **reciprocity fee** upon entry to citizens of the following countries: $140 for the U.S., $61 for Australians, $132 for Canadians, and $23 for Mexicans. Visitors from the U.K. and New Zealand do not pay a fee. The one-time fee is good for the life of a traveler's passport, and is charged when entering through the **Santiago airport only.** Travelers crossing over land do not pay this fee. You may pay this fee at the airport counter (to the left of Customs) with your credit card.

Before entering Chile, you'll need to fill out a tourist card that allows visitors to stay for 90 days. **Do not lose this card,** as you will need to present it to Customs when leaving the country. Also, many hotels waive Chile's 19% sales tax applied to rooms when the guest shows this card and pays with U.S. dollars or a credit card. The easiest (and free) way to renew your 90-day stay is to cross the border and return. For $100, tourist cards can be renewed for another 90 days at the **Extranjería,** San Antonio 580, second floor, in Santiago (© **2/600/626-4222**), open Monday through Friday from 8:30am to 2pm (be prepared for long lines), or at any Gobernación Provincial office in the provinces. The extension must be applied for 1 month before the visa's expiration date. Bring the original card, your passport, and photocopies of the two.

Contact the Chilean consulate closest to you for information about children under age 18 traveling alone, with one parent, or with a third party. Child abduction awareness is on the rise, and there have been cases of customs agents forbidding parents from traveling solo to or from Chile with children. Play it safe and travel with a written authorization by the absent parent(s) or legal guardian granting permission, which must be notarized by the consulate or a reputable notary.

LOST DOCUMENTS

If you lose your tourist card outside Santiago, any police station will direct you to the Extranjería police headquarters for that province (usually the nearest principal city). In Santiago, go to the **Policía Internacional,** Departamento Fronteras, General Borgoño 1052 (© **2/565-7863** or 2/565-7941; note that it may take time for someone to answer), open Monday through Friday from 9am to 5pm.

If you lose your passport, you can get a passport replacement at your country's embassy. See p. 435 for a list. The embassy might require you to file a *constancia* with the police, but without Spanish skills, this can be difficult; call ahead and ask if this document can be waived. It is imperative that you carry a **photocopy of your passport** with you and another form of ID to facilitate the process.

Customs

WHAT YOU CAN BRING INTO CHILE

Any travel-related merchandise brought into Chile, such as personal effects or clothing, is not taxed. Visitors entering Chile may also bring in no more than 400 cigarettes, 500 grams of pipe tobacco, or 50 cigars, and 2.5 liters of alcoholic beverages per adult (ages 18 and up).

WHAT YOU CAN TAKE HOME FROM CHILE
U.S. Citizens
Returning U.S. citizens who have been away for at least 48 hours are allowed to bring back, once every 30 days, $800 worth of merchandise duty-free. You will be charged a flat duty fee for the next $1,000 worth of purchases. Beyond that, any dollar amount is dutiable at whatever rates apply. On mailed gifts, the duty-free limit is $200. Be sure to have your receipts or purchases handy to expedite the declaration process. *Note:* If you owe duty, you are required to pay upon arrival in the United States by cash, personal check, government or traveler's check, or money order, and in some locations, by Visa or MasterCard.

To avoid having to pay duty on foreign-made personal items you owned before you left on your trip, bring along a bill of sale, insurance policy, jeweler's appraisal, or receipt. Or register items that can be readily identified by a permanently affixed serial number or marking—think laptop computers, cameras, and CD players—to avoid problems with Customs. Take the items to the nearest Customs office or register them with Customs at the airport from which you are departing. You will receive, at no cost, a Certificate of Registration, which allows duty-free entry for the life of the item. There is little chance that Customs will seriously question personal items, but it's better to be safe than sorry.

For specifics on what you can bring back and the corresponding fees, download the invaluable free pamphlet *Know Before You Go* online at **www.cbp.gov**. (Click on "Travel," and then click on "Know Before You Go! Online Brochure"). Or contact the **U.S. Customs & Border Protection (CBP),** 1300 Pennsylvania Ave. NW, Washington, DC 20229 (✆ **877/287-8667**), and request the pamphlet.

Canadian Citizens
For a clear summary of Canadian rules, order the booklet *I Declare,* issued by the **Canada Border Services Agency** (✆ **800/461-9999; www.cbsa-asfc.gc.ca**).

U.K. Citizens
For information, contact **HM Customs & Excise** at ✆ **0845/010-9000** (020/8929-0152 from outside the U.K.), or consult the website at **www.hmce.gov.uk**.

Australian Citizens
A helpful brochure available from Australian consulates or Customs offices is *Know Before You Go.* For more information, call the **Australian Customs Service** at ✆ **1300/363-263,** 612/6275-666 from outside Australia, or log on to **www.customs. gov.au**.

New Zealand Citizens
Most questions are answered on the **New Zealand Customs** website at **www. customs.govt.nz**, or by calling ✆ **04/473-6099**.

GETTING THERE & AROUND
Getting to Chile
BY PLANE
Many major airlines serve Santiago's **Arturo Merino Benítez** airport (SCL) with direct flights from Miami, Atlanta, New York, Dallas–Fort Worth, Los Angeles, San Francisco, and Toronto. Fares vary throughout the year but are highest during from December to March and June through August. Nearly all flights are night flights arriving early in the morning.

There are two airline passes available to travelers seeking to visit several destinations in South America: the **Oneworld Visit South America Pass** (www.oneworld.com) and **LAN's South America Airpass** (www.lan.com). Oneworld is an alliance of 12 airlines that include LAN and American, and the South America Pass allows you to custom-plan your itinerary with set flight prices based on the miles covered between destinations. The problem is that travelers must contact each airline separately to book rather than buying through the Oneworld website. LAN's Airpass can be cheaper depending on the time of year, so do a little digging before reserving. LAN's Airpass does not permit open-ended travel whereas the Oneworld pass does, so travelers seeking convenience over price might opt for the latter option.

See the "Fast Facts: Chile" chapter on p. 434 for additional help in booking your air travel to Chile.

FROM NORTH AMERICA The country's national air carrier **LAN Airlines** (℃ 866/435-9526; www.lan.com) has daily flights to Santiago from New York and Los Angeles, and nonstop flights from Miami. Check its website on Wednesdays for cheap, last-minute (and heavily restricted) fares from Miami. **American Airlines** (℃ 800/433-7300; www.aa.com) has daily nonstop flights from Miami and Dallas–Fort Worth, with connections from Vancouver, Toronto, and Montreal. **Delta** (℃ 800/221-1212; www.delta.com) offers nonstop daily flights from Atlanta. Costa Rica's **Lacsa** airline, of the parent company Taca (℃ 800/535-8780; www.taca.com), has flights from San Francisco, Los Angeles, New York, or Miami with a stopover in Costa Rica or El Salvador. **Air Canada** offers nonstop service from Toronto to Santiago (℃ 888/247-2262; www.aircanada.com). *Tip:* The airline with the most gracious service and the best planes (domestically and internationally) is LAN Airlines, by a long shot.

FROM EUROPE & THE U.K. LAN Airlines (℃ 0800/977-6100 in the U.K.; www.lan.com) serves London to Santiago via Madrid, in partnership with Iberia and British Airways, or try booking directly with **Iberia** (℃ 800/772-4642 in the U.S., or 0870/609-0500 in London; www.iberia.com) or with **British Airways** (℃ 0844/493-0777; www.ba.com). **Air France** (℃ 0871/663-3777; www.airfrance.com/uk) has daily flights from London to Santiago via Paris. **KLM** (℃ 0871/231-0000; www.klm.com) and **Lufthansa** (℃ 0871/945-9747; www.lufthansa.com) also serve Santiago.

FROM AUSTRALIA & NEW ZEALAND Qantas (℃ 13-13-13 in Australia, or 0800/808-767 in New Zealand; www.qantas.com) works in conjunction with LAN, offering daily flights from Sydney and Auckland to Santiago. **Aerolíneas Argentinas** (℃ 2/9234-9000 in Australia, or 9/379-3675 in New Zealand; www.aerolineas.com) has five weekly direct flights from Sydney and Auckland to Buenos Aires, Argentina, with a connecting flight to Santiago aboard LAN.

Getting Around
BY PLANE
Given Chile's length, travelers, especially those short on time, must fly if planning to visit several destinations. **LAN Airlines** (℃ 866/435-9526 in the U.S., or 600/526-2000 in Chile; www.lan.com) is the leader of the airline pack in terms of destinations, frequency, and quality of service. LAN serves Arica, Iquique, Calama, Antofagasta, Concepción, Temuco, Valdivia, Osorno, Pucón (Dec–Feb only), Puerto Montt, Coyhaique (Balmaceda), and Punta Arenas. **Sky Airline** (℃ 600/600-2828; www.sky airline.cl) is another Chilean domestic carrier, with daily flights to all major cities.

If you're planning to visit several countries within South America, remember to check out LAN's **South America Airpass,** which allows travelers to custom-book one-way flights around the continent and within Chile, for typically lower prices. See p. 33 for info.

BY CAR

Car rentals for Santiago are totally unnecessary, but they do offer a lot of freedom if you're wine tasting, traveling in the Lake District, or seeing the coast. Weekly rates for a compact vehicle, rented from and returned to the Santiago airport, average about $400 to $485. Prices include basic insurance with no deductible and unlimited mileage, although some companies include full insurance in the price, with the exception of the theft of car accessories such as a stereo. Each company sets its own policy, so comb carefully through the contract before signing it.

You may find cheaper rates by booking via an agency's website before you arrive. Most major American rental-car companies have offices in Chile, which are listed under the appropriate chapter for each company's location. To make a reservation from the United States, call **Alamo** (© **800/906-5555;** www.alamo.com), **Avis** (© **800/3331-1212;** www.avis.com), **Budget** (© **800/472-3325;** www.budget. com), **Dollar** (© **800/800-3665;** www.dollar.com), or **Hertz** (© **800/654-3001;** www.hertz.com). If you haven't made a reservation, you can still rent from an agency kiosk at the airport.

Don't overlook a few of the local car rental agencies for cheaper prices; you'll find their booths at major airports. *Note:* Taking a rental car across the border to Argentina requires advance notification up to 10 days in advance, and a permit that costs C$148,000 and lasts for 1 to 30 days.

You don't need an international driver's license to rent a vehicle—your current driver's license suffices. On major highways and, less frequently, on city streets, police (*carabineros*) set up "control" checkpoints and randomly stop vehicles, but they simply check driver's licenses and registration, and then motion you along.

Driving in Santiago is better than driving in some other capitals, but you'll find more considerate motorists outside of the capital. Drivers use their horn and indicators constantly to signal where they are turning or that they are passing another vehicle—you should, too. On the highway, car and especially truck drivers signal to advise you that it's safe ahead to pass, but don't put your entire faith in the other driver's judgment, and give yourself ample space, as Chilean drivers have lead feet. The concept of "merging" is entirely foreign to Chilean drivers—you'll need to be a little aggressive to get into another lane, or wait until all traffic passes by to enter. Right turns on red are forbidden unless otherwise indicated.

Outside Santiago, especially on roads off Ruta 5 (also called the Pan-American Highway or *Carretera Panamericana*), your major concern will be keeping an eye out for bicyclists and farm animals along the road. Ruta 5, like nearly all major highways in Chile, was expanded and modernized during the last decade, but now **periodic tollbooths** charge *peajes* (fees) that can be quite expensive if driving long distances, ranging from C$400 to C$3,400. Also, tolls are higher from 5pm on Friday to midnight on Sunday. Many country roads are dirt, either smoothed with gravel or washboard bumpy and pothole-scarred. Gasoline is sold in liters and is called *bencina,* and comes in three grades: 93, 95, and 97.

Car-rental agencies provide emergency road service. Be sure to obtain a 24-hour number before leaving with your rental vehicle. The **Automóvil Club de Chile** also offers services to its worldwide members, including emergency roadside service. For more information, contact the offices in Santiago, at Av. Andrés Bello 1863 (© 2/431-1000, or toll-free in Chile 600/464-4040; www.automovilclub.cl).

Good maps can be found at service stations such as the **Copec** *Rutas de Chile,* or reference Copec's website for online maps at **www.chileturcopec.cl**. Rental agency maps are often too basic, or you can pick up a map in the airport when you arrive. The sites **www.mapcity.com** and **www.mapadechile.cl** provide travelers with maps of major Chilean cities.

BY TRAIN

The company **Empresa de los Ferrocarriles del Estado (EFE)** offers high-speed train service from Santiago to Chillán aboard comfortable coaches, stopping along the way in Rancagua, San Fernando, and Talca, and passing through beautiful, pastoral landscapes along the way. Call EFE or check the website for updated information (© 2/585-5000; www.efe.cl), or check with your travel agent or hotel for a reservation.

BY BUS

Traveling long-distance by bus is very common in Chile, and there are many companies to meet the demand. Most Chilean buses are clean and efficient and an excellent transportation alternative, although longer distances, Santiago to Calama for example, can be excruciating, so reevaluate taking a flight, and check www.lan.com for last-minute flights or the cheaper Sky Airline if price is an issue. The main bus companies in the country are **Pullman** (© 600/320-3200; www.pullman.cl), **Tur Bus** (© 600/660-6600), and **Expreso Norte** (© 2/596-1100; www.expresosnorte.cl).

Standard buses go by the name *clásico* or *pullman*. An *ejécutivo* or *semi-cama* is a little like business class: lots of legroom and seats that recline farther. At the top end of the scale is the *salón cama,* which features seats that fold out into beds. A *salón cama* is an excellent way to get to a region such as the Lake District, as riders sleep all night and arrive in the morning. Fares are moderately priced and seats fill up fast, so buy a ticket as far in advance as possible. Ask what is included with your fare, and whether they serve meals or if they plan to stop at a restaurant along the way.

BY FERRY & LOCAL CRUISES

Navimag offers an exceptionally beautiful (some say monotonous) 3-day journey from Puerto Montt (Lake District) to Puerto Natales (Patagonia) or vice versa aboard a passenger/cargo ferry that introduces travelers to remote, virgin fjordland unseen outside of Norway. The journey is very popular with backpackers with a lot of time on their hands and who enjoy the camaraderie that often develops among passengers during the journey. Navimag is not a luxury liner, but there are pricier berths that provide enough standard comfort for even finicky travelers.

Naviera Sur has cargo ferries for vehicles that link Puerto Montt and Chiloé with the Carretera Austral (Chaitén). **Cruce Andino** (operated by Andino del Sud) offers a popular full-day cruise between Argentina and Chile in a boat-bus-boat combination through Vicente Pérez Rosales near Puerto Varas and Parque Nacional Nahuel Huapi Lake at Bariloche, Argentina.

Skorpios has 4- and 7-day cruises from Puerto Montt or Puerto Chacabuco, stopping at Castro and Quellón in Chiloé before or after the Laguna San Rafael Glacier; they also have a dock in Puerto Natales that takes passengers to Pío XI Glacier (the only advancing glacier off the Southern Ice Field) and the remote village Puerto

Eden. **Cruceros Australis** offers an unforgettable journey through the untouched wilderness of Tierra del Fuego. The 3- or 4-day journey begins in Punta Arenas and ends in Ushuaia, Argentina, or vice versa, stopping at Cape Horn (weather permitting). Most travelers do this trip as a one-way journey only, visiting both Chile and Argentina. For more information, see "Ferry Journeys Through the Fjords to Laguna San Rafael," near the end of chapter 12.

MONEY & COSTS

THE VALUE OF THE CHILEAN PESO VS. OTHER POPULAR CURRENCIES

Chilean Peso	US$	Can$	UK£	Euro (€)	Aus$	NZ$
C$475	$1	C$.96	£.61	€.70	A$.97	NZ$1.3

Currency

The unit of currency in Chile is the **peso.** The value of the peso has risen sharply and at press time was 475 pesos to the American dollar and 730 pesos to the British pound. Most prices in this book are listed in pesos, however we have listed prices for hotels and some tour packages in dollars primarily because most hotels show prices in dollars, but also because foreigners are exempt from paying the **19% IVA** (*Impuesto al Valor Agregado*) tax on hotel stays and vacation packages when paying in dollars. In Chile, the peso is indicated with "$" while amounts in U.S. dollars are preceded by "US$." In this book, pesos are listed with the symbol C$ and U.S. dollars are simply preceded by $.

Newly designed in a rainbow of colors, Chilean currency comes in denominations of 1,000, 2,000, 5,000, 10,000, and 20,000 pesos. There are currently six coins in circulation, in denominations of 1, 5, 10, 50, 100, and 500 pesos; however, it's unusual to be issued 1 peso or even 5 pesos. In colloquial Spanish, Chileans call 1,000 pesos a *luca,* as in "It cost *cinco lucas*" (5,000); a 500-peso coin is a *quina.*

Although foreigners are exempt from the IVA tax when paying in dollars for hotel rooms and vacation packages, you might find this is not the case with low-budget hotels and hostels that only take pesos. Do a little math when offered a price in dollars as the peso rate might be cheaper due to a proprietor's improper or inflated exchange rate.

Carry small peso bills and coins with you when traveling around Chile, as corner shops, taxis, kiosks, and other small businesses rarely have change for anything over 5,000 pesos. Also consider keeping the change separate from your larger bills, so that it's readily accessible and you'll be less of a target for theft.

ATMs

A Chilean ATM is known as a *cajero automático,* or more commonly as a **Redbanc,** which is advertised on a maroon-and-white sticker. You'll find ATM Redbancs in banks, grocery stores, gas stations, and pharmacies throughout the country. Redbancs are compatible with a variety of networks, including Visa/Cirrus and MasterCard/PLUS. Before you travel, be sure your ATM can be used overseas and that you know your daily withdrawal limit. **Note:** Chilean banks do not charge a fee to use their ATMs, but check your bank's policy as many charge fees for international transactions.

	US$	UK£	A$	C$
Cup of coffee	3.15	2.05	3.20	3.20
A movie ticket	8.00	5.18	9.40	9.40
Taxi from airport	30	20.45	32.16	32.15
Gallon of gas	5.75	3.70	5.85	5.85
Price of moderate, 3-course dinner for one sans alcohol	31.75	20.45	32.15	32.15

Traveler's Checks

Traveler's checks are something of an anachronism these days—they're accepted at larger hotels but few other places, though they can be changed in most cities and towns. Some travelers feel safer carrying a few traveler's checks just in case, and they can be bought at most banks in denominations of $20, $50, $100, $500, and sometimes $1,000. Generally, you'll pay a service charge ranging from 1% to 4%. Try **American Express** (© **800-528-4800,** or 800/221-7282 for cardholders; the latter number accepts collect calls, offers service in several foreign languages, and exempts Amex gold and platinum cardholders from the 1% fee); **Visa** (© **800/732-1322** or 866/339-3378, where AAA members can obtain Visa checks for a $9.95 fee for checks up to $1,500); and **MasterCard** (© **800/223-9920**). MasterCard also offers a pre-paid **Travel Card** in lieu of traveler's checks. Keep a record of the serial numbers separate from your checks in the event that they are stolen or lost. You'll get a refund faster if you know the numbers.

Traveler's checks, dollars, and euros can be exchanged at a *casas de cambio* (money-exchange houses) for a small charge; *casas de cambio* are generally open Monday through Friday from 9am to 6pm (closed 1–3pm for lunch), and Saturday until 2pm, and there are exchange houses open all day and on weekends at the shopping malls Parque Arauco and Alto las Condes.

Credit Cards

Visa, MasterCard, and American Express are widely accepted throughout Chile, and Diner's Club isn't far behind. Many Chilean businesses are charged a 2% to 4% service fee and will pass that cost on to you, so expect cheaper deals with cash. *Note:* Some hostels and rural hotels and restaurants might not accept credit cards, so it is advisable to always carry pesos if you're planning on visiting these kinds of establishments.

You can withdraw cash advances from your credit cards at banks or ATMs (provided you know your PIN), but this is an expensive option considering that you'll pay interest from the moment of your withdrawal, even if you pay your monthly bills on time. Also, note that many banks now assess a 1% to 3% "transaction fee" on *all* charges you incur abroad (whether you're using the local currency or your native currency).

3

PLANNING YOUR TRIP TO CHILE

Money & Costs

STAYING HEALTHY

Chile poses few health risks to travelers, and no special vaccinations are required. In fact, there are no poisonous plants or animals in Chile. Nevertheless, standard wisdom says that travelers should get tetanus and hepatitis boosters before leaving.

DIETARY AILMENTS Few visitors to Chile experience anything other than run-of-the-mill traveler's stomach in reaction to unfamiliar foods and any microorganisms in them, but even this is uncommon. As a general rule, it's best to eat shellfish only in reputable restaurants or those that are near the sea and receive fresh supplies daily.

In many large cities and towns, Chile's tap water is clean and safe to drink. Seek local advice, if you are in doubt; or, to be on the safe side, drink bottled water—it's widely available throughout Chile. In San Pedro de Atacama, *do not drink tap water,* as it contains trace amounts of arsenic.

ALTITUDE SICKNESS Altitude sickness, known as *puna,* is a temporary yet often debilitating affliction that affects about a quarter of travelers to the northern *altiplano,* or the Andes at 2,400m (7,872 ft.) and up. Nausea, fatigue, headaches, shortness of breath, sleeplessness, and feeling "out of it" are the symptoms, which can last from 1 to 5 days. If affected, drink plenty of water, take aspirin or ibuprofen, and avoid alcohol and sleeping pills—or avoid the condition and acclimatize by breaking the climb to higher regions into segments.

SUN & THE OZONE LAYER Do not take this lightly. Chile's ozone layer, especially in the southern region and Patagonia, is thinner than in the U.S. or Europe, and you'll burn a lot faster here, especially if you're in high altitudes. In Patagonia, "red alert" days (Sept–Nov) mean that fair-skinned visitors can burn within *10 minutes.* Protect yourself with sun block, a long-sleeved shirt, a wide-brimmed hat, and sunglasses. Slap sunscreen on even when at the beach in Viña.

GENERAL AVAILABILITY OF HEALTH CARE

Contact the **International Association for Medical Assistance to Travelers** (**IAMAT**; ✆ **716/754-4883** or, in Canada, 416/652-0137; www.iamat.org) for tips on travel and health concerns, and for lists of local, English-speaking doctors. The U.S. Embassy in Santiago (✆ **2/330-3000;** http://chile.usembassy.gov) also has a list of English-speaking doctors that you can download from the website. The United States **Centers for Disease Control and Prevention** (✆ **800/232-4636;** www.cdc.gov) provides up-to-date information on health hazards by region or country and offers tips on food safety. The website **www.tripprep.com**, sponsored by a consortium of travel medicine practitioners, may also offer helpful advice on traveling abroad. You can find listings of reliable clinics overseas at the **International Society of Travel Medicine** (www.istm.org).

WHAT TO DO IF YOU GET SICK AWAY FROM HOME

Medical care in Santiago is world-class, and many doctors are English-speaking. In smaller towns, always visit a private clinic instead of a public hospital. Some rural areas have only a basic clinic, and you'll need to travel to the nearest large town for more complicated procedures. Numbers for **hospitals** and **emergencies** can be found in "Fast Facts" throughout this guide.

If you suffer from a chronic illness, consult your doctor before your departure—especially if planning to visit high altitudes. Pack **prescription medications** in your carry-on luggage, and carry them in their original containers, with pharmacy labels—otherwise they won't make it through airport security. Carry the generic name of prescription medicines, in case a local pharmacist is unfamiliar with the brand name.

Travel insurance is a must. See "Insurance," on p. 434.

CRIME & SAFETY

Chile is one of the safest countries in Latin America, with little political unrest, corruption, or violent crime. A traveler's principal concerns are pickpockets and break-ins, which are on the rise in cities like Santiago. Never leave valuables in your rental car, and always keep a close eye on your belongings when in public.

Police officers wear olive-green uniforms and are referred to as *carabineros*, or colloquially as *pacos*. Never, ever, think about bribing a police officer—you'll be taken straight to the *comisaría* (police station). Chile's police force is highly respected and courteous to travelers, if just not very effective when it comes to petty crime. If you've been robbed, your insurance company will most likely ask for a police report, called a *constancia*, which you can get at any police station.

Chile is prone to earthquakes, yet major quakes such as the 8.8 quake in 2010 are uncommon, taking place every 20 years or so. If you feel an earthquake begin to rattle, keep the following safety tips in mind. Try to stay where you are; studies show most injuries and deaths occur when fleeing outdoors or trying to move too far from your location. If you are indoors, take cover under something sturdy such as a desk or table or other heavy furniture, or if you are near a load-bearing doorway, stand under that. Stay put until the shaking stops, and then make your way outside as carefully as possible as many are injured from falling debris when taking their first step outside. Do not even think of taking an elevator, since electricity often shorts after an earthquake and you may get trapped inside. If you are outdoors, move away from streetlights, wires, buildings, and anything else that could fall on you. If you're near the coast, consider the very real possibility of a tsunami, and remember the Chilean saying "if an earthquake is strong enough to knock you off your feet, then run for higher ground."

SPECIALIZED TRAVEL RESOURCES

Travelers with Disabilities

There are more options and resources out there than ever before for travelers with disabilities, and here in Chile it is increasingly common to see hotels and restaurants that are wheelchair-accessible. It's best to call ahead (especially with restaurants) to inquire about an establishment's facilities.

Many travel agencies offer customized tours and itineraries to Chile for travelers with disabilities. Among them are **Flying Wheels Travel** (© 877/451-5006; www.flyingwheelstravel.com) and **Accessible Journeys** (© 800/846-4537 or 610/521-0339; www.disabilitytravel.com). **Avis Rent a Car** has an "Avis Access" program that offers such services as a dedicated 24-hour toll-free number (© 888/879-4273) for customers with special travel needs; special car features such as swivel seats, spinner knobs, and hand controls; and accessible bus service.

Organizations that offer assistance to travelers with disabilities include **MossRe-hab** (www.mossresourcenet.org); the **American Foundation for the Blind** (© 800/232-5463; www.afb.org); and **SATH** (Society for Accessible Travel & Hospitality; © 212/447-7284; www.sath.org).

Air Ambulance Card (© 205/297-0060; www.airambulancecard.com) has now partnered with SATH and allows you to preselect top-notch hospitals in case of an emergency.

For more information and resources on travel for those with disabilities, see www.frommers.com/planning.

LGBT Travelers

Gays and lesbians visiting Chile will most likely not encounter any prejudice or outward intolerance. Still, public displays of affection between same sexes are rare, even in metropolitan cities such as Santiago. Attitudes toward gays and lesbians, especially those of Chilean men, are not very liberal, owing in part to the conservative nature of their society. Homosexual relationships have only recently been declared officially legal, and many gays and lesbians are not actively open about their orientation outside their own circles. In Santiago, the two most gay-friendly neighborhoods are Bellavista and Parque Forestal (also known as Bellas Artes).

The best source for information is the website **www.santiagogay.com**, a resource directory that covers gay issues and provides information about travel, gay-oriented businesses and bars, employment, and more. **The International Gay and Lesbian Travel Association** (**IGLTA**; © 954/630-1637; www.iglta.com) is the trade association for the gay and lesbian travel industry, and offers an online directory of gay-and lesbian-friendly travel businesses; go to the website and click on "Members."

For more gay and lesbian travel resources visit www.frommers.com/planning.

Senior Travelers

Seniors, referred to in Chile as *tercera edad*, or "third age," will find plenty of discounts at museums and attractions, but not much else. Members of **AARP,** 601 E St. NW, Washington, DC 20049 (© 888/687-2277; www.aarp.org), get discounts on hotels, airfares, and car rentals. AARP offers members a wide range of benefits, including *AARP The Magazine* and a monthly newsletter. Anyone over 50 can join.

Many reliable agencies and organizations target the 50-plus market. **Elderhostel** (© 800/454-5768; www.elderhostel.org) arranges thought-provoking study programs in Chile for those ages 55 and over. **ElderTreks** (© 800/741-7956; www.eldertreks.com) offers small-group tours to off-the-beaten-path or adventure-travel locations, restricted to travelers 50 and older. **INTRAV** (© 800/456-8100; www.intrav.com) is a high-end tour operator that caters to the mature, discerning traveler (not specifically seniors), with trips around the world that include guided safaris, polar expeditions, private-jet adventures, and small-boat cruises down jungle rivers.

For more information and resources on travel for seniors, see www.frommers.com/planning.

Family Travelers

Chileans are kid-friendly, and family-style lodging and children's specials are the rule, not the exception. Many hotels feature playgrounds, swimming pools, child care, and attached rooms or space for additional beds, and some resorts offer full-scale kids' activities, giving parents a breather and a little "adult time." To locate accommodations, restaurants, and attractions that are particularly kid-friendly, refer to the "Kids" icon throughout this guide. For special travel requirements for children, see "Passports & Visas" earlier in this chapter.

When choosing lodging, check to see if a suite is cheaper than booking two connecting rooms. Most suites have a sofa bed, or at the very least the hotel can add an extra cot-style bed. A good bet for families spending several days in a destination is an *apart-hotel* or a *cabaña*, which are self-catering units with living areas and kitchens—these options are frequently less expensive than a hotel room. Hotel chains such as the Radisson and the Sheraton occasionally offer specials for families with kids, but as a general rule, kids are either free when sharing a room with their parents, or are charged a minimal fee for an extra bed.

For a list of more family-friendly travel resources, visit www.frommers.com/planning.

Women Travelers

Chilean men are more "macho" than Americans or Europeans, but their introverted nature means they aren't prone to whistle and make boisterous comments to women the way that Argentine men do. Some Chilean men do have the annoying, some say creepy, habit of leering. Most women advise to just ignore it rather than say something that will most likely antagonize the situation or egg them on. Hitchhiking in rural areas by single women is common, but exercise caution. A lift up to a ski resort or into a national park that does not have public transportation is usually safe, but longer trips up and down the Pan-American Highway are best undertaken aboard one of the country's cheap and plentiful long-distance buses.

For general travel resources for women, go to www.frommers.com/planning.

Student Travelers

You'd be wise to arm yourself with an **International Student Identity Card (ISIC),** which offers substantial savings on plane tickets and entrance fees in Chile. It also provides you with basic health and life insurance and a 24-hour help line. The card is available from **STA Travel** (© **800/781-4040** in North America; www.sta.com or www.statravel.com; or www.statravel.co.uk in the U.K.), the biggest student travel agency in the world. If you're no longer a student but are still under 26, you can get an **International Youth Travel Card (IYTC)** from the same people, which entitles you to some discounts (but not on museum admissions). **Travel CUTS** (© **800/592-2887** in the U.S. or 866/246-9762 in Canada; www.travelcuts.com) offers similar services for both Canadians and U.S. residents. Irish students may prefer to turn to **USIT** (© **01/602-1906;** www.usitnow.ie), an Ireland-based specialist in student, youth, and independent travel.

For more information on traveling as a student, go to www.frommers.com/planning.

Single Travelers

On package vacations, solo travelers are often hit with a dreaded "single supplement" to the base price. To avoid it, you can agree to room with other single travelers or find a compatible roommate before you go, from one of the many roommate-locator agencies.

Travel Buddies Singles Travel Club (© **800/998-9099;** www.travelbuddies worldwide.com), based in Canada, runs small, intimate, single-friendly group trips and will match you with a roommate free of charge. **TravelChums** (www.travel chums.com) is an Internet-only travel-companion matching service with elements of an online personals–type site, hosted by the respected New York–based Shaw Guides travel service.

For more information on traveling single, go to www.frommers.com/planning.

RESPONSIBLE TOURISM

The principal environmental problems that confront Chile are deforestation and air, water, and land pollution. Currently the loudest protest by environmentalists in Chile involves the struggle against proposed hydroelectric dams on the Baker and Pascua rivers, two of the wildest and most beautiful rivers in the country, located in Patagonia. The group **Patagonia Sin Represas** (Patagonia Without Dams; www.patagoniasin represas.cl) is a powerful collection of national and international environmental groups who are fighting against the Chilean company proposing the dams, HidroAysén. Apart from staunching the flow of the rivers, the company plans to install mammoth power towers and lines that would stretch north to Santiago and beyond, passing through protected areas and creating an eyesore. At presstime, these plans had been approved but were being fought in court.

Santiago's notorious smog problem has been waning as of late, and in 2010 the city reached its lowest levels of smog in 14 years. Still, on heavily polluted days, which typically occur during the winter months due to cold air creating an inversion layer, young children and the elderly are advised to stay indoors. Indoor fires are prohibited in Santiago, and on "pre-emergency days," which occur several times a year, the government regulates car traffic by prohibiting certain license plate numbers from circulating for a day.

Chile is home to more than 50% of the southern hemisphere's temperate forests, yet indiscriminate logging has caused widespread deforestation. Over the past century the forests of the Valdivian Coastal Range have been reduced by 50%. The most publicized case of illegal logging, which has been taken up by environmental agencies that include Greenpeace, is that of the rare *alerce* tree, which can live to 3,500 years and is often called the "South American Sequoia." The *alerce* is similar to Californian redwood trees in its robustness and impermeability, which make it an extremely valuable commodity. Under Pinochet, logging of the *alerce* reached its nadir, and while new laws introduced in 1974 have protected the species under international law, logging still exists due to a loophole that allows for the extraction and commercialization of trees that were cut before the law was passed.

A handful of Chile's 91 mammals are threatened with extinction, such as the Andean Cat (*Felis jacobita*), and many more are vulnerable, such as the *huemul,* a deer that is, along with the condor, the national animal of Chile. About 5% of Chile's 298 breeding bird species are threatened with extinction, most notably the tundra peregrine falcon, the Chilean woodstar, and the ruddy-headed goose. Also threatened are four types of freshwater fish and over 250 plant species. On the other hand, Chile's waters have been designated a whale sanctuary and thus scientists are beginning to see a comeback in whale populations, including humpback and blue whales.

Chile has only recently moved toward thinking green when it comes to designing and running hotels. At the very least, many hotels are turning to solar panels to heat water and provide electricity, while some are striving towards total sustainability. Patagonia, the Atacama, and to a lesser extent Easter Island, have several environmentally friendly hotels and lodges. Hotels in the Patagonia region are some of the

GENERAL RESOURCES FOR responsible travel

In addition to the resources for Chile listed above, the following websites provide valuable wide-ranging information on sustainable travel.

o **Responsible Travel** (www. responsibletravel.com) is a great source of sustainable travel ideas; the site is run by a spokesperson for ethical tourism in the travel industry. **Sustainable Travel International** (www. sustainabletravelinternational.org) promotes ethical tourism practices, and manages an extensive directory of sustainable properties and tour operators around the world.

o **Carbonfund** (www.carbonfund. org), **TerraPass** (www.terrapass. org), and **Cool Climate** (http:// coolclimate.berkeley.edu) provide info on "carbon offsetting," or offsetting the greenhouse gas emitted during flights.

o **Greenhotels** (www.greenhotels. com) recommends green-rated member hotels around the world that fulfill the company's stringent environmental requirements. **Environmentally Friendly Hotels** (www.environmentallyfriendly hotels.com) offers more green accommodation ratings.

o **Volunteer International** (www. volunteerinternational.org) has a list of questions to help you determine the intentions and the nature of a volunteer program. For general info on volunteer travel, visit **www.volunteer abroad.org** and **.idealist.org**.

most innovative on the continent when it comes to sustainability. The striking **Remota Hotel** (p. 391) in Puerto Natales has natural grasses planted on rooftops, simplified heating from appropriate sun exposure, energy-efficient lighting, and low-consumption water systems. At press time, the **explora Salto Chico Hotel** (p. 402), in nearby Torres del Paine, is expected to receive the prestigious LEED certification from the United States Green Building Council in 2011. In 2009, the **explora's Posada de Mike Rapu** (p. 424) in Easter Island became the first hotel in Latin America to attain LEED certification from the U.S. Green Building Council and is the 13th in the world to achieve this distinction. Construction followed LEED recommendations while protecting the delicate surroundings of the island.

Nearby, **Indigo Patagonia** (p. 391) includes an advanced insulation system that requires no central heating for most of the spring and summer, and bright natural solar lighting that reduces the need for bulbs. Inside the hotel, there's extensive recycling. **Patagonia Camp** (p. 403) was built completely on stilts so as to have a minimal impact, and houses a gray-water treatment system and solar-powered lighting. In the Atacama Desert, the hotels **Alto Atacama Desert Lodge & Spa** and **Awasi** are eco-friendly models that contribute to the local community, too. See the website **www.itsagreengreenworld.com** for a list of green hotels in the country.

With their near-nothing eco-footprint, the colorful domes at **EcoCamp Patagonia** (p. 405), inside Parque Nacional Torres del Paine, have been awarded the rigorous Swiss-based ISO 14001 certification. It's the only property in Patagonia to garner this award for its eco-efforts, including using alternative energy, waste water processing, and compost toilets.

As the popularity of **Antarctic tourism** has boomed over the past few years, so have concerns about the safety of both the local ecology and the tourists who are venturing to see the continent. A handful of incidents involving expedition ships sinking, running aground, or hitting rock or ice in Antarctic waters have set off alarm bells. Beginning in August 2011, a new law passed by members of the Antarctic Treaty will enact stricter regulations, including a ban on ships carrying more than 500 passengers, and a limit on the number going ashore at any time to 100. These regulations are voluntary under international law, however, since Antarctica has no internationally recognized governance body.

See "Volunteer Opportunities" under "Special-Interest & Escorted Trips" (p. 44) for info on volunteer trips to Chile.

SPECIAL-INTEREST & ESCORTED TRIPS

Language Classes

There is no shortage of Spanish language schools in Santiago and with the beach and mountains a short ride away, the city provides a great base for an active student life. Most of the city's reputable language schools are located in the residential areas of Providencia and Las Condes and offer total immersion programs with homestays that are usually a 20- to 30-minute journey on public transport from the school. Tuition and accommodation prices are considerably more expensive than other countries in Latin America; expect to pay between $2,500 and $3,000 per month, including lessons (4–6 hr. per day) and accommodations in a private room with a host family, with two meals daily.

AmeriSpan (✆ 800/879-6640; www.amerispan.com) is well established in South America and takes the hassle out of planning; the school, lodging, airport pickup, and other services are all prearranged. Their Santiago school is located in a renovated 18th-century building in Providencia and group classes are limited to seven people. Prices also include organized activities per week. Another big player with a strong reputation is **Spanish Abroad** (✆ 888/722-7623; www.spanishabroad.com). Their school is also in the quiet neighborhood of Providencia, a few blocks from the Metro. Four classes are run daily, with a maximum of six students per class. **Bridge Abroad** (✆ 866/574-8606; www.bridgeabroad.com) offers 4 hours of group lessons and 2 hours of private lessons at their school in Providencia; they also host family accommodations and can arrange a number of activities and excursions. Lastly, the local agency **Chile Inside** (✆ 954/762-7607; www.chileinside.cl) offers Spanish courses in Santiago, Valparaíso, and Pucón.

Volunteer Opportunities

There are literally hundreds of volunteer organizations operating in Chile. Most opportunities are aimed at gap year students and young adults taking work sabbaticals. Opportunities range from teaching English in small towns (TEFL certificates are usually required) to working in orphanages, building schools, community development, environmental conservation, and wildlife and research programs. Accommodations and meals are usually included.

South American Explorers (www.saexplorers.cl) is a wonderful nonprofit organization that has earned cult status among seasoned backpackers, especially those traveling solo with its outreach community feel and volunteer programs. Offices throughout South America provide fact sheets (available online) detailing hotels, transport information, entry requirements, travel advisories, and tour ideas. You are required to become a member of the club ($60 single or $90 for a couple), but if you are a regular visitor to the continent or just an armchair travel junkie, it's well worth it.

Also check out the following websites for details on volunteer programs in Chile:

o Chile Inside (www.chileinside.cl)
o ELI (www.eliabroad.org)
o Mondo Challenge (www.mondochallenge.org)
o United Planet (www.unitedplanet.org)
o VE Global (www.ve-global.org)
o Volunteer Abroad (www.volunteerabroad.com)
o Volunteer Adventures (www.volunteeradventures.com)

STAYING CONNECTED

Telephones

Public phones are not as ubiquitous as they once were, but they do still exist in shopping areas and gas stations, and occasionally on the street. Most phone boxes accept coins, but you will often find them jammed; it's much more efficient to buy a **phone card,** available from newsstands or Metro stations. **Call centers** are also common in Santiago and larger cities; they are often much cheaper and more comfortable than using a public phone, especially if they are privately operated. A local phone call requires 100 pesos; phone cards sold in kiosks offer better rates. Phone cards have individual instructions on long-distance dialing, and phone booths at telephone centers will provide instructions on dialing according to the carrier they use.

To place a call from your home country to Chile, dial the international access code (011 in the U.S. and Canada, 0011 in Australia, 0170 in New Zealand, 00 in the U.K.) plus the country code (56), plus the Chilean area code, followed by the number. For example, a call from the United States to Santiago would be 011+56+2+000+0000. **To place a local call within Chile,** dial the number; for long-distance national calls, dial a carrier prefix, then the area code, and then the number. (To place a collect call, dial a prefix and then 182 for an operator.) **To place a direct international call from Chile,** dial a carrier prefix followed by 0, then the country code of the destination you are calling, plus the area code and the local number.

Cellular numbers are seven digits with a prefix of **9, 8,** or **7.** Here's the tricky part. When dialing from a local landline to a cellphone, you must dial an additional prefix of 09 (for example, 099+000+0000); but this is not the case when dialing from cellphone to cellphone (for example, 9+000+0000). If dialing a cellphone from outside Chile, you'll need an additional prefix of 9 instead of 09 (011+56+9+000+0000). To dial a landline from a cellphone, you must first dial 0 plus the area code (Santiago for example is 02+000+0000).

For tips on calling between Chile and Argentina, see p. 374 in chapter 13.

Cellphones

Chile's two largest phone companies, Entel and Telefónica, operate on a GSM 1900 MHZ frequency. Any dual or multiband GSM cellphone will work in Chile, but you'll pay expensive roaming rates; check with your cellphone company before leaving. (In the U.S., T-Mobile and AT&T/Cingular use this quasi-universal system; in Canada, Microcell and some Rogers customers are GSM.)

If your cellphone does not have this capability, you can rent a phone before you leave home. Pre-departure, North Americans can rent a phone from **InTouch USA** (*©* **800/872-7626;** www.intouchglobal.com) or **RoadPost** (*©* **888/290-1616** or 905/272-5665; www.roadpost.com). InTouch will also, for free, advise you on whether your existing phone will work overseas; simply call *©* **703/222-7161** between 9am and 4pm EST, or go to **www.intouchglobal.com/travel.htm**.

It is difficult to rent a phone in Chile; instead consider buying a cheap prepaid phone from **Entel** or **Telefónica-Movistar** for between C$10,000 and C$15,000 that comes with C$10,000 to C$20,000 worth of minutes already charged to the phone. Both **Entel** and **Movistar kiosks** are located on the departure level at the Santiago airport and have stores around the city.

Internet Access

Nearly every hotel in Chile has an Internet station, but if for some reason they don't, **cybercafes** are commonplace and clustered around all commercial areas in every city's downtown area. Midrange and upscale hotels have Wi-Fi even in remote destinations (some use satellite phone systems that can be slow), but you'll often need to use it in common areas rather than your room. See individual "Fast Facts" throughout this book for recommendations of Internet cafes.

TIPS ON ACCOMMODATIONS

In most cities and towns throughout Chile you will find a broad range of accommodations choices, but one thing is clear: hotel rates have shot through the roof during the past couple of years. Even hotels that are nothing more than high-end hostels are charging upwards of $100 without the service and amenities a traveler would expect for such a high price tag. On the low end, hostel options start at $40 for a shared bathroom and $60 for an en-suite room, and about $15 to $20 for a shared room with bunks. There are several great-value gems listed in the guide, but for the most part expect small rooms and a paucity of services. Midrange hotels run about $80 to $160 and offer a more salubrious aura, dapper service, and plusher rooms. Expensive hotels run $160 to $250, and luxury hotels will set you back $250 to $400 per night, including locally owned properties and chains such as the Ritz Carlton and the Grand Hyatt. A new wave of charming adobe-style lodges and decadent spas also provides a perfect fusion of style and substance. Boutique hotels that had been curiously missing from the Chile hotel scene are now gaining a foothold, especially in Valparaíso.

It is imperative that you consider Chile's high season when planning your trip, as prices are sky-high and reservations are hard to come by without advance planning. High season runs from December to the end of February, as well as Easter week and a 2-week school holiday in July. Hotels in tourist regions may extend their high season to include November and March. Hotels drop their prices from 15% to 50% in the off-season. Hotel price ranges listed in this guidebook reflect low- to high-season rates.

The prices listed in this book are also **rack rates**—that is, a hotel's standard or advertised rate. Don't be shy about negotiating a discount with a hotel. Owners are accustomed to paying a 20% commission to tour operators, so they will often consider dropping the price slightly during the off-season (or for multiday stays). Alternately, check a hotel's website or simply ask if there is a promotion or package deal being offered that you're not aware of. Remember that if you pay in Chilean pesos for a room that's quoted in U.S. dollars, you'll often have to pay an IVA tax. Sometimes euros may also be accepted, but don't expect to be able to pay in any other foreign currency. See "Currency" above for more information.

A sales tactic that is creeping its way into the cheap hotelier's lingo is the "bed-and-breakfast," but don't buy it. The term is redundant because every hotel, with the exception of the dirt-cheap hostel, includes breakfast in its price. Expect a continental breakfast at inexpensive and moderately priced hotels and an "American" or buffet breakfast at larger, high-end hotels.

Note: Air-conditioning is not necessarily a given in many hotels throughout the country. In general, this is not a problem. Cooler nights and a well placed ceiling fan are often more than enough to keep things pleasant.

Hotel Options

APART-HOTEL   This amalgam is exactly what it implies: an "apartment-hotel," or a hotel room with an additional living area and kitchen. Found primarily in Santiago and other large cities, they offer a wider range of services than a *cabaña*. Some are bargains for their price and come with maid service. However, some are nothing more than a hotel room with a kitchenette tucked into a random corner.

CABAÑAS   *Cabañas* are a versatile lodging option. They are commonly found in resort areas and are popular with families and travelers seeking an independent unit. They resemble cabins or chalets and range from bare-bones to deluxe, although all come with fully equipped kitchens, and most have maid service, a swimming pool, and a BBQ area.

HOSTERÍAS   An *hostería* is a guesthouse or hotel attended by its owner, typically found in a country setting.

RESIDENCIALES & HOSTELS   These lodging options are for budget travelers. *Residenciales* are private homes whose owners rent out rooms, and they range from simple, clean rooms with a private or shared bathroom to ugly spaces with creepy bathrooms. In towns that see more tourists, a hostel can be a hip and very comfortable place run by foreigners or Chileans, typically from Santiago. Some hostels are private homes that use their living area as a common area, and some of them can be very comfortable, but they are almost always full of backpackers and younger travelers.

REFUGIOS   *Refugios*, which are common in Patagonia, are remote and rustic lodges that are similar to cabins. They are wonderful places to mix and mingle with fellow trekkers, and allow you to hike without a heavy pack loaded with a tent. Still, you'll want to bring your own sleeping bag, and book your bunk at *refugios* months ahead of time to secure your spot.

SUGGESTED CHILE ITINERARIES

Chile is home to a staggering array of formidable landscapes, each beautiful in its own way and offering a broad spectrum of otherworldly attractions and adrenaline-infused activities that will live long in the memory.

Chile has it all: gorgeous wine country framed by an Andean backdrop; wild whitewater rapids; sea kayaking; country lanes perfect for biking; trekking and skiing in the stunning Andean peaks; surreal cityscapes in poetic Valparaíso; lunarlike desert landscapes, and so much more.

Although the country is South America's adventure travel capital, Chile is laid-back and many travelers find equal pleasure in relaxing with a good book in truly breathtaking surroundings, wine tasting, taking long walks along the beach, or in sightseeing drives or "photo safaris." There are some travelers who come for a specific sport and plan their entire journey around it, such as skiing, rafting, or fly-fishing. Some lodges take the guesswork out of trip planning with all-inclusive packages that include excursions, transportation, and meals, although most of these lodges are luxurious and pricey. A cheaper option is to book your own lodging directly and arrange day activities with local operators.

Chile is one heck of a long country, and so flying makes the most sense to get around, especially if you are short on time. Increased flight service by the country's two domestic airlines as well as new direct routes have cut down on travel time, but still plan on losing a half-day to a full-day traveling. Whatever your destination, it is recommended that visitors spend at least 1 night and a full day in Santiago to visit historical attractions, and to witness the many changes unfolding in Chile's capital. The city also works as a base for wine-tasting, day jaunts to the coast, and day ski trips.

Independent travelers will find driving to the coast or to wine country quite straightforward, but make certain you carry good maps and directions to your destination. The Lake District provides many photo-worthy sightseeing drives. DIY travelers who are not planning to take long hikes can also rent a vehicle in Punta Arenas and explore southern Patagonia on their own. You'll never need a vehicle in Santiago. See "By Car" under "Getting Around Chile," in chapter 3, for more information about driving in Chile.

The following itineraries are blueprints for memorable vacations that can be adhered to explicitly, modified according to your desires and likes, or even expanded if you're lucky enough to have a longer vacation.

REGIONS IN BRIEF

Sandwiched between the Andes and the Pacific Ocean, Chile's lengthy, serpentine shape at first glance seems preposterous: nearly 4,830km (3,000 miles) of land stretching from the arid northern desert to the wild desolation of Patagonia, and a width that averages 180km (112 miles). Chile encompasses such a breathtaking array of landscapes and temperate zones (the only zone not found here is tropical), it is hard to believe such variation can exist in just one country.

SANTIAGO & THE CENTRAL VALLEY The central region of Chile, including **Santiago** and its environs, features a mild, Mediterranean climate. This is Chile's breadbasket, with fertile valleys and rolling fields that harvest a large share of the country's fruit and vegetables; it is also Chile's main wine-producing region. Santiago's proximity to ski resorts, beach resorts, and the idyllic countryside, with its campestral and ranching traditions and colonial estates, offer plenty for the traveler to see and do. The character-rich port town of **Valparaíso,** an hour west of Santiago on the Pacific Coast, makes a fascinating base for your stay in the middle part of the country, an alternative to Santiago altogether. It's just south of the posh resort city of **Viña del Mar.** See chapter 7.

LA SERENA & THE ELQUI VALLEY Known as the "Norte Chico," or the small north, this region is best-known for **La Serena,** a resort town that boasts long, golden beaches and is popular with Chilean summer vacationers. It is also one of Chile's oldest cities and its colonial heritage is very much in evidence. High up in the Andes, the **Elqui Valley** is well-known for its astronomical observatories, some of which are open to the public, and a general New-Age vibe that might remind some of Sedona. See chapter 8.

THE DESERT NORTH This region claims the world's driest desert, a pastel-colored "wasteland" set below a chain of rust-colored volcanoes and high-altitude salt flats. The sun-baked **San Pedro de Atacama,** a pueblo typical of the region, is the main oasis, and the best place to base your trip. Some of the finest lodges in the country are located here. Nearby are plentiful and well-preserved Indian ruin sites. The arid climate and the geological forces at work in this region have produced far-out land formations and superlatives such as the highest geyser field in the world. See chapter 9.

THE LAKE DISTRICT Few destinations in the world rival the lush scenery of Chile's Lake District. This region is packed with a chain of conical, snowcapped volcanoes; glacier-scoured valleys; several national parks; thick groves of native forest; hot springs; and, of course, many shimmering lakes. Temperatures during the summer are normally warm and pleasant, but winter is characterized by overcast days and drizzling rain. It's an outdoor lover and adventure seeker's paradise, especially in **Pucón** and **Puerto Varas.** See chapter 10.

CHILOÉ Chile's enigmatic island Chiloé is made of emerald, rolling hills, tiny fishing villages, antique Jesuit wooden churches, and a way of life notably different from the Chilean mainland, due to nearly 300 years of virtual isolation. A visit to Chiloé often feels like stepping a century back in time with most residents still employing old-fashioned farming methods and using animals in all factors of life. Mythology also plays into the local psyche here. See chapter 11.

THE CARRETERA AUSTRAL Chile's Southern Highway, or the Carretera Austral, stretches nearly 1,000km (620 miles) from Puerto Montt to Cochrane in northern Patagonia. From here, it is only possible to reach southern Patagonia via Route 40 in Argentina as Chile breaks into hundreds of islands and is impassable by vehicle. The half-paved, half-dirt Southern Highway winds through virgin rainforest and rugged terrain, and is visited by relatively few travelers. It could be one of Chile's best-kept secrets. One of the region's major attractions is the Parque Nacional Laguna San Rafael, but this is visited by boat or cruise line. See chapter 12.

PATAGONIA & TIERRA DEL FUEGO Also known as the Magellanic Region, this part of the southern end of the continent has soared in popularity over the past 15 years, drawing visitors from all over the world to places such as **Parque Nacional Torres del Paine.** Chilean Patagonia officially begins in the south of the Lakes District, but Patagonia is really characterized by vast, open steppe; the colossal Northern and Southern ice fields and the glaciers that descend from them; the rugged peaks of the Andes as they reach their terminus; and a myriad of fjords and sounds that wind around thousands of uninhabited islands. Chilean Tierra del Fuego's principal town is **Porvenir,** but this is just a windswept village with little to interest tourists; Tierra del Fuego's major destination and port of call is Ushuaia, on the Argentine side. **Puerto Williams,** located on Isla Navarino on the Beagle Channel, is the world's southernmost town and a military base and port. See chapter 13.

EASTER ISLAND Easter Island ("Rapa Nui" to locals) is the world's most remote island, about a 5-hour flight from Santiago. Annexed by Chile in 1888, the island is famous for its *moai* sculptures. The entire island is a veritable living museum, known for its two white-sand beaches, scuba diving in the island's crystal-clear, periwinkle blue water, wild horses at every turn, and a people whose Polynesian culture is thriving despite having been nearly decimated. This is a destination that will exceed expectations, but bring a hang-loose attitude. See chapter 14.

CHILE IN 1 WEEK

Travelers with just 1 week in Chile are well advised to choose one major destination (Patagonia, the Lake District, the Atacama, or a weeklong cruise through fjordland) and plan for a 2-day visit to Santiago, a wine region, or the coast. Alternatively, travelers may spend a week in Chile's Central Valley and divide their time among the many activities the region presents.

Day 1: Santiago

Arrive and get settled in **Santiago.** Chances are your flight arrived early in the morning; once you've rested and freshened up, head to **Cerro San Cristobal** and its **Metropolitan Park** (p. 107) for sweeping views of the city and to get your bearings. Afterward, take a stroll around the bohemian Barrio Bellavista and pay a visit to **La Chascona** ★★★ (p. 108), the former home of Pablo Neruda and now a museum. Head to "el centro" and the **Plaza de Armas** (p. 101) and tour the city's historical quarters, with a visit to the colorful **Mercado Central** ★★★ (p. 107). Walk back toward the Alameda and take a peek

Chile in 1 or 2 Weeks

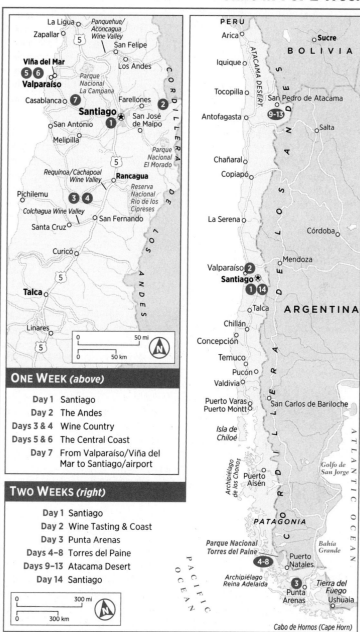

ONE WEEK (above)

Day 1 Santiago
Day 2 The Andes
Days 3 & 4 Wine Country
Days 5 & 6 The Central Coast
Day 7 From Valparaíso/Viña del Mar to Santiago/airport

TWO WEEKS (right)

Day 1 Santiago
Day 2 Wine Tasting & Coast
Day 3 Punta Arenas
Days 4–8 Torres del Paine
Days 9–13 Atacama Desert
Day 14 Santiago

at the **Palacio de la Moneda** ★★★ (p. 103). If you aren't exhausted and still have time, stroll up to the **Bellas Artes** neighborhood and take a load off with an ice-cream cone at **Emporio La Rosa** ★★ (p. 91). Later that evening, order a frosty pisco sour and dine on traditional Chilean bistro food at **Bar Liguria** ★★★ (p. 117).

Day 2: The Andes

During the summer, there's no shortage of adventurous activities, especially in the mountain valley **Cajón del Maipo,** located between 45 minutes and 2 hours (depending on how far up the valley you travel) from Santiago. Raft the Class III and IV rapids on the Maipo River, pretend you're Butch Cassidy or the Sundance Kid and horseback ride along Andean ridges that open out to sweeping views, or put on a pair of hiking boots and trek to a glacier in **Parque Nacional El Morado** (p. 152). Oenophiles will want to include a stop at the **Concha y Toro** (p. 166) winery that is near the mouth of the valley. During winter, grab a shuttle and ride 1 to 1½ hours up to nearly 3,000m (9,840 ft.) in the **Andes Mountains** for a day of skiing or snowboarding at **Valle Nevado** (p. 183), **La Parva** (p. 185), or **El Colorado** (p. 186). Gear rental is available at all three resorts.

Whatever you decide to do during the day, head back to your hotel in Santiago to indulge in an exquisite dinner at one of the city's finest restaurants, such as **Opera** (p. 93) or **La Mar** (p. 100).

Days 3 & 4: Wine Country

The **Colchagua Valley** is Chile's "Napa Valley," with good hotels (some very luxurious) and a well-structured wine tasting circuit. Leave early from Santiago for a scenic 2½-hour drive that features outstanding Andes views. Before entering Santa Cruz, stop at one of the region's oldest wineries, **Casa Silva** ★★ (p. 174), where you can sample excellent wines paired with a delicious lunch. Alternatively, consider visiting **Viña Viu Manent** (p. 176), which offers carriage rides and horseback riding, and **MontGras** (p. 175), which has biking. After spending the late afternoon strolling around the typical rural town of **Santa Cruz** (p. 173), lodge and dine at the **Hotel Santa Cruz Plaza** ★ (p. 178). If you really want to splurge, stay at the luxurious **Clos Apalta** ★★★ (p. 174), one of the world's most talked about wineries, and revel in the luxurious facilities and fabulous array of activities on offer. Whether you stay or not, do book a visit here to wine taste on day four. Have lunch at **Vino Bello** ★ (p. 180), then visit **Montes** ★★ (p. 175) winery for a tour and tasting.

Days 5 & 6: The Central Coast

Your fifth day involves driving north and then west from Santa Cruz to **Valparaíso** ★★★ (p. 133), a 3½- to 4-hour drive. Along the way, you have the option of stopping just outside of San Fernando for a wine tasting at **Casa Silva** ★★ (p. 174) if you didn't stop here on the way in. Spend the afternoon getting lost along the kooky, twisty streets of Valparaíso, soaking up the old port town ambience, and reveling in sublime views over a light lunch at **Café Turri** ★★ (p. 145). Then visit **La Sebastiana** ★★ (p. 137), the former home of Pablo Neruda. If it's the weekend, have dinner at the city's best restaurant, **Pasta e Vino** ★★★ (p. 146); otherwise enjoy a romantic meal with sparkling panoramas at **Montealegre** ★★ (p. 146). If you are enticed by the notion of a lively beach scene, you will want to spend your next day in **Viña del Mar** (p. 122), or even spend the night at the fabulous **Hotel Del Mar** ★★★ (p. 127).

Day 7: Valparaíso or Viña del Mar to the Airport

On your last day, rest up for your flight back at the beach in Viña, take a scenic coastal drive, or, if you haven't already had your fill of Chilean wine, stop at the **Viñedos Orgánicos Emiliana** ★★ (p. 164) and **House of Morandé** ★★ (p. 166) wineries on the road back to the airport. Arrive in time for your evening flight out of Santiago.

CHILE IN 2 WEEKS

Travelers with 2 weeks and a well-planned itinerary can squeeze in several of Chile's highlights and still travel at a pace that allows for some relaxation. The exception to this is a journey that includes all long-distance destinations such as Patagonia, Easter Island, and the Atacama, in which case you'll spend a lot of time traveling and little time actually visiting. The itinerary laid out below is geared toward both the adventurous traveler and the low-key traveler, and it is a classic journey in the sense that it takes you to Chile's extremes in terms of distance, culture, and landscapes. If it seems too ambitious, low-key travelers might consider following the 1-week itinerary described earlier and combining it with a visit to one long-distance destination. Seriously active travelers will find a home in Pucón; the sheer variety of active excursions here can keep you busy for more than a week. This itinerary includes Patagonia, the Lake District, and the Atacama Desert, but the Atacama could easily be replaced with a 4-day journey to Easter Island. Another option for this itinerary would be to drop the Lake District and add extra days to your Atacama and Patagonia visit.

Day 1: Santiago

Spend as described in "Chile in 1 Week: Day 1," earlier.

Day 2: Sip Wine & See the Coast

Head west from the capital, stopping first for some wine tasting in the **Casablanca Valley** (p. 162). Then, continue on to colorful **Valparaíso** ★★★ (p. 133) for lunch and a walking tour of Chile's most storied port town. Finish the day with a pisco sour by the beach at **Viña del Mar** (p. 122). Return to Santiago, or spend the night at an oceanfront hotel in Viña or a cozy B&B in Valparaíso.

Day 3: Punta Arenas or Penguins

After breakfast by the sea, head to the Santiago airport and catch a midday flight south to **Punta Arenas** ★ (p. 374). Spend the late afternoon touring the city, including the Alice-in-Wonderland city cemetery, the Strait of Magellan port, and the Museo Braun Menéndez. Or if you're visiting from October to March, plan for a 5pm visit to a **penguin rookery** (p. 382) to watch these amusing birds waddle out to sea. In the evening, dine on the region's specialty, king crab, at **Damiana Elena** (p. 385).

Days 4-8: Parque Nacional Torres del Paine

Head out early from Punta Arenas to **Torres del Paine** (p. 394), Chile's breath-takingly beautiful national park. Spend the following days hiking, horseback riding, or touring the park by van. Hotels, such as explora and Patagonia Camp, offer all-inclusive packages that include lodging, meals, and day tours with bilingual guides. Or plan to backpack the "W" trail, sleeping in tents or in comfortable *refugios* (shelters). Either way, don't miss **Glacier Grey** and, if you can hack it, the 6-hour **Towers hike** to the granite spires that give the park its name. Your final day is mostly spent driving back to Punta Arenas for an afternoon flight to Santiago, connecting to Calama, before arriving in **San Pedro de Atacama ★** (p. 218).

Days 9-13: Explore the Enigmatic Atacama Desert

Wake up in the driest desert in the world. Spend the day lazily strolling the dirt streets of charming San Pedro de Atacama, and visit one of the best pre-Columbian museums in South America, the **Museo Arqueológico Padre le Paige** (p. 221). Book a nighttime astronomy tour; these are the some of the clearest skies in the world. During the next few days, hike or bike to **Atacama Indian ruins** (p. 217); visit the Salt Lake at **Laguna Cejar** (p. 222) and take a dip; drive up to lofty, turquoise Altiplanic lakes and salt flats; view the world's highest geyser field at sunrise; and finish the day with a soak in a hot spring. On your final day, book a midday flight back to the Santiago airport, spending the night in a different neighborhood than at the beginning of your trip. If you've been to Las Condes, try the gorgeous **Aubrey hotel** (p. 85) in Bellavista.

Day 14: Back in Santiago

Spend the day shopping for gifts at **Pueblo los Dominicos** (p. 112) or at **Patio Bellavista** (p. 112). Visit any attractions you were unable to see on your first day in Santiago, or head up to the city's burgeoning **Vitacura** neighborhood and its excellent **Fashion Museum** (Museo de la Moda, p. 109). Also go for a bike ride in Vitacura's **Parque Bicentenario,** or visit any of the happening new art galleries that now crowd the streets here. Later that evening, head to the airport for your flight home.

CHILE FOR FAMILIES

Chile is a veritable traveler's paradise for families. Chileans love kids, and the tourism industry goes out of its way to cater to families, including offering children's rates, kids' menus, jungle gyms, and scheduled activities; many larger resorts offer free babysitting for young children. While the long-distance travel can be tiring, Easter Island is a fun place for children, with its easy walks, beaches, and ocean water that is noticeably warmer than Chile's coast, fun forays to visit moai sculptures, caves to explore, and snorkeling. To include Easter Island in the following itinerary, spend Day 1 in Santiago, Days 2 to 4 in Pucón, Day 5 in transit from Pucón to Easter Island, and Days 6 to 8 on the island; return to Santiago on Day 9, and see the city's sights on Day 10 before catching your evening flight home.

Chile for Families & Wine Lovers

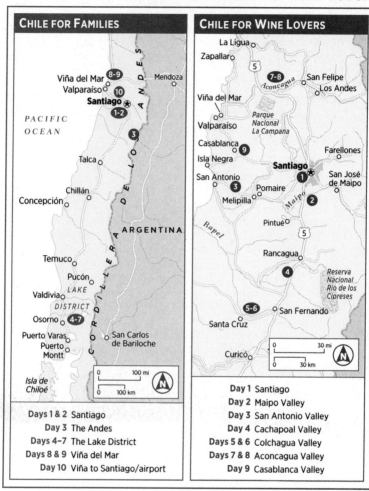

CHILE FOR FAMILIES

Days 1 & 2 Santiago
Day 3 The Andes
Days 4–7 The Lake District
Days 8 & 9 Viña del Mar
Day 10 Viña to Santiago/airport

CHILE FOR WINE LOVERS

Day 1 Santiago
Day 2 Maipo Valley
Day 3 San Antonio Valley
Day 4 Cachapoal Valley
Days 5 & 6 Colchagua Valley
Days 7 & 8 Aconcagua Valley
Day 9 Casablanca Valley

Days 1 & 2: Santiago

Arrive and get settled in **Santiago.** If it is summer, stay in a hotel with a swimming pool, or head up to the **Metropolitan Park** at Cerro San Cristobal (p. 107), which has lovely public pools for summertime swimming. Kids love the park's funicular and especially the city's zoo, the **Jardín Zoológico** (p. 108). Here your kids can view animals endemic to Chile, such as the puma, condor, and guanaco. Next, kids should get a kick out of checking out the weird seafood displayed at the **Mercado Central** ★★★ (p. 107); after lunch or an early dinner there, you can visit **Parque Quinta Normal** (p. 108) with its kid-friendly museums and beautiful gardens. For more kid-oriented activities in Santiago, see "Especially for Kids" in chapter 6.

Day 3: The Andes

A trip to Chile wouldn't be complete without heading high into the famous **Andes Mountains** that tower above Santiago. If it's winter, grab a shuttle and head up to one of the three ski resorts that lie within 1 to 1½ hours of the city: **Valle Nevado** (p. 183), **La Parva** (p. 185), or **El Colorado** (p. 186). You can rent gear when you get there, and resorts offer ski lessons tailored to kids. During the summer, there's no shortage of kid-friendly activities, especially in the mountain valley **Cajón de Maipo** (p. 166), located roughly 45 minutes or 2 hours (depending on how far up the road you travel) from Santiago. Raft the Class III rapids section of the **Maipo River,** or horseback ride along **Andean ridges** that open out to sweeping views. If it's warm out, spend the night at a cabin at **Cascada de las Animas ★** (p. 153), which has an outdoor pool, horses, and hiking trails.

Days 4–7: The Lake District

Hop on a flight to Temuco, gateway to the idyllic mountain village **Pucón** (p. 261). During January and February, Pucón is packed to the rafters with vacationing families, and though it's busy during this time, there are certainly a lot of other kids for your children to meet. Book a self-catering *cabaña,* rent a car, and spend your days taking easy to moderate hikes through lush forest, bike riding around town, relaxing and swimming at **Lake Villarrica's** beach (p. 266), or visiting a fun hot spring such as **Termas Geométricas ★★★** (p. 277). Three activities your kids will love are Pucón's canopy adventure; a horseback ride and farm visit at **Fundo Huifquenco ★★★** (p. 260); and rafting the **Trancura River** (p. 265). The beauty of Pucón is that you can do as little or as much as you'd like, and there are plenty of outstanding restaurants and shops. Full-service hotels such as the **Gran Hotel Pucón** (p. 266) and **Las Cabañas Metreñehue ★** (p. 268) have children's activities and are located next to the lakeshore.

Days 8 & 9: Viña del Mar

Kids love the beach any time of the year, and 2 days in **Viña del Mar** (p. 122) gives you a chance to relax; visit a couple of kid-friendly museums, such as the **Museo de Arqueología e Historia Francisco Fonck ★★** (p. 126); take a buggy ride; or play in a park. The **Hotel San Martín ★★** (p. 128) has reasonably priced suites that work well for families, or pay a little extra for the **Hotel del Mar ★★★** (p. 127), which has a children's entertainment center and on-site day care.

Day 10: From Viña to the Airport

Viña is a convenient last-day destination, since the airport lies on the highway back to Santiago, allowing you to max out your day with fun (and tire your kids out), in preparation for the flight home in the evening.

CHILE FOR WINE LOVERS

Chile's wine tourism industry has gone from the dark age to the enlightened age in just a decade. Wineries have built hotels and B&Bs; opened gourmet restaurants, spas, and tasting facilities with normalized operating hours; and created such complementary activities as horse-and-buggy rides through vineyards, bicycling, and hiking.

Prices are only slightly less than in comparable wine regions such as Napa Valley; however, in Chile you can still enjoy wine tasting without the crowds and savor the antique charm and slow pace of the colonial towns for which the Central Valley is known. The following 10-day itinerary covers the top wine-growing regions, concentrating on wineries that currently produce the best varieties in Chile.

Day 1: Santiago

Arrive and get settled in **Santiago**—this will be your base for the next 3 nights. Spend the first part of your day as described in "Chile in 1 Week: Day 1," earlier. Before heading back to your hotel, take a stroll through picturesque **Parque Forestal** (p. 106). Enjoy a fine Italian meal and excellent service at **Pasta e Vino** ★★★ (p. 146), in the lovely environs of **The Aubrey** (p. 85) hotel.

Day 2: Maipo Valley

Begin where it all started, at the **Maipo Valley** (p. 166), where Chile's first vines were planted in the mid-1500s. Drive or hire a cab to visit **Concha y Toro** ★★★ (p. 166), Chile's largest and best-known winery, now offering tastings of its full range of wines. Also book an appointment to visit the Concha y Toro and Baron Rothschild joint venture **Almaviva,** the Maipo Valley's star winery (p. 168). Later, head to Chile's oldest winery, **Cousiño Macul** ★★ (p. 168), where you can appreciate one of the Maipo Valley's most characteristic wines while you take in the stunning estate with French-style gardens. In the evening, continue the old-world theme and dine at **Europeo** ★★★ (p. 99), in Vitacura, one of Santiago's most elegant restaurants, with a very knowledgeable sommelier.

Day 3: San Antonio Valley

This full-day journey visits Chile's newest wine-growing valley, **San Antonio** (p. 162), home to top boutique wineries located near the coastal city of the same name and producers of whites and cold-weather reds. Plan to visit **Matetic Vineyards** ★★ (p. 165) first, producer of highly rated syrahs and an architectural gem to boot. After your tour, have a gourmet lunch at their restaurant. Continue west to **Viña Casa Marin** ★★ (p. 164), the winery closest to the coast and producer of the country's top rated sauvignon blanc. Head back to Santiago for your final night there and dine at **Opera** ★★★ (p. 93), followed by cocktails upstairs at the hip **Catedral** ★ (p. 93).

Day 4: Cachapoal Valley

Arrange a tour or, if you're feeling adventurous, rent a vehicle and journey south to the **Cachapoal Valley** (p. 170), spread at the foot of the Andes. Bring along a picnic lunch. Arrive for your 10:30am wine-tasting tour at **Altaïr** ★★★ (p. 170), a unique winery launched to craft a distinctively Chilean grand cru. Enjoy your picnic (let them know you're bringing one when you book), and then carry on to **Anakena** ★★ (p. 170). Your accommodations this evening are at the **Hotel Il Giardino** ★★ (p. 172), a tastefully decorated, country-French-style B&B with spacious lawns and an outdoor pool. If you'd like to stay a little closer to the Colchagua Valley, opt instead for **Hotel Casa Silva** (p. 177), a gorgeously restored old home that is now a luxury hotel near San Fernando.

Days 5 & 6: Colchagua Valley

Head to the **Colchagua Valley** (p. 173), Chile's best-developed wine region for tourism. Before you arrive in Santa Cruz, stop outside San Fernando for a wine tasting at the lovely **Casa Silva** ★★ (p. 174). Carry on to just before Santa Cruz and stop next at **Viña Viu Manent** ★★ (p. 176) for a gourmet lunch, followed by a wine tasting and a horse-and-buggy ride through their vineyards. If you have kids in tow, you may prefer to spend a few hours touring Viña Santa Cruz, the Disneyland of the Chilean wine world, with its mock indigenous village and astronomical facilities. Check into your room at the **Hotel Santa Cruz Plaza** ★★ (p. 178), and spend the late afternoon strolling around the typical rural town of Santa Cruz or lounging by the pool; dine that night at **Vino Bello** (p. 180) on the edge of town.

The following day, tour the state-of-the-art winery **Clos Alpalta** ★★★ (p. 174), soak in the pastoral scenery, and taste their award-winning blends. Visit the **Montes** winery ★★ (p. 175) for a tour and tasting of this well-known producer of fine varietals. Later that afternoon, visit the **Colchagua Museum** (p. 176).

Days 7 & 8: Aconcagua Valley

Leave early in the morning for the 4-hour drive to the **Aconcagua Valley** (p. 160), with its stunning Andean views and tiny colonial villages. If you'd like to stay in town, lodge in Los Andes at the **Hotel Inca** ★ (p. 161); or stay at the luxury spa outside town **Termas de Jahuel Hotel & Spa** ★★ (p. 162), and spend the afternoon visiting **Von Siebenthal** ★ (p. 161) winery. Dine at your hotel, and the next morning visit the venerable **Errazuriz** ★★ (p. 161) winery, with its striking *bodega* trellised terraces and historic winery. Book lunch in advance at Errazuriz and enjoy divine country views. Then drive to **Valparaíso** ★★★ (p. 133) to spend the night at the boutique hotel **Casa Higueras** ★★★ (p. 142), or alternatively, stay in **Viña del Mar** (p. 122); spend the afternoon exploring one of the two towns.

Day 9: Casablanca Valley

The following morning, pick up your exploration of either Viña or Valparaíso, pack your bags for the last time, and head back toward Santiago, stopping in the **Casablanca Valley** (p. 162) on the way. Here, you'll enjoy a lengthy tasting at **Viñedos Orgánicos Emiliana** ★★ (p. 164), an organic winery with excellent guides and winemakers who serve cheese and nuts while walking you through a relaxing tasting. Follow this visit with lunch at **Morandé** ★★ (p. 166) just down the road, then make a final stop at the slick **Veramonte** ★ (p. 163) winery to taste their specialty white wines. Then it's on to the airport, where you'll catch your flight back home. Pick up a couple of bottles to take home with you at the **La Vinoteca** store inside the departure gate in the airport (p. 74).

THE ACTIVE VACATION PLANNER

C hile is an active travel mecca. There are few countries where you can trek through primordial rainforests, ascend some of the world's highest peaks, kayak pristine lakes and fjords, raft one of the world's top-rated rivers, mountain bike on hushed country lanes lined with tall poplar trees, ski or snowboard where the powder lasts for days, not hours; climb a smoking volcano, or gallop across the Patagonian pampa like a true gaucho. Further boosting Chile's kudos as a breathtaking land of natural highs, many of Chile's national parks and reserves are so underrated and underappreciated that they are, for the most part, empty.

Adventure and active travel journeys can be pieced together as day excursions or your trip can be planned from start to finish by a tour operator. The latter option is often more expensive, but undoubtedly these planned journeys put far more emphasis on personalized attention and service than a run-of-the-mill day-tour operator. A handful of all-inclusive resorts and lodges also plan daily excursions that are sometimes included in the price of a room. Some of these resorts have their own horses, guides, and/or equipment, while others subcontract a local outfitter.

ORGANIZED ADVENTURE TRIPS

The advantages of traveling with an organized group are plentiful, especially for travelers who have limited time or for those who are traveling solo and are seeking companionship. Tour operators take the headache out of planning a trip by including guides, transportation, accommodations, gear, and sometimes meals in one price. Having a tour guide can help transcend any cultural and linguistic barriers as well as interpret the culture and history of Chile and the natural surroundings of your destination. Independent travelers tend to view organized tours as antithetical to the joy of discovery and too prescriptive, but many tour operators now offer journeys that take travelers off the beaten path or that work with local agencies and associations to provide a more in-depth experience.

There are several potentially major downsides to organized tours that should be considered beforehand. Shoddy service provided by a mediocre or inexperienced guide is a common complaint. Ask about your guide and his or her qualifications, background, and even age, to avoid being paired with a guide who is either not interested in the job or even one who is bent on simply having a good time rather than providing an informative journey. Also ask about the other people on your trip; if you are a middle-aged adult, chances are you won't want to spend your entire trip with a group of students who happened to book the same tour you did. Lastly, ask about extra costs for meals, tips, entry fees to attractions, and even day tours, which might not be covered in the package price.

The best tours limit group size to 10 to 15 people, which allows for personal attention and a bit of breathing room—this is appreciated after a week on the road together. For a higher price, most tour operators can organize a custom trip for a family or small group. Ask about difficulty levels when you're choosing a tour. Most tours are focused on "soft" adventure, with light excursions that are suitable even for couch tubers; be truthful with yourself when considering more difficult journeys. A multiday adventure that includes trekking through virgin jungle might look great on paper, but are you physically up to it? Tour operators are responsible for their clients' well-being and safety, but that doesn't let you off the hook in terms of your own personal responsibility. For more adventurous journeys, you'll want to inquire about your guide's outdoor experience, safety record, and insurance policy. Remember, no adventure trip is 100% risk-free.

International–Based Tour Operators

These agencies and operators specialize in well-organized, 7- to 15-day tours that allow travelers to pack a lot of action into a short period of time. (*Tip:* There's really no point in booking a tour that takes you to an all-inclusive lodge with its own guides and transportation, unless you just want someone to solve any glitches from start to finish.) A few of the operators include luxury accommodations and gourmet dining as part of the travel itinerary, and are therefore *very* expensive. Remember, the tours shown below do not include international or internal airfare. Solo travelers in most cases will be charged the dreaded single supplement fee that can run an additional 30% to 80% of the per person cost. For more specific activity-oriented tours, such as biking, see "Activities A to Z." Destination-specific chapters list local guide services or tour operators.

o **Abercrombie & Kent** (© 800/554-7016; www.abercrombiekent.com) caters to the luxury market (world-class hotels and gourmet dining), and offers mostly set trips to different regions of Chile or trips that might combine Argentina or Brazil with Chile; they also offer tailored trips for families and independent groups. The "Wonders of Chile, Argentina, and Brazil" tour takes travelers from Santiago to Puerto Montt, Bariloche, Buenos Aires, Iguazú Falls, and Río de Janeiro for $9,860 per person; the "Signature Chile Series" includes wine tasting and stops in Patagonia and the Lake District for $8,060 per person.

o **Gap Adventures** (© 416/260-0999; www.gapadventures.com) is a Canadian company that provides adventurous travelers with journeys that are economically priced, and include lodging in mostly 3-star hotels. The outfit caters to younger travelers (their YOLO trips are designed specifically for travelers 18 to 30 years old) and offers solo travelers the option to pay a single rate or be matched with another solo traveler to share a room and cost. The 14-day "Essential Patagonia" begins in Santiago and ends in Punta Arenas, stopping in the Lake District along the way and sailing aboard the *Navimag* ship from Puerto Montt to Puerto Natales, with trekking in Torres del Paine. All other journeys include visits to Argentina, Brazil, or Peru. The cost is $2,399.

o **Journey Latin America** (© 020/8747-8315; www.journeylatinamerica.co.uk) is the U.K.'s largest Latin American tour operator specialist, offering a plethora of tours. Check their website for ideas, which can be "Discovery Journeys," "Classic Journeys," and "Tailor Made." Apart from the many guided tours, which can include visits to Argentina and Brazil, the operator offers independent travelers the "Freedom of the Road" self-drive trip, an 18-day journey from Santiago to wine country, including stops at the rainforest of the Southern Highway and in southern Patagonia. The cost for the 18-day journey is $5,042 per person, based on double occupancy, and includes domestic flights, car rental, lodging, and some meals.

o **Knowmad Adventures** (© 877/616-8747; www.knowmadadventures.com) is one of the best U.S. tour operators in this category. The owners, an American husband-and-wife team, have spent considerable time on the ground in Chile researching destinations and activities, and they work with top local operators. Journeys run the length of Chile and are organized in small groups with preset dates and customized tours. Their "Countryside, Culture & Coast" packages (7 days, $1,880 per person) put together walking tours through Valparaíso, a night at Matanzas with an optional surf lesson, a Santiago bike tour, and wine tasting with a Chilean BBQ.

o **Mountain-Travel Sobek** (© 888/831-7526 or 510/594-6000; www.mtsobek.com) are the pioneers of organized adventure travel; their trips involve a lot of physical activity and combine camping with hotel stays, with an average of 12 nights. Sample trips include the 10-night "Trekking the Paine Circuit," which costs, per person, $4,195 for 5 to 7 guests, and $3,995 for 8 to 14 guests. Sobek is a pricey outfitter, but the guides carry gear and set up camp for guests, and it's known for its knowledgeable and competent guides.

o **Myths and Mountains** (© 800/670-6984; www.mythsandmountains.com) is an innovative tour operation that focuses on cultural themes, seeking ways to give travelers a more "in-depth" experience. The company offers trips to standard destinations such as the Atacama and Patagonia, and a unique journey to the Lake District's Vicente Perez Rosales Park, an 8-day trek through rainforest, with lodging in *refugios* and at campsites. Weeklong to 10-day journeys cost $2,100 to $3,995 per person.

o **Southern Explorations** (© 877/784-5400; www.southernexplorations.com) is a reputable organization that works with top local operators to provide authentic and interesting journeys to Patagonia, mostly in the Torres del Paine region. The "Patagonia Multisport Tour" runs for 12 days and includes trekking, horseback riding, and kayaking in and around the national park for $3,600 to $4,355 per person, depending on group size. Southern Explorations can also put together a multi-destination ski trip.

o **Wilderness Travel** (© 800/368-2794 or 510/558-2488; www.wildernesstravel.com) is a well-respected company with 31 years of experience planning unique journeys that go beyond the usual tried-and-true destinations and lodging options. The operator offers private journeys and small group trips to mostly Patagonia destinations, such as a wonderful multisport journey in northern Patagonia's Futaleufu region, with opportunities for hiking and wildlife spotting, and accommodation in hotels and remote lodges. The cost, per person, is $3,995 for 8 days.

CHILE-BASED TOUR OPERATORS

International tour operators without their own local offices must subcontract local tour agencies and services or book stays in all-inclusive hotels. Operators based in Chile typically offer a wider variety of tours here—after all, they operate within their own country. The following operators run a multitude of trips throughout the country; also see "Activities A to Z," later, for specialized tour operators.

o **Altué Expediciones** (📞 2/235-1519; www.altue.com) is the oldest and most respected tour outfitter in Chile. Their specialties are rafting (rivers Futaleufú, Maipo, and what's left of the Bío-Bío) and horseback riding (Central Andes, Parque Nacional La Campana, Patagonia), as well as their terrific kayaking operation/lodge based in Chiloé (with trips around Chiloé and Parque Pumalín). They have exceptionally friendly guides, a solid operation, and very reasonable prices. At print time, Altue's website was woefully out-of-date, so contact them directly for updated info and prices.

o **Azimut Expediciones** (📞 2/235-3085; www.azimut.cl), a French- and Chilean-run operation with 20 years experience, is a top choice for adventure travel and traditional tours with an "avant-garde" itinerary—that is, travel that takes you to off-the-beaten-path locations and overland tours. Some trips are planned in conjunction with lodging at their properties the Terra Luna in northern Patagonia, and the Codpa Valley Lodge in the Atacama Desert. Climbing, trekking, rafting, and bike trips are Azimut's specialties.

o **Cascada Expeditions** (📞 800/901-6987 in the U.S. or 2/923-5950; www.cascada.travel) is the most comprehensive tour operator in Chile, offering soft and hard adventure trips such as rafting and mountain climbing, and more traditional excursions such as wine tasting and cultural visits to areas outside of Santiago. Cascada runs its Torres del Paine trips from their EcoCamp dome camp in that national park, and they run a horseback riding and rafting outfit from Cascada de las Animas in the Cajon del Maipo, near Santiago.

o **Santiago Adventures** (📞 802/904-6798 in the U.S. and 2/244-2750 in Chile; www.santiagoadventures.com) offers, in spite of its name, journeys throughout Chile, with special emphasis on day and multiday mountain bike trips to the coast, remote areas of Patagonia, and boutique wineries; backcountry ski trips; and trekking and horseback riding around the Central Valley. Santiago Adventures has the best of both worlds with an American owner who is familiar with the U.S. market, and a local base that keeps them more in touch with the local pulse and new trip ideas. This is a good operator to contact when booking a Chile ski holiday and seeking add-on trips around the country.

OTHER GENERAL-INTEREST TOUR AGENCIES & PACKAGE DEALS

o **Chile Discover** (℡ 800/791-6520; www.chilediscover.com) puts together "Self-Guided" tours, whereby they book the car rental, hotels, and any other reservations; provide you with a map; and send you on your way on an independent tour. Research the hotels that they suggest as part of their itinerary—they may not be the best available.

o **LADATCO Tours** (℡ 800/327-6162 or 305/854-8422; www.ladatco.com) organizes custom tours only to all regions of Chile, including theme-oriented tours such as wine tasting, fly-fishing, glaciers, and more. LADATCO has operated as a Central and South American tour operator for 30 years. The epic, 25-day "Ultimate Chile" tour includes luxury accommodations and costs $14,995 to $15,600 per person based on double occupancy.

o **LatinTrip** (℡ 800/811-3077; www.latintrip.com) has an inconsistent and outdated website, but it's a good place to check out (or call for) cheaper deals for popular locations throughout Chile, especially hotel rates and daily tours. Half-day city tours of Santiago and half-day tours to wineries in the Maipo Valle run $45 to $55 per person.

ACTIVITIES A TO Z

This section is divided by activity, with listings of the prime destinations in Chile for practicing each activity, and the tour operators and outfitters who tailor their trips around each activity. Tour operators bring with them local knowledge, and more importantly, they provide guides and in most cases equipment. If you are planning to focus your trip to Chile around one specific activity, these tour operators and outfitters are your best bet. The companies listed under "Chile-Based Tour Operators" above offer outstanding trips based around many of the following activities, so check them out and note that some of the following activities will refer you to the specific region for more information about outfitters.

Adventure travel carries risks, and travelers should be well aware of dangers before participating in any activity. The tour operators mentioned in this chapter have been chosen for their safety and reputation, but ask questions on your own. For example, if your adventure involves trekking, how strenuous are the trails? What safety gear will be carried along, and what experience do your guides have? Tour operators in Chile have had their share of accidents, either fatal or just serious, and you'll want to know the background details of said accidents and make your decision to book accordingly.

Biking

Biking has grown exponentially in Chile, and there are now several tour companies offering bike journeys throughout the country and within Santiago. There are a few factors about biking in Chile to consider. First, many roads in Chile are dirt, and obstacles include horseback riders, livestock, and potholes. Chileans like to speed and pull out of lanes without signaling, so ride with caution around blind curves. Throughout **Patagonia,** frequent summer gales can make bicycling a nearly impossible undertaking. Tourism-oriented towns such as Pucón and San Pedro de Atacama have bicycle rental shops with maps and information for bicycle routes in their region, which are listed in regional chapters within this book.

In **Santiago** a popular and safe bike-riding area is the Cerro San Cristobal/Parque Metropolitano, with winding paved roads and spectacular views, however the terrain is uphill and downhill only. Other parks include Vitacura's Parque Bicentenario, Providencia's Parque de las Esculturas, and Parque Forestal; all of these parks are flat and have public art works and views of the Andes and the Mapocho River. As part of its Bicentennial celebration, Santiago is paving 690km (421 miles) of bike paths throughout the city by the end of 2012; much has already completed and paths can be found along major avenues and city streets. **La Bicicleta Verde,** Avenida Santa Maria 227 (© **2/570-9338;** www.labicicletaverde.com), rents recreational bikes, mountain bikes, and tandem bikes from its office in Bellavista, and offers day bike tours and a nighttime tour (7:30–10:30pm; C$30,000 per person). **Paseos en Bicicleta** (© **956-3075;** www.paseosenbicicleta.cl) offers a night tour, too, and has a more complete city tour that takes visitors to little-known places such as Barrio Brasil and the Parque Quinta Normal. Their wine-and-bike tour cruises through the tony neighborhoods of Vitacura and Las Condes and finishes with a wine tasting at the city's best wine shop. Tours last an average of 5 to 6 hours and cost between C$45,000 and C$60,000 per person.

The tour operator **Santiago Adventures** (see above) organizes bike trips to the southern Lake District and Carretera Austral, traveling along remote dirt roads to view rainforest, glaciers, tiny villages and little-known mountain valleys. **Expediciones Chile** (© **888/488-9082;** www.exchile.com) organizes mountain-bike trips centered around its base area in the Futaleufu region, which can be combined with rafting and kayaking; they also offer trips around Valle del Elqui in the Norte Chico region.

Bird-Watching

In Latin America, countries such as Panama or Brazil overshadow Chile when it comes to bird-watching, but Chile truly delights bird lovers for its nearly 300 species that include unusual birds such as the ostrichlike rhea and the Andean condor, pink flamingos, Magellanic woodpeckers, black-necked swans, torrent ducks, and Chilean flickers. Patagonia, especially **Torres del Paine,** is the perfect venue for bird-watching and home to the aforementioned birds. **Seno Otway** and **Isla Magdalena,** near Punta Arenas, are two sanctuaries for the amusing Magellanic penguins, who gather at both locations from September through March; the best viewing time, however, is November through January. Humboldt penguins can be viewed at the **National Humboldt Penguin Reserve** near La Serena, at the coast at **Maitencillo,** and at the penguin reserve at **Chiloé.** The Chilean Sea is rich with nutrients thanks to the Humboldt Current, attracting sea birds and such pelagic birds as boobies, albatrosses, and oystercatchers; you can see these birds virtually anywhere along the **Central Coast.**

The **Carlos Anwandter Nature Sanctuary** near Valdivia, renowned for its wetlands that teem with birds such as grebes, ducks, and wigeons, took a major hit in 2005 when a pulp mill devastated its formidable black-necked swan population; you can still see these elegant birds and dozens of other marsh species at the nearby **Río Cruces Nature Sanctuary,** wetlands that remain prime marsh bird–viewing sites. In the *Nothofagus* forests of the Lake District, especially in parks such as **Puyehue** and **Pumalín,** bird-watchers may spot (or hear the distinctive cluck of) a tapaculo called the *chucao,* and even clap eyes on a Magellanic woodpecker. The Lake District and Chiloé draw splendid ringed kingfishers and flocks of noisy ibis and wigeons.

Other birding hot spots include the pink flamingo sanctuary at the **Atacama Salt Flat,** near San Pedro de Atacama, and **Parque Nacional Lauca.**

Few hotels, even those that are geared toward nature, offer bird-watching as a regular activity, but with some advance planning, your hotel should be able to hire a bird-watching guide for you. You might want to contact a Chile-based bird-watching tour operator to arrange your own trip. The American-owned company **Alto Andino Nature Tours** (© 9/282-6195; www.birdingaltoandino.com) specializes in the northern region, including Parque Nacional Lauca and day trips from San Pedro de Atacama, and even offers ornithology courses. Farther south, try **Hualamo** (no phone; www.hualamo.cl) for day trips and custom multiday trips that center around the Central Andes and coast, the Río Cruces Nature Sanctuary, and the Lake District. In Patagonia, **Fantástico Sur** (© 800/656-1806; www.fsexpeditions.com) takes birders in and around Torres del Paine, including Tierra del Fuego, with day and multiday tours with bilingual guides. The U.S.-based **Field Guides** (© 800/728-4953 or 512/263-7295; www.fieldguides.com) is a specialty bird-watching travel operator with highly esteemed and friendly guides. Its all-inclusive program, "The Heart of Chile," covers Santiago to Chiloé, while its more comprehensive 21-day program spans northern Chile to Patagonia and costs $7,475 per person, including internal flights; the maximum group size is 14.

For more information on Chile's birds, see chapter 17.

Cruising & Yachting

No single activity has taken off in Chile like cruising, with scores of travelers hopping aboard for a circumnavigation of the southern cone. Most large cruise lines begin in Valparaíso or farther north in Peru and end in Buenos Aires or even Río de Janeiro. In Chile, stops typically include Arica, Valparaíso, Puerto Montt, Puerto Chacabuco, and Punta Arenas.

Of course, as a cruise-ship passenger you won't spend a lot of time getting to know Chile, but there is something to be said for experiencing the lush Chilean fjords, and some cruises visit the Laguna San Rafael glacier and sail around Cape Horn. Also, if you begin or end your trip in Valparaíso, you can tack on a couple of extra days and visit Santiago, the coast, or wine country.

MAINSTREAM CRUISE LINES These cruise lines offer something for everyone: **Celebrity Cruises** (© 800/647-2251; www.celebritycruises.com); **Holland America** (© 877/932-4259; www.hollandamerica.com); **Norwegian Cruise Lines** (© 866/234-7350; www.ncl.com); **Oceania Cruises** (© 800/531-5619; www.oceania cruises.com); **Orient Lines** (© 800/333-7300; www.orientlines.com); **Princess Cruises** (© 800/774-6237; www.princess.com); and **Royal Caribbean** (© 866/562-7625; www.rccl.com).

LUXURY LINERS Options include: **Crystal Cruises** (© 866/446-6625; www.crystalcruises.com); **Regent Seven Seas Cruises** (formerly Radisson; © 877/505-5370 or 954/776-6123; www.rssc.com); **Seabourn Cruise Line** (© 800/929-9391; www.seabourn.com); and **Silversea Cruises** (© 954/759-5098; www.silversea.com).

SPECIALTY CRUISES Lindblad Expeditions (© 800/397-3348; www.lindbladexpeditions.com) has educational cruises that focus on culture and the environment.

Travel agencies and tour operators that specialize in cruises buy in bulk and are often capable of offering lower rates than those advertised by cruise lines, and they stay on top of special deals and promotions. Try the **Cruise Company** (⏻ 800/289-5505; www.thecruisecompany.com) or **World Wide Cruises** (⏻ 800/882-9000; www.ww-cruises.com).

CHARTER YACHTS   Inter Yacht Charter (⏻ 212/461-4637; www.interyacht charter.com) has four charter ships located at Puerto Williams that are available for weeklong journeys around Patagonia and Tierra del Fuego. **Cascada Expeditions** (⏻ 800/901-6987 in the U.S. or 2/923-5950; www.cascada.travel) offers a 4-day excursion around the coast of Chiloé aboard a character-rich "Chilote" boat for eight people maximum; the all-inclusive cost is $1,950 per person, double occupancy.

CHILE-BASED SMALL CRUISES & YACHTING

Travelers experience a more intimate journey aboard cruise lines based in Chile rather than aboard one of the long-haul cruise lines mentioned above. Smaller ships foster more personalized attention, and smaller crowds allow guests to interact more closely with their natural surroundings.

Navimag Ferries is the cheapest option for sailing the Patagonia fjords, with comfortable but cramped accommodations (mostly quadruple bunks) popular with backpackers and budget travelers. The Chilean company's most popular route is its passenger and freight ferry that sails for 3 days from Puerto Montt to Puerto Natales and vice versa. If you have a lot of time on your hands, this is a worthwhile way to get from the Lake District to Patagonia. Navimag offers a 5-day journey from Castro, Chiloé to the Laguna San Rafael that is popular with Chilean travelers. See p. 364.

Small cruise operations based in the Chilean fjords include **Patagonia Express** (p. 354), which works in conjunction with the Puyuhuapi Lodge & Spa (formerly known as Termas de Puyuhuapi), leaving from Puerto Chacabuco and including a 2-night stay at the hotel and 1 night in Puerto Chacabuco. Contrasted with Navimag, it's a premium excursion, but it's not as luxurious as they might suggest. **Skorpios Cruises** is a deluxe (but not luxury) operation with three routes in Patagonia: the Aysén region, with visits to Chiloé and the fjords; Laguna San Rafael; and the Pío XI glacier, leaving from Puerto Natales. Cruises run from 4 to 7 days; see p. 366. **Catamaranes del Sur** (p. 364) is a catamaran service to Laguna San Rafael that works in conjunction with the Hostería Loberías del Sur hotel in Puerto Chacabuco. It offers packages that include a stay here, or 1-day journeys for travelers not lodging at the hotel. Catamaranes also has their own private park, Aikén del Sur, which is visited as part of 2- to 3-night packages.

The **Nomads of the Seas** cruise puts a different spin on luxury adventure cruising in the Chilean fjords—and in the world. It's not cheap, but given the tony interiors, degreed guides, onboard helicopter to reach out-of-the-way trout rivers and take fly-overs, and gourmet cuisine, it's worth every penny. Though the cruise focuses on fly-fishing, they cater to all outdoor pursuits; see p. 336.

The *Antarctic Dream* (⏻ 877/238-7477; www.antarctic.cl) is a Chilean-owned ship that has won praise for its small vessel trips to the Antarctic.

Fishing

Chile is a world-class fly-fishing destination renowned for its trout-rich rivers, with shores that are blissfully empty of other anglers. Famous actors, such as Robert Redford and Harrison Ford, are fly-fishing fans who've thrown in lines here in Chile, and with so many outstanding fly-fishing lodges and quality tour operators, it's an easy trip to plan. Rivers and lakes suitable for fly-fishing can be found in the southern Lake

District and Patagonia, centered around the Carretera Austral area. Lodges are not cheap, but they are attuned to the most demanding of tastes, offering highly qualified guides, deluxe lodging, and gourmet meals. See chapter 12 for a full guide to lodges and guides, and be sure to check out Chile's fly-fishing venture under "Chile-Based Small Cruises & Yachting" above, for **Nomads of the Seas,** a luxury yacht that specializes in this sport.

FISHING LODGES

Chucao Fishing Lodge ★★ (© 801/415-9617 in the U.S. or 2/201-8571 in Chile; www.chucaolodge.cl) is a newer lodge just 45 minutes from Chaitén, on the shore of the Yelcho Lake, and it is owned by Chilean Gonzalo Cortés, who authored the book *Fly Fishing in Chilean Patagonia.* The rough-hewn wood lodge offers comfort and views, and outstanding fly-fishing opportunities, given its location at the mouth of the Yelcho River. It costs $3,990 per week, including all meals and drinks.

El Patagon Lodge ★★ (© 866/881-9215 in the U.S. or 65/212030 in Chile; www.elpatagonlodge.com) is the "backcountry" version of the Yankee Way Lodge, located in a remote area south of Futaleufú, which puts anglers closer to the goods for longer fly-fishing days. High-quality service and more rustic accommodations in wooden cabins, with a yurt dining room and outdoor hot tub, are the hallmarks of this lodge. El Patagon has a 10-day camping adventure program that includes hiking, horseback riding, and rafting that costs $3,000.

Tierra del Fuego Lodge ★★ (© 2/196-0624; www.tierradelfuegolodge.cl) is perfectly suited for adventurous fishermen seeking an utterly remote lodge. The lodge was founded by American Mark Kniprath, an expert fly-fisherman and Alaska bush pilot who has spent years fly-fishing in Chile. Kniprath takes guests to nearby rivers and on overnight jaunts to Fagnano Lake and Azopardo River for brook, rainbow, and brown trout. Lodging consists of three log cabins with rustic yet contemporary decor, a common chimney-heated lounge, and warm, family-style service.

Isla Monita ★★★ (© 800/245-1950 in the U.S.; www.islamonita.cl) is an English-run lodge that caters to distinguished clientele. It has access to some of the most diverse fly-fishing conditions found in Chile, and it's located on an exclusive island in the beautiful Yelcho Lake. Prices are $4,495 per person, per week, or $3,295 for non-anglers. Check the website for great deals during their off-season.

Cinco Rios Lodge ★ (© 866/378-5006 in the U.S; www.cincorioschile.com) is just 10 minutes from Coyhaique, allowing for more time spent fishing rather than traveling far into the backcountry. The newer lodge overlooks the Simpson River, the lodge's primary fishing spot, and is run by Sebastian Galilea, who does an impressive job providing outstanding guided services, gourmet cuisine, and a warm and comfortable lodge experience.

Yankee Way Lodge ★★ (© 866/881-9215 in the U.S. or 65/212030 in Chile; www.yankeewaylodge.com) is a luxurious option, and its location at the foot of conical, snowcapped Volcán Osorno and fronting Lake Llanquihue can't be beat. The lodge offers more creature comforts than its peers and soothes the senses with chalets and bungalows, a small spa, and gourmet dining. In addition to its renowned fly-fishing, accessed by boat or horseback, the lodge offers multisport packages.

Golf

The beauty of playing golf in Chile lies in its Andean backdrop; the golf courses Coya and Pucón undoubtedly offer some of the most stunning views from any golf course in the world. However, golf in Chile is an exclusive sport played by the country's elite on private courses, and few tour operators are able to organize package excursions with the exception of **Chile Golf Tours** (no phone; www.chilegolftours.com), an upstart American-Chilean operation that puts together custom tours.

Public courses include the often mosquito-heavy **Golf Mapocho** (© 2/476-4800; www.golfmapocho.cl), just outside of Santiago, near the airport; **Marbella Resort** (© 32/277-2020; www.marbella.cl), at the coast near Maitencillo, which has ocean views; **La Serena Golf** (© 51/276037; www.laserenagolf.cl), a coastal resort, which is farther away from Santiago than Marbella but offers a better and more beautiful course; and Pucón's **La Peninsula** 8-hole course (© 45/443965), which is open to the public and a good way to gain access to the sweeping views from the privately owned peninsula.

Horseback Riding

Chile was settled on horseback and horseback riders as famous as Butch Cassidy and the Sundance Kid have ridden trusty steeds here—they rode through the Andes while on the run from the law. *Huasos* from the Central Region, and *baqueanos* or *gauchos* in Patagonia, are Chile's answer to the cowboy, and much of these regions' culture is centered on these two groups of wild and weathered Chileans.

Horseback riding hot spots include the **Atacama Desert, Central Andean Region, Colchagua Valley, Lake District,** and **Patagonia.** Two excellent lodges specialize in horseback riding. One is **Hacienda los Andes** (© 53/691822; www.haciendalosandes.com), located near La Serena and run by Austrian Manuela Paradeiser and German Clark Stede, offering visitors a chance to envelop themselves in Chilean culture and a hacienda lifestyle. You can choose from 4- or 8-day riding adventure packages or just book a room in the lovely hacienda on a nightly basis. Manuela also operates **Ride Chile** (© 53/691822; www.ridechile.com), which specializes in 2- to 10-night horseback-riding trips in the Central Region and Patagonia. The second lodge is **Estancia Cerro Guido** (© 2/196-4807; www.cerroguido.cl), located outside Parque Nacional Torres del Paine and within a working *estancia* (ranch), with day trips around the area that provide spectacular, sweeping views. The two **explora Hotels** in the Atacama and Torres del Paine also have stables and include horseback riding as part of their activities.

You'll find horseback operations in nearly every destination within Chile, so check each chapter for contact information. The following are a few of the best picks (the quality of the horses varies considerably; and experienced riders may be frustrated if the ride is geared toward beginners), and they usually can put together multiday trips for riding fanatics. In San Pedro de Atacama, contact **Rancho Cactus** (© 51/851506; www.rancho-cactus.cl), which offers day and overnight trips through stunning desertscapes. In Pucón, the two companies to contact are: **Campo Antilco** (© 9/9713-9758; www.antilco.com), a German-run business with day rides and 5- to 7-night trips to hot springs and Andean heights; and the **Huifquenco Fundo** (© 45/412200; www.fundohuifquenco.cl), a working ranch with family-friendly farm tours and day rides paired with a Chilean-style barbecue. In Puerto Varas, visit the stunning **Campo Aventura** (© 65/232910; www.campo-aventura.com), offering day rides and overnight trips, from 2 to 10 nights, based out of their modest lodge nestled in the rainforest near Parque Nacional Vicente Pérez Rosales. The trips also offer opportunities for rafting and canyoning. Two outfitters, **Cascada de las Animas** and **Altué Expediciones,** offer day horseback-riding trips in the Andes just outside of Santiago that are easy-going lopes up to lookout points with sweeping views of the Santiago Valley. See "What to See & Do" in section 4 of chapter 7.

Kayaking & Whitewater Rafting

It shouldn't come as a surprise that Chile has world-class rafting and kayaking, given the hundreds of pristine rivers that descend from the Andes and the country's Pacific Coast border. One of the most captivating and wildest rivers to raft in the world is the renowned **Futaleufú,** which means "Big River" in local indigenous Araucaria, and sports Class III to Class V rapids with such daunting names as the Terminator and Hell Canyon. Local and international tour operators organize multiday rafting journeys based around mountain refuges and camping, and can be found in chapter 12. Just 45 minutes from Santiago at the Cajón de Maipo, the **Maipo River** is a quick city escape for moderate, Class III rafting from November to February, and tamer floats suitable for families the rest of the year; see "Chile-Based Tour Operators" earlier in this chapter. The **Petrohué River** with Class III and IV rapids is equally spellbinding for its impossibly emerald waters and the majestic Volcán Osorno that rises high in the distance. To raft this river, contact **Alsur Expeditions** (✆ 65/232300;** www.alsurexpeditions.com).

While cruising the hushed Chilean fjords is a memorable experience, kayaking puts you closer to nature and the feeling of being enveloped in an emerald wonderland. Paddling journeys take travelers past cascading falls, along picturesque coves at Chiloé, and past sea lion rookeries, often stopping at a natural hot springs along the way. **Altué Expediciones** (✆ 2/235-1519;** www.altue.com) pioneered sea kayaking in this region; their modest but cozy lodge based at Chiloé has dynamite views, and their support vessel takes travelers wherever they want to paddle. **Yak Expeditions** (✆ 8/332-0574;** www.yakexpediciones.cl) specializes in low-impact trips with overnights in tents in natural settings, and they can also plan day trips around the lakes near Puerto Varas. The "official" tour operator for Parque Pumalín is **Alsur Expeditions** (✆ 65/232300;** www.alsurexpeditions.com), which has a support vessel, a traditional Chiloé boat, and kayak tours around the park, with overnights in tents. Note that while tent camping is a dream for nature lovers, a downpour, common in this region, can be uncomfortable, and support vessels are not usually large enough to accommodate groups indoors. If you're not specifically seeking out kayaking but would like to include the sport in your trip, check out the cruises offered by **Austral Adventures** (✆ 65/625977;** www.austral-adventures.com).

The company **Kayak Australis** (✆ 2/334-2015;** www.kayakaustralis.com) offers dozens of river and sea kayak courses and trips throughout the length of Chile.

Motorcycling

The romance of Che Guevara's epic journey through South America has enticed legions of travelers to Chile, seeking to follow Guevara's famous route. But don't be too swept away by the romance of the movie and book *The Motorcycle Diaries:* many of the roads in Patagonia are unpaved and rife with potholes. Lengthy motorcycle trips are for those with a true spirit for adventure and who are mentally and physically up to the challenge, and reservations must be made far in advance for organized journeys. The Texas-based company **MotoDiscovery** (✆ 800/233-0564 in the U.S.; www.motodiscovery.com) has a 24-day tour that begins in Viña del Mar, and winds through the Lake District and Patagonia in Argentina and Chile, before finishing in Tierra del Fuego.

Skiing

Chile's awesome Andean terrain and world-class resorts are no longer just a summer refuge for ski fanatics and foreign ski teams—it's now a hot destination for even recreational skiers, especially in August. A guide to Chile's ski resorts can be found in chapter 7 ("Ski Resorts in the Central Andean Region" and "Chillán & Termas de Chillán Resort"). With the exception of the Snowcat-serviced resort Ski Arpa, the resorts listed on these pages are the country's largest, and pull in the lion's share of foreign skiers. But adventurous skiers and snowboarders are finding that heliskiing (p. 185) lets them put tracks down where no one has before, and others are striking out and visiting the country's unsung, smaller resorts such as Corralco (p. 258), where they find intimate settings and a more "Chilean" experience. **PowderQuest Tours** (© **888/565-7158** toll-free in the U.S.; www.powderquest.com) offers 7- to 12-day resort and backcountry ski and snowboard tour packages with highly qualified guides who know Chile's terrain and conditions intimately and where to find the goods; they offer snowboard and heliski camps, too. The group maximum is eight skiers; their 9-day "Chile Snow Adventure Tour" costs $3,995 per person and includes lodging, lift tickets, transportation, and most meals. **Casa Tours** (© **888-311-2272;** www.casatours.com) offers similar ski and snowboard trips that cater to more budget-minded travelers, with lodging in low or mid-range hotels and hostels. The 8-day "Classic Shortie" visits the Three Valleys near Santiago and spends several days in Nevados de Chillan, for $2,995 per person, including lodging, lift tickets, transportation, and most meals.

For trip planning, call expert South America ski tour operators **Ski Organizers** (© **800/283-2SKI** [283-2754]; www.skiorganizers.com); **Rocky Mountain Getaways** (© **866/764-3829;** www.rockymountaingetaways.com); or **Ski.com** (© **800/908-5000;** www.ski.com). All three are specialists in ski and snowboard vacations in Chile and can put together an entire package that includes flights and transfers, and add-on trips around Chile.

Spas

Chile's geographic faults produce geothermal activity and mineralized, naturally hot water that has given birth to a long tradition of facilities offering *baños termales* (thermal baths). Some of the country's century-old facilities have been renovated to appeal to modern spa tastes; others offer a historical traipse back in time, with their marble tubs and vigorous massages. Count on nearly every world-class hotel to provide guests with services such as massage, a gym, a sauna, and sometimes a steam room. Following are a few of Chile's best spas.

In Santiago, try the sleek spa **Balthus,** in Vitacura (© **2/410-1411;** www.balthus.cl), a spa within the city's toniest gym. For a Santiago getaway, try the Viña's luxury hotels, the **Sheraton Miramar** (which has a Balthus spa; p. 127) or the **Hotel del Mar** (p. 127). Outside Pucón, the **Termas de Hulfe** (p. 273) offers a variety of massage and body treatments.

Puyuhuapi Lodge & Spa ★ (© **888-898-7334** in the U.S. or 2/225-6489 in Chile; www.patagonia-connection.com) is perhaps the best-known spa destination in Chile. The lodge's truly breathtaking location on the shore of the Puyuhuapi fjord is the major draw here, as is sitting in an outdoor pool surrounded by rainforest and mist, however the "spa" experience could be upgraded as service is not up to the level most foreigners are used to. It takes time to get here, but the remote location is close enough to cruise to the Laguna San Rafael glacier, which the spa features as part of its package. A 4-day "body and soul" package costs from $1,670 to 1,820 per person, double occupancy.

Termas de Cauquenes (*©* **72/899010;** www.termasdecauquenes.cl) draws visitors more for its award-winning restaurant, antique hacienda-style architecture, and lovely alpine setting than its spa facilities and guest rooms. The 200-year-old spa is Chile's oldest, having hosted the likes of Charles Darwin, and it was inspired by France's Vichy Spa. While the spa's Gothic-designed thermal pavilion is striking, the ancient marble tubs do not inspire a soak.

Termas de Chillán ★★ (*©* **2/233-1313;** www.termaschillan.cl) is located at the ski resort Nevados de Chillán, and is a full-service hotel nestled in a lovely valley of beech forests and craggy peaks. The hotel boasts a complete spa with massage, aromatherapy, facials, and other body treatments, and outdoor thermal pools. Beyond the spa, the hotel has skiing, a golf course, hiking trails, horseback riding, and a casino.

Termas de Puyehue ★ (*©* **64/331400;** www.puyehue.cl) draws mostly Chileans for its large indoor thermal pool; herbal, mud, sulfur, and marine salt baths; massage; and family-friendly activities such as horseback riding and farm tours. The grand facade of the hotel reminds visitors of a traditional European spa. The services are not as modern as those found elsewhere in the country, although the perk during the winter is its proximity to the Antillanca ski resort.

Termas Geométricas ★★★ (*©* **2/214-1214;** www.termasgeometricas.cl) is undoubtedly Chile's most beautiful hot springs complex, and consists of a series of slate-tiled pools that descend through a jungle-draped ravine. It's an utterly divine and exotic attraction and well worth the 45-minute drive from Pucón.

Surfing

The powerful swells and consistent breaks off the Pacific Ocean along Chile's 4,186km (2,600-mile) coast draw surfers from around the world—but it's *cold* swimming out there, and you'll need a wetsuit (⅓mm during the winter, ½mm during the summer), booties, and even a hood when surfing from the Central Region to the south. Surfing is good year-round, and a majority of left-breaking waves makes Chile a goofy-foot paradise. In the north, expect a few beach breaks but mostly board-breaking, Hawaiian-style reef breaks; here the best spots for surfing are Iquique and Arica. The Central Region's best (and most popular) spots for surfing include Chile's surfing mecca Pichilemu, with three surfing areas: La Puntilla, a 2-minute walk from town; Infernillo, which, when conditions are right, can produce a 2.4m-plus (8-ft.-plus) tube; and Punta de Lobos, considered Chile's most consistent break and a long left break with mixed conditions producing tubes and powerful waves. Lastly, Puertocillo is a renowned point break that's fast and has excellent tubes. Though this rustic spot is closed to the public without a permit, you can access this beautiful cove by booking a room at the **Aquí y Ahora Eco Lodge** (*©* **9/919-1085;** www.ecolodgepuertecillo.cl); they offer surf classes and trips to surf spots around the area, and are open year-round. The **Surazo Lodge** at Matanzas (*©* **9/277-8706;** www.surazo.cl) is a stylish wood-and-glass lodge with eight airy rooms that come with ocean views and a deck, and surf and windsurf classes available for C$20,000 (private) and C$15,000 (group). With a pristine beach, hot tub, hammocks, and delicious cuisine, Surazo is really an ideal lodge for kicking back on the beach even if you do not surf.

Wellness Activities

The yoga center and wellness retreat **Canal Om** (② 2/232-2452; www.canalom. com) lies 2½ hours north of Santiago in Ensenada, near Los Vilos, and is a lovely, tranquil retreat with rates that include lodging, one yoga class per day, use of their sauna and swimming pools, and other amenities; there are also additional services such as massage, and the center often hosts wellness retreats with visiting yoga gurus. The acclaimed **Bío Bío Expeditions** (② 800/246-7238; www.bbxrafting.com) offers a comprehensive 9-day "Yoga Adventure Patagonia" program, with eco-camp style accommodation options in both Argentina and Chile. At around $3,300 per person, there is nothing very Zen-like about the price, however. **Expediciones Chile** (② 888/488-9082 in the U.S., 2/570-9885 in Chile; www.exchile.com) offers a 9-day program (for $2,195) based on the Futaleufú river, which includes yoga, rafting, sea kayaking, hiking, and horseback riding. The trip is more of a well-rounded trip for couples and friends with varied interests rather than a retreat for yoga devotees.

SANTIAGO

Santiago, one of South America's most sophisticated cities, is a thriving metropolis that's home to more than five million people, or a third of Chile's population. Travelers have for years categorized it as a "gateway" city to destinations like Patagonia and the Atacama Desert, but that moniker no longer holds ground. Situated at one of the most stunning locations imaginable at the foot of the towering Andes, the city has become a fashionable megalopolis that is home to chic galleries and new cultural centers and museums, and the country's 2010 Bicentennial has spawned a host of infrastructure upgrades. The restaurant scene has never been better, with a wave of innovative chefs working culinary magic at restaurants throughout town. Santiago also offers both leisure and business travelers close access to ski resorts, wineries, and even the coast, making this clean, safe, and very modern city a convenient base for travelers seeking to pack a lot of action into just a few days.

Much of the development has a downside, however, which is that unchecked growth in the construction industry has quickly replaced many lovely antique homes and buildings with boxy, bland condominium buildings. Earthquakes have flattened many of Santiago's colonial-era buildings, and what remains has been left to decay to the point that tearing down an antique mansion is cheaper than restoring it to its former glory. Thus, it isn't uncommon to see a glitzy skyscraper or cracker-box apartment building towering over a 100-year-old relic, or to see cobblestone streets dead-end at a tacky 1970s shopping gallery. Some neighborhoods look as though they belong to entirely different cities.

This nearly 250-square-mile city frankly has outgrown its sleepy, old-fashioned, and dictatorial past and is virtually unrecognizable from 15 years ago. At the turn of the 20th century, Santiago city life was concentrated around its city center and the Plaza de Armas, however today major businesses and the upper-class have migrated north to newer neighborhoods such as Las Condes, Vitacura, and La Dehesa. Nearly 640km (390 miles) of new bike paths around Santiago and cheap bike rentals have brought residents out into the streets, as have the development of new parks such as the Parque Bicentenario in Vitacura and the multimillion-dollar renovation of the Metropolitan Park and the Quinta Normal. Most importantly, the city is experiencing historically low levels of smog (present during winter months mostly from May to October, except around rainy periods).

ORIENTATION

Essentials

GETTING THERE

BY PLANE   Santiago's **Comodoro Arturo Merino Benítez Airport** (SCL; ℭ 2/ 690-1752; www.aeropuertosantiago.cl) is served by LAN and Sky Airline (formerly Aerolíneas del Sur), and most major international carriers. **Currency-exchange** kiosks can be found inside the customs arrival area, outside in the public arrival area, and near the international departure gate (before entering Customs). To the left and right of the passenger gate are cash machines.

Depending on traffic, your Santiago destination, and how you get there, the city can be reached in 20 to 45 minutes. Most hotels offer a private car or van pickup for about C$16,635. An **official taxi** costs C$15,000 to C$16,000 one-way, but if you book your return ride with the official taxi, that price drops to C$13,000 to C$14,000 each way. Hotels can also arrange transportation but often this option is more expensive than a regular official taxi. More economical options are the minivan transfer shuttles **TransVip** (ℭ 2/677-3000; www.transvip.cl) and **Tur Transfer** (ℭ 2/677- 3600; www.turtransfer.cl) that charge, per person, C$6,000 for Providencia and C$6,700 for Las Condes. Tickets can be purchased in both the domestic and international arrivals areas. For outbound passengers leaving Santiago for the airport, both companies prefer reservations to be made 1 day in advance. The drawback with this service is that you may stop at several other destinations before arriving at your own.

Cheaper yet are bus services that depart from the far ends of the arrival curb and drop passengers downtown, from where they can take the Metro or a taxi. The blue bus **Centropuerto** leaves every 10 minutes from 6am to 11:30pm and drops passengers at Los Héroes Metro station on the main avenue Alameda, for C$1,400 one-way and C$2,500 roundtrip (ℭ 2/601-9883). **Tur Bus** (ℭ 2/822-7741) leaves every 30 minutes from 5:30am to midnight, also dropping passengers off at the Los Héroes Metro station. The cost is C$1,700 one-way and C$2,900 roundtrip.

BY BUS   There are four **bus stations** in Santiago. The station for international arrivals and departures to and from destinations in southern Chile is **Terminal Buses Estación Central,** formerly known as the Terminal Santiago and not to be confused with the actual Estación Central train station and Metro stop; it's located at Alameda 3848 (ℭ 2/376-1750; Metro: Universidad de Santiago). The **Terminal Alameda** next door at Alameda 3750 is the terminal for the Pullman and Tur Bus companies, two well respected, high-quality services. For departures to northern and central Chile, you'll go to **Terminal San Borja,** San Borja 184 (ℭ 2/776-0645; Metro: Estación Central). The smaller **Terminal Los Héroes,** Tucapel Jiménez 21 (ℭ 2/420-0099; Metro: Los Héroes), has service to a variety of destinations in both northern and southern Chile as well as a clutch of international destinations.

BY TRAIN   Santiago is serviced by the state-owned **Empresa de los Ferrocarriles del Estado (EFE),** which provides modern and comfortable service to Chillán, stopping first in Rancagua, San Fernando, and Talca, and passing through beautiful, pastoral landscapes. Prices are C$3,600 to C$4,800 from Santiago to Chillán one-way. Tickets purchased online are 10% cheaper. There is a snack and beverage service car. Call EFE or check the website for updated information (ℭ 600/585-5000; www.efe.cl), or check with your travel agent or hotel for a reservation.

The best time to visit Santiago is from December to March, when the weather is balmy and restaurants open their doors to outdoor seating. Most Santiaguinos leave the city for vacation during February and sometimes January, and so traffic is light during this period. Summertime also brings about street fairs and events, such as the huge International Theater Festival (Santiago a Mil) and other street music and sporting events.

VISITOR INFORMATION

The **National Tourism Service (Sernatur)** office is at Av. Providencia 1550 (© 2/731-8310; www.sernatur.cl; Metro: Manuel Montt), open Monday through Friday from 9am to 6:30pm, and Saturday from 9am to 2pm. Sernatur also has a small information desk in the international area with hotel information and maps, open daily from 8:15am to 8pm (© 601-9320). The Santiago Municipality has an **Oficina de Turismo** in a kiosk in the Plaza de Armas (© 2/713-6745), with information about downtown Santiago attractions. The Oficina de Turismo also offers free English-language tours leaving from the kiosk: "Santiago Step by Step" leaves every Monday, Wednesday, and Friday at noon, and the "Walking Tour of El Centro" leaves every Saturday and Sunday at 11am. Another **Oficina de Turismo** (© 2/664-4216) can be found at Cerro Santa Lucia on the Neptuno terrace; beginning in early 2011 they will offer English-language walking historical tours of the Cerro Santa Lucia. The **Yellow Pages** has detailed maps of the entire city of Santiago, or you can pick up a pocket guide to the city, called **Map City** (www.mapcity.com), sold at newsstands and kiosks, for C$3,000.

City Layout

Santiago incorporates 32 *comunas,* or neighborhoods, although most visitors will find they spend their time in just a few. **Downtown,** or *el centro,* is the political and historic center of Santiago, although it is older and grittier and has been losing clout as more of the financial wealth of Santiago has relocated. **Providencia** and **Las Condes,** and the tiny area that separates the two, **El Golf** (also known as El Bosque, or colloquially as "San-hattan" in reference to its glitzy high-rises), are upscale, modern neighborhoods, with residential areas centered on a bustling strip of shopping galleries, restaurants, and office buildings. Although *el centro* is older and scruffier, the exception is the charming **Lastarría/Parque Forestal/Bellas Artes** micro-neighborhood, an up-and-coming arts and cafe community. Although *el centro* may not be easy on the eye or the nerves, it remains the city's microcosm and the most rewarding place to get under the skin of Santiago's urban matrix.

The well-heeled residential neighborhood **Vitacura,** north of Las Condes and south of the Mapocho River, and spliced by the thoroughfare Avenida Kennedy, is home to many of Santiago's posh boutiques and gourmet restaurants. The sleepy, middle-class residential communities **Ñuñoa** and **La Reina** offer few attractions and are not commonly visited by travelers.

Santiago is bisected by the Río Mapocho; on the northern side rises **Cerro San Cristóbal,** an 880m (2,886-ft.) forested park and recreation area. At the foot of the hill is the bohemian neighborhood **Bellavista,** another restaurant haven and happening night spot. Santiago's principal avenue that runs through the city changes names

Downtown Santiago Accommodations, Dining & Attractions

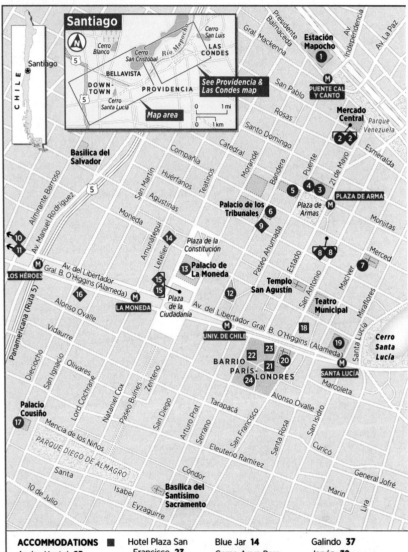

ACCOMMODATIONS ■
Andes Hostel **25**
Hotel El Patio **33**
Hotel Foresta **30**
Hotel Fundador **22**
Hotel Galerias **18**
Hotel París Nuevo **21**

Hotel Plaza San
Francisco **23**
The Aubrey **41**

DINING ◆
Ambrosía **8**
Azul Profundo **38**
Barandiaran **34**
Bar Nacional **9**

Blue Jar **14**
Como Agua Para
Chocolate **36**
Confitería Torres/
Café Torres **15, 16**
El Hoyo **10**
El Toro **27**
Etniko **39**

Galindo **37**
Japón **32**
Opera & Catedral **28**
Patagonia Café **31**
Squadritto **30**
Zully **11**

ATTRACTIONS ●

Barrio París-Londres **24**

Basílica de la Merced **7**

Biblioteca Nacional **19**

Calle Dieciocho and
Palacio Cousiño Macul **17**

Calle Nueva York & the
Bolsa de Comercio **12**

Casa Colorada &
Santiago Museum **8**

Catedral Metropolitana **5**

Centro Cultural Palacio
La Moneda **15**

Cerro San Cristóbal **42**

Correo Central and
Museo Postal **4**

Estación Mapocho **1**

Iglesia, Convento y Museo
de San Francisco **20**

La Chascona **40**

Mercado Central **2**

Museo Chileno de Arte
Precolombino **6**

Museo de Artes Visuales
(MAVI) / Museo
Anthropología **29**

Museo de Bellas Artes
& Museo de Arte
Contemporaneo **26**

Palacio de la Real Audiencia/
Museo Histórico Nacional **3**

Palacio La Moneda **13**

Patio Bellavista **35**

6 | Accommodations, Dining & Attractions in Providencia & Las Condes

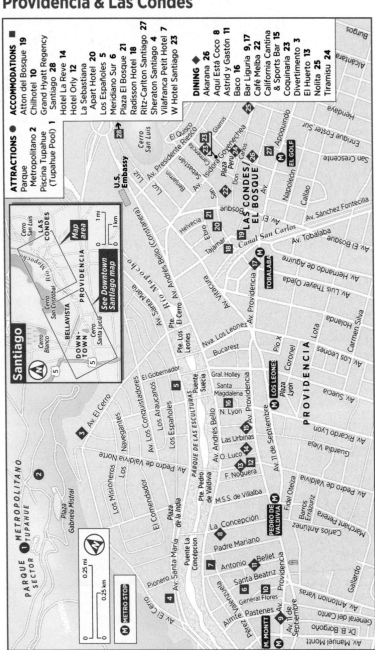

ATTRACTIONS ●
Parque Metropolitano **2**
Piscina Tupahue (Tupahue Pool) **1**

ACCOMMODATIONS ■
Atton del Bosque **19**
Chilhotel **10**
Grand Hyatt Regency Santiago **28**
Hotel La Reve **14**
Hotel Orly **12**
La Sebastiana
Apart Hotel **20**
Los Españoles **5**
Meridiano Sur **6**
Plaza El Bosque **21**
Radisson Hotel **18**
Ritz-Carlton Santiago **27**
Sheraton Santiago **4**
Vilafranca Petit Hotel **7**
W Hotel Santiago **23**

DINING ◆
Akarana **26**
Aquí Está Coco **8**
Astrid y Gastón **11**
Baco **16**
Bar Liguria **9,17**
Café Melba **22**
California Cantina & Sports Bar **15**
Coquinaria **23**
Divertimento **3**
El Huerto **25**
Nolita **24**
Tiramisu **24**

three times (Av. Apoquindo in Las Condes; Av. Providencia and Av. 11 de September in Providencia; and Av. Alameda in downtown—although the latter is officially named Ave. Libertador Bernardo O'Higgins, locals call it Alameda).

GETTING AROUND

By Metro

Cheap, clean, and efficient, the **Metro** subway (© 2/937-2000; www.metro santiago.cl) is by far the fastest and most agreeable way to get around the city. It's also an attraction in its own right—stations are adorned with murals painted by some of Chile's most important artists. Unfortunately, it is now the most congested transport option, especially during rush hour from 7 to 10am and 5 to 7pm, when critical mass reaches an estimated six users per square meter. The Metro is considered to be generally safe; however, pickpocket incidents are on the rise with the new influx of passengers, so keep a sharp eye on your belongings.

There are five Metro lines. Line 1 is the principal Metro line for travelers, as it runs from Las Condes to attractions and bus stations downtown. Line 2 transfers from Line 1 at Los Heroes and stops at Cal y Canto (near the Mercado Central). Lines 4 and 4a are residential lines connecting Avenida Alameda with La Reina. Line 5 takes travelers transferring at Baquedano to Plaza de Armas and the Quinta Normal park. **Note:** Lines 3 and 6 are not scheduled for completion until 2015.

Rides on the Metro can be purchased individually at each station, or riders purchase a *bip* card for multiple rides. The *bip* card is the only form of payment on public buses (see below). *Bip* cards can be purchased at Metro stations, various banks (Banco de Chile and Banco Santander), various commercial locations throughout the city, and designated *Punto bip* centers. The minimum *bip* credit is C$1,000, plus an initial C$1,250 to buy the card. A one-way Metro fare costs between C$480 and C$600 depending on the time of day. If you then transfer from a bus to the Metro, you will be required to pay an additional C$400.

See the inside front cover of this guide for a map of the city's Metro system.

TRANSANTIAGO: mass transit mayhem

Arguably the most loathed word in the Chilean lexicon, Transantiago, the integrated transport system introduced in February 2007, provoked chaos on an unprecedented scale. The most ambitious transport reform undertaken by a developing country, Transantiago was introduced via a "big bang" approach rather than as a gradually phased-in scheme. The ensuing mayhem was reflected in then-president Michelle Bachelet's approval rating, which fell from 55.2% to 42.7% in the month following the system's introduction. With decreased bus routes, an increased route network, and insufficient infrastructure to deal with the complexities of a prepay system, travelers have opted to use the more efficient Metro. Since 2007, the Metro has been overwhelmed by increased passenger numbers (riders jumped from 1,300,000 to 2,200,000 that year). Government initiatives imply that the flaws in the system will be gradually smoothed out, but at press time, not much had been accomplished to disperse the congestion and improve bus service.

By Bus

The **Transantiago** (© 800/733-0073; www.transantiago.cl) lime-green and white coaches that race through the city streets do not come with maps or bus schedules; this can obviously be confusing, however you can visit their website and enter your route from start to finish, and the site will tell you which bus to take and how long on average the trip is. Transantiago requires payment via a *bip* card (see "By Metro" above for info).

By Taxi

Taxis are plentiful and reasonably priced when compared to rates in North America and Europe. Taxis are identifiable by their black exterior and yellow roof; a light in the corner of the windshield displays a taxi's availability. Always check to see that the meter is in plain view, to avoid rip-offs. Drivers do not expect tips. Do not confuse taxis with *colectivos,* which are similar in appearance but without the yellow roof—these local, shared taxis with fixed routes are too confusing to visitors to recommend taking (there are a few exceptions listed in this book).

The starting taxi fare is C$250, then C$100 for every subsequent 200m (656 ft). Count your change after paying as drivers often shortchange unwary passengers. Go to **www.taximetro.cl** and enter points A and B and the site will advise you of the best route to take and the approximate cost.

By Car

Do not rent a vehicle if you only plan to stay within metropolitan Santiago, but consider doing so if you are an independent traveler seeking to visit the coast, Cajón de Maipo, or wine country. Santiago's slick new Costanera Norte (an express transit tunnel that runs from La Dehesa and Las Condes to the Pan-American Hwy. and the airport) has entrances and exits along the Mapocho River, but finding one can be confusing, so check out the website **www.costaneranorte.cl** for a map, or ask your rental agency or hotel to guide you. The city's "TAG" system (TAG stands for an automatic toll that is charged electronically to the vehicle) is included in the rental price. Stay out of downtown Santiago during weekdays due to extreme congestion, and drive defensively—buses and other drivers steadfastly refuse to let other vehicles merge into their lane, so be prepared to turn or exit any highways.

RENTALS   At the airport, you'll find most international rental agencies, such as **Alamo** (© 2/655-5255; www.alamochile.com), **Avis** (© 600/368-2000; www.avis.cl), **Budget** (© 600/441-0000; www.budget.cl), **Hertz** (© 2/360-8600; www.hertz.cl), and local agency **Rosselot** (© 2/690-1374; www.rosselot.cl). All agencies have downtown or Providencia offices. Generally, Rosselot and Dollar are lower in cost. Many hotels also offer competitive rates and can pick up and drop off the car.

DRIVING TIPS   Yellow lanes on the right-hand side of major streets and avenues, especially the Alameda/Providencia/Apoquindo avenues, are for buses and taxis specifically and you may only enter when preparing to make a right-hand turn. Take care with speed limits (100–120kmph/62–75mph) on the main highways out of town, especially Ruta 5 where *carabineros* (police officers) wield radars and purvey hefty fines.

Maps are sold at most gas stations, and your rental agency should be able to provide you with one.

PARKING   Every hotel, with the exception of budget hostels, offers on-site and sometimes free valet parking. There is no street parking downtown except Saturdays

Accommodations, Dining & Attractions in Vitacura 6

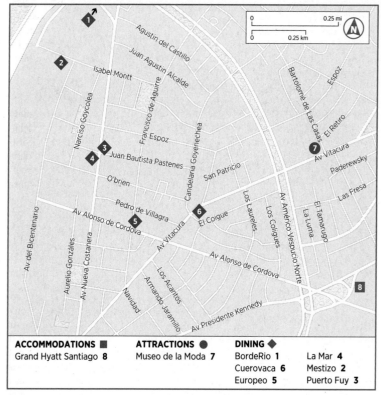

ACCOMMODATIONS ■	ATTRACTIONS ●	DINING ◆	
Grand Hyatt Santiago **8**	Museo de la Moda **7**	BordeRio **1**	La Mar **4**
		Cuerovaca **6**	Mestizo **2**
		Europeo **5**	Puerto Fuy **3**

and Sundays, although there are underground lots called *estacionamientos* that are recognizable by a blue sign marked with a giant E. In Providencia, along Avenida Providencia, you'll find a series of expensive underground lots. Santiago meters busy streets in Providencia and Bellavista, which is done by an official meter maid who waits on the street and times and charges drivers—he or she will leave a white ticket on your windshield. On commercial streets where there is no meter maid, you'll find the *cuidador,* an unofficial, ragtag "caretaker" who will "watch" your car for you. You're expected to give him or her a tip of C$100 to C$300 when you leave your space. *Cuidadores* can be aggressive if you elect not to pay them.

Do not leave valuable items in your car if you park on the street; break-ins are common when items are in view. Car theft is common, too, so always park your vehicle in a lot overnight.

On Foot

Santiago is not laid out on a perfect grid system; however, the neighborhoods most visitors stick to run along the length of the Mapocho River, making the river a good point of reference. Always carry a map with you. Saturday afternoons and Sundays are quieter days to explore neighborhoods such as downtown. Pedestrians should be alert at all times and never stand too close to sidewalk curbs because buses roar by dangerously close to sidewalks. Drivers are not always polite enough to give the right of way to pedestrians, so cross streets quickly and with your eyes wide open.

[FastFACTS] SANTIAGO

American Express
The American Express office is at Av. Isidora Goy-enechea 3621, Piso 10 (𝄐 2/350-6700); it's open Monday through Friday from 9am to 2pm and 3:30 to 5pm. Twenty-four-hour customer service in the U.S. is available at 𝄐 800/545-1171 (Gold Card) and 𝄐 800/570-0089 (Plati-num Card), although you will be charged for the call if you dial from outside the United States.

Banks Banks are open from 9am to 2pm Monday through Friday, and closed on Saturday and Sunday. ATMs, called "Redbancs," are found in banks, phar-macies, gas stations, and shopping malls, and accept Visa/PLUS and MasterCard/Cirrus.

Business Hours Com-mercial business hours are Monday through Friday from 10am to 7pm, closing for lunch between 1 and 1:30pm and reopening between 2:30 and 3pm. Most stores are open from 10am to 2pm on Saturday and closed on Sunday, with the exception of shopping malls.

Currency Exchange
All major banks exchange currency, but most charge a commission that is higher than a money-exchange house (casa de cambio). In

downtown, there are numerous exchange houses clustered around Agustinas between Ahumada and Bandera pedestrian walk-ways; try Guinazu Transfer (𝄐 2/469-5303) at Matías Cousiño 170 or Calle Ban-dera 585. In Providencia, exchange houses are found around Avenida Pedro de Valdivia at Avenida Provi-dencia. In Las Condes, there are a couple on Avenida El Bosque Norte near Avenida Apoquindo. Exchange houses are generally open Monday through Friday from 9am to 2pm and 4 to 6pm, and Saturday from 9am to 1 or 2pm; on Sun-days the shopping malls Parque Arauco and Alto las Condes have open currency exchange offices. Hotels exchange dollars at an unfavorable rate.

Emergencies For a **police** emergency, call 𝄐 133. For **fire**, call 𝄐 132. To call an **ambulance**, dial 𝄐 131.

Hospitals The American Embassy can provide a list of medical specialists in Santiago. The best hospitals in Santiago are private: **Clínica Las Condes**, Lo Fontecilla 441 (𝄐 2/210-4000); **Clínica Alemana**, Vitacura 5951 (𝄐 2/210-1111); and **Clínica Indisa Santa María,** Av. Santa María 01810 (𝄐 2/362-5555).

Internet Access
Almost every hotel has a computer with Internet access for its guests; some offer free or paid Wi-Fi ser-vice. For Wi-Fi service on your laptop, try **Starbucks** or **Valdéz** coffee shops, or libraries such as the **Cafe Literario Bustamante** near the Metro Baquedano (𝄐 2/381-2231) at Busta-mante 335; it's open every Monday to Friday from 9am to 8pm and Saturday to Sunday from 10am to 8pm.

Outdoor Equipment
Parque Arauco mall has a **North Face** clothing store (𝄐 2/592-0810) and a shop within the W Hotel in Las Condes (p. 89). Locally produced, high-quality out-door gear company **Doite** (𝄐 2/570-5300) is in the Alto los Condes mall; **Pata-gonia Sport** is in Providen-cia at Almirante Simpson 77 (𝄐 2/222-9140). The best outdoor equipment and info can be found at **La Cumbre,** Apoquindo 5220 (𝄐 2/220-9907; www.lacumbreonline.cl), which is open Monday through Friday 11am to 8pm and Saturday from 11am to 4pm.

Pharmacies Pharmacies are ubiquitous in Santiago, and can even be found in gas stations along major highways. They're generally open from 8am to mid-night; however, the following branches are open 24 hours: **Farmacias Ahumada** (📞 600/222-4000; Av. Apoquindo 2782) and **Farmacias Salco Brand** (📞 600/360-6000; Av. Padre Hurtado, at Av. Las Condes). Both of these pharmacies deliver for a nominal fee.

Post Office The main post office is on Plaza de Armas (Mon–Fri 8:30am–7pm; Sat 8:30am–1pm). There are other branches at Moneda 1155, in downtown, and Av. 11 de Septiembre 2239, in Providencia. **FedEx** is at Av. Providencia 1951, and in the Dimacofi center at Moneda 792 (📞 2/361-6000; Mon–Fri 9am–7pm).

Telephones Tourists are offered cheaper rates from phone centers than from their hotels. The centers are predominately run by **Entel** (at Morandé btw. Huérfanos and Compañía) and **Telefónica CTC Chile** (found inside the Metro stations Universidad de Chile and Moneda, and in Providencia at the Mall Panorámico at Av. 11 de Septiembre 2155). Most phone centers have fax service and Internet access as well. Alternatively, you can buy a phone card at any kiosk, gas station, corner store, or telephone center, but ask your hotel if you are charged for the local connection—chain hotels can really stick it to you even though you're using a phone card. Also see the "Telephones" section on p. 45.

WHERE TO STAY

Given Santiago's mélange of architectural styles and socioeconomic levels, where you stay could very well shape your opinion of the city. The cheapest accommodations are in the downtown area, *el centro,* but the neighborhood is congested and older, with the exception of the antique, lovely Lastarría neighborhood (also called Parque Forestal or Bellas Artes) on the east side of Cerro Santa Lucía. The Lastarría neighborhood has a handful of stylish, **temporary apartment rentals** in studios, one to two bedrooms, and lofts, which can be booked for the night or for longer-term stays. These "apart-hotels" come with kitchens and are fully furnished, feature maid service, and there is usually a front desk clerk. Check the website **www.barriolastarria.com** for a list of these properties, or try our pick, **Lastarría 43** (📞 2/638-3230; www.santiagoapartment.cl), which has rooms that go for, per night, $65 to $80 for a studio, and $80 to $110 for a loft. Weekly rentals receive a 10 to 15% discount.

Depending on your perspective, you'll either enjoy the upscale ambience of Las Condes, or find it antiseptic and devoid of local color. The Metro system quickly connects travelers to the downtown area, and taxi rides take between 15 and 30 minutes depending on traffic. Providencia is a happy medium between the two, with leafy streets, restaurants, and shops, and Metro access. Energetic types can also reach downtown on foot from Providencia by heading directly east along Avenida Providencia (around 45 min.). Boutique hotels have finally taken hold in this city, and are found mostly in Providencia and Bellavista. See the maps on p. 76, 79, and 81 to locate the hotels reviewed below.

Parking at Santiago hotels is free unless otherwise indicated below. High season is generally October through March, yet many hotels offer cheaper deals in January and February.

EXPENSIVE

Hotel Plaza San Francisco ★★ 🏅 Following a $5-million renovation in 2008, rooms at the Plaza are now comfortable, if rather homogenous—all sport neutral tones and Pottery Barn–esque furnishings. While it may not exude the class and style of its luxury peers, the prices here are more affordable than the competition. The

Plaza is on noisy Avenue Alameda, but behind the hotel lie the tranquil pedestrian streets of the Barrio París-Londres micro-neighborhood, and guest rooms have double-paned windows. The hotel's proximity to downtown attractions and the shops and cafes of the Lastarría Street area is a definite perk, if you are only in town for a day or two, but the neighborhood isn't especially attractive at night. The hotel has a long list of amenities, but note that their "spa" is really a fitness center with a sauna and massage services. The **Bristol Restaurant** has been lavished with national gastronomic awards.

— Alameda 816. ℂ **2/639-3832.** Fax 2/639-7826. www.plazasanfrancisco.cl. 155 units. $174 double king bed; $224 junior suite. AE, DC, MC, V. Metro: Univ. de Chile. **Amenities:** Restaurant; bar; concierge; heath club; indoor heated pool; room service. *In room:* A/C, TV, minibar, free Wi-Fi.

MODERATE

Hotel Fundador 💧 Since being taken over by the Brazilian Blue Tree Hotels chain, this classic European-style hotel in the lovely París-Londres neighborhood has stepped back into the spotlight. Its total renovation brought a flashy—some might say quirky—new style to the older part of the city. Rooms are still small, but the new decor (including lime-green sofas, hand-painted murals, and wooden floors) brightens things up. It's popular with tour groups and the area in general can be noisy. Rack rates are listed below, but the secret is to book via their website, which offers up to 40% off the regular rate, year-round.

Paseo Serrano 34. ℂ **2/387-1200.** Fax 2/387-1300. www.hotelfundador.cl. 147 units. $190 double standard; $110 double standard (if booked on website). AE, DC, MC, V. Valet parking. Metro: Univ. de Chile. **Amenities:** 2 restaurants; bar; babysitting; concierge; health club; indoor pool; room service; sauna. *In room:* A/C, TV, hair dryer, minibar, Wi-Fi (free).

Hotel Galerias ★ ☺ This mid-range hotel is a delightful oasis on a rather hectic street of downtown, close to the Plaza de Armas and Avenida Alameda. The hotel has a heavy dose of themed decor in its public spaces that represents the various cultures and regions of Chile from faux Easter Island moai to Mapuche Indian sculptures. The guest rooms, renovated several years ago, are modern and functional with double-paned windows and a pared-down style colored in varying earth tones, and soft beds are topped with crisp white duvets. Rooms are spacious and suites are double the size, with a sofa bed for kids. The hotel has a vast, atrium-like atmosphere with 12 floors whose interior balconies wrap around the lounge. Like the Fundador, this hotel charges rack rates to walk-ins that are twice the price of their Internet rate, so book ahead online.

San Antonio 65. ℂ **2/470-7400.** www.hotelgalerias.cl. 162 units. $308 double, $143 double (if booked on website). AE, DC, MC, V. Rates include breakfast. Metro: Santa Lucía. **Amenities:** Restaurant; bar; outdoor pool; sauna. *In room:* A/C, cable TV, hair dryer, minibar, free Wi-Fi.

INEXPENSIVE

Andes Hostel ★★★ 🎒 If you thought your hostelling days were over, it may be time to think again. Located at the pumping heart of the fashionable and energetic Lastarría neighborhood, the hostel is within walking distance to downtown historical attractions and Bellavista. There are dorm rooms that sleep four to six guests (with communal bathrooms) or single and double rooms with shared or private facilities. The spic-and-span, folksy rooms are a cut above most hostels, with embroidered sheets and duvets; all sheets and towels are provided and daily cleaning is included. The inviting communal living room feels like an art-house cafe with a vibrant retro mélange of leopard print rugs, pop art, and postmodern furnishings. There's also a rooftop deck with a BBQ for guests' use.

Monjitas 506. ℂ **2/632-9990.** www.andeshostel.com. 16 units. $17–$18 per person shared room sleeping 4–6; $42 single/double with shared bathroom; $58 double with private bathroom. AE, DC, MC, V. Metro: Bellas Artes. **Amenities:** Cafe; bar; room service. *In room:* A/C, TV, hair dryer, minibar, free Wi-Fi.

Hotel Foresta ★   Housed in an antique building that feels like an old home, this quirky budget hotel has a prime location in the Lastarría neighborhood facing Cerro San Lucía. In spite of the hotel's charming exterior, the rooms—though clean—are dated, with furniture that looks like it was purchased at a flea market. But it's about what you'd expect for the price, and a continental breakfast is included in their upper-story restaurant that looks out over the park. Stay away from the single rooms, which are gloomy and Lilliputian; opt instead for a "matrimonial" double, which is large enough to be a junior suite and has views of the park. Quieter rooms can be found facing the interior air shafts, but they offer drab views and aren't as picturesque as those facing the street.

Victoria Subercaseaux 353. ℂ **2/639-6261.** Fax 2/632-2996. hforestsa@terra.cl. 35 units. $66 double matrimonial; $45 single. AE, DC, MC, V. Metro: Univ. de Chile. **Amenities:** Restaurant; bar; free Wi-Fi in lobby. *In room:* TV, minibar.

Hotel París Nuevo ★   Stick with a room in the newer wing of this European-style budget hotel. Rooms in the older wing are resolutely for backpackers. The Hotel París is old and atmospheric, a mansion-turned-hotel with rooms of differing sizes and lots of winding stairs; some rooms feature Oriental rugs and mahogany molding. When booking, ask for a room with a terrace because they are the same price. Continental breakfast costs an extra C$1,500.

París 813. ℂ **2/664-0921.** Fax 2/639-4037. carbott@latinmail.com. 50 units. $38 "backpacker-style" double; $42 to $55 newer wing double. AE, DC, MC, V. Parking across the street C$5,000 per day. Metro: Univ. de Chile. **Amenities:** Cafe. *In room:* TV, no phone (lower-end rooms only).

Bellavista
VERY EXPENSIVE

The Aubrey ★★★ 📷   Upping the wow factor with a trendy yet elegant tone, this new boutique hotel, located in the heart of Bellavista at the foot of the Metropolitan Park, has finally brought pizzazz to the hotel scene in Santiago. Two historic mansions were masterfully renovated as one to create the property. A cobblestone patio leads up to the hotel's slick outdoor Jacuzzi pool, with views stretching over Bellavista. Every detail has been addressed, from the imported fixtures to laptop-sized safes to Italian ceramics and Sommier beds. Every room is differently sized and decorated; the most luxurious is the Art Deco suite with a private entrance, and the San Cristobal suite is the most romantic. Top-floor doubles have low, angular ceilings in what once was the attic, and Terraza Rooms come with a terrace patio and a view. Breakfast is outstanding and can be served in your room at no additional charge.

Constitución 317. ℂ **2/940-2800.** www.theaubrey.com. 15 units. $240–$350 double; $450 suite. AE, DC, MC, V. Limited parking. Metro: Baquedano. **Amenities:** Restaurant; lounge; concierge; outdoor heated pool. *In room:* A/C, TV, hair dryer, minibar, MP3 docking station, free Wi-Fi.

MODERATE

Hotel El Patio ★   The 11 rooms of the Hotel El Patio are spaced around the second floor of a 19th-century building that is part of the charming Patio Bellavista shopping/dining center. With creaky wood floors, antique plaster walls, and a winding staircase that you climb once the front desk has buzzed you in, El Patio is more an upscale hostel than a boutique hotel. Rooms are on the darker side but appointed with colorful contemporary duvets and minimal decor. The staff is courteous and knowledgeable, without being intrusive. A delicious healthy breakfast is served on a tiny rooftop terrace that overlooks the Patio de Bellavista, which is an enjoyable way to spend your first hour of the day, but the outdoor social scene and construction in the area is very bothersome to weary travelers and light sleepers, in spite of the double-paneled windows.

Pío Nono 61. ℂ **2/732-7571.** www.hoteldelpatio.cl. 11 units. $122 double standard; $143 double superior. AE, MC, DC, V. Metro: Baquedano. **Amenities:** Cafe; bar. *In room:* Fan, TV, hair dryer, free Wi-Fi.

Providencia
VERY EXPENSIVE

Sheraton Santiago ★ Crystal chandeliers, marble floors, and a voluminous lobby give this hotel a hint of glamour. The Sheraton, one of the first upscale hotels to open in Santiago decades ago, is actually two hotels: the older Sheraton with standard rooms, and the more luxurious **San Cristóbal Tower ★★★** with conference centers and executive rooms. The upside to the Sheraton is its spectacular views of Santiago and the Andes (book any room on the 10th floor and up), but the downside is that the hotel feels cut off from Providencia by the Mapocho River and a busy thoroughfare, although really it's just a 15-minute walk to the heart of Providencia. It is recommended that travelers only consider rooms in the San Cristóbal Tower due to the worn state of the standard rooms in the older wing. The Sheraton occasionally sells out to visiting conventioneers.

Av. Santa María 1742. ℂ **2/233-5000.** Fax 2/234-1066. www.sheraton.cl. 379 units. Sheraton: $189 double standard; San Cristóbal Tower: $279 double, $529 deluxe executive suite. AE, DC, MC, V. Metro: Pedro de Valdivia. **Amenities:** 3 restaurants; bar; babysitting; concierge; outdoor and indoor pools; sauna; tennis courts. *In room:* A/C, TV, hair dryer, minibar, stereo, Wi-Fi (C$7,125 per day).

EXPENSIVE

Hotel Le Rêve ★★★ Opened in May 2010, Le Rêve is impeccably designed, and immensely comfortable, with a tailored, French Provençal decor and homey touches such as a cheery blue-tiled kitchen that guests may use to make beverages or indulge in the hotel's nightly "midnight snack" of cakes and coffee. The hotel, housed in a renovated mansion, is conveniently located and steps from good restaurants, and its individual antiques, pleasing art, and fine detailing are a departure from the cookie-cutter decor commonly found in Santiago hotels. Room sizes vary, but are on the whole smaller than one would expect for the price. There are, however, plenty of soothing spaces to sit and relax here, especially a pebble-filled interior patio shaded by an enormous tree. The best rooms are 210 and 211, which open onto small terraces.

Orrego Luco 023. ℂ **2/757-6000.** Fax 2/757-6010. www.lerevehotel.cl. 31 units. $239 double standard; $289 double with terrace; $339 suite. AE, DC, MC, V. Metro: Pedro de Valdivia. **Amenities:** Cafe; kitchen for beverages. *In room:* A/C, TV, hair dryer, minibar, free Wi-Fi.

Radisson Hotel ★★ The Radisson Hotel is housed within the glitzy World Trade Center building in the area known as "San-hattan" for its financial clout. The location is very convenient for tourists and business travelers alike because it is close to Las Condes district businesses and the El Bosque restaurant row, and still just a few blocks from the heart of Providencia. Best of all, the guest rooms have a fresh and contemporary decor thanks to recent renovations. The gentlemanly and plush lobby seems out of step with the hotel's glass high-rise exterior. Get a room that faces the Andes (seventh floor and up). The health club and small pool on the rooftop have panoramic views.

Av. Vitacura 2610. ℭ **800/333-3333** in the U.S., or 2/203-6000 in Santiago. www.radisson.cl. 159 units. $170 double. AE, DC, MC, V. Metro: Tobalaba. **Amenities:** Restaurant; 2 bars; babysitting; concierge; Jacuzzi; indoor pool; sauna. *In room:* A/C, TV, hair dryer, minibar.

MODERATE

Hotel Orly ★★ 🏆 A European-style midrange hotel that's a good value, the Orly is close to absolutely everything, and the staff here is very welcoming. The hotel is housed in a renovated mansion with French-influenced architecture. The somewhat stuffy lobby has a few places to sit and relax and a small, glass-roofed patio; there's also a bar and a dining area where the staff serves a hearty buffet breakfast and courtesy snacks throughout the day. The interiors are a restful white and decorated with country manor furnishings. Room sizes vary; doubles come with two twins or a full-size bed and are of average size; a few singles are decidedly not for the claustrophobic.

Av. Pedro de Valdivia 027. ℭ **2/231-8947.** Fax 2/334-4403. www.hotelorly.cl. 28 units. $130 double; $130-$140 junior suite. AE, DC, MC, V. Metro: Pedro de Valdivia. **Amenities:** Cafe; bar; room service. *In room:* A/C, TV, hair dryer, minibar.

Los Españoles ★ This is a good hotel for travelers seeking generic comfort. Los Españoles is part of the Best Western chain, although it has been run by the same family for 30 years—in fact, the hotel is their old family home, and their friendliness really makes you feel at home yourself. The rooms are spotless and comfortable, and feature a country-style decor; each is sized differently and some are dark and smaller, so let them know what kind of room you want. The front desk staff is very helpful with information about what to do and see, and their buffet breakfast is hearty and varied. This hotel sits near the Mapocho River in a quiet residential area that is a 10-minute walk to the commercial center of Providencia and the closest Metro station, but best of all the hotel faces a lengthy park that's a good place for a run or a walk.

Los Españoles 2539. ℭ **2/232-1824.** Fax 2/233-1048. www.losespanoles.cl. 50 units. $130 double; $150 suite. AE, DC, MC, V. Metro: Pedro de Valdivia. **Amenities:** Restaurant; bar; babysitting; room service; sauna. *In room:* A/C, TV, hair dryer, minibar, free Wi-Fi.

Meridiano Sur ★★ 🧳 What travelers love about this newer inn is how well the vibe blends with what brings travelers to Chile in the first place: peace and nature. The friendly innkeeper and her cheery staff provide personalized attention that extends to more than just restaurant reservations; they seem eager to help with just about everything. The inn is located in a Providencia area with old homes that have been adapted into offices, so at night it is dead quiet. The Meridiano, too, is in a refurbished home made of stucco and decorated with upscale touches such as marble bathrooms, modernist furniture, poetry painted on the walls, and artisanal weavings hanging in the hallways. Standard doubles are tiny, so pay the additional $10 for a Doble Meridiano. The top floor loft sleeps five and is great for families.

Santa Beatriz 256. ℭ **2/235-3659.** www.meridianosur.cl. 8 rooms. $125-$135 double; $260 loft. AE, DC, MC, V. Metro: Manuel Montt. **Amenities:** Cafe; lounge w/TV. *In room:* A/C, TV, free Wi-Fi.

Vilafranca Petit Hotel ★★★ 🧳 One of Santiago's original B&B-style hotels, the Vilafranca is housed in a superbly refurbished old mansion and provides travelers with a more personalized lodging option brimming with character and coziness, at a price that's reasonable. As with any B&B, the feeling that you're bunking in an old home is clearly evident, yet the interiors are bestowed with a French Provençal design, and lovely old antique armoires and nightstands, fresh white linens, and walls painted in soothing tones of ecru and decorated with dried sprigs of flowers and simple sketch art. It's a great value for this neighborhood, but then many rooms are very small. Service is delightful. Common areas include a living room with over-stuffed sofas and a cobblestone patio fringed in greenery.

Perez Valenzuela 1650. ℰ **2/232-1413.** www.vilafranca.cl. 8 units. $98–$105 double AE, DC, MC, V. Metro: Manuel Montt. **Amenities:** Cafe. *In room:* A/C (some rooms), TV, hair dryer, free Wi-Fi.

INEXPENSIVE

Chilhotel ☺ ✦ Price and a convenient location are the major draws for this functional, no-frills lodging, tucked away on a quiet street. A medley of basic rooms, which vary from prissy to spartan, are woven through the labyrinthine corridors of an eccentric, rambling old house. While certain areas of the place could do with upgrading (like the carpets), the sizeable rooms are all crisp, clean, and comfortable. The common areas are more akin to a hostel than a hotel, with travelers hanging out and exchanging stories over beer and pisco sours. Ask to see a few rooms before you commit; and, if you are noise sensitive, be sure to request a room overlooking the tranquil courtyard. Rooms come in four sizes, each with a private bathroom, and sleep up to five people.

Cirujano Guzmán 103. ℰ **2/264-0643.** Fax 2/264-1323. www.chilhotel.cl. 32 units. $75 double standard. Rates include breakfast. AE, DC, MC, V. Metro: Manuel Montt. **Amenities:** Cafe. *In room:* A/C (superior rooms only), TV, fridge, free Internet (superior rooms only).

Las Condes & El Golf

VERY EXPENSIVE

Grand Hyatt Regency Santiago ★★ The Grand Hyatt is a 24-story atrium tower with two adjacent wings and four glass elevators that whisk guests up to split-level rooms and terraced suites. Inside it feels as spacious as an airport hanger, but it exudes a sense of chic glamour lacking in so many high-end hotels. What sets this hotel apart is the flawless service provided by the staff and peerless amenities, amply spacious guest rooms with views of the Andes (rooms with an eastern orientation from the 10th floor up), its lush palm-and-fern-fringed pool, and the best gym/spa of any hotel in Santiago. Guests in suites enjoy their own 16th-floor private lounge for lingering over breakfast and soaking up the spectacular view. On the down side, you'll always need to take a taxi because the location at a crazy traffic loop makes it difficult and too far away to walk anywhere from here. Cheaper deals can be found when booking on their website.

Av. Kennedy 4601. ℰ **2/950-1234.** Fax 2/950-3155. www.santiago.grand.hyatt.com. 310 units, 26 suites. $250–$299 grand deluxe (double); $310–$399 Club King. AE, DC, MC, V. **Amenities:** 3 restaurants; bar; babysitting; concierge; exercise room; free Internet (in lobby); Jacuzzi; outdoor pool; room service; sauna; tennis courts. *In room:* A/C, TV, hair dryer, minibar, Wi-Fi (C$7,125 per day).

Ritz-Carlton Santiago ★★★ Expect to be pampered here. Though the exterior of the Ritz-Carlton is remarkably plain, it is one of Santiago's finest hotels. The interiors are plush and luxurious in the Ritz-Carlton fashion, and there is a fabulous rooftop swimming pool with a glass-dome ceiling. The Ritz is near restaurants and the thriving economic hub of Santiago, making this a more convenient choice than the Hyatt. But what really stands out here is the gracious, attentive service. The guest rooms are deluxe but in a homespun, floral kind of way; still, each spacious room is quiet, spotless, and blessed with heavenly beds. The hotel's lobby, which has a two-story rotunda and floors made of imported marble, sets a plush, mature tone. Note that the Ritz in Santiago is more economically priced than many of their other hotels, and they offer special packages on their website.

El Alcalde 15. ✆ **800/241-3333** from the U.S., or 2/470-8500 in Santiago. Fax 2/470-8501. www.ritzcarlton.com. 205 units. $358 deluxe room; $390–$458 club room. AE, DC, MC, V. Metro: El Golf. **Amenities:** 3 restaurants; bar; babysitting; concierge; exercise room; Jacuzzi; indoor rooftop pool; room service; sauna. *In room:* A/C, TV, hair dryer, minibar, Wi-Fi (C$12,000 per day).

W Hotel Santiago ★★ Like all W hotels, the decor here is over-the-top trendy, ideal for fashionistas and the chic set seeking a little style with their stay. Each floor is individually decorated, with a stunning fourth-floor lobby lounge and bar wrapped in mirrors and backed by an endless loop of chill-out music. The number-one feature is the hotel's rooftop bar lounge and swimming pool with truly beautiful views of Santiago's La Dehesa district and the towering Andes behind it; you could easily while away an entire afternoon here. As with all W hotels, the vocabulary here is a bit cheeky—the concierge is called "Whatever Wherever" and staff are known as "W insiders," and although the staff here is friendly, sharper service can be found at other luxury hotels in Santiago. All guest rooms are spacious and have floor-to-ceiling windows, and deluxe mattresses and sheets. The restaurants, from the covered terrace at Terraza to the Asian-Peruvian fusion at Osaka, are popular with the local Blackberry-and–high heels crowd.

Isidora Goyenechea 3000. ✆ **2/770-000.** Fax 2/770-0003. www.whotels.com. 196 units. $539 "Wonderful Room," $719 "Fantastic Suite". AE, DC, MC, V. Metro: El Golf. **Amenities:** 3 restaurants; bar; concierge; exercise room; free Internet (in lobby); pool. *In room:* A/C, DVD player, hair dryer, minibar, Wi-Fi (C$7,125 per day).

MODERATE

Atton del Bosque ★ 💣 Just steps from the sidewalk cafes of El Bosque, this 5-year-old midrange hotel provides standard rooms at very good rates. In fact, it's the best priced hotel in the area and appeals to many business travelers on more limited expense accounts. Rooms are decorated with earthy tones like rust and mustard yellow. All have plasma TVs and sterile bathrooms, which may remind you of a hospital. It may be a bit lackluster, but it's practical. This hotel is particularly friendly to those with mobility problems, from the rooms to the small wheelchair-accessible rooftop pool.

Roger de Flor 2770. ✆ **2/947-3600.** www.atton.com. 240 units. $140 double, $160 junior suite. AE, DC, MC, V. Metro: El Golf. **Amenities:** Restaurant; bar; small exercise room; free Internet (in business center); pool; free Wi-Fi. *In room:* A/C, hair dryer.

La Sebastiana Apart Hotel ★ ☺ 💣 A relative newcomer in the Las Condes neighborhood, this apart-hotel is just what it says: hotel rooms with living areas and kitchens. It's attractive, fresh, and decorated with inexpensive but trendy furniture and store-bought art. Rooms come in three sizes: studios, one-bedrooms (standard), and a two-bedroom (superior), the latter of which has a sofa bed for a total of six guests. It's an ideal place for long-term visitors (who pay a discounted rate for stays of 2 weeks or longer), and families with young children; and you can't beat the price or the location close to shops and restaurants, nor the outdoor, rooftop pool (available during summer only).

San Sebastian 2727. ✆ **2/658-7220.** www.lasebastiana.cl. 45 units. $72 studio; $105 studio; $125 standard; $185 superior; discounts given for longer stays. AE, DC, MC, V. Metro: Tobalaba. **Amenities:** Outdoor pool; free Wi-Fi (at shared computer). *In room:* A/C, cable TV, CD player, kitchenette, minibar.

Plaza El Bosque ★★ Catering to business travelers seeking a pied-à-terre during a lengthier stay in Santiago, the Plaza el Bosque offers very spacious one- and two-bedroom "suites" with living areas and a kitchenette. The hotel is classy and contemporary, a blend of Asian decor with stuffier oriental rugs and glossy floors, and centrally located next to services and restaurants. But the perk here is really the hotel's chic 17th-floor restaurant with an outdoor terrace that affords city views backed by the Andean skyline. The hotel is less suited for young children, but their billiard room is a great bonus for teens. Friendly and attentive service makes you feel at home. Located in the heart of El Bosque, the hotel's entrance is on a quiet tree-lined street and not on the main drag.

Ebro 2828. © **2/498-1800.** Fax 2/498-1801. www.plazaelbosque.cl. 179 units. $135–$165 standard suite; $160–$185 superior suite. AE, DC, MC, V. Metro: Tobalaba. **Amenities:** 2 restaurants; bar; babysitting; concierge; exercise room; rooftop pool; room service; sauna; spa. *In room:* A/C, TV, hair dryer, kitchenette (in executive suites), minibar.

WHERE TO DINE

Santiago's gastronomic scene has undergone a culinary revolution during the past decade, with an influx of ethnic restaurants and trendy eateries serving fusion-style, creative cuisine commonly known as *cocina de autor*. The culinary scene is now fertile enough to persuade the city's most talented chefs to stay rather than flee to Europe or the U.S. High-end, haute-cuisine restaurants are predominately springing up in the eastern edge of Santiago's swanky Vitacura neighborhood north of Las Condes. While it's gratifying to see young Chileans study to become "chefs" rather than "cooks," Santiago restaurants in general have a ways to go before reaching the caliber of other world class cities.

Downtown eateries cater principally to office workers, meaning they're open for lunch only and closed on weekends (there are several exceptions in the Lastarría neighborhood, on the east side of Cerro Santa Lucía). Travelers seeking to dine well at lunch and on a tight budget should always opt for the *menú del día, menú ejecutivo,* or *colación* for C$3,500 to C$7,000 that includes an appetizer, main course, beverage, coffee, and dessert. Restaurants advertise their daily fixed-price lunches on chalkboards or on signs posted near the front door.

In the peculiar Chilean fashion of concentrating similar businesses in one neighborhood, restaurant "clusters" have been popping up like mushrooms around the city. Bellavista is perhaps the best neighborhood to see this phenomenon, with its mind-boggling number of artsy restaurants (most of which come and go every 2 years or so) that range from Chilean to Mexican to Mediterranean to Asian. Both Avenida El Bosque Norte and its sister street, Avenida Isidora Goyenechea, are lined with a mélange of upscale eateries and American chain restaurants, and now the Lastarria/ Parque Forestal and Vitacura neighborhoods are forging ahead as the new dining hot spots. A few of the local favorites from these neighborhoods are listed below, but you could really just stroll the streets until something strikes your fancy. Don't overlook dining in one of the city's 5-star hotels, either. Chefs at the Ritz-Carlton's **Adra** restaurant, the Sheraton's **El Cid,** and the W Hotel's **NoSo** are impressing foodies with their new takes on Chilean cuisine, which has been rather unfairly denigrated for quite some time.

Santiago is not a cafe or bar society. The reason Starbucks is now popular in Santiago is that nothing existed like it before. Cafes are mostly found in the Lastarria area, and there's also **Café Tavelli** (© **2/481-5315;** www.tavelli.cl), a Chilean chain with good pastries, ice cream, and sandwiches. Tavelli can be found at Andres de Fuenzalida 36 in Providencia, with outdoor seating in an artsy shopping area; in Las Condes at Isidora Goyenechea 2891; and downtown within the beautiful Teatro

Municipal building at Tenderini 168. There are many cafes in the Lastarría neighborhood (see below).

See the maps on p. 76, 79, and 81 to locate the restaurants reviewed below.

Downtown

Restaurants in the Lastarría neighborhood offer evening dining if you are staying downtown and would rather not wander too far. Lastarría, also known as Parque Forestal or Bellas Artes, is a burgeoning artsy, cafe-oriented neighborhood that has undergone a revival in the past few years, and it is undoubtedly the most charming neighborhood in Santiago. Outstanding homemade ice cream and sandwiches can be found at **Emporio La Rosa** (corner of Monjitas and Merced; ✆ **2/638-9257;** Mon–Wed 8am–9pm and Thurs–Sun 9am–10pm), with outdoor seating; **Zabo** (Plaza Mulatto Gil de Castro; ✆ **2/639-3604;** Mon–Wed 1pm–midnight, Thurs–Sat 1pm–1am), which serves sushi and cocktails in a pretty cafe with outdoor seating; and **"R"** (Plaza Mulatto Gil de Castro; ✆ **2/664-9844;** Mon–Fri 11:30am–1am and Sat 7pm–2am), a cozy spot for wine and conversation, although the ambience is far better than the food. **Mosqueto Café** (corner of Villavicencio and Lastarria; ✆ **2/639-1627;** daily 8:30am–10pm), serves coffee, cakes, and sandwiches in a gorgeous, meticulously restored antique building that also houses the cultural center and crafts shop El Observatorio (see "Shopping," p. 111). You can park your rental car in the garage at Merced 317.

EXPENSIVE

Zully ★★ 🔲 INTERNATIONAL   Chic, yet true to the utterly charming, historical neighborhood in which it is located, Zully is a fun place to dine. The American-owned restaurant covers four floors of a lovingly restored old mansion and boasts a wine-tasting cellar, an interior patio, and trendily decorated dining rooms. For a memorable, even romantic, evening, you may sacrifice quality (especially considering the expensive price). No matter, you won't be sorry you taxied over when you lay eyes on this architectural gem. It's best to take a taxi here at night; during the day, take the Metro to the República stop, walk out the north exit, head east 1½ blocks to Calle Concha y Toro, and turn left.

Concha y Toro 34. ✆ **2/696-1378.** www.squadrittoristorante.cl. Reservations recommended for dinner. Main courses C$12,900–C$17,500. AE, DC, MC, V. Mon–Fri 1–4pm and 8pm–1am; Sat 8pm–2am (or when the last guest leaves). Metro: República.

MODERATE

Ambrosía ★★ 🍴 INTERNATIONAL   Tucked behind the Casa Colorado Museum (enter the museum and cross the patio to get here), Ambrosía is a chic little eatery and quiet haven from the boisterous downtown street outside. The menu features an eclectic offering of Peruvian, Asian, and Italian dishes; examples include blue-cheese salad with prosciutto and sunflower seeds, sole filet with passion fruit and arugula, osso buco with goat cheese gnocchi, and risotto with shrimp, scallops, and shitake mushrooms. There is a daily fixed-price menu for C$13,000 including an appetizer, main course, dessert, beverage, and coffee, which they update on their website daily. With its patio dining, this restaurant is ideal for summer days. Service is friendly, too, in a way common with family businesses.

Merced 838 A. ✆ **2/697-2023.** www.ambrosia.cl. Main courses C$7,500–C$8,500. AE, DC, MC, V. Mon–Fri noon–4pm. Metro: Plaza de Armas.

Bar Nacional CHILEAN   Bar Nacional is an institution in downtown Santiago, having drawn locals for more than 50 years for simple, hearty Chilean fare in timeworn, dinerlike atmosphere. On Calle Bandera and Paseo Huérfanos, both are relatively identical. This is where to try Chilean favorites such as empanadas, *cazuela* (a hearty chicken soup), *pastel de choclo* (a meat-and-corn casserole), and the cholesterol-boosting *lomo a lo pobre* (steak and fries topped with sautéed onions and a fried egg).

Bar Nacional 1: Huérfanos 1151. © **2/696-5986.** Bar Nacional 2: Bandera 371. © 2/695-3368. Main courses C$2,900–C$6,400; sandwiches C$1,950–C$3,200. AE, DC, MC, V. Mon–Fri 7:30am–11pm; Sat 7:30am–4pm. Metro: Plaza de Armas.

Blue Jar ★★★ INTERNATIONAL

Owned and operated by a British expat, the Blue Jar is arguably the best restaurant in the civic center area, serving divine gourmet cuisine that is neither fussy nor pretentious, yet artfully prepared and served by a cheery staff. The restaurant could easily fit into New York or London, with its contemporary decor and large black-and-white photos that adorn the walls. The fixed-price luncheons are a good value (around C$7,000 for a three-course meal), but diners here often opt for their delicious gourmet burgers, a fresh salad, or a bowl of homemade pasta. Take advantage of their happy hour from 5pm to 9:30pm after a long day of sightseeing, with two-for-one drinks and snacks such as charcuterie and cheese platters or fish tacos.

Almirante L. Gotuzzo 102. © **2/699-8399.** www.bluejar.cl. Main courses C$7,200–C$10,500; sandwiches C$5,200–C$5,800. AE, DC, MC, V. Mon–Fri 8:30am–9:30pm. Metro: Moneda.

Confitería Torres ★★ 📷 CHILEAN

Saved from the wrecker's ball, Confitería Torres, Santiago's oldest restaurant, first opened its doors in 1879, and has been splendidly reborn as a contemporary eatery serving a sophisticated crowd. This restaurant was the haunt of intellectuals, writers, politicians, and poets for decades, including former president Barros Luco (for whom the eponymous melted cheese and slab of steak sandwich served throughout Chile is named) and poets Rubén Darío and Vicente Huidobro. The Chilean couple who invested in this project rescued the original Art Deco style and have spruced up what was once a rather fatigued ambience. The cuisine is influenced by century-old recipes such as beef marinated in cilantro, and conger eel with a barnacle sauce—simple but tasty. On Fridays and Saturdays, the restaurant has live tango music; in the afternoon, the restaurant is a good bet for tea and cakes. Confitería Torres also has a **restaurant/cafe** within the Centro Cultural (p. 104), offering the same menu but in a more masculine, modish ambience. It's an attractive place for lunch, but for the real deal, visit their locale on Avenida Alameda.

Alameda 1570. © **2/688-0751.** www.confiteriatorres.cl. Main courses C$3,500–C$6,200. AE, DC, MC, V. Mon–Sat 11am–midnight (later Fri–Sat). Metro: Univ. de Chile.

Japón ★★ SUSHI/JAPANESE

This is hands-down Santiago's best restaurant for sushi, principally because of the quality and freshness of their fish, and the fact that they don't run out of harder-to-get varieties such as tuna. Owned and operated by Japanese immigrants, this is Chile's oldest Japanese restaurant. On any given day, at least some of the clientele are visiting Japanese—a good sign that the food hits the mark. Also on offer are udon soups, tempura, teriyaki meats, and so on. The restaurant has a handsome sushi bar and table seating. To get here, from the Baquedano Metro station, head south on Vicuña Mackenna and turn right on Baron Pierre De Coubertin street.

Baron Pierre De Coubertin 39. © **2/222-4517.** Main courses C$3,200–C$7,500. AE, DC, MC, V. Mon–Sat 12:30–3:30pm and 7:30–10:30pm (Fri–Sat until midnight). Metro: Baquedano.

Opera & Catedral ★★★ CONTEMPORARY FRENCH/CHILEAN   These two eateries each have a sleek look that would fit in nicely in a city like New York or London, and accordingly, both are popular with the young glitterati of Santiago, and discerning customers who enjoy a little more sophistication in their dining experience. Opera is a polished fine-dining establishment, with exposed brick walls and white-linen tablecloths. Upstairs at moderately priced Catedral, the look is minimalist, with gun-battle-gray walls, wicker chairs, and a couple of leather couches, and there is also a rooftop terrace for summer evenings. Opera pays homage to French cuisine, serving fabulous dishes such as delicate foie gras, chicken breast poached in broth and served with truffles, and a "tasting" of five kinds of crème brûlée. Catedral serves modern takes on Chilean classics, with a few Asian-influenced dishes, gourmet sandwiches, and a very tasty *crudo*, or steak tartare. The owners of Opera & Catedral recently opened Cafe del Opera next door, a casual place for a coffee, sandwiches, and ice cream.

Both at the corner of Merced and José Miguel de la Barra. ⓒ **2/664-3048.** www.operacatedral.cl. Reservations required at Opera; reservations not accepted at Catedral. AE, DC, MC, V. Opera: Main courses C$8,000–C$12,000. Mon–Fri 1–3:45pm and 8–10:45pm; Sat 8–10:45pm. Catedral: Main courses C$5,000–C$7,500. Mon–Thurs 1pm–3am; Fri–Sat 1pm–5am. Metro: Bellas Artes.

Patagonia Café ★★ ARGENTINE   This unpretentious eatery is warm and inviting, with rough-hewn wood interiors and a floor-to-ceiling wine rack boasting excellent varieties. During warmer days, you can't beat their sidewalk seating for dining on simply prepared yet surprisingly tasty and hearty food and catching a few rays. The *parrilla* (BBQ) for two, which comes with a platter of grilled meats and vegetables, plus a bottle of wine, costs C$21,000 and could easily feed three. The menu focuses on meats, seafood, and delicious sandwiches prepared with Patagonian-style recipes and exotic meats such as wild boar and venison. Their lamb is quite good, as is the king crab ravioli and the stuffed trout. On weekdays, there is a fixed-price lunch from noon to 4pm for around C$5,500. This restaurant fills up quickly during the lunch hour, so arrive early or late.

Lastarria 96. ⓒ **2/664-3830.** www.patagoniarestobar.cl. Reservations not accepted. Main courses C$5,600–C$6,500. AE, DC, MC, V. Daily 10am–midnight. Metro: Univ. Católica.

Squadritto ★ ITALIAN   Squadritto, one of the older restaurants in the Lastarria neighborhood, has an elegant, Tuscan-style dining room that is accented with dark wooden furnishings, ochre-painted walls, plants, and ambient lighting. The well-executed menu pays homage to classic northern Italian staples with menu stalwarts such as fried calamari and eggplant parmesan followed by seafood risotto and king crab ravioli. The dishes are rather rich, with cream making its way into many of the pasta entrees but, then again, the pasta portions are hardly monumental—though they can easily be split as an appetizer should you wish to sample one of their fish-and-meat specialties as an entree. These fish-and-meat dishes change according to the season and tend to be simpler in presentation.

Resal 332. ⓒ **2/632-2121.** Reservations recommended. Main courses C$6,800–C$8,900. AE, DC, MC, V. Mon–Fri 1–4pm and 7pm–midnight. Metro: Univ. Católica.

INEXPENSIVE

El Hoyo ★★ 🄾 TRADITIONAL CHILEAN   A haven for foodies searching for the quintessential "Chilean" meal, this century-old restaurant is Santiago's best "picada," a dive-like restaurant whose slogan is *chicha, chancho, y pipeño*, a reference to three classic specialties: fermented fruit juice, pork, and a fruity, young white wine.

The host of the show *No Reservations,* Anthony Bourdain, called this his favorite restaurant in Chile, but then the average diner might not love the meat-heavy menu (think innards and boiled ham hocks). Highlights are the *arollado* (seasoned pork rolled in a thin layer of pork fat and boiled), the *plateada* (stewed beef), and *porotos granados* (broad-bean and corn stew). The restaurant is located fairly far from the Plaza de Armas, so a taxi ride here is a good idea. The decor is spartan, and waiters in stiff white shirts and bow ties provide perfunctory service.

San Vicente 375. ℂ **2/689-0339.** www.elhoyo.cl. Reservations not accepted. Main courses C$3,100–C$7,200. AE, DC, MC, V. Mon–Fri 11am–11pm and Sat 11am–9pm.

Bellavista

The streets Constitución and Dardignac are packed door-to-door with restaurants, but there is also a bounty of dining options (20 eateries and counting) within the **Patio Bellavista** complex between Pío Nono and Constitución streets, the best of which are **Barandiaran** (reviewed below); **Le Fournil,** a French bistro with good onion soup and set meals (ℂ **2/248-9699**); and **La Bota,** with Italian cuisine (ℂ **2/248-9747**).

MODERATE

Azul Profundo ☺ SEAFOOD   A popular seafood restaurant for its variety and nautical decor, Azul Profundo, or "Deep Blue," serves a lengthy list of Chilean fish, including yellowfin tuna and vidriola from Easter Island. Order your fish *a la plancha,* and it will arrive sizzling on a cast-iron plate; add just a squeeze of lemon or choose one of five sauces. If there are two of you, you might opt for a shared dish such as *curanto,* the surf-and-turf stew from Chiloé, or a Tabla Marina, a selection of shellfish and salmon served with grilled vegetables. The cozy nautical decor—fish nets, a wooden siren hanging from a mock ship's bow, and bathroom doors that look like they lead to a sailor's bunk—lend a theme park vibe to the restaurant, which makes this a gem of a place for young families.

Constitución 111. ℂ **2/738-0288.** Main courses C$7,900–C$9,000. AE, DC, MC, V. Daily 1–4:30pm and 7:30pm–12:30am (Fri–Sat until 1:30am). Metro: Baquedano.

Barandiaran ★★ PERUVIAN   Peru is widely regarded as home to the best cuisine in Latin America after Mexico, and one of the best places in Santiago to sample the country's spicy, delicious concoctions is Barandiaran. The eponymous Chef Marco Barandiaran launched his career as the chef in residence at the Peruvian embassy before graduating to become a charismatic TV personality in addition to an acclaimed gastro entrepreneur. This is the third and the newest Barandiaran restaurant, and the best in terms of service, its attractive yet casual ambience, and location. Because it is tucked away in the Patio Bellavista market, you can shop till you drop and then refuel on superbly prepared *ceviche,* fried calamari, *parihuela* (sea bass stew), or tender lamb in a cilantro puree. There's also lots of patio seating. The pisco sours will knock your socks off.

Constitución 38 (inside Patio Bellavista). ℂ **2/737-0725.** Reservations not necessary. Daily noon–11:45pm. Main courses C$4,500–C$7,900. AE, DC, MC, V. Daily 1pm–midnight. Metro: Baquedano.

Como Agua Para Chocolate ★ NUEVO LATINO   Inspired by the romantic whimsy of the famous novel (*Like Water for Chocolate*) with the same name, this is not your average restaurant. The menu aims to spark passions, with aphrodisiac options like the Passion and Vigour Beef and a seafood sampler known as the Lover's Sigh. Lovers can also share the Diego (Rivera) and Frida (Kahlo) Stew. The decor is a dreamy renovation of two old homes. The food is not always as heart-throbbing as the setting, but the service is lovely and the entire experience fun and light-hearted.

Constitución 88. ℂ **2/777-8740.** www.comoaguaparachocolate.cl. Main courses C$6,500–C$8,000. AE, DC, MC, V. Reservations recommended. Tues–Sat 12:30–5pm and 8pm–1am; Sun 12:30–5pm and 8pm–midnight. Metro: Baquedano.

Divertimento ★★ TRADITIONAL CHILEAN   Santiago's best restaurant for lunch on a balmy summer day, Divertimento sits at the base of the Cerro San Cristobal and is enveloped in greenery from grand, towering trees that provide a refreshing and delightful ambience for outdoor seating. The restaurant specializes in Chilean cuisine and also serves traditional Italian pastas; standout items include chicken stewed in cognac, beef ribs braised in red wine, roasted pork ribs, and sea bass with cilantro shellfish. Service is absent-minded and harried, however Divertimento isn't the kind of place you visit in a hurry, so take it in stride. Divertimento is a good lunch spot following a hike up and down the Metropolitan Park (located near the Pedro de Valdivia entrance). Always make a lunch reservation if you want to sit outside, otherwise the wait can be up to an hour.

Avenida El Cerro at Pedro de Valdivia Norte. ℂ **2/233-1920.** www.divertimento.cl. Reservations recommended. Main courses C$7,400–C$8,800. AE, DC, MC, V. Mon–Sat 1–11:30pm and Sun 1–10pm. No Metro access.

El Toro ★ CHILEAN/LIGHT FARE   An enduring favorite among hipsters and artists, El Toro is the kind of restaurant you expect to see in San Francisco's Mission District, or London's Shoreditch. The ambience is laid-back, service is friendly, and a whimsical 1970s decor with disco balls, paper menus, and crayon graffiti scrawled on the walls sets the irreverent mood. The international culinary repertoire won't win any medals for originality, but each dish, ranging from bountiful Caesar salads to crepes oozing with mushroom and cheese and simply grilled salmon, is flavorful and satisfying.

Bellavista location: Loreto 33. ℂ **2/737-5937.** Providencia location: Santa Beatriz 280. ℂ **2/235-5012.** Reservations recommended for parties of 4–6. Main courses C$5,200–C$6,800. AE, DC, MC, V. Mon–Sat 1–4pm and 7:30pm–midnight. Metro: Baquedano.

Etniko ★★★ ASIAN/SUSHI   Etniko is one of Santiago's hippest restaurants, serving Asian-influenced cuisine in a trendy and sophisticated space frequented by Santiago's stylish young adults and expats. Soberly attired waiters will guide you through the menu's eclectic selections, but regulars laud the many varieties of sushi (don't miss the Easter Island tuna). Also on offer are Japanese tempura and Chinese and Vietnamese stir-fries, and a *ceviche* bar. Etniko has an open-air atrium dining area, and the bar is a lively, fun place for a cocktail. As the evening accelerates, the dining room pulsates to the modern beat of house music played by talented resident DJs, and diners tend to head to the adjoining disco-bar afterwards and make a night of it. The front door is usually shut, so ring the bell to enter, and don't expect the place to fill up until 9 or 10pm.

Constitución 172. ℂ **2/732-0119.** www.etniko.cl. Reservations recommended. Main courses C$5,200– C$8,000. AE, DC, MC, V. Mon–Sat 8pm–midnight (Fri–Sat until 2am). Metro: Baquedano.

INEXPENSIVE

Galindo TRADITIONAL CHILEAN   Galindo is a local institution and a hit for its reasonable prices and its *comida casera*: simple, hearty dishes like your mother used to make—if your mother were Chilean, that is. Virtually any kind of typical meal served in Chilean homes can be found here, including *pastel de choclo* (a ground beef and chicken casserole) and *cazuela* (chicken soup with vegetables). The atmosphere is folksy and casual; in the evening, the restaurant serves as a meeting place for writers, artists, and other locals to share a bottle of wine and good conversation. There's additional seating outside on the sidewalk, and it's open late into the evening, even on weekdays.

Dardignac 098. ✆ **2/777-0116.** Main courses C$4,500–C$6,200. AE, DC, MC, V. Mon–Sat 10am–2am. Metro: Baquedano.

Providencia

In addition to fine dining, avenues Providencia and 11 de Septiembre are chock-a-bloc with fast-food restaurants and cheap eateries such as *fuentes de soda* and *schoperías*, which serve draft beer, burgers, and hot dogs. Providencia offers the most variety in cuisine of any neighborhood in Santiago, plus plenty of cafes and sandwich shops; the best here is **Dominó**, at Avenida Pedro de Valdivia 28, Avenida Providencia 2304, or at Avenida Providencia 1355 (✆ **600/411-0600;** www.domino.cl). A very popular sandwich chain, Dominó is known for its hefty sandwiches and especially its *churrasco* (meat, green beans, and tomatoes) and its messy *italiano* hot dog with avocado, tomato, and mayonnaise.

EXPENSIVE

Astrid y Gastón ★★★ INTERNATIONAL   If you're looking to blow your budget, this is your place. Peruvian celebrity chef Gastón, his wife Astrid, and his kitchen staff have created a wonderfully provocative menu filled with delicious flavor combinations using luxurious ingredients in unexpected ways. The ambience is brightly lit, elegant, and better for a meal among friends than a romantic date. The service at Astrid y Gastón is flawless, with a sommelier and one of the city's most interesting and varied wine lists. Try the fresh goose liver, or my favorite, king crab ravioli. Dessert orders must be placed early so that the kitchen staff can make each one from scratch. If you are on a budget, come in for *ceviche* and a pisco sour.

Antonio Bellet 201. ✆ **2/650-9125.** Reservations required. Main courses C$7,500–C$10,000. AE, DC, MC, V. Mon–Fri 1–3pm and 8pm–midnight; Sat 8pm–midnight. Metro: Pedro de Valdivia.

MODERATE

Aquí Está Coco ★★ SEAFOOD   Aquí Está Coco, one of Santiago's most famous seafood restaurants, reopened in 2010 like a phoenix from the ashes following a devastating fire that destroyed the restaurant. The rebuilt restaurant is decidedly more attractive and classy, but thankfully still exudes the same "elegant kitsch" it's always had, making this a fun place to dine. The restaurant serves outstanding seafood dishes that are artfully prepared but not too overly conceptual: king crab empanadas, sautéed conger eel with hot pepper and cilantro, and abalone risotto are a few examples. The Barra Chilota—a bar made from a Chiloé fishing boat—has a selection of tasty appetizers and *ceviches*, or you could splurge and order a fresh king crab for two. The restaurant boasts an excellent selection of fine piscos, and there is a gift shop on-site, too.

La Concepción 236. ✆ **2/410-6200.** www.aquiestacoco.cl. Reservations recommended. Main courses C$7,200–C$9,800. AE, DC, MC, V. Mon–Fri 1–3pm and 7–11pm, Sat 8am–11pm. Metro: Pedro de Valdivia.

Baco ★★ FRENCH/CHILEAN   The smartly decorated and well attended Baco is an excellent value and offers an unusually cozy and agreeable ambience, including year-round outdoor seating. In fact, this little French bistro seems to be everyone's favorite place to dine these days, in part because the eatery offers such an outstanding selection of wine by the glass. Diners familiar with French bistros will recognize many of the dishes on the menu, including onion soup, steak tartar, duck magret, and a tender filet mignon with *pomme frites* and béarnaise sauce; order these or the *bacalao* (dried and salted cod), cheese plates, and the salmon tartare, and finish it off with a creamy crème brûlée.

Calle Nueva de Lyon 113. © **2/231-4444.** Reservations recommended. Main courses C$5,400–C$7,900. AE, DC, MC, V. Daily 12:30pm–midnight. Metro: Los Leones.

Bar Liguria ★★★ ◙ CHILEAN/BISTRO   The city's two convivial Bar Ligurias are vibrant, warm, and eternally popular with actors, writers, businesspeople, and just about everyone else who comes to soak up the kitschy, bohemian atmosphere. Do not miss dining here once while in Santiago. The eclectic clientele chat and philosophize loudly at rickety tables draped with red-and-white check tablecloths surrounded by a gallery of floor-to-ceiling posters, paintings, maps, and memorabilia. At lunchtime and on weekends after 9pm, you'll usually have to wait 10 to 15 minutes at the bar before you get a table. The Manuel Montt location has two bars and three dining areas, but manages to remain cozy. A fleet of bow-tied waiters provides entertaining and prompt service. The Liguria serves ample portions of emblematic Chilean meat and seafood dishes that change weekly, in addition to a handful of Italian dishes such as lasagna and ricotta ravioli, as well as hefty sandwiches (try either the fish or beef *plateada* sandwiches) and salads. Don't miss a visit here.

Ojeda location: Luis Thayer Ojeda 019. © **2/231-1393.** Providencia location: Av. Providencia 1373. © **2/235-7914.** Reservations not accepted. Main courses C$4,800–C$7,900. AE, DC, MC, V. Mon–Sat noon–1am (Fri–Sat until 3am). Metro: Los Leones (Ojeda branch), and Manuel Montt (Providencia branch).

INEXPENSIVE

California Cantina & Sports Bar ★ AMERICAN   If you've had it with Chilean fare and have a hankering for American cuisine, or just want things easy with waiters serving you in fluent English, head here. The food is quite tasty, with Tex-Mex tacos, burritos, nachos, and quesadillas, and 12 kinds of half-pound burgers named after California regions. Huge salads, and lots of appetizers to share such as buffalo wings, spinach dip, and fried calamari, go well with the Cantina's 42 kinds of beer, and they're open very late if you're looking for a midnight snack.

Las Urbinas 56. © **2/361-1056.** www.californiacantina.net. Tacos and burgers average C$3,500. AE, DC, MC, V. Mon–Fri 12:30pm–3am; Sat 1:30pm–3am; Sun 1:30pm–1am. Metro: Pedro de Valdivia.

El Huerto ★ VEGETARIAN   With its organic decor, peaceful ambience, and creative vegetarian dishes, El Huerto is the culinary equivalent of a pair of Birkenstocks. For all its natural kudos, it offers a hip, metropolitan dining experience with a wonderful outdoor terrace on a quiet leafy street in the heart of Providencia. Breakfast features omelets, granola, fruit smoothies, and freshly baked bread, and the lunch and dinner menu offers traditional veggie staples that are reinvented with panache, including burritos, wok-sautéed vegetables, eggplant gratin, soups, and salads. El Huerto is known for its delicious desserts.

Orrego Luco 054. © **2/233-2690.** www.elhuerto.cl. Main courses C$4,500–C$6,000. AE, DC, MC, V. Daily noon–11:30pm. Metro: Los Leones.

Las Condes/El Bosque Norte

The streets El Bosque and Isidora Goyenechea have it all: Chilean, French, seafood, steakhouses, fast-food courts, and more. Virtually every business on these two streets is a restaurant, food shop, or cafe. There are several American chain restaurants here, such as **Ruby Tuesday's,** at Isidora Goyenechea 2960 (📞 **2/361-1803**).

EXPENSIVE

Akarana ★★ 🍴 ASIAN FUSION   I can't think of a more delightful place in Las Condes to dine alfresco than on this restaurant's wraparound patio, and Akarana's contemporary, all-white interiors are chic, fresh, and airy. A globetrotting menu boasts touches of Pacific Rim, Mediterranean, Middle Eastern, and Indian flavors, and the restaurant offers interesting small dishes perfect for sharing among a couple or group of friends. Main courses include thin-crust pizzas, grilled fresh tuna with chile and lime *beurre blanc,* lamb shanks with vegetable marmalade, and good ol' fish and chips. Good to point out, too, are the outstanding quality of Akarana's cocktails and wine list, one of the best in the city.

Reyes Lavalle 3310. 📞 **2/231-9667.** Reservations recommended. Main courses C$8,000–C$10,500. AE, DC, MC, V. Daily noon–midnight. Metro: El Golf.

MODERATE

Café Melba ★★ INTERNATIONAL   This bustling yet unassuming cafe is simply *the* best spot in El Bosque for lunch, the reason why you'll have to wait 15 minutes or so for a table if you arrive after 1:30pm. On any given day, at least a quarter of the clientele are American or British expats who come for Café Melba's inventive meals and good-natured ambience. The restaurant also serves American/English-style breakfasts, a rarity in Santiago, and doors open early at 7:30am on weekdays, and 8:30am on weekends. More thought is put into the lunch menu here than at nearby competing restaurants, with a seasonally changing menu that features pastas, salads, meats, and seafood. There's an Internet cafe and a covered outdoor seating area.

Don Carlos 2898. 📞 **2/232-4546.** Reservations not accepted. Main courses C$4,100–C$5,800. AE, DC, MC, V. Mon–Fri 8am–3pm, and Sat–Sun 8:30am–3:30pm. Metro: El Golf.

Coquinaria ★★★ INTERNATIONAL   An innovative concept in Santiago dining, the brand-new Coquinaria is much more than just a restaurant, it is a gastronomic experience, consisting of both an indoor-outdoor dining area and a gourmet market. The brainchild of British expat Kevin Poulter, Coquinaria serves wonderfully prepared and reasonably priced breakfasts and weekend brunches, casual fare such as baguette sandwiches, burgers (made with regular or Kobe beef with foie gras), and organic salads, and simply prepared gourmet cuisine such as grilled tuna with an herb crust, creamy seafood risotto, or "surf and turf" steak with shrimp. An open-air kitchen gives the restaurant a lively atmosphere, and you won't want to miss a trip around the market to pick up a local gourmet goodie to take home with you.

Av. Isidora Goyenechea 3000. 📞 **2/245-1934.** Reservations recommended for dinner. Main courses C$5,700–C$8,900. AE, DC, MC, V. Mon–Fri 8:30am–11:30pm; Sat 9:30am–11:30pm, and Sun 9:30am–9:30pm. Metro: El Golf.

Nolita ★ ITALIAN/AMERICAN   Taking its cue from Northern Italy and New York (yes, its name was borrowed from the NYC neighborhood), Nolita specializes in cuisine from the former and style from the latter. The El Bosque neighborhood is often referred to as "San-hattan," and so a restaurant like Nolita only makes sense with its cosmopolitan atmosphere, generous service, and refined cuisine created by a chef with roots in the U.S. What I like about Nolita is that the chef is adept at creating haute cuisine that isn't so haute that it leaves you yearning for comfort food. Try a rich pasta such as king crab cannelloni, or even better, the shellfish platter, a veritable Roman feast of smoked salmon, crab legs, scallops, shrimp, and *ceviche,* and save room for one of their delectable desserts. As prices shoot through the roof at other high-end eateries, Nolita remains reasonable for a restaurant of this caliber. You'll need reservations booked days in advance on weekends.

Isidora Goyenechea 3456. ✆ **2/232-6114.** Reservations recommended. Main courses C$6,000–C$12,500. AE, DC, MC, V. Daily 1–3:30pm; Mon–Thurs 8–11pm; Fri–Sat 8pm–midnight. Metro: El Golf.

INEXPENSIVE

Tiramisu ★ PIZZA/ITALIAN   This gourmet pizzeria began as a hole-in-the-wall but spread into three dining areas to accommodate the growing throngs of admirers—during lunch you should come early or make a reservation. Tiramisu serves thin-crust pizzas (that are large enough for two when accompanied by a salad) baked in a stone oven and served in a delightful wood-and-checkered-tablecloth atmosphere. There are dozens of combinations, from traditional tomato and basil to arugula with shaved Parmesan and artichokes, as well as hearty calzones, delicious salads, and desserts that of course include tiramisu. The restaurant offers ample outdoor dining.

Av. Isidora Goyenechea 3141. ✆ **2/335-5135.** www.tiramisu.cl. Pizzas C$4,500–C$7,000; salads C$3,000–C$6,000. AE, DC, MC, V. Daily 1–4pm and 7pm–midnight. Metro: El Golf.

Vitacura

The apex of Santiago's booming gourmet scene is here in the Vitacura neighborhood, known for its art galleries, Rodeo Drive–style shopping, expensive homes, and prime real estate bordering the Mapocho River. In fact, the restaurant complex **BordeRío** (Av. Monseñor Escrivá de Balaguer 6400; ✆ **2/218-0100;** www.borderio.cl) means just that, "bordering the river." BordeRío is a cluster of 11 upscale chain restaurants housed in a modern, Spanish-style complex. There are a few fine restaurants, but the place feels slightly prefabricated, like a shopping center. To get here, you'll need a taxi (there is no Metro service available in Vitacura).

EXPENSIVE

Cuerovaca ★★ STEAK   A top Santiago steakhouse, Cuerovaca puts great emphasis on providing carnivores with the finest cuts of meat available in Santiago, including *wagyu,* the Japanese-origin Kobe beef, Magellanic lamb, and Angus and Hereford beef. If you're not squeamish, start your meal with an appetizer platter of entrails that includes blood sausage, sweetbreads, and kidneys. Non-meat eaters can choose from grilled fish specializing in Easter Island imports and locally produced salmon. The ambience is urban-contemporary, with flagstone walls and lots of wood and glass, and they feature an excellent wine list. All meats and fish can be accompanied by salads, potatoes, or even mashed pine nuts (sides are an additional price). Note that the owners recently opened **Cuernovaca Cívico,** a second branch downtown within the Centro Cultural La Moneda (✆ **2/671-4260**).

El Mañío 1659. ✆ **2/206-3911.** www.cuerovaca.cl. Reservations recommended. Beef cuts C$7,200–C$11,700; Kobe beef cuts C$11,900–C$19,900; seafood courses C$6,600–C$8,600. AE, DC, MC, V. Daily 1–4pm and 8–11:30pm.

Europeo ★★ CONTINENTAL   Prestigious food writers heap accolades and awards every year on Europeo, ranking it as the best or second-best restaurant in the city, but outrageous prices may give visiting diners pause to wonder if it's all really worth it. Europeo draws Santiago's elite for European-influenced cuisine, although native Swedish chef Carlos Meyer has expanded his global range by adding a dab of Asia here and there to liven things up. You'll find dishes such as steak tartare on rye, duck ravioli in port sauce, sea bass with stuffed artichokes and lobster sauce, as well as more classic steak and lamb specialties, artfully arranged and a delight to look at before diving in. The dining area is polished and sophisticated, yet its compact size and individual hanging lamps create warmth and intimacy. The restaurant has a superb on-site sommelier.

Alonso de Córdova 2417. ✆ **2/208-3603.** Reservations recommended. Main courses C$9,500–C$17,000. AE, DC, MC, V. Mon–Fri 1–3pm and 8–10:30pm; Sat 8–11pm.

La Mar Cebicheria ★★★ PERUVIAN/SEAFOOD   With seven locations in the Americas (including San Francisco, California, and Sao Paolo, Brazil), La Mar Cebicheria strives to spread the word about Peru's ubiquitous "cebicherias," restaurants dedicated to the country's love affair with *ceviche,* the tangy concoction based on raw seafood marinated with lemon juice. Critics love La Mar, but the restaurant is a favorite place to dine for locals, too, because of the lively, light and airy ambience and outdoor seating. If you've never tasted ceviche, try a sampler appetizer, or you might try the outstanding *tiradito,* delicate strips of raw fish that pack a punch with hot chili sauces. For a heartier dish, there are *anticuchos* (meat or shellfish brochettes), shellfish brochettes; wok-sautéed rice and shellfish dishes; and *sudados* (seafood stews). Start off your meal with one of their terrific pisco sours.

Nueva Costanera 3922. ✆ **2/206-7839.** www.lamarcebicheria.com. Reservations recommended. Ceviche appetizers C$8,600–C$14,600; main courses C$8,200–C$12,800. AE, DC, MC, V. Lunch Mon–Fri 1pm–3:30pm; Sun 1–4pm; dinner Mon–Wed 8–11pm, Thurs–Sat 8pm–midnight.

Puerto Fuy ★★★ 📷 SEAFOOD   Fancy foodies not afraid of the price must make the trip to this slick establishment, named for a remote outpost in the temperate rainforest of the Chilean Lake District. Star chef Giancarlo Mazzarelli is a fan of molecular cuisine, which he deftly works into seafood dishes such a sesame tuna with puréed onions and sea urchin dumplings, or his famous abalone raviolis with champagne foam. Both pair well with a sauvignon blanc from the very long wine list. A seven-step tasting menu, for a cost of C$29,000, starts with abalone carpaccio and ends with a lemon parfait, and may be the best splurge in town.

3969 Nueva Costanera. ✆ **2/208-8908.** Reservations highly recommended. Main courses C$12,500–C$13,000. AE, DC, MC, V. Mon–Sat 1–3:30pm and 8–11:20pm.

WHAT TO SEE & DO

Visitors with little time can pack in a lot of attractions in even just 1 day, given that most of the city's highlights are found in a localized area that runs along the length of the Mapocho River. Visitors might begin in *el centro,* the city's historic center and home to museums, cathedrals, cultural centers, and civic institutions. Pick a few attractions that pique your interest, then walk over to the Barrio París-Londres neighborhood. Cross back over Avenida Alameda to the Cerro Santa Lucía hilltop park, and take a stroll through the charming streets of Parque Forestal, Santiago's burgeoning arts-and-cafe neighborhood. From here, it is just a short walk across the Mapocho River to the bohemian Bellavista neighborhood and the Cerro San Cristóbal Metropolitan Park.

Now, if you do indeed have only 1 day, you're going to have to hustle and get a very early start, or narrow attractions down to only those that really interest you. Travelers with 2 or 3 days can take this tour at a more leisurely pace, and visit the chic Vitacura area and more off-the-beaten-track attractions such as the Quinta Normal Park or Barrio Brasil.

If you're lucky enough to visit during the **last weekend in May,** all of Chile's governmental buildings are open to the public during its Día de Patrimonio Cultural (Day of Cultural Patrimony), but be prepared for long lines.

See the maps on p. 76, 79, and 81 to locate the attractions reviewed below.

Downtown Historic & Civic Attractions

PLAZA DE ARMAS

Begin your tour of Santiago at the grand **Plaza de Armas** ★★★ (Metro: Plaza de Armas). Pedro de Valdivia, who conquered Chile for the Spanish crown, founded this plaza in 1541 as the civic nucleus of the country and surrounded it with the Royal Court of Justice (now the Natural History Museum), the Governor's Palace (now the Central Post Office), the Metropolitan Cathedral, and the venerable homes of early Chile's movers and shakers. The square became the epicenter of public life and the stage for markets, festivals, and even bullfights. In the mid-1800s, the somber plaza was spruced up with gardens and trees, creating a promenade that became a social center for fashionable society. Though fashionable society has since moved uptown, the plaza still ranks as one of Santiago's most enjoyable areas to sit and watch the world go by. Between the hustle and bustle of city workers, there is an eclectic mix of characters that spend the better part of their day here: soap-box speakers and shoe shiners, comedians and preachers, garrulous old men playing chess, young couples embracing on park benches, and street photographers and artists hawking paintings.

Catedral Metropolitana ★★   Santiago's grand cathedral spans a city block and is the fifth cathedral to have been erected at this site due to earthquake damage. The cathedral was also the subject of intrigue in 2005 when renovations unearthed the lost body of Diego Portales, the principal ideologist for the Chilean Constitution of 1833. The cathedral, designed by the Italian architect Joaquín Toesca in a neoclassical-baroque style, took nearly 30 years to complete, and was finished in 1780. Of most interest here are the hushed, cavernous cathedral interiors, with columns that soar high to arched ceilings, and an ornate altar made of marble, bronze, and lapis lazuli, and brought from Munich in 1912.

Paseo Ahumada, on the west side of the plaza. (C) **2/696-2777.** Free admission. Mon–Sat 9am–7pm; Sun 9am–noon. Metro: Plaza de Armas.

Correo Central and Museo Postal   The Central Post Office was built in 1882 on the remains of what was once the colonial Governor's Palace and the post-independence Presidential Palace. After the building succumbed to fire in 1881, workers rebuilt it, incorporating several of the old building's walls. In 1908, architect Ramón Feherman added a third floor and an extravagant glass cupola. Unless you have postcards to mail or a fondness for Renaissance-period architecture, there isn't much to see here.

Plaza de Armas 983. (C) **2/956-5145.** Free admission. Mon–Fri 9am–5:30pm. Metro: Plaza de Armas.

Palacio de la Real Audiencia/Museo Histórico Nacional ★   This excellent museum is a must-see for history buffs and travelers seeking insight into Chile's past, from the conquest to present day, presented in a way that doesn't feel overwhelming. The museum is housed in the elegant, lemon-colored Palacio de la Real, where Chile held its first congress following independence. Displays wind around a central courtyard, beginning with the Conquest, and finishing with a photo montage depicting modern political turmoil and literary and artistic accomplishment in Chile. Along the way, visitors can view weapons, agricultural tools, traditional costumes, household

Coffee with Legs

Downtown Santiago is home to a curious phenomenon known as *Café con Piernas* ("Coffee with Legs"), cafes manned by waitresses done up in skimpy ensembles and thick makeup, serving ogling businessmen from behind a stand-up bar. **Café Haiti** (© 2/737-4323; locations at Ahumada 140, Huérfanos 769, and Bandera 335) and **Café Caribe** (© 2/695-7081; locations at Ahumada 120 and Huérfanos 812, and 1164) are local institutions and tamer affairs than otherwise raunchier versions (recognizable by darkened windows and men sheepishly slinking in or out the door). Café Haiti and Café Caribe are patronized by women as well as men.

appliances, oil paintings depicting early Chile, and reproductions of home life during the 18th and 19th centuries. There are, unfortunately, no tours in English, and all interpretative information is in Spanish; however, most displays are self-explanatory. Plan to spend 30 minutes to 1 hour here.

Plaza de Armas 951. © **2/411-7010.** Admission C$600 adults, C$300 children 17 and under; free Sun and holidays. Tues–Sun 10am–5:30pm. Metro: Plaza de Armas.

NEAR THE PLAZA DE ARMAS

Paseo Ahumada, at the southwest corner of the Plaza de Armas, and its sister street **Paseo Huérfanos,** which bisects Paseo Ahumada a block away, are bustling pedestrian walkways that offer the visitor a good feel for downtown Santiago and the people who work there. Musicians and street performers entertain passersby who race to and fro the almost continual line of shops, newspaper kiosks, and restaurants. It can get frenzied during the lunch hour here; when it does, keep an eye on your belongings.

Basílica de la Merced ★★ First built in 1566 by the Order of the Blessed Virgin Mary of Mercy (Mercedarians) who arrived with the first discovery expedition to Chile, this church succumbed to earthquakes in 1647 and 1730, and was rebuilt in 1760. Today the church is an architectural gem built in the neo-Renaissance style with two bell towers and a stunning Bavarian baroque pulpit, but what's really interesting here is the image of the Virgin Mary brought to Chile by Mercedarians in 1544, and the tiny sliver under glass encasing said to have originated from the actual cross of Jesus. Several of Chile's earliest luminaries are buried here, including Inés de Suarez, the first Spanish woman to arrive in Chile and the central character of Isabel Allende's *Ines of My Soul.* The **Museo de la Merced** has a highly variable collection of religious and archeological artifacts that include Easter Island art and a rongorongo tablet, as well as kitschy Jesus figurines in bell glasses.

MacIver 341, corner of Merced. © 2/633-0691 (church); © 2/664-9189 (museum). Admission: Church free; museum C$600 adults, C$300 students. Church hours: Mon–Fri 6:30am–1:30pm and 3–8:30pm; Sat–Sun 9:30am–1:30pm and 6–9pm. Museum hours: Mon–Fri 10am–1:30pm and 3–9pm; Sat 10am–1pm. Metro: Plaza de Armas.

Casa Colorada & Santiago Museum The Casa Colorada (Red House) is regarded as the best-preserved colonial structure in Santiago, having survived devastating earthquakes and the whims of modern developers. The structure was built between 1769 and 1779 as a residence for the first president of Chile, Mateo de Toro y Zambrano. Inside, the missable (unless you have kids to entertain) Santiago Museum depicts the urban history of the city until the 19th century using amateurish scale models. Still, it's worth checking out Casa Colorada if only for its architecture, and you can grab lunch or a coffee at Ambrosía (p. 91) behind the museum.

Merced 860. © **2/639-7903.** Admission free. Tues–Sun 10am–6pm. Metro: Plaza de Armas.

Museo Chileno de Arte Precolombino ★★★   Heading back on Merced and past the plaza to Bandera, you'll find the notable Chilean Museum of pre-Columbian Art, housed in the elegant 1807 ex-Royal Customs House. This is one of the better museums in Chile, both for its collection of pre-Columbian artifacts and its inviting design. There are more than 1,500 objects on display here, including textiles, metals, paintings, figurines, and ceramics spread throughout seven exhibition rooms. The collection is encompassing but not as extensive as, say, the Anthropological Museum of Mexico, but the exhibition does offer a vivid exhibition of indigenous life and culture before the arrival of the Spanish. There's also a well-stocked bookstore that sells music, videos, and reproductions of Indian art, textiles, and jewelry. Docents offer tours in English at 1 and 5pm from Tuesday through Friday and at 10am and 2pm Saturday, but visitors must call ahead for a reservation. If you have time for just one museum in downtown Santiago, make it this one.

Bandera 361. © **2/928-1510.** www.museoprecolombino.cl. Admission C$3,000 adults, C$1,000 students; kids 13 and under are free; Sun and holidays free for all. Tues–Sun 10am–6pm; holidays 10am–2pm. Metro: Plaza de Armas.

Museo de la Memoria y Los Derechos Humanos ★★★   Created as an educational center to explore and understand the effects of Chile's military dictatorship and the price its victims paid, this museum was also conceived as a way to ensure that such a human rights tragedy never again occurs in Chile. Housed within a sober yet architecturally striking and linear building of glass and cement, the museum was suggested by ex-president Michelle Bachelet, herself a victim of torture during the dictatorship, as a Bicentennial project. Through thousands of photos, letters, personal objects, stories, and newspaper clippings, visitors are taken on a thought-provoking journey that is at once terribly sad yet fundamental in terms of understanding contemporary Chile's societal mores and structure.

Matucana 501. © **2/365-1165.** www.museodelamemoria.cl. Free admission. Tues–Sun 10am–6pm; holidays 10am–2pm. Metro: Quinta Normal.

PLAZA CONSTITUCION & THE COMMERCE CENTER

Santiago's historic presidential building, the graceful **Palacio de la Moneda ★★★**, is considered one of the finest neoclassical structures in Latin America. Located between Plaza de la Constitución and Plaza de la Libertad and extending for an entire block, it was built between 1784 and 1805 by revered Italian architect Joaquín Toesca to house the royal mint. In 1848, it became the residential palace for the presidents of Chile starting with Manuel Bulnes and ending with Carlos Ibáñez de Campo in 1958, when it became the official seat of government rather than the president's home.

The palace's harmony and symmetry are best viewed from Plaza de la Constitución's northern side. The building's regularity—the same set of windows is repeated 14 times along the length of the main facade, each divided by uniform columns—and the overarching feel is of order and stability rather than grandeur. Fittingly, this is the only presidential headquarters in the world that allows civilians to simply stroll through the main archway and wander around the inner courtyards (bring your passport to show the guards for entry). Patio de los Cañones is named for the two centerpiece 18th-century canons while the Moorish-style Patio de los Naranjos is more reminiscent of the Alhambra Palace in Granada, with a cluster of orange trees surrounding a serene 17th-century fountain. Take a walk inside; you may not see the president but it's quite an experience to glimpse the rush of ministers and journalists. There are also several art and sculpture exhibitions inside. Try to plan your visit at 10am to watch Chilean soldiers perform a somber **changing of the guard** to the Chilean national anthem; it takes place every other day.

Beyond aesthetic appreciation, the palace has symbolic and historic resonance. Most infamously, the Palacio was the site of the 1973 Pinochet-led coup that ousted Salvador Allende. For several generations of Chileans, the scratchy black-and-white images of La Moneda being blitzed by General Pinochet on September 11, 1973, ushered in a brutal period in the history of Chile. Today, it is the presidential palace and offices of Chile's president Sebastián Piñera. See p. 12.

Calle Nueva York & the Bolsa de Comercio ★   Walk east on Moneda Street from the Plaza Constitución, and you'll immediately notice a marked increase in business suits—this is the financial apex of Santiago, home to the city's Stock Exchange (Bolsa de Comercio). The Stock Exchange occupies one of Santiago's most architecturally interesting buildings, a 1917 triangular stone French-style edifice, built of Roman pillars and topped with an elegant dome cupola. If by some lucky stroke you know a trader or if you own stock in a Chilean company that is publicly traded, you may enter the Stock Exchange; if not, it is closed to the public. Surrounding the Bolsa are the sinuous, cobblestone streets of Nueva York, La Bolsa, and Club de la Unión— if you're downtown, you won't want to miss a stroll through these picturesque streets.

Calle Nueva York. ✆ **2/399-3000.** www.bolsadesantiago.cl. Free admission. Mon–Fri 9am–5pm. Metro: Plaza de Armas.

Centro Cultural Palacio La Moneda ★★   Chile's 5-year-old cultural center hosts a revolving-door of exhibits ranging from modern art and literature to design and cultural heritage; unfortunately, however, the center is perpetually underfunded and exhibit changes sometimes force entire wings to be closed for more than a week. The center is located underground between the Alameda and the Palacio (Citizen's Plaza) and can be accessed by walking down a ramp at either Teatinos or Morandé streets. The space is worth a visit as a sensational example of urban-contemporary design. The center also has an art-house cinema, library, educational center, and a sleek cafe. Check their website for upcoming exhibitions and events, and plan to spend about 30 minutes here.

Plaza de la Ciudadanía (underground). ✆ **2/355-6500.** www.ccplm.cl. Admission is free Mon–Fri until noon and all day Sun; other times C$1,000 adults, C$500 students and seniors. Tues–Sun 9am–9pm. Metro: La Moneda.

ATTRACTIONS OFF THE ALAMEDA

The formal moniker of Santiago's principal avenue is Avenida Libertador Bernardo O'Higgins, but everyone calls it *La Alameda*. O'Higgins is Chile's founding father, and his remains are buried under a monument dedicated in his honor across from the Plaza de la Ciudadanía. La Alameda is a congested and harried thoroughfare, characterized by throngs of people and screeching buses, and there are few crosswalks— remember that you can cross the avenue via an underground Metro station. The following attractions can be found on or just off the Alameda.

Barrio París-Londres ★★   This incongruous neighborhood oozes faded charm, with winding cobblestone streets and pretty 1920s-era facades, but is just a few blocks in diameter and surrounded by the hustle and bustle and hodgepodge 1970s architecture of downtown Santiago. The *barrio* was built on what once were the gardens of the adjoining Iglesia San Francisco, land that Jesuits were forced to sell to pay off debts. A handful of prominent architects designed the neighborhood's rows of elegant stone mansions, yet the project as a whole was the visionary idea of one Ernesto Holzmann, who sought to create an aesthetically pleasing neighborhood modeled after Europe for residents who wanted to be close enough to downtown to walk to work each day.

The streets btw. Prat and Santa Rosa, walking south of Alameda.

Biblioteca Nacional   The principal attraction of the country's National Library is the French neoclassical stone building that houses it, which spans an entire city block. Inside its handsomely painted interiors are over six million works, as well as historic archives and a map room, though admittedly the building could really use an upgrade. The lovely Jose Medina reading room offers a glimpse into an early-20th-century library, with antique books stacked in tiers, leather-topped reading desks, and a giant spinning globe.

Av. Bernardo O'Higgins 651. ✆ **2/360-5310.** Free admission. Mon-Fri 9am-7pm; Sat 9:10am-2pm. Metro: Cerro Santa Lucía.

Calle Dieciocho and Palacio Cousiño Macul ★   During the turn of the 20th century and before Santiago's elite packed it up and moved away from the downtown hubbub, Calle Dieciocho ranked as the city's toniest neighborhood. The tourism board touts Calle Dieciocho as a step back in time, but neglect has taken its toll, and the only site really worth visiting here is the **Palacio Cousiño Macul,** once the home of Chile's grandest entrepreneurial dynasties, the Goyenechea-Cousiño family. Unfortunately, the museum was closed at press time due to earthquake damage and isn't slated to reopen until mid 2012, so call ahead to see if renovations have been completed, or simply view the Palace from the outside. A visit provides a unique opportunity to appreciate how Santiago's elite lived during the late 1800s. Once completed in 1878, the palace dazzled society with its opulence: lavish parquet floors, Bohemian crystal chandeliers, Italian hand-painted ceramics, and French tapestries. Much of the building was destroyed by fire in the 1960s but what remains provides a dizzying insight into the excellence of European craftsmanship at the turn of the 19th century. To get here, walk from Avenida Alameda down Calle Dieciocho for 15 minutes, until you reach the Palace. Also, take a 10-minute detour around the corner from Cousiño Macul (east on San Ignacio) to Parque Almagro, a scruffy park that nevertheless affords a view of the little-known, almost Gaudiesque **Basílica del Santísimo Sacramento** church, constructed between 1919 and 1931 and modeled after the Sacre Coeur in Montmartre, Paris; the church is not currently open.

Dieciocho 438. ✆ **2/698-5063.** Admission C$200 for adults and kids. Bilingual tours Tues-Fri 9:30am-1:30pm and 2:30-5pm; Sat-Sun 9:30am-1:30pm. Metro: Toesca.

Iglesia, Convento y Museo de San Francisco ★★   The Church of San Francisco, built between 1586 and 1628, is the oldest standing building in Santiago, having miraculously survived three devastating earthquakes. At the altar sits the famous *Virgen del Socorro,* the first Virgin Mary icon in Chile brought to Santiago by Pedro de Valdivia, the country's conquistador. Valdivia claimed the icon had warded off Indian attacks. The highlights, however, are the museum and the convent, the latter with its idyllic patio planted with flora brought from destinations as near as the south of Chile and as far away as the Canary Islands. The garden, with its bubbling fountain and cooing doves (including a peacock that struts about the courtyard), is so serene you'll find it hard to believe you're in downtown Santiago. The tiny museum houses a collection of one of the largest and best-conserved examples of 17th-century art in South America. A sizable percentage of colonial-period furniture, keys, paintings, and other items on display were crafted in Peru, when it still was the seat of the Spanish government in Latin America. Also on display are personal items from writer and Nobel laureate Gabriela Mistral's life.

Av. Bernardo O'Higgins. © **2/638-3238.** Admission to convent and museum C$1,000 adults, C$500 kids; free church admission. The museum is open Mon–Fri 9:30am–1:30pm and 3–6:15pm; Sun 10am–2pm. Church open Mon–Fri 10am–1pm and 4–8pm, Sat 10am–1pm.

CERRO SANTA LUCÍA & PLAZA MULATO GIL DE CASTRO

Materializing as if out of nowhere on the edge of the city's downtown limits, the **Cerro Santa Lucía** ★★★ is a lavishly landscaped hilltop park and one of the more delightful attractions in Santiago. Native Mapuche Indians called this hill Huelén (Pain) until conqueror Pedro de Valdivia seized the property and planted the Spanish flag in 1570, thereby founding Santiago. In the late 1800s, Governor Benjamin Vicuña envisioned the hill as a recreation area and transformed Santa Lucía into an extravagant labyrinth of gardens, fountains, and flagstone promenades that gently spiral up to a 360-degree view of the city. At one point, the city's Dissident's Cemetery (cemetery for non-Catholics) could be found here until it was moved to the Cementerio General. The park is open daily September through March from 9am to 8pm, and April through August from 9am to 7pm; admission is free, though you'll be asked to sign a guest registry. At the top of the hill is the Castle Hidalgo, which operates as an event center.

Santiago's burgeoning arts-and-cafe scene centers around the tiny **Plaza Mulato Gil de Castro** ★★, located at José Victorino Lastarría and Rosal streets. The fine examples of early 1900s architecture at the plaza and the handful of streets that surround it provide visitors with a romantic step back into old Santiago. From Thursday to Sunday, antiques and book dealers line the plaza, but the highlights here are the **Museo de Artes Visuales (MAVI)** ★★★ and the **Museo Antropología (MAS)** ★★ (© 2/664-9337; www.mavi.cl; admission C$1,000 adults, C$500 students and seniors [one admission price gets you into both]; Tues–Sun 10:30am–6:30pm). Many of Chile's most promising contemporary artists exhibit their work at MAVI. The MAS offers archaeological displays of artifacts produced by indigenous peoples throughout the length of Chile. The collection at MAS is extensive, but the museum is small and takes no more than 10 minutes to peruse.

PARQUE FORESTAL

This slender, manicured park, landscaped in 1900 with rows of native and imported trees, skirts the perimeter of the Río Mapocho from Vicuña Mackenna at the Metro station Baquedano to its terminus at the Mapocho station. The winding path takes walkers past several interesting attractions and makes for a pleasant half-hour to 1-hour stroll, especially on a sunny afternoon when the air is clear. If you plan to walk the entire park, try to finish at the Mercado Central (see below).

Estación Mapocho ★   Built in 1912 on reclaimed land formed by the canalization of the Río Mapocho, this beautiful, Beaux Arts building served as the train station for the Santiago-Valparaíso railway until the late 1970s, and it was built as part of the country's centennial celebration. After a decade of abandonment, the Chilean government invited architects to sketch a renovation of the building as part of a contest, and it was redesigned as a four-story, grand cultural center with a 40-ton copper, marble, and glass roof and seats made of Oregon pine. The center hosts events such as rock concerts and the International Book Fair, and within its handful of salons, visitors can view exhibitions of local art. There's also an arts-and-crafts store and two cafes. The Metro station Cal y Canto is right nearby, making this a perfect stop before visiting the Mercado Central.

Bandera and Río Mapocho. ⓒ **2/787-0000.** www.estacionmapocho.cl. Daily 9am–5pm; other hours according to events. Metro: Cal y Canto.

Mercado Central ★★★   It's the quintessential tourist stop, but the colorful, chaotic Mercado Central is nevertheless a highlight for visitors to Santiago. A large share of Chile's economy depends on the exportation of natural products such as fruits, vegetables, and seafood, and the market here displays everything the country has to offer. Lively and staffed by pushy fishmongers who quickly and nimbly gut and fillet while you watch, the market displays every kind of fish available along the Chilean coast. Depending on your perspective, the barking fishmongers and waitresses who harangue you to choose *their* zucchini, *their* sea bass, *their* restaurant can be entertaining or somewhat annoying. Either way, don't miss it, especially for the market's lofty, steel structure that was prefabricated in England and assembled here in 1868. If you're here during lunch, stop off for a rich bowl of *caldillo de congrio* (a thick conger eel soup) or a tangy *ceviche* (see "Where to Dine," earlier in this chapter).

Ismael Valdes Vergara and Av. 21 de Mayo. No phone. www.mercadocentral.cl. Daily 7am–5pm (some stalls stay open later). Metro: Cal y Canto.

Museo Nacional de Bellas Artes (MNBA) & Museo de Arte Contemporaneo (MAC) ★★   The Palacio de Bellas Artes is the city's fine arts museum, housed in a regal, neoclassical building inaugurated on the eve of Chile's centennial independence day in 1910. The palace has a noteworthy glass cupola that softly lights the vast lobby. The museum's permanent collection showcases Chilean art from the colonial period to the 20th century only. Each year the museum also hosts temporary exhibitions of international artists such as Damian Hirst, Henri-Cartier Bresson, and David Hockney, to name a few, so it's worth stopping by to see what is on offer. Within the same building, but entering from the back, is the Museo de Arte Contemporaneo (MAC), the city's modern art museum and part of the University of Chile. This museum hosts temporary exhibitions of national and international modern art, yet such heavyweights as Hirst are typically shown in the Fine Arts Museum.

Parque Forestal, by way of Jose Miguel de la Barra. MNBA: ⓒ **2/499-1600.** www.mnba.cl. MAC: ⓒ **2/977-1741.** www.mac.cl. Admission MNBA C$300 adults, children under 13 are free; MAC C$600 adults, students C$400 (visitors must pay separately for each museum), free for all Sun. Hours MNBA Tues–Sun 10am–7pm; MAC Tues–Sat 11am–7pm and Sun 11am–6pm. Metro: Bellas Artes.

BARRIO BELLAVISTA ★★★ & PARQUE METROPOLITANO (CERRO SAN CRISTOBAL) ★★★

One of the city's more enigmatic neighborhoods, Bellavista is Santiago's bohemian quarter and positively buzzes with a sense of excitement and creativity. The neighborhood has come into its own of late, with new restaurants, hotels, and boutiques springing up within the confines of mansions and colorful one-story homes that dominate the area. Pablo Neruda, Chile's most famous poet, had a home here that is now a do-not-miss museum. The shopping/dining area **Patio Bellavista** (see "Shopping," later) is a pleasant place for a stroll or to plop down after a day exploring the city. In the evening, Bellavista pulses to the beat of music pouring from its many discos and bars. On weekends, there is an evening handicrafts market that runs the length of Pío Nono.

La Chascona ★★★ Bellavista's prime attraction is one of three homes once owned by Chile's most famous literary artist, the Nobel Prize–winning poet Pablo Neruda. Located a block east of the Plaza Caupolican (the entrance point to the Parque Metropolitano), Neruda lived here with his third wife, Matilde Urrutia (the woman with the red, tousled hair for whom the house was named) between 1955 and 1973. As with Neruda's other two homes, La Chascona was built to resemble a ship, with oddly shaped rooms that wind around a compact courtyard. It's fascinating to wander through Neruda's quirky home and observe his collection of precious antiques and whimsical curios collected during his travels, many of which are backed by a soulful story or historical tale that really brings you into Neruda's world. The library holds the antique encyclopedia set he purchased with a portion of his earnings from the Nobel Prize. The home is headquarters for the Fundación Pablo Neruda, which provides bilingual guided tours.

Fernando Márquez de la Plata 0192. *©* **2/777-8741.** www.fundacionneruda.cl. Admission C$2,500 tours in Spanish; C$3,500 tour in English; C$1,000 seniors. Jan–Feb Tues–Sun 10am–7pm; Mar–Dec Tues–Sun 10am–6pm. Call to make a reservation; if you just show up, you may need to wait until a guide is free. Metro: Baquedano.

Parque Metropolitano ★★★ The Parque Metropolitano is a 730-hectare (1,803-acre) park and recreation area atop **Cerro San Cristobal** (the park is often referred to as such) with swimming pools, walking trails, a botanical garden, a zoo, picnic grounds, restaurants, and children's play areas. Beginning in 2011, the park will receive a multimillion-dollar upgrade with new botanical gardens planted with diverse flora from all of Chile and a new cable car *teleférico* (the current cable car has been decommissioned until a new system is installed). The park is divided into two sectors, Cumbre and Tupahue, both of which are accessed by car, cable car, funicular, or foot. On a clear day, the sweeping views of the city render this attraction as the best in the city, but it can be disappointing on a particularly smoggy day. During the summer, the Tupahue and Antilén swimming pools, not your average YMCA-style pools but rather attractively landscaped pools with sweeping city views, are refreshing ways to cool off. To get here, go to the Plaza Caupolican at the end of Calle Pío Nono, where you'll encounter a 1925 **funicular** that lifts visitors up to a lookout point that is watched over by a 22m-high (72-ft.) statue of the **Virgen de la Inmaculada Concepción** a few dozen steps up. Along the way, the funicular stops at the **Jardín Zoológico** ★★ (*©* **2/777-6666**), a surprisingly diverse zoo with more than 200 species of mammals, reptiles, and birds, including native condors, pumas, and guanacos. It's also possible to take a *colectivo* taxi to the top; pick one up at the Pío Nono entrance.

Cerro San Cristóbal/Parque Metropolitan. *©* **2/730-1300.** www.parquemet.cl. Daily 8:30am–9pm. Free admission to the park. Metro: Baquedano. Funicular: Mon–Fri 10am–8pm, Sat, Sun, and holidays 10am–8:30pm. One-way prices C$950 adults, C$500 children. Admission for vehicles C$2,500. Pools (no phone); Nov 15–Mar 15 Tues–Sun 10am–7pm; Admission Tupahue pool C$5,000 adults, C$3,500 children; Antilén pool C$6,000 adults, C$3,500 children. Zoo hours Tues–Sun 10am–6pm; admission C$650 all ages.

PARQUE QUINTA NORMAL

The Quinta Normal Park was established in the mid 1880s as an acclimatization nursery for imported species of plants and trees and an agricultural study center when the area was still outside the boundaries of Santiago. The park today measures 40 hectares (99 acres) and incorporates grassy lawns; splendid mature examples of Monterey pine, Douglas firs, Sequoias, Babylonian willows, and more; sporting facilities; and a lagoon with paddle boat rental. The park recently received a face-lift with new lawns and upgraded pavement and plazas, and the opening of a Metro station (Metro Quinta Normal) has made getting here a whole lot easier.

The park is ideal for families for its a handful of kid-friendly museums, including the **Natural History Museum** ★★ (*C* **2/680-4624;** www.mnhn.cl), open Tuesday through Saturday from 10am to 5:30pm, and Sunday from 11am to 5:30pm. The museum, the oldest natural history museum in Latin America, was unfortunately heavily damaged by the 2010 earthquake and was closed for repairs at press time. It is slated to fully reopen in January 2012, however some exhibits are on display in a small salon. Consult their website for updates.

Worth a visit is the **Artequín Museum** ★★, Av. Portales 3530 (*C* **2/681-8656;** www.artequin.cl), open Tuesday through Friday from 9am to 5pm, and Saturday, Sunday, and holidays from 11am to 6pm. The museum is closed throughout February; admission is C$800 adults, C$500 students and children, and free on Sundays. Housed in a cast-iron building accented with a kaleidoscope of colorful glass, it was first used as the Chilean exhibition hall at the 1889 Parisian centenary of the French Revolution. Workers took the building apart, shipped it to Santiago, and reassembled it here. The museum displays only reproductions of famous paintings by artists from Botticelli to Rubens, Picasso to Monet, and even Andy Warhol's *Marilyn* and Francis Bacon's *Study after Velázquez's Portrait of Pope Innocent X.* The idea is to introduce kids to important works of art.

A popular museum with kids here is the **Museo de Ciencia y Tecnología (Museum of Science and Technology)** ★★ (*C* 2/681-6022; www.corpdicyt.cl), whose engaging, interactive, and hands-on displays provide a worthy initiation into the basic precepts of astronomy, geology, and physics. It is open Tuesday through Friday from 10am to 6pm, Saturday and Sunday from 11am to 6pm; admission is C$800 adults and C$650 students. At the southern end of the park, on Avenida Portales, is the fourth museum here, the **Museo Ferroviario (Railway Museum)** ★ (*C* 2/681-4627; www.corpdicyt.cl), with railway exhibits that feature 14 steam engines and railway carriages, including the train that once connected Santiago with Mendoza until 1971. It's open Tuesday through Friday from 10am to 6pm, Saturday and Sunday from 11am to 6pm; admission is C$800 adults and C$650 students.

VITACURA

Vitacura is shaping up to become the new Santiago destination for travelers, especially those seeking to surround themselves with luxury and high-brow culture. Previously known for its Rodeo Drive–style shopping, Vitacura is now home to more upscale art galleries than any other neighborhood in Santiago (see "Shopping," p. 111).

Museo de la Moda ★★★ 📱 Santiago's Fashion Museum is extraordinarily well designed and so chic it could easily exist in London or Paris. Founded and run by the wealthy son of a textile magnate, Jorge Yarur, the museum is in Yarur's old family home, a gem of mid-century design. Upon entrance, travelers first pass by something of a shrine to his past, with a living area, bar, and his mother's old vanity (her impeccable style inspired Yarur to found the museum) set up with period furniture just as it would have been in the 1960s. Low-lit, temperature-controlled salons display a treasure trove of historic and couture costumes from the 20th century, in changing thematic displays such as "The 80s," or "War Fashion." Madonna's cone bra and Princess Di's strapless black taffeta gown are just two examples of the 8,000-plus pieces the museum owns, however costumes are revolved periodically and so only a fraction of the collection is on display at any one time.

Avenida Vitacura 4562. © **2/219-3623.** www.museodelamoda.cl. Admission C$3,500; C$1,800 on Wed. Bilingual tours available daily at 10:30am, 11:30am, 12:30pm, 2:30pm, 3:30pm, and 4:30pm. Tues-Fri 10am–6pm; Sat-Sun 11am–7pm. No Metro access.

Especially for Kids

In addition to the following recommendations, the Parque Metropolitano Zoo, the Museum of Science and Technology, the Artequín Museum, and the Railway Museum described earlier are all ideal for kids.

The spacious **Parque Bernardo O'Higgins** is a tired, worn-down park frequented by blue-collar Santiaguinos who come to fly kites and barbecue on the weekends; there's nothing worth seeing here except the modern amusement park **Fantasilandia,** corner of Beaucheff and Tupper streets (© **2/476-8600;** www. fantasilandia.cl; Metro: Parque O'Higgins). Admission is C$7,900 for adults or C$3,800 for children. It's open April 1 through November 9 on Saturday, Sunday, and holidays only from noon to 7pm. It's the largest amusement park in Chile, with four stomach-churning roller coasters, a toboggan ride, and a haunted house. If you are in town, the Halloween theme night is not to be missed.

The **Museo Interactivo Mirador (MIM)** ★★ and the **Santiago Aquarium** ★★ (two entrances: Sebastopol 90 and Punta Arenas 6711; © **2/828-8000;** www.mim.cl; admission to MIM is C$3,900 for adults or C$2,600 for children; Wed are half-price; a combo ticket with the aquarium costs C$5,300 for adults, or C$4,300 for children) are neighbors within an 11-hectare (27-acre) park in the La Granja barrio in the Parque Brasil. Inaugurated in 2000, MIM dedicates itself to providing children with an introduction to the world of science and technology. Adults will be fascinated by MIM, too. The ultramodern museum has more than 300 exhibits, mostly interactive displays that cover the range of paleontology, computer animation, robotics, and 3-D cinema. In 2008, MIM proudly unveiled its latest permanent exhibition, "Protecting the Ozone Layer." You could spend nearly a full day here if you choose to check out the aquarium which, while far from world class, has over 200 species of primarily Chilean marine life and an eternally crowd-pleasing sea lion show. Buy a combo ticket for both if you have enough time. To get here, the Metro Line 5 drops you off at the Mirador stop, but then you'll have to walk 9 blocks, or you can take the *colectivo* taxi #9001 that will drop you off at the Sebastopol entrance.

Organized Tours

Major hotels work with quality tour operators and can recommend a tour even at the last minute. Better to plan ahead and reserve a tour with an operator who can show you a more interesting side to Santiago or who is more attuned to foreign guests' desires or needs (and a guide who is truly bilingual).

Santiago Adventures (© 2/244-2750; www.santiagoadventures.com) is a premiere operation with more than a decade of experience in Santiago tours. Tours include a standard, 4-hour city tour with a van and bilingual guide for C$25,175 per person; a 5- to 6-hour bike tour through the lovely old Barrio Brasil and Yungay neighborhoods for C$48,925 per person; and a culinary tour that includes visits to local markets, a wine tasting, and lunch prepared at the private home of a Chilean who is the past executive chef for LAN Airlines, for C$52,725 per person for a party of four.

Paseos en Bicicleta (© 956-3075; www.paseosenbicicleta.cl) offers day and night tours on bicycle such as a wine-and-bike tour that pedals through the tony neighborhoods of Vitacura and Las Condes and finishes with a wine tasting at the city's best wine shop; and a more physically demanding afternoon–night tour that rides up the steep road to the top of San Cristobal hill. Tours last an average of 5 to 6 hours and cost between C$45,000 and C$60,000 per person, for a minimum of two people.

Bicicleta Verde (✆ 2/570-9338; www.labicicletaverde.com) is an upstart venture by a couple of young bicycle enthusiasts who offer tours aimed more at the casual backpacker crowd. Their 3-hour day tour includes stops at the La Vega market and historical downtown and costs C$17,100 per person; and a 3-hour night tour along the Mapocho River costs C$28,500 per person.

Spectator Sports & Recreation

HORSE RACING Two racetracks hold events on either Saturday or Sunday throughout the year: the recommended **Club Hípico,** Blanco Encalada 2540 (no phone; www.clubhipico.cl), and the **Hipódromo Chile,** Avenida Vivaceta 2753 in Independencia (✆ 2/270-9200; www.hipodromo.cl). The Hípico's classic event, El Ensayo, takes place the first Sunday in November and always provides a colorful Chilean spectacle as attendees arm themselves with grills and barbecue meat in the middle of the racetrack oval. The Hipódromo's classic St. Leger is the second week in December, but it takes longer to get to than the Club Hípico.

POOLS Your best bet are the public pools **Tupahue** and **Antilén,** atop Cerro San Cristóbal; see "Barrio Bellavista & Parque Metropolitano" above for details.

SKIING For information about skiing in the area, see chapter 7.

SOCCER (FOOTBALL) Top *fútbol* (as soccer is called here) games are held at three stadiums: the Universidad de Chile play at the **Estadio Nacional,** Avenida Grecia 2001 (✆ 2/238-6477); Colo-Colo plays at **Estadio Monumental,** Maraton 5300 (✆ 600/420-2222; www.colocolo.cl); and Universidad Católica plays at **Estadio San Carlos de Apoquindo,** Camino las Flores 13000 (✆ 2/412-4400; www.lacatolica.cl). Check the sports pages of any local newspaper for game schedules.

SHOPPING
Shopping Centers

American-style megamalls are scattered all over Santiago, but the two most convenient are: **Parque Arauco,** Av. Kennedy 5413 (✆ 2/299-0629; www.parquearauco.cl), and **Alto Las Condes,** Av. Kennedy 9001 (✆ 2/299-6965; www.cencosudshopping.cl); both are open daily from 10am to 9pm but are closed on major holidays. Both offer national brands and well-known international chains, junk-food courts, and multiscreen theaters. Parque Arauco has the edge with its "Boulevard" shopping area with hip shops and (unbelievably) some of Santiago's better restaurants. The best way to get to Parque Arauco is by cab (about C$3,000–C$3,500). On weekends, Santiago's malls heave with shoppers. There are no Metro stops near Alto Las Condes or Parque Arauco.

Like most Latin American nations, Chile has many shopping *galerías,* labyrinthine mini-malls with dozens of compact shops that independent vendors can rent for considerably less money than a regular storefront. Most are cheap to midrange clothing stores, upstart designers with fun styles but so-so fabrics, or importers of crafts, antiques dealers, tailors, and so on. A vibrant, bustling example is the **Mall Panorámico,** Avenida 11 de Septiembre 2155 (Metro: Los Leones), with 130 shops and a department store across the street. Also see **Drugstore** under "Fashion" below.

Crafts Markets

Crafts markets in Santiago are either permanent installations or weekly events. Two permanent markets stand out for their high-quality crafts and souvenirs from every region of Chile. The perk with these two markets is that they are very large and diverse, and you could do all your shopping in one fell swoop. The beautifully designed **Patio Bellavista** (btw. Constitución and Pío Nono sts. and Avenida Bellavista and Dardignac; ✆ **2/249-8700;** www.patiobellavista.cl; shops are open Sun–Wed 10am–9pm and Thurs–Sat 10am–10pm; restaurants are open Sun–Wed noon–2am, Thurs–Sat noon–4am) is a collection of shops hawking high-quality arts and crafts, jewelry, woolens, and woodwork, centered around a cobblestone patio with a couple of cafes and outstanding restaurants. There is street parking and more expensive 24-hour indoor parking at Bellavista 052. Farther away, but just as fun to visit, is the **Pueblito de los Domínicos ★★**, at Apoquindo 9085. Los Domínicos is a folksy, mock colonial village with shops selling hand-knit sweaters, lapis lazuli, arts and crafts, expensive antiques, and traditional Chilean clothing such as ponchos. Los Domínicos is your best bet for good-quality traditional souvenirs, and there are more than 100 stalls so you could spend more than an hour or two here. To get here, take the Metro to the Domínicos stop, or grab a taxi (about C$3,000). The Pueblito is open Tuesday to Sunday from 10:30am to 8pm.

The cheapest place for locally produced crafts is the **Feria Santa Lucía,** at Cerro Santa Lucía (on the other side of Alameda; Metro: Santa Lucía). The outdoor market can be recognized by its soaring billboards and sprawl of stalls hawking clothing, jewelry, and arts and crafts—even some antiques and collectibles. Hours vary, but it's generally open Monday through Saturday (sometimes Sun) from 11am to 7pm.

Shopping from A to Z

ANTIQUES

The antiques stalls at **Antiguedades Parque los Reyes,** Brasil 1157 at Mapocho (✆ **2/688-1348;** www.antiguedadesparquelosreyes.cl; daily 10am–late afternoon) sell a huge selection of refurbished and as-is antique furniture, paintings, sculptures, jewelry, and one-of-a-kind keepsakes at usually affordable prices. For large, heavy items, always check shipping costs (which can be excruciatingly expensive) before you buy; many stallholders will be able to arrange shipping. The market is within the confines of one huge red warehouse on the other side of the Panamericana, so a taxi here is about C$2,000 from the Plaza de Armas; or take the Metro to Santa Ana station, head west on Catedral Street for 3 blocks to Avenida Brasil, turn right, and walk north 8 blocks until you reach Mapocho Street.

On Saturdays and Sundays, the parallel streets of Bío-Bío and Franklin are transformed into a cluttered, crowded flea market with a seemingly never-ending supply of antiques and plain junk. If you have the patience and luck, amid the bric-a-brac you can often discover eclectic pieces and handicrafts. Take the Metro to Franklin and then walk north to the intersection with Victor Manuel.

A collection of antiques stores can be found clustered around Malaquias Concha and Caupolican streets, between Condell and Italia avenues. Considering that there are only a few shops, however, I recommend visiting only if you have a lot of time or are seeking an enjoyable walk; the neighborhood here is old-fashioned and a pleasant place for a stroll. In Vitacura, at Candelería Goyenechea 3820, the ground floor of the Anfiteatro Lo Castillo has two dozen antiques stores with beautiful European antiques at astronomical prices and more than a whiff of pretentiousness. Another pricey collection of antiques shops can be found at Calle Bucarest and Avenida Providencia, selling paintings, china, furniture, and nearly every knickknack imaginable. Lastly, the Plaza Mulato Gil de Castro, on Lastarría Street at Rosal, has a small antiques fair (mostly china, purses, and jewelry) that runs from Thursday to Saturday from about 10am to 8pm (closing earlier during winter).

ARTS & CRAFTS

Artesanías de Chile (☎ 2/777-8643; www.artesaniasdechile.cl) is the public face of the Chilean Crafts Foundation, which promotes and sells the work of local artisans. The store offers simply stunning arts and crafts and other handiwork, including intricate hand-woven textiles from the Aymara Indians, clay pottery from Pomaire, Mapuche silver jewelry, hand-woven baskets, and woodcarvings. The main Artesanías store is located at Av. Bellavista 0357, and there is a stand at the Pueblito los Domínicos (see above), plus a sizeable shop in the Centro Cultural La Moneda (p. 104) with interpretative information and a small store.

Two stores specializing in less-traditional *artesania,* with arts and crafts produced by contemporary artists, are **Observatorio Lastarría,** at Lastarría 395 (☎ 2/632-4588; www.elobservatorio.cl), and **Ona Chile,** at Victoria Subercaseaux 295, across from Cerro Santa Lucía (☎ 2/632-1859; www.onachile.com). Driven by a commitment to cultural and environmental conservation, the Observatorio has books, clothing made from local fibers, and ceramics for the home, and the shop is part of a larger arts center that often features temporary exhibitions, a sleek cafe, and "La Cava," a wine cellar offering tastings and workshops. Ona has a beautiful range of high-quality and unique artesanía, including alpaca shawls, *cacique* ponchos, ceramics, paintings, sculptures, jewelry, and other Patagonia and Ona Indian–themed art pieces.

BOOKS

The largest selection of English-language books can be found at the **Librería Inglesa** (www.libreriainglesa.cl), which sells literature, nonfiction, and children's books in shops at Av. Pedro de Valdivia 47 (☎ 2/232-8853); Paseo Huérfanos 669, Local 11 (☎ 2/632-5153); and Vitacura 5950 (☎ 2/413-1704). For the largest selection of books in Spanish, the **Feria Chilena del Libro,** Paseo Huérfanos 623 (☎ 2/345-8315), is your best bet, and it sells local and national maps. It has a smaller branch in Providencia at Santa Magdalena 50 (☎ 2/345-8346). Magazines from the U.S. can only be found at the airport, however there is a kiosk on Paseo Ahumada between Avenida Alameda and Estado that sells a limited number of international publications.

FASHION

Designer clothing and jewelry, both internationally recognizable brands and Chilean and Argentine brands, can be found in boutique shops along the streets Alonso de Córdova and Nueva Costanera in the neighborhood of Vitacura. Funky, handmade clothing by young local designers is sold at shops around the Bellavista neighborhood and within the Patio Bellavista complex. In the Parque Forestal neighborhood (also called Bellas Artes), you'll also find young designers selling quirky clothing in tiny shops around Merced St and José Miguel de la Barra, but the best place is **Hall Central,** José Victorino Lastarria 316 (no phone; www.hallcentral.cl), with six local designers selling their creations within a stately 20th-century mansion. **Tampu,** Av. Merced 327 (☎ 2/638-7992), presents modern renditions of the traditional weaving techniques of the Mapuche, Aymara, and Ona tribal cultures, with a funky range of sweaters and jewelry. Another good place for clothing made by local designers is at

Drugstore, Avenida Providencia 2124 (no phone; www.drugstore.cl) in the Providencia neighborhood and featuring a dozen mid-range shops with men's and women's fashions. Otherwise, Chileans shop for clothing in one of the city's many shopping malls.

FINE ART

Paintings, sculptures, and conceptual pieces by Santiago's contemporary artists can be found in the Vitacura neighborhood at galleries such as **Galería Animal,** Av. Alonso Córdova 3105 (℅ 2/371-9090; www.galeriaanimal.com) and **Artespacio,** Alonso de Córdova 2600 (℅ 2/206-2177; www.artespacio.cl). Animal has an extensive collection of art for sale; Artespacio sells primarily sculpture. Art by more established Chilean artists can be found at **Galería Patricia Ready,** Espoz 3125 (℅ 2/953-6210; www.galeriapready.cl) and **Galería Isabel Aninat,** Espoz 3100 (℅ 2/481-9870; www.galeriaisabelaninat.cl); both have sleek cafes and good bookshops, too. Downtown, visit the **Galería Moro** at Merced 349 #12, in Parque Forestal (℅ 2/633-8652; www.galeriamoro.cl), a hip gallery that displays and sells photography in addition to paintings. In Providencia, visit **Galería D21,** Nueva de Lyon 19, departamento 21 (℅ 2/335-6301; www.departamento21.cl), a large gallery located in a second-story apartment, which recently had an exhibit by Gonzalo Diaz, the National Art Award winner for 2010.

FOOD & WINE

Foodies and travelers looking for Chilean food products to bring home as gifts should not miss a stop by the wonderful **Coquinaria,** Santiago's best gourmet market (Av. Isidora Goyenechea 3000, in the W Hotel building; ℅ 2/245-1934; www.coquinaria.cl). Among the vegetables, cheeses, and charcuterie you'll find Chilean marmalades, chocolates, pâtés, smoked salmon, olive oil, and much, much more, as well as imported goods. If you're planning a picnic, this is your place to pick up supplies, and you can buy food to go to take back to your hotel.

Santiago's top wine shop is **Wain** in the Vitacura neighborhood, Av. Costanera 3955 (℅ 2/953-6290; www.wain.cl). Though it's a rather silly play on words, this is a shop that takes its wine seriously. There are three floors with wine divided into kinds of varietals and quality, as well as fine liquors, beer, and wine accoutrements and fun wine toys. It can seem overwhelming at first, but a truly knowledgeable and friendly English-speaking staff can help you pick out just what you're looking for. They'll also let you sample wine. Call ahead to participate in one of their regular wine tastings or cooking demonstrations. Wain's sister store, **Vinoteca,** Av. Manuel Montt 1452 (℅ 2/829-2200; www.vinoteca.cl), is smaller but no less diverse, selling boutique wines that are hard to find back home, and at reasonable prices. The jumbo **El Mundo del Vino** at Av. Isidora Goyenechea 3000, in the W Hotel building; (℅ 2/584-1173; www.elmundodelvino.cl), has an extensive selection and is more convenient for people lodging in the Las Condes area. For tips about shipping wine or bringing wine back with you on the plane, see p. 167 in chapter 7.

SANTIAGO AFTER DARK

Residents of Santiago, especially young Chileans, adhere to a vampire's schedule, dining as late as 10 or 11pm, arriving at a nightclub past 1am, and diving into bed before the sun rises. But there are many early-hour nighttime attractions if you can't bear late nights. The best place to find out what's happening is to visit **www.santiago magazine.cl**, the English-language *Santiago Times* entertainment site with a complete guide to nightlife and other events. *El Mercurio* publishes an event guide supplement called "Wiken," or you can visit their "Panoramas" site at www.wiken.emol.com.

The Performing Arts

Santiago is known for its theater, including large playhouses and small-scale, independent theater groups. Rarely do newspapers give reviews and descriptions of theater productions, so it might be difficult to find a production that interests you. Ask around for recommendations, or ask the staff at your hotel.

The most exciting development in the country's performing arts world is the recent opening of the **Centro Gabriela Mistral (GAM),** Alameda 227 (✆ **2/566-5500;** www.gam.cl), a cultural center for theater, music, and dance located within a monstrous structure that was once a military building and a symbol of political repression. After a wing of the building was destroyed by fire, the property was converted into a cultural center in celebration of Chile's bicentennial.

Well-established theaters with high-quality, contemporary productions and comedies include **Teatro Bellavista,** Dardignac 0110 (✆ **2/735-2395;** Metro: Baquedano) and **Teatro Alcalá,** Bellavista 97 (✆ **2/732-7161**). As the name implies, the nearby **Teatro La Comedia,** Merced 349 (✆ **2/639-1523;** Metro: Univ. Católica), hosts comedy, but it is better known for cutting-edge productions. The cultural center **Estación Mapocho,** at the Plaza de la Cultura s/n (✆ **2/787-0000;** Metro: Cal y Canto), hosts a large variety of theater acts, often concurrently. The **Centro Mori,** Constitución 183 (✆ **2/777-6246;** www.centromori.cl; Metro Baquedano), hosts well-respected, avant-garde theater acts that change weekly, and occasionally, live music; the center's restaurant, **Bar Restaurant Mori** (✆ **2/737-3398**), fronts the theater. The newer **Teatro Nescafe de las Artes,** Manuel Montt 032 (✆ **2/236-3333;** www.teatro-nescafe-delasartes.cl) boasts outstanding dance, opera, and concert performances in an intimate setting.

Realistically, if you do not speak Spanish, even the city's current hit production is going to be a waste of your time and money. Stick to something more accessible, such as a symphony, ballet, or opera at the city's gorgeous, neoclassical **Teatro Municipal ★**, located downtown at Agustinas 749 (✆ **800/471000;** www.municipal.cl; Metro: Univ. de Chile). The Teatro is worth a visit alone to marvel at the lavish interior, dripping with marble, red velvet, and crystal. The National Chilean Ballet holds productions from April to December, including contemporary and classic productions such as *The Nutcracker*. There are musical events and special productions throughout the year; the best way to find out what's on is to check the theater's website. You can **reserve and buy tickets** on the website, and select a seat from a diagram. Tickets are also sold over the phone Monday through Friday from 10am to 6pm, or can be bought in person at the theater itself from Monday through Friday from 10am to 7pm, and Saturday and Sunday from 10am to 2pm. Tickets are sold beginning 1 month before the show's starting date.

Visiting orchestras, the Fundación Beethoven, and contemporary acts play at the **Teatro Oriente,** Av. Pedro de Valdivia 099 (✆ **2/231-2173;** www.teatrooriente.cl); buy tickets at the theater or via Ticketmaster (see below). **Teatro Universidad de Chile,** Av. Providencia 043 (✆ **2/978-2480;** www.teatro.uchile.cl), hosts ballet and symphony productions, both national and international, throughout the year. You may buy tickets at the theater near Plaza Italia or by phone. **Ticketmaster** sells tickets for nearly every act in Santiago at CineHoyts cinemas, at Falabella department stores, via their website www.ticketmaster.cl, or by calling ✆ **2/690-2000** from 10am to 7pm.

Santiago a Mil Theater Festival

Santiago's largest summer festival, Festival Teatro a Mil, draws international theater troupes, clowns, mimes, and puppeteers from around the world in January to participate in a month-long celebration of the performing arts.

Special productions take place in more than 15 playhouses, and the cost is an average of C$4,000 for national productions and C$10,000 for international productions. Visit www.santiagoamil.cl for a list of events and venues.

Live Music

Crowd-pulling national and international megabands play in the **Estadio Nacional,** the **Movistar Arena,** the **Estación Mapocho,** and lately the **Club Hípico.** The **Espacio Riesco** hosts electronic music festivals such as Creamfields and SUE (Santiago Urbano Electrónico); the venue is located on the road to the airport about a 15-minute drive from Las Condes, with no public transportation, so you'll need a taxi. You'll find listings for concerts on the English-language site www.santiago magazine.cl, in newspapers, or on the *El Mercurio's* website, **www.emol.com,** under "Pasatiempos."

As an all-around nightlife spot, Bellavista is a good bet. Try **La Casa en el Aire,** Antonia López de Bello 0125 (© 2/735-6680; www.lacasaenelaire.cl), for a candlelit ambience and nightly live music on weekdays and Saturdays at 10pm and Sundays at 9pm. The **Patio Bellavista** between Constitución and Pío Nono streets has frequent live music in its center patio. The restaurant **Le Fournil** (© 2/248-9699; www.lefournil.cl) has a jazz club and **Backstage** (no phone; www.bks experience.com) has nightly live music; both venues are free if you buy a drink. The Patio's **El Cachafaz** has live tango music and tango dancing and classes; check out the Patio's website at www.patiobellavista.cl for a calendar of events. The recommended jazz club **El Perseguidor,** Antonia López de Bello 0126 (© 2/777-6763; www.elperseguidor.cl), offers strong performances in an intimate lounge setting, starting around 11pm.

There are smaller music venues spread across the city, but the two that attract the highest quality national and international bands are **Teatro Caupolicán,** San Diego 850 (© 2/699-1556; www.teatrocaulpolican.cl), in the downtown area, and **La Batuta,** Jorge Washington 52 (© 2/274-7096; www.batuta.cl), in the Ñuñoa neighborhood about a 10- to 15-minute taxi ride from downtown and Providencia. The atmosphere and crowds at these two venues depends on which band is playing that evening. The **Club de Jazz,** Santa Rita 1153 (© 2/274-1937; www.clubdejazz.cl), has been jamming since 1939, and it's one of the city's more traditional night spots, although earthquake damage forced it to move to another venue, located in the Casa de la Cultura de La Reina. The club pulls in talented acts from around Latin America and the world. Live music happens on Fridays only at 8:30pm, with cover charges ranging from C$2,500 to C$4,000.

Nightclubs

Santiago's club scene caters to an 18- to 35-year-old crowd, and it all gets going pretty late, from midnight to 6am, on average. If you like electronica music, you might check out *fiestas* publicized in the weekend entertainment sections of newspapers that list 1-night-only raves and live music, or check out **Amanda Cultural Center,** Embajador Doussinague 1767 at Los Cobre de Vitacura (© **2/218-5420;** www. amanda.cl), which has weekly *fiestas* with DJs spinning house, trance, and sometimes 80s and 90s classics, depending on the evening. Amanda is located in a funky 70s shopping area in Vitacura and requires a taxi ride to get there. In Bellavista, try **La Feria** at Constitución 275, in an old theater, open Thursday through Saturday. Another recommended club in Bellavista for dancing and the occasional live act is **El Clandestino,** Bombero Nuñez 363 (© **2/735-3655**). **Blondie,** Alameda 2879 (© **2/5-8433;** www.blondie.cl), is a goth/'80s revival/electronic dance club, depending on the night.

The Bar Scene

Chilean law requires that bars sell food (that's why you'll see the term "resto-bar" frequently), and so Santiago is bereft of true bars—the city instead passes establishments off as restaurants by day and bars by night, often without actually featuring a "bar." Bars that feature live music as an attraction are reviewed earlier. Most bars have happy hours from around 5 to 8pm.

DOWNTOWN

Downtown bars are concentrated around the Parque Forestal/Lastarría/Bellas Artes area near Cerro Santa Lucía. The newest hot spot is **Bar The Clinic,** Monjitas 578 (© **2/639-9548**), launched by the popular satirical newspaper *The Clinic* and frequented by a mélange of hipsters and office workers. The upmarket, trendy **Catedral** (p. 93) is a happening downtown bar, but get there early, before 9pm, or prepare yourself to wait forever for a table or a place at the bar. Catedral has outdoor seating on the rooftop patio. Nearby, Lastarría Street is lined with cafes and restaurants that are popular for a quiet drink and light conversation. Near the Plaza Mulatto Gil de Castro is **Bar Berri,** Rosal 321, a pub frequented by locals and college students; for a more romantic ambience, walk a block down the dead-end street off Rosal 346-C (called "Rosal Interior" and a half-block from Lastarría) for **Café Escondido** (© **2/632-7356**), a "hidden" cafe/bar with cozy, rough-hewn wood interiors and soft music.

PROVIDENCIA

In Providencia, the wildly popular **Bar Liguria ★**, with two locations at Luis Thayer Ojeda 019 (© **2/231-1393**) and Av. Providencia 1373 (© **2/235-7914**), is without a doubt the best nightspot given its broad appeal to a variety of ages; also see the review under "Where to Dine" earlier. Both branches are open until 2am on weeknights, until 5am on weekends, and are closed Sunday, and they serve food practically until closing time. Expats love to hang out at the American-owned **California Cantina and Sportsbar,** Las Urbinas 56 (© **2/361-1056**). **Santo Remedio,** Roman Díaz 152 (© **2/235-0984;** www.santoremedio.cl), provides one of the funkier atmospheres in Santiago, and it is the one of the few bars open on Sunday nights.

Bellavista's Pío Nono street is best avoided as it draws mobs of teens and university students hanging out at cheap beer joints and clubs, but 1 block away on quieter Constitución street is **Etniko** (p. 95), a standby yet a recommended bar for its lively, sophisticated crowd. Etniko has live DJ music, a full bar, an airy atrium for dining on sushi or *ceviche,* a new disco-bar with electronica music and a dance floor, and an open-air ceiling perfect for balmy summer nights. **Constitución,** at Constitución 61

(© **2/244-4569**), is the place where industry night owls head when they hang up their aprons for the night. With its casual, chic ambience, theatrical bartenders, quality live musicians, and guest DJs, it's the epitome of Bellavista bohème. As mentioned above, the **Patio Bellavista** has plenty of restaurants and bars within its complex and it's an entertaining area to sit outdoors and have a drink.

Tip: Do not heed the recommendation to visit the "Suecia" neighborhood for its dozens of clubs and bars. Long known as a tacky tourist rip-off and party-animal scene, the neighborhood has grown dangerous and is taking its last breath since property developers are eyeing the area for new condo developments.

LAS CONDES & VITACURA

The **W Hotel's** lounge (p. 89) is the latest Las Condes hot spot for the fashionable to see and be seen, and their roof-top deck (open beginning at 7pm) offers dazzling city views. The stuffier **Ritz-Carlton Bar** (p. 88) boasts bartenders who are cocktail experts, and offers more than 100 varieties of martinis. The **Hotel Plaza el Bosque** (p. 89) is a good "adult" spot for reasonably priced happy hours and dynamite city views from their 17th floor, with indoor and outdoor seating. **Flannigans's Geo Pub,** Encomenderos 83 (© **2/233-6675**), is an Irish pub with beer on tap that's a hit with expats and the Santiaguinos who like to rub shoulders with them. It's open until midnight on weeknights, 2am on weekends. One of the best alfresco drinking spots is on the patio of **Akarana** (p. 98), which has an outstanding wine list, well-made cocktails, and mellow live (or DJ) music.

If it's a summer evening and you're looking for a calming place to have a cocktail with a crowd in their 30s and up, head to **Zanzibar,** in the restaurant complex BordeRío at Avenida Escrivá de Balaguer 6400 (about a C$3,000 taxi ride from Las Condes; © **2/218-0118**). This Mediterranean/Moroccan restaurant and bar has an outdoor, candlelit terrace on the second floor furnished with pillows and banquettes, and a relaxing ambience with light chill-out music. Reservations are recommended; Zanzíbar is open from Monday to Saturday from 6:30pm to 1am (until 2am Fri–Sat).

Cinemas

Megaplexes such as CineHoyts and Cinemark, with their multi-screened theaters, feature the widest variety of movies and a popular Monday-to-Wednesday discount price. More avant-garde and independent films can be found in "Cine Arte" theaters, such as **Cine Alameda,** Alameda 139 (© **2/664-8821**), **El Biógrafo,** Lastarría 181 (© **2/633-4435**), and **Cine Arte Tobalaba,** Providencia 2563 (© **2/231-6630**). The entertainment sections of *El Mercurio* and *La Tercera* newspapers list titles, times, and locations, or check www.emol.com.

AROUND SANTIAGO: THE CENTRAL VALLEY, PEAKS & COASTAL REGION

S antiago is an excellent jumping-off point for a wealth of distinctive attractions and destinations: Fine beaches, an eccentric port town, nature preserves, serrated mountains, hot springs, and wineries are just a few examples of what's nearby. You'll also find a multitude of outdoor activities, including skiing at world-renowned resorts, hiking, rafting, biking, horseback riding, and more. Although some of the destinations listed in this chapter require an overnight stay, most attractions are within a half-hour to 2-hour drive from Santiago, meaning it is possible to pack a lot of action into just a few days.

This chapter proposes ideas for 1-day or multiday adventures outside of Santiago. You'll find information about where to find the best ski resorts, where to go wine-tasting, where to see Chile's rural traditions and old-world haciendas, and where to take a soak in a hot spring or visit a spa.

Exploring the Region

Many wineries, ski resorts, and coastal communities are close enough to Santiago to be explored on day trips, but your travel experience will be enriched if you opt to spend the night high in the Andes at a ski resort, or at a cozy B&B in the wine country. This way you'll spend less time in a vehicle and more time enveloping yourself in truly beautiful natural environments. A rental car provides a lot of freedom to explore at your own pace, especially if you are heading to the coast or visiting wineries. Chile has a first-rate highway system and roads are usually well marked, although a good road map is essential.

Taking a bus is not a bad option either—in fact, Santiago's national coach system is better than that of the U.S. Buses are modern and clean,

AFTER THE earthquake

The catastrophic 8.8-magnitude earthquake that hit south-central Chile on February 27, 2010 was one of the strongest in recorded history. It resulted in approximately 525 deaths and severe damages to a number of cities and valleys. About 800,000 were left homeless and economists have pegged the reconstruction costs at upwards of $30 billion.

The hardest hit areas were around the city of Concepción, Chile's second-largest metropolis, about 564km (350 miles) south of Santiago. The majority of this area is far from the regular tourist path and isn't covered in this book. In Santiago, older homes, churches, and buildings were randomly affected, although even as this book goes to print there are a handful of museums and other attractions that are still being repaired. Otherwise, travelers to Santiago will most likely not see any evidence of earthquake damage. Tourist-favorite destinations such as Torres del Paine, the Atacama Desert, and the Lakes District were not affected.

The Chillán and Colchagua areas (p. 173) were also hit hard, but repairs began almost immediately, and most services were up and running within days. The ski resort Nevados de Chillán opened without any incident during its 2010 ski season, and all roads and bridges in the Central Valley have been repaired. Unfortunately, however, the many lovely, century-old adobe homes and buildings of the Colchagua area are either going to be demolished or will undergo lengthy and costly renovations, and some will most likely just sit unattended until they rot. Nevertheless, the area is fully functional and all wineries are open and have been since late 2010.

In February 2011, a 6.8 aftershock shook off the coast of Concepción close to the epicenter of the 2010 quake, and although no damage was reported it did much to jangle the nerves of a population already worn down after having experienced hundreds of aftershocks since the 8.8 quake.

It is important to keep in mind that Chile enforces strict building codes that are designed to withstand major quakes, the reason why so few of Santiago's buildings underwent damage. By comparison, the earthquake that affected Haiti in 2010 registered 7.0 on the Richter scale and caused widespread death and destruction. Chile's prevention measures, strong emergency response services, and experience with earthquakes allowed the country to pull through considerably less scathed.

and there are usually a dozen or so daily departures to most major destinations. Bus terminals are located downtown and can by reached by Metro, although some major companies provide service leaving from their offices in Providencia. Taxis wait at regional bus terminals to deliver you to your hotel or wherever you need to go.

THE COASTAL REGION

Beach retreats are Chileans' favorite weekend getaway, and this chapter covers, in depth, Chile's better-known coastal cities: **Viña del Mar** and **Valparaíso.** Other smaller villages that dot the coast have their own strongly defined characteristics (and clear-cut socioeconomic levels), and visitors with a rental car will take pleasure in discovering each new village around the bend. You can also arrange a tour to coastal destinations that are not part of the "usual" itinerary.

Around Santiago & the Central Valley

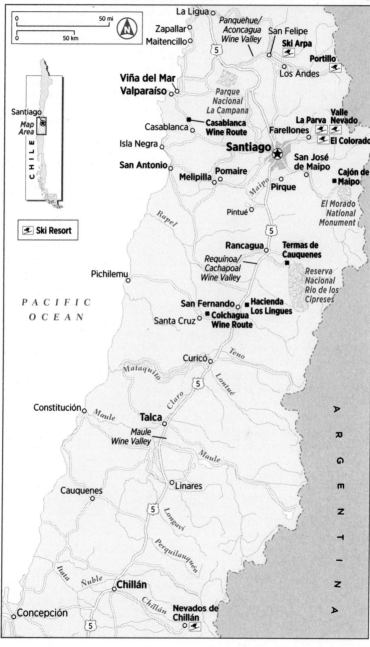

La Ligua
Zapallar
Maitencillo
Panquehue/ Aconcagua Wine Valley
San Felipe
Ski Arpa
Los Andes
Portillo

Viña del Mar
Valparaíso
Parque Nacional La Campana
Casablanca
Casablanca Wine Route
La Parva **Valle Nevado**
Farellones **El Colorado**
Isla Negra
Santiago
San Antonio
Melipilla **Pomaire**
San José de Maipo
Cajón de Maipo
Pirque
Maipo
Pintué
El Morado National Monument
Rapel
Rancagua **Termas de Cauquenes**
Requínoa/ Cachapoal Wine Valley
Reserva Nacional Río de los Cipreses
Pichilemu
P A C I F I C
O C E A N
San Fernando **Hacienda Los Lingues**
Santa Cruz **Colchagua Wine Route**
Teno
Curicó
Mataquito
Claro
Lontué
Constitución
Maule
Talca
Maule Wine Valley
Maule
A R G E N T I N A
Linares
Cauquenes
Longaví
Perquilauquén
Ñuble
Itata
Chillán
Chillán
Concepción
Nevados de Chillán

0   50 mi
0   50 km

Santiago
Map Area
CHILE

✈ **Ski Resort**

Zapallar is home to Chile's moneyed elite, and it's the prettiest cove in the region. **Cachagua** and **Maitencillo** are where many upper-middle and middle classes own second homes and apartments. **Con Con** is where you'll find the cheapest—and the freshest—seafood restaurants; **Reñaca** is where the young and gregarious socialize and loll in the sun. Farther south is another middle-class hub, **Algarrobo,** and **Cartagena,** the oldest seaside resort in Chile, which has now fallen out of favor (Chileans commonly use the phrase "tackier than a honeymoon in Cartagena"). The coastal village **Isla Negra** is popular for the Pablo Neruda museum, located in his former home (p. 149), which you can visit in conjunction with a stop at the San Antonio wine valley nearby.

VINA DEL MAR

120km (74 miles) NW of Santiago; 8km (5 miles) N of Valparaíso

Viña del Mar is Chile's largest and best-known beach resort town. The city was founded in 1874 as a weekend retreat and garden residence for the wealthy elite from Valparaíso and Santiago, and it has remained a top destination for Santiaguinos ever since, although the ultrafashionable are now electing to build their second homes in less-developed and therefore more exclusive coastal areas such as Tunquen and Quintay. Viña's manicured lawns, monolithic 1960s apartment buildings, and sandy beaches filled with sunbathers are an extreme contrast to the ramshackle streets of Valparaíso. Most Chileans call Viña del Mar simply "Viña"; you'll call it "chaos" if you come any time between December and late February, when thousands of vacationers arrive, crowding beaches and snarling traffic. On the other hand, there exists a heightened sense of excitement during these months with so much activity happening in the area. If the lure of the ocean is compelling for you, remember that Viña is certainly no beach paradise—the ocean is icy and a bit rough for swimming. But, having said that, if you enjoy the overarching indulgence and expectation that such resorts imbue, a couple of days in Viña may be to your liking—especially if you reside for a night at the superlative Hotel del Mar.

Better beaches for sunbathing can be found at nearby Reñaca, about 6km (3¾ miles) north of Viña (see "What to See & Do," later in this section). If you plan to spend a long day on the sand, bring plenty of sunblock and an umbrella as the sun is unusually strong along Chile's coast. The sea is very cold due to the Humboldt Current that travels up the coast from Antarctica, but you may be able to brave a swim during the summer from December to February.

Viña is divided into two sectors: downtown and the beachfront, which are separated by a river. Travelers are usually happiest lodging near the beach for access to the oceanfront promenade and plenty of restaurants.

Essentials
GETTING THERE

BY CAR Viña is 122km (76 miles) from Santiago and is reached by the highway Rte. 68. Driving to Viña from Santiago is quite easy: Simply hop onto the Costanera Norte headed west, and follow it all the way to the coast (the Costanera turns into Rte. 68). There are two tolls along the way that each cost C$1,500 from Monday to 5pm on Friday, and C$2,200 from 5pm Friday to Sunday. Note that **street parking** in Viña is scarce in January and February.

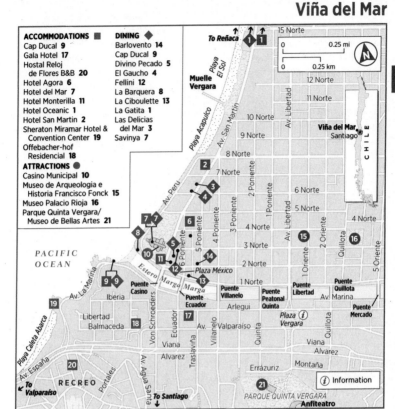

BY BUS   Tur Bus (© 600/660-6600; www.turbus.cl) and **Pullman** (© 600/320-3200; www.pullman.cl) leave from the Terminal Alameda in Santiago, located at Av. Alameda 3750 (Metro: Univ. de Santiago), every 15 minutes from 6:30am to 10:30pm (Tur Bus), and 6:10am to 10:10pm (Pullman). The cost on Pullman is C$11,000 one-way, and C$3,400 one-way on Tur Bus. During weekends, especially December through March, it is strongly recommended that you buy your ticket in advance from any Tur Bus or Pullman office in Santiago (your hotel can give you the address of the nearest office). The trip takes around 1½ hours. The bus terminal in Viña is located at Avenida Valparaíso and Quilpué, near the main plaza, and there are taxis available.

BY TRAIN   The **Metrotren** (also known as the "Merval"; © 32/252-7500) connects Viña with Valparaíso, leaving every 5 to 10 minutes from 7:30am to 10pm during weekdays, and every 15 to 20 minutes from 9:30am to 9pm on Saturdays, Sundays, and holidays. To ride the train, you must first make a one-time purchase: a rechargeable card for C$1,200 that you then charge with enough money to cover the cost of your trip. If you're with friends or family, you need only purchase one card for your group.

GETTING AROUND

All attractions in Viña can be reached on foot with streets organized according to a grid layout that is easy to navigate. Taxis are inexpensive and are available either by hailing one in the street or calling **Radio Taxi Viña del Mar** (© **32/271-4711** or 9/323-1346; www.radiotaxisvinadelmar.cl). Viña is divided into two parts by the Marga Marga estuary; north of the Marga Marga, you'll find the beachfront resort area with 3.5km (2.1 miles) of coastline fronted by monolithic condominiums, hotels, restaurants, and bars, primarily catering to tourists. The area south of the Marga Marga is the "downtown," dominated by Avenida Valparaíso, a principal shopping area punctuated with familiar global brand stores and fast-food outlets. Sleek designer stores and shopping malls are concentrated along the 5 blocks west of Plaza Vergara; just walk west toward the ocean as far as Calle Ecuador. A taxi to Valparaíso costs around C$7,500 if hailed on the street, or slightly more if ordered to your hotel. A couple of blocks south, the exotic Quinta Vergara Park is a lovely place for an afternoon stroll.

VISITOR INFORMATION

The **Oficina de Turismo de Viña** is on Plaza Vergara, next to the post office near avenidas Libertad and Arlegui (© **800/800830** toll-free in Chile; www.visitevinadel mar.cl). Hours are weekdays from 9am to 2pm and 3 to 7pm; Saturday and Sunday from 10am to 2pm and 3 to 7pm. The helpful staff speaks English and can provide visitors with maps, event details, and accommodations information, including private cabin rentals. The **Sernatur office,** located on the third floor (office no. 302), at Av. Valparaíso 507 (© **2/268-3355;** www.sernatur.cl), is also helpful and has information and maps on the entire region. It's open Monday through Thursday from 8:30am to 5:30pm, and Friday from 8:30am to 4:30pm.

SPECIAL EVENTS   Every third or fourth week of February, Viña plays host to the **Festival de la Canción,** a weeklong gala event held at the Quinta Vergara Park amphitheater. It's Chile's largest music festival, drawing nearly 30,000 spectators nightly who collectively form "The Monster," so-called for the crowds' ability to tear apart so-so performers with thunderous whistles and boos. Apart from national and international Latin acts such as Chayanne and Fito Paez, past festivals have booked international acts such as Tom Jones, Marc Anthony, and Franz Ferdinand. Viña bursts at the seams during this event, and hotel reservations are imperative.

During the second or third week of November, Viña hosts the acclaimed **Festival Cine Viña del Mar** film festival (www.cinevina.cl). Nearly 90% of films showcased during this event are of Latin American origin and in Spanish and Portuguese only.

[FastFACTS] VIÑA DEL MAR

Banks   Most major banks can be found on Avenida Arlegui, and although they're open Monday through Friday from 9am to 2pm only, nearly all have ATMs (Redbancs).

Car Rentals   Try **Alamo,** Agua Santa 402 (© 32/215-6525; www.alamochile.com); **Rosselot,** Av. Libertad 999 (© 32/238-2373; www.rosselot.cl), and Av. Alvarez 762 (© 32/314-0350); **Hertz,** Av. Quillota 766 (© 32/238-1025; www.hertz.cl); or **Verschae Rent A Car,** Av. Libertad 1045 (© 600/500-0700; www.verschae.com). Daily rental prices average C$27,000 per day for a compact car, and C$30,000 for a mid-range vehicle.

Currency Exchange   *Cambios* (money-exchange houses) are open in the summer Monday through Friday from 9am to 2pm and 3 to 8pm, and Saturday from 9am to 2pm; and in winter Monday through Saturday 9am to 2pm and 4 to 7pm, and Saturday from 9am to 2pm. Several *cambios* can be found along Avenida Arlegui.

Emergencies For **police,** dial © **133;** for **fire,** dial © **132;** and for an **ambulance,** dial © **131.**

Hospital For medical attention, go to **Hospital Gustavo Fricke** on calles Alvarez 1532 at Simón Bolívar (© **32/257-7600** or 32/257-7602; www.hospital fricke.cl).

What to See & Do
THE COASTLINE

Just south of the Marga Marga, the whimsical **Castillo Wulff,** with its Bavarian-style turrets, is quite the architectural anachronism. Built for coal baron Gustavo Adolfo Wulff in the early 20th century, the Maritime Museum that was housed here for many years has been transformed into a cultural center; it's worth taking a stroll around inside to view the eccentric interior. Just south, **Playa Caleta Abarca** beach is in a protected bay near the entrance to Viña del Mar, next to the town's poster-child "flower clock," a meticulously landscaped flower-bed with working dials and flanked by exotic palms. On weekends, the Playa Caleta beach is an animated scene but certainly not the prettiest of beaches in the area; here groups of friends and families set up shop for the day with picnic tables, barbecues, and boom boxes.

In the northeast, fronting rows of terraced high-rise apartment buildings, you'll find **Playa Acapulco, Playa Mirasol,** and **Playa Las Salinas** (the latter is near the naval base). The sea here tends to be too rough for swimming; also these beaches are packed towel-to-towel with throngs of vacationers and families in the summer, and could qualify as a vacationer's nightmare. Better to go to **Reñaca,** just 6km (3.7 miles) up the coast. The first stretch of the beach is popular with families, while the end is the "cool" spot frequented by the young for its sleek cocktail bars and ebullient discos. There are several glass-enclosed beach cafes along the principal road here for a snack and plenty of cheap seafood restaurants. Because Chileans party late into the night, you won't see many people on any beach until about noon. To get here, take a taxi (about C$5,500 one-way) or a bus (nos. 302 and 602 at Av. Libertad and 15 Norte).

It's also worth taking a drive north for 10km (6.2 miles) to **Concón,** for splendid coastal views and a chance to see fat sea lions sunning themselves on the rocky shore. Follow the coastal road Avenida San Martín until it becomes Avenida Jorge Montt, and continue along the winding, two-lane road as it hugs the shore. When you tire of the drive, simply turn around and head back the same way. This run-down fishing village, overlooked by smug, pristine villas and mansions, makes for a fascinating contrast to the airs of Viña. It's worth strolling down to the frenetic quay here, La Boca, where *marisquerías* purvey über fresh fish, shellfish, and crustaceans.

THE TOP ATTRACTIONS

Casino Municipal ★ Built in 1930, the Casino Municipal was the most luxurious building in its day and is worth a visit even if you're not a gambler. The interior has been remodeled over time, but the facade has withstood the caprices of many a developer and is still as handsome as the day it opened. Semiformal attire is required to enter the gaming room: no T-shirts, jeans, or sneakers. Minimum bets of C$5,000 may deter some budget travelers, although there are slot machines and video poker. The casino holds periodic art exhibits on its second floor, and there are bars and a discotheque if you're looking for nightlife that's a step up from the teen clubs in Viña.

Av. San Martín 199. ✆ **32/284-6084.** www.enjoy.cl. Hours vary, but generally in winter game room Mon–Thurs noon–4am, Fri–Sun 24 hr.; in summer daily 24 hr.

Museo de Arqueología e Historia Francisco Fonck ★★

Founded in 1937, this highly recommended natural history museum is named after German doctor Francisco Fonck (1830–1912), a pioneer in the archaeological exploration of Central Chile, who bequeathed his extensive collections of artifacts from Chile, Peru, and Ecuador to the Chilean government. The natural history display at the Museo Fonck spans the entire second floor, but what really warrants a visit here is the museum's 1,400-piece collection of Rapa Nui (Easter Island) indigenous art and archaeological artifacts, including one of the only six moai sculptures found outside the island (the others are in England, the U.S., Paris, Brussels, and La Serena in Chile). This monumental piece brought from Easter Island in 1950 stands majestically in the garden by the museum's entrance. The display is more complete than the archaeological museum on Easter Island itself. Also on display are art and archaeological remnants of all cultures in Chile, and the size of the museum is just right to not grow tiresome—you'll need about 45 minutes here. There is also an on-site store selling jewelry, Easter Island art replicas, woolen goods, and more.

Av. 4 Norte 784. ✆ **32/268-6753.** www.museofonck.cl. Admission C$1,800 adults and C$300 children. Mon–Fri 10am–6pm; Sat, Sun, and holidays 10am–2pm (Oct–Mar Sat 10am–6pm).

Museo Palacio Rioja ★★

The lushly landscaped grounds that surround this grand Belle Epoque stone mansion are only a fraction of what they once were when wealthy Spaniard banker Fernando Rioja took residence in 1910. Originally spanning 4 blocks, with a classical facade dominated by stout Corinthian columns, this palace took opulence to a new level during its time. It's well worth taking one of the daily tours (around 30 min., in Spanish only) to absorb the grandeur of elite life during the early 20th century. The rich interiors, made of oak and intricately carved stone, feature a split double staircase and baroque, rococo, and Chesterfield furniture imported from Spain and France. The palace hosts a range of classical concerts and theater performances in addition to screening movies.

Quillota 214. ✆ **32/248-3664.** Admission C$600 adults and C$300 children. Tues–Sun 10am–1:30pm and 3–5:30pm.

Parque Quinta Vergara/Museo de Bellas Artes ★★

A compact but lovely park, the Quinta Vergara pays homage to the future with its spaceshiplike music amphitheater, and to the past, with its converted 1910 Venetian-style palace, the former home of historical heavyweights the Alvarez/Vergara family, now converted into a fine arts museum. Quinta Vergara was originally the site of an early 19th-century hacienda, which was acquired by Portuguese shipping magnate Francisco Alvarez and his wife Dolores in 1840. Dolores was a keen botanist and in between bouts of pre-Raphaelite languor, she transformed the gardens into an exotic Eden featuring many plants brought from Europe and Asia by her seafaring son, Salvador. Taking center stage in the park, the striking Italianate Palacio Vergara was built in 1906 by Blanca Vergara, Salvador's granddaughter. When Blanca's mother married José Francisco Vergara, the man who founded Viña del Mar in 1874, two of Chile's most influential families were united. The mansion now houses the family's collection of baroque European paintings, as well as oil paintings of Chilean VIPs during the 19th and early 20th century. Every February, this park fills with music lovers who come for the annual Festival of Song, which features largely Latin pop boy bands hotly pursued by cadres of screaming groupies. The rest of the year the park is an idyllic spot for a quiet stroll.

Errazuriz 563. Museum: ☏ **32/226-9431.** Admission C$300 adults, C$100 children. Tues-Sun 10am–1:30pm and 3–5pm. Park: Free admission. Daily 7am–6pm (until 7pm in summer).

Where to Stay

Lodging options in Viña lean toward large hotels and a mixed bag of smaller inns and hostels, whereas Valparaíso is known for its intimate boutique hotels. The best options are hotels that face or are near the beach for access to restaurants, the casino, and the beach and its long promenade. The ambience here is decidedly less urban than Valparaíso, too.

VERY EXPENSIVE

Hotel del Mar ★★★ ☺ 📷 The Hotel del Mar, part of the Enjoy hotel and casino chain, is the finest hotel in the region, designed with exquisite taste and offering superlative amenities. The cream-colored hotel is evocative of Greco-Roman style and was designed to match the 1930s-era casino that adjoins the hotel, and so it lacks the cookie-cutter feel that is more prevalent at the Sheraton nearby. The central location near restaurants and fronting the beach is the best of any hotel in town. Viña's beach is overcrowded during the summer, but guests here can bask in the sun, glamorously, on terraces with ocean views, and there is a glass-enclosed indoor pool that affords panoramic views of the ocean. The guest room aesthetic is sober and understated, decorated in neutral tones; standard and deluxe rooms are on the north and south ends of the hotel with city/sea views, while suites are in the center, offering a wide-open view of the sea. All rooms have balconies. The city's best restaurant, Savinya (see "Where to Dine," later) is here, and there is a discotheque in the casino, bars, and kids activities. Service is more on the formal side but polite. The hotel's website offers rates that are 30 to 50% off rack rate.

Av. San Martín 199. ☏ **32/770-5190.** Fax 32/250-0801. www.hoteldelmar.cl. $477–$667 double. 60 units. AE, DC, MC, V. Valet parking. **Amenities:** 4 restaurants; bar; babysitting; children's game room; health club; indoor pool; room service; solarium. *In room:* A/C, plasma TV w/pay-per-view movies, DVD and CD player, hair dryer; free Wi-Fi.

Sheraton Miramar Hotel & Convention Center ★★★ With the most stunning location of any hotel in Viña, this Sheraton offers sweeping ocean views, a state-of-the-art spa and fitness center, a delightful outdoor pool, and an endless range of high-end services. The hotel hugs the shore and is across from Viña's famous flower clock, about a 10-minute walk to beachfront restaurants and stores. The Sheraton glitters in white-and-glass minimalism, yet the hotel's sleek packaging and voluminous public spaces accented with little or no furniture creates an air of emptiness. The service is quite friendly, but this is not a place where you will experience personalized service. The guest rooms are attractive in a Sheraton chain way, and are impeccably clean and decorated in blues, white, and cherrywood tones; beds have silky cotton sheets and bathrooms have marble inlaid sinks and rain showers. All rooms come with floor-to-ceiling windows and ocean views, with small terraces; if you can afford a suite, the corner views are breathtaking. Rates listed below are rack rates during high season; check their website for real-time prices that are usually around half the price of rack rates.

Av. Marina 15. ☏ **32/238-8600.** www.starwoodhotels.com/sheraton. 142 units. $470 classic double; $745 suite. AE, DC, MC, V. Valet parking. **Amenities:** 2 restaurants; bar; babysitting; concierge; state-of-the-art health club & spa; indoor and outdoor pools; room service. *In room:* Plasma TV, minibar, hair dryer, Internet (C$7,125 per day).

EXPENSIVE

Gala Hotel   The high-rise Gala hotel is a contemporary if not utilitarian hotel within walking distance of the beach, offering a myriad of facilities that facilitate affordable pampering. The rooms are your average beachside rooms with generic art and flimsy, IKEA-style furnishings, but they are light, breezy, and kept spotlessly clean. Most travelers find that the array of facilities, as well as the location and price, compensates for the generic overtones. The hotel often plays host to large conferences, which precludes a sense of intimacy and escapism; also the swimming pool is too tiny to be fully enjoyed.

Arlegui 273, Viña del Mar. ☎ **32/232-1500.** Fax 32/268-9568. www.galahotel.cl. 64 units. $157 standard double; $195 suite. AE, DC, MC, V. **Amenities:** Restaurant; bar; babysitting; outdoor heated pool; sauna. *In room:* A/C, cable TV, hair dryer, minibar.

Hotel Oceanic ★   The Oceanic boasts a privileged location perched on a rocky promontory with dramatic coastal views of the ocean crashing against the shore. If you're looking for a hotel with sea views but the Sheraton is too pricey, consider this independently run hotel, but note that the hotel's isolated location means you'll need to take a 5-minute taxi ride to get to Viña. The hotel is by no means luxurious, and service can be hit-or-miss, but this is one of the few hotels in town with a pool, and the coastal walkway along the shore makes for a good stroll. Four rooms face the road and are a whopping $63 cheaper, but it seems pointless to get a room without a view here, and traffic noise is noticeable. For more space, consider a superior junior suite that costs $21 more than a standard double.

Av. Borgoño 12925. ☎ **32/283-0006.** Fax 32/283-0390. www.hoteloceanic.cl. 28 units. $123 double street view; $184 street view; $202 superior junior suite. AE, DC, MC, V. **Amenities:** Restaurant; bar; babysitting; outdoor pool; sauna. *In room:* Cable TV, hair dryer, minibar, free Wi-Fi.

Hotel San Martín ★   The Hotel San Martín's spotless guest rooms bear a whiff of '50s modern with clean lines, polished wood, and chrome fixtures, paired with salmon pink or floral bedspreads and coordinated drapery; it's a little too fusty but clean and accommodating. Double rooms are small; if you need a lot of room, consider paying extra for the terracotta-hued suites, which are more sophisticated and spacious, or consider lodging elsewhere. Light sleepers should book a "sea view" room that is quieter, but the name is a misnomer as the views are minimal; "poniente" rooms overlook a pretty garden. Polished parquet floors with carpet runners and halogen lighting lend the hotel's public spaces coziness. The hotel has five rooms adapted to wheelchair users. The central location is very convenient and although there is no pool, you have the beach at your feet. Note that prices shown on the website are often incorrect, so it's better to call or email for a price quote.

Av. San Martín 667. ☎ **32/268-9191.** Fax 32/268-9195. www.hotelsanmartin.cl. 160 units. $200 double standard; $290 junior suite; $325 suite. AE, DC, MC, V. **Amenities:** Restaurant; bar; tiny exercise room; room service; sauna. *In room:* Cable TV, hair dryer, minibar, free Wi-Fi.

MODERATE

Cap Ducal ★   Built to resemble a ship moored to the shore, this offbeat hotel has been a Viña institution since 1936. The hotel's location perched above the coastline affords views of the pounding surf from all of its 25 rooms, which cantilever out over the ocean. Balconies afford prime viewing territory for the rich profusion of birdlife and sea lions. Inside, the nautical theme continues, with narrow halls with wood-paneled walls and brass handrails; the low-slung rooms look and feel much like a ship's berth. On the downside, potential irritations do lurk beneath the hotel's overarching coziness. The hot water can be sporadic and the hotel's age clearly shows in its worn furnishings; the carpet could stand to be replaced and some rooms reek of smoke (ask for a nonsmoking room). Still, it's an overall welcoming place to spend the night and the beach is a 10- to 15-minute walk away. The restaurant is well known for its seafood dishes.

Av. Marina 51, Viña del Mar. © **32/262-6655.** Fax 32/266-5471. www.capducal.cl. 25 units. $120 standard double; $180 junior suite. AE, DC, MC, V. **Amenities:** Restaurant; cafe. *In room:* Cable TV, minibar.

Hotel Monterilla ★★ 🛏️   This delightful, family-run boutique hotel, located near the beach and casino, is an excellent value and one of the best-kept secrets in Viña del Mar. Cheerful service and a central location are definite draws, but the hotel's contemporary decor—and recently renovated guest rooms—is what really makes the Monterilla special. The eye-catching, postmodern rooms are styled with chromatic furniture contrasted against white and orange walls, striped bedspreads, and artwork by Chilean artists, and the feeling is of freshness and comfort. There is one apartment with a kitchenette for four guests; the Monterilla has also added four new rooms and two meeting salons in a new wing, as well as a patio terrace. Singles are the cheapest option but smaller in size. Despite the hotel's central location, it is quiet. The Monterilla offers a promotion for cruise ship passengers for $336 for two that includes airport pick-up, lodging and breakfast, a welcome cocktail, and transportation to the ship's port in Valparaíso.

2 Norte 65, Plaza México, Viña del Mar. © **32/297-6950.** Fax 32/268-3576. www.monterilla.cl. 28 units. $159 standard double; $183 superior double. AE, DC, MC, V. **Amenities:** Cafeteria; bar. *In room:* Cable TV, hair dryer, minibar, free Wi-Fi.

INEXPENSIVE

Hostal Reloj de Flores B&B ★ 🍴   Dollar for dollar, the Hostal Reloj de Flores offers decent value. There's nothing fancy about the place, but guest rooms, especially those with private bathrooms, are clean, comfortable, and brightly decorated. It's just a hop, skip, and a jump to Caleta Abarca Beach (but a healthy walk to restaurants along the beachfront). As a converted home, rooms are differently sized and decorated—some are contemporary, with colorful duvet comforters, and others have antique headboards. Two rooms have shared bunks, and some private rooms have shared bathrooms. Try to nab their only room with a balcony, as it is the same price. As with most B&Bs, service is exceptionally friendly, and there's a shared kitchen and barbecue area. The staff will also help to arrange tours in the area.

Calle Los Baños 70, Caleta Abarca. © **32/296-7243.** Fax 32/248-5242. www.hostalrelojdefloresbb. com. 13 units. $48–$52 for double with shared bathroom; $59–$64 double with private bathroom; $79–$86 superior double with private bathroom. No credit cards. **Amenities:** Cafe; shared kitchen; babysitting. *In room:* Cable TV, no phone, free Wi-Fi.

Hotel Agora ★   This budget hotel is a paradigm of tasteful simplicity and low-cost chic tucked away on a peaceful street just a 15-minute walk to the ocean. With its stark, rectilinear form and white and pastel color scheme, it creates the immediate impression of a tropical playground. Rooms are a blaze of hallucinogenic color with acid greens, ocean blues, and egg-yolk yellows contrasting with polished wooden floors and minimalist bed frames. All are discreetly appointed with TVs, minifridges, and reading lights.

Poniente 253, Viña del Mar. © **32/269-4669.** Fax 32/269-5165. www.hotelagora.cl. 16 units. $85 standard double. AE, DC, MC, V. **Amenities:** Cafeteria; bar. *In room:* Cable TV, minibar, hair dryer.

Offenbacher-hof Residencial ★ Housed in a Victorian house dating to 1905 and perched high atop Cerro Castillo, the Offenbacher has sweeping views of the city and the hills beyond, and a splendid glass-enclosed patio. It is by far one of the more interesting and best value places to lodge, and its location on this historic hill puts you near some of the city's oldest homes—but guests must either grab a taxi to reach the beach, or hoof it. The mix-and-match decor is on the funky side, but it's hard to balk at the flea market furniture when you consider the panoramic views. Superior doubles are worth the extra $11 for better views and substantially more space. The three doubles that open onto the patio are darker and less private. The German-Chilean family that runs the Offenbacher is cheerful, helpful, and always on hand to provide comprehensive information on cultural tours and activities throughout the region.

Balmaceda 102, Cerro Castillo, Viña del Mar. © **32/262-1483.** Fax 32/266-2432. www.offenbacher-hof. cl. 15 units. $74–$80 double twin; $84–$93 superior double. AE, DC, MC, V. **Amenities:** Cafe; bar; airport transfers; bikes; exercise room; Jacuzzi; sauna. *In room:* Cable TV, free Wi-Fi.

Where to Dine

Valparaíso has taken the lead as the gastronomic nucleus of the central coastal region, leaving Viña in the dust. Frankly, it's a mystery as to why there are so few good restaurants here considering its importance as a tourism destination. Expect a lot of fast-food joints, beer gardens, and theme restaurants with loud music and wine-barrel decor. Most restaurants in Viña are centered on Avenida San Martín along the coast.

If you're spending a few days in town, I recommend you take a drive up the coast one afternoon to Concón (16km/10 miles from Viña) or one of the tiny hamlets before it—this is where locals go for fresh seafood in one of the many *picadas* (something like a dive, with cheap but hearty and delicious food). One of the best *picadas* is **La Gatita,** Avenida Borgoño in Higuerillas (© **32/281-4235;** Sun–Wed noon–4pm and Thurs–Sat noon–midnight), a wildly popular restaurant with an agonizingly long wait if you arrive any time between 1:30 and 3pm on weekends. There is no street number, so look for a small fish market on the left-hand side of the road just after passing the yacht harbor (when driving north). Try Chile's famous *caldillo de congrio* (conger eel soup) here. Another local favorite is **Las Delicias,** Av. Borgoño 25370, in Concón (no phone; daily 11am–5pm), which specializes in greasy but good fried empanadas, such as one filled with crab, shrimp, and delicious *macha pino,* or razor clams sautéed in onions.

EXPENSIVE

La Ciboulette ★ 📖 BELGIAN/CHILEAN An altogether unwelcoming facade keeps tourists away from this tiny restaurant, but La Ciboulette is a local favorite and has won various culinary awards for its home-style, Belgian/French-influenced cuisine prepared by old-fashioned restaurateurs who are passionate about the delicate balance of each dish; ask for a substitution at your peril. The brief menu changes seasonally so that every element is very fresh, and their wine list is quite varied. Each dish is flavorful and transcends the type of food served at traditional Belgian bistros; menu items include snails drenched in a rich sauce of Camembert and almonds, grouper in a Provençal sauce, and duck confit with pear and red wine sauce. For dessert, try the juicy strawberries laced with pepper and served with homemade ice cream.

1 Norte 191-A. © **32/269-0084.** www.laciboulette.cl. Reservations recommended. Main courses C$8,900–C$11,500. AE, DC, MC, V. Mon–Sat 1–3:30pm and 8pm–midnight, Sun 1–3:30pm.

Savinya ★★★ INTERNATIONAL Savinya is part of the Hotel del Mar and is known for its outstanding haute cuisine—the restaurant was recently rated the #1 regional restaurant by the annual *Guia Culinary*. It's Viña's most refined and expensive restaurant, and the place to go if you're looking to blow your budget on a special meal; though when compared to restaurants of the same caliber in the U.S. or Europe, the prices at Savinya could be considered reasonable. The menu changes seasonally, but what doesn't change is the chef's impeccable technique and presentation of each dish, blending uncommon flavors and textures that work surprisingly well together, with a list of complementary palate-pleasing wines. A white truffle infusion here and a foie gras sliver there add a lavish decadence that transforms an otherwise hearty Mediterranean staple into haute cuisine. For purists, the unadulterated meat dishes provide intense flavors and a silken texture. Attentive, agreeable service comes with the price, as does an elegant-chic ambience, and gigantic picture windows offer a gorgeous view overlooking the ocean.

Av. Perú and Los Héroes. © **32/250-0800.** www.hoteldelmar.com. Reservations recommended for dinner. Main courses C$9,500–C$12,500. AE, DC, MC, V. Daily 12:30–4:30pm and 8:30pm–midnight.

MODERATE

Barlovento ★ MODERN CHILEAN   Barlovento is a perfect distillation of Viña's modern night scene. What Barlovento does best is casual and light meals and especially tapas, but this latter term really refers to a wide selection of platters heaped with meats, charcuterie, and cheese. The resto-bar also serves panini sandwiches, salads, and pizzas. Cocktail lovers will like that the bartenders here really know how to make a proper cosmopolitan, dry martini, and a Bloody Mary, a skill not often well honed in Chile. Barlovento's minimalist look of cement, steel, glass, and wraparound windows is somewhat of an architectural anachronism in an area replete with chain-style restaurants. Live DJ music happens on weekends and draws a lively crowd of young professionals.

2 Norte 195. © **32/297-7472.** www.barlovento.cl. Reservations accepted for groups. Sandwiches and wraps C$3,500; platters C$4,500–C$9000. AE, DC, MC, V. Daily 6pm–2am.

Cap Ducal SEAFOOD   This Viña del Mar institution is notable for one reason only: an intimate, candlelit dining experience with a view of the sparkling coastline and the crashing surf. The restaurant is designed to resemble a ship moored against the cliff, and it has been a fixture in the Viña dining scene since 1936. However, the ambience outshines the food, which is not bad but does lack creativity. The focus here is on Chilean cuisine and international style seafood. Try the classic Chilean razor clams with Parmesan cheese.

Av. Marina 51. © **32/262-6655.** www.capducal.cl. Main dishes C$4,800–C$7,000. AE, DC, MC, V. Daily 1pm–midnight.

Divino Pecado ★★ ITALIAN   Cozy and centrally located, this chef-owned restaurant combines all the elements of an enjoyable dining experience: a pleasant wait-staff, delectable fresh pastas and seafood, and a trattoria-style dining area that's cheery during the day, and romantic at night. For an aperitif, order a pisco sour—this restaurant is known for its delicious Peruvian variety. Also, the wine list is extensive and offers excellent value for the price. Don't expect traditional Italian home-style cooking; each dish promises to be a taste sensation with interesting and unusual combinations of traditional Italian ingredients infused with ethnic herbs and spices and some modern European twists. "Black" raviolis are made with calamari ink and stuffed with curried shrimp, while the fettuccine with lamb is garnished with aromatic clumps of rosemary. Divino Pecado specializes in "boutique" fish such as sole, the delicate *mero* (grouper), and Easter Island tuna, and there are meats such as filet mignon.

Av. San Martín 180 (in front of casino). ✆ **32/297-5790.** divinopecado@terra.cl. Reservations recommended. Main courses C$8,000–C$9,000. AE, DC, MC, V. Daily 12:30-3:30pm; Mon–Fri 8–11pm; Sat–Sun 8pm–1am.

El Gaucho ★ ARGENTINE/STEAK   Carnivores will find a home at El Gaucho, which dishes out succulent cuts of just about any kind of meat, served sizzling off their huge indoor *parrilla* (grill). The Argentine-style "interiors" appetizers include blood sausage, sweetbreads, and crispy intestines. If that doesn't make your mouth water, try starting with grilled provolone cheese with oregano. Entrees include beef loin, ribs, chicken, sausages, and other grilled items and salads. Wood floors and brick walls create a warm, comfortable ambience.

Av. San Martín 435. ✆ **32/269-3502.** Main courses C$7,500–C$9,500. AE, DC, MC, V. Daily 1-3:30pm, and 8-11:30pm.

Fellini ★ ITALIAN   A Viña del Mar stalwart, Fellini recently introduced changes to its menu and took a previously dated repertoire of dishes up a notch in quality and style. The cuisine is hearty and flavorful without being too pretentious, and bow-tied waiters provide old-fashioned service, usually greeting local patrons by name. Pastas are the mainstay here—you can build your own pasta dish or order 1 of 10 varieties of lasagna. The risotto with Ecuadorian shrimp, vegetables, and scallop oil is quite good, as are Fellini's seafood entrees, including a Capitan's Fish Stew. This is a good restaurant for fussier eaters, since most of the pasta, fish, and meat dishes can be individually "designed" from a variety of sauces.

3 Norte 88. ✆ **32/297-5742.** www.fellini.cl. Reservations recommended for dinner. Main courses C$6,500–C$8,900. Daily 1-4pm and 8pm-midnight.

Las Delicias del Mar ★ SEAFOOD   Las Delicias serves inspired seafood dishes in a comfortable, plant-filled environment, with attentive service. The restaurant is one of the best bets in town for fresh fish dishes, which former TV chef Raúl Madinagoitía executes with flair and imagination. Each recipe has a story; the *crema de almejas* soup is an homage to a humble Hamptons clam chowder, while the Corvina Dicaprio—sea bass steamed with crab, mussels, shrimp, and white wine—was baptized in honor of Leonardo following his visit. The excellent paella, prepared according to a centuries-old traditional Spanish recipe, is always a hit. The wine list is also one of the most discriminating in Viña and the classic desserts, such as the crème brûlée, have the power to stir heavenly rapture. A sister restaurant is in Reñaca.

Av. San Martín 459. ✆ **32/290-1837.** www.deliciasdelmar.com. Main courses C$7,600–C$12,000. AE, DC, MC, V. Daily 12:30-4pm and 7pm-midnight.

INEXPENSIVE

La Barquera ★★ INTERNATIONAL   The best alfresco dining venue in Viña is at this open-air deck restaurant, where you can eat with the sea breeze in your face and a cold glass of chardonnay in your hand. The restaurant is part of the Hotel del Mar (see above), but it is located across the street on the beach. The main courses strive for gourmet caliber, but never quite achieve that; instead, the best bet here is the pizza or salad bar. There are also sandwiches, burgers, and an ice-cream parlor. The restaurant is always open, from the early morning until the wee hours, and they host live music on weekends.

Av. Peru 100. ✆ **32/268-7755.** Main courses C$4,000–C$8,000. AE, DC, MC, V. Sun–Wed 7am–1am; Thurs–Sat 7am-3 or 4am.

VALPARAÍSO ★★★

Valparaíso is Chile's most captivating city, and, accordingly, it is the most popular coastal destination and an obligatory cruise ship port of call. During the 19th century, Valparaíso ranked as a port town of such wealth that few others in the world could compare, but in the years following the completion of the Panama Canal, Valparaíso sunk into poverty. Like a penniless aristocrat, the city clung for decades to its glorious past, yet only traces of the architectural splendor and riches the city once knew could still be seen. Today, especially on hills such as Cerro Concepción and Cerro Alegre, the city's run-down buildings are experiencing a rebirth, with a boom in gourmet restaurants and boutique hotels. The city has also launched the Proyecto Puerto Viejo, a $30 million renovation plan that will give new life to the gritty port area around Plaza Echaurren, including the long-awaited restoration of the 1902 Hotel Reina Victoria on Plaza Sotomayor and the transformation of the city's old jail on Cerro Cárcel, which once housed Chile's worst criminals, into a modern cultural center in late 2011. The historic importance of this city, paired with the vibrant culture of local *porteños,* is far more intriguing than Viña—a reason why UNESCO designated Valparaíso a World Heritage Site in 2002.

Much like San Francisco, the city is made of a flat downtown surrounded by steep hills, but unlike that city, the irregular terrain in Valparaíso presented far more challenges for development. The jumble of multicolored clapboard homes and weathered Victorian mansions that cling to sheer cliffs and other unusual spaces are testament to this, and you could spend days exploring the maze of narrow passageways and sinuous streets that snake down ravines and around hillsides. Given the lack of towering high rises on the hillsides, the city is frequently described as having "stadium seating"—providing breathtaking views no matter where you are.

Valparaíso has spawned generations of poets, writers, and artists who have found inspiration in the city, including the Nobel Prize–winning poet Pablo Neruda, who owned a home here. The city is also known for its bohemian and antiquated bars that stay open into the wee hours of the morning. But the real attraction here is the city's streets, where you can admire the angular architecture that makes this city unique, and ride the century-old, clickety-clack *ascensores,* or funiculars, that lift riders to the tops of hills. If you're the type who craves character and culturally distinctive surroundings, this is your place.

Essentials

GETTING THERE

BY BUS **Tur Bus** (© 600/660-6600; www.turbus.cl) and **Pullman** (© 600/320-3200; www.pullman.cl) leave from the Terminal Alameda in Santiago, located at Av. Alameda 3750 (Metro: Univ. de Santiago), every 15 minutes from 6:10am to 10pm (Tur Bus), and 6:10am to 10:10pm (Pullman). The trip takes about 1 hour and 15 minutes, depending on traffic, and costs C$3,200 (Tur Bus) and C$11,000 (Pullman). In Valparaíso, you'll disembark at the terminal at Avenida Pedro Montt; taxis are available and a good idea at night—it's possible to walk to the Cerro Concepción funicular in approximately 20 to 30 minutes, but the neighborhood surrounding the bus depot is pretty grimy. Microbuses and collectives also run frequently from outside the station to the city center for C$300. During weekends, especially from December to March, it is strongly recommended that you buy your ticket in advance from any

Tur Bus or Pullman office in Santiago (your hotel can give you the address of the nearest office).

BY CAR   Valparaíso is reached by Ruta 68, a four-lane highway in excellent condition. Driving to Valparaíso from Santiago is quite easy: Take the Costanera Norte headed west, and follow it all the way to the coast (the Costanera turns into Ruta 68). There are two tolls along the way that each cost C$1,500 from Monday to 5pm on Friday, and C$2,200 from 5pm Friday to Sunday. At Km 105, follow the signpost for Valparaíso, taking Avenida Santos Ossa. You'll enter Valparaíso and turn onto Avenida Argentina, then turn onto Avenida Pedro Montt, which will take you to downtown. Hotels offer street parking only. If visiting for the day, park in the underground garage on Calle Errázuriz, across from the Plaza Sotomayor, or at Avenida Brasil and Bellavista. Do not leave possessions in your car if you park it on the street at night, as break-ins are common.

BY TRAIN   The very sleek **Metrotren** (also known as the "Merval"; ℭ **32/252-7500**) connects Viña with Valparaíso (Plaza Sotomayor), leaving every 5 to 10 minutes from 7:30am to 10pm during weekdays, and every 15 to 20 minutes from 9:30am to 9pm on Saturdays, Sundays, and holidays. To ride the train, you must purchase a rechargeable card for C$1,200, which you then charge with enough money to cover the cost of your trip. If you're with friends or family, you need only purchase one card for your group. During summer, you can also purchase a *Tarjeta Turista* (C$4,990) which grants unlimited travel on the "Merval" for 3 days; after those 3 days, you may charge trips as you would with a regular card.

GETTING AROUND

Walking is really the only way to see Valparaíso; hilltop streets are confusing and very tight to drive, so park downtown and ride a funicular up. The only exception, considering the strenuous uphill walk, is the Pablo Neruda museum (La Sebastiana) and the City Cemetery. There are 15 *ascensores* (funiculars) that operate daily from 6am to 11pm and cost between C$100 and C$300, although only 6 are currently running. The most transited *ascensores* are: **Ascensor Cerro Concepción,** which runs from Calle Prat, opposite the Turri clock tower, to the gilded residential enclave of Paseo Gervasoni; **Ascensor El Peral,** which runs from Plaza Sotomayor to Paseo Yugoslavo; **Ascensor Artillería,** which runs from Plaza Aduana to Paseo 21 de Mayo, and usually packs in tourists with mouths agape at the sublime vistas; and the vertiginous **Ascensor Polanco,** which runs from Calle Almirante Simpson to Calle Latorre.

VISITOR INFORMATION & TOURS

Valparaíso's municipality has a good website packed with information in English at **www.ciudaddevalparaiso.cl**, and there are four **tourist information kiosks** around the city: at the Prat Pier near the Plaza Sotomayor, at Plaza Anibal Pinto in the business district, at the city's bus station, and on Cerro Bellavista at the corners of Blanco and Bellavista streets. The **Municipal Tourism Department's** main office is at Condell 1490 (ℭ **32/293-9262;** www.ciudaddevalparaiso.cl). The kiosks are open Monday through Friday from 10am to 2pm and 3:30 to 5:30pm, and Saturdays and Sundays from 10:30am to 5:30pm.

The British-Chilean run **Darwin's Trails,** based out of Viña del Mar at Montenegro 110 (ℭ **32/319-3478;** www.darwinstrails.com) are expert tour operators in the region; the agency tends to plan custom-made tours for travelers rather than act as a drop-in shop, so it is a good idea to contact them well in advance of your visit. A typical full-day "Heritage Tour" that explores the history of the city and its architecture

Valparaíso

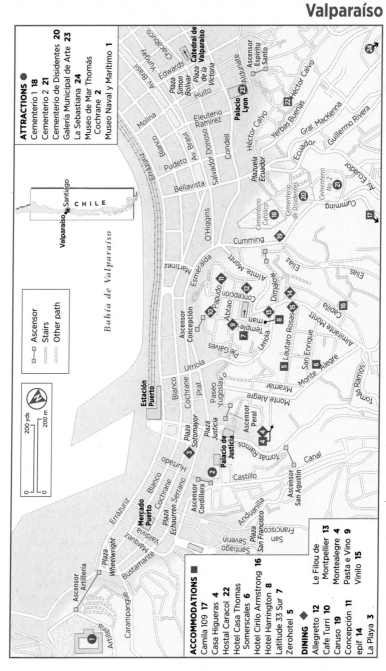

ATTRACTIONS ●
Cementerio 1 **18**
Cementerio 2 **21**
Cementerio de Disidentes **20**
Galería Municipal de Arte **23**
La Sebastiana **24**
Museo de Mar Thomás
Cochrane **2**
Museo Naval y Marítimo **1**

CHILE
Valparaíso • Santiago

Bahía de Valparaíso

Ascensor
Stairs
Other path

200 yds
200 m

Catedral de
Valparaíso

Plaza
de la
Victoria

Palacio
Lyon

Plaza
Simón
Bolívar

Ascensor
Espíritu
Santo

Héctor Calvo

Yerbas Buenas

Gral. MacKenna

Guillermo Rivera

Av. Ecuador

Cumming

Cementerio
No. 2

Cementerio
de Disidentes

Cementerio
Católico

Cumming

O'Higgins

Bellavista

Pudeto

Blanco

Molina

Av. Brasil

Av. Yungay

Edwards

Chacabuco

Huito

Eleuterio
Ramírez

Salvador Donoso

Condell

Av. Brasil

Plazuela
Ecuador

Héctor Calvo

Ecuador

Elías

Elías

Esmeralda

Martínez

Almte. Montt

Concepción

Dimalow

Papudo

Abtao

Templo

Urriola

Lautaro Rosas

San Enrique

Monte Alegre

Capilla

Almirante Montt

Ascensor
Concepción

Estación
Puerto

Blanco

Cochrane

Prat

Plaza
Sotomayor

Plaza
Justicia

Palacio de
Justicia

Paseo
Yugoslav

Ascensor
Peral

Monte Alegre

Miramar

Tomás Ramos

Tomás Ramos

Castillo

Canal

Ascensor
San Agustín

Anduanilla

Ascensor
Cordillera

Mercado
Puerto

Blanco

Cochrane

Echaurren Serrano

Plaza
Hurtado

Valdivia

Plaza
Severín

Santiago
Severín

San Francisco

Plaza
San Francisco

Errázuriz

Márquez

Plaza
Wheelwright

Bustamante

Carampangue

Ascensor
Artillería

Artillería

**Mercado
Puerto**

ACCOMMODATIONS ■
Camila 109 **17**
Casa Higueras **4**
Hostal Caracol **22**
Hotel Casa Thomas
Somerscales **6**
Hotel Cirilo Armstrong **16**
Hotel Harrington **8**
Latitude 33 Sur **7**
Zerohotel **5**

DINING ◆
Allegretto **12**
Cafe Turri **10**
Caruso **19**
Concepción **11**
epif **14**
La Playa **3**
Le Filou de
Montpellier **13**
Montealegre **4**
Pasta e Vino **9**
Vinilo **15**

costs C$77,000 for two people. Another, more economical, option is **Turis Tour** (© **2/488-0444;** www.turistour.com), which runs tours from Santiago to Valparaíso and Viña for approximately C$33,000 and up. Given the efficiency, frequency, and comfort of bus transportation from Santiago to the coast, however, you may prefer to travel to both cities on your own. See the "Walking Tour" later for information about picking up a detailed walking guide.

The **Art Path** (© **32/212-5269;** www.talleresdevalparaiso.cl), a new tour developed by the Valparaíso Artist's Atelier Agency, takes visitors on a tour of local artists' workshops and homes. The cost is a bit steep at C$33,000, but it does include transportation and an English-speaking guide.

Plentiful **banks** and **currency exchange offices** can be found along Calle Prat and Esmeralda Street. Hours are generally from 9am until 4pm. Most ATMs (*cajeros automáticos*) are open 24 hours. For medical emergencies, **Hospital Carlos Van Buren** is at Av. San Ignacio 725 (on the corner of Colón; © **32/236-4000**).

SPECIAL EVENTS Valparaíso's famed **New Year's Pyrotechnic Festival** is an event so spectacular even Chileans consider it something they must see at least once in their lives. Thousands of partiers crowd the streets and hilltops to take in the radiant lights that explode over the shimmering bay. You'll want to arrive early to stake out your "corner" atop one of the hills, or at the very least make a hotel reservation early— some hotels sell out 3 to 6 months ahead and charge hefty rates. Savvy Chileans arrive in the early afternoon and bring chairs, barbecues, and a day's ration of food and drink to save their viewing platform for the nighttime fireworks display.

The city builds up to New Year's with the frenetic **Cultural Carnival,** which since 2001 has grown into a massive 3-day festival with international and national artists, musicians, theater acts, and dancers flooding the streets of distinct neighborhoods of Valparaíso.

The first weekend of October heralds the **Carnaval Mil Tambores** (Thousand Drums Festival), an anything-goes street festival celebrating the alternative art scene—with musicians, dancers, and free spirits running through the streets in body paint and tossing confetti, among other spontaneous street acts.

What to See & Do

The city's **Natural History Museum,** Av. Condell 1546 in the Palacio Lyon (© **32/254-4844**), is now closed for major renovations until mid-2012. The **Galería Municipal de Arte** (© **32/22-0062**), in the basement level of the Natural History Museum/Palacio Lyon at Av. Condell 1550, features paintings and sculptures by regional artists, usually arranged thematically and related to the Valparaíso area. It's open Tuesday through Sunday, 10am to 7pm; admission is free.

Cementerio 1, 2 & De Disidentes ★★ A walk through Valparaíso's cemeteries is not only worthwhile for its utterly fascinating, baroque antique mausoleums, but it also provides visitors with some of the best views in the city. Focus your visit on the Cementerio de Disidentes; this is where the tombs of British and European immigrants lie, having been shunned from the principal cemeteries for not being Catholic (the reason why it is called the Cemetery of the "Dissidents"). This cemetery is by far more intriguing than the other two for its matter-of-fact gravestones spelling out often dramatic endings for (usually very young) adventurers who arrived during the 19th century. It's a short, but hearty, walk up Ecuador Street to get here, and worth the effort—or just grab a cab.

Btw. Av. Ecuador and Cumming (Cerro Panteón). No phone. Free admission. Daily 10am–5pm.

La Sebastiana ★★★ ☺ La Sebastiana is one of poet Pablo Neruda's three quirky homes that have been converted into museums honoring the distinguished Nobel laureate's work and life. Neruda is Chile's most beloved poet, and the country's most famous literary export. Even if you haven't familiarized yourself with Neruda's work, this museum is worth visiting to explore this eccentric home and view the whimsical knickknacks he relished collecting while traveling in Africa, Asia, and Europe. Neruda searched for poetry in the most mundane of objects. From a carousel horse brought from Paris to a chest of drawers wrenched from a ship, Neruda developed a collector's zeal for what most people would view as junk. The poet called himself an "estuary sailor"; although terrified of sailing, he nevertheless was spellbound by the sea, and he fashioned his homes to resemble boats, complete with porthole windows. Neruda named the house after its architect, a "poet of construction" Sebastián Collado, who had searched relentlessly for a site that would afford a panoramic view of the city. When Collado died, Neruda bought the house and in September 1961 it became the home where he would spend a great deal of time during the last decade of his life. The organized chaos that characterizes this home is a perfect microcosm of Valparaíso itself. What sets this museum apart from Neruda's other former residences at Isla Negra and Santiago is that here visitors are able to wander freely with self-guiding information sheets. A cultural center is here too, with a gallery and a gift shop.

The walk from Plaza Victoria is a hike, so you might want to take a taxi. From Plaza Ecuador, there's a bus, Verde "D," or the *colectivo* no. 39.

Calle Ferrari 692 (Cerro Bellavista). ℂ **32/225-6606.** www.fundacionneruda.org. Admission C$3,000. Mar–Dec Tues–Sun 10am–6pm; Jan–Feb Tues–Sun 10:30am–6:50pm.

Museo de Mar Thomás Cochrane ★ The main reason for visiting this maritime museum, built to house the impressive display of model ships that belonged to British navy hero Lord Cochrane, is to revel in one of the best panoramic views in the city. High atop Cerro Cordillera, this stately mansion, now a national monument, was built by one Juan Mouat, an English immigrant who designed the house in 1841 in colonial style with all the trimmings. The residence even had its own observatory—the first in Chile.

Calle Merlet 195 (via the Ascensor Cordillera). ℂ **32/293-9486.** Free admission. Tues–Sun 10am–6pm.

Museo Naval y Marítimo ★★★ This museum merits a visit even if you do not particularly fancy naval and maritime-related artifacts and memorabilia. The museum is smartly designed and divided into four salons: the War of Independence, the War against the Peru-Bolivia Confederation, the War against Spain, and the War of the Pacific. Each salon holds antique documents, medals, uniforms, and war trophies. Of special note is the Arturo Prat room, with artifacts salvaged from the *Esmeralda,* a wooden ship that sank while valiantly defending Valparaíso during the War of the Pacific.

Paseo 21 de Mayo, Cerro Artillería. ℂ **32/243-7651.** Admission C$700 adults, C$300 children 11 and under. Tues–Sun 10am–6pm.

WALKING TOUR: **FROM THE PORT TO THE HEIGHTS OF VALPARAÍSO**

START:	**Muelle Prat (Prat Pier).**
FINISH:	**Ascensor Concepción or Calle Esmeralda.**
TIME:	**1 to 3 hours.**
BEST TIMES:	**Any day except Monday, when most museums and restaurants are closed.**

The **Fundación Valparaíso** has done an exceptional job of mapping out a "Bicentennial Heritage Trail," a looping 30km (19-mile) walking tour divided into 15 thematic stages. I urge visitors to pick up a copy of the trail guide to supplement the walking tour described below. The guide can be found at the **Gato Tuerto bookstore,** at Héctor Calvo 205 (Espíritu Santo Funicular), or bookstores (if you are cruising, you may find the book at the Baron's Pier shopping gallery); the cost is C$5,000. Each stage takes approximately 90 minutes to 3 hours to walk, and the guide provides historical data, literary gossip, architectural information, and fun anecdotes about the city. To help you navigate, the *fundación* has placed arrows on the street at various stages of the trail. For visitors with limited time in the city, the walking tour outlined below will take you to the city's finest viewpoints and top attractions.

---

1 Muelle Prat (Prat Pier)

Begin at the Prat Pier. There is quite a bit of hullabaloo at the dock here, with skippers pitching 20-minute boat rides around the bay to tourists aboard one of their rustic fishing skiffs. It's not a very professional operation, but for C$2,000 per person, what do you have to lose? There are few places in the world where you can get so close to commercial ships (docked here in the harbor). Valparaíso has changed little in the past century, and to view the city from this perspective is to see the city as many a sailor did when arriving here for the first time after a long journey around Cape Horn. A row of curio shops lines the dock, which are packed with tourists when a cruise ship docks in Valparaíso. There is an information kiosk here, too.

Head away from the pier and cross Errázuriz to reach:

2 Plaza Sotomayor

Until the late 1800s, the sea arrived just a few feet from the edge of this plaza, lapping at the gates of the Naval Command Headquarters on the west side of the plaza. Built in 1910, the grand neoclassical building was once the summer residence for several of Chile's past presidents. At the plaza's entrance you'll encounter the **Monument to the Heroes of Iquique.** The heroes of the War of the Pacific—Prat, Condell, and Serrano—are buried underneath this monument. This tremendous battle in 1879 pitted Chile against a Peru-Bolivia confederation, and Chile's victory against the two resulted in the capture of the mineral-rich northern territory, cutting Bolivia off from the sea and extending Chile's size by nearly a third (to learn more about the war, visit the Naval Museum). Underneath the plaza, where you now stand, are shipwrecks and remains of the old pier, which you can view at the tiny underground museum (at the plaza's center, daily 10am–6pm; the museum suffered damages from the 2010 earthquake but is expected to reopen in mid 2011). The pier and artifacts

Walking Tour: From the Port to the Heights of Valparaíso

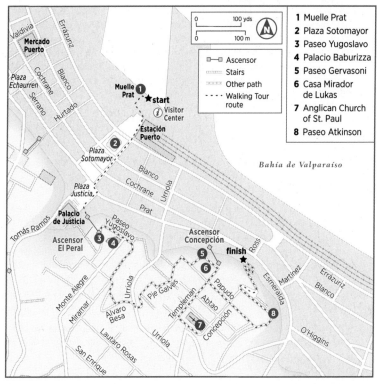

1 Muelle Prat
2 Plaza Sotomayor
3 Paseo Yugoslavo
4 Palacio Baburizza
5 Paseo Gervasoni
6 Casa Mirador de Lukas
7 Anglican Church of St. Paul
8 Paseo Atkinson

such as anchors, ballast, and cannons were discovered while excavating land to build the parking garage at the northeast edge of the plaza. Next to the old post office is the "American Fire House," the first volunteer fire station in Latin America. Cross the plaza toward the Justice Palace.

To the left of the plaza, next to the Palacio de Justicia, ride the Ascensor Peral (ca. 1902) for C$100 to the top of Cerro Alegre and there you'll find:

3 Paseo Yugoslavo

Nitrate baron Pascual Baburizza built this pretty terrace walkway and dubbed it Yugoslavian Promenade in honor of his heritage.

Continue along the terrace until you pass:

4 Palacio Baburizza

This Art Nouveau palace was built in 1916 for Ottorino Zanelli and later sold to nitrate baron Pascual Baburizza, who lived here until his death in 1941. The palace is a fine display of the best European handiwork available during the early 1900s; and today, after nearly a decade of closure, the first floor houses the city's Fine Arts Museum with a collection of 19th- and 20th-century Chilean and

European paintings. The museum is most interesting for its paintings of early Valparaíso by local artists Juan Mauricio Rugendas and Thomas Somerscales. Hours are Tuesday through Sunday from 10am to 6pm, and admission is free.

Continue along Paseo Yugoslavo, past the La Colombina restaurant. The road curves to the right around a tiny plaza; follow it until you reach Calle Alvaro Besa. Take Alvaro Besa as it winds down the hill, or take the shortcut down Pasaje Bavestrello, a cement stairway at the left. Continue until you reach Calle Urriola, which you'll cross, then walk up 20m (66 ft.) and turn left into another stairway, Pasaje Gálvez. The narrow walkway twists and turns, passing the colorful facades of some of the most striking homes in Valparaíso. At Calle Papudo, climb the stairway and turn left into:

5 Paseo Gervasoni

Another of Valparaíso's characteristic promenades, this *paseo* fronts a row of stately 19th-century mansions.

At the end of the walkway, you'll find Café Turri, a popular Valparaíso restaurant and a good spot for a snack or coffee. Before the cafe, to the right, is the:

6 Casa Mirador de Lukas

This museum is dedicated to the much-loved "Lukas," aka Renzo Pecchenino, a brilliant cartoonist and satirist who worked for years for the newspaper *El Mercurio*. Lukas dedicated his career to drawing Valparaíso and the eccentric characters found here; a collection of his drawings is available for sale, *Apuntes Porteños*, which makes an excellent Valparaíso souvenir. The museum is open Tuesday through Sunday from 11am to 7pm; admission is C$1,300 for adults and C$700 for children 5 and over. It is possible to terminate the walking tour here and descend via Ascensor Concepción, but I recommend that you keep walking.

Continue around Gervasoni until you reach Papudo. You can take a detour here 2 blocks up Calle Templeman to visit the:

7 Anglican Church of St. Paul

Built in 1858, this Anglican church was not officially recognized until 1869, when the Chilean government repealed a law banning religions other than Catholicism. The church houses a grand organ donated by the British in 1901 in honor of Queen Victoria. You can hear this magnificent instrument at work at 12:30pm every Sunday.

Double back to Calle Papudo, head southeast (turning right if returning from the church) until reaching:

8 Paseo Atkinson

At the entrance to Paseo Atkinson, you'll pass the city's Lutheran church, built in 1897 for the large German population here in the early 19th century. Paseo Atkinson is another lovely pedestrian walkway, bordered by antique homes with zinc facades and guillotine windows popular with the British in the early 20th century. Continue down the pedestrian stairway until you reach Calle Esmeralda and the end of the walk. You can also descend by doubling back and riding the Ascensor Concepción to Calle Prat.

Additional Walking Tours

At the southwest corner of the Anglican church, walk up Templeman and turn left on Urriola. Just past the El Desayunador cafe on the left is a barely perceptible promenade, called Dimalow. Halfway down the esplanade, you will encounter one of the **best viewpoints** in Valparaíso, a truly spectacular vista of the bay, the tall steeple of the Lutheran church, and the colorful, tumbledown homes clinging to the hills. Bring your camera. The Queen Victoria Funicular is here, and you can ride it down to Cumming Street; then head left 1 block to the Plaza Aníbal Pinto and down Esmeralda until reaching the Plaza Sotomayor.

The coastline of Valparaíso, accessible at Muelle Baron (parking C$600 per hour), has an attractive jogging/walking path that hugs the shoreline, offering splendid views for visitors seeking a little exercise. Also at Muelle Baron is **Puerto Deportivo** (✆ **32/259-2852;** www.puertodeportivo.cl), which offers 2-hour sailing trips in the bay for C$15,000 per person, kayak rental for C$10,000 for 3 hours, and a 1½-hour Sunset Cruise for groups of up to 6 for C$600,000, including champagne.

The Port Neighborhood   Begin at the north of town at Plaza Wheelwright at the end of Cochrane and Calle Carampangue, at the **Customs House (Aduana).** The Aduana was built in 1854 and is the oldest public building in Valparaíso, influenced by post-colonial North American architectural style. To the right, you'll find the **Ascensor Artillería,** built in 1893; the admission fee is C$300. The wobbly contraption takes visitors to the most panoramic pedestrian walkway in Valparaíso, **Paseo 21 de Mayo.** Don't miss the view of the port from the gazebo. Follow the walkway until reaching the **Museo Naval y Marítimo** (described in "What to See & Do," earlier). To return, double back and descend via the *ascensor,* or head down the walkway that begins at the cafe, and take a left at Calle Carampangue.

Ruta Bellavista: From Plaza Victoria to the Casa de Pablo Neruda (La Sebastiana)   The recent incarnation of the "Ruta Bellavista—Culture and Poetry" is the result of businesses, artists, and the Fundación Valparaíso on Cerro Bellavista banding together to offer a mapped walking route that incorporates some of the city's highlights, including La Sebastiana (described in "What to See & Do," earlier), and Plaza Victoria, where in the late 1880s elegant society met, and whose grand trees, trickling fountain, and sculptures imported from Lima recall that era's heyday. The Ruta also includes the **Open Air Museum,** a public art display featuring more than 20 murals painted on cement retainer and building walls along winding streets. Pick up a brochure with a map at most restaurants, hotels, or at the visitor kiosk on Plaza Sotomayor or Plaza Aníbal Pinto.

Really, the best way to walk this route is downhill (unless you need the exercise—Calle Ferrari is Valparaíso's steepest street), beginning high up at La Sebastiana and continuing down along Ferrari, veering left onto Héctor Calvo and taking a quick duck left onto Temuco to see the Villa Hispania castles. Continue down Héctor Calvo until reaching the outstanding **Gato Tuerto bookstore** and arts-and-crafts shop at the Fundación Valparaíso (Héctor Calvo 205); there is also Internet service here and a cafe. Turn right on Pasteur and make an immediate right onto Guimera for the Open Air Museum, which continues down along Rudolph, looping back onto Ferrari, where, if you head left, you'll end up at the Plaza Victoria at Edwards and Independencia. The **Ascensor Espíritu Santo** allows you to ride up to simply catch a glimpse of the Open Air Museum, and can be found on Calle Aldunate; take a left after getting off and continue the walk at Rudolph Street (as earlier).

Shopping

Valparaíso's labyrinthine streets are full of independent shops selling locally produced *artesanía,* the best of which are **Del Rio al Mar,** San Enrique 338 on Cerro Alegre

(© **32/317-8592;** www.delrioalmar.cl), with handsomely produced arts and crafts and plenty of items for children, too; **Alpaca Samka,** Papudo 450 (© **32/296-6919;** www.alpacasamka.com), with high-fashion coats, shawls, and ponchos made of alpaca wool, accessories, and jewelry; **Kipu,** Paseo Gervasoni 408 (© **32/259-1149**), which has handmade crafts and clothing for adults and children, including sweaters, ponchos, shawls, and jewelry; and **Viña Crea,** Concepción 194 (© **32/223-8108;** www.vinacrea.cl), with funky, locally produced arts and crafts and children's toys. The **Galería de Arte Bahía Utópica,** Almirante Montt 372 (© **32/273-4286;** www.bahia.utopica.over-blog.com), features paintings by Chileans, mostly local artists, on display and on sale.

For books, guides, and maps, head to the Fundación Valparaíso's **Gato Tuerto Café & Bookstore,** Héctor Calvo 205 (© **32/222-0867;** Espíritu Santo Funicular), which also has a small arts-and-crafts store. **Design For Valparaíso,** Concepción 154B (© **32/259-1868**), has original designs of textiles and clothing woven from natural fibers found in Chile.

If you are visiting on Saturday or Sunday, don't miss the **La Merced Antique and Book Fair** on Plaza O'Higgins, close to the Congreso Nacional, a flea market purveying all manner of collectibles ranging from knickknack memorabilia to books, homemade jams, Neruda-themed souvenirs, and electrical items. It's generally open from 10am to 7pm.

Where to Stay

Just a decade ago, lodging was so scarce in Valparaíso that even the city's own tourism board recommended that travelers lodge in Viña del Mar. Today Valparaíso has blossomed into an epicenter of stylish boutique lodging, whereas Viña continues to offer resort-style lodging and full-scale hotels with all the bells and whistles and beach access. Valparaíso hotels are not cheap; they all seem at least 20% pricier than they should be. However, the pleasure of awakening in this eclectic and colorful city and being absorbed into its rhythm is worth the price, so consider a room with a view. At press time, the brand-new boutique **Hotel Palacio Astoreca** was in the final stages of development and is slated to be the city's toniest and most stylish lodging option, located in the center of it all on Cerro Alegre, next to the Palacio Baburizza.

EXPENSIVE

Casa Higueras ★★★ 🖼 Housed in a magnificently restored 1920 mansion that clings to the hillside on Cerro Concepción, Casa Higueras is not only the best hotel in Valparaíso, it is one of the finest in Chile. A true boutique hotel in every sense of the word, with an infinity pool, lush gardens, and luxe guest rooms, it serves as a 5-star refuge from the chaotic mosaic that is Valparaíso. Star designer Paula Gutiérrez leaned toward a more masculine decor for the hotel's interiors, with dark wood flooring and paneling; cream-colored walls adorned with photos of Valparaíso life; and minimal designer furniture. All rooms except the "traditional" rooms come with panoramic views, and most have private terraces (if yours doesn't, do not fret as there are plenty of outdoor lounges around the hotel, including a spectacular rooftop lounge with 360-degree views). Rooms are individually decorated yet all follow a common monochromatic style with just a touch of color from heavy curtains and bed throws, bathrooms with whirlpool tubs and glass-tiled walls, 300–thread count sheets on heavenly soft beds, and amenities galore. After a long day tromping around the city, the hotel offers a sanctuary in which to relax and be pampered, with a minispa that includes massage, a sauna, and a Jacuzzi. On Saturdays and Sundays, the hotel offers a 1½-hour walking tour through Valparaíso for C$7,500 per person.

Higueras 133, Cerro Concepción. ☎ **2/249-7900.** www.hotelcasahigueras.cl. 20 units. $203–$248 traditional room, $238–$289 premium room, $315–383 suite. AE, DC, MC, V. **Amenities:** Restaurant; outdoor pool; room service; minispa. *In room:* Plasma TV/DVD, hair dryer, minibar, free Wi-Fi.

Zerohotel ★★★ 🛎 Relatively indistinguishable from its residential neighbors due to its tiny sign and soft lilac facade, this is another of Valparaíso's top lodging options—a boutique hotel that effectively blends a contemporary, whimsical decor with lovingly refurbished antique ceilings, wall panels, and parquet floors. Breakfast is served in the light and airy winter garden conservatory from which steps lead down to three heavenly terraces, which invite relaxation with sun loungers and a small pool. The location is ideal and close to restaurants. The rooms, like the Casa Higueras (see above), feature high-end amenities and Egyptian cotton sheets. But the style here is decidedly more young and funky than at Casa Higueras. Rooms that face the hillside are considerably cheaper than rooms with a port view, so if you're not planning to spend a lot of time in your room, the views from the terrace will suffice.

Lautaro Rosas 343, Cerro Alegre. ☎ **2/211-3113.** www.zerohotel.com. 9 units. $240 street view, $340 port view. AE, DC, MC, V. **Amenities:** Bar; room service. *In room:* Cable TV, hair dryer, free Wi-Fi.

MODERATE

Harrington B&B ★★ The Harrington is a spruce and squeaky-clean B&B located in a 2-story renovated 1920 home, with a cheery yellow, corrugated facade. The location near restaurants is a perk, and the amiable French couple who run the place take pride in maintaining a fresh environment. All rooms are on the second floor and are reached by a stairwell; three rooms face an interior light well and two are more spacious and luminous as they face the street. Sharp decor and linens make the Harrington more chic than classic, with slate-tiled bathrooms, colorful flower photography, and blond furniture made from recycled wood.

Templeman 535, Cerro Concepción. ☎ **32/212-1338.** www.harrington.cl. 5 units. $114 double. No credit cards. **Amenities:** Cafeteria. *In room:* TV, free Wi-Fi.

Hotel Casa Thomas Somerscales ★★ This exquisite hotel is housed in the former home of Valparaíso's most famous painter, Thomas Somerscales, renowned for his portraits of the city and the War of the Pacific. It's old enough to be on the National Heritage Registry, and its historical focus and the lovingly restored interiors makes the Somerscales one of the most unique places to stay in Valparaíso. Guest rooms are immaculately clean and fresh, and feature crisp white linens and curtains, 19th-century antiques, and period ornaments. The stairwell is cheerfully lit by a two-floor stained-glass window, and the front patio sports black-and-white checkered tiles. If you consider a luxury hotel too impersonal and a typical B&B too homespun, this is a happy medium. Guests often get to know each other over breakfast, but you can always sleep in and have it served to you in bed.

San Enrique 446, Cerro Alegre. ☎ **32/233-1006.** www.hotelsomerscales.cl. 8 units. $166 double; $253 double with terrace and bay view. AE, DC, MC, V. **Amenities:** Cafeteria. *In room:* TV, minibar, Wi-Fi (free, not available in 2 rooms).

Hotel Cirilo Armstrong ★ 🔥 Although the Cirilo was built new from the ground up, in a space left bare by a burnt-down home, this 12-room hotel blends seamlessly into its residential surroundings. The hotel features 2-floor "suites" that are apartment-style units with a kitchenette, which in reality seem better suited for heating up water than cooking a meal. There are lots of luminous spaces with floor-to-ceiling windows, and most suites open onto a terrace with views of a kaleidoscope of colorful homes. The owners, a designer and an architect, have opted to use lots of battle-gray corrugated steel and glass trimmed in wood. Rooms are narrow and a staircase leads up to a loftlike bedroom. While the decor, with stylish touches like locally produced woolen blankets and pillows, is attractive, some of the construction details seem slightly on the cheap side. For the price, however, the hotel is a good value.

Cirilo Armstrong 12, Cerro Alegre. *32/318-7257.* www.ciriloarmstrong.com. 11 units. $110 double. AE, DC, MC, V. **Amenities:** Cafeteria; Internet station. *In room:* Cable TV, free Wi-Fi.

Latitud 33 Sur ★ ☺ ✦   At the end of the delightful and brightly painted interior street near Calle Templeman, just steps from restaurants and tightly curving passageways, Latitud 33 clings to a cliff and, like most hotels in Valparaíso, is located within a refurbished old home. That means it's a bit quirky (amplified rooms have the plaster removed but the beams remain) and certainly not noise-proof. But it has contemporary charm and rooms are clean and nicely finished with carpet or parquet floors and cheap but stylish furnishings. Rates vary according to room size, the miniscule room 5, for example, is $67 a night, and the larger triple room no. 7 is spacious and $111 a night. Staff members are very helpful. One room is wheelchair-friendly, and two of the rooms on the top floor (including one with a bunk bed) share a bathroom, making them a good choice for families or groups.

Pasaje Templeman 183, Cerro Concepción. *32/211-7983.* www.hotellatitud33sur.cl. 10 units. $67 single; $107–$116 double. AE, MC, V. **Amenities:** Cafeteria; Internet station. *In room:* TV, free Wi-Fi.

INEXPENSIVE

Camila 109 ★★ ⬛   Valparaíso's best B&B is stylish and intimate and provides warm, personalized service from a very hospitable owner. Precipitously located on Cerro La Loma, next to the fine arts school, this modern home with huge picture windows has sweeping views over the bay from its rooftop terrace. The three double rooms are impeccable and very urban in feel with minimalist furnishings, polished wooden floors, and huge windows. Red and blue linen adds a flash of vibrancy to an otherwise Zen simplicity. From the crisp linens to the delicious coffee, quality and simplicity are the overarching themes. For travelers keen to explore beyond the more manicured areas of town, this is a great base and, because of its proximity to La Sebastiana, a raw, artistic vibe prevails.

Calle Camila 109, Cerro la Loma. *32/249-1746.* www.camila109.cl. 3 units. $76–$84 double. AE, DC, MC, V. **Amenities:** Babysitting. *In room:* Cable TV, hair dryer (ask front desk), free Wi-Fi.

Hostal Caracol ★★   This gem of a hostel is a good walk up the Cerro Bellavista (though conveniently close to the Pablo Neruda Museum) and located within a refurbished antique home whose common areas are bestowed with old-world interiors such as vaulted ceilings and early 20th-century decorative floor tiles. The hostel is ideal for independent travelers on a shoestring, because it comes with a shared kitchen and a sunny patio garden with a barbecue grill for guests' use. The five ensuite rooms are quite simple and colorfully painted (each room is named for its color) and have parquet floors. Some have closets and others an old trunk with a padlock for storing personal items. There is one dorm room with seven beds and a shared bathroom.

Hector Calvo 371, Cerro Bellavista. *32/239-5817.* www.hostalcaracol.cl. 6 units. $59 double, $17 per person dorm. AE, DC, MC, V. **Amenities:** Kitchen. *In room:* Cable TV, no phone, free Wi-Fi.

Where to Dine

Valparaíso's bohemian flair, its concentration of talented young chefs, and its constant supply of adventurous and demanding diners have all combined to inspire a synergistic food culture found in few regions of Chile. Instead of restaurants serving just fish-and-fries fare, which reigned in this city for decades, you'll have your choice of bistros, intimate eateries housed in recycled old Victorians that are typically owner-attended and offer inventive cuisine. Of course, you won't want to miss dropping into one of the century-old establishments in Valparaíso that have played host to generations of revelers, if only for the antique architecture and a whiff of the city's formidable and colorful history. One such museumlike restaurant, **Casino Social J. Cruz M.** (located in a tiny alley way at 1466 Condell Ave.; ℂ **32/221-1225;** open Mon–Thurs noon–2am; Fri–Sat noon–3:30am; Sun 1pm–2am) is a hole-in-the-wall dive draped in cluttered antiques, photos, and port memorabilia. J. Cruz serves just two dishes: steak sandwiches and the Valparaíso institution *chorrillana,* a greasy stir-fry of fries, meat, and eggs. Just come before 10pm as the tiny restaurant fills up fast.

Valparaíso has quite a few charming cafes for a snack or *onces,* Chile's famous afternoon tea, best served at **Cafe Con Letras** (Almirante Montt 316; ℂ **32/223-5480;** Mon–Sat 11am–10pm and Sun 4–10pm). The **Café del Poeta** (Plaza Anibal Pinto #1181; ℂ **32/222-8897**), has outdoor seating, an in-the-thick of it location downtown, and an ample menu with a reasonably priced lunch. The folksy restaurant **El Desayunador** (Almirante Montt 399; ℂ **32/236-5933**; open Mon–Sat 8:15am–9:45pm and Sun 8:30am–8pm) specializes in breakfast and inexpensive organic salads and sandwiches, but not friendly and fast service.

EXPENSIVE

Vinilo ★ CHILEAN BISTRO   I love Vinilo's easy-going, cozy ambience and retro kitsch decor, as well as its long granite bar and good wine list; it's the kind of place I always want to stop in and grab a coffee, drink, or snack any time of the day. The restaurant is expanding to include an eventual B&B, and they recently began serving cuisine that is surprisingly gourmet for such a funky little cafe (but, alas, with gourmet prices), prepared only with regional Chilean specialties mail-ordered from around the country. Expect *arrollado* (spiced pork roll), stewed beef with wheat risotto, salmon with local pine nut crust, and even avocado ice cream. For beer, Vinilo only serves its own delicious microbrew. Main course prices are a tad steep, however.

Almirante Montt 448 (Cerro Alegre). ℂ **32/223-0665.** www.cafevinilo.cl. Main courses C$9,000–C$10,000. AE, DC, MC, V. Mon–Thurs 9am–11:30pm; Fri–Sat 9am–12:30am; Sun 4pm–12:30am.

MODERATE

Café Turri ★★★ 📷 FRENCH/CHILEAN   Valparaíso's emblematic restaurant changed ownership several years ago and the nasty waiters and awful food are thankfully a thing of the past. This restaurant has always reigned as the city's can't-beat spot for outdoor dining, and it's well located at the top of the La Concepción funicular and close to other points of interest. It's the kind of place I always fall back on for lunch, just for the sun-drenched patios and the sweeping views. Cafe Turri's new owners preserved the restaurant's lovely antique interiors but gave the place a fresh, contemporary update. They also hired a cheery waitstaff. Cafe Turri's French-influenced fare features staples such as duck confit, steak tartare, and onion soup, as well as an outstanding tuna tartare and delectable rabbit in port sauce. The restaurant has one of the best wine and bar menus in Valparaíso. For a primo table, make a reservation.

Calle Templeman 147 (Cerro Concepción; take the Concepción lift). ℭ **32/225-2091.** www.cafeturri.cl. Reservations recommended for outdoor seating. Main courses C$5,000–C$9,500. AE, DC, MC, V. Mon-Thurs noon–11pm; Fri–Sat noon–midnight; Sun noon–3:30pm. Closed Mon for dinner Apr–Sept; 5–7pm cafe service only.

Caruso ★★ CHILEAN   Chef Tomás Olivera of the Santiago Ritz Carlton's famed Adra restaurant opened this pet project in 2010, keeping the name of the former Caruso but switching the focus from Peruvian to Chilean cuisine. The restaurant is located on the newly gentrifying hill Cerro Cárcel, in a corner building 2 blocks downhill from the cemetery. The ambience isn't as relaxed as the old Caruso (the tone is now decidedly minimalist, with a dozen tables and whitewashed walls), but the food shines. Chef Olivera is a fervent promoter of traditional Chilean cuisine, and here he keeps it simple but uses fresh and high-quality ingredients. The razor clams broiled with parmesan delight with a drizzle of basil oil; his *cazuela* beef stew is healthy and light; the bean stew with stewed beef is a hit; and the *calugas*, or lightly battered and fried fish pieces, come with a tomato and onion salad and is large enough to split between two diners.

Av. Cumming 201, Cerro Cárcel. ℭ **32/259-4039.** www.caruso.cl. Reservations recommended on weekends. Main courses C$6,200–C$7,500. AE, DC, MC, V. Tues–Sat 1–4pm and 8–11pm, Sun 1–4pm.

Concepción ★★ INTERNATIONAL   One of the newest restaurants in Valparaíso, Concepción also has a pretty garden patio and second-floor deck for dining while looking out at the twinkling lights along the coast. The enviable port views and a something-for-everyone menu make this a wonderfully relaxing place and a good spot for a romantic dinner. The mood hits the right note between casual and elegant, with a conscientious staff but informal ambience. The bread service, which includes doughy home-baked bread served with herb-infused olive oil and tapenade, is a treat in itself. The eclectic menu is slanted toward seafood, with excellent *ceviche* and sashimi on order, along with large green salads dressed with hunks of goat cheese, olives, and pearly shrimps. Other standout items are the stewed beef ribs and the king crab ravioli. The only downside is that the restaurant is open for dinner only, 3 nights a week.

Papudo 541, Cerro Concepción. ℭ **32/249-8192.** www.restaurantlaconcepcion.cl. Reservations recommended during summer. Main courses C$8,500–C$10,000. AE, DC, MC, V. Thurs–Sat 8:30pm–midnight.

Montealegre ★★★ INTERNATIONAL   Casa Higueras' elegant-chic restaurant not only has a spectacular view, especially at night as the cruise ships pull out of the bay and the hillside is transformed into a dazzling cascade of twinkling lights, but it also has the advantage of being open on Sundays and Mondays when most other places are closed. The gourmet cuisine is also flawless and the service attentive and friendly without being fawning. As at Cafe Turri, the alfresco dining terrace here is the kind of place you want to linger for hours. A short but varied menu offers well executed flavor combinations; the menu changes seasonally and can include a barnacle salad and king crab casserole, slivers of foie gras perched atop silky veal, plus fresh seafood bought daily from the city's fish market. The pasta dishes, especially the goat cheese and pancetta tortellini, are tasty and are best as a shared appetizer as the servings are insubstantial for a main course, and there is a fig cheesecake and lúcuma mousse for dessert.

Higueras 133, Cerro Concepción. ℭ **2/657-3950.** www.casahigueras.cl. Reservations recommended during summer. AE, DC, MC, V. Main courses C$7,500–C$10,300. Daily 1–3pm; 8–11pm.

Pasta e Vino ★★★ 🍴 CONTEMPORARY ITALIAN   The day Pasta e Vino opened its doors to the public, it became immediately clear what Valparaíso had been missing all these years: a warm, intimate ambience, fabulous and ultra-fresh cuisine, and personal service. Pasta e Vino virtually launched the culinary metamorphosis in Valparaíso, and it remains one of the best restaurants in this city—you'll need to make reservations days in advance. The restaurant is the brainchild of executive chef and owner Verónica Alfageme, who really understands flavor combinations and technique and leans toward using ingredients that are in season. Apart from a few seafood-inspired appetizers, the menu features only pasta; standout menu items include gingery clams, chili-cream shrimp, duck ravioli with port and plums, and squid-ink ravioli stuffed with curried shrimp and chestnuts. The ambience is low-lit, sophisticated chic with exposed brick walls, but wooden tables and a lively atmosphere keep the restaurant down-to-earth.

Templeman 352. ✆ **32/249-6187.** www.pastaevinoristorante.cl. Reservations recommended. Main courses C$8,500–C$10,000. AE, DC, MC, V. Tues–Sat 1–4pm and 8pm–midnight.

INEXPENSIVE

Allegretto ★ DELI/PIZZERIA   A cheery, retro ambience reminiscent of an old emporium, a jukebox that spins old rock and English punk, wooden booths, and friendly service make Allegretto a truly enjoyable place for a casual meal. The large stone-baked, thin-crust pizzas, which can be customized with a medley of ingredients, are the highlight of the menu; however they also serve gnocchi and risotto dishes. What's great about Allegretto is that you can get out the door having spent less than C$11,875 for two, with wine included. They even deliver. Allegretto has a selection of packaged specialty foods from around Chile for sale, too. Come for the locally brewed draft beer, but skip the premade pisco sours.

Pilcomayo 529 (Cerro Concepción). ✆ **32/296-8839.** Pizzas C$4,000–C$5,500. No credit cards. Daily noon–4pm and 7–11pm.

epif VEGETARIAN   Veggies and vegans will find a home at epif, located a few steps from the top of the Reina Victoria funicular. The young Chilean-American couple who own epif (which is short for epiphany, by the way) are great fun and very friendly—probably because they gave up Boston for Valparaíso and couldn't be happier. The dining area is funky and antiques-filled, with an interior patio. It's a very relaxed environment, and most diners come as much for the inexpensively priced veggie burgers, gazpacho, and tofu burritos as they do for its lively nightlife.

Calle Dr. Grossi 268 (Cerro Concepción). ✆ **32/259-5630.** www.epif.cl. Main courses C$2,400–C$3,800. AE, DC, MC, V. Tues–Thurs 7pm–1am; Fri–Sat 8pm–2am.

La Playa ★ CHILEAN   As young restaurateurs scramble to open the next "it" gourmet restaurant on Cerros Alegre and Concepción, La Playa restaurant, located on the edge of downtown's Plaza Sotomayor, keeps drawing a steady clientele of diners and drinkers just like they have for more than 100 years. It's one of Valparaíso's oldest bars/restaurants, and no other establishment in this city oozes more old-world, bohemian charm, with its long oak bar, marine memorabilia, lofty ceilings, antique mirrors rescued from the Seven Mirrors brothel that shut down decades ago, and new tables (auction-bought from the defunct Cafe Riquet). While digging into an inexpensive meal of crab soup or steak *a la pobre,* it's easy to sense the ghosts of sailors past who frequented this restaurant during the city's heyday. After 10pm, the restaurant converts into a pub popular with young adults and college students (see p. 148).

Serrano 568. ✆ **32/259-4262.** Reservations not accepted. Main courses C$3,500–C$6,000. AE, DC, MC, V. Mon–Wed 10am–10:30pm; Thurs–Sat 10am–5am.

Le Filou de Montpellier ★ 🍴 FRENCH   Le Filou is a bastion of French gastronomic ingenuity, a local favorite and one of the first restaurants that opened on Cerro Concepción. Le Filou, owned by a French immigrant from Montpellier, started out serving a Saturday lunch special that grew so popular that the owner opened the bistro full-time. The dining room is casual and buzzes with chatter, a reflection of the gregarious spirit of the charming owner—who may even be your waiter for lunch. The bistro offers reasonably priced, fixed-price meals that change frequently but always feature well executed, simple, and truly authentic Gallic delicacies. Try a Parma ham salad followed by melt-in-your-mouth medallions of beef tenderloin in a Roquefort sauce, and a gooey chocolate crepe for dessert. Dinner is served on Fridays and Saturdays only.

Almirante Montt 382. (✆ **32/222-4663.** www.lefiloudemontpellier.cl. Reservations recommended Sat-Sun. A la carte menu available Fri-Sat. Fixed-price lunch C$4,600 Tues-Fri, fixed-price lunch Sat-Sun and dinner C$7,500. No credit cards. Tues-Sun 1-4pm; Fri-Sat dinner 8-10:30pm.

Valparaíso After Dark

Valparaíso is nationally famous for its bohemian pubs and bars where poets, writers, tango aficionados, sailors, university students, and just about everyone else spend hours drinking, dancing, and socializing well into the early morning hours. In fact, most restaurants and bars do not adhere to a set closing hour, but instead close "when the candles burn down."

That said, given that Valparaíso University is here, a lot of these nighttime watering holes draw a disproportionate amount of young adults. The **Cinzano,** facing Plaza Aníbal Pinto on Calle Esmeralda (✆ **32/221-3043**), is one exception. This traditional and unabashedly kitschy bar/restaurant is known for its kooky tango singers who break out the mic Thursday through Saturday after 10pm. But you need to get here earlier, or you'll end up waiting for a table. **La Colombina** (✆ **32/223-6254**) is frequented by an adult/young adult crowd for its comfortable ambience, live jazz, and bolero music, and view of the glittering lights of Valparaíso that spread out below; take a cab or the funicular Ascensor Peral and walk down Paseo Yugoslavo. The **Brighton Bed & Breakfast** (✆ **32/259-8802**) has live music on Fridays and a bar ambience most nights on their hanging terrace. **La Playa,** Serrano 568 (✆ **32/259-4262**), is one of Valparaíso's legendary bar/restaurants, and it draws an eclectic mix of characters who come to eat, drink, and listen to live music or poetry readings well into the early morning (See "Where to Dine" above).

My pick for a venue dedicated to nightlife action is **La Piedra Feliz** ★★, Av. Errázuriz 1054 (✆ **32/225-6788**). This bar/dance club is housed within the old storehouse of a shipping company, and it has something for everyone: a trendy subterranean lounge and club with DJs (lounge Thurs–Sat), a salsa room, tango room, pub, and a stage for live music. Twenty- and thirty-somethings sweat to electronic music at the ultracool **Mundo Pagano,** Blanco 236 (✆ **32/223-1118;** www.mundopagano.cl), which has nightly dance parties and occasionally live music. On Cerro Concepción, one of the hippest bars is **Gremio,** Pasaje Gálvez 173 (✆ **32/222-8394;** www.paganoindustry.cl), with periodic arts exhibitions and snacks. **Bitácora,** Cumming 68 (✆ **32/200-0601**), is a popular bar with young adults featuring a second-story salon dedicated to art displays; the bar also serves Chile's famous *terremoto* drink of young white wine and pineapple ice cream.

EXCURSIONS OUTSIDE VALPARAÍSO & VIÑA DEL MAR

Isla Negra

125km (78 miles) W of Santiago

Isla Negra is mostly known as "the place where Pablo lived"—Pablo Neruda, that is. His third—and favorite—home is here, perched high above the sand and sea that inspired him, and it is now a museum. The endearing little town is about 1½ hours south of Valparaíso, and anyone planning to spend the night in that city might consider this recommended destination as a first stop. Another idea is to include a visit to Isla Negra before or after a tour of the San Antonio wine region (see p. 162). After lunch here at one of two good restaurants, you can head north for a beautiful coastal drive to Valparaíso.

The **Casa Museo Pablo Neruda ★★★**, at Calle Poeta Neruda s/n (© 35/461284; www.fundacionneruda.org), has been afforded quasi-mythical status by many Chileans. Larger than Neruda's other two homes, ethereally perched on a cliff overlooking the crashing waves of the Pacific, it harbors a remarkable depository of travel mementoes: glass bottles, wooden sirens salvaged from ships' bows, butterflies, shells, African masks, Hindu carvings, ships-in-bottles, and more. Neruda, it seems, when not penning verse, liked to travel, hunt out treasures, and spend a lot of cash. The museum is a wonderful place to visit, and kids love it, too. The tomb of Neruda and his wife is also on view here. Tours in English cost C$3,500, and reservations must be made in advance. It's open March to December Tuesday through Sunday from 10am to 6pm, and January to February Tuesday through Sunday 10am to 8pm.

At the back of the museum is **Café del Poeta** (© 35/461774), with pleasant outdoor seating and a direct view of the rocky beach and crashing waves below. You'll find good pisco sours, seafood dishes, and fixed-price lunches here. If you are tempted to stay, **Hostería La Candela,** Calle de la Hostería 67 (© 35/461254; www.candela.cl), is a charming, rustic little hotel and restaurant owned by a local filmmaker and his musician wife. Neruda photographs and memorabilia line the walls of the lobby and stand as testament to the author's time here. The rooms are all decorated differently, to match the themes of Neruda's "20 Poems of Love"; a few have balconies with sea views and fireplaces. The restaurant is open all day and serves primarily simply prepared seafood.

The coastal strip of Isla Negra has been declared a *Zona Típica* (Heritage Zone) to preserve the area from becoming overrun by multistoried apartment buildings. You can get here from Valparaíso by bus with **Tur Bus** (© 600/660-6600; www.turbus. cl) and **Pullman** (© 600/320-3200; www.pullman.cl), which leave from the Terminal Alameda in Santiago, located at Av. Alameda 3750 (Metro: Univ. de Santiago). I recommend that visitors rent a car, stop along the way in Pomaire (see "Pomaire: The Clay Village," on p. 156) or wine taste, visit Isla Negra, and return to Santiago or head up to Valparaíso. To get here by car from Valparaíso, drive back out toward Santiago on Rte. 68 and follow the sign to Algarrobo (Isla Negra is south of Algarrobo); the trip should take about 2 hours.

Zapallar, Maitencillo & Colchagua

Zapallar 169km (105 miles) from Santiago, Maitencillo 161km (99 miles) from Santiago, Cachagua 183km (113 miles) from Santiago

Continuing north along the coast road, some 80km/50 miles from Viña del Mar you will reach Zapallar, which is a refuge of Chile's moneyed elite. The stalwart residents who have lived here over the past century have lobbied successfully to keep the riffraff out and construction to a minimum. Accordingly, it is the loveliest residential cove along the shore of the Central Coast. Each home flourishes with exotic land-scaping, and the beach is so pristine, it looks as though it has been raked with the meticulousness of a Zen master.

All this aside, Zapallar is also where you'll find one of the region's most popular restaurants, **El Chiringuito ★★** (*(C)* 33/741024). Birthed from humble beginnings, Chiringuito serves the same tasty but simply pre-pared seafood dishes it always has, so bring your bourgeois manners and your prole-tarian bite; the crashing sea views and outdoor seating here encourage you to linger for a long lunch. Credit cards aren't accepted, and reservations are strongly recom-mended for weekends and during the summer. The place to spend the night here is the **Hotel Isla Seca,** Rte. F-30 E, no. 31 (*(C)* 33/741224; www.hotelislaseca.cl), which has 38 handsome, comfortable guest rooms, two swimming pools, and a full-service restaurant. Rates are $175 to $206 for a standard double, or $267 to $316 for a double with a terrace and ocean view.

Neighboring Zapallar is Colchagua and farther south, Maitencillo, two middle-class weekend retreats for Santiaguinos. In this region, individual private cabins and weekend homes are really the only lodging options, with one exception: **Cabañas Hermansen,** one of the more interesting places to bunk for the night (Av. del Mar 592; *(C)* 32/277-1028; www.hermansen.cl). These self-catering, Swiss Family Rob-inson–style cabins are handcrafted to be individually different and are scattered amid thick foliage on a hilly slope. The guest rooms (for two to six people) were recently renovated and are perfectly comfortable, and a hit with kids. You'll need a rental car if you want to get around the area. The cost is $76 for two people March 16 to December 14, and $109 from December 15 to March 15.

A few attractions in this area stand out. At the northern end of the beach in Cachagua, there is a rocky pathway that takes visitors past the **Island of Cachagua Nature Sanc-tuary,** where you can view Humboldt penguins and sea lions (try to bring binoculars if you can). In Maitencillo, at Playa Caleta, there is a **fishermen's market** with a dozen stands hawking fish just pulled from the sea. This is as fresh as it gets: Order a plate of raw clams or live scallops, and watch the fishmongers expertly fillet the catch of the day.

Parque Nacional La Campana ★

110km (68 miles) northwest from Santiago

Parque Nacional La Campana is located in the dry coastal mountains, close enough for a day visit or as a stop on the way to or from Valparaíso. Immortalized by Charles Darwin in *Voyage of the Beagle,* the park's jagged peaks afford the most spectacular views in Chile as well as a rich profusion of Palma Chilena (*Jubaea chilensis*), the southernmost species of palm tree in the world. It was from the summit of the 1,800m-high (5,904-ft.) Cerro La Campana that Darwin professed that he never so thoroughly enjoyed a day as the one he spent atop this summit. It does indeed offer the best 360-degree summit lookout point in the central region, but it's a *strenuous* hike to get to it (see later for more info).

While Parque Nacional La Campana may not offer the diverse array of activities that you find in Cajón del Maipo, it is wonderful hiking territory. There are three sectors with separate entrances. **Sector Ocoa** has the largest concentration of palms and is a lovely day hike winding through palm groves and ending at a 30m (98-ft.) waterfall. The trail is mostly flat and about 6km (3.75 miles) long. The stout-trunk palms that you see here grow very slowly and live as long as 800 years. Hundreds of thousands once blanketed the central region, but they were nearly harvested to extinction for their sap, which was used to make *miel de palma,* something like a pancake syrup. You can reach this sector from the Pan-American Highway; the signs for the park exit are very visible.

In the Sector **Cajón Grande,** the Sendero Plateau is a 4.2km (2.6-mile) trail through oak groves (best viewed in the autumn) that is easy to moderate and takes around 2 hours to complete. Also in the Cajón Grande sector, the Sendero Portezuelo de Ocoa is a 5.5km (3.4 miles) trail that meanders through magical woods with *miradores* that overlook the valley.

Far and away the park's most popular sector is **Granizo,** where you'll find Sendero Andinista, the trailhead for Darwin's climb to Cerro La Campana. The trail is very steep in parts, especially the last 90 minutes, and can be slippery due to loose rock; if you can hack it, the vista at the end is breathtaking, with sweeping views of the Andes mountain range and the coast. The trail is 7km (4.25 miles) and takes approximately 8 hours to complete. For a more tranquil ramble, the Sendero Los Peumos is a 4km (2.6 miles) walk through lush woodlands, which connects with the Sendero Portezuelo de Ocoa Sector in the **Cajón Grande** sector. The CONAF station at Granizo is the most equipped, with knowledgeable rangers providing comprehensive, well designed information. Both sectors Grande and Granizo are in the park's southern region, with both entrances close to the pleasant town of Olmué. There are campsites in all three sectors, which cost $13 per night for one to six people. If you plan to stay for a couple of nights, you'll find more creature comforts at the immaculate and kid-friendly **Hostería Copihue,** Diego Portales 2203 (✆ **33/441544**), which has pleasant rooms nestled in manicured grounds with swimming pools, a gym, children's play area, and a good restaurant, and there are massages services and horseback riding tours; rates are $160 per double, or $202 with half-board.

Admission to the park is C$1,500 for adults and C$500 for children; it's open year-round Saturday to Thursday from 9am to 5:30pm, and Friday from 9am to 4:30pm. Call ✆ **33/443067** for more information. It is possible to reach the park by taking a bus from Santiago, Valparaíso, and Viña del Mar. From the San Borja terminal in Santiago, *Golondrinas* run daily services every 30 minutes to Olmué, which connect with the local *Agdabus* bus service every 10 minutes—this will drop you off at the park entrance at Granizo. From Valparaíso, the route is much more direct with *Ciferal* Express services running every 2 hours, leaving from Playa Ancha and 1 Norte in Viña del Mar and dropping you off less than half a kilometer from the park entrance at Granizo. For more freedom, rent a car, or contact **Santiago Adventures** (p. 160), which runs day tours.

CAJÓN DEL MAIPO

San Alfonso: 65km (40 miles) E of Santiago

Cajón del Maipo is part *huaso* cowboy, part artists' colony, part small-town charm tucked into a valley in the foothills of the Andes. From Santiago, it's less than 1 hour to the heart of the Cajón, the reason so many city denizens come to exchange the city smog and cement for the area's rugged, pastoral setting of towering peaks, freshly scented forest slopes, and the roar of the Maipo River as it descends along its route to the sea. If you have a day and would like to get a feel for the Andes and its rugged beauty, I highly recommend a visit here.

The highlight of this area is **Parque Nacional El Morado,** which offers ideal opportunities for day hiking, but it is certainly not a requisite destination. Cajón del Maipo boasts a wide array of outdoor activities, such as rafting, horseback riding, hiking, climbing, and more, but it also offers a chance to linger over a hearty lunch or picnic, stroll around the area, and maybe even lay your head down for the night in one of the charming little hotels or *cabañas* that line the valley.

The well paved road through this valley follows the path of the Maipo River. Along the way you'll pass dozens of stalls set up by locals who sell fresh bread, honey, *küchen* (a dense cake), empanadas, *chicha* (cider), and chocolate to passersby.

Then you'll pass the tiny hamlets of Vertientes and San José de Maipo, the principal city of the area, founded in 1792 when silver was discovered in the foothills. Colonial adobe homes and an 18th-century church still stand at the traditional plaza in the center of town. Continuing southeast, the road curves past San Alfonso and eventually reaches a police checkpoint where drivers register before continuing on the dirt road to El Morado. About a half-hour farther (due to the condition of the road), there are fabulous clay-pool hot springs surrounded by soaring alpine peaks. **Note:** The weekends are packed with day-trippers, the hot springs are overflowing with people, and traffic on the way back is horrible. Plan to come on a weekday, if you can.

Getting There

BY BUS & METRO   Getting here by bus is cheap, but takes forever. First you'll need to take the Metro Line 4 toward Puente Alto and get off at the Las Mercedes station. You'll come out on Avenida Concha y Toro, and from here buses pass by every 10 minutes for San Jose de Maipo only; if you're headed to San Alfonso, you can take a *taxi colectivo* (shared black taxis) from San Jose for C$500 once you get there.

BY TAXI   This is a faster option than the bus. Take the Metro as stated above; outside the Metro station await the *taxis colectivos,* which leave every 10 minutes from 7am to 8pm and cost C$1,700 per person. Regular taxis (with the yellow roof) from the Mercedes Metro station can run anywhere from C$10,000 to C$12,000 depending on your destination in the Cajón. Always negotiate a price with the driver beforehand.

BY CAR   The fastest and easiest way from Las Condes or Providencia is to take Avenida Vespucio Sur and head south until the avenue turns into a highway. Exit at Las Torres and continue straight along the lateral road and make your first left, heading under the freeway. After turning left, get in the right lane and veer right immediately onto Avenida La Florida. Continue along this road for 12km (7½ miles) until you see the road fork at Puente Alto; head left at the sign pointing toward San José de Maipo. If you are downtown, follow Vicuña Mackenna Street until you hit Departamental, and head left (east) until you run into Avenida La Florida. Take a map and count on snarling weekend traffic. If you plan to go to El Morado, note that there is a police checkpoint where drivers are sometimes asked to show their documents, including a passport.

What to See & Do

El Morado National Monument   This 3,000-hectare (7,410-acre) park is 90km (56 miles) from Santiago. It takes its name from the sooty-colored rock of the Morado mountain (*morado* means "purple" or "bruised"). At 5,060m (16,596 ft.), the views at El Morado are stunning, and a relaxing spot to take in all this beauty is the Tyrolean mountain lodge **Refugio Lo Valdés ★★★**, San José de Maipo (© **9/220-8525;** www.refugiolovaldes.com). The *refugio* (meaning "refuge," but really a rustic lodge made of stone) serves truly delicious food and a fixed-price lunch and dinner. This is hands-down my favorite place for lunch in the Cajón del Maipo, since you can sit out on their stone patio and gaze out at the snowcapped peaks. The *refugio* is owned by the same people as La Cumbre mountain store in Las Condes (see "Fast Facts: Santiago" in chapter 6), and they offer outdoor activities such as day hiking or overnight climbing trips, horseback riding, mountain biking, visits to the hot springs, nature tours, and even fossil hunting. There are clean, simple accommodations (all bathrooms are shared; bring your own towel) should you decide to spend the night, including three doubles with a queen-size bed, four doubles, three triples, and a few bunk rooms, and a cozy dining area warmed by a wood stove. Rates are $36 per adult, $29 per child 10 to 15 years old, and $21 per child 3 to 9 years old; breakfast is included.

You'll find the CONAF park ranger hut at the **Baños Morales.** The park is open daily October through April from 8:30am to 6pm, and costs C$1,500 to enter. There is just one trail, which runs for 8km (5 miles) and varies between easy and intermediate terrain, eventually passing by an alpine lake and a glacier with a profile view of the El Morado mountain. This is a first-rate day hike (about 6 hr. average round-trip), and there is a place to camp near the lake. The reserve provides a haven for an array of bird species, including hummingbirds, austral thrush, and the cometocino. The raggedy little village of Baños Morales has several hot spring pools open daily from 8:30am to 8pm during the summer and from 10am to 4pm April through September, but they are not particularly inviting, and they're crammed with Santiaguinos during the peak of summer. Better natural hot springs are at **Termas de Colina,** in the form of clay pools descending a slope; its expansive alpine setting adds a sense of grandeur to the experience. It takes time to get here due to the condition of the road; continue past Lo Valdés for 12km (7½ miles). If you don't have a car, **Manzur Expediciones** (© **2/777-4284**) offers round-trip transportation for C$14,000 per person, which includes the entrance fee, leaving Santiago at 7:30am and returning at 8pm. However, they operate only on weekends, and that is when the hot springs are at maximum capacity; otherwise Manzur offers private transportation for C$80,000 roundtrip. The entrance fee is C$4,000 per person.

RAFTING Rafting the Maipo River is very popular among Santiaguinos and foreigners alike, and it's really remarkable that this activity exists so close to a major metropolitan city. Although the season runs from September to April, the river really gets going from November to February, when rafters can expect to ride Class III and IV rapids. Two companies offer half-day rafting excursions: **Cascada de las Animas** (© **2/861-1303;** www.cascadadelasanimas.cl) is based in the Cajón, and they arrange rafting trips from their tourism complex in San Alfonso (see "Where to Stay," later), but it's best to reserve beforehand. Another highly respected, and much friendlier, outfitter is **Altué Expediciones,** in Santiago, Encomenderos 83 (© **2/232-1103;** www.altue.com). They are based in Santiago and can arrange transportation for you to the Cajón del Maipo.

HORSEBACK RIDING The same two companies above offer horseback riding in the Cajón del Maipo, either for the day or for multiday riding (with themes such as "Following Darwin's Footsteps"). I can't express enough how enjoyable a horseback ride in the Andes is: the sweeping views from high, the grassy meadows, galloping home . . . There is an indefinable magic about crossing the Andean peaks the way Butch Cassidy and the Sundance Kid did. Cascada de las Animas has tours through its own private chunk of the Andes (see later), but verify that your guide is bilingual when booking as they sometimes pair you with an old ranch hand who just lopes quietly along with you. Horseback rides are suitable for families and even those with little experience.

Where to Stay

Cascada de las Animas ★ ☺ This tourism center is run by the Astorga-Moreno family, who own a monster swath of land outside San Alfonso. Within their complex are 80 campground and picnic sites scattered about a lovely wooded hillside. There are also eight log cabins set amid sylvan, leafy surroundings and uniquely built with carved wood details; they're rustic but enchanting, with fully equipped kitchens and wood-burning stoves. Owned by the same family, the tiny **Hostal La Casa Grande** in San Alfonso (Vicuña Mackenna 90; (✆ **2/222-7347;** www.hostalcasagrande.cl), just 4 blocks from the entrance to their complex, offers tasteful simplicity in a welcoming hostel housed in a renovated 1930s home and surrounded by greenery. While the cabins are great for a group of four to six, the hostel is more economical (at $63 for a double with private bathroom) for a couple, and rooms are brightly painted, spotless, and very comfortable. Only two of the four rooms are en suite. Breakfast is included at the hostel, but not for the cabins; however, guests in both lodging options receive a discount on excursion prices (see "What to See & Do"). From April to August Monday through Thursday, there is a 20% discount for cabins.

There is a small grocery store in San Alfonso, and Cascada has a restaurant with dynamite views overlooking the Maipo River. The food is tasty, with lots of vegetarian options, but my major caveat with Cascada is that their staff seems unenthusiastic to the point of being aloof, and service is agonizingly slow.

Camino al Volcán 31087, San Alfonso. (✆ **2/861-1303.** www.cascadadelasanimas.cl. 8 units. $101 *cabaña* for 1–4 people; $202 for 8. AE, DC, MC, V. **Amenities:** Restaurant; outdoor pool; sauna. *In room:* Kitchenette (cabins), no phone.

Hotel Altiplánico San Alfonso ★★ Good for travelers who want more comfortable lodging without losing the funky, artsy feel that pervades through this Andean valley, the Altiplánico looks vaguely Tolkien-esque with shingled exteriors, adobe interiors, and a healthy dose of ethnic furnishings. The location is divine, with manicured gardens, stone walkways, and 360-degree views of the surrounding peaks, and the complex sits next to the fast-flowing Maipo River. The sharply landscaped outdoor pool is ideal for hot summer days, and the hotel can book excursions such as horseback riding, rafting, and wine tours to the Maipo Valley with a local agency. A truly relaxing destination, it features lots of patios and outdoor lounges for resting, and there is a hot tub. Rates include gourmet meals in their smartly designed restaurant, which is open to the public with a previous reservation.

Camino al Volcán 29955. (✆ **2/861-2078.** www.altiplanico.cl. 8 units. $140 per person, double occupancy, including meals. AE, MC, V. **Amenities:** Restaurant; Jacuzzi; outdoor pool (summer only). *In room:* Cable TV, no phone, free Wi-Fi.

La Bella Durmiente Located at the end of a steep dirt road, these *cabañas* seem as if they've jumped out of the tale *Sleeping Beauty,* which is what the name means— but the word *durmiente* also refers to the thick wooden railroad planks used in the cabins' construction. Each *cabaña* is distinct, but all are handcrafted from wood and stucco and set among a grove of trees. While they may not offer many creature comforts, they are cozy idyllic places to relax a couple of nights. Each cabaña has a kitchen and barbecue, which can prove cost effective for independent travelers. Given the setting and amenities, such as the lovely palm-fringed swimming pool and games room with ping-pong and pool, the cabins are especially popular with young Chilean families. Try to get the "honeymoon" cabin—it's the best here.

Calle Los Maitenes 115, San Alfonso. © **2/861-1525.** www.labelladurmiente.cl. 6 units. $88 cabin for 2, $120 cabin for 4. AE, MC, V. **Amenities:** Restaurant; outdoor pool (summer only). *In room:* TV, kitchenette.

Lodge Andino El Ingenio ★★★ 💼   The gorgeous Lodge Andino is the Cajon del Maipo's upscale lodging option, located well into the valley about 65km (40 miles) from Santiago, and providing perhaps the most stunning Andean views of any property here. What makes the lodge especially delightful is that it is family run, and hosts Magdalena Frugone and Juan Eduardo Oyanedel are bilingual and couldn't be more gracious and welcoming; they even like to invite guests into their adjoining home for an evening cocktail to chat. The lodge is surrounded by ornamental gardens and is close to the family's working ranch and bakery; there are three smaller rooms in a converted wing of the family's ranch home, and four luxurious and spacious rooms that sit above the home, with large picture windows, flagstone floors, custom-made furniture, and crisp linens. Meals are included and served family-style, and there is a lush lawn and garden with a swimming pool. A long list of excursions is available, including heliskiing during the winter, and hiking and horseback riding excursions are included in the price. The lodge will often customize excursions with a traveler's tastes in mind.

Camino al Volcán, Km 66, 6km (4 miles) past San Alfonso. © **2/861-3176.** www.lodgeandino.cl. 7 units. Prices are per person and include meals and excursions: $220 double occupancy in home; $320 in newer luxury rooms. AE, MC, V. **Amenities:** Dining room; Jacuzzi; outdoor pool (summer only). *In room:* Free Wi-Fi.

Where to Dine

Casa Bosque Restaurant ★★ ☺ STEAK   If you don't eat at Casa Bosque, stop here quickly anyway to check out the restaurant's fabulously outlandish architecture. The local artist who designed Casa Bosque has left his mark on many buildings in Cajón del Maipo, but none as dramatically as here: Polished, raw tree trunks are kept in their natural shape, forming madcap door frames, ceiling beams, and pillars; oddly shaped windows and stucco fill in the gaps. It's pure fantasy, and adults will love it as much as kids. Casa Bosque is a *parrilla*, and it serves succulent grilled beef, chicken, and sausages from a giant indoor barbecue, which you can pair with fresh salads, creamy potatoes, or a grilled provolone cheese, along with a few vegetarian dishes. During the weekend lunch hour, this restaurant can get packed, mostly with families with lots of kids, and service can be absent-minded and slow.

Camino el Volcán 16829. © **2/871-1570.** www.casabosque.cl. Main courses C$7,500–C$9,000. AE, DC, MC, V. Mon–Thurs 12:30–6pm; Fri–Sat 12:30pm–11pm; Sun 12:30–7pm.

La Petite France Restaurant & Hotel ★ 💼 BISTRO   The walls of La Petite France's restaurant, with its Edith Piaf posters and ads for French products, are pure kitsch. In spite of its incongruity here in the Chilean Andean foothills, locals love this little restaurant, especially for its pastries and winter garden dining area. La Petite blends classic French bistro fare with flavorful Chilean and international dishes. On offer are dishes such as filet mignon in a puff pastry with Roquefort sauce, and turkey

POMAIRE: THE clay VILLAGE

Every region in the Central Valley has a specialty good that it produces with pride, and Pomaire's is ceramic pottery. Pomaire is a small, dusty village 65km (40 miles) west of Santiago that was known as a *pueblo de indios,* a settlement the Spanish created for Indians. The area is rich in brown clay, and the main street (almost the only street here) overflows with shops hawking vases, funny little figurines, decorative pieces, and pots, plates, and other kitchen crockery—all at reasonable prices. This is also the place to sample homespun, country cooking (try San Antonio or Los Naranjos restaurants) such as the stews *cazuela* and *charquicán,* and Pomaire's famous half-kilo empanada; some restaurants even have *cueca* shows, highlighting the national dance of Chile.

Most tour companies offer an excursion here, or you can rent a car or take **Buses Melipilla** (℅ **2/776-2060**), which has several daily trips for C$3,000 from the San Borja Terminal in Santiago at San Borja 184. The bus will leave you at the end of the road to Pomaire, where you'll have to take a *colectivo,* or shared taxi, into town. To get here by car, take the Pan-American Highway to the turn-off for Rte. 78 to San Antonio; follow the highway until you see the sign for Pomaire 3km (1¾ miles) before Melipilla. Note that Pomaire is shut down on Monday, and weekends are crowded.

breast stuffed with almonds, plums, and apples in a cactus sauce. Of course, there's also pâté, escargot, and croque monsieur. During teatime on weekends, mouthwatering desserts are laid out enticingly across a long table: Tarte tatin, crème brûlée, and chocolate layer cake are just a few choices.

La Petite also runs a small hotel above the restaurant—a level high enough to provide guest rooms with sweeping views of the mountains. The nine rooms, while simple, are perfectly comfortable and have private bathrooms and TVs (but no phone). Amenities include an outdoor pool and Internet access; guest rooms are C$40,000 for double occupancy.

Camino el Volcán 16096. ℅ **2/861-1967.** www.lapetitefrance.cl. Main courses C$3,325–C$5,225. AE, DC, MC, V. Tues-Sun noon–6pm and 8pm–midnight.

Trattoria Calypso ★★ ITALIAN   Owned and operated by a Genovese family who immigrated to this region more than a decade ago, Trattoria Calypso serves delicious homemade pastas and, on Saturdays and Sundays only, crispy stone oven–baked pizzas. Everything is made using organic and local farm ingredients, such as the mozzarella bought from a family in Cajón del Maipo and smoked here at the restaurant. Pastas include ravioli, cannelloni, fungi fettuccine, and pesto lasagna, but you might want to nibble an antipasti platter with fresh focaccia bread. The cozy restaurant has indoor and outdoor seating at wooden tables; the staff gives a warm welcome to all who pass through the doors. It's open Friday through Sunday only, but if you're in the area during one of these days, don't miss a stop here.

Camino el Volcán 9831, El Manzano. ℅ **2/871-1498.** www.trattoriacalypso.cl. Main courses C$4,500–C$7,900. No credit cards. Daily 12:30–10pm.

WINE, SPAS & RURAL TRADITION IN THE CENTRAL VALLEY & ACONCAGUA REGIONS

A few miles outside the city limits of Santiago, the scenery opens into a patchwork of poplar-lined agricultural fields and grapevines, and tiny towns hearken back to a quieter, colonial era where it is common to see weathered adobe homes, horse-driven carts, and dirt roads. This is Chile's breadbasket, a region that boasts a mild, Mediterranean climate, fertile soil, and plenty of irrigation thanks to the Andes, and testament of this natural bounty can be seen at the myriad of roadside stands hawking fresh fruit and vegetables and unbelievably cheap prices.

There is much to see and do here, but what travelers really come to do is tour vineyards, the reason why this section is divided into the main wine regions, featured geographically from north to south, and encompassing hotels, spas, and rural and colonial historical highlights found within each area.

Wine in Chile: The Facts

The international popularity of Chilean wine has exploded over the past 15 years principally because Chile produces high-quality wines that are an extraordinary value. Chilean wine also has moved up the ladder and into the premium and ultra premium bracket, winning awards and catching the eye of many wine connoisseurs around the world. Chile's wine tradition dates back to the days of the Spanish conquest, although modern winemaking techniques and technology were only introduced in the late 1970s, when the Spanish winemaker Miguel Torres imported the first stainless-steel wine tanks. Yet given this long tradition of winemaking, the Chileans themselves have been slow to appreciate their wines, and consequently many winegrowers export the bulk of their product to Europe, the United States, Canada, and Asia.

Chile is a winemaking paradise. Mother Nature has blessed the country with a natural geography that creates the perfect *terroir*—that is, a combination of local climate and geology. Central Chile's Mediterranean-like climate produces lots of luminosity and minimal but sufficient rainfall outside the winter months. During the past few years winemakers have learned which grapes grow better and produce better wines in which valleys. For example, white grape production has been moved from the Colchagua Valley to the Casablanca Valley, a cooler region that has produced far superior sauvignon blancs and chardonnays, and vintners have identified which micro-regions are ideal for producing premium wines, such as Apalta.

What is unique about Chilean wine is that vintners imported their rootstock from Europe more than a century ago, long before European roots were affected with *phylloxera*, a pest that nearly wiped out the whole of the European wine industry. Chilean rootstock, having not been affected by this plague, is therefore the oldest original European rootstock in the world. Another unique fact is that Chileans only discovered the **carmenère** grape in 1994, intermingled with its merlot vines. Outside Chile there are very few hectares of carmenère planted in the world due to the difficulty in growing the grape and its late harvest. Carmenère is now Chile's flagship grape variety, even though it is more commonly used in blends.

Today, Chile receives direct foreign investment and has partnerships with American and European companies, such as Grand Marnier, Château Lafite, Baron Philippe de

reservations AT WINERIES

Only a few wineries are open to anyone who walks through the door between 9am and 5pm. Most wineries require reservations for English-speaking tours, or even just to pay a visit. Wineries also charge a fee for tastings; the higher-end wineries producing icon (premium) wines charge up to C$23,750 per person for a tour and tasting, and the tasting is not much more than a half glass of wine. It's unfortunate that some of the country's wineries extort grand fees; in this respect Argentina is handling wine tourism better, since a visit to Mendoza often is cheaper (but not as beautiful as the lush Central Valley). Some wineries work hard to provide visitors with a memorable experience, but the industry as a whole will begin to lose wine tourism if prices continue to climb and wineries do not adopt a more professional attitude toward their visitors.

Call to confirm if you have your heart set on visiting a certain winery, and keep in mind that reservations at small wineries can occasionally be canceled at the last minute. More popular wineries such as Concha y Toro can accommodate tour groups of up to 30 people, yet other wineries limit the number of guests to create a more intimate experience. If you'd like a personalized tour, ask to have one set up for you; it will cost extra, but it is usually worth it.

Rothschild, and Kendall Jackson, who have recognized Chile's ideal growing conditions and cheaper land and labor costs as a potential to produce world-class wines.

THE REGIONS IN BRIEF

In 1994, the Chilean government defined specific viticultural regions, known as appellations, and their sub-regions: **Atacama** (Copiapó and Huasco valleys); **Coquimbo** (Elqui, Limarí, and Choapa valleys); **Aconcagua** (Aconcagua, Casablanca, and San Antonio valleys); **Central Valley** (Maipo, Rapel, Curicó, and Maule valleys); and the **South** (Itata, Bío-Bío, and Malleco valleys).

Of Chile's five grape-producing regions, currently the two most important in winemaking are the **Aconcagua** and **Central Valley** regions, beginning about 100km (62 miles) north of Santiago and stretching south past Talca, a little less than 300km (186 miles) from Santiago. Within these two regions lie seven sub-regions (or appellations), composed of the Aconcagua, Casablanca, San Antonio, Maipo, Rapel, Curicó, and Maule valleys. Within these valleys, finer distinctions have been divided into sub-appellations and even micro-valleys. Such is the case of the Rapel Valley being split into the Cachapoal and Colchagua valleys.

The traditional wineries of Chile (Cousiño Macul and Concha y Toro) and a few up-and-coming boutique wineries are within 35km (22 miles) of Santiago, meaning it is possible to spend a day wine-tasting without having to travel very far. Even the Casablanca Valley is less than an hour away. The **Colchagua Valley,** Chile's answer to Napa Valley, is a 5-hour roundtrip drive that can be feasibly done in 1 day, but it is recommended that travelers opt to spend the night in or around Santa Cruz.

Touring the Wine Country & the Rural Heartland

A good place to get your Chilean wine country bearings and research enotourism offers is the **Wines of Chile Experience** website (www.chilewinetourism.com), which has interactive maps showing Chile's wine regions and winery locations, and descriptions and contact info. The essential guide for wine lovers visiting Chile is the English-language *Guía de Vinos,* a 400-page ratings guide that comes with basic maps and descriptions of the different wine valleys, but not much travel information other than address and telephone numbers of wineries. You can order a copy online at www.puro-wine.com, or pick up a copy at the **Puro Chile** shop in New York City (221 Centre St.; ✆ **212/925-7876;** www.puro-chile.com). The guide, as well as wine region maps in general, are sold in Chile at bookstores and wine shops. *Note:* MasterCard and Visa are accepted in all wineries, and in most local stores in the wine country.

WINE ROUTES

Attempts have been made to join wineries together in each region and form an established "wine route," yet this concept has achieved only moderate success and really only three regions, Colchagua, Casablanca, and Maule, have a truly established "Wine Route" with guided tours and transportation. Wineries in all regions are well signed on main highway and auxiliary roads; most can be recognized by a chocolate brown sign with white lettering and a "Ruta del Vino" logo.

○ **Ruta del Vino de Casablanca,** Punta Arenas 46, Casablanca (✆ **32/274-3755;** www.casablancavalley.cl), offers the convenience of transportation to and from your Santiago hotel to the valley. As a newer wine route, the organizers are still building momentum, and they've yet to promote this route as strongly as the Colchagua Valley. The Casablanca Wine Route includes the wineries **William Cole, Morandé, Matetic, Kingston, Viña Mar, Indómita, Casas del Bosque, El Cuadro, Veramonte, Santa Emiliana,** and **Catrala.** The Wine Route offers seven distinct tours that are priced differently according to length (half-day or full-day), and the level of wine included in the tasting; a half-day Casablanca Reserva tour costs C$25,000 per person and includes a visit to two wineries. Transportation to and from Santiago costs C$90,000 for two.

○ **Ruta del Vino de Colchagua,** whose office is located at Plaza de Armas 298 in Santa Cruz (✆ **72/823199;** www.rutadelvino.cl; click on "buscar" on the right-hand side and "English" will appear on the left side, for the English version), incorporates most wineries in the valley: **Viña Montes, Casa Silva, Casa Lapostolle, Viña Santa Helena, Viña Bisquertt, Viña MontGras,** and **Viña Hacienda Araucano.** The Ruta del Vino books wine tours, but doesn't include a bilingual guide (wineries provide their own English-speaking guides for winery tours); a guide costs an extra C$30,000 for a half-day, and C$50,000 for a full day. Full-day tours include a set-menu lunch at either Casa Silva or Panpan Vinovino. If you have your own transportation, you'd really be better off planning your own journey via email with wineries, so I've listed prices that include transportation only here. Tours come in three price ranges for "wine lovers," "connoisseurs," and "fanatics," which essentially refers to the cost and the caliber of wines offered for tasting: varietals and reserve wines; grand reserve and premium; and ultra premium/icon wines. Tours cost, per person and based on two people, C$48,000 to C$99,000 for a half-day, and C$84,500 to C$159,000 for a full day. A full-day tour can include visits to three wineries, or two wineries and a stop at the **Museo de Colchagua** (p. 176).

○ The **Ruta del Vino Valle del Maule** office is at 1 Sur 4 Oriente, at the Plaza Cienfuegos in Talca (✆ **8/157-9951;** www.valledelmaule.cl). This is the southernmost established wine route, working with the wineries **Balduzzi, Via,**

TerraNoble, Gillmore, J. Bouchon, Valle Frio, Calina, Corral Victoria, Reserva de Caliboro, Hugo Casanova, Casa Patronales, and **Chilean Wines Company.** The association is updating its website to provide better details for visitors so check the site for more information, especially about full-day tours that can include a special lunch at a winery. In general, Maule tours come with a bilingual guide who sticks with the group during the entire tour. Tours for one to four people are C$40,000 per person, and C$25,000 per person for groups of four to eight.

GUIDED WINE TOURS

Guided tours make a lot of sense here. Travelers leave the logistics and planning to someone else, which is especially helpful in terms of transportation (you can also drink wine without worrying about driving). Tour operators also offer "private" tours that can provide an insider's view; often this can mean a visit with the actual winemaker and/or a visit when a winery is otherwise closed to the public. Multiday and 1-day tours are available to all wine regions.

Santiago Adventures (© 802/904-6798 in the U.S., 2/244-2750 in Santiago; www.santiagoadventures.com) specializes in unique tours with visits to little-known boutique wineries such as Corcoran Gallery or Viña VIK, and active wine journeys bicycling between wineries; they also book ski trips to places like Valle Nevado or Ski Arpa in combination with wine visits. What also makes Santiago Adventures special is that the business is located in Chile and run by an American who has established special relationships with wineries and can, for example, organize overnights at exclusive properties, many of which are usually not open to the public. Santiago Adventures can work with travelers on any kind of budget. A 2-day trip to the Colchagua Valley, including transportation, an English-speaking guide, lodging, visits to four wineries, two winery lunches, a wine map, and bottled water is $619 per person, double occupancy.

VM Elite Viajes (© 2/893-7532; www.vmelite.com) is run by a Canadian who spends the majority of her time in Chile, and who has been guiding wine tours around the country since 2004. VM specializes in custom-designed wine trips to all valleys, including the Elqui Valley. Some wine tours can be paired with adventure activities such as skiing or surfing, in English, French, or Spanish for groups of 2 to 12 people.

Robertson Wine Tours (© 707/927-4167; www.robertsonwinetours.com) is a highly regarded wine tour operator run by a Scottish expat based in Uruguay. Robertson Tours are directed toward wine connoisseurs who seek to make wine touring and tasting the focal point of their Chile journey; most travelers with Robertson in fact combine visits to wineries in Chile, Argentina, and Uruguay. Robertson offers no set trips; instead, they work with travelers to tailor private journeys according to individual budgets and interests. Chile wine tours average 6 nights, and combination trips run about 2 weeks; call or e-mail for prices, which vary according to the aggressiveness of the itinerary and standard of accommodation.

The Aconcagua Valley

Spread across the feet of the Andes, this is the narrowest wine-growing valley with the steepest slopes, offering visitors one of the most stunning wine country tours in terms of scenery. The Aconcagua is characterized by winter rains and cool breezes entering from the Pacific Ocean, and is particularly well adapted for growing syrah, or blends based on syrah. The Aconcagua is ideal for visitors headed to Argentina or skiers visiting Portillo or Ski Arpa resorts, and there is a spa and lots of picturesque rural adobe architecture that was spared damage from the 2010 earthquake. Beyond the restaurants listed below, note that the Portillo resort is open year-round for lunch, and is worth the extra 1½-hour round-trip drive from Los Andes for its majestic Alpine views.

Errazuriz ★★★   One of Chile's oldest and most respected wineries, Errazuriz was founded in 1870 by Don Maximiano Errazuriz, a member of one of Chile's most illustrious families whose members included four presidents and a number of diplomats and writers. The particular appeal of this lovely winery resides in its Spanish-style architecture that dates to 1850, and there are sweeping views of the valley and the Andes and an impressive underground barrel cellar. Launched in 2010, the winery's striking new *bodega* with private tasting rooms and wine tank storage seamlessly blends with the traditional style of the winery. This vineyard is renowned for its natural techniques and delicate production methods, which are employed to create complex and elegant wines. Errazuriz's Don Melchor cabernet sauvignon is widely considered the best "Bicentennial Wine" if not one of the best wines ever produced in Chile, and in 2010 the winery's Kai icon wine, a carmenère, won first place at the Berlin Tasting. There are three tours available, and it is highly recommended that you book your tour to be followed by lunch on the winery's patio (at least 48 hours in advance). The Tour Histórico visits the cellar and estate (C$12,000), and the Tour Mirador adds a walk to the top of La Cumbre for views (C$15,000). The winery also offers horseback riding and bicycle rental with advance reservation.

Calle Antofagasta s/n, Panquehue. © **34/590139.** www.errazuriz.com. Reservations required. Tours offered Tues–Sat 10am–6pm.

Von Siebenthal ★ ⛏   One of the Aconcagua Valley's upstarts, this oak-and-wood boutique winery was founded by Swiss attorney Mauro Von Siebenthal in the late 1990s. Mention Von Siebenthal in local wine crowds and you will get a consistent thumbs-up on the overall quality of the vineyard's cabernet sauvignon, merlot, and carmenère to cabernet franc, petit verdot, and syrah. Varied soils allow the winery to grow all its grapes on site. Given the winery's limited production, its top wines include the super premium Montelìg, premium Carabantes and Parcela #7, and carmenère reserva, which won the prestigious Concours Mondial de Bruxelles award. Von Siebenthal's sommeliers provide the sort of personalized attention most visitors crave.

Av. O'Higgins s/n, Panquehue. © **34/591827.** www.vinavonsiebenthal.com. Reservations required. Tours daily 9am–5pm. From Los Andes, located on the road to San Esteban at Km 77.

WHERE TO STAY & DINE

Hotel Inca ★★ ❀   The highly recommended Hotel Inca is located on the edge of Los Andes about 8 blocks from the main plaza, and the property is the first four-star hotel to open in this rural city. The Inca offers plush comfort and brand-new facilities, and is geared mainly toward business travelers, but leisure travelers always leave content with their stay. The hotel's smart decor, a rustic-chic style that seems to be the boilerplate design for nearly every new hotel in Chile these days, is principally wood, glass, and stone, with Pottery Barn-esque furniture and couches draped in beige linen. The monochromatic beige-brown-chocolate decor carries on in the guest rooms, which have hardwood floors but are immensely comfortable, and have beds with downy comforters and full amenities. The Inca Hotel has the hippest lounge in Los Andes and an attractive Peruvian restaurant, **Mikuy,** a cafe called **Tambo,** and the semi-central location makes it easy to get out and explore the town.

Avenida Argentina Oriente 11, Los Andes s/n, San Felipe. © **34/345500.** www.incahoteles.cl. 45 units. $124 double standard. AE, DC, MC, V. **Amenities:** 2 restaurants; bar. *In room:* TV, hair dryer, minibar, free Wi-Fi.

La Table de France ★ 📖 The service can be languid and the food inconsistent, but the sweeping pastoral views from the terrace of this restaurant can make you overlook just about anything. La Table de France, opened by a French expat nearly a decade ago, pays homage to that country with a menu that offers classic dishes like pâté, French onion soup, and coq au vin (recommended), and an ample selection of Chilean-style seafood such as turbot in orange sauce and meats such as curried pork and lamb ragout. During colder months, there is a comforting fireplace indoors, so come early to nab a table next to it.

Camino Internacional, Km 3, Located at the "T" of the Camino Internacional to Argentina and the Los Andes bypass. ✆ **34/406319.** www.latabledefrance.cl. Main courses C$5,400–C$8,900. AE, DC, MC, V.

Termas de Jahuel Hotel & Spa ★★ ☺ Central Chile's spa tradition dates back to the turn of the 20th century, but Termas de Jahuel is the only antique spa resort that has renovated its facilities for the 21st century. Nestled in the forested foothills of the Andes near San Felipe, Termas de Jahuel was built in 1912 with Oregon Pine that had been used as ballast in cargo ships sailing to Valparaíso from the U.S. Charles Darwin spent 5 days here in 1834 and quite liked his experience, claiming the "atmosphere is of an extraordinary purity." The grounds are lovely as are the light and airy public spaces, which feature a preponderance of glass and carved wood. The resort is very popular with weekender Santiaguinos who come to enjoy the salubrious setting, book spa treatments, and lounge by the Olympic-sized outdoor pool filled with cool mineralized water (undoubtedly one of the best swimming pools in all of Chile). Some rooms are better than others; be certain to specify that you do not want a room facing the *cerro* or hill, since those rooms are smaller and dark. Superior rooms have terraces, and "VIP" rooms are just $25 more and worth the extra splurge. Rates include meals and use of their facilities. The spa resort has activities oriented towards kids and a game room, as well as horseback riding, biking, and walking/trekking on short trails that lead to stunning views of the valley.

Jahuel s/n, San Felipe. ✆ **2/411-1720** or 2/411-1721. www.jahuel.cl. 82 units. Rates shown are for 2 people sharing a room and include breakfast, lunch, and dinner: $434 classic double; $476 superior double; $499 VIP double. AE, DC, MC, V. **Amenities:** 3 restaurants; bar; bikes; outdoor and indoor heated thermal pools; full-service spa. *In room:* Satellite TV, CD player, hair dryer, minibar.

The Casablanca & San Antonio Valleys

The Casablanca Valley and its neighbor the San Antonio Valley are often compared to California's Sonoma and Russian River valleys. Casablanca flanks both sides of the Rte. 68 highway that connects Viña del Mar and Valparaíso with Santiago and is therefore very convenient to visit while traveling out to the coast. Until recently, the region mostly consisted of dairy farms. Winemaker Pablo Morandé saw parallels here to California's Carneros region, and in 1982 he planted 20 hectares (49 acres) of chardonnay, riesling, and sauvignon blanc. His hypothesis proved right: Today Casablanca is considered *the* great discovery in wine valleys in the modern era of winemaking, and although the valley now produces a large share of Chile's white wines, cold-weather reds like pinot noirs and syrahs are making a foothold, too. Both the Casablanca and San Antonio valleys are widely considered two of the world's most reliable sauvignon-growing regions.

San Antonio is the newest, tiniest, and most "happening" wine appellation in Chile, with just four boutique wineries that focus on quality, not quantity, producing fine pinot noir, sauvignon blanc, and syrah. Plan your visit here in conjunction with a visit to Pablo Neruda's museum in Isla Negra.

Casas del Bosque ★ Founded in 1993 by Chilean businessman Juan Cuneo Solari, this boutique winery produces just 75,000 cases of wine a year and is dedicated to the production of high-quality wines. Located just 19km (12 miles) from the Pacific, the winery is widely applauded for its delicious and citrusy sauvignon blanc, and chardonnay. Although the house specialty is white wine, their creative winemaking team was the first in the valley to plant merlot. Casas del Bosque is open daily and year-round, and you can just drop in for a tasting that includes four wines for C$5,000. A 1-hour tour includes a walk though the vineyard and cellars with tastings of five reserve wines; while it is best to reserve a tour, especially with a group, tours in both English and Spanish also are offered on a drop-in basis at 10:30am, 12:30pm, 3pm, and 4:30pm. Finish off your tour with a gourmet lunch in their **Tanino Restaurant** (see "Where to Dine" below).

Alejandro Galvaz s/n. ✆ **2/377-9431.** www.casasdelbosque.cl. Jan–Apr daily 10am–6pm; May–Dec daily 10am–5:30pm. Exit at the Casablanca/Lo Vasquez sign, cross over the hwy., and continue to Alejandro Galvaz. Turn right and drive about 1km (⅔ mile) until you see the winery on the left-hand side.

Matetic Vineyards ★★★ ☺ Located within its own 11,000-hectare (27,000-acre) valley not far from the Pacific, Matetic's state-of-the-art, multimillion-dollar, gravity-flow winery sinks into a sloping hill, and it is one of the most architecturally avant-garde wineries in Chile. They are experts in determining just the right *terroir* to produce Chile's EQ and Corralillo syrahs, which are consistently rated above 90 points in a variety of guides and specialized magazines, and it's believed that the winery's young vines will only continue to produce better wine as time marches along. Matetic is also a strong proponent of organic and biodynamic wines. The actual vineyards and winemaking facility are more than a mile from the winery's **Matetic Guesthouse & Restaurant** (see "Where to Stay," later). For a treat, have lunch at the gourmet restaurant (Tues–Sun) where chef Matías Bustos creates innovative recipes using the freshest local ingredients. Apart from wine tours, Matetic's agro-tourism offerings include horseback riding, harvest tours, and blueberry picking, making this winery a good bet for kids. Tours take place daily and last 1 hour; Tour 1 costs C$10,000 for a tasting of the Corralillo line and one premium EQ wine, and Tour 2 costs C$16,000 for tastings of two Corralillo reserve wines and two EQ premium wines. Visitors have the option of adding on a lunch or a country-style BBQ (the latter requires a minimum of 10 people) for C$28,000 to C$34,000 per person.

Fundo Rosario, Lagunillas. ✆ **2/232-7191** for reservations Mon–Fri, and 2/585-8197 for reservations Sat–Sun. www.matetic.cl. Reservations required 24 hr. in advance. Tours daily at 11am, 12:30pm, and 3:30pm (Tour 1), and 11:30am and 3pm (Tour 2). From road to Algarrobo, take Lagunillas exit and continue to Rosario, where you'll see the winery's sign.

Veramonte ★ The owners of this large winery, the Hunees family, have roots in Napa Valley—in fact, Veramonte's first vintages (1995–97) were bottled in California. More than 85% of their wine is exported to the U.S. Veramonte's vineyards are designed for mechanical harvest, and their state-of-the-art facility is capable of crushing 75 tons of grapes per day, sauvignon blanc being their mainstay. Wine tours begin out in the vineyards with a detailed explanation of the characteristics of the grapes and the features of the terrain before proceeding to an explanation of the manufacturing process, and finishing in a somewhat industrial-looking tasting room that has a soaring rotunda and glass walls that let you peek into the barrel caves below. It's a "stand-up" winery that's better for a quick tasting, not a tour, so consider just dropping in and heading back out on the road. Tours, which last 45 minutes, cost C$4,000 and include three tastings; or you can try individual wines for C$1,000 (two tastings),

C$1,500 (one tasting of Primus), C$4,500 (seven tastings), or C$6,000 (for sampling three wines and cheese).

Rte. 68, Km 66, Casablanca. © **32/232-9999.** www.veramonte.cl. Tasting room Mon–Fri 9am–5:30pm, Sat–Sun 9am–2pm. Tours Mon–Fri 10:30am, 12:30, and 3pm; Sat–Sun 10:30am and 12:30pm.

Viña Casa Marin ★★★ 🏨 Casa Marin holds the distinction of being the winery that sits closest to the Pacific Ocean. It is also the proud producer of Chile's best sauvignon blanc (Los Cipreses 2009), quite a victory for a winery that has been around only since 2003. Casa Marin is the brainchild of winemaker María Luz Marin, ex-head of production at the gargantuan Viña San Pedro. Marin's pet project focuses exclusively on pinot noir and white varieties such as its sauvignon blanc and riesling, as well as gewürztraminer and sauvignon gris. The vineyards here are slope-planted and take advantage of varying soils and orientations—producing outstanding results. A tour and tasting of three premium wines is C$18,000, or C$32,000 for the tour, including lunch with the Marin family in their home. Casa Marin recently opened a tiny and very simple **guesthouse** that has spectacular views and is perched high on a hill overlooking the vineyard; prices are C$80,000 for two people including breakfast and a winery tour, or C$200,000 for two including a visit to Pablo Neruda's museum in Isla Negra, lunch on the beach, a tour, breakfast, and lodging.

Camino Lo Abarca s/n. © **2/334-2986.** www.casamarin.cl or www.casamarinlife.com. Reservations required. Tours Mon–Sat. From Rte. 78 toward San Antonio, turn right at the Malvilla exit.

Viñedos Orgánicos Emiliana ★★★ Chile's pioneer in organic and biodynamic wines prides itself on service-oriented tastings, and there is a lot on offer here. Like Veramonte, it's one of the few wineries in Chile where you can just walk in during open hours, yet it's best to call ahead for the full, sit-down wine-tasting with organic cheese, or to take the hour-long tour, during which Emiliana's guides take visitors on a walk through their gardens and vineyard and explain the concept of biodynamic wines, and how all aspects of nature play a role in this kind of winemaking. Emiliana's main winery and cellar is located in Colchagua, which is temporarily closed to visitors, but here at their Casablanca vineyard the winery has a contemporary, glass-and-wood tasting facility and wine shop surrounded by a grassy park. Groups of 10 or more can book a gourmet lunch with a 2-week advance reservation (call for prices), or reserve 2 days ahead for an organic picnic of fresh bread, cheeses, dried fruits, and a bottle of their Novas wine (C$28,000 for two). Emiliana's premium wine, Coyam, is one of the highest-rated assemblages in the country, and their recently released Gê is the country's only biodynamic icon wine. Basic hour-long tours with tastings are C$7,700 and individual tastings only run C$1,000 to C$2,300 per glass; there are also blind tastings for C$9,500 per person with tastings of seven wines.

Rte. 68, Km 61, Casablanca. © **9/327-4019.** www.emiliana.cl. Tasting room daily 10am–5pm April–Nov and daily 10am–6pm Dec–March. Tours Mon–Thurs 10:30am, noon, 2:30pm, and 4pm; Sat–Sun 10am, 11am, 12:30pm, 2:30pm, and 4pm.

WHERE TO STAY

Hotel Casablanca Spa & Wine ★ 🍷 The newest arrival to the Casablanca wine tourism scene is a more rustic, homespun hotel that feels somewhat like a lodge, with whitewashed adobe walls, weathered wood and large ceiling beams, and wine-barrels-as-art. The hotel, and two log cabin–like independent cabins for five, wraps around a large swimming pool; the cabins come with a kitchenette. A basic spa offers wine-based treatments, massage services, and a wine-bath whirlpool. Check their website as they often offer weekend packages that include lodging, meals, a relaxation massage, and a guided wine tour in the Casablanca Valley.

Ruta 68 at Tapihue, Casablanca. © **32/274-2711.** www.hotelrutadelvino.cl. 8 units; 2 cabins. $147 double; $168 cabin for 5. AE, DC, MC, V. **Amenities:** Restaurant; spa. *In room:* Hair dryer, no phone.

Matetic Guesthouse & Restaurant ★★★ ▣ The Matetic Guesthouse is one of the finest wine-country hotels in Chile and a delightful experience that blends tradition with modern luxury. The hotel occupies an early 20th-century colonial-style hacienda that wraps around a fragrant garden and looks out toward a lap pool flanked with mesh-draped lounge "beds." Inside are seven French country-chic guest rooms, replete with parquet floors, antique furniture, and French doors that open onto a patio terrace on both sides. The three original guest rooms are considered suites and have spacious bathrooms and Jacuzzi tubs. I can't say enough about the beds, which are soft and downy and difficult to vacate in the morning. At night, the friendly staff serves welcome cocktails in one of the hotel's elegant lounges. The guesthouse operates on an all-inclusive basis: prices include lodging, a tour of their winery and a wine tasting, bicycles and use of the swimming pool, a hearty breakfast, and a gourmet dinner with a bottle of premium wine—served in a gorgeously preserved dining room swathed in crimson wallpaper and heavy dark wood furniture (or outdoors on the patio if the weather permits). Optional add-ons include horseback riding and tours to the Pablo Neruda Museum in Isla Negra.

Matetic's **Equilibrio Restaurant** serves gourmet cuisine for day-trippers (located near the hotel, not the winery) headed by chef Matías Bustos, who is a pro at creating innovative meals featuring local ingredients and artful presentation. The restaurant is closed on Mondays.

Fundo Rosario, Lagunillas. © **2/232-3134.** www.matetic.com. 7 units. $400 double; $500 double superior. AE, DC, MC, V. **Amenities:** Restaurant; bikes; pool. *In room:* Hair dryer, TV, minibar; free Wi-Fi.

WHERE TO DINE

Botha ★ Unlike the sleek-and-chic restaurants of the Casablanca Valley, Botha aims for something a little more homey. Cobbled together with odds and ends of recycled wood and glass, it's the kind of restaurant you'd expect to see surfers at, not polo players. And that is the charm of this rustic, bright red restaurant, owned and run by a very friendly couple who moved to Chile just several years ago and who are originally from South Africa (hence the name). The informality is refreshing: there is no wine menu, instead the owner lines up bottles of what he is offering that week so you can see the bottle and label rather than pick a name off a list. The menu changes daily according to what's fresh and in season, but always includes grilled meats, fish, and pastas. There is also a gift shop on site with locally produced arts and crafts.

Rte. 68, Km 63. © **7/431-2040.** www.casabotha.cl. Main courses C$6,000–C$8,000. AE, MC, V. Sun-Wed 10am–4:30pm, and Thurs-Sat 10-2am.

El Sauce ★★ ⏳ Some say this little hole-in-the-wall serves the best pork in all of Chile, which I'm inclined to believe. Mouthwatering, spiced to perfection, and finger-licking, the pork comes to you on a heaping platter as either ribs, tenderloin, or as an *arrollado,* the Chilean classic of chopped pork wrapped in its own fat. For those who eschew pork, El Sauce barbecues chicken and beef. Most order the ribs with a side of spicy mashed potatoes and a salad, preferably *ensalada chilena,* or tomatoes and onions. You might consider splitting a meal since the lumberjack portions are difficult for one to finish alone. El Sauce is ideal for lunch after visiting Casa Marin, and they have a decent wine list with varieties from the Casablanca Valley.

Juan Palominos 15, Lo Abarca. © **35/437206.** www.elsauceloabarca.cl. Main courses C$6,500–C$8,400. No credit cards. Daily 12:30–10:30pm.

House of Morandé ★★★ Viña Morandé's stylish eatery is right off Rte. 68 at Km 61, and is therefore a convenient stopping point for lunch. There is a glass-and-wood indoor dining area, and pleasant patio dining overlooking a grassy expanse and grapevines. What's enjoyable about the restaurant is its tasting menus and its wine-pairing suggestions with each dish. For C$13,900 you may order an appetizer sampler with items like rabbit empanadas, *ceviche,* tuna tartar, and surf-and-turf sautéed in garlic. Main courses are well balanced and are reinvented takes on Chilean cuisine, with dishes such as Kobe beef pot roast, grilled tuna with hearts of palm and pea puree, or salmon raviolis with capers. The restaurant follows up with a dessert tasting menu to share with your friends for C$9,900. The staff is all smiles, and they are well educated about their wines. Although House of Morandé offers a tour through their winery, a far better way to sample their varieties is over lunch, and they have an on-site wine shop if you want to take home a bottle.

Rte. 68, Km 61. © **32/275-4701.** www.morande.cl. Reservations not necessary. Main courses C$7,900–C$8,900. AE, DC, MC, V. Tues–Sun 11am–5pm.

Restaurante Viña Indómita ★★ 📷 You can't miss Indómita—just look for the giant white castle perched on a knoll above a spread of grapevines. Chef Oscar Tapia's gourmet cuisine is above par and arguably the best in the Casablanca Valley, and the sweeping views are outstanding. And the wine? Well, two out of three ain't bad. Start with a crab ravioli or creamy baked clams, and follow with pinot-noir–braised osso buco served with coriander gnocchi, or grilled grouper with papaya confit and mashed squash. The airy, sophisticated ambience is surprisingly comfortable. During week-days, service can be absent-minded and clumsy, although things pick up on weekends when there are more diners.

Rte. 68, Km 63. © **32/275-4400.** www.indomita.cl. Main courses C$6,000–C$9,000. AE, MC, V. Daily 12:30–4:30pm.

The Maipo Valley

Chile's "classic" valley is home to the most traditional wineries in the country, including heavyweight winemaker Concha y Toro. The huge advantage of visiting wineries here is their proximity to Santiago. In fact, you can simply taxi over to wineries like Concha y Toro or Cousiño Macul. The Maipo is the king of red wine production, with cabernet sauvignon occupying more than 70% of the total hectares planted here. This valley was recently divided into the sub-appellations **Alto Maipo** and **Isla de Maipo.**

For a taxi to Concha y Toro or Cousiño Macul, call a private radio taxi with executive vehicles, such as **Radio Taxi Chile** (© **2/713-2000**), or ask your hotel concierge to call one rather than flagging down a street cab. Often you'll need the bare minimum of Spanish, as drivers do not speak English. Rates cost approximately C$45,000 for roundtrip transportation and a driver who will wait for up to 3 hours.

Concha y Toro ★★★ Chile's largest and best-known winery produces the lion's share of export wines—from inexpensive table reds to some of Chile's high-end, traditional cabernet sauvignons such as Don Melchor, which is considered one of the best wines produced in Chile today. Founded in 1883 by the eccentric mining magnate Don Melchor Concho y Toro, this gorgeous estate, which resembles an English country manor, is part of the attraction, with gardens large enough to require eight

SHIPPING & carrying wine BACK HOME

Ever since the ban of liquids on flights, many visitors aren't sure how to get their wine home. Here are several points to consider.

- First, check to see if you can buy the wine at home for less money. Chilean wines are often cheaper in the U.S., for instance, as the VAT (sales) and alcohol tax exceeds 35% in Chile. Generally speaking, though, you won't find boutique gems outside of Chile.

- Shipping wine is expensive: more than C$118,750 per 12-bottle case. Most wineries that ship abroad by air use **Hot Express** (℡ **2/410-7000;** www.hot express.cl), who are experts in shipping wine and have special wine cases fitted with Styrofoam to protect bottles, which you can pick up at their office or coordinate to have dropped off at your hotel. Plan ahead at least 2 or 3 days, and, if you're an American, check with Hot Express to see if your state prohibits wine shipments from Chile (they have an updated list).

- Despite the myth, corks do not explode, and bottles will not break if some care and common sense are taken when packing. If you can't get your hands on a Hot Express Styrofoam case, any sturdy 12-bottle cardboard wine case will do. Pack each bottle firmly in bubble wrap (or your underwear and socks) and place in the case so that they don't move. For 6 bottles in a 12-bottle case, for example, stagger the bottles with an open place between them so they don't bang against each other. Close and reinforce with packing tape. Put your name, address, and a "fragile" label on the box. You can shrink-wrap your box at the airport if it gives you peace of mind. Check the box as a normal piece of luggage.

- While you may be able to get wine out of Chile, make sure you can get it *into* your home. In the U.S., some states like Pennsylvania and Arizona have stringent alcohol laws. In some cases you will have to pay duty, and in some states your wine may be confiscated. U.K. residents can take home a maximum of 4 liters of still table wine (per adult) without paying customs duty. New Zealand residents can enter with 4.5 liters of wine, while Australian residents are limited to 2.25 liters of duty-free alcohol total. Canadian travelers may return from Chile with just 1.5 liters of wine, *or* 1.14 liters of liquor, *or* 24 12-ounce cans or bottles of beer or ale, including beer coolers over 0.5% alcohol. For updated information, check your home country's customs regulations before you travel.

- Once your wine is safe in your home, you'll need a couple of weeks to let it rest. Wine gets "stressed" when traveling, and it can actually taste off if you don't give it time to let the molecules settle.

full-time gardeners, a sculpted lake, eucalyptus-lined pathway and antique *bodegas* whose interiors include the famous "Castillero del Diablo," a folkloric tale featuring a cellar haunted by a devil, invented to scare workers away from stealing the owner's prize wines. There is a huge wine shop with wine, souvenirs, arts and crafts, and books, too. If you want to skip the tour, Concha y Toro's smart wine bar has tastings of all wines, including Almaviva (see later), paired with appetizers, and is open Monday through Saturday from 10am to 6pm. Group tours cost C$7,000 and include a souvenir glass. You can even take the Metro here: Ride to the Tobalaba station, transfer to Line 4, and ride it to Plaza de Puente Alto station; from here, a taxi gets you there in 5 minutes.

Virginia Subercaseaux 210, Pirque. © **2/476-5269.** www.conchaytoro.com. Wine tour and tasting C$7,000 per person. English tours available with previous appointment. Daily 10am–5pm, closed holidays.

Cousiño-Macul ★★   The first vines in Chile were planted here in 1546, but the winery itself was founded by the Cousiño family in 1856. Of its peers established at the same time (such as Concha y Toro, earlier), Cousiño Macul is the only one that continues in the hands of the original founding family, now in its sixth generation. In 2010, *Wines & Spirits* magazine chose the winery's 2006 Lota icon wine as one of the best cabernet blends of the year, and the winery's riesling is receiving rave reviews, too. Using entirely estate-grown grapes, Cousiño-Macul's wines are known around the world for their distinctive Maipo characteristics and fruit. The absolutely beautiful estate, with its lush, French-designed gardens, is worth a visit to see this grand original in the history of Chilean wine. Tours cost C$7,000 and include a souvenir wine glass and tastings of two wines.

Av. Quilin 7100, Peñalolen. © **2/351-4135.** www.cousinomacul.cl. Tours Mon–Fri at 11am, noon, 3pm, and 4pm; Sat 11am and noon. To get here, head south on Américo Vespucio until the Rotunda Quilin; from here, head east toward the Andes. The winery is on the left-hand side.

Odfjell Vineyards ★   A newcomer to the Isla de Maipo scene, this winery is the creation of Norwegian shipping magnate Dan Odfjell and his son, an architect who sketched out the winery's stylish, minimalist look and narrow ceiling, which gives the sensation of being in a ship's hull. Although "boutique" by Chilean standards, Odfjell is by no means a small operation, producing 50,000 cases per year in different price ranges and lines. In 2008, Odfjell purchased a new 7-hectare (17-acre) vineyard of cabernet sauvignon and carmenère grapes in the Colchagua Valley. The wines routinely score high on the *Wine Spectator* scale, but it's the sylvan setting, design, quirkiness of the winery, and Mrs. Odfjell's Norwegian ponies that make this a worthwhile visit. There is a terrace with a sprawling view of the vineyard and the Andes. The basic tour costs C$12,000 and the advanced tour with higher caliber wine tasting is C$20,000; both last between 1 and 2 hours.

Camino Viejo a Valparaíso 7000. © **2/811-1530** or 2/876-2830. www.odfjellvineyards.cl. Reservations required. Tours Mon–Fri by appt. only. Follow the Camino Melipilla west until crossing under Américo Vespucio. Continue for 14km (8⅔ miles) until you see the sign for Odfjell on the right.

Viña Almaviva ★★   A world-class joint venture between Baron Philippe de Rothschild and Viña Concha y Toro, Almaviva produces an exceptional Franco-Chilean premium wine under the concept of the French grand cru. The winery's slick design for its cellars and tank areas reminds one vaguely of Opus One in Napa. Almaviva produces just one blend of carmenère, cabernet franc, and cabernet sauvignon, and is consistently rewarded with 93 to 95 points by *Wine Spectator*. It is worth the visit just to try a glass of this nectar, and the tours are very sleek and Americanized, but then again the price has shot through the roof and Almaviva now charges C$25,000 per person for a tour and *one* tasting, so those on a budget might opt for a visit to Concha y Toro instead.

Av. Santa Rosa, Paradero 45, Puente Alto. ☎ **2/270-4225.** www.almaviva.cl. Reservations required at least 1 week in advance. Tours Mon–Sat 10:30am–3:30pm, except holidays. Take Américo Vespucio to Santa Rosa exit, head south just past Paradero 45; you'll see Almaviva on your left near the Shell station.

Viña Santa Rita ★★★ 📷 Founded in 1880, this is one of Chile's oldest wineries and highly recommended both for its convenient location just 1 hour from Santiago and for its lovely antique architecture. Santa Rita produces award-winning wines, too, and the grounds here are fragrant and lush. The winery, Chile's third-largest, is an important historical site. The *hacienda* was originally founded in the 18th century by Doña Paula Jaraquemada, who offered refuge for liberator Bernardo O'Higgins' 120 soldiers following a failed attempt to conquer the Spanish. One of Chile's most popular "cheap and cheery" wines is Santa Rita's 120 series line, which commemorates the event. Santa Rita is highly regarded for producing good value wines such as their Casa Real and Medalla Real cabernet sauvignon and chardonnays, and in 2010 *Wines & Spirits* magazine named Santa Rita Chile's Winery of the Year and Value Brand of the Year. Santa Rita is now trying its hand at ultra premium wine with its Triple C line.

Tours here take visitors down to the winery's original cellars, which are outstanding examples of the ancient *cal y canto* stone laying method, and whose vaulted ceilings have been designated a national monument. The tour includes tastings of two premium wines and a complimentary wine glass, as well as a visit to the winery's newish Museo Andino, a private collection of pre-Columbian artifacts collected by Santa Rita winery owner Juan Claro, and including 1,800 pieces from Easter Island, northern and central Chile (museum open 1–5pm Tues–Sun, admission free). Unfortunately, the tour does not include a visit to the old hacienda home; it is now a hotel (recommended, see below) and to see it you'll need to stay the night.

Camino Padre Hurtado 0695, Alto Jahuel. ☎ **2/362-2520,** 2/362-2590 (on weekends). www.santarita. com. Wine tasting and tours cost C$8,600 per person. Reservations necessary. Tours available Mon–Fri 11:30am and 4pm, closed holidays.

WHERE TO STAY

Villa Virginia Fundación Origen ★ This is the only decent place to spend the night in the Maipo Valley. The charming, country-style boutique hotel is part of the Fundación Origen, a non-profit agro-ecological school in Pirque that offers training for local youth and adults. The hotel grounds feature a sprawling lawn and garden with towering Chilean Araucaria and purple Jacaranda trees that frame a shimmering pool. There are two sleeping options: the main house, a 100-year-old villa, or in a more modern pagoda-style building. The hotel focuses on de-stressing via their hot tub, visits to the ecological school, a meditation room, and yoga classes. But be prepared to be jolted awake with an early wake-up call, courtesy of a local rooster.

Virginia Subercaseaux 2450, Pirque. ☎ **2/853-1818.** 24 units. www.fundacionorigen.cl. $105 double. AE, DC, MC, V. **Amenities:** Restaurant; Jacuzzi; outdoor pool; yoga room. *In room:* No phone.

Viña Santa Rita Hotel Casa Real ★★★ 📷 Occupying the original manor home of Domingo Fernández Concha, who founded the Santa Rita winery in 1880, this gorgeous hotel seamlessly pairs antique loveliness with modern comfort. The hotel is surrounded by a 40-hectare (100-acre) garden designed by a French landscape artist in 1882, and the grounds feature a central patio with an ornate fountain, as well as an 1885 neo-Gothic chapel. The hotel's public spaces include a game room with an imported pool table from England, and salons that are impeccably restored and replete with antiques, crystal chandeliers, and 19th-century artwork and grand mirrors. The opulent guest rooms feature antiques, polished parquet floors, soaring ceilings, and French doors. Stays include a full breakfast and tour of the vineyard, as well as access to mountain bikes. The winery also boasts an elegant restaurant, **Doña Paula,** serving gourmet Chilean cuisine. Dishes include recipes popular a century ago in rural Chile, including lamb kidneys with port, king crab with cilantro sauce, and even Rocky Mountain oysters canapé. Prices, surprisingly, are quite reasonable, with main courses averaging C$6,500 to C$8,000.

Camino Padre Hurtado 0695, Alto Jahuel. © **2/821-9966** (hotel), and 2/362-2594 (restaurant). www. santarita.com. 16 units. $350 double standard. AE, DC, MC, V. **Amenities:** Restaurant; bikes. *In room:* Hair dryer, TV; free Wi-Fi.

Cachapoal Valley

This valley was for years grouped together with the Colchagua Valley, but split when differences between the two valleys' climate and topography became too distinct to ignore. The Alto Cachapoal near the Andes produces world-class cabernet sauvignon with a freshness and natural elegance derived from its alluvial, infertile soils and cool breezes. To the west, carmenère has thrived, achieving a perfect maturity. Other grapes that are producing interesting results are viognier, syrah, merlot, and cabernet franc. In addition to wine, the Cachapoal Valley is home to a couple of interesting attractions such as Sewell, a UNESCO Heritage site and abandoned mining town; Teniente, the deepest copper mine in the world; and an old-world spa modeled after Vichy. The drive from Ruta 5 (Panamericana) up to Termas de Cauquenes along the "Copper Highway" offers utterly spectacular views of the Andes.

Altaïr ★★★ Situated in the foothills of the Andes in Alto Cachapoal, Altaïr is a joint venture between Viña San Pedro and France's Château Dassault, launched in 2001 to craft a uniquely Chilean grand cru. The winery itself is understated yet majestic, made of natural stone culled from the surrounding area, and their "quincho" (pavilion) and tasting room boast a 360-degree view of the patchwork valley below and the hills. This is a top-tier winery in the Cachapoal Valley and has produced some of this valley's finest varietals; both their Altaïr and Sideral cabernet blends are elegant yet powerful. All Altaïr wines have been rated over 90 points by *Wine Advocate*. The winery's basic tour, including a visit to the vineyard and a tasting of their Altaïr wines, costs C$18,000. A far more unique tour is the winery's Terroir & Cosmos night tour on horseback, which follows a triangular path inspired by the constellations Altaïr, Deneb, and Vega; the cost is C$36,000 and the tour is only available during a full moon at 8pm. Daytime horseback rides cost C$32,000 and are available at 10:30am and 3pm. A full-day tour with a horseback ride and a BBQ lunch is C$72,000 per person and is available daily from 9am to 6pm.

Fundo Totihue, Requínoa. © **2/477-5555.** www.altairwines.com. Reservations required. Tours daily at 10am, noon, 3, and 5pm. From the Panamericana, exit at Requínoa and head left until you reach a dead-end intersection; turn right and follow the road until Camino a Pimpinela, turn left and continue 10km (6 miles).

Anakena ★★ Launched in 1999 by two school friends, Anakena features vines that are scattered around four different wine valleys, but their flagship winery is here in Cachapoal and it is their largest, offering lovely views of the Andes. The winery produces 400,000 cases a year, and is known for producing good value wines such as the excellent but low-cost viognier and pinot noir; their premium ONA line is well regarded. Anakena is committed to the environment more so than most wineries and a tour explains the importance of creating fine wines in an environmentally sensitive

A COPPER MINE & a nature reserve

Chile's mining industry recently received a lot of exposure with the rescue of 33 miners from a collapsed subterranean shaft near Copiapó in late 2010 (see p. 12 for info). If the news coverage made you want to see some of the country's mines up close, you have an excellent opportunity to do so south of Santiago. Near Rancagua (87km/53 miles south of Santiago), **El Teniente** is the world's largest underground copper mine and a supremely fascinating journey into the bowels of the earth. El Teniente began in 1905 and once employed 15,000 workers, who, at the time, lived at the mine in the town **Sewell** (www.sewell.cl). Dubbed the "city of stairs" for its location on a mountain slope, it is now a ghost town and a UNESCO World Heritage Site, and a superb example of old company towns that fused know-how from industrialized nations with local labor. Many of the old homes have been restored as interpretive museums. About 3,000 Chileans still work at El Teniente in shifts, 24 hours a day, and a tour here puts you in safety gear and shows you how they do their job. You will be awed by the immense size of this mine; however, claustrophobia sufferers should think twice about this tour. The minimum age is 14. **VTS Tours** (☏ 72/210290; www.vts.cl) has Spanish-only tours and transportation on Saturdays and Sundays leaving from the Parque Arauco shopping center at 9am (from the Turistik kiosk); call for pick-up times and location if you're in the Cachapoal area, since VTS also stops in Rancagua. The tour visits both the mine and Sewell; the cost is C$26,000 for adults and C$21,000 for 14- to 24-year-olds, as well as seniors 60 and over.

While in the area, you'll want to pay a visit to the underrated **Reserva Nacional Rio Los Cipreses,** a little-known nature reserve 14km (8¾ miles) from Termas de Cauquenes (see below). It's open daily from 8:30am to 6pm; admission is C$2,000 for adults and C$1,000 for children. There is a park administration center with information, including trails and a guide to the flora and fauna of the reserve. Here it is possible to watch wild parrots swoop from trees and tiny caves high on cliffs; there are also rabbitlike *vizcachas* and red foxes, and, of course, a blanket of cypress trees. You'll need your own car to get here or, if you plan to stay at Termas Cauquenes (see "Where to Stay & Dine" below), have them plan a visit for you.

manner. One-hour tours here include a walk through their vineyard to a lookout point to sample a sauvignon blanc, followed by a visit to the bodega and winemaking facilities and another tasting in their shop; the cost is C$8,000 for reserve wines, and C$12,000 with premium wines. Better yet, book a tour with a 1-hour horseback ride included for C$27,900 per person; or book ahead for a cheese picnic that includes a bottle of wine (C$24,000 for two with a picnic and tour). Visitors may also drop in and simply taste Anakena's wines for C$4,000 to C$9,000 depending on the caliber of wine.

Camino Pimpinela s/n, Requínoa. ☏ 72/954203. www.anakenawines.cl. Reservations required for tours, Mon–Sat 10:30am, noon, 3, and 4:30pm, and Sun and holidays 10:30am and noon. Boutique de Vino daily 10am–8:30pm. For directions, see Altaïr above; the winery is next door.

Viña VIK ★★★ 📷 When Norwegian businessman Alexander Vik set out to indulge in viticulture with his own 10,500-acre winery in 2006, he didn't aim to make the best wine in Chile, rather the best wine in the world—a feat he very well might accomplish when the 2010 varietal matures and hits the market in 2012. This is one of the most unique wineries a traveler to Chile can experience; it gives visitors a chance to see a winery that seems to get everything right even though it's just starting out. A mind-boggling amount of investment has been made here: Its winemakers grafted phylloxera-resistant roots to Chilean vines and spent several years testing syrah, merlot, cabernet franc, and cabernet sauvignon varieties in the valley's distinct microclimates, searching for foolproof growing conditions that will eventually be blended into an icon wine. VIK strives to produce "Holistic Wine" in which technology, know-how, environmental sensitivity, solid social practices, and advanced science merge to create fabulous wine. The property is also set in one of the loveliest valleys in Chile's Central Valley, untouched by development and magical in nature, with bountiful bird life and flitting butterflies, drooping willow trees alongside country lanes, and locals who get to and fro on slow bicycle rides. Wine tours here are C$30,875 per person, but the tour is private and led by a supremely knowledgeable enologist, followed by a sample of their first wine, a 2009. They also offer a lunch with wine in their lodge for C$57,000 per person; both tours and lunch must be booked in advance.

Road to Millahue s/n. © **2/248-2218.** www.vik.cl. Tours C$30,875 per person, and by appointment only.

WHERE TO STAY & DINE

The Central Valley's famous **Hacienda los Lingues,** one of the oldest and best-preserved haciendas in Chile, was heavily damaged in the earthquake of 2010, but plans are afoot to reopen it in late 2011 or early 2012. King Phillip III bestowed the hacienda to the first mayor of Santiago in 1599, and it has remained in the same family for 400 years. The hacienda is literally brimming with decorative pieces, family photos, collector's items, and fascinating odds and ends, and there is an antique chapel, a patio with a bubbling fountain shrouded in greenery, an organic garden, a library, and a rodeo ring. If you are visiting Chile in late 2011, call ahead and see whether Los Lingues has reopened, and plan a stop here for a tour or an overnight stay.

Hotel Il Giardino ★★ ♦   There are few hotels in Chile with an interior design as tasteful and beautiful as Il Giardino's, let alone ones that are such a deal. Tucked behind a brick wall, with a sizable garden centered around an outdoor pool, this boutique hotel is frequented more by traveling businessmen in the wine and copper industry than by tourists, which is odd given that the hotel is so perfectly suited as a base when exploring the area. From the outside, it's the spirit of rural Chile, but on the inside it is a blend of modernism and French country: A soothing muted palette of cream and soft beige offsets the mahogany bed frames, fluffy white duvets, toile curtains, and velvet settees. The view's better up at Cauquenes, but the rooms are 50 times better down here. A copious breakfast is included and afternoon high tea, served on the terrace, makes for a very civilized ritual. The property's expansive lawn is great for kids.

Carretera del Cobre, Km 7. © **72/281301.** www.hotelilgiardino.cl. 9 units. $131 superior suite; $157 executive suite; $202 suite Il Giardin. AE, DC, MC, V. **Amenities:** Restaurant; bar; outdoor pool. *In room:* A/C (some rooms), TV, hair dryer, minibar, free Wi-Fi.

Termas de Cauquenes   Chile's oldest spa resort is tucked away in the foothills of the Cachapoal Valley in a gorgeous alpine setting, and it is a historical landmark established more than 200 years ago. The architectural splendor of the property is apparent the minute you arrive. The spa's style was inspired by France's Vichy; its centerpiece is a lovely, Gothic-designed thermal pavilion offset with colorful stained glass, marble floors, and antique marble soaking tubs. But in spite of the spa's exterior beauty, it is a mystery as to why the guest rooms have not been renovated in more than a decade. Expect very basic comfort, midrange quality beds, and frumpy, cheap furniture—if you're looking for luxury, look elsewhere. On weekends, the spa offers massage and other beauty services to guests and the public by advance reservation, but their swimming pool is for guests only. Note that the original soaking tubs are tiny and ancient, but they also have a few modern whirlpools with mineralized water.

The owner of Termas de Cauquenes is Swiss and a professional chef, and the spa's restaurant is hailed by critics for its fine cuisine. In my opinion, the food is quite good, but their ranking as an epicenter of gourmet cooking is a touch overrated. The changing menu features fresh seafood and meats that embrace regional recipes, and the voluminous, old-world dining area, flooded with light from the floor to ceiling windows, makes for an interesting option for lunch if you're just touring the area.

Road to Cauquenes, near Rancagua. ✆/fax **72/899010.** www.termasdecauquenes.cl. 50 units. $254 per person double for full pension and use of spa baths; $149 per person double for breakfast only and spa baths. AE, DC, MC, V. **Amenities:** Restaurant; bar; outdoor pool (guests only). *In room:* TV, minibar.

Viña VIK ★★★ 📷   No other hotel in wine country, with the exception of Casa Lapostolle's *casitas*, boasts a more spectacular view than this upstart winery's new, four-room "lodge." The nearly 360-degree-view stretches from the snowcapped Andes to the winery's lush valley, with its neat rows of vines and poplar-lined country roads, and an estuary that draws a rich assortment of bird life. The current lodging facility is a precursor to what will eventually be a full-service tourism destination, with a boutique hotel to open in 2012, and it must be made clear that the current property might feel to some visitors like the winery's guesthouse rather than a proper hotel. Still, it's difficult to imagine a more awe-inspiring setting, and the lodge is a haven of minimalist Scandinavian design encouraged by the winery's Norwegian owner. The room that you'll want to book is the principal suite; its floor-to-ceiling panoramic window frames the breathtaking view and encourages you to stay put in your room. The other three rooms are standard doubles that are on the smallish side. There are two large outdoor decks, and an indoor kitchen and dining area for homemade meals.

Road to Millahue s/n. ✆ **2/248-2218.** www.vik.cl. 4 units. $450 per person suite; $350 double; prices include meals, wine, mountain biking, horseback riding, and a private vineyard tour. AE, DC, MC, V. **Amenities:** Restaurant; bikes. *In room:* A/C, hair dryer, minibar, free Wi-Fi.

Colchagua Valley

The Colchagua Valley has been compared by many to Napa Valley in California, and it is home to many of Chile's top red wines and the most developed tourism infrastructure. Colchagua's hot climate is due to the steep hills surrounding both sides of the valley that extend from the Pacific Coast east to the Andes. These hills block the cool breezes entering from the Pacific, trapping the daytime heat, and making Colchagua a paradise for "big" red wines, and, in particular, carmenère, a variety that needs a lot of heat and sun to mature correctly. Syrah, cabernet, and malbec have also found their home in the valley. All these grape varieties express themselves quite differently than in other valleys, with ripe flavors, high alcohol levels (here they can top 15 degrees), and tannins with a firm, silky feel that is almost like chocolate candy. However, beyond Santa Cruz, vintners like Montes are now exploring cooler areas to the west near the coast in Lolol and Marchihue, and trying new plantings such as pinot noir.

GETTING THERE
BY BUS   **Pullman Sur** (✆ 2/776-2426) leaves from the **Estación Alameda** (Metro: Universidad de Santiago), every hour for Santa Cruz until 6:45pm, for C$4,000 one-way.

BY CAR Leaving Santiago, take the Pan-American Highway (Rte. 5) and drive south toward San Fernando for 142km (88 miles). There is one C$2,200 toll on Rte. 5 along the way. Pass the first exit for San Fernando and exit on the road to Pichilemu, or the "Carretera del Vino," (Wine Hwy.). Pay a C$300 toll and continue toward Santa Cruz for 37km (23 miles).

BY PLANE The Ruta del Vino (© 72/823199; www.rutadelvino.cl) works with **ChileAereo** and **AirAdventure** to provide 1-day wine tours to the Colchagua Valley via a small private plane leaving from Santiago's Tobalaba Aerodrome. The tour leaves at either 8:30am or 2:30pm (contact the Ruta directly for a custom tour or full-day tour), and includes hotel-aerodrome transfers, flights (less than an hour each way), and a 3-hour wine tour with a bilingual guide to two wineries of your choice. The cost ranges from C$727,500 for one person to C$202,500 per person for a group of four (maximum five guests).

TOURING THE WINERIES

Casa Lapostolle (Clos Apalta) ★★★ 🄾 Few wineries in Chile have been talked about more than the Clos Apalta facility, and rightfully so. It took Casa Lapostolle, the parent of this icon wine, 4 years to blast tons of granite bedrock on a sloping hillside in order to build a $10-million, six-story, gravity-flow winery that descends deep underground. Spanning five levels, the winery is entirely gravity-fed. Three levels have been chiseled from the granite hillside to create a naturally cool environment for cellaring and ageing. The winery's spiral staircase, reminiscent of the Guggenheim in New York, was made to resemble wine swirling in a glass. The pundits have certainly made their opinions clear; Clos Apalta consistently ranks 93 to 95 points in *Wine Spectator* and is considered one of the top wines made in Chile today (in 2008 *Wine Spectator* elected Clos Apalta 2005 its Wine of the Year).

Clos Apalta is a highlight on any wine connoisseur's tour. Basic tours cost a very steep C$20,000 (minimum four people) and private tours cost C$35,000 per person, and include tastings of Clos Apalta and other lines of the Casa Lapostolle brand. For a splurge, enjoy a gourmet lunch on their terrace along with the tour for C$40,000 per person with Cuvée Alexander wine, or C$60,000 per person with Clos Apalta wine. The Clos Apalta lodge (p.174), located at the winery, has four *casitas* designed in harmony with the winery.

Hijuela Villa Eloisa, Camino San Fernando a Pichilemu, Km 36. © **9/533-60100.** www.casalapostolle. cl. Reservations required. Tours daily at 10am, noon, and 3:30pm. On the road to Santa Cruz from San Fernando, turn right just after the Casa Lapostolle winery at the sign for the Apalta valley.

Casa Silva ★★★ Casa Silva wines are known for their excellent price-quality ratio and consistency. Originally founded and planted by the Frenchman Emilio Bouchon in 1892, this winery has some of the oldest vines in Colchagua. The Silva family grew bulk wines until the 1990s, when the family son Mario Pablo Silva had an idea to revolutionize the winery to focus on fine bottled wines. The winery's vineyards are dispersed around the Colchagua Valley, but it is here in Los Lingues that the Silva family established its beautiful wine-tasting facilities and idyllic B&B and restaurant (see "Where to Stay" below) that sport whitewashed adobe walls, red-tiled roofs, and old-world ceramic patterned floors. Hour-long tours to visit the winery's lovely facilities, including the bodega and winemaking area, cost C$16,000 and include a tasting of three wines, or you may skip the tour and simply taste wine for C$3,000 for reserva, C$4,000 for premium, or C$10,000 for an icon wine. Guests lodging at the Casa Silva hotel receive a free tour and tasting.

Wine Tasting in the Colchagua Valley

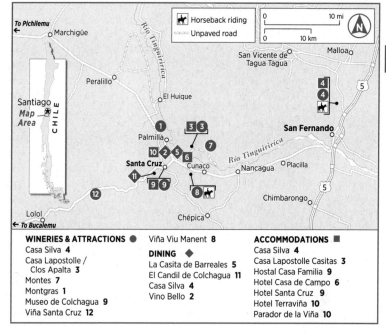

WINERIES & ATTRACTIONS ●
Casa Silva **4**
Casa Lapostolle / Clos Apalta **3**
Montes **7**
Montgras **1**
Museo de Colchagua **9**
Viña Santa Cruz **12**

Viña Viu Manent **8**

DINING ◆
La Casita de Barreales **5**
El Candil de Colchagua **11**
Casa Silva **4**
Vino Bello **2**

ACCOMMODATIONS ■
Casa Silva **4**
Casa Lapostolle Casitas **3**
Hostal Casa Familia **9**
Hotel Casa de Campo **6**
Hotel Santa Cruz **9**
Hotel Terraviña **10**
Parador de la Viña **10**

Hijuela Norte, Casilla 97, San Fernando. © **72/710180.** www.casasilva.cl. Reservations required. Tours daily at 10:30 and 11:30am, 12:30, 3, and 4pm.

Montes ★★　Montes is a true Chilean winery success story. A little more than 20 years ago four partners with little capital and a big dream set out to make premium wines, something unheard of at the time in this country. Today it is one of the best-known premium wines outside of Chile. Montes struck gold here in the Apalta micro-valley, benefiting from an ideal climate and soil that bestowed the winery with spectacular reds—particularly their Montes "M," Folly, and the cultish Purple Angel, a carmenère–petit verdot blend. The Apalta valley is more temperate than the rest of the Colchagua valley and produces cabernet sauvignon, syrah, merlot, carmenère, petit verdot, cabernet franc, and mourvèdre. The tour here is one of the most informative and entertaining, leading visitors through the winery's gravity-flow facilities, followed by a tractor ride through the sloping vineyards to an observation deck with a panoramic view, and finally back in the tasting room to try four different wines, including the Alpha (C$12,000). Montes has a botanical trail to a lookout point with sweeping views, which will appeal to visitors who need a little vigorous exercise. Visitors short on time or not looking to invest an hour and a half in a tour can try Montes' wine with a quick lunch in their new Cafe Alfredo.

La Finca de Apalta, Parcela 15, Apalta. © **72/817815.** www.monteswines.com. Reservations recommended. Tours daily at 10:30am, noon, 3, and 5pm.

MontGras ★　MontGras wines, while decent, pale alongside those of Montes or Casa Lapostolle, however the winery's tours are so welcoming, and they offer more than just the same old barrel-and-bodega tour that most wineries adhere to. Perhaps the most enjoyable thing on offer here is the "Make Your Own" activity that gives budding oenophiles a chance to blend, bottle, and cork their own wine, with the help of experts (C$20,000). From February to March, visitors may participate for 2 hours in the yearly harvest, picking grapes and learning firsthand about wine production (C$20,000), or take a tour and then take a horseback ride for 1½ hours (C$25,000 per person for groups of two to six), or rent a mountain bike (C$20,000 for unlimited hours). Reservations are not necessary for tastings and basic tours (see hours below), but 24-hour notice is necessary for horseback rides, and harvest and wine-blending activities.

Camino Isla de Yáquil s/n, Palmilla. ⓒ 72/822845. www.montgras.cl. Tours Mon–Fri 10:30am, 12:30, 3, 4, and 6pm, Sat–Sun 10:30am, 12:30, 3:30, and 4:30pm.

Viña Santa Cruz ☺   Sprawled across a valley on the edge of the picturesque village Lolol, this Disneyland-esque winery is one of the most curious wineries in the world: It's a mock indigenous village, observatory, and museum all wrapped up into one. Launched in 2006 by local entrepreneur and one-man promoter of Santa Cruz, Carlos Cardoen, the Viña Santa Cruz focuses less on wine than most vineyards, to the chagrin of wine enthusiasts but to the relief of young families. The tour begins with a cable car ride—or as they like to call it, the "time machine"—that transports visitors to a hilltop to tour reproductions of the typical houses of the Mapuche, Aymara, and Rapa Nui indigenous groups of Chile. (Do not visit this winery after the Colchagua Museum to avoid artifact overkill.) Later, the guide herds the group through the gift shop, and then for a brief tasting. The winery's small observatory boasts the most powerful telescope in private hands in Chile; and, on Friday and Saturday nights, Viña Santa Cruz offers a highly recommended "tour through the cosmos," which allows visitors to star-gaze through the winery's high-powered telescopes.

Fundo El Peral s/n. ⓒ 72/941090. www.vinasantacruz.cl. Reservations required for observatory tour only. Tours daily 10am–6pm; observatory tours begin at 9:30pm. From Santa Cruz, take Rte. 72 southwest toward Lolol to Km 25.

Viña Viu Manent ★★   Viu Manent was one of the first wineries to see the potential in wine tourism, and they still offer visitors one of the most enjoyable experiences. Viu Manent was founded more than 70 years ago, and their house specialty is malbec, a wine normally associated with Argentina. In fact, their *gran reserva* wines are perennial favorites, and their lauded Viu 1 wine is Chile's only malbec icon wine. You can just drop in for a tasting, or take a 1-hour tour through the vineyard on a horse-drawn carriage, stopping at the winemaking facility to try wine straight from the barrel, or you may rent one of their bicycles for a spin through the vineyards, finishing off with lunch. Horseback rides and riding lessons are available through their on-site equestrian club for C$20,000 per person (24-hour advance reservation required). A basic tour with carriage ride costs C$14,000 with a tasting of four to five wines, or C$7,000 for a simple tasting of seven wines without the tour. *Note:* At press time, Viu Manent's principal wine-tasting facility and restaurant had just reopened after finishing repairs on its main building following major damage from the 2010 earthquake. The winery also has a tasting room inside their restaurant La Llaveria, next to their cafe (see "Where to Dine" below).

Road to Santa Cruz, Cunaco. ⓒ 72/858350. www.viumanent.cl. Tours 10:30am, noon, 3, and 4:30pm.

HISTORICAL ATTRACTIONS
Museo de Colchagua ★★★ ☺   Arguably the best museum in Chile for its scope and attractive design, you'll be flabbergasted when you consider that this is the

collection of one man, Carlos Cardoen, who also owns the Hotel Santa Cruz and the Viña Santa Cruz. Cardoen is a controversial figure wanted by the FBI for arms trading, and to bide his time while he's prohibited from leaving Chile, he's launched a mind-boggling spending spree that has doubled the size of this museum over the past 5 years. Wander the halls and admire exhibits that include paleontology, pre-Columbian artifacts from all of Latin America, colonial household items, indigenous clothing, and colorful *huaso* ponchos. The Pavilion of Arms presents the country's finest and broadest collection of weapons, which span the pre-Columbian epoch through to World War II and includes arms used by the Third Reich. The Jewels from the Andes collection is a dazzling display of Maya, Olmec, Aztec, and Inca jewels. Step outside to view the collection of carriages—the 1800s funeral carriage is simply astonishing—as well as farm machinery. This is a don't-miss attraction that should be given 1 to 2 hours to explore. Audio guides are available in Spanish and English at an additional cost of C$2,138.

Av. Errazuriz 145. © **72/821050.** www.museocolchagua.cl. Admission C$4,000. Daily 10am–6pm.

OUTDOOR ACTIVITIES

BIKING   **MontGras** (p. 175) has bicycle rentals that include a helmet, bottle of water, tour of the winery, and insurance for C$20,000 per person (unlimited hours).

HIKING   **Montes** (p. 175) offers a botanical trail with more than 100 species of native flora for hiking, with guided tours leaving at 9am every day, and lasting about 4 hours total. Plan this hike with a tasting upon your return—you've earned it.

HORSEBACK RIDING   **Viña Viu Manent** (© **72/858350;** www.viumanent.cl) boasts a certified equestrian club, and they offer a 1½-hour horseback ride around their vineyards in Peralillo for C$20,000 per person, with professional riding guides who are members of the club. Rides must be booked at least 24 hours in advance.

   MontGras (p. 175) has horseback rides through their vineyards and up to a ridge with a vantage point boasting sweeping views for C$25,000 per person, based on a group of two to six people.

WHERE TO STAY
Expensive

Casa Lapostolle Casitas ★★★ 📷   Built by Alexandra Marnier Lapostolle, of the family responsible for Grand Marnier liquor, the Casa Lapostolle is the Colchagua Valley's most luxurious and exclusive lodging option. It's hard to imagine a more bucolic, peaceful surrounding than Clos Apalta's four *casitas*, which are small individual units nestled on a hillside near their winery. The casitas are elegantly appointed and modern in decor, with lots of dark wood, white and ecru-colored fabrics, freshly cut flowers, plush bathrooms, and wooden decks that afford truly magnificent, wide-open views of the Apalta Valley. Prices include meals served at the property's "guesthouse" nearby, where there is an infinity pool and lounge spaces; also included are horseback rides, wine tours, and a bottle of their superb Clos Apalta wine. Come for romance and indulgence.

Hijuela Villa Eloisa, Camino San Fernando a Pichilemu, Km 36. © **72/953360.** www.lapostolle.com. $500 per person, double occupancy first night, $400 per person thereafter; includes breakfast, lunch, dinner, and wine, bike rental. AE, MC, V. **Amenities:** Gourmet restaurant; bikes; outdoor pool; room service. *In room:* Minibar, free Wi-Fi.

Casa Silva ★★★ 🛏   This enchanting B&B is a wistful paradigm of French country chic. The Silva family left the infrastructure of this old hacienda as is and spruced up its interiors with restrained elegance, leaning heavily on the white, distressed-paint wood look with all of its beams, pillars, and furniture, and outfitting the interiors with crystal chandeliers, four-poster beds, oriental carpets, and overstuffed couches. Guest rooms are spacious and homely without sacrificing style or flair. They are each decked out in a different color, such as lime, ruby, or with gingham-check wallpaper. Room 4 is particularly well conserved and features high ceilings. Considering its location, this B&B is more suitable for visitors with a rental car, as it is a 30-minute drive to Santa Cruz and not within walking distance to anything. Also, their **Casa Silva Restaurant** (see "Where to Dine" below) has moved 1km (⅔ mile) from the hotel to the polo field, but the hotel will order a taxi for visitors without transportation. Guests of the hotel receive a courtesy tour of the winery with a tasting of three reserve wines. There is an outdoor pool, too.

Rte. 5, Km 128. ✆ **72/913091.** www.casasilva.cl. 7 units. $260 double, $295 king deluxe. AE, DC, MC, V. **Amenities:** Restaurant; outdoor pool. *In room:* Cable TV, hair dryer, minibar, free Wi-Fi.

Hotel Santa Cruz ★ ☺ This hotel's handy setting on the main plaza is convenient, but the hotel itself has grown too big, losing its charm in the process. There are now more than 110 rooms and endless meeting space, but then some travelers will enjoy the hotel's surplus of services that include a good-value spa, casino, two restaurants, a swim-up bar, gift shops, and a museum. The hotel has the look of a colonial villa, with terracotta tiles, peach-colored walls, and lots of wrought iron and heavy doors. Guest rooms are decorated in a country style and are well kept and comfortable, but the rooms and bathrooms, especially in the older wing, are really too small for the asking price. The hotel's location means you can walk anywhere around Santa Cruz, and enjoy the rhythm of the town plaza in the afternoon. Also, the Colchagua Wine Route is next-door and convenient if you've arrived without a vehicle, and the hotel has an on-site tour agency that can plan any kind of wine tour or activity in the area.

The hotel's **Restaurante Los Varietales** serves mostly Chilean fare, with a few international dishes, and it's undoubtedly one of the most popular restaurants in town; guests lodging at the hotel are treated to a huge breakfast spread in the morning that's included in the price. It's open daily from 1 to 4pm and 8pm to midnight.

Plaza de Armas 286, Santa Cruz. ✆/fax **72/821010.** www.hotelsantacruzplaza.cl. 113 units. $330 double, $380 junior suite. Rates include breakfast. AE, DC, MC, V. **Amenities:** Restaurant; babysitting; outdoor pool; spa. *In room:* A/C, cable TV, minibar, free Wi-Fi.

Moderate

Hotel Casa de Campo ★★ Sitting alongside the busy main road just before arriving to Santa Cruz, this idyllic little hotel is actually quite serene given that rooms are set back behind tall trees and a babbling creek, and face out overlooking a bucolic pastoral landscape. The colonial style of the hotel has whitewashed walls, rough wood beams, terracotta roof tiles and lots of potted flowers, and there is a swimming pool and lush gardens with a bubbling fountain. The guest rooms are some of the best in Colchagua for their ample size and rural-style yet smart furnishings; they come with picture windows and plush beds, and they all have small terraces. The friendly family that runs the hotel has added environmentally friendly aspects such as using recycled materials in the construction of the building and solar panels for heating.

Fundo Santa María de Viego no. 2, Santa Cruz. ✆/fax **72/823-5400.** www.hotelcasadecampo.cl. 11 units. $149–$175 double. AE, DC, MC, V. **Amenities:** Cafe; outdoor pool. *In room:* Cable TV, hair dryer, minibar, free Wi-Fi.

Hotel Terraviña ★ 🎁   Blending seamlessly with the vineyards that surround it, this new midlevel lodge is a great value. All rooms are tastefully decorated with contemporary style and wooden armoires and higher-end amenities, and each room has a small balcony facing out onto the boutique vineyard next door. Bathrooms are compact but tidy, with colorful tiles. There's a nice pool in the garden and a huge swath of lawn, and one of the best breakfasts in Chile is offered. The inn is close to town but it would be a good long walk to get there. The hotel is run by a Danish-Chilean couple who are more than happy to help you sort out wine tour options.

Camino Los Boldos s/n, Barreales, Santa Cruz. ℂ **72/824696.** www.terravina.cl. 18 doubles, 1 suite. $140 double; $250 master suite. **Amenities:** Restaurant; outdoor pool. *In room:* A/C, TV.

Parador de la Viña ★   The Parador de la Viña, located across the road from the Terra Viña about a 5-minute drive from town, is reasonably priced but doesn't skimp on service or quality. The hotel is within a converted adobe hacienda built in 1930. Most rooms are on the small side, but they're clean and fresh, with floral bedspreads and whitewashed walls. The best room here is the "suite," a large double with views of the vineyard, and it is the same price as a regular double so be sure to request it. It's pricier than the Hostal Casa Familia, but the Parador de la Viña has a quiet, natural ambience surrounded by vineyards, grassy areas for kids, and a swimming pool, and a free minibar with soft drinks and wine.

Camino Los Boldos s/n. ℂ **72/825788.** www.paradordelavina.cl. 6 units. $95 double. AE, DC, MC, V. **Amenities:** Cafeteria; outdoor pool. *In room:* TV, hair dryer, minibar, no phone, free Wi-Fi.

Inexpensive

Hostal Casa Familia ★★ ✦   Budget travelers will adore this pretty little hostel, which has been recently renovated with such care that one would now lean toward calling it a B&B rather than a hostel. Located in a converted home just 4 blocks from the plaza and in a residential area, the Casa Familia is fresh and clean, and guest rooms have decorative painting, antique armoires and lamps, and embroidered bedspreads. Some rooms have terraces and there is one more spacious junior suite. As the name states, the Casa Familia is a family-run operation and the mostly Spanish-speaking staff provides a welcoming ambience and help with transportation and tours.

Los Pidenes 421. ℂ **72/825766.** www.hostalcasafamilia.cl. 10 units. $76 double; $114 junior suite. No credit cards. **Amenities:** Breakfast cafe. *In room:* Cable TV, hair dryer, no phone, free Wi-Fi.

WHERE TO DINE

In addition to the restaurants listed below, the **Hotel Santa Cruz** has a restaurant specializing in *criollo* cuisine (hearty, *campestrale*, or country style, dishes) served in a colonial-style dining area (see "Where to Stay" above). Along the road to Santa Cruz at Km 31.5, between Nancagua and Santa Cruz, the **Casa Valdés** (ℂ **72/858757**) has delicious empanadas and a specialty food store that is ideal for picking up picnic supplies and other regional gourmet foods to bring back home.

Casa Silva ★★★ CHILEAN GRILL 📷   Heavy earthquake damage to the Casa Silva's original restaurant had one positive outcome: the winery elected to relocate from a windowless barrel room to their clubhouse in the middle of the leafy vineyard, a whitewashed building with outdoor terrace seating and views of a lush, emerald polo field. At this new location, diners often are treated to a game of polo or equestrian training and jumping, which only adds to the already gorgeous sylvan setting. Casa Silva's restaurant serves simple but gourmet-quality cuisine, with grilled Angus and Kobe beef, grilled fish, sandwiches, soups such as a rich clam chowder, and tapas. The interior setting, like the winery's hotel, is rustic chic with weathered white

Wine, Spas & Rural Tradition

furniture and polo-themed decor. To get here, enter at the winery's gift shop area and drive through the vineyard to the end of the road.

Ruta 5, Km 128, near entrance to San Fernando, Colchagua. ✆ **72/710180.** www.casasilva.cl. Reservations recommended on weekends. Main courses C$6,800–C$16,800. AE, DC, MC, V. Mon–Thurs 12:30–3:30pm and 7:30–9:30pm, Fri–Sat 12:30–3:30pm and 7:30–11:30pm, and Sun 12:30–3:30pm.

El Candil de Colchagua ★ SPANISH/STEAK   True to the Colchagua Valley's *campestrale* roots, El Candil serves thick cuts of barbecued meats and sports a country-style feel with clunky wooden tables and chairs and cowhide decor. The restaurant also features more sophisticated fare with meat and seafood dressed in *jerez* and *vizcaina* sauces and prepared with other Spanish and Basque touches; there's a vegetarian lasagna for non carnivores. El Candil also has a lengthy tapas menu ideal for sharing along with a good bottle of wine; tapas include broiled oysters, Spanish omelets, abalone chowder, cured meats, empanadas, and even lamb testicles. The restaurant has more than 120 wines from the Colchagua Valley.

La Lajuela, Km 4, Santa Cruz, Colchagua. ✆ **9/395-1576.** www.elcandildecolchagua.cl. Reservations recommended on weekends. Main courses C$4,500–C$9,200. AE, DC, MC, V. Tues–Sat 12:30–4pm and 7pm–midnight, Sun 12:30–4pm.

La Casita de Barreales ★ PERUVIAN   La Casita is regarded as one of the best Peruvian restaurants in the Central Valley, owned by a Chilean but with a kitchen staffed by Peruvians. Skip the dusty barnlike smoking section and opt for the cozier interior area with whitewashed stucco walls and candlelit tables. The menu is quite extensive and offers traditional Peruvian fare such as *lomo saltado* (beef tenderloin with fried potatoes and tomatoes) and *ají de gallina* (stewed creamy chicken with rice), and outstanding *ceviches,* from which there are several types to choose. On the downside, dishes come out of the kitchen too quickly, even though service can be inattentive and slow.

Camino Barreales s/n, Santa Cruz, Colchagua. ✆ **72/824468.** www.lacasitadebarreales.com. Reservations recommended on weekends. Main courses C$5,400–C$7,600. AE, DC, MC, V. Tues–Sat noon–4pm and 7-11pm.

Vino Bello ★★ ITALIAN   Located just on the edge of town in a converted hacienda-style colonial building, Vino Bello has a splendid sunny patio with large white sunshades and looks out onto the vines of neighboring Laura Hartwig winery. The restaurant specializes in gourmet, homemade Italian fare with fresh pastas and stone-oven baked pizzas, and heartier dishes such as stewed beef ribs with polenta and roasted osso buco with gnocchi. Appetizers are limited to a list of antipasti platters, but there are green salads, too. The lasagna, cannelloni, and blood sausage ravioli with shrimp are rich and flavorful. Waiters here are friendlier than normally found at most Chilean restaurants, and this, coupled with the restaurant's antique decor and bright outdoor dining, causes diners to linger long after lunch and soak up the relaxing surroundings.

Barreales s/n, Santa Cruz, Valle de Colchagua. ✆ **72/822755.** www.vinobello.cl. Reservations recommended on weekends. Main courses C$4,400–C$10,500; pizzas C$4,900–C$6,900. AE, DC, MC, V. Mon–Sat 11:30am–3pm and 7:30–11:30pm, Sun 11am–4pm.

Maule Valley

Along with the northern Limarí Valley, the Maule Valley is striving to establish itself as a wine tourism destination but is still one of the least-visited, principally due to its distance nearly 300km (185 miles) south of Santiago and long distances between wineries within the valley itself. Carmenère is an important grape here but lately the

Carignan grape, previously considered a second-rate variety, has established itself and is used frequently in blends.

VIA Wines ★★ The winery is known for its Oveja Negra (Black Sheep) varietal, a cheap and cheery wine with a cheeky name, and they offer a fun way to experience a wine tour with a "make your own" activity that allows amateur visitors to blend their own variety. An expert begins with a tasting of four reds used in the blend, along with an informative look into the winemaking process and discussion of things to consider before crafting your own wine, which you'll take with you when finished with your own label (C$14,500 per person). You might also opt for a food and wine-pairing course, and follow it up with a picnic on the winery's truly lovely grounds, or take a spin on a bicycle or via horseback like one of the valley's local cowboys.

Fundo la Esperanza s/n, San Rafael. © **71/415500.** www.viawines.com. Reservations necessary. Tours available daily.

Viña Balduzzi ★ The Balduzzi winery's history stretches back to the 19th century with Albano Balduzzi, an Italian immigrant and descendent of 2 centuries of winemakers, who established his winery here in the Maule Valley and the turn of the last century, eventually passing the tradition down through three generations. Great-grandson Jorge Balduzzi is at the helm today, producing Carmenère and Cabernet Sauvignon reserve wines of note, and inviting visitors to tour the winery's centenary park full of stately oaks and monkey puzzle trees, and its colonial-style winemaking facility via a traditional tour or a more technical tour with a winemaker (C$4,750 for regular tours, C$17,575 for the technical tour with premium wines). Balduzzi offers an adventurous overflight tour of the winery and the Maule Valley with a local air charter company for C$136,325 per hour (3 people maximum) and traditional Chilean barbecues for groups of 10 or more. The winery is one of the few in the region that does not require reservations for basic tours and tastings.

Ave. Balmaceda 1189, San Javier. © **73/322128.** www.balduzziwines.com. Reservations not necessary for basic tours. Tours available Mon–Sat 9am–6pm.

Viña Gillmore ★★ Located in the Loncomilla Valley, this family-run winery offers an enjoyable experience that goes beyond the average wine tour, and it's a good detour for a break when heading south. The winery, known for boutique red wines, offers standard tours and tastings, and they even offer longer programs for amateur winemakers who are more serious about understanding the winemaking process. A small museum and a zoolike collection of regional animals (including pumas and a *pudú*, or miniature deer) are all part of the property. If you'd like to unwind, spend a night at the winery's **Tabonko Hotel & Spa,** take a mountain bike ride or a nature walk, and indulge in a wine bath or another grape-based body treatment, the lodge's specialty. The lodge's seven rooms are elegantly appointed and contrast with the rather whimsical architecture—the building was constructed using recycled materials such as old fermentation tanks.

Camino a Constitución Km 20, San Javier. © **73/197-5539.** www.gillmore.cl and www.tabonko.cl. 15 units. Reserved required at least 2 days in advance. $180 double. AE, DC, MC, V.

SKI RESORTS IN THE CENTRAL ANDEAN REGION

It's no longer just a summer getaway for skiing fanatics in search of the endless winter—increasingly even recreational skiers are packing their gear during July and

August to head to the Andes. The allure? Andean skiing delivers a combination of world-class terrain, glorious weather, and an exotic journey that is without peer. The novelty of skiing from June to October does have some cachet, but skiers have also discovered that the Andean terrain has everything from easy groomers to spine-tingling steeps, and with so few people on the slopes here, that powder lasts for days, not hours. There are few lift lines, and passes are generally 50% cheaper than ski resorts in the U.S., Canada, or Europe. The ambience is relaxed and conducive to making friends and waking up late. For families, the kids are on vacation, and most resorts offer reduced rates or free stays for kids under 12. Beware, however, that during the school holidays in July, prices can soar by as much as 80% and resorts are overrun with young kids.

The major resorts in Chile are top-notch operations with modern equipment and facilities. Resorts centered on the Farellones area, such as Valle Nevado, La Parva, and El Colorado, can be reached in a 1- to 1½-hour drive from Santiago or the airport, and can be visited for the day. At a little over 2 hours from Santiago, the classic resort Portillo is a bit far for the day; instead most visitors book 7-night all-inclusive stays. Termas de Chillán is a short flight and a 1½-hour transfer shuttle south of Santiago, or a 4½-hour train ride followed by a 1-hour transfer; this resort offers tree skiing, a casino, and an extensive spa. Looking for wild adventure? Check out the box "Backcountry Bliss" on p. 185 for ideas about out-of-the-ordinary ski and snowboard adventures.

GETTING TO THE RESORTS   Portillo organizes transfers through its own company, Portillo Tours & Travel, when you reserve. If you've booked a reservation for any resort through a U.S.-based tour operator (see chapter 5), they'll book your transportation for you. You do not need to rent a vehicle if you are planning to spend the night at any of the resorts listed in this chapter. **Ski Total** (*©* **2/246-0156;** www.skitotal. cl) has daily transfer shuttles to El Colorado, La Parva, and Valle Nevado for C$8,550 round-trip per person. The shuttles leave at 8am from their offices at Av. Apoquindo 4900, no. 42 (in the Omnium shopping mall in Las Condes, or at the Mall Sport parking area at Av. Las Condes 13500—there's no Metro station nearby, so take a taxi), and no reservation is required. Round-trip transportation with hotel pickup costs C$15,675 per person, and requires a reservation made 24 hours in advance; pickup time for this service is between 7am and 7:30am. All return shuttles leave from the resorts at 5pm. Transfer shuttles to Portillo are C$15,675 and leave from the Omnium office, or there is a 7am hotel pickup to Portillo for C$22,800 per person for one of their 8:30am shuttles (round-trip same day).

Ski Portillo

Internationally famous, Portillo is South America's oldest resort and one of the more singular ski destinations in the world. The resort is set high in the Andes on the shore of Lake Inca, a little more than 2 hours from Santiago and near the Argentine border. Unlike most ski resorts, there is no town at Portillo, just one sunflower-yellow lodge and two more economical annexes. Although open to the public for day skiing (call ahead—they're open to the general public only when conditions are optimal), Portillo really operates as a Saturday-to-Saturday, all-inclusive resort. The ski area is smaller than Valle Nevado and Termas de Chillán; however, Portillo is known for its steep terrain. Portillo is billed as a "boutique resort" with a maximum of 450 people, giving visitors the sensation of skiing in their own private resort. Indeed, camaraderie can grow over the course of the week as it would at a summer camp.

Portillo is not for everyone, specifically groups with a member who does not ski. There is also not a lot of terrain here suitable for intermediates, and when conditions are not optimal there isn't anywhere to go but the lodge. The grand yet rustic hotel forgoes glitz for a more relaxed atmosphere encouraged by its American owners. Rooms are on the small side but comfortable; the best rooms are the suites and sixth-floor doubles because they come with balconies and larger bathrooms. The Octagon annex has rooms with four bunks and a private bathroom; the Inca annex is for backpackers and has Lilliputian rooms with four bunks and a common bathroom. The Octagon and the Inca annexes offer a special price for only three people per room; otherwise, if you're less than four, you might share with strangers. The main dining area features hearty staples and is for hotel and Octagon guests only; Inca guests dine in the cafeteria or at the mountainside restaurant or snack bar on the slopes. Portillo loves a party, and on some nights the fiesta really cranks up with live music in the hotel bar, a thumping disco, and an off-site *cantina*.

There are 14 lifts, including 5 chairs, 5 Poma lifts, and 4 "slingshot" lifts that tow skiers to the top of vertiginous chutes. Heliskiing costs C$147,250 per person for the first run, and C$80,750 for the second run, based on four guests.

WHERE TO STAY Hotel Portillo's 7-day packages include lodging, lift tickets, four meals per day, and use of all facilities. Per person rates are: $1,850 to $3,500 double with a lake view; $2,400 to $5,200 for suites; $1,450 to $2,590 for family apartments (minimum four people). Children under 4 stay free, kids 4 to 11 pay half-price, and kids 12 to 17 pay about 25% less than adults.

For more information or to make reservations, contact the resort's office at Renato Sánchez 4270 in Santiago (℃ **2/263-0606;** fax 2/263-0595; www.skiportillo.com), or call the toll-free lines at ℃ **800/829-5325** in the U.S., or 800/514-2579 in Canada. Lift tickets cost C$21,500 to C$35,000 for adults, and C$16,000 to C$20,000 for children 5 to 12. Amenities at the resort include an outdoor heated pool, fitness center, sauna, child-care center, salon, massage, a full-court gym, disco, cybercafe, and theater.

Valle Nevado

Valle Nevado sits high above Santiago, near El Colorado and La Parva resorts, surrounded by jaw-dropping Andean views, and it is the only resort in the Three Valleys area that offers a full-service tourism infrastructure. The resort complex is not a town, but there are clothing, gear, and souvenir shops, seven restaurants, bars, a disco, and a full-service spa, making Valle a good destination for nonskiing guests accompanying their family or friends. The French-designed resort is Chile's answer to Les Arcs, with three hotels and five condo buildings that straddle a ridge. The entire complex was renovated in 2009, including guest rooms and public spaces, and today offers the most contemporary and upscale accommodations of any resort in Chile. The wallet-friendly Hotel Tres Puntas is a perfectly comfortable lodging option, but quads are tight. The Hotel Puerta del Sol has connecting rooms and other family-friendly setups, but for not much more money you can upgrade to the deluxe Hotel Valle Nevado. Valle also boasts the most modern lift system, and will install a gondola in late 2011, all part of a major development plan that will eventually cause it to develop into a minivillage by 2022. The terrain is large enough to entertain skiers for days, and they can purchase an interconnect ticket for an additional cost and traverse over to La Parva and El Colorado, for nearly 7,000 acres. The steeper runs are at Portillo, yet Valle is larger and the runs longer, and there's more variety with the interconnect pass.

Of all the resorts in Chile, Valle is the most snowboard-friendly, offering a terrain park, and there is a lot of intermediate and advanced off-*piste* terrain here, whereas most off-*piste* terrain at Portillo is for advanced skiers only.

Valle Nevado has a more Chilean feel since many Santiaguinos visit Valle Nevado on weekends—note that traffic up the hill on Saturdays and Sundays is one-way up from 9am to 3pm, and one-way down from 3pm to 8pm. Saturdays and Sundays can bring more crowded slopes in the morning, but everyone calls it a day after lunch and the runs in the afternoon are gloriously people-free. Weekdays are also devoid of many people and the lift wait is never more than 1 minute.

There are 12 lifts, including 5 chairs, and 8 surface lifts. Heliskiing here is considered the best of any operation in Chile, and costs C$90,250 to C$498,750 depending on the amount of runs and the quality of terrain, and is based on four guests.

WHERE TO STAY   Valle Nevado offers all-inclusive packages that include lodging, lift tickets, breakfast, dinner, and après ski (lunch is an additional cost), access to the resort's gym and outdoor pool, daycare for children 3 to 7, ski lockers, and Wi-Fi. Valle Nevado's more economical hotel Tres Puntas has shared rooms but only between private parties, not strangers, and doubles are more akin to a regular hotel room. Prices are per person, double occupancy. Valle Nevado offers Friday-to-Friday weeklong packages with a cheaper per night cost, and slightly more expensive nightly rates for "miniweeks" that run from Friday to Tuesday (4 nights) or Tuesday to Friday (3 nights). The elegant ski-in/ski-out **Hotel Valle Nevado** costs per person, per night, $265 to $484 for a standard double, and $300 to $539 for a suite. Hotel Valle Nevado guests receive more personalized service, take breakfast in the gourmet restaurant La Fourchette, and guests staying 7 nights also receive a free 25-minute massage.

The midrange **Hotel Puerta del Sol,** which is popular with families for its "double-double" connected rooms and "atillo" lofts for four, sells two rates: "north" side rates are more expensive for their terraces than the "south" side rooms, which face over the valley and parking lot but have sunset views and bay windows. The cost per person, per night, is $207 to $392 for a south double and $223 to $421 for a north-facing double.

Hotel Tres Puntas has rooms with either two twins or four-bed bunks; they are great values for their private bathrooms and nicely renovated lounge and restaurant. The hotel is popular with ski bums, younger guests, and families looking to spend less. Note that the four-bed bunk rooms are very tight, however, and better suited for young skiers. Rates are, per person, per night, $175 to $280, double occupancy. In bunk rooms, two guests pay the double rate and the third and fourth pay $105 to $168 per person.

The **Valle de los Cóndores** building has condos for two to six guests (studio apartments for two are not worth it; the hotel rooms are better, and the one- and two-bedroom units are quite attractive). The cost for 7 nights in a two-bedroom unit that can sleep up to six people is $429 to $1,115. The price does not include lift tickets and meals, but these can be purchased separately as a package. The units come with fully equipped kitchens, but you'll need to stop at the Líder supermarket on the way up beforehand to shop; most transportation companies are accustomed to this and can stop and allow guests to shop before heading up to the resort. There is a small kiosk with very limited supplies at Valle Nevado, so you'll need to bring all groceries with you.

For more information or to make reservations, contact the resort's office at Av. Vitacura 5250, no. 304, in Santiago (© **2/477-7700;** fax 2/477-7736; www.valle nevado), or call toll-free © **800/669-0554** in the U.S., or 888/301-3248 in Canada.

backcountry BLISS

Skiing beyond the cordoned-off limits of a commercial resort and into the backcountry is an awesome experience that every skier and snowboarder should try at least once in his or her life (with an experienced guide, of course). Here in Chile, it's just you, the spectacularly rugged Andean Mountains, condors soaring overhead, and lots of virgin powder snow. There are several options for backcountry skiing and snowboarding near Santiago, but you've got to be at least an intermediate/advanced level skier to join in. By far the best heliskiing is at **Valle Nevado** (see above), with more runs and vertical drops than any other resort-based operation in Chile. The resort will often give a 5% discount on heli-runs to skiers lodging in their all-inclusive hotels. **Powderquest** and **Casa Tours** (see p. 70) are two operators that visit multiple resorts, many of them smaller, local resorts, focusing much of the day on backcountry touring with a knowledgeable guide. **Santiago Adventures,** who also manages reservations, transportation, and lodging for Ski Arpa (see contact info below), offers heliski packages that conveniently leave from Santiago and head to the Three Valleys, the Aconcagua Valley, or the Cajon del Maipo. The cost runs from $1,290 to $1,875 per person, based on four people, for three to six runs, and includes lunch and all safety gear.

Ski Arpa (© **802/904-6798** in the U.S.; 2/244-2750 in Santiago; www.ski arpa.com), located just outside San Esteban, about 2 hours north of Santiago and owned by Austrian Toni Sponar, has two Snowcats based at a picturesque mountain refuge at 2,700m (8,825 ft.), which carry skiers up to altitudes as high as 3,750m (12,500 ft.). At the top, Mt. Aconcagua, the highest in the Americas, rises in the near distance. Ski Arpa offers day trips from Santiago, and multiday trips with lodging at the Hotel Inca or Termas de Jahuel (p. 162); the cost for a day trip is $324 per person, based on four people for a total of four runs, and includes roundtrip transportation from Santiago.

Lift tickets cost C$25,000 to C$33,000 for adults, and C$18,000 to C$23,000 for children under 11. Valle Nevado has a full-service spa, gym, outdoor heated pool, a child-care center, a Wii room for kids, room service, a full-court gym, a small cinema, and a shopping gallery with brand-name ski and snowboard equipment.

La Parva

La Parva caters to Santiago's well heeled skiers and snowboarders, many of whom have condos or chalets here. For visiting travelers, La Parva rents mediocre apartments that have not been updated since the 1970s, and there isn't the kind of infrastructure for tourism that you'll find at Valle Nevado. However, on weekends the center seems to take on the feel of a small village, and the ski center offers good off-*piste* skiing conditions and steep inbound terrain. Also, La Parva is closer to Santiago, if you're heading up only for the day.

There are 4 chairs and 10 surface lift runs, such as T-bars, and several on-slope cafes for lunch and a few at the base of the resort, including the fondue-style restaurant **La Marmita de Pericles, El Piuquen Pub** for pizzas, and the **St. Tropez** for breakfast, fine dining, and a bar with excellent pisco sours.

La Parva's condos have kitchens, living areas, and TVs, and the cost varies depending on the season and the amount of rooms; prices for the 2011 season were unavailable at press time, so contact their offices for information. Prices in 2010 were an average of $1,700 to $2,600 for six people, $2,700 to $3,650 for eight people; with maid service an additional $30 per day. You'll need to buy groceries in Santiago. For more information, contact the resort (© **2/431-0420** in Santiago, or 2/220-9530 direct; fax 2/264-1575; www.laparva.cl).

7 | El Colorado & Farellones

Farellones is a sprawl of chalets and small businesses spread across a ridge below the ski area El Colorado, which is quickly growing into a village. El Colorado, and specifically lodging in the Farellones area, is the economical option for skiers and snowboarders in the Three Valleys area; it's also more of a party scene with several restaurants and bars. For kids there is a tubing area, too. The cone-shaped El Colorado has a wide variety of terrain, but a more outdated lift system than Valle Nevado. Still, the resort is home to world-class backcountry runs on Santa Teresita, which deposit skiers at the road to Valle Nevado, so you'll need a rental vehicle or some other form of transportation to get you back to the resort.

El Colorado has 4 chair lifts and 16 surface lifts. At the base (sometimes called Villa Colorado) there is the **El Colorado Apart-Hotel,** a simple but modern and clean condo with two- and three-bedroom units with kitchenettes for $240 to $410 per person, double occupancy, including breakfast and dinner (prices are cheaper with larger groups). For more information, contact the resort (© **2/245-3401;** www. skiandes.cl). In Farellones there are several lodging options, including the **Lodge Andes,** Camino La Capilla 662 (no phone; www.lodgeandes.cl), with private double rooms with shared bathrooms ($126) and shared rooms with four and eight beds, including an all-female dorm for eight with a private bathroom ($63 per person) that includes breakfast and dinner. The Lodge, formally known as the Refugio Aleman, is rustic but recently refurbished, and has beautiful views. The **Posada Farellones,** at the entrance to Farellones (© **2/248-7672;** www.farellones.cl), is a cozy lodge with doubles, triples, and rooms with two bedrooms for $108 to $175 per person (double occupancy, including breakfast and dinner and transport to El Colorado or La Parva). The Posada has a Jacuzzi and satellite TV, a large living area with board games, and a ski locker room.

CHILLÁN & TERMAS DE CHILLÁN RESORT

407km (252 miles) S of Santiago

Chillán is a midsize city located 407km (252 miles) south of Santiago, and it is the gateway to the popular **Termas de Chillán** thermal spa and recreational area, and **Nevados de Chillán,** one of South America's largest and most complete ski resorts. A rustic but tidy city of 145,000, with five spruce plazas and hodgepodge, utilitarian architecture, bustling streets with open storefronts, and street dogs, Chillán looks like any other Chilean city in the Central Valley.

There is really only one reason to stop here when heading south on the Ruta 5 highway, the **Feria de Chillán ★★**, one of the largest and most colorful markets in Chile, where you'll find baskets, *huaso* clothing and saddles, chaps and spurs, pottery, knitwear, blankets, caged birds, and Jurassic size fruit and vegetables. Bargaining is futile unless your Spanish is at the very least proficient. The Feria is located between Maipón, Arturo Prat, 5 de Abril, and Isabel Riquelme streets; across Maipón Street is the food market, with everything from pickled vegetables to dried fruit to Chillán's famous sausages.

Like Farellones, the Nevados de Chillán ski resort has a tiny village, **Las Trancas,** about a 10-minute drive from the resort base. Many choose to stay here rather than up at the resort, given that there are pubs and restaurants, independent lodging in *cabañas,* and inexpensive lodging options that are more flexible with shorter stays.

Essentials

GETTING THERE

BY PLANE   Chillán is served by the **Aeropuerto Carriel Sur** (CCP; ℂ **9/282-9579;** www.carrielsur.cl) in Concepción, about an hour away. There are direct flights here from Santiago several times daily via **LAN** and **Sky** airlines; see the "Airline Websites" section of chapter 15 for phone numbers. If you've made hotel reservations at Termas de Chillán, their transfer service can arrange to pick you up and take you directly there. If not, you must take a taxi to the bus terminal, where buses for Chillán leave every 20 minutes; a taxi costs around C$7,000.

BY BUS   **Línea Sur** (ℂ **2/481-8877**) and **Tur Bus** (ℂ **600/660-6600**) offer daily service from most major cities, including Santiago. The trip from Santiago takes about 5 to 6 hours and costs C$8,400 for a regular seat or C$13,700 for a fully reclining seat. The bus terminal in Chillán is located at Av. O'Higgins 010, and from there you can grab a "RemBus" (ℂ **42/229377**) for the Termas.

BY TRAIN   EFE (Terrasur) offers an enjoyable 4½-hour train journey from Santiago, leaving from the Estación Central, and arriving in Chillán at the station at Calle Brasil (ℂ **600/585-5000;** www.efe.cl). This modern train speeds through scenic orchards and farmland, much of it still tilled by horse, with changing views of the Andes. One-way fares cost C$8,500 to C$9,500 for a *salón* coach, and C$12,000 to C$14,000 for a *"preferente"* coach with reclining seats. There are three to five daily trips, and a dining car with snacks, sandwiches, and beverages.

VISITOR INFORMATION

Sernatur can be found at 18 de Septiembre 455 (ℂ **42/223272**); it's open Monday through Friday from 8:30am to 1:30pm and 3 to 6pm, and closed on weekends.

Where to Stay & Dine

Few foreign visitors spend the night in Chillán (visitors to Termas de Chillán do not stay here and drive up daily), unless they're looking for a place to rest after driving along the Pan-American (Ruta 5) Highway. During the day, great local color and cheap prices can be found in abundance at the **Municipal Market** across the street from the Feria de Chillán, where simple restaurants serve seafood and local dishes, some featuring Chillán's famous sausages. Be forewarned of pushy waitresses who stalk the passageways and practically clobber you over the head and drag you into their restaurant; it can be very entertaining but a little overwhelming. The market is open every day. Cheap, hearty meals and hefty sandwiches are served at the **Fuente Alemana** (ℂ **42/423565**), on the pedestrian walkway next to the Hotel Isabel Riquelme.

Gran Hotel Isabel Riquelme ★★   This hotel sat ignored and unloved for so many years, it was difficult to remember that it was, in its day, a "Gran" hotel. After a rebirth, its bar/restaurant fills with friends chatting over coffee and businessmen shaking hands and smoking cigars, and even the waiters just seem thrilled to be a part of such a lively center in this dreary old town. The lobby gleams, and the common areas are surprisingly stylish, with flagstone walls, ambient lighting, leather and wood furniture, and contemporary art, and the guest rooms are handsome in their shades of chocolate and beige, with floor-to-ceiling drapes and squeaky-clean bathrooms. If you don't stay here, eat here, as their restaurant serves creatively prepared Chilean food, and they have lighter fare and a decent wine list.

Constitución 576, Chillán. ℂ **42/434400.** Fax 42/211541. www.hotelisabelriquelme.cl. 70 units. $146 double; $220 suite. AE, DC, MC, V. **Amenities:** Restaurant; bar; room service. *In room:* Cable TV, free Wi-Fi.

Hotel Paso Nevado ★   If you just need a clean and reasonably priced place to put your head down after long hours on the road, this is a good bet. Country furnishings, comfortable guest rooms, a pleasant outdoor patio for enjoying the continental breakfast (included in the price), and amicable service can be expected. Ask for a discount, as the hotel will often grant one. The hotel is located 3 blocks west of the main plaza.

Libertad 219. ℂ **42/237666.** Fax 42/211541. www.hotelpasonevado.cl. 70 units. $95 double. AE, DC, MC, V. **Amenities:** Cafeteria; bar. *In room:* Cable TV, hair dryer, free Wi-Fi.

Termas de Chillán

The star attraction in the Chillán area is **Termas de Chillán,** a full-season resort hotel and **Nevados de Chillán,** one of Chile's three largest ski resorts, both 80km (50 miles) from the city of Chillán. Foreign visitors principally visit during the winter, but the resort area is open year-round and offers good hiking, biking, and horseback riding opportunities in the summer. Visitors to Chile normally head to Pucón, Puerto Varas, or even Patagonia for those kinds of summer-season activities because they offer more uniquely beautiful landscapes than Chillán, but then again, a deluxe spa and a 5-hour drive from Santiago are appealing factors.

The tiny village Las Trancas, the resort hotel Termas de Chillán, and the ski resort Nevados de Chillán are nestled in a forested valley under the shadow of the 3,212m (10,535-ft.) Chillán Volcano. Unlike ski resorts in the north, this resort has a fair amount of tree skiing. The mountain feels monumental in size and the terrain is more suited to intermediates with trails winding along the volcano's ridge. There is also ample off-*piste* terrain, and chutes and tight canyons due to the volcanic terrain. It can often snow more here than in the north; however, snow conditions change quickly throughout the day given its lower altitude.

Note: Before planning a winter ski trip to Chillán, it is important that visitors are aware of a major dispute taking place in the region that, if it's still happening by the time you read this, will have a profound effect on your experience. Several years ago the hotel Termas de Chillán lost the ski resort concession to a new operator, who changed the name of the ski resort to Nevados de Chillán, and took charge of the resort's base hotel, the ex-Pirigallo, changing its name to the Hotel Nevados. Termas de Chillán has sued, and in the meantime has halted operation of two chair lifts the hotel installed as a private venture, essentially reducing the skier lift capacity and shutting down a portion of the resort. The ski area's facilities are already in sore need of an upgrade and visitors complain intensely about the astronomical prices that local hotels and restaurants charge for third-rate service and facilities. Check the status of the resort before booking here, and keep in mind that both the spa hotel and the ski resort have a tendency to deliberately mislead travelers about the resort's operational status and snow conditions.

The two major hotels here, as mentioned, are the deluxe **Gran Hotel Termas de Chillán** with 120 rooms, and the **Hotel Nevados** with 48 rooms. Closer to Las Trancas is the midrange **Hotel Pirimahuida,** with free—but scheduled—transportation to and from the resort. The Gran Hotel has a full-service spa and indoor/outdoor thermal baths produced by natural geothermal fissures. The spa offers hydrotherapy, aromatherapy, mud baths, and massages, and is open to the general public during the ski season until 2pm, with access to the spa available thereafter to Gran Hotel guests only. Termas also has a new casino, significantly boosting what once was a rather tame nightlife scene.

Weeklong stays at the Gran Hotel include half board, lodging, and access to the thermal pools for $1,400 to $2,300 per person, double occupancy, for a room with a resort view, and do not include lift tickets. The Hotel Nevados de Chillán offers weeklong packages that include lodging, lift tickets, half board, and access to their outdoor thermal pool for $1,340 to $1,800 per person, double occupancy.

The Hotel Pirimahuida is an attractive option for its low cost and proximity to the restaurants and bars in tiny Las Trancas. Rates include lodging and half-board only, not lift tickets, and cost $750 to $1,150 per person, double occupancy. The Pirigallo has an outdoor thermal pool; otherwise, guests must pay extra to use the Gran Hotel's facilities.

You might try one of the **condominium units** at the resort base for four to six guests. A four-person condo costs $1,400 to $1,575 for 1 week, but this does not include meals or lift tickets, although it does include daily maid service. There is a small grocery store (bring specialty items with you from Santiago) in Las Trancas, or you can dine a la carte in the resort's restaurant or buy an additional meal plan. Day lift tickets (2010 rates are shown here) cost C$15,000 for adults and C$10,000 for children.

LODGING OUTSIDE THE RESORT

Before reaching the resort, you'll pass through Las Trancas, a scattering of hotels, *cabañas,* restaurants, gear-rental shops, and other small businesses dependent on tourism. The party is rowdier here than the relatively tame nightlife at the resort, and prices are cheaper than at the resort. None of the 10 or so restaurants is particularly memorable, so you might find renting a cabin with a kitchen a better proposition; but double-check before you rent that there's a dining and living area, or you'll have only a bed to kick back on. Also, hardly any property in Las Trancas has transportation to the resort, so verify this or else you'll be taking the once-a-day bus or be forced to rent a car or hitchhike.

Cabañas and Restaurant Rucahue ★ ☺　Here you'll find comfortable cabins for 2 to 10 people, with kitchens and living areas. The best thing about these cabins is that they are part of a complete service complex, including a game room with video games and pool tables, a cybercafe, and a general store, and they also have the best restaurant in town, the **Restaurant Rucahue,** serving international and vegetarian dishes.

Km 72, Las Trancas. ☏ **42/236162.** www.rucahueescalador.cl. 6 units. $74 cabin for 4. AE, DC, MC, V. **Amenities:** Restaurant; cybercafe. *In room:* TV.

Hotel Robledal ★　This hotel is surrounded by oak and beech trees and serenaded by a babbling creek. It is a good choice "hotel" option for lodging outside the Termas de Chillán ski resort if you can't get a room at Termas de Chillán's Las Trancas–based Hotel Pirimahuida. The Robledal has a heated pool, although the pool is covered by a plastic bubble, making it one hot, stuffy swim. The entrance is flanked on one side by an airy, comfortable lobby with a copper fireplace and bar, and on the other by a restaurant. Guest rooms feel like condominiums, starkly decorated but brightly lit by an abundance of windows; some have terraces.

8km (5 miles) from Termas de Chillán. ℂ/fax **42/214407.** www.hotelrobledal.cl. 22 units. $63–$116 per person, includes breakfast and dinner. AE, DC, MC, V. **Amenities:** Restaurant; bar; babysitting; Jacuzzi; outdoor pool. *In room:* Cable TV, minibar.

Mission Impossible Lodge ★★ 🎁 This is my favorite place to stay outside of the Termas de Chillán ski area. The young owners of MI Lodge, a French trio, found their home here in Las Trancas and built a lofty yet cozy and bright lodge for people who love to snowboard and ski, and kick back and enjoy warm camaraderie at night. The 360-degree views from here are the best in Las Trancas, and there is a wood fire–heated hot tub, swimming pool, snowmobiles, a climbing wall, skate ramp, and other toys. However, it is a long walk to the road, and you'll need to either have a car or rely on the lodge's transportation to get to Las Trancas (an additional cost). This is a good place to have a rental vehicle. Solo travelers may or may not feel lonely here, depending on the lodge's occupancy at any given time, which often hosts pro snowboarders and many foreigners. Wood-paneled rooms have comfortable beds and quad rooms for groups. The friendly, knowledgeable staff is the best in the area for tips on secret powder stashes and backcountry terrain, and you can hire a guide to lead you around for a day on the slopes. Prices include breakfast and dinner, and use of their facilities. There is also a snowboard/ski shop on the premises, with rentals.

Fundo Los Pretiles, Parcela 83, Sector C, Las Trancas. ℂ **9/321-7567.** www.misnowchile.com. 9 units. $95 per person, double occupancy. AE, DC, MC, V. **Amenities:** Restaurant; bar; babysitting; Jacuzzi; outdoor pool; Wi-Fi (free in common area). *In room:* No phone.

LA SERENA & THE ELQUI VALLEY

B etween the Mediterranean climate of Santiago and the bone-dry Atacama Desert runs a roughly 500km (310-mile) stretch of arid territory that Chileans call Norte Chico, or Little North. Though less famous overseas than the far north, the area surrounding La Serena, Chile's sole remaining colonial Spanish city, features much more in the way of beach fun, along with penguins and dolphins up the coast and a unique fog-fed mini–cloud forest to the south.

Get away from it all in the rustic Elqui Valley and sample its spirits—both pisco brandy and its esoteric retreats. With 300 nights a year of some of the world's clearest skies, astronomers from around the globe are drawn to the region, a hub of state-of-the-art telescopes. With few travelers and a clutch of good value, holistic lodges, and plenty of outdoor activities ranging from hiking to horseback riding, it's a place to truly unwind and revel in the beautiful landscape. Norte Chico's most alluring attraction might be the *desierto florido* (flowering desert), which occurs only every few years, when above-average winter rainfall triggers a springtime explosion of wildflowers that turn the dusty desert into a multicolored feast for the eyes.

LA SERENA ★

474km (295 miles) N of Santiago

Founded in 1544 on a bluff just south of the Elqui River's entry into the Pacific, La Serena is Chile's second oldest city (the oldest is Santiago, established in 1541). Now home to some 190,000 inhabitants, it alone among the country's larger cities still sports more than just a few memories of Spanish architectural heritage; low-slung colonial houses, beautifully restored churches, and kaleidoscopic crafts markets are all on offer. La Serena is by far the most harmonious city in the entire country; and, with the bucolic and mystical delights of the Elqui Valley less than an hour's drive away and nature preserves both to the south and to the north, La Serena is a worthy destination in its own right.

Chile was one of Spain's poorest, remotest colonies, limiting what could be spent on architecture, and much of what at first glance appears old in La Serena in fact was built rather recently. The town's architecture fails to match the beauty of the colonial gems of the Andean countries, Mexico, or Cuba, but art fans will love the few, attractive Mannerist-style (late Renaissance) stone churches that survived multiple pirate raids. Most of the city was built during the silver boom times of the 19th century or after 1950 in imitation baroque style, in the wake of the 1948 "neocolonial" plan hatched by President Gabriel González Videla, who hailed from the city. Church spires dominate the skyline, and even the shopping mall respects the traditional style.

For several years, construction companies have been pushing for the right to build high-rises downtown. Fortunately, so far at least, city planners have resisted. La Serena has seen notable improvement in the past few years—many of those ugly electrical and phone cables that mar so many towns have, at least in the city center, been buried under new stone paving—and nowhere else in the country will you get a better impression of what it was like in the old days. Plus, the beaches are among Chile's finest—having eclipsed Viña del Mar in terms of beach scene cachet—and in season, you'll find plenty of activities.

Essentials

GETTING THERE

BY PLANE La Serena's **Aeropuerto La Florida** (LSC; © **51/200900**), 5km (3 miles) from downtown on Rte. 41, is served by **LAN** (© **600/526-2000**; www.lan.com) with up to three daily flights from the capital. A taxi to downtown costs around C$5,000; airport transfer vans cost C$2,000 per person to downtown, C$2,500 to beachfront hotels on Avenida del Mar.

BY BUS It takes close to 7 hours to reach La Serena by bus from Santiago. You can make it an overnight trip, but that means a crack of dawn arrival as no buses leave Santiago later than shortly before midnight. **Tur Bus** (© **600/660-6600**; www.turbus.com) departs from Santiago's Terminal Alameda at Av. Alameda 3750 (Metro: Univ. de Santiago); prices for the five daily *semi-camas* are C$12,100 one-way, C$17,900 for a *salón cama,* and C$26,300 for *premium.* Note that if you want to head back to Santiago, you might prefer to board a bus that starts off in La Serena rather than way up north, because these are frequently delayed. **Pullman Bus** (© **600/320-3200**; www.pullman.cl) leaves eight times daily from Estación San Borja (Metro: Estación Central). Prices for a *semi-cama* are C$11,000 one-way and C$16,600 for *salón camas.* In general, prices are lower during the off-season. La Serena's bus terminal is just south of downtown at El Santo and Amunátegui.

BY CAR A car is the best transportation in the Elqui Valley. You won't need a 4×4, though the drive out to Punta Choros is a little rough.

The trip up from Santiago takes between 5 and 6 hours on Ruta 5 Norte, a toll road (the trip will cost around C$9,600). The speed limit is 120km (73 miles); beware of police radars. Coming from the south, stop and put some fuel in your tank at Pichidangui or Los Vilos, as the next station is at Socos, which is quite far away and often has long gas lines. If you're renting, it might make more sense to pick up your car in La Serena than in Santiago.

The airport has rental kiosks for **Avis** (© **600/368-2000** or 51/200921; www.avischile.cl), **Budget** (© **600/441-0000**; www.budget.cl); and **Hertz** (© **600/360-8666** or 51/200922; www.hertz.cl). Downtown, you'll find **Avis** on Av. Francisco de Aguirre 63 (© **51/545300**; laserena@avischile.cl); **Budget** at Av. Francisco de Aguirre 15 (© **51/218272**); and **Hertz** at Av. Francisco de Aguirre 225 (© **51/226171**).

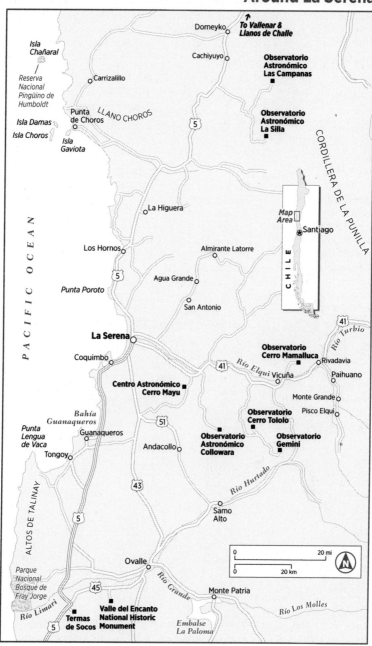

Domeyko
To Vallenar &
Llanos de Challe

Cachiyuyo

Observatorio
Astronómico
Las Campanas

Isla
Chañaral

Reserva
Nacional
Pingüino de
Humboldt

Carrizalillo

Punta
de Choros

LLANO CHOROS

Observatorio
Astronómico
La Silla

Isla Damas

Isla Choros

Isla
Gaviota

5

CORDILLERA DE LA PUNILLA

La Higuera

Map
Area

Santiago

Los Hornos

Almirante Latorre

CHILE

5

Agua Grande

Punta Poroto

San Antonio

41

Río Turbio

La Serena

Observatorio
Cerro Mamalluca

Coquimbo

41

Río Elqui

Rivadavia

Vicuña

Paihuano

Centro Astronómico
Cerro Mayu

Bahía
Guanaqueros

51

Monte Grande

Pisco Elqui

Punta
Lengua
de Vaca

Guanaqueros

Observatorio
Cerro Tololo

Tongoy

Andacollo

Observatorio
Astronómico
Collowara

Observatorio
Gemini

ALTOS DE TALINAY

43

Río Hurtado

5

Samo
Alto

0   20 mi

0   20 km

Ovalle

Parque
Nacional
Bosque de
Fray Jorge

45

Río Grande

Monte Patria

Río Los Molles

Río Limari

5

Termas
de Socos

Valle del Encanto
National Historic
Monument

Embalse
La Paloma

PACIFIC OCEAN

ORIENTATION

La Serena's square-grid colonial center lies on a bluff about a mile from the ocean, with the main square just a block from its western fringe and all the sights within easy walking distance. You'll need a taxi to travel to and from the beachfront hotels, which run north–south 12km (7½ miles) all the way down to the port of Coquimbo.

VISITOR INFORMATION

Sernatur operates a visitor center with a very friendly and helpful staff (who speak some English) at Matta 461 on the west side of the plaza between Prat and Cordovez, almost across from the cathedral (☎ 51/225199; www.turismoregiondecoquimbo. cl). In January and February, it's open daily from 9am to 9pm; the rest of the year, it's open Monday through Friday from 9am to 5:30pm, and Saturday from 10am to 2pm.

[FastFACTS] LA SERENA

ATMs & Currency Exchange Options include **AFEX,** Balmaceda 413 (☎ 51/217751; www.afex.cl); **Cambios Inter,** Balmaceda 431 (☎ 51/225199); and **Fides,** Balmaceda 460 no. 7 (☎ 51/214554), all open Monday through Friday from 9am to 6:30pm and Saturday from 10am to 2pm. You'll find plenty of ATMs in the banks and pharmacies on Cordovez and Prat, as well as a shopping center west of downtown and a mall near the bus station.

Hospital The city's hospital is at Balmaceda 916 (☎ 51/333424). For emergencies, dial ☎ 131.

Internet Access There are plenty of Internet cafes downtown, including **Infernet,** Balmaceda 412 (daily 10am–midnight); **Netcafé,** Cordovez 285 (daily 11am–11pm); and **CyberCaféBar,** Matta 611 (daily 10am–10pm).

Laundry Some Laundromats to try in town are: **Lavaseco Supremo,** Balmaceda 851 (☎ 51/225195); **Nevada Lavaseco,** Los Carrera 635 (☎ 51/216607); and **Lavandería y Lavaseco Vicky,** Juan de Dios Peñi 363-A (☎ 51/211904).

Post Office **Correos de Chile** is at the corner of Prat and Matta (☎ 51/420910). It's open Monday through Friday from 9am to 6:30pm.

What to See & Do

Many tour operators offer excursions in and around La Serena, including transportation to the observatories (see later). Check with your hotel regarding quality as tour company guides come and go and the level of service may change for the better or worse over time. For day tours of the city or 2- or 3-night specialist packages, including visits to vineyards, nature preserves, and archaeological monuments, as well as a pisco tasting and astronomy lessons, check with **Ingservtur,** Matta 611 (☎ 51/484008; www.ingservtur.cl), or **Ovitravel,** Balmaceda 1126 (☎ 51/340541; www.ovitravel.cl). For more athletic activities, including horseback riding, surf camps, ocean kayaking, mountain biking, and camping, contact **Chilesafari,** Matta 367 (☎ 09/8769-7686; www.chilesafari.com). There's also the little **Poisson** surfing school (☎ 9/138-2383; www.poisson.cl) right on the beach on Avenida del Mar 1001.

CHURCHES

La Serena's most recent urban renewal includes expensive, bilingual (Spanish/English), but ridiculously illegible glass historic markers on its main landmarks, including the most important of its 30-odd churches. Most, including the 1844–56 cathedral,

La Serena

ACCOMMODATIONS ■
Hostal El Punto **16**
Hotel Francisco
    de Aguirre **3**
Hotel Fuente del Mar **13**
Hotel Los Balcones
    de Aragón **9**

DINING ◆
Café Centenario **15**
Café Colonial **7** ●
Café El Patio **5**
Café Morocco **8**
Coffee Express **6**

ATTRACTIONS
Kokoro No Niwa **1**
La Recova **10**
Museo Arqueológico **12**
Museo Histórico
    Gabriel González
    Videla **4**
San Agustín church **11**
San Francisco church **14**
Santo Domingo church **2**

ⓘ Information
✉ Post office

ACCOMMODATIONS ■
Hotel La Serena Plaza **17**
Hotel Mar de Ensueño **18**
La Serena Club Resort **20**
Hotel Campanario
    del Mar **24**
Hotel de la Bahía Enjoy **26**

DINING ◆
Porota's Resto-Bar **19**
La Mia Pizza **21**
Martin Fierro **22**
Resto-Bar
    Huentelauquén **23**
Tololo Beach **25**

date back to the 19th-century silver mining boom. Three attractive stone colonial churches bear special mention; admission is free but opening hours are irregular.

The Mannerist, late-16th-century **San Francisco church ★★** at Eduardo de la Barra and Balmaceda, was the only religious building to survive the destruction wreaked by English pirate Bartholomew Sharp in 1680. Supported by meter-thick walls, the stone facade (stone churches are a rarity in Chile) is beautifully carved with ornate Baroque flourishes.

Rebuilt in the mid-18th century in the wake of pirate Edward Davis's 1685 raid, **Santo Domingo church ★★** is located on a small square on Cordovez just off the main plaza. It boasts a simple, airy interior, a 16th-century baptismal font, and an attractive courtyard; an ill-fitting, neo-Renaissance bell tower was attached in the early 20th century.

Following the expulsion of the Jesuits in the late 18th century, the Augustinians laid claim to **San Agustín church ★**, across from the Recova market on Cienfuegos. It has a similar Italian Renaissance style to that of Santo Domingo and was restored between 1985 and 1995 according to the original 17th-century plan.

MUSEUMS

Museo Arqueológico ★★ This smallish, crescent-shaped building houses a top-notch collection of pre-Columbian pottery from the Diaguita people who, originally from across the Andes, lived in the Norte Chico from around the year 1000 until largely disappearing in the wake of the Spanish conquest. The pottery alone makes it a must-see local attraction, but it also boasts a real *moai*—a giant anthropomorphic head from Easter Island—which was donated to the museum in 1952 as a result of the not-so-subtle persuasion of President Videla. The museum does a good job of tracing Chile's pre-Columbian history, and in early 2011 was completing renovations, which were sorely needed. The museum sells an odd assortment of expensive archaeology books and pottery, including clay dinosaurs and T-shirts.

At Cordovez and Cienfuegos. ✆ **51/224492.** Admission C$600 adults, C$300 children and seniors. Tues–Fri 9:30am–5:50pm; Sat 10am–1pm and 4–7pm; Sun 10am–1pm.

Museo Histórico Gabriel González Videla This museum, located in a lovely two-story mansion on the Plaza de Armas—is the former home of President Videla. Along with modest contemporary Chilean painting and temporary exhibitions, the collection of course focuses on the museum's namesake and city's native son. The display of photographs, letters, and paintings related to the man responsible for exiling Chile's greatest poet, Pablo Neruda, is misleadingly positive and rather dull. Of course without that exile, we wouldn't have had the charming 1994 Italian movie, *Il Postino (The Postman)*. If you're short on time, you might want to skip this place.

Matta 495, on the Plaza de Armas. ✆ **51/217189.** Admission C$600 adults, C$300 children and seniors. Mon–Fri 10am–6pm; Sat 10am–1pm.

A JAPANESE GARDEN

Kokoro No Niwa ★ "Garden of the Heart," as the name translates, is a delightful, unique park whose manicured lawns, ponds, waterfowl, and Japanese pagodas and bridges are in stark contrast to the derelict Parque Pedro de Valdivia next door and its depressing zoo. Japanese architect Akira Ohira designed the 2.6-hectare (6½-acre) grounds in honor of La Serena's 450th anniversary.

Entrance off Av. Juan Bohón. ✆ **51/217013.** Admission C$1,000 adults, C$300 children and seniors. Daily 10am–6pm.

SHOPPING

One of Chile's best-known city markets, **La Recova** ★, lies on the square at the corner of Prat and Cienfuegos just 3 blocks from the plaza. Many of the handicrafts are pretty tacky and most feature goods imported from Peru or Bolivia, but you can sample some of the local sweets and liquors for an authentic taste of the area. You'll also find items in lapis lazuli and combarbalite, a unique, gray-green semi-precious stone found only around Combarbalá, a village to the south. In January and February, it's open Monday through Saturday from 10am to 10pm and Sunday from 10am to 5pm; during the rest of the year, Monday through Saturday from 10am to 9pm, and Sunday from 10am to 3pm.

Downtown, the main shopping area includes Cordovez and Prat streets departing from the plaza. You'll find several handicraft stalls selling local honey and folkloric dolls and knickknacks along Cordovez. A shopping mall straddles La Serena's colonial center to the south next to the bus station, while a large strip mall lies to its west just across the train tracks, each keeping the neocolonial style and each featuring retail chains common in Chile, including clothing and athletic goods stores. There's a Jumbo supermarket of a similar ilk to Costco, with a little more polish—it's a convenient place to stock up on food or camping equipment. They also sell some electronics, such as memory cards and cellphone batteries, as do several stores in the downtown shopping district.

Where to Stay

If you'd like to step outside your hotel in the evening, I recommend you stay on the beach, particularly if you're looking for a more upscale hotel; downtown, pickings in those categories are slim and nightlife is as serene as the city's name implies. The 6km (3¾-mile) string of accommodations running down Avenida del Mar isn't particularly attractive, but rooms are comfortable, and they're directly across the street from the beaches. The cuisine in this area by far outshines that offered downtown, too, and here you'll be able to sip a sunset cocktail on the beachfront.

EXPENSIVE

Hotel de la Bahía ★★★ 🎣 Of all the hotels and resorts along the beachfront, this is as good as it gets. The gorgeous, swanky hotel, owned and operated by the chain Enjoy, sits just on the edge of La Serena, where the coastal avenue crosses into Coquimbo, and so it's farther from the downtown area. However, the hotel is self-contained with three restaurants, a casino, deluxe spa, tour desk and concierge, nightclub and salon with evening performances, and a large outdoor pool, so chances are you won't travel too far once you check in. The hotel has a minimalist exterior made of lots of glass and concrete, and is in a semi-circular shape so that all guest rooms have ocean views, as do all restaurants. Some rooms have balconies but guests can only try to get one when checking in, not in advance. The lobby, like the rest of the hotel, is elegant yet very trendy, with lots of wicker furniture, beige linen, bold geometric carpets, and colorful mosaic tiles; and guest rooms are tidy and handsome, with dreamy beds and full amenities. Given all you get, the hotel is a great value.

Av. Costanera 5351, Coquimbo. ⓒ **600/700-6000** or 51/423000. 111 units. www.enjoy.cl. $217 double standard. AE, DC, MC, V. **Amenities:** 3 restaurants; bar; club; babysitting; room service; deluxe spa; casino. *In room:* A/C, TV, hair dryer, minibar, free Wi-Fi.

Hotel La Serena Plaza ★ Don't be put off by the plain exterior of this hotel, which belies a pretty interior that is shaded by large palm trees and a good-size pool.

Its conservative, tangerine and yellow rooms are a 1970s throwback and range from smallish singles to big quadruple and junior suites. The rooms vary considerably in terms of polish and some are much more faded than others; be sure to ask for a nonsmoking room. While it's just across from La Serena's landmark faux lighthouse on Avenida del Mar, the stretch of beach closest to this hotel is neither particularly clean nor safe, so you'll need to walk a fair distance before you reach a good spot for a dip in the waves. The staff is friendly and helpful. The Plaza also has one of the biggest and best-equipped gyms of any hotel in Chile, but you'll have to share it with local members of the Pacific Fitness chain.

Av. Francisco de Aguirre 0660, La Serena. ⓒ **51/226913.** www.hotelserenaplaza.cl. 58 units. $95 double standard, $135 junior suite. AE, DC, MC, V. **Amenities:** Restaurant; bar; outdoor pool; free Wi-Fi in lobby area. *In room:* TV, small fridge, hair dryer, Internet.

Hotel Mar de Ensueño ☺ This almost 20-year-old hotel looks a bit odd: The four-story main building is covered in thatch, as are the 10 family cabins on the grounds, while the large grassy garden around the pool has practically no shade and faces the avenue directly. The location does give all rooms an ocean view, most with a balcony, and all rooms except doubles and triples have kitchenettes with refrigerators. The upside of this hotel is the range of amenities included in the price, including a "beach kit" with towels and umbrellas. The hotel seems geared more toward families with kids, but they do see a fair share of business travelers who typically stay on the fourth floor, which features rooms with slightly more sober decor than the hotel's tropical-style guest rooms. Service is bend-over-backwards friendly.

Av. del Mar 900, La Serena. ⓒ **51/222381.** Fax 51/226177. www.hotelmarensueno.com. 50 units and 10 4-person cabins. $90–$150 double; $210 cabin. AE, DC, MC, V. **Amenities:** Restaurant; bar; bikes; children's playground; gym; pool. *In room:* TV, hair dryer, minibar, free Wi-Fi.

La Serena Club Resort ★★ ☺ This was the fanciest resort on the beachfront until the Hotel de la Bahía came along, but it's still quite enjoyable, especially since the resort renovated its guest rooms in 2010. It bears the contemporary style of the architects who designed the upscale Casa Piedra convention center in Santiago. Guest rooms come with either faux wood floors or carpeting, and are bathed in tones of brown, with ecru walls and coffee-colored drapes, and touches of Asian decor. Suites can be booked together with doubles to connect rooms for families, and there are apartments with two bedrooms and two bathrooms, plus a living area. Suites have terraces and views from the fourth floor. Most rooms look over the central lawn and palm-lined pool, which has chaise longues and a swim-up bar. During the summer, the resort often plans activities with entertainment and aerobics on the beach. The only downside to the resort is that there are lots of large, empty spaces around the hotel that are used for conventions and events, and it doesn't lend much intimacy to the place. However, the competent, attentive staff may well be the best in La Serena.

Av. del Mar 1000, La Serena. ⓒ **51/221262.** Fax 51/217130. www.laserenaclubresort.cl. 95 units. $170 double standard, $227 suite. AE, DC, MC, V. **Amenities:** Restaurant; bar; barbecue area; outdoor pool; small spa; clay tennis courts. *In room:* TV, minibar, hair dryer.

MODERATE

Hotel Campanario del Mar ★★ The Campanario del Mar is the most intimate hotel on the beachfront. The hotel was built in Spanish colonial style, with tiled roofs below the namesake little belfry and an interior courtyard enlivened by a fountain. All rooms, including a triple and two suites, are on the second floor, have a view of the Pacific, and are re-carpeted every season. Rooms are decorated in a blue-and-white nautical color scheme with spartan furnishings including metal-framed beds and dressers. The white-tiled bathrooms with tubs are sterile but clean and quite spacious. The suites and superior rooms have kitchenettes and minibars. The restaurant offers open-air terrace seating with a view of the beach.

Av. del Mar 4600, La Serena. ℂ **51/245516.** Fax 51/245531. 14 units. www.hotelcampanario.cl. $111–$143 double, $135–$172 suite. AE, DC, MC, V. **Amenities:** Restaurant; bar. *In room:* TV, kitchenette, minibar, free Wi-Fi.

Hotel Francisco de Aguirre ✋
In theory, this is the top place in the downtown area, in a historic neoclassical three-story building a block from the main plaza. It promises upscale accommodations and a range of good amenities, but the hotel has been undergoing major noisy remodeling that won't be completed until late 2011. The current renovations are taking place on the west-facing newer wing; the hotel's older wing is now remodeled with new carpets and drapes, but nothing very fancy or eye-catching. The best rooms here are the superior doubles facing the interior pool area in the older wing.

Cordovez 210, La Serena. ℂ **51/222991.** www.dahoteles.com. 102 units. $137 double standard; $160 double superior. AE, DC, MC, V. **Amenities:** Restaurant; bar; small outdoor pool. *In room:* TV, minibar, free Wi-Fi.

Hotel Los Balcones de Aragón
This downtown, midrange hotel has aged somewhat and still has a strong whiff of the 1970s, but it is immaculately clean and tidy, and the service makes up for the fact that it is a little on the expensive side for what it offers. The rooms are adequately sized but not huge and have fresh white bedspreads and new carpets, but rather spongy beds. Rooms facing a pleasant courtyard are quieter and newer than the rooms facing the noisy street. The hotel recently opened a simple spa offering massage services, manicures, and other body treatments.

Cienfuegos 289, La Serena. ℂ **51/212419.** Fax 51/211800. www.losbalconesdearagon.cl. 26 units. $105 double. AE, DC, MC, V. Rates include a modest breakfast. **Amenities:** Restaurant; bar; spa. *In room:* TV, minibar, free Wi-Fi.

INEXPENSIVE

Hostal El Punto ★★★ 🎒
This charming German-owned little hostel, located just beyond downtown, is extremely well run and oozes character. In many respects, El Punto is a much more appealing prospect than La Serena's bland midrange options, with exceptionally clean, whitewashed guest rooms with comfy, wood-framed beds. The six cheapest rooms share three bathrooms, while the most expensive have private bathrooms. El Punto's most endearing feature is its attractive garden courtyard with tables and chaise longues, providing a shady spot to relax and read or enjoy a snack amid the flowers and colorful Mediterranean arches. Activities such as yoga add to the hostel's serene allure; the helpful and friendly staff plan excursions around La Serena and to the Valle del Elqui. It's also very convenient for those schlepping luggage from the bus station 2 blocks away.

Andrés Bello 979, La Serena. ℂ **51/228474.** 15 units. www.hostalelpunto.cl $53 double with private bathroom; $34 double with shared bathroom. No credit cards. **Amenities:** Cafe; yoga room. *In room:* TV, no phone, free Wi-Fi.

Hotel Fuente del Mar
This family-run property is a more homespun alternative to the Hostal El Punto (see above). You'll be surprised at the height of the plant-filled courtyard inside as the 1940s-style hotel appears much smaller from the outside. The cream-colored rooms are bright and quiet, but very spartan and simply decorated;

also, this is an old home rather than a proper hotel and has more of a guesthouse feel. The hotel is about a 3-block walk to the Recova market.

Vicuña 635, La Serena. © **51/219768.** 10 units. $53–$63 double. AE, DC, MC, V. **Amenities:** Breakfast area; airport transfers (for a fee). *In room:* TV, free Wi-Fi.

Where to Dine

Dining in the downtown area is limited to simple restaurants that do not necessarily merit recommendation, as well as fast food and chain restaurants. There are a couple of good cafes listed below with snacks and sandwiches, otherwise the best place to dine in the downtown area is at the **Recova market,** where many second-floor restaurants prepare fresh seafood and hearty Chilean stews (*cazuelas*). The dining areas here, which perch above the colorful market, also exude a bit more ambience. The **Café Centenario** (© **51/212659**) is well located on the plaza and within a beautiful antique building, with coffee, pastries, and sandwiches. The small **Café Morocco ★**, Prat 566 (© **51/550444**), serves what may well be Chile's best *cortados* (espressos with milk) set in a lightly Arab-themed, intimate setting of wood-inlaid tables and exposed brick walls. It also has a few sidewalk tables, as does the larger, less stylish **Coffee Express** on the corner of Prat and Balmaceda (© **51/221673**). Half a block away on Balmaceda 475, **Café Colonial** (© **51/216373**) has vegetarian dishes and offers set lunches for C$2,375. **Café El Patio,** in a courtyard at Prat 470 (© **51/210759;** www.cafeelpatio.4mg.com), is something of a jazz bar indoors, with outdoor seating and a cheap set menu (usually C$2,500) at lunch. None of these cafes is open on Sundays.

EXPENSIVE

Martín Fierro ★ ARGENTINE   Tired of fish? This is the place to go for hearty meat dishes. Martín Fierro specializes in Argentine beef cuts—the jolly waitstaff are very happy to provide guidance on the various cuts of meat served—as the owners sought to make clear when naming the large restaurant after the legendary gaucho hero. Pork and lamb dishes along with homemade pasta also please a large appetite at a fair price. For the less carnivorous, there are several well-prepared fish dishes including sea bass, conger eel, and salmon carpaccio, which are served with a choice of different sauces and accompaniments. The restaurant has an average selection of Chilean wines to accompany meals. It also has a small playground.

Cuatro Esquinas and Av. Pacífico. © **51/219002.** www.martinfierro.cl. Main courses C$4,500–C$10,100. AE, DC, MC, V. Daily 11:30am–4:30pm and 7pm–midnight.

MODERATE

La Mia Pizza ★ ITALIAN/PIZZERIA   This cozy, casual restaurant is a favorite among La Serena locals, and it therefore tends to fill up quickly. As the name indicates, the restaurant is known for its wide selection of pizzas, which are some of the best in the entire Norte Chico region, and very crisp and flavorful. There is other Italian fare, too, such as good pasta dishes and grilled meats, and fresh salads. Service is attentive and friendly. Arrive early to grab a window seat with a view.

Av. del Mar 2100. © **51/212232.** Main courses C$3,500–C$8,000. AE, DC, MC, V. Jan–Feb daily 11am– 1:30am, rest of year Tues–Sun 1pm–1:30am.

Porota's Resto-Bar ★★ INTERNATIONAL/CHILEAN   The closest beachfront restaurant to downtown has a few outdoor tables and a more elegant and warm interior dining area, along with a varied, imaginative menu interspersed with Asian influences. There are meat dishes, but the restaurant is better known for its ultra-fresh fish dishes, which are very well prepared and a good value given the portions. Try the grouper and calamari with risotto seasoned with olives from the Elqui Valley, or the deliciously light and flavorful grilled conger eel with abalone and fava beans. The waitstaff is prompt and friendly, and are more than happy to alter a dish according to your likes. The pisco sours aren't the best but there is a good wine list.

Av. del Mar 900b. ✆ **51/210937.** www.porotas.cl. Main courses C$7,100–C$8,000. AE, DC, MC, V. Jan-Feb daily 11am–2am, rest of the year daily noon–4pm and 7:30pm–midnight.

Resto-Bar Huentelauquén ★★ ☺ ITALIAN   This laid-back, ebullient restaurant has an extensive Italian menu served in a cozy and artistic setting. The dining area sits in a semicircular space built around several polished tree trunks and a central steel fireplace. Illuminated at night under conical lamps, most tables have windows facing the ocean, but you can also sit outside, either on top of the building itself or facing the sea. It's the imaginative varieties of oven-baked pizzas that draw the crowds, but the salads, which are composed of a bounty of fresh ingredients from the Elqui Valley, are as wholesome as they are delicious. The homemade pastas are decent, if rather rich. The restaurant gets its name from a unique cheese produced in the hamlet of Huentelauquén, about 200km (125 miles) to the south, and it's a great addition to all the Italian dishes. Huentelauquén is also very kid friendly; children will love to clamor on the playground's wooden ship in between munching on pizza and tasty empanadas.

Av. del Mar 4500. ✆ **51/233707.** Reservations recommended in high season for dinner. Main courses C$4,300–C$8,900. AE, DC, MC, V. Daily 1pm–2am in summer; rest of year Tues–Thurs 6:30pm–midnight, Fri 6:30pm–2:30am, Sat–Sun 1pm–2am.

INEXPENSIVE

Tololo Beach ★★★ INTERNATIONAL/CHILEAN   If you want to dine on fresh seafood with the sand between your toes, this is the place. The restaurant has the best beachfront ambience, really, of any restaurant in La Serena, with tables and chairs in the sand that are flanked by small palms, and a vaguely oriental-style and chic terrace lounge with wicker couches and white umbrellas that offers a view of sunbathers and pelicans diving into the Pacific. The food, while a little on the expensive side, is exceptionally good, with a varied selection of native fish like vidriola and rollizo that you won't often find elsewhere. Beyond fresh seafood, the restaurant's slow-braised beef ribs are fall-off-the-bone tender and large enough to split between two when ordering a couple of side dishes. There are also omelets, risottos, pizzas, sandwiches, and hamburgers. The bartender shakes up some of the best cocktails served anywhere in Chile; try a margarita or their delectable berry sour.

Av. del Mar 5200. ✆ **51/242656.** www.tololo.cl. Main courses C$6,500–C$9,500, sandwiches C$3,750–C$4,600. AE, DC, MC, V. Daily noon–3am in summer; rest of year daily noon–midnight.

Near La Serena

Coquimbo, a gritty, tough port city of 150,000, has beautifully renovated its **Barrio Inglés,★,** a neighborhood named for the mostly English immigrants who built the houses near the port during the 19th-century. Visitors will be reminded of Valparaíso, with lovely old mansions built by the finest craftsmen during the city's mining heyday, many of which have now been turned into restaurants and bars. It's quite a little swanky enclave but surrounded by the seedy port and dirty streets of Coquimbo.

Annually, Coquimbo hosts Chile's biggest popular festival, *La Pampilla,* during Independence Day festivities from September 18 to 20. It's a massive, utterly Chilean folk event with popular concerts, but it might be a little rough for those who are annoyed by heavy drinking. There's also a string of beachfront villages farther south, including **Guanaqueros** and **Tongoy,** popular for their wide, sandy beaches and seafood.

Coquimbo's sights include a small, restored 19th-century **fort** at the end of the peninsula, with an 1868 English cannon and a cafe; the **church** designed by famed French engineer Alexandre Gustave Eiffel in the Guayacán neighborhood; the **English cemetery** in the same neighborhood; and the 36m-tall (118-ft.) **mosque.** The mosque was built by Moroccan craftsmen at the behest of ex-mayor Pedro Velásquez and funded by King Mohammed VI of Morocco, though few Muslims actually live in town. It's near the bus station (**Rodoviario Coquimbo,** Av. Varela 1300; © 51/ 326651). The biggest and ugliest of Velásquez's latest projects is the gigantic hilltop **Cross of the Third Millennium,** a sculpture that was built to commemorate 2,000 years of Christianity and that now dominates the skyline.

THE OBSERVATORIES

The Norte Chico's dry and clear skies rank as one of the best places in the world for stargazing, and a cluster of observatories, some of the most advanced in the world, have established themselves in the area. Some hotels and resorts also offer telescopes or their own private observatory as an added attraction. It goes without saying that viewing the stars simply with the naked eye is best when there is no moon, so check the lunar calendar if you plan to make stargazing an important facet of your visit. It is possible to visit a scientific observatory base, but it is very time-consuming and difficult to plan, the reason why most travelers settle with a visit to an observatory geared more toward tourism. Individual reservations requirements and restrictions are listed below. Also, see the site **www.turismoastronomico.cl** for general information about stargazing in the area.

Near Vicuña are the scientific bases **Observatorio Cerro Tololo** (© 51/205200; www.ctio.noao.edu/tourism; Sat 9am–noon and 1–5pm; reservations must be made 1 month in advance) and **Observatorio Gemini** (© 2/205600; www.gemini.edu; no scheduled tours, visits are by appointment only and must be made 2 months in advance). The difficulty with Tololo and Gemini is that the observatories require you to pick up a visitor's card 1 week before your scheduled visit date and their offices are in La Serena; otherwise you won't be allowed access. North toward Domeyko are **Observatorio Astronómico La Silla** (© 2/463-3100; www.ls.eso.cl; contact recepstg@eso.cl), open September through June on Saturday from 1:30 to 4:30pm, and **Observatorio Astronómico Las Campanas** (© 51/207301; www.lco.cl), open Saturday from 2:30 to 5pm. Both Las Campanas and La Silla are quite a distance from La Serena—around a 90-minute drive.

You might prefer to look through a telescope yourself, and you can at the following tourist observatories. The closest to La Serena is the **Centro Astronómico Cerro Mayu,** 27km (17 miles) east of La Serena (© 8/249-7337; www.cerromayu.cl; Tues–Sat 6pm–midnight); admission is C$2,500. If you are staying in Pisco Elqui or Vicuña, your best option is **Observatorio Cerro Mamalluca** (© 51/411352; www.mamalluca.cl; daily 9am–8pm except Oct 30, Dec 24–25 and 31, and Jan 1); tours in English or Spanish cost C$3,500 for adults and C$1,500 for children and seniors. Tours are geared toward those with a basic knowledge and begin at 8:30pm and last for 2 hours (minibus transfers leave from Vicuña each night at 8pm for C$1,500 per person). Tour groups are rather large (often as many as 30 people), which means that there is a lot of standing around in the cold while you await your turn to look through the telescope. Near Andacollo, 60km (37 miles) southwest of La

Serena, is **Observatorio Astronómico Collowara** (℗ 51/432964; reserve at Urmeneta 599 in Andacollo); it costs C$3,500 for adults, C$2,500 for children, and tours are in Spanish only. The cabin complex **Refugios la Frontera** (℗ 8/805-7104; www.refugioslafrontera.cl) has three observatories on its properties that travelers can visit with an advance reservation. The cost is $7,500 per person.

RESERVA NACIONAL PINGUINO HUMBOLDT ★★

Three rocky islands in the Pacific 110km (68 miles) north of La Serena form the **Reserva Nacional Pingüino de Humboldt,** a small 860-hectare (2,125-acre) preserve remarkable for its abundant marine wildlife, such as its namesake species of penguin, sea lions, sea otters, and bottlenose dolphins (admission C$1,600 adults, C$600 children; daily 8:30am–5:30pm). Other cetaceans have also been sighted on occasion, including fin and blue whales and other species of dolphins. You can disembark on one of the islands, Isla Damas, which has two beautiful beaches and a small campsite (reserve at **CONAF** in La Serena; ℗ 9/544-3052).

The friendly fishermen in **Punta de Choros** offer boat trips to the island, and the desert hamlet offers pleasant accommodations, including the rustic **Cabañas Amarilis** (℗ 9/447-5200; www.ananucas.cl), charming, well equipped cabins close to the main square and the beach. **Memo Ruz** (℗ 9/534-3644; www.memoruz.cl) is a tourist center that organizes activities, including diving tours, and also has several sturdy, modern beachside cabins with terraces for rent. Tour agencies in La Serena offer day trips to the preserve. You can book a multiday sea-kayaking, scuba diving, or fishing trip to the islands through **Kayak Australis** (℗ 2/334-2015; www.kayak australis.cl) or **Yak Expediciones** (℗ 9/299-6487; www.yakexpediciones.cl); book early as dates for these trips are limited. Note that trips in the winter months can be very windy, making for choppy water.

DESIERTO FLORIDO ★★★

The phenomenon known as the **Desierto Florido,** or flowering desert, occurs when enough rain falls in the winter months to trigger an explosion of colors, carpeting hundreds of square kilometers of parched, barren desert with endemic wildflowers that appear almost hallucinogenic in color. There is really no way to predict when this will happen, especially because winter rainfall seems to be decreasing annually, but a rough guess would put the chances at every 4 or 5 years. Some 70 species, including the rare red lion's claw—protected in the **Parque Nacional Llanos de Challe**—the violet guanaco's foot, or the blue field sigh, brighten the drab desert near **Vallenar,** a town 187km (116 miles) north of La Serena. They crop up with at least 35mm (1⅓ in.) of water; a good year demands some 55mm (2¼ in.). When the desert blooms, you'll have from late July to October to visit, with flowers closer to the coast opening their petals later than those in the Central Valley.

Tours are available in season from La Serena, or drive north on the Pan-American Highway (Rte. 5), remembering to fill your tank before departing. From Vallenar, loop to the west to the coast, head north to Parque Nacional Llanos de Challe, then back southwest to Vallenar.

PARQUE NACIONAL FRAY JORGE ★

In an otherwise arid area, plants have clutched enough moisture from the desert fog (*camanchaca*) that regularly rolls in from the ocean to form vegetation amazingly similar to Patagonian rainforests. A UNESCO World Biosphere Reserve, Parque Nacional Fray Jorge is actually a remnant of those same forests that has held on from the end of the last ice age. Sadly, since its discovery in 1627 by Franciscan friar Jorge, settlers

PAN DE azúcar

Northern Chile's Parque Nacional Pan de Azúcar is an arid desert park with a varied vegetation that grows thanks to Chile's coastal phenomena, a heavy mist called *camanchaca*. The park, located 31km (19 miles) from Chañaral and 180km (112 miles) north of Copiapó, is also known for its diversity of animal species, and is divided into two areas that include the coastal Taltal sector and the Sierra Vicuña Mackenna sector farther inland, which is characterized by steppe. Pan de Azúcar is home to herds of *guanacos,* the cousin of the llama, as well as Humboldt penguins and sea otters that live on Pan de Azúcar Island near the coast, and which can be reached by boat (local fishermen provide this service for C$5,000 per person, leaving from the Caleta Pan de Azúcar).

Visitors will want to arrive in their own rental vehicle in order to explore the park and possibly camp on a stretch of the park's long and lovely beaches, in one of four areas that include Caleta Pan de Azúcar, Piqueros, Soldado, and Piqueros Norte; the latter two are less crowded. The best time to visit is during the spring (Oct–Dec) when cactus and other plants are in bloom, and ideally after a rain shower that, while uncommon, unleashes the "Flowering Desert," when usually dormant plants burst with colorful flowers. The park, measuring 43,769 hectares (108,156 acres), is open every day from 8am to 6pm, and admission costs C$3,500 per adult, and C$1,500 for children. Camping is C$3,500 per person, per night, and there are general services such as bathrooms and showers. Rustic beach *cabañas* cost C$20,000 to C$40,000 per night.

chopped down much of the original forest, leaving just 400 wooded hectares (990 acres) out of a total 9,959 hectares (24,610 acres) protected in the national park. Beyond a visitor center, a short hilltop trail leads through the forest and offers views of the steep drop to the Pacific. The best time to visit is late October and November, when its flowers bloom. Park wildlife includes birds of prey, hummingbirds, guanacos, gray and culpeo foxes, along with sea otters and Humboldt penguins along the shore. Fray Jorge is about 100km (62 miles) due south from La Serena on the Pan-American Highway. Tours are available from La Serena. The park is open daily from 9am to 4:30pm, and an hour later in January and February. Admission for adults is C$1,600 and C$600 for children.

As the limited trail means your visit to Fray Jorge will likely be short, I recommend you combine it with a visit to the **Valle del Encanto National Historic Monument ★**, 14km (9 miles) from the Pan-American Highway. The park holds 30 petroglyphs chiseled into the stones by the El Molle culture from around A.D. 700, though objects dating from as far back as 2000 B.C. have been found. The park is open daily from 8am to 4:30pm; admission is C$500 for adults, and C$300 for children. A pleasant stop here, too, is the **Termas de Socos,** a hotel and more traditional spa with thermal baths and very reasonably priced massages and other body treatments. The thermal baths are really just small tubs in individual rooms, but there is a refreshing swimming pool with mineralized water, and a decent restaurant serving Chilean cuisine (at Km 370 on the Ruta 5; ✆ **53/198-2505;** www.termasocos.cl; double rooms including breakfast cost C$33,400–C$36,200).

Farther inland from Fray Jorge are **Ovalle,** whose museum holds a very good collection of Diaguita pottery, and **Andacollo,** a mining village that hosts one of Chile's main religious celebrations. In honor of the Virgin Mary, an astounding 400,000 pilgrims congregate here on December 26, following a tradition begun in 1584. Including Fray Jorge, this 318km (197-mile) loop can be done in a day with a rental car, but it will be a long one as roads to Andacollo are not all paved and some have hairpin mountain turns. You might want to consider an overnight stay at Socos.

THE ELQUI VALLEY ★

Pisco Elqui: 104km (65 miles) SE of La Serena; 578km (359 miles) N of Santiago

A long, green valley in the arid Andes, enfolded by stunning mountains streaked with improbable hues of pink, silver, beige, and blue, the tranquil Elqui Valley faces the challenge of safeguarding its rural *huaso* soul amid expanding agro-industrial fruit production, distilleries, and an influx of Santiaguinos fleeing the capital's urban ills. Until recently, the area was still something of a backwater, but the road is now paved beyond the picturesque village of Pisco Elqui and more and more tourists are discovering the valley's unspoiled nature and clear, bright skies. Still, the valley rates as one of the most lovely and underrated destinations in Chile. A string of wholesome villages comprising colorful low-slung adobe houses punctuates its serpentine roads, which weave through mountains where locals gather to sell fresh fruit and other food.

The valley's salubrious aura, wonderful healthy food, and humbling natural setting will certainly relax you, and you'll be safe from the clamor of ringtones and other urban distractions. Most hotels can arrange treatments and therapies to soothe your spirit, such as massages, meditation, and yoga. If meditating isn't your thing, hiking, mountain biking, and horseback riding will keep you busy, while pisco distilleries offer spirits of another kind. It can get very crowded in February at the height of the travel season, but the gentle climate makes the valley a great place to visit year-round.

Essentials

GETTING THERE

BY CAR The journey from La Serena to Vicuña takes around 45 minutes on the excellent Rte. 41. To reach Pisco Elqui, turn south on Rte. 485 just past Rivadavia; it takes another 30 minutes along a serpentine mountain road. Vicuña has the only fuel station (Shell, on Rte. 41, just before the turnoff to town) beyond La Serena, as well as the last bank and ATM (often out of service). It's a relatively short trip on good roads, and a rental car is convenient as attractions are pretty far apart. For rental locations, see "Getting There: By Car" in "La Serena" on p. 192.

BY BUS For buses to La Serena, see "Getting There: By Bus" on p. 192. To get to Vicuña or Pisco Elqui, take a bus with either **Via Elqui** or **Sol del Elqui** from La Serena's bus terminal (C$1,800 to Vicuña and C$2,500 to Pisco Elqui). Buses leave every 45 minutes Monday through Sunday from 6:30am to 8:30pm; some continue on to Alcohuaz at the end of the Claro Valley.

ORIENTATION

The area popularly called Valle de Elqui actually includes the three valleys of the Elqui, Claro, and Cochiguaz rivers. **Vicuña,** 55km (34 miles) east of La Serena, is the main town, with services, a rural hospital, and four small museums, one in honor of Nobel Prize–winning poet Gabriela Mistral.

A string of villages continues on up to the higher reaches of the Claro, including (north–south) **Paihuano, Monte Grande** (Mistral's birthplace), and **Pisco Elqui,** a quaint, hillside place on the left bank of the river. All are easily navigable on foot but poorly lit in the evenings.

VISITOR INFORMATION

In Vicuña, the municipality operates a **visitor center** in the landmark faux-medieval tower **Torre Bauer** on the plaza (© 51/209125). In January and February, it's open daily from 8:30am to 7:30pm; the rest of the year, it's open Monday through Saturday from 8:30am to 5:30pm, and Sunday from 9:30am to 2pm. In Pisco Elqui, your best bet for travel info and to book excursions is **Turismo Migrantes,** Calle O'Higgins s/n (© 51/451917; www.turismomigrantes.cl; Tues–Sun 9am–2pm and 4–10pm).

What to See & Do

For at least 400 years, people in what are now Chile and Peru have distilled a brandy from wine called **pisco,** named after the Peruvian port of the same name through which it was shipped to Spain. Still popular in both countries—particularly in the ubiquitous cocktail called pisco sour—the debate rages on regarding which side can actually claim the rights to the name. Nevertheless, to underscore the authenticity of Chile's claim, in the 1930s González Videla (you'll remember him from La Serena) pushed for the renaming of the village of La Unión to Pisco Elqui.

The valley produces most of Chile's pisco, and you can visit several distilleries. Two kilometers (1¼ miles) east of Vicuña is the somewhat touristy **Capel,** one of Chile's largest producers of pisco. The plant is within a pretty colonial estate, and includes a **Pisco Museum** (© 51/411251); it's open daily from 10am to 12:30pm and 2:30 to 6pm, and in January and February daily from 10am to 6pm; the cost for the tour and museum is C$1,000, and C$500 for the museum alone. The tour includes a tasting of two pisco lines and a brief explanation of pairing pisco with food. About 8km (4¾ miles) from Vicuña at the village El Arenal is **Pisco Aba** (© 51/411039), a "boutique" pisco production facility that makes just 15,000 bottles a year, and which still employs antique methods in its pisco production. The visit is free but call ahead to verify opening hours and days.

Pisco Elqui is home to the attractive **Destileria Pisco Mistral,** located on the plaza (© 51/451358; www.piscomistral.cl), with 1-hour tours showing how pisco is made, and with an explanation of the antique method and the implements and techniques used a century ago, as part of the facility's small museum. Along with Capel, Mistral is one of the largest pisco production facilities in Chile, recently having purchased the **Tres Erres** pisco line, considered to be one of the finest. Tours cost C$5,000 per person and happen every hour on the hour (noon–7pm) daily during January to February, and March to December every hour on the hour from 11am to 5pm, except Mondays. Lastly, the facility **Los Nichos** (© 51/451085) is the oldest in the valley and the only one to continue to make pisco organically. The facility is located 3km (2 miles) south, is open March through October daily from 10am to 1pm and 2 to 6pm, and November and December daily from 11am to 7pm, and is free.

Travelers will no doubt notice the plethora of businesses and sites named after **Gabriela Mistral,** one of Chile's best-known writers and the first woman to win the Nobel Prize for Literature, in 1945. Mistral, born in Monte Grande in 1889 (her tomb can be visited in that town), is honored at the attractive **Museo Gabriela Mistral,** Calle Gabriela Mistral 759, Vicuña (© 51/225398; www.dibam.cl; open

Jan–Feb Mon–Fri 10am–7pm, Sat 10:30am–6pm, and Sun 10am–6pm, rest of year Mon–Fri 10am–5:45pm, Sat 10:30am–6pm, and Sun 10am–1pm), with a sizeable and interesting collection of Mistral's personal and professional items, a timeline, and even the chair and wooden board she used. Note, however, that the museum is entirely in Spanish.

If you have time after visiting the Gabriela Mistral museum, the simple **Casa Museo el Solar de Los Madariaga** (✆ 51/411220; 10am–2pm and 3–6pm every day except Mondays) at Gabriela Mistral 683 offers a look within one of Vicuña's 19th-century homes. The old *casona* is fitted with period antiques, most of it imported from the U.S. and Europe, and the charming family that runs the place can provide info (in Spanish only). It's a spartan affair and will take no more than 30 minutes to see. The cost is C$600 for adults, or free for children, and it's open January to February daily from 10am to 7pm, closing at 6pm on Sundays; and March to December Monday to Friday from 10am to 5:45pm, Saturday from 10:30am to 6pm, and Sunday from 10am to 1pm.

OUTDOOR ACTIVITIES

An excellent **hike** if you don't mind the steep, 2,000m (6,560-ft.) climb is the 6.5km (4-mile) *Cumbres de Elqui* or Elqui Peaks, departing from Pisco and marked by three statues on the way up; register with the police before setting out. Alternatively, for a more accessible, less challenging hike from Pisco, take Calle Baquedano (just north of the main square on the road to Alcohuaz) and follow the dirt track through the mountains. You are unlikely to pass another soul other than the odd herd of lonely goats, a few wild horses, and a couple of lone *huesos*. Experiencing the silent grandeur of the mountains with the flourishing valley below is a soulful way to spend a couple of hours. Take plenty of water, as cool mornings soon give way to torrid midday heat. Hotels often offer **horseback riding** throughout the valleys, and you can try your hand at **trout fishing** in the rivers. Winds over the artificial lake **Puclaro** west of Vicuña make it a great area for **watersports** such as wind or kite surfing; check at your hotel (El Tesoro de Elqui, reviewed later, is best). An entertaining spectator sport is the Chilean-style **rodeo,** held annually on September 19 in the rickety-looking *media luna* or crescent stadium near Horcón.

SHOPPING

A government-sponsored investment scheme has helped local craftsmen set up a market in the hamlet of **Horcón** 10km (6 miles) past Pisco Elqui. The vendors offer a wide range of goods from herbs, honey, and jams to musical instruments and crafts made of quartz, metals, and wood. The market is open January and February daily from 12:30 to 8:30pm, and during the rest of the year Tuesday through Friday from 12:30 to 6:30pm, Saturday and Sunday 12:30 to 8pm.

Where to Stay

You'll find plenty of campgrounds and *cabañas* catering to domestic tourists throughout the valley. Standards are improving and most hotel staff will be able to help you book excursions or relaxation therapies.

EXPENSIVE

Elqui Domos ★   One of the more futuristic and memorable accommodations choices in Chile, Elqui Domos is composed of six canvas geodesic domes that look like a hillside observatory. These are no ordinary tents. The split-level domes, which have been freshly renovated, are large with a living room and bathroom on the first level and a bedroom complete with a detachable ceiling. Each dome can sleep up to four people. The domes are airy and the decor is minimalist—white lounge chairs, a futon, and a quilted bed—and each dome has a terrace with deck chairs. On the downside, most but the highest are a bit close for comfort, and the domes by nature are hot in the summer and chilly in the winter, in spite of an electric heater. The property also now offers four new wood cabins for two, located a steep walk up from the main complex but with better views than the domes. Telescopes are available in a common area near the restaurant, and horseback riding can be arranged.

Sector Los Nichos s/n, 3.5km (2 miles) S of Pisco Elqui. © **51/211453.** www.elquidomos.cl. 10 units. MC, V. $120–$145 double. **Amenities:** Barbecues; bikes; yoga; meditation room; swimming pool; free Wi-Fi. *In room:* Small fridge, hair dryer upon request.

La Casona Distante ★★★   If you are looking for peace and quiet in a stunning setting with plenty of activities like horseback riding on hand, this "secluded ranch" is worth the journey. This is the best hotel in the valley and, as its name indicates, one of its most remote, all the way at the high end of the valley near Alcohuaz (11 miles) beyond Pisco Elqui. The owners have transformed the three-story 1940 hacienda, nestled amid 25 hectares (63 acres) of lush valley, into a gorgeous eco-lodge in adobe, bay, and poplar. Rooms have high wooden ceilings, earthy adobe walls, and comfortable beds. Bathrooms are fancifully rustic and stylish, and the outdoor pool is beautiful. Thick walls help keep the rooms cool in summer. All meals are included and the dining area and kitchen are integrated, so you can watch or participate—you can even cook your own trout from the river.

Fundo Distante s/n, Alcohuaz. © **9/226-5440** or 9/320-9686. www.casonadistante.cl. 8 units. $168 per person double standard, $189 per person double superior, includes meals and bike rentals. No credit cards. **Amenities:** Restaurant; bar; bikes; outdoor pool; massage room; TV room. *In room:* TV, hair dryer, minibar (by request).

MODERATE

El Quimista ★★ 🧳   Independent travelers will adore these adobe-style cabins, perched on a steep slope replete with scented fruit trees and offering truly spectacular views of the Elqui Valley. The cabins were built and are now run by a young Chilean couple that live on the property, as well as their mother, the warm and very friendly Ximena Carey (all speak fluent English). The cabins are about a 5-minute walk to the plaza of Pisco Elqui. Rustic but cosmopolitan, the cabins have full kitchens, wide picture windows, outdoor decks, and barbecue areas; indoors the walls are clay-colored and decorated with colorful throws and gorgeous furniture and art imported from Bali. There are three cabins with room for two to four guests, and one old adobe home (the "Aphrodita") with three bedrooms, a Jacuzzi tub, and a long deck. Guests share use of the swimming pool. The owners offer workshops in bio-architecture, reiki, and weaving, so inquire ahead if interested. Stock up at the Jumbo supermarket before coming here if you plan to cook your own meals.

Callejon Aurora s/n. © **51/451185** or 9/721-0313. www.elquimista.cl. 4 units. $84–$116 cabin for 2; $126–$158 cabin for 4; $158–$206 house for 6. AE, DC, MC, V. **Amenities:** Outdoor pool. *In room:* TV, minibar, no phone.

Hostería Vicuña ★ ☺   This is a hacienda-style hotel with a 40-year history, which also means it could use a little sprucing up. Pricey but still the best hotel in Vicuña, it has relatively few rooms considering the size of the complex, which includes a swimming pool and a kiddie pool, tennis courts, and palm-lined grounds with pet llamas. Rooms are large and have high ceilings, with huge windows looking out on the pool and comfortable beds covered in flowery bedspreads.

Sargento Aldea 101, Vicuña. © **51/411301.** www.hosteriavicuna.cl. 15 units. $114 double. AE, DC, MC, V. **Amenities:** Restaurant; bar; large outdoor pool; wading pool; tennis courts. *In room:* TV, minibar, no phone.

Hotel El Galpón ★

La Serena artist Marcos Ramos has decorated this hotel with vaguely Mayan elements to reflect the mystical, esoteric side of the valley, with symbols for light, water, earth, and sun both on the outside of the main building and inside the rooms. The hotel gardens are a blaze of color and surround a good-size pool, which has plenty of chaises for sunbathing and sits at the foot of the mountains. The rooms are simple and more traditional, and not very large, with white, thick adobe walls of natural stone, and beds with metal or wood frames. There are also five spacious, terraced cabins for two to four people spread about a grassy area that features a small kitchenette for heating water and making coffee. On the downside, it is a dark 15-minute walk at night along a mountain road to get to Pisco Elqui, so most guests tend to dine at the hotel.

1km (½ mile) N of Pisco Elqui on the main hwy. © **51/198-2554.** www.elgalpon-elqui.cl. 6 units, 7 cabins. $105–$137 double, and $126–$158 cabin for 2. AE, DC, MC, V. Children are not accepted. **Amenities:** Restaurant; lounge w/fireplace; free Internet. *In room:* TV, hair dryer, minibar.

Hotel Halley

This colonial hotel close to the Plaza de Armas has old-fashioned rooms with Victorian-style furnishings and 1950s adornments. High ceilings and large windows alleviate the fussy trimmings. The main allure lies in the building's charming original features such as wrought-iron balconies and a verdant courtyard with a small pool, and the reasonable tariff. On the downside, the beds are rather soft and spongy, rooms facing the street are noisy, and you don't always get service with a smile.

Gabriela Mistral 542, Vicuña. © **51/412070.** 12 units. $82 double. AE, DC, MC, V. **Amenities:** Small outdoor pool. *In room:* Free Wi-Fi.

Hotel Las Pléyades ★★ 🎒

Owner Soledad Donoso has elegantly transformed a large old house into the valley's only boutique hotel. Rooms are large and, like the living and dining areas, sport a fine but rustic decor—plenty of wood and stone, and no two rooms are alike. The property features an outdoor pool and a private beach on the river. Show Ms. Donoso this Frommer's guide and she'll give you a discount (as much as a 50% discount in the off-season). Monte Grande is 4km (2½ miles) from Pisco Elqui.

Calle principal s/n, Monte Grande. © **51/451107.** www.valledeelqui.cl/laspleyades.htm. 5 units. $116 double. No credit cards. Children are not allowed. **Amenities:** Dining area; outdoor pool. *In room:* Hair dryer.

Misterios de Elqui ★★ 🎒

Tasteful and utterly relaxing, this Santa Fe–style adobe hotel is a heavenly place to spend a couple of nights in the Elqui Valley. At the foot of the mountains, spacious cabins with jaw-dropping views are woven through lush gardens that brim with color. The attractively designed cabins have white cotton bedspreads, hand-carved bed frames, cream linen sofas, and chairs made of logs, and well-appointed bathrooms with rainforest shower heads and slate tile showers. There are no TVs in the rooms, just wide-open views of star-studded skies. The pool area affords beautiful mountain views and has sun loungers surrounded by verdant gardens, a barbeque, a putting green, and even a bustling little brook. The stylish reception area has a small bar and TV area and is decorated with local arts and crafts. The intimate restaurant is one of the best in the area. Convivial owner Jaime is helpful and as likely to be sunbathing next to you on the terrace as he is working the reception desk.

Arturo Prat s/n. ☏ **51/451126.** www.misteriosdeelqui.cl. 7 units. $116–$126 cabin for 2, $137–$147 cabin for 4. AE, DC, MC, V. Rates include large breakfast. **Amenities:** Restaurant; outdoor pool; TV room.

INEXPENSIVE

El Tesoro de Elqui ★ ☺ 🦤 The beauty of its gardens sets this hotel apart from others in Pisco Elqui, and the place was designed with foreign tourists in mind. Its 10 *cabañas* and two double rooms vary widely, though all have their own bathrooms except for the dorm-type room. They also all have warm, milk chocolate–colored adobe walls with stone trim, knotty wooden floors or ceramic tiled flooring, and small terraces with chairs and hammocks. You can view them all on the hotel's trilingual website. My favorite is the cozy, sky lit *Suspiro* (Sigh) that allows you to stargaze. The staff can organize kite surfing on the Puclaro lake as well as other excursions around the area. The view of the Andes from the figure-eight pool is simply lovely.

Arturo Prat s/n, Pisco Elqui. ☏ **51/451069.** www.tesoro-elqui.cl. 10 units. $78 cabin for 2, $95 cabin for 4. AE, DC, MC, V. **Amenities:** Restaurant; bar; outdoor pool.

Hotel Elqui ★ 🦤 This centrally located hotel in a classic mansion is the oldest in Pisco Elqui, with 5 decades under its belt. It's still run by the friendly Áviles family who give it a welcoming, homey atmosphere. It has eight simply decorated rooms sharing five clean bathrooms. It's a steal considering its amenities: attractive gardens with three pools to cool off in, balconies in some rooms, and hammocks. Plus, it has one of the better restaurants for traditional Chilean fare.

O'Higgins s/n (off the square), Pisco Elqui. ☏ **51/451130.** www.valledeelqui.cl/mainhotelelqui.htm. 8 units. $21 per person. No credit cards. **Amenities:** Restaurant; 3 pools. *In room:* TV by request.

Refugios La Frontera ★ The La Frontera cabins are for independent travelers with a rental vehicle who really want to get away from it all. Located nearly at the end of the road in Alcohuaz, the cabins come with a big perk: three on-site observatories with a stargazing session with astronomer Mako offered for an additional C$7,500 per person. There are six very attractive wood-and-stone cabins for two to eight people, some with split levels and soaring ceilings, and all with a full kitchen and dining area, wood-burning stove, living room, and outdoor deck with a soak pool and barbecue. All are sufficiently far enough apart to give privacy, and the cabins for two are hidden in a grove of willow trees along a small creek.

Camino a Alcohuaz s/n. ☏ **8/805-7104** or 9/279-8109. www.refugioslafrontera.cl. 6 units. $116 cabin for 2, $168 cabin for 5. No credit cards. **Amenities:** Restaurant; soak pools; barbecue area. *In room:* Cable TV, no phone.

Where to Dine

MODERATE

Destileria Mistral ★★ CHILEAN Part of the Mistral pisco production facility and tour center, this is Pisco Elqui's loveliest and most relaxing place to dine, because of its patio seating under trellised vines that faces out toward panoramic views. The restaurant is backed by a 19th-century adobe building, part of the pisco distillery, and has antique machinery and other items scattered about. There is also a long bar where the restaurant shakes up its dynamite pisco sours made with interesting combos such as cedron, avocado, and cranberry. At night (summer only), the ambience is candlelit and romantic, and is popular as a low-key bar. Chilean specialties include homemade beef empanadas and slow-cooked pork ribs with a pisco sauce, and there's homemade ice cream for dessert. You might consider dining here following a tour of the pisco facility (see "What to See & Do" above).

At the plaza in Pisco Elqui. ✆ **51/451338.** Main courses C$4,500-C$7,800. AE, DC, MC, V. Jan-Feb daily 11:30am-midnight, and rest of the year 10:30am-6pm.

El Durmiente Elquino ★ CHILEAN In Pisco Elqui, this adobe building with terra-cotta walls decorated with local artworks and an outdoor terrace complete with a roaring fire pit is a heart-warming setting to try old-fashioned Chilean specialties, snack on decent thin-crust pizzas, or sample healthy salads made from local products such as quinoa and goat cheese from Horcón. If you are in the mood for a hearty staple, try the pork ribs or stewed beef *carne mechada*. As for libations, there is a well conceived selection of regional wines and, of course, the fitting precursor for any meal in Chile, a feisty pisco sour.

Las Carreras s/n, Pisco Elqui. ✆ **8/906-2754.** Main courses C$4,200-C$7,000. AE, DC, MC, V. Tues-Thurs noon-midnight, Fri and Sat noon-2am, and Sun noon-midnight.

Hacienda Miraflores ★★ 📷 CHILEAN This is one of the few remaining family-owned haciendas in the valley, though the owners have switched from making their own pisco to exporting grapes. The Miraflores has splendid views through enormous windows. Its high-quality spit-roasted meats will tempt all except for vegetarians, but it also serves pasta dishes. They offer good desserts, and it's one of a few places in the valley with real espresso. You can also head down to the river on the property, or spend a pleasant evening on the terrace (open for dinner in Jan–Feb only). It is popular with tour groups, especially at lunchtime, so reservations are highly recommended.

Rte. 485, 2.5km (1⅝ miles) past Pisco Elqui. ✆ **51/285901.** Reservations recommended. Main courses C$8,000-C$10,000. AE, DC, MC, V. Jan-Feb daily 1-10pm, rest of year lunch only Tues-Sun 1-5pm.

INEXPENSIVE

Los Jugos ★ CHILEAN More a pub than a restaurant, this is Pisco Elqui's main nightlife hot spot. The restaurant burned to the ground in 2010 but was nicely rebuilt, this time with a spacious booth-only restaurant, small bar, and second-story outdoor terrace that is pleasant on warm evenings. Famous for its fruit juices, hence the name, the restaurant also serves La Serena sours, and pisco with papaya rather than lemon juice. Los Jugos offers mostly pizzas, a couple of meat and cheese platters to share, and a set menu for C$6,000 that includes either grilled salmon, beef, or chicken as a main course, as well as an appetizer and dessert.

Centenario s/n (on the main square), Pisco Elqui. ✆ **51/212182.** Set menu pizzas C$3,500-C$4,000, shared platters C$7,000 for two or C$12,000 for four. AE, DC, MC, V. Tues-Sat noon-2am.

THE DESERT NORTH

9

Almost a third of Chile's 6,000km (3,720-mile) length is the driest desert in the world; the Atacama is an area of red sand and stone so dry that NASA once used the region to conduct experiments for Martian exploration as some areas are practically devoid of any life at all. Death Valley is moist by comparison. Still, several rivers descend from the Andes—including Chile's longest, the Loa—and oases dot the region, giving life to picturesque villages steeped in native and colonial Spanish tradition, including, most famously, San Pedro de Atacama.

In this desert, you'll find literally breathtaking high-altitude landscapes, abundant wildlife, archaeological and architectural heritage, and multiple activities for sports enthusiasts. San Pedro's burst onto the travel scene has led to many improvements in infrastructure: The dusty village itself boasts some of the best hotels in the country amid a relaxed, laid-back atmosphere easily accessible to those with limited time. But the area also holds many more remote jewels to entice adventuresome travelers.

Exploring the Region

Calama, a scrappy boomtown served by frequent flights from Santiago, is the gateway to San Pedro de Atacama. Calama is best experienced by travelers only from an airplane window. It's generally regarded as one of Chile's ugliest cities, and so it's not surprising that most visitors make a hasty exit and head to the more picturesque oasis town of San Pedro. Really, the only reasons to spend the night in Calama are to visit the immense Chuquicamata copper mine and to use it as a springboard to the border with Bolivia at Ollagüe. From **San Pedro,** you can take part in a multitude of day trips ranging from close encounters with ethereal natural phenomenon to quiet wanderings amid the colonial villages that dot the central desert. Plan for at least 4 days to visit this region's highlights, or 6 to 7 days to really explore it, especially if you're a fan of active travel. With a plethora of adobe-style accommodations, convivial restaurants where travelers gather around fire pits under star-studded skies, and an artsy laissez faire vibe, it's easy to yield to San Pedro's wild mysticism.

Arica, the coastal city on the border with Peru and home to the world's oldest mummies, is your first stop on the way to spectacular **Parque Nacional Lauca** and its unique villages, but it's also a fine place to unwind on the beach. The city and immediate environs can be explored in a day. While Lauca is less than 200km (124 miles) from Arica, take it

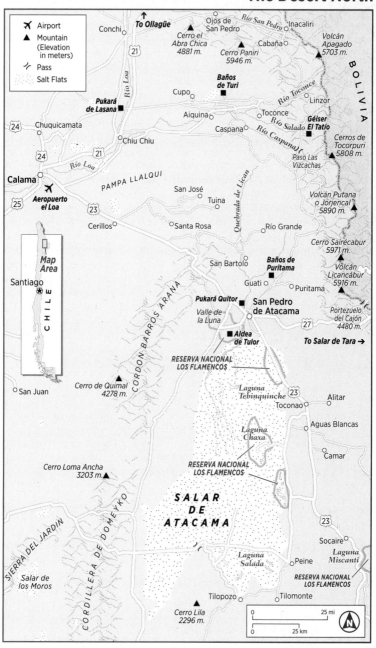

easy because of the high altitude and allot at least 2 days for your visit, with an overnight stay in the pretty Aymara village of **Putre.**

A few tour operators offer multiday excursions to a variety of additional locations that might not be highlighted in this book. Reasonably priced day tours render a vehicle unnecessary, unless your intrepid spirit demands the freedom and spontaneity that a vehicle affords. In this case, safety considerations are imperative. For obvious reasons, solo travel is *not* the ideal way to explore Chile's northern desert region. Also, **bring plenty of water**—a gallon per person per day—and extra food, as well as sunscreen, a hat, sunglasses, warm clothing, and even a thick blanket or sleeping bag (in case you have to spend a chilly night on the road). If driving to remote areas, take at least one extra tank of gas; few places outside cities sell fuel, and then only at exorbitant prices. Your rental agency will provide you with a phone number for breakdowns and emergencies; however, even if you are carrying a cell phone, the signal will likely not be in range while on the road. *Always* double-check the state of any spare tires. Be certain to give at least one person your planned itinerary, even if it's the car-rental agency.

In addition, **land mines** left over from the paranoid Pinochet era still endanger some areas. Keep this threat in mind and ask locals before heading to remote areas—shifting sands mean some warning signs may not be accurate, even if they're written in Spanish, English, and German. Another consideration is **flash floods.** Though the region receives only a few days of rainfall each year, it can come in a torrential downpour known as the "Bolivian Winter," which impedes travel and drowns the region in flash floods causing substantial damage to roads and bridges. Bad weather can strike anywhere during the summer between December and early March.

CALAMA & THE CHUQUICAMATA COPPER MINE

1,574km (976 miles) N of Santiago; 98km (61 miles) NW of San Pedro de Atacama

Originally a desert way station, Calama has grown into a city of roughly 140,000 serving the gigantic copper mines in its vicinity. While the city is unattractive and hodgepodge and has a nasty reputation for crime and prostitution, its downtown commercial heart is safe enough and unemployment has almost disappeared. Its sole real attraction is slightly to the north, the Chuquicamata copper mine, whose huge tailings—hills of extracted dirt—form a partial backdrop to the city. The pre-Inca fortress **Pukará de Lasana** and the villages of **Chiu Chiu, Ayquina,** and **Caspana** are close to Calama, though they can also be visited from San Pedro via the Tatio Geysers. Adventurers can take the trip farther northeast toward **Ollagüe** on the border with Bolivia by train or bus.

Essentials

GETTING THERE

BY PLANE   Calama's **Aeropuerto El Loa** (CJC; © 55/367100) is served by **LANExpress** (© 600/526-2000; www.lan.com), **Sky Airline** (© 600/600-2828; www.skyairline.com), and **Aerolíneas del Sur** (© 800/710-3000). LAN has up to five daily flights from Santiago weekdays and three on weekends; Sky has two daily flights, and Aerolíneas del Sur has one Sunday through Friday. A taxi to Calama costs between C$5,000 and C$6,000. To get to San Pedro de Atacama, **Transfer Licancabúr** (© 55/334194) offers transfer services that cost C$10,000 per person from 7am to 9pm, and C$12,000 from 9pm to 7am (roundtrip fare is C$18,000 if traveling between 7am and 9pm). Services are scheduled to coincide with each plane's arrival from Santiago, so you shouldn't have to wait long to be on your way. You will also be dropped off at your hotel, making a taxi ride an unnecessary expenditure; a taxi will cost about C$30,000—be sure to fix a price before leaving the airport.

BY BUS   Unless you are time rich and money poor, the 21-hour bus journey from Santiago to Calama, plus another hour to get to San Pedro, is a torturously long ride that is best avoided. True enough, buses cost about half the cheapest plane fare, but even a *salón cama,* with reclining seats, hardly mitigates this painstaking journey. **Tur Bus** (© 600/660-6600) has service to Calama that carries on to San Pedro, leaving from Santiago's Terminal Alameda and Terminal San Borja; **Pullman** (© 600/320-3200;** www.pullman.cl) leaves from Terminal San Borja but does not go on to San Pedro, so you'll need to transfer in Calama. Buses to Calama leave about five times per day. Prices for a *salón cama* are C$36,000 one-way on Pullman and C$41,000 on Tur Bus to San Pedro.

BY CAR   It takes more than 20 hours to drive to Calama from Santiago. The final 12 hours of the journey beget a mind-altering landscape of surreal, barren landscapes. If you do choose to rent, rental cars are available at the Calama airport and in town. Roadside service is available from rental agencies, but without any services or phones on most roads, you will have to flag someone down for help—if someone comes along, that is. If you stay on main routes, you should have no problem, but outside of that, be prepared for the worst, and bring extra water and food and warm clothes in case you must spend the night on the road. A 4×4 is unnecessary, unless you plan an expedition along poorly maintained roads.

   The airport has rental kiosks for **Avis** (© 600/368-2000; www.avis.cl), **Budget** (© 600/441-0000; www.budget.cl), and **Hertz** (© 600/360-8666; www.hertz.cl). Rates include insurance. **Alamo** (© 2/655-5255 or in Calama 55/556802; www. alamochile.com) is the cheapest, but you may want to check with a local agency when you arrive at the airport for deals. *Tip:* Fill your gas tank in Calama. The sole pump in San Pedro charges at least 30% more.

BY TRAIN   One of Latin America's great remaining railway journeys links Calama with Uyuni in Bolivia. It's a rustic, fascinating trip along beautiful salt lakes and smoking volcanoes, but it's also grueling, and officially scheduled to take between 18 and 20 hours, with frequent delays. Trains leave Calama Wednesdays at 10pm, in theory reaching the border village of Ollagüe at 6:50am. The station is at Balmaceda 1777 (© 55/348900); the cost is C$7,000. Bring warm clothing as there is no heat on the train and temperatures at night are frigid.

Visitor Information

For maps and information about the entire Atacama region, an excellent source in Calama is the **Corporación de Cultura y Turismo,** Latorre 1689 (© 55/531707; open daily from 8am–1pm and 2–6pm). The main **hospital** "Dr. Carlos Cisternas" is on the street of the same name (© 55/655742; dial 131 for emergencies).

What to See & Do

The following tour operators offer excursions around the Calama area and trips to the Tatio Geysers and San Pedro de Atacama: **Atacama Indómita,** Av. La Paz 988

(✆ **55/347564;** www.atacamaindomita.com), or **Chuqui Tour,** Latorre 1512 (✆ **55/340190**). Your hotel in Calama can also put you in touch with a reputable tour operator.

CHUQUICAMATA COPPER MINE

Ghost towns throughout the northern desert bear traces of Chile's nitrate-mining glory days, but the copper-mining industry is alive and well, as evidenced by Calama's Chuquicamata mine, the largest open-pit mine in the world. Few wonders generate the visual awe a visitor experiences when gazing into this gigantic hole in the ground; in fact, the mine is so vast it can be seen from space, though morning dust often limits visibility. Workers still call it *El Cerro*—the mountain—which it was when begun in 1910 by the U.S. Guggenheim brothers, but today, the mine's main pit measures 4km (2½ miles) across and more than half a kilometer deep—everything at its bottom looks tiny, including the four-story giant trucks. Now run by government-owned Codelco and together with nearby Radomiro Tomic, it produces almost a million tons of copper per year. Codelco has finalized the transfer of Chuquicamata's 13,000 residents to modern housing in Calama, due to environmental and health concerns, but also to expand mining operations. Additionally, plans are underway to take the mine underground within the next decade.

Tours run every weekday, except holidays, from 2 to 3pm; you must be at the Chuquicamata office at the mine (Av. Tocopilla and José Miguel Carrera) at 1:30pm. For reservations (at least 1 day in advance), call ✆ **55/322122** or 55/345345, or e-mail visitas@codelco.cl. To get to the office, take an all-yellow *colectivo* taxi signed CALAMA CHUQUI from the corner of Ramirez and Abaroa in the plaza for C$1,200, or hire a regular taxi for about C$4,000 one-way. The mine tour is free, but donations to a foundation for underprivileged kids are encouraged. For safety, wear trousers, long-sleeved shirts, and closed shoes.

OTHER ATTRACTIONS

The **shopping mall** in Calama, Av. Balmaceda 3242 (www.mallplaza.cl; daily 10am–9:30pm), brandishes all the usual chain stores, which are useful if you need supplies from shoes and bathing suits to cameras and electronics, and has a cinema with mostly dubbed or subtitled U.S. films.

Where to Stay

Hotel El Mirador ★★   Steeped in an aura of bygone elegance, the El Mirador is far and away Calama's most colorful choice. Elegantly housed in a late-19th-century English home built by a cattle baron of that era, the hotel exudes charm with its graceful living area brimming with antiques and historical memorabilia, a plant-filled patio, and a sun-drenched terrace. Spotless, comfortable rooms are immaculate and tastefully decorated and the gleaming bathrooms feature claw-foot tubs and French-style windows. The hotel provides excellent, amiable service and can organize several tours around the area, including to Chuquicamata, and is close to shops, banks, and other services.

Sotomayor 2064, Calama. ✆/fax **55/340329.** www.hotelmirador.cl. 15 units. $84. double. AE, DC, MC, V. **Amenities:** Restaurant. *In room:* TV, free Wi-Fi.

L&S Hotel   This impeccable little hotel sets itself apart from its peers with its pristine and tasteful character. The owners of the L&S take great pride in providing value for your money, and the hotel has been thoughtfully designed according to a philosophy of budget chic and feng-shui. Each spacious guest room is decorated in a comforting palette of cream and beige with hard beds and minimalist IKEA-style furniture. The surgically clean white-tiled bathrooms surpass the medieval dimensions and cantankerous facilities of Calama's often seedy budget hotels. A light breakfast is included and served with a smile by the young, largely non-English speaking staff who are eager to please. The hotel is ideally situated, just 3 blocks from the plaza.

Vicuña Mackenna 1819, Calama. ℂ **55/361113.** www.lyshotel.cl. 20 units. $103 double. MC V. **Amenities:** Cafe. *In room:* TV, free Wi-Fi.

Park Hotel ★★ 🍴 On the deluxe end, Calama's Park Hotel offers dependable, high-quality accommodations and free airport pickup. The hotel interiors are a soothing mix of pastels and understated desert style; you can also cool off in the outdoor pool. Rooms are spacious and comfortable, and the restaurant is the best in town. The hotel, which is on the road to the airport, offers excursions with its onsite agency Atacama Park Adventure, with tours to the Chuquicamata mine and nearby destinations such as the Pukará de Lasana.

Alcalde José Lira 1392, Calama. ℂ **55/715800.** www.parkplaza.cl. 102 units. $107 double. AE, DC, MC, V. **Amenities:** Restaurant; bar; free airport transfers; health club; outdoor pool; room service; sauna; tennis court. *In room:* A/C, TV, minibar, free Wi-Fi.

Where to Dine

The **Club Croata,** Abaroa 1869 (ℂ **55/342126**), is midrange in terms of price and culinary inspiration. On the higher end, there's fine international cuisine at the **Park Hotel's Restaurant Parinas,** Alcalde José Lira 1392 (ℂ **55/715800**), with breakfast and a buffet at lunch and dinner for C$16,500 per person.

Nearby Excursions to Colonial Villages & Pukaras

These agricultural colonial-era villages and 12th-century Atacama Indian ruins merit a stop on the return trip to the airport, after an early morning visit to the Tatio Geysers (p. 223). That said, this can be an exhausting journey, considering the 4am wake-up call and the long drive thereafter (some all-inclusive hotels in fact no longer offer this combination excursion for this reason). If you can't muster the stamina, try a day visit from Calama.

The tiny village **Chiu Chiu,** founded as a missionary site by the Spanish around 1610 in what once was a popular trading route, is home to one of Chile's oldest churches, **San Francisco de Chiu Chiu,** erected in the mid-17th-century. The whitewashed adobe walls of this weather-beaten gem are 120cm (47-in.) thick, and its doors are made of cedar and bordered with cactus, displaying the Atacama style unique to the extreme north of Chile and Argentina. But what's most unusual are the church's two towers, and the ceiling made of chañar and algarrobo wood and held together with leather ropes instead of nails (the church is open from Tues–Sun 9am–2pm and 4–7pm). Just north, explore the ruins of the **Pukará de Lasana,** a 12th-century Indian fort abandoned after the Spanish occupation and restored in 1951. You'll want to spend some time wandering the labyrinthine streets that wind around the remains of 110 two- to five-story buildings built alongside the Loa river gorge, taking in the views toward the Andean peaks.

Another fortress due east, the **Pukará de Turi** was the largest fortified city built in the area; archaeological evidence shows the site was inhabited from the 9th century through almost 1600, when it was abandoned in the wake of the Spanish conquest. The scale of these 4-hectare (10-acre) ruins, with their circular towers and wide streets, is impressive, though those at Lasana are in better shape.

A bit to the south, **Ayquina** takes in part of a small valley formed by the Salado River, an affluent to the Loa River, with the church and cemetery at its bottom surrounded by gray limestone houses largely covered in straw, as tradition dictates from before the Spanish conquest. Only about 100 people still inhabit the village as people have left to find work in the copper mines, but it returns to life as some 40,000 people—including some 30 groups of costumed native dancers—converge on September 8 to celebrate the **Virgin of Guadalupe,** the patron saint of Chuquicamata's miners, to whom its lovely 17th-century church is dedicated. Walk to the arch east of the church to take in the view over the Salado and its lush valley.

While maps mark a road southeast from Ayquina to Caspana, it's been washed away at a river crossing. Take the road farther south, doubling back toward Calama to reach the engaging village of **Caspana,** surrounded by a fertile valley cultivated in a terraced formation like a sunken amphitheater. The village is characterized by its rock-wall and thatched-roof architecture. In the center, there is a tiny museum dedicated to the culture of the area and a crafts shop selling textiles made from alpaca. Cactus lampshades sold here do indeed give off a pretty flickering light, but pass them up because the species is endangered. Caspana also boasts a colonial-era church, **San Lucas,** completed in 1641 of stone, cactus, and mortar, and covered in adobe.

SAN PEDRO DE ATACAMA

98km (61 miles) SE of Calama; 1,674km (1,038 miles) N of Santiago

Quaint, unhurried, and built of adobe brick, the oasis town of San Pedro de Atacama lies in the midst of a region replete with bizarre land formations, giant sand dunes, jagged canyons, salt pillars, boiling geysers, and one smoking volcano. It seems better to call it a moonscape rather than a landscape. Certainly there is no other place on the planet like the Atacama Desert, which is the driest in the world, and it rates as one of Chile's star attractions. The region was the principal center of the Atacama Indian culture, and relics such as Tulor, an ancient village estimated to have been built in 800 B.C., still survive. There's also a fine museum of ancient artifacts well preserved by the bone-dry climate. Adventure travelers can pack a week full of activities here, including hiking, mountain biking, sandboarding, and horseback riding.

Know Before You Go

At just over 2,400m (8,000 ft.), the **altitude** in San Pedro will slow you down at first, though few are gravely affected by it. Don't plan on undertaking any grand expeditions to extreme altitudes during your first 2 days in San Pedro. Instead, allow yourself to acclimatize slowly. (See the "Health" and "Safety" sections in chapter 3 for more information.) There is just one small medical clinic in town, and no hospital. **Do not drink tap water** here (unless your hotel filters its tap water, which many now do) or in other altiplano villages, as the local supply contains trace amounts of arsenic. A **flashlight** could come in handy as many streets off the main drag are not lit at night.

San Pedro de Atacama

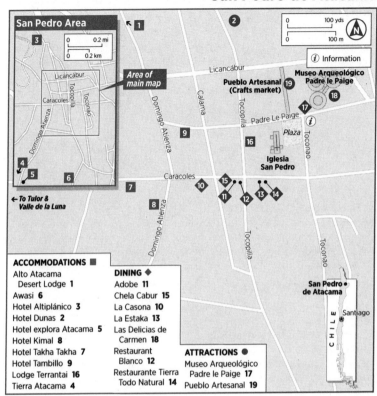

San Pedro Area

To Tulor & Valle de la Luna →

ACCOMMODATIONS ■
Alto Atacama
  Desert Lodge **1**
Awasi **6**
Hotel Altiplánico **3**
Hotel Dunas **2**
Hotel explora Atacama **5**
Hotel Kimal **8**
Hotel Takha Takha **7**
Hotel Tambillo **9**
Lodge Terrantai **16**
Tierra Atacama **4**

DINING ◆
Adobe **11**
Chela Cabur **15**
La Casona **10**
La Estaka **13**
Las Delicias de
  Carmen **18**
Restaurant
  Blanco **12**
Restaurante Tierra
  Todo Natural **14**

ATTRACTIONS ●
Museo Arqueológico
  Padre le Paige **17**
Pueblo Artesanal **19**

San Pedro's tiny, three-by-four street center has a pleasant bohemian vibe. The town has grown this past decade to cater to a growing number of visitors, but in spite of the new streetlights along Caracoles street and a proliferation of hostels, travel agencies, and arts and crafts stores, San Pedro still maintains its mellow charm. Its location almost exactly on the Tropic of Capricorn (which means no drastic changes in the length of daylight hours) and a stable climate make any time of the year a good time to visit here. But if you dislike the cold, June through September can be uncomfortable when temperatures plummet at night. Also, if you want to avoid the crowds, steer clear of high season, since you might feel overwhelmed by the number of tourists if you come from December through February, mid-July, or Chile's Independence and Armed Forces' Days of September 18 and 19.

Essentials

GETTING THERE

BY CAR   From Calama, head southeast on the route marked "San Pedro de Atacama," and continue for 98km (61 miles).

BY BUS   For Santiago buses to San Pedro, see "Getting There" in the Calama section. Several bus companies provide service to San Pedro from Calama: **Buses**

Atacama, Abaroa 2106 (© **55/316664**), has three trips per day at 8:15am, 1:15pm, and 6pm for C$2,000; and **Tur Bus,** Av. Balmaceda 1852 (© **600/660-6600**), has five trips to San Pedro daily for C$2,300 to C$3,100.

ORIENTATION

San Pedro de Atacama is divided into several *ayllus,* or neighborhoods; however, the principal area of the town can be walked in about 10 or 15 minutes. As more businesses pop up, residents are beginning to use street numbers, but many cling to citing "s/n" for *sin número,* or without number. The town's main axis that funnels east to the explora hotel and west to the Quitor archaeological site is Calle Domingo Atienza. The thoroughfare and dining and shopping epicenter is the north–west Calle Caracoles. Note that the street Antofagasta becomes Padre Le Paige (also known as Gustavo Le Paige) closer to the plaza. Several sights are within walking or biking distance, such as Quitor and Tulor, and it is possible to bike to the Valley of the Moon and through Devil's Canyon. But you'll need a tour to get to the Tatio Geysers, altiplanic lakes, or Laguna Cejar and the Atacama Salt Flat.

VISITOR INFORMATION

Sernatur operates a small visitor center at the plaza on the corner of Gustavo Le Paige and Toconao (© **55/851420**). Hours are Saturday through Thursday from 9:30am to 1:30pm and 3 to 7pm. The best site for information is **www.sanpedro atacama.com**, in English and Spanish, however it is not updated frequently.

What to See & Do

The boom in tourism has given birth to a dozen tour operators that line the streets of San Pedro, and which can be classified into two divisions: traditional tours and active expeditions (although a few offer both). Always try to book a reservation ahead of time, especially during the summer. Tour operators have minimum group sizes, but if you've made a reservation they will usually take you regardless of the group size being under the minimum.

If you can afford it, I strongly recommend hiring a private guide. A private guide will take you on uncommon tours, such as the remote salt flat Salar de Tara, and can adapt to your whims. Many are ex-guides from luxury hotels, with years of experience and insider contacts around town, but turnover is high, so check with Sernatur to contact a registered guide. The professional outfitter **Azimut 360** (© **2/235-1519;** www.azimut.cl), based in Santiago, offers weeklong customized adventure trips throughout Chile and Argentina and classic day trips around San Pedro which extend to the far reaches of the desert north. It can guide climbers up one of the four volcano routes in Chile and Bolivia. Costs vary; normally, a private guide charges one fee, around C$28,500 to C$38,000 per day for two to four people, and C$47,500 for six. Extras, including lunch, a car and driver, and entrance fees, can push the daily cost up to around C$109,250 for a group of two to four people.

For traditional tours (Valle de la Luna, the Salar de Atacama, Tatio Geysers, and archaeological tours), the following are tried and true: **Atacama Connection,** Caracoles and Toconao (©/fax **55/851421;** www.atacamaconnection.com); **Incahuasi,** Toconao 441 (© **55/851407;** www.bbincahuasi.cl); **Desert Adventure,** corner Caracoles 174 (©/fax **55/851067;** www.desertadventure.cl); and **Vulcano Expediciones,** Caracoles 317 (© **55/851023;** www.vulcanochile.com). Average prices are, per person: Valle de la Luna, C$10,000; Tatio Geysers, C$20,000; Laguna Cejar C$17,000.

STARGAZING The Atacama Desert boasts optimal conditions for astronomy and amateur stargazing (in the next decade two of the most important observatories in the world will be located here: Atacama Large Millimeter Array [ALMA] and the Extremely Large Telescope [ELT]). The Atacama's high altitude, infrequent cloud cover, and low-level light pollution allow travelers to clearly make out important constellations in the southern hemisphere such as Orion, the Southern Cross, and the Tarantula Nebula. The hotels **Alto Atacama Desert Lodge** and **explora Atacama** have installed Meade 16" telescopes with observatory platforms on their properties and offer evening stargazing sessions (except during and around full moon periods). Another truly enjoyable way to see the stars is an evening excursion with **Space** (San Pedro de Atacama Celestial Explorations), a French/Chilean-run outfit located at Caracoles 166 (© **55/851935;** www.spaceobs.com). Space currently has the largest collection of large-diameter telescopes available for public use in South America, and they run 2½-hour tours nightly except for periods around the full moon. The cost is C$15,000 per person and includes transportation, use of telescopes, and an easy-to-understand interpretation of the stars using a green-light laser as a guide. Tours in English are not always available so try to reserve a couple of days in advance, and bring warm clothing.

IN TOWN

Artisans ply their goods from many shops along the streets of San Pedro, but much of it seems to be of the same mid-range quality, and many items are really imported from Peru and Bolivia. A daily souvenir and crafts fair begins at the plaza, between the Municipal Building and the museum.

Museo Arqueológico Padre le Paige ★★★ Founded in 1957 by the Belgian missionary priest Padre Gustavo le Paige, this museum near the plaza is a regional highlight. Because the Atacama Desert is extremely arid, the nearly 400,000 artifacts on display here are exceptionally well preserved, and include ceramics, textiles, tablets used for the inhalation of hallucinogens, tools, gold and silver ceremonial masks, and more, all clearly displayed according to time period. The museum originally displayed several mummies, including "Miss Chile," a female mummy with her legs curled up to her chest as in contemplative repose, but since 2007 the mummies have been removed and stored after the local community objected to the ethical implications of displaying a dead human as a curiosity piece. Still, there is a creepy display of skulls that clearly demonstrates the ancient elite's penchant for self-imposed cranial deformation as a show of wealth. Often a side hall features artwork by local artists.

Gustavo Le Paige 380. © **55/851002.** Admission C$2,500 adults, C$1,000 children. Mon–Fri 9am–noon and 2–8pm, Sat–Sun 10am–noon and 2–6pm.

RESERVA NACIONAL LOS FLAMENCOS: THE SALAR DE ATACAMA, VALLE DE LA LUNA & THE SOUTHERN ALTIPLANIC LAKES

The **Reserva Nacional Los Flamencos (National Flamingo Reserve)** is divided into seven sectors and distributed over a vast area of land, including portions of the **Salar de Atacama (Atacama Salt Flat) ★**. A trip to the Salar is among San Pedro's most accessible destinations (as is Valle de la Luna). The Salar is a tremendous 100km-long (62-mile) mineralized lake with no outlet, and it is covered nearly completely by saline minerals and dust that combine to form a putty-colored crust; the salt crystals are formed by the evaporation of saline water that is unable to escape from the basin. The salt flat is the largest in Chile, and it is home to 40% of the world's lithium reserves. In some areas, lagoons peek out from under the crust, such as at Laguna Chaxa, the traditional stop at the Salar due to the CONAF interpretative center here; the center is open daily 8am to 7:30pm and there's a C$2,500 park entry fee. But it is difficult to see flamingos at Chaxa, and as destinations go, it is a fairly boring stop.

Most tour companies also run afternoon excursions to the far more interesting **Laguna Cejar** ★, some 19km (12 miles) from San Pedro, and/or visit the visually stunning, turquoise-blue **Laguna Tebinquinche** ★★, quite possibly the best place to watch the sun set and the colors of the Atacama basin flit from pink to orange to purple. Often tour companies will stop midway at two round swimming holes called **Ojos del Salar;** visitors can swim in both Cejar and the Ojos. Laguna Cejar affords a remarkable swimming experience of floating in water so saline it is virtually impossible to sink (Cejar contains even greater levels of salt and lithium than the Dead Sea). Shards of protruding, jagged salt crests can prove lethal, so flip flops or sandals are essential, and bring a couple of large bottles of fresh water to rinse yourself off with afterward. Renting a bike to come here is an option, but it's a long ride and some parts of the road are very sandy and tricky to pedal through; you also won't want to ride here in the afternoon since you won't find your way back in the dark. Bring a sweater or fleece as there generally is a steady breeze here in the afternoon.

Valle de la Luna (Valley of the Moon) ★★ is easily San Pedro's most popular destination. It's known for its eerie land formations and salt-encrusted peaks sculpted by wind and occasional floods, creating a truly ethereal landscape of textures and colors. Visitors frequently come to watch the sunset from here at a *mirador* that looks out over a massive sand dune pinned between two ridges (earthquake activity in 2007 dropped the level of the dune and visitors are unfortunately prohibited from walking across it, until the dune rebuilds itself). Tours here usually include a 15-minute walk through the Cordillera de Sal (Salt Hill Range) where one can hear cracking noises as the salt hills expand or contract due to temperature. The dune lookout point is a popular place to watch the sunset, so be prepared to share the view with dozens of other tourists, especially during high season. For an unforgettable night, come on the night of a full moon, when ghostly light casts shadows on an already spooky landscape. The Valley is 15km (9¼ miles) from San Pedro and can be reached by bicycle or car. To get here, head west on the street Licancabúr toward Calama, and follow the left-turn sign for Valle de la Luna. At the entrance is a small visitor's center. The Valle is open daily from 9am to 7pm, and the cost is C$2,000 per person.

Heading south 38km (24 miles) from San Pedro, you will reach the oasis towns of Toconao, Camar, and Socaire. These three towns are not as picturesque as their counterparts in the Atacama Desert, so you might want to just continue on. What you should head for are the high altiplanic lakes, **Laguna Miscanti** and **Laguna Miñeques,** two stunning cobalt-blue lakes at the foot of their respectively named peaks, and the **Salar de Talar** ★★★ and the **Laguna de Tuyajto,** where it is easier to spot flamingos than at the Salar de Atacama. This journey is recommended in order to view high-altitude lakes on a less strenuous trip than the **Salar de Tara** ★★★, near the Argentina/Bolivia/Chile border. More adventurous types are better off visiting Tara because the reserve is larger, the salt flat's colors are more intense, and there are no other tourists. The Salar de Tara (also part of the Flamingo Reserve) rates as one of the most memorable journeys in the Atacama area, but few visitors are aware of it. The trip requires a round-trip 200km (124-mile) drive with a total 1-hour ride on a bumpy road, and altitudes that reach upwards of more than 4,200m (14,000 ft).

GEYSERS DEL TATIO/BAÑOS DE PURITAMA ★★★

One of the major highlights in the Atacama Desert is the **Geysers del Tatio (Tatio Geysers),** located 95km (59 miles) north of San Pedro. The geysers excursion is nonetheless not the easiest—there's not a lot of physical activity required, but tours leave around 5 to 5:30am (the geysers are most active around 6–8am). At 4,321m (14,173 ft.), these are the highest geysers in the world, and it is a marvelous spectacle to watch thick plumes of steam blow from holes in such a windswept, arid land. Interspersed between the geysers, bubbling pools encrusted with colorful minerals splash and splutter—but exercise extreme caution when walking near the thin crust; careless visitors burn themselves here frequently. Grazing about the periphery are herds of *vicuñas,* the smallest camelid, and it is common to see *vizcachas,* hare-like rodents that like to warm themselves on rocks. There is a basic hot springs pool at the geyser site, but a more deluxe option is the Baños de Puritama (see later) on the way back to town. Leave your rental car in San Pedro and opt for a tour here instead (many include breakfast at the geyser site). The partially paved road to the geysers has made the journey less difficult, but it is still easy to get lost in the dark. All tours stop at the charming village Machuca on the way back, where locals sell llama-meat shish kebabs, empanadas, and local artisanal crafts.

Due to the high altitude at Tatio, this journey is not recommended as your first-day excursion; head here on day 3 or later. On the way back to town from Tatio, many opt to stop for a dip at the **Baños de Puritama,** a sybaritic hot springs oasis composed of attractive rock pools fringed with greenery that descend down a gorge, about 60km (37 miles) from the geysers (or 28km/17 miles from San Pedro, heading out on the road that borders the cemetery). They are run by the luxury Hotel explora (see "Where to Stay," later) and cost a steep C$10,000 to enter, but it's worth it (a discounted rate of C$5,000 per person is available from 2pm to 5:30pm on weekdays, excluding holidays). Puritama is open daily from 9:15am to 5:30pm. You may want to tote a picnic and a bottle of wine to enjoy while there. There are changing rooms and bathrooms on the premises.

PUKARÁ DE QUITOR ★★

The Pukará is a 12th-century, pre-Inca fortress that clings to a steep hillside some 3km (1¾ miles) outside San Pedro in the Catarpe Valley (near the Alto Atacama Lodge; see "Where to Stay.") Although formidable, the fortress was no match for the Spanish who, in spite of numbering just 30 men, conquered hundreds of Atacama there in 1540 with the use of horses and steel swords. Beyond its strategic purpose, the fortress was inhabited and many of the unmarked terraced enclosures—which number over 200—would have been living spaces, patios, and kitchens. It requires a healthy imagination to visualize the site as a powerful defensive fortification, but there is a palpable energy about the place that invites soulful contemplation. It takes a further 15 minutes (a moderate climb) to reach the top of the fort. This is an ideal bike ride from San Pedro but a searing hot walk during the middle of the day.

There are information boards in English and a small information office with facilities. Entrance to the site is C$2,000. If you're riding a bike, continue north from the Pukará up through the valley for a truly enjoyable ride along a dirt road for 2km (1¼ miles). There, a short scramble up the eastern, right-hand ridge will take you to the tiny Inca ruin of **Catarpe.** It's a quiet, pensive spot with a beautiful view of Licancabúr and other Andean peaks.

If you need a visa for Bolivia, the **Bolivian consulate** is on Sotomayor 1959, second floor, office 6. It's open Monday through Friday from 9am to 4pm (ℂ 55/341976). The visa costs C$47,500 and can be obtained within 24 hours with luck, but you'll need to present documents such as your Bolivian hotel reservation, your roundtrip bus or plane ticket, a credit card, and your itinerary when in Bolivia.

ALDEA DE TULOR ★★

Tulor, Atacama's oldest pueblo, is a fascinating attraction, if only because of its age, estimated to have been built around 800 B.C. The site remained intact in part because it had been covered with sand for hundreds of years, and today it is possible to see the walls that once formed the structures of this town. There are a few reconstructed houses on view as well. Tulor is 9km (5½ miles) southwest of San Pedro.

BOLIVIA'S LAGUNA VERDE ★★

Why not visit Bolivia for the day? Early afternoon journeys to the shimmering turquoise lakes on the backside of Volcán Licancabúr put travelers in a high-altitude wonderland including a hot springs pool. This is an easy journey, but perhaps not as grand as the Salar de Tara. Rental vehicles may not cross the border; if you have your own vehicle, you'll need to register at Customs on the road out to Bolivia and pay an entrance fee at the Bolivian border. Better still, go with a Bolivian tour operator out of San Pedro. Try **Colque Tours,** at the corner of Caracoles and Calama (ℂ 55/851109; www.colquetours.com). They can also take you deeper into Bolivia to the fantastic, snow-white salt flat **Uyuni,** the largest in the world.

OUTDOOR ACTIVITIES

BIKING   The Atacama region offers excellent terrain for mountain-bike riding, including the Quebrada del Diablo (Devil's Gorge) and Valle de la Muerte (Death Valley); however, it is also enjoyable to ride across the flat desert to visit sites such as Tulor. Bike rental shops can be found along Caracoles, and they all are the same in terms of quality and charge about C$5,000 to C$6,000 per day.

HORSEBACK RIDING   Horseback riding is a quiet, relaxing way to experience the Atacama and view Indian ruins that are inaccessible by bike. If you are adept at galloping, fulfill your Lawrence of Arabia fantasies and race across a sand dune. **Rancho Cactus,** Toconao 568 (ℂ 55/851506; www.rancho-cactus.çl), and **Rancho La Herradura,** Tocopilla 406 (ℂ 55/851956; www.atacamahorseadventure. com), offer short and full-day rides to a variety of destinations; the cost is C$15,000 for 2 hours, and C$30,000 for 5 hours. Full day rides cost C$57,000 and include lunch. They also plan overnight trips; consult each agency for details and prices.

SANDBOARDING   Sandboarding is the sand-dune version of snowboarding. Several places in San Pedro rent boards, and the place to head is Valle de la Muerte. It's best to go by bike or car. The more similar the bindings on your board to snowboard bindings, the easier it will be to keep your balance. Also, take the more tapered, slightly longer boards instead of those short, wheel-less skateboards some places offer. No ski lifts here—don't forget to take water and sunblock on this excursion, as you'll spend lots of time climbing back up the steep dunes in the heat.

VOLCANO ASCENTS   Climbing one of the four volcanoes in the area requires total altitude acclimatization and good physical condition. It is a heart-pounding hike up, but if you can hack it, the sweeping views and the experience in itself are exhilarating. The most popular is the 5,400m (17,712 ft.) ascent up the active Volcán Láscar, about a 4-hour climb; climbing groups leave San Pedro before sunup. However, recent activity means this climb may not be available. Volcán Licancabúr is also popular, but it requires an overnight stay at a rustic *refugio* just across the border and a Bolivian guide. Many tour companies offer these excursions; among the best is **Azimut 360** (© 2/235-1519; www.azimut.cl).

Where to Stay

San Pedro de Atacama is packed with lodging options but what the town lacks is moderate accommodations. Hostels and economic hotels abound, but then it's a steep climb to expensive options, and even budget accommodations are pricey for what you get. Any double room under $60 will most likely come with a shared bathroom. During the colder months, make certain your hostel has heat, as some budget-friendly options still lack this very important amenity. Most lodging in San Pedro (even at the top of the range) does not come with televisions, and many rooms do not have phones. Do not underestimate the luxury of a swimming pool, especially during the summer. Most hotels do not have air-conditioning, though the architectural design that is prevalent in San Pedro features dark and cool interiors, and some hotels have ceiling fans. For camping, the **Takha Takha Hotel** (see below) has a pleasant, shady campground with a BBQ dining area and hot showers for $17 per person.

VERY EXPENSIVE

Alto Atacama Desert Lodge & Spa ★★★ 📷   The Alto Atacama, located in the Catarpe Valley near the Pukará de Quitor ruins, boasts the most stunning landscape of all the luxury properties in the region, and its distance from the village (about 3km/1¾ miles away) provides guests with absolute silence and tranquillity. The Alto also deserves kudos for its dedication to sustainability and cultural consciousness; architects designed the low-slung lodge to blend into the mountains that back the property, with colors and textures that mimic its natural surroundings. The lodge has six oasis-like swimming pools, a full-service spa, and an alfalfa patch grazed by llamas and alpacas, as well as indoor and outdoor dining areas and lounges warmed by crackling fires. Its handsomely decorated guest rooms are kept cool with dark adobe walls and a fresh breeze, and each room opens onto a private patio with sweeping views of the valley. As at the explora, there's a professional telescope and observatory for stargazing. Many of the staff members here are indigenous, and the service is wonderfully friendly. All-inclusive packages include delicious cuisine, but the hotel also offers lodging only (with breakfast) for $400 to $500 double per night.

Camino a Quitor s/n, San Pedro de Atacama. © **2/982-3945** (local); **2/957-0300** in Santiago (reservations). www.altoatacama.com. 32 units. All-inclusive rates (including excursions, meals, open bar, and airport transfers), double occupancy, per person: 3 nights $1,339–$1,711; 4 nights $1,696–$2,168; 5 nights $2,009–$2,567. Reduced rates available for children and teens. AE, DC, MC, V. **Amenities:** Restaurant; bar; babysitting; 6 outdoor pools; spa; free Wi-Fi. *In room:* Hair dryer, minibar.

Awasi ★★★   This exclusive hideaway opened in 2007 and was promptly heaped with accolades by the travel industry. Of all the luxury hotels in San Pedro, the Awasi feels closest to "boutique," with just eight private cottages constructed in wood, adobe, and stone, and that look straight from the pages of a glossy designer magazine, with simple but luxurious fabrics, and decor swathed in tones of beige and cream.

Guests find the Awasi's main perk to be its privately guided tours, meaning you will not share a tour or vehicle with other guests, and the staff-to-guest ratio is two to one, providing personalized, attentive service. That said, the compact premises, with its tiny pool and public spaces, put you in close contact with other guests, but few seem to mind this. Perhaps the only other caveat is that the Awasi does not have views, and some rooms require a key to get into the main lounge area. Yet, in spite of that, the Awasi is a marvelous experience that pampers its guests with finery. The gourmet cuisine, too, is divine and deserves special mention.

Tocopilla 4, San Pedro de Atacama. © **55/851460** (local), or 888/880-3219 in the U.S. and 2/233-9641 in Santiago (reservations). www.awasi.com. 8 units. All-inclusive rates (including excursions, meals, open bar, and airport transfers), double occupancy, per person: 3 nights $1,887–$2,350; 4 nights $2,510–$3,020; 5 nights $3,140–$3,775. Reduced rates available for children and teens. AE, DC, MC, V. **Amenities:** Restaurant; bar; babysitting; outdoor pool; sauna; free Wi-Fi.

Hotel explora Atacama ★★ The internationally acclaimed Hotel explora pioneered the 5-star, all-inclusive hotel experience in the Atacama in 1998. Although the hotel faces a lot of competition these days, the explora's "Hotel de Larache," as it is known, is still one of the most deluxe hotel options in the region. Explora's concept is rustic elegance and active travel, perhaps more active than other hotels; in fact, explora offers "Travesías," a series of truly memorable and adventurous add-on trips (at an additional cost) to Salta, Argentina, and Uyuni, Bolivia, with overnight luxury camping. Whereas Awasi is intimate, explora is lofty and expansive, with a light and airy wraparound public area that includes an art gallery, an excellent excursion room with maps and reference literature, a bar, and a lounge with plenty of couches and spaces to relax. This lounge and the hotel's outdoor pool area (with four swimming pools, a Jacuzzi, and sauna) are the property's principal selling points, as is its on-site stable for horseback riding enthusiasts. Of the top luxury hotels, explora's guest rooms are perhaps more youthful in decor than elegant, with dashes of whimsical colors, checkered bedspreads, and Crate and Barrel–style furniture. Rooms, however, do come with lovely views.

Domingo Atienza s/n, San Pedro de Atacama (main office: Américo Vespucio Sur 80, Piso 5, Santiago). © **55/851110** (local), or toll-free 866/750-6699 in the U.S. www.explora.com. 50 units. All-inclusive rates (including excursions, meals, open bar, and airport transfers), double occupancy, per person: 3 nights $1,920–$2,895; 4 nights $2,560–$3,860. Reduced rates available for children and teens. AE, DC, MC, V. **Amenities:** Restaurant; bar; babysitting; bikes; Jacuzzi; 4 outdoor pools; sauna. *In room:* Hair dryer, free Wi-Fi.

Tierra Atacama ★★ This all-inclusive retreat, a 10-minute walk from the center of San Pedro, is the modernist alter ego of the Portillo ski resort (see p. 182 in chapter 7). A more holistic approach is also on display here—the owners have utilized natural materials to create a striking contemporary design that blends harmoniously with the landscape. An airy dining area and public space is scattered with animal skin rugs and Scandinavian-style furniture mixed with local art and Andean textiles. Guest rooms are painted with soft cream and earth tones and are decorated with crushed seashells. Some of the rooms have four-poster beds. Sheaths of glass framed with steel provide picture window views of the Licancabúr Volcano (request a room facing east), and rooms with bathtubs face the other direction; each room has a delightful private bamboo patio. The cuisine, a daily set menu, is superb, and many of the ingredients are grown in the hotel's 4-hectare (10-acre) garden. In many ways the hotel feels like a luxury commune and guests are encouraged to kick off their shoes and mingle in the lounge area, bar, and library.

Calle Séquitor s/n, Ayllú de Yaye. San Pedro de Atacama. ℂ **55/555977** (local), or 800/829-5325 in the U.S. www.tierraatacama.com. 32 units. All-inclusive rates (including excursions, meals, open bar, and airport transfers), double occupancy, per person: 3 nights $1,290; 4 nights $1,600; 5 nights $1,900. Reduced rates available for children and teens. AE, DC, MC, V. **Amenities:** Restaurant; bar; babysitting; bikes; Jacuzzi; outdoor pool; sauna. *In room:* Hair dryer, free Wi-Fi.

EXPENSIVE

Hotel Altiplánico ★ The Hotel Altiplánico, a 15-minute stroll from town toward the Pukará de Quitor, offers stylish architecture and comfortable guest rooms without the price tag of the Awasi or explora. It's not all-inclusive and so it's a good option for independent travelers seeking to plan their own excursions and dine according to their whims, either at the hotel or in town. The very spacious property is pleasantly landscaped with river rock patios and straw roofs, as well as a large swimming pool surrounded by shaded adobe seating and hammocks. Guest rooms are simply adorned, with adobe walls and thatched roofs, and all come with small patios and some with an outdoor fire pit. The drawbacks are that the walk back from town at night is very dark, and service, while friendly, can be lackadaisical. Also, for the price, the hotel is lacking in amenities such as a minibar and phones in the rooms, and wake-up calls sometimes don't materialize—bring an alarm clock and a flashlight to be on the safe side.

Domingo Atienza 282, San Pedro de Atacama. ℂ **55/851212.** Fax 55/851238. www.altiplanico.cl. 29 units. $232 double standard, $263 double superior (includes breakfast). AE, DC, MC, V. **Amenities:** Cafeteria; bar; Jacuzzi; large outdoor pool. *In room:* No phone, free Wi-Fi.

Hotel Kimal ★★ 🎁 The Hotel Kimal is one of the longest-operating hotels in San Pedro and while it doesn't have the bang and prestige of other luxury hotels in the area, it does offer a slice of tranquillity and a central location. The Kimal also recently opened a new property across the street called the Hotel Poblado Kimal, with 21 cabin-style independent units connected by wooden walkways and featuring its own outdoor swimming pool. The rooms in the Poblado are comfortable but a bit sparse and do not feature finer detailing as does its flagship hotel, which explains the $32 difference in price. The Hotel Kimal's rooms are softly lit by skylights and have wooden floors and crisp cream-colored and beige linens, and rooms are fringed outside by pimiento trees and stone walkways. Most rooms have a little seating area outside. Like the Altiplánico, guests plan excursions and dine independently.

Domingo Atienza 452 (at Caracoles), San Pedro de Atacama. ℂ **55/851152.** Fax 55/851030. www. kimal.cl. 19 units (Hotel Kimal); 21 units (Hotel Poblado Kimal). $232 double Hotel Kimal; $200 Hotel Poblado Kimal (includes breakfast). AE, DC, MC, V. **Amenities:** Restaurant; bar; outdoor pool. *In room:* Minibar, free Wi-Fi.

Lodge Terrantai ★★ This smartly decorated and elegant little boutique hotel is located smack in the middle of San Pedro yet is a quiet oasis. The Terrantai is housed in a lovely century-old home that was renovated by a well-known Chilean architect who employed ancient building techniques during the preservation of the building's flat-fronted facade, adobe walls, and thatched roof. The interiors are very style-conscious and exude pure minimalism, with every inch of the interior hallways and many of the room walls fortified with stacked river rock. Two room types are available: the larger Andina with better views of the interior garden and pool area; and the smaller Intiwasi with plain white adobe walls, small windows, and skylights. Rooms are quite cozy with down comforters and colorful throws, and soft reading lights. There is a restaurant for breakfast, lunch, and dinner, and a new reading room lounge and expanded swimming pool.

Tocopilla 411, San Pedro de Atacama. © **55/851045.** Fax 55/851037. www.terrantai.com. 21 units. $160–$198 Intiwasi double room; $180–$200 Andina double room. AE, MC, V. **Amenities:** Restaurant; outdoor pool. *In room:* Free Wi-Fi.

INEXPENSIVE

Hotel Dunas   Unlike most Atacama hotels, the Dunas is run by a local couple who give the hotel a family feel. The hotel is located just 3 blocks from the main Caracoles street, with eight guest rooms situated in a long motel-like layout with a central foyer/lobby. Given that it opened in 2006 the Dunas is in good shape for an economy hotel and kept trim and neat. Rooms are simple yet strive for a pinch of style with the local penchant for river-rock and adobe walls.

Calle Tocopilla 313, San Pedro de Atacama. © **55/851989.** www.hoteldunas.cl. 8 units. $80 double. AE, DC, MC, V. **Amenities:** Cafe. *In room:* No phone.

Hotel Tambillo   The Tambillo is a decent option in this price range, with a tranquil central patio and indoor parking. Its 15 units are spread along an adobe and inlaid stone-walled building, although the rooms forego the Atacama style for a more generic hotel decor. Solar-powered units have arched windows and doors, high ceilings, and basic furnishings, which rather than being unappealing, create an atmosphere that is natural and fresh. A vaguely indigenous ascetic continues through the lobby and bar. Breakfast can be purchased for an additional C$1,500 per person, served inside the hotel's spacious cafe. It's a 4-block walk to the main street.

Gustavo (Padre) Le Paige 159, San Pedro de Atacama. ©/fax **55/851078.** www.hoteltambillo.cl. 15 units. $80 double. No credit cards. **Amenities:** Cafeteria. *In room:* No phone.

Takha Takha Hotel ★   A San Pedro stalwart with a central location, the Takha Takha has taken it up a notch with newly renovated, hostel-like accommodations and campground facilities. Rooms with private bathrooms for one to four people are spartan in style, with average beds, a nightstand, and lamp; the double "superiors" come with more space and attractive decor for about $15 more. Although one could expect a bit more for $65 to $95 for a double with a private bath, the rooms are clean, the premises are leafy and delightful, and the service is usually reliable. Rates include a simple continental breakfast and there are dining areas with BBQ pits; a swimming pool is slated for installation in 2011.

Caracoles 101-A, San Pedro de Atacama. © **55/851038.** www.takhatakha.cl. 23 units. $41 double with shared bath; $78–$95 double with private bath. AE, DC, MC, V. **Amenities:** Cafe; BBQ and dining area. *In room:* No phone.

Where to Dine

Many restaurants fill up quickly after 8:30pm when dusty, weary travelers arrive back from their daily excursions. Arrive early or consider making a reservation if the restaurant accepts them. Most restaurants are casual and some offer both a day and an evening fixed-price menu that is a good value, otherwise it can be pricey to dine out at night. Menus tend to be all things to all diners, featuring a selection of pasta, pizza, sandwiches, salads, and meat dishes of varying quality in cozy, unpretentious settings that are often situated around nightly bonfires.

Competition has drawn waiters onto the street to harangue for business, but your choices aren't too overwhelming. A popular pub for drinking and light meals, as well as televised sporting events, is **Chela Cabur,** Caracoles 211 (© **55/851576**). For dessert lovers, **Las Delicias de Carmen,** Calama 370 #B (© **9/089-5673**), offers apple and lemon pie, walnut tarts, strudel, and several kinds of cakes made to order or to try there at the restaurant. The restaurant also offers pizza, delicious empanadas, and inexpensive Chilean-style fixed-price meals (C$1,800–C$4,000). Also recommended for dinner is the Hotel Kimal's **Restaurant Paacha** (see earlier), with a quiet, intimate environment, set menus for lunch and dinner, and outstanding pisco sours—and they'll let visiting diners take a dip in their pool either before or after the meal.

MODERATE

Adobe ★★ CHILEAN   Adobe is one of the most enjoyable and cozy places to dine and unwind in San Pedro. What sets the mood here, though, is the blazing bonfire, around which diners sit at wooden tables under a semi-enclosed thatched roof. Adobe sticks to what it does best: stone-baked, thin crust pizzas, spaghetti, quesadillas, and satisfying meat dishes served with quinoa and salads or "a lo pobre" style (enough to feed a starving man), beef or chicken served on a well-oiled mountain of chunky french fries and then topped with a fried egg. Good-looking waiters dressed in black provide attentive service. Live music serenades diners beginning at 9pm, and although Adobe serves dinner only until 11:30pm, the restaurant converts into a bar with light snacks thereafter.

Caracoles 211. ℂ **55/851164.** www.cafeadobe.cl. Main courses C$6,000–C$9,500. Reservations recommended for groups. AE, DC, MC, V. Daily 11am–1am.

La Casona ★★★ CHILEAN   La Casona has been around for years but new ownership has reinvented this amicable restaurant and turned the focus to serving traditional Chilean cuisine in a more refined atmosphere. If you've been to the Bar Liguria in Santiago (p. 97), you can't help notice its influence on La Casona's cuisine and the decor, with huge kitschy chalkboard menus, wood tables, and hanging mirrors. La Casona is as warm and inviting as at Adobe (see earlier) but the ambience is less rustic. The dining area takes up the better part of an old colonial building, with soaring ceilings and whitewashed adobe walls. Dishes are authentic and hearty and include *pastel de choclo*, a corn and meat pie; empanadas; grilled meats; *arrollado*, a delicious pork roll with spices; and seafood dishes that include *chupe de loco*, or abalone casserole. Hungry diners might opt for a sizzling mini BBQ "parrillada" brought to the table with slabs of meat; the cost for two is C$18,000 but it can feed three people.

Caracoles 195. ℂ **55/851337.** Main courses C$4,500–C$7,000. AE, DC, MC, V. Daily noon–4pm and 7pm–midnight.

La Estaka ★ INTERNATIONAL/CHILEAN   Owned by the same people as Adobe, La Estaka has become a local institution, the place where young hotel managers like to indulge when they clock out. The cavernous, semi-outdoor dining room with a thatched roof, tiled floor, and rustic wooden tables is decorated with local artwork and is usually packed by 9pm. The laid-back staff flits among the tables with a functional friendliness. The menu is small but the chefs have clearly mastered each dish—all are artfully presented and heartily proportioned. If you are in the mood for rich Italian food, the bubbling cannelloni filled with fresh seafood and the decadently cheesy risotto with shrimp are two of the best entrees in town.

Caracoles 259-B. ℂ **55/851164.** www.laestaka.cl. Main courses C$4,800–C$6,900; sandwiches C$3,500–C$4,600. AE, DC, MC, V. Daily 9am–1am.

Restaurant Blanco ★★ CHILEAN/INTERNATIONAL   Blanco completes the trilogy of restaurants under the same wing as Adobe and La Estaka. True to its name, the atmosphere is almost entirely white and minimalist with molded banquettes and flickering candles. It's a simple—some would argue sterile—backdrop for the experimental cuisine, which attempts to inject more intriguing flourishes into the region's standard meat and fish specialties. Try their gingery salmon with pears and ricotta potatoes or the beef tenderloin with mushrooms and drizzled with pesto oil, accompanied by a bottle of carmenère wine selected from their impressive wine list.

Caracoles 195. ✆ **55/851939.** www.blancorestaurant.cl. Main courses C$5,200–C$8,500. AE, DC, MC, V. Daily 6–11pm.

INEXPENSIVE

Restaurante Tierra Todo Natural ★ HEALTH FOOD This winning little restaurant expanded recently and now there are plenty of tables for diners seeking healthy, well-prepared meals using organic produce, and creative vegetarian cuisine. The restaurant still serves its mainstay of delicious whole-grain empanadas and sandwiches with bread made from scratch, as well as fresh fruit juices. Now on the menu are meatless dishes such as veggie lasagna and salads, as well as simple meat dishes, crepes, and pastas. This is an excellent spot for a continental-style breakfast, with fresh bread and juice, and strong coffee.

Caracoles 271. ✆ **55/851585.** www.restaurantetierratodonatural.cl. Empanadas and sandwiches C$1,800–C$2,200; main courses C$4,200–C$6,400. AE, DC, MC, V. Daily 8:30am–midnight.

ARICA ★★

2,062km (1,281 miles) N of Santiago; 614km (382 miles) NW of Calama

Chile's northernmost city, just 19km (12 miles) south of the border with Peru, Arica lies on a large bay dominated by the massive Morro, the landmark desert hill that almost juts into the Pacific Ocean alongside the city's main square. Founded in 1565 and seized from Peru in 1880 during the War of the Pacific, the city was the exit harbor for the massive silver exports to Spain from Potosí in what is now Bolivia; its port handles much of Bolivia's present-day trade. With a year-round, springlike climate and string of pleasant beaches, Arica has become a popular area for vacationing Chileans and Bolivians. For most travelers, however, Arica's main draw is its location as the gateway to world-class ancient treasures in the pleasant and lush Azapa and Lluta valleys and the Parque Nacional Lauca.

Though its colonial heritage has been wiped away by successive natural disasters, this city of roughly 180,000 residents exudes stately pride with graceful, palm-studded squares from the cathedral to the port and brightly painted houses jutting against the Morro. It's also one of Chile's most ethnically varied cities, with the presence of Peruvians and Bolivians adding an indigenous mysticism to Arica's provincial quaintness. Development has been rapid and ill thought out; the pretty cast-iron cathedral just manages to escape being overshadowed by ugly 1970s government buildings, and monolithic high-rises are springing up along the Chinchorro beach in the northern suburbs.

Essentials

GETTING THERE

BY PLANE Arica's **Aeropuerto Chacalluta** (ARI; ✆ **58/213416**) is served by **LAN Express** (✆ **600/526-2000;** www.lan.com) and **Sky Airline** (✆ **600/600-2828**). LAN has three daily flights from Santiago to Arica; Sky has two, however neither airline has service to Arica from Calama or Antofagasta (you'll need to travel

to Iquique for a flight to Arica). A taxi to Arica costs around C$8,000, or you can take the shuttle service **Arica Service Tour** (© 58/222899) for C$2,500 per person. There is an ATM at the airport.

BY BUS   Several bus companies provide service to Arica from Santiago, a grueling 28-hour trip (C$35,000 for a *salon cama*), and a flight booked well in advance might not be that much more expensive than a good seat on a bus. Connections throughout the far north are readily available from the domestic terminal, Terminal Rodoviario Diego Portales 948, north of downtown. From here, **Tur Bus** (© 600/660-6600) offers service to San Pedro and **Pullman Bus** (© 58/227146) to Calama with connections to San Pedro for between C$11,000 and C$12,500; travel time is 8 hours to Calama and 9 hours to San Pedro.

The international bus terminal next door at Diego Portales 1002 has connections to nearby Peru and Bolivia; buses on the La Paz route can drop you off at Lake Chungará in Parque Nacional Lauca, but you'll need to pay full fare and you're not guaranteed to be picked up again (you can try to flag down a coach, as they will sometimes stop). **Buses Transalvador** (© 58/246064) has service to La Paz for C$8,000 oneway leaving at 2:30pm and 1am. **La Paloma,** Germán Riesco 2071 (© 58/222710), runs to Putre for C$3,000; travel time is 2.5 hours with trips leaving daily and only at 7am. For bus service in Peru, the best option is to cross the border to Tacna, and take the bus line "Buses TEPSA" from there.

BY CAR Unless you're in Chile on a road trip and with considerable time and tolerance, you won't drive here from Santiago, which takes 3 days with 24 hours behind the wheel. Distances can be deceiving; even Calama is about a day's drive south of Arica. However, renting a car can be a rewarding and convenient way to visit sights near Arica. While the city is pretty easy to negotiate and roads are in good condition, consider the inconvenience of driving at high altitudes around Parque Nacional Lauca before rushing off. You can reach Lago Chungará with a regular vehicle, but you'll need 4×4 transportation on roads south of Surire, and this trip should not be risked in poor weather. Surire is far more remote than San Pedro, so seriously consider taking it easy and instead book a guided altiplano tour in Arica or Putre for less stress and more of a holiday.

The airport has rental kiosks for **Avis** (② 600/368200; www.avischile.cl), **Budget** (② 58/258911; www.budget.cl), and **Hertz** (② 58/219186; www.hertz.cl). Downtown, you'll find **Avis,** at Chacabuco 314 (② 58/214671); **Budget,** in the Hotel Arica on San Martín 599 (② 58/258911); and **Hertz,** at Baquedano 999 (② 58/231487). Regular vehicles rent for about C$50,000 per day, and 4×4 trucks for an average of C$75,000. You can also shop around with smaller agencies for cheaper prices (and usually older models): **Cactus,** Baquedano 666 (② 58/257430; cactusrent@latinmail.com) and **Klasse Rent a Car,** General Velásquez 760 (② 58/252954). Rental vehicles cannot be taken over the border to Peru or Bolivia.

BY TRAIN Sadly, passenger travel to the Andean highlands and as far as La Paz has been suspended for several years now, however there is talk of possibly reinstating the service sometime in 2012. You can take a train to **Tacna** in Peru, however, with trains departing daily from the Ferrocarriles Arica-Tacna station just north of the port (② 58/231115). Tickets are a rock-bottom C$1,300 Monday to Friday, and C$1,600 Saturdays, Sundays, and holidays. Buy your tickets at least a day in advance; the ticket office is open daily from 10am to 5:30pm. Departures from Arica are at 9am and 8pm; from Tacna, return trips are at 5pm.

ORIENTATION

Arica's main squares, Plaza Colón and Vicuña Mackenna, almost jut against the Morro in the southwest corner of downtown, which is otherwise laid out in a typical colonial Spanish square grid that one can easily walk. A pedestrian area extends for 5 blocks to the east, away from the port, and the ever-present hilltop serves as an excellent orientation marker. The main avenues leading east from downtown will take you to two roundabouts that each offer exits to the Azapa Valley. The airport and border with Peru are to the north; along the way, Hwy. 11 branches off toward the altiplano and Bolivia. The main beaches are well north of downtown and just south of the Morro.

VISITOR INFORMATION

Government tourism body **Sernatur** (② 58/252054; infoarica@sernatur.cl) operates a visitor center near Plaza Colón on San Marcos 101. It's open Monday through Thursday from 8:30am to 5:30pm, and Fridays from 8:30 to 5pm; in peak season (Jan–Feb), hours are Monday through Friday from 8:30am to 7pm and weekends from 10am to 2pm. The staff can provide detailed maps of the region and helpful, objective information on the levels of professionalism of various tour operators (see later for a list of recommended outfitters). Somewhat removed from downtown, the **CONAF** forestry service has an office where you can make reservations for their shelters in the region's national parks—a must if you want to stay there. It's at Av. Vicuña Mackenna 820 (✆ **58/201201;** www.conaf.cl), and is open Monday through Thursday from 8:30am to 5:30pm, and Fridays from 8:30am to 4pm.

[FastFACTS] ARICA

Bolivian Consulate The Bolivian consulate in Arica is at Patricio Lynch 298, on the corner of Sotomayor (✆ **58/583390**). See p. 224 for information on how to apply for a visa, which is necessary to enter Bolivia.

Currency Exchange Try **Yanulaque,** Colon 392 (✆ **58/232839**), open from Monday to Saturday from 9:30am to 2:30pm and 4pm to 8pm. You'll find plenty of ATMs in the banks and pharmacies on pedestrianized 21 de Mayo.

Hospital The city's Hospital Juan Noe is at 18 Septiembre 1000 (✆ **58/204500**). For emergencies, dial ✆ **131.**

Internet Access Internet cafes abound downtown on 21 de Mayo and its side streets. There are also several close to the bus terminals. **CiberCentro** at the corner or Bolognesi and Sotomayor (✆ **58/253156**) is open daily from 9am to 6pm.

Laundry Try **La Moderna,** 18 de Septiembre 457 (✆ **58/232006**).

Post Office Correos de Chile is at Prat 305 (✆ **58/255075**), and is open Monday through Friday 8:30am to 2pm and 3:30 to 6:30pm, and Saturday 9am to 12:30pm.

What to See & Do

The Arica region holds fantastic sights, but it's still a bit away from the mainstream attention that has engulfed San Pedro and its infrastructure is still somewhat lacking. Plan to spend at least a night at higher ground before heading to the Parque Nacional Lauca—make it a fantastic, not a head-splitting and nauseating, experience (see the "High Altitude Health Warning" box on p. 242). I can't recommend a day trip to the park, though these are readily offered. Check with the tour operators in Putre; they can be cheaper for a small group of three to four people, and also offer a high standard of service. Consider also that you can easily visit the Azapa Valley on your own, which most agencies include in multiday programs.

In Arica, reputable outfits include Belgian-run **Latinorizons,** Bolognesi 449 (✆ **58/250007;** www.latinorizons.com), which offers tours throughout the altiplano and Parque Nacional Lauca in addition to railways tours to the Lluta valley, a 4-hour train ride primarily aimed at cruise-ship passengers. **Raíces Andinas,** at Heroes del Morro 632 (✆ **58/233305;** 98/792-0415; www.raicesandinas.com), emphasizes sustainable and ethnic tourism, often arranging tours that include visits to the homes of locals in tiny villages of the altiplano. Raíces Andinas also owns **Parinacota Expediciones,** located in the same office but with a different website (www.parinacota expediciones.cl), which specializes more in trekking and adventure travel. A classic, 2-day journey to Parque Nacional Lauca with an overnight in Putre costs C$86,000 per person (based on two people) and includes meals, lodging at a Putre hostel, transportation, and a guide. Check the websites for longer excursions of up to 2 weeks.

THE WAR OF THE pacific

Also called the Saltpeter War, the 1879–84 war was one of the few major international conflicts in Latin America after independence from Spain. It had major consequences for Chile and its opponents, Bolivia and Peru.

Post-colonial borders were a constant issue between the new republics, and overlapping claims were the rule. The sovereignty of Bolivia over the area around Antofagasta and Calama and that of Peru over Arica were never in question, however. At the same time, Chilean entrepreneurs, supported in part by British financiers in Valparaíso, were the first to exploit the area's nitrate deposits. Contrary to border treaties, fiscally strapped Bolivia hit the Chilean companies with export taxes in February 1879. Chile retaliated by occupying Antofagasta, leading Bolivia to declare war. More than a month later, Chile declared war on Peru when it refused to remain neutral, linked as it was to Bolivia in a defensive pact. Neither side was particularly well equipped to go to war.

Victory hinged on dominance of the sea. Capturing Peru's modern Huáscar monitor late in the year allowed Chile to secure the supply lines, letting it more easily transfer troops to the north. Winning the battle of Tacna in May 1880, Chile forced Bolivia out of the war, and began to push Peru's troops back toward Arica, which it took 3 weeks later. Renewed failure to agree on redrawn borders kept the war alive, and Chilean troops captured and looted Lima in early 1881. It took a long time to find an exit strategy, but one was finally found in 1883, and sealed with peace and border treaties years later.

Chile's victory left it with the Peruvian province of Tarapacá, including Arica, and stripped Bolivia of key nitrate and copper deposits and blocked it from direct access to the Pacific Ocean, a painful loss for the Bolivian psyche that remains a cause of tension between South America's richest and poorest countries. More than 100 years after the war, the issue of sovereign access to the sea for Bolivia still festers and won't be easily solved.

THE MORRO & DOWNTOWN

Three pleasant, palm-studded squares lie just south of the Morro (see below). On the eastern end of Plaza Colón stands the small but unique **San Marcos Cathedral ★**. The 1876 neo-Gothic church was prefabricated by the company of noted French engineer Alexandre Gustave Eiffel and shipped to Arica to replace the cathedral destroyed by the 1868 tidal wave. The three-nave church with a single, octagonal spire ends in a point made entirely of iron (touch the tracery to believe it) and is well proportioned, though it could use a touch of new paint in parts. A 17th-century baroque crucifix adorns the high altar.

Eiffel was also responsible for the old **Customs House** across from the white port authority building 2 blocks away, built in 1872 to 1874 largely from materials shipped overseas from France. With coral-and-white horizontal stripes, the distinctive Customs House is now a cultural center that hosts regular art, sculpture, and photographic exhibitions, open Monday through Friday from 8:30am to 4:30pm. You'll also see the 1913 **railway building** fronted by an old German steam locomotive, though the building is closed to the public until further notice. Even if you're not hungry for seafood, I recommend you walk a little farther on the port side of Máximo Lira until you reach the **fishermen's port,** where you'll find sea lions basking near the railings, along with plenty of pelicans and stray cats and dogs amid stalls selling fish and shellfish. There are boat trips from there to see a penguin and sea lion colony on the rocky coast to the south. Some traditional houses have been restored or at least repainted recently, notably the sky-blue former Peruvian consulate **Casa Bolognesi** at Colón and Yungay, which now hosts cultural events.

El Morro de Arica ★★   Visible from everywhere in town, at 130m (430 ft.), this buff-colored hill fortress is Arica's most distinguishing feature. Geologically, it marks the end of the coastal range that runs the entire length of the country. Chilean troops captured the hill on June 7, 1880, in a dawn attack on a surrounded Peruvian garrison that had refused to surrender. Cannons and other pieces of artillery mark the site, along with a large statue of Christ, adorned with the coats of arms of both nations, asking for reconciliation. You can walk to the summit from near the end of Colón, or drive or take a taxi (C$3,000 one-way). From there, you'll be able to see all the way to the border, taking in the panorama of the city, port, and Azapa Valley, and it's certainly worth a trip back to take in the view at night.

The army owns and operates the Morro's commemorative museum that explains the siege and combat in great detail, along with displaying uniforms and weapons of the war. Though former dictator Augusto Pinochet himself placed several plaques there that remain on display, it's not offensively nationalistic, but it also doesn't make much of an effort to explain the war itself.

Museo Histórico y de Armas. ℂ **58/254091.** www.museomorrodearica.cl. Admission C$600 adults, C$300 children. Daily 9am–8pm.

Museo del Mar ★   In a pretty restored house, this "museum of the sea" is a bit misleadingly named as it focuses almost entirely on seashells alone. That said, it has some gorgeous specimens. The brainchild of a local private collector, the museum holds a 1,000-species collection of seashells, including fossils, many from Chile, others imported. It also has an aquarium featuring sea anemones.

Sangra 315. www.museodelmardearica.cl. Admission C$1,000 adults, C$500 children. Mon–Sat 11am–7pm.

Museo de Sitio Colón 10 ★★★   When architect Fernando Antequera began demolishing an old home on Colon St. at the foot of the Morro, with the intent to build a three-story hotel, workers lifted the floorboards and found a surprise: a Chinchorro graveyard with nearly a hundred cadavers ranging in age from infants to adults and estimated to have been buried between 4,000 to 5,000 years ago. Hotel plans were halted and the University of Tarapacá instead developed the site into an interpretative museum displaying the bodies *in situ* and under transparent acrylic glass that visitors can actually walk over and see the gravesites from above. Many of the bodies still have hair and teeth, along with clothing and other decorative items and tools. The well-designed museum shows 48 cadavers, but it's estimated that there are hundreds more buried beneath them. Sitio 10 is especially interesting because it is the only museum in the Americas to show pre-Hispanic cadavers in their original gravesites and, chillingly, it shows that much of the area that skirts the Morro is actually one massive gravesite paved over by the city of Arica. The second story deck offers splendid views of Arica.

Colon 10, Arica. ℂ **58/205041.** www.momiaschinchorro.cl. Admission C$2,000 adults, C$1,000 children. Daily 10am–6pm.

SHOPPING

With its proximity to Bolivia and Peru, a local Aymara Indian community, and thousands of years of history, you won't be surprised that Arica showcases plenty of Andean handicrafts. Stalls clog Bolognesi downtown, and a Bolivian-Peruvian market runs along Máximo Lira, between the entrance to the port and the Tacna train station. Higher-quality local products, albeit a reduced selection, are available at the **Pueblo Artesanal,** spread out in a 12-hut replica of Parinacota. Crafts include textiles, sculptures, alpaca knitwear, leather goods, and ceramics. The village entrance is at Hualles 2885, near the road entries to the Azapa Valley; it's open Tuesday through Sunday from 9:30am to 1pm and 3:30 to 7:30pm. Around the corner on the Carretera Panamericana Sur is the **Terminal Agropecuario ★★**, a massive market stretching several long blocks and selling all manner of goods from clothing to household items to tools. The highlight, especially for foodies, is the colorful vegetable and fruit market, on the north side of the avenue in a mustard-yellow building with Coca-Cola flags. Here Chilean, Bolivian, and Peruvian vendors sell local and imported foods and products.

BEACHES

Arica's tourism is still principally geared toward domestic visitors and those from southern Peru and La Paz, who flock to its beaches mid-December through February. It certainly has plenty to offer at a noticeably warmer water temperature than that of the frigid ocean of the rest of Chile. Oddly, beachfront accommodations are comparatively rare and overpriced, with most hotels and small *residenciales* downtown.

North of downtown, the long **Chinchorro** beach will give you plenty of room for sunbathing, swimming, or in-season jet ski rental, and there are restaurants, cafes, parks, and an Olympic-size pool—it's open Tuesday through Sunday from 9am to 2pm and costs C$1,000. Farther north, the undertow makes **Las Machas** too dangerous for swimming, but the waves are good for surfing. You might see the rusting remains of the U.S. steamer *Wateree* that an 1868 tidal wave ripped from anchorage in the harbor and shoved inland. It was little damaged and subsequently found use as a building, but the next tidal wave in 1877 destroyed it.

South of downtown are four popular beaches safe for swimming. *Micro* buses run along the length of Avenida San Martin. The closest to the center, just a 20-minute walk away, and the most populated, is **El Laucho,** a pleasant cove that has undergone an overhaul and now features a rock jetty and an artificial beach, a renovated boardwalk, and additional food stands and other services. The second and smaller cove, popular with families, is **La Lisera,** about 20 minutes from downtown, followed by **Playa Brava,** and finally the dark sand expanses and curvaceous dunes of **Playa Arenillas Negras,** which has the benefit of being the quietest stretch, but the disadvantage of having ocean views marred by fish-processing plants. Farther south there are wilder, rockier beaches with a few cheap restaurants, which can be reached on an asphalt road that runs along the coast for 6km (4 miles) from the Morro. Where it ends, an easy, hour-long walk along the rocky shore will take you to a sea lion colony. You can camp and fish near the shore, but it's too dangerous for swimming.

THE AZAPA & LLUTA VALLEYS

The lush valleys of fruit orchards and olive groves east of the city offer refuge from the dusty dryness of the Atacama and Arica's urban bustle. Enormous geoglyphs adorn the sandy hillsides, along with ruins of several native fortresses. Hundreds of mummies—the oldest found *anywhere*—have been unearthed and placed in the care of an excellent museum. The oldest artifacts found in Azapa date from 9000 B.C. But poor protection threatens these treasures just as they begin to capture the international spotlight.

Geoglyphs ★★★ Orange or yellow obelisks with red Indian symbols mark several archaeological sites in the Azapa and Lluta valleys, including gravesites, *pukarás* (pre-Columbian fortresses), and geoglyphs, giant depictions of people or animals scratched into the mountain or assembled in stones. Peru's Nazca Lines (200 B.C.–800 A.D.), some 800km/496 miles north, are the world's best known geoglyphs. More varied and covering a greater area, between Chug-Chug (near Calama) and Nazca in Peru, the Atacama geoglyphs were thought to have been built much later, between 600 A.D. and 1500 A.D., and in addition to possessing ritual and symbolic significance, these geoglyphs also served as route markers for desert caravans.

The geoglyphs of the Lluta Valley are the best preserved; the closer they are to Arica, the more they've been vandalized, grimly proving the fragility of the sites and their lack of protection. Binoculars are handy for viewing geoglyphs in the Lluta Valley, high above the valley floor. You can get much closer to the geoglyphs in the Azapa Valley and see them more clearly. Across the valley from the museum (see later), foundations remain of a *pukará* or village from the Tiahuanaco period, with a great view of the emerald valley contrasting with the reddish desert.

Travelers who can't head to the Andean highlands for health reasons are able to do this excursion easily by booking a tour in Arica, but the Lluta geoglyphs will also be seen above the highway (Rte. 11) by those en route to Putre and the Parque Nacional Lauca—just use the obelisks for orientation.

Near Arica, at the mouths of the Azapa and Lluta valleys E and NE of town, respectively, and visible from a long distance away above the roads. For more specific information, ask at Sernatur downtown or the Museo Arqueológico San Miguel de Azapa (reviewed below).

Museo Arqueológico San Miguel de Azapa ★★★ For anyone with even a minimal interest in history and archaeology, this museum, spanning 10,000 years of history, is one of the top attractions in all of Latin America. It outlines the entire history of pre-Columbian cultures in the Arica area through Tiahuanaco and the Inca periods with displays featuring textiles, tapestries, pottery, and weapons, but the standout attraction is the mummies on display. Around 5000 B.C.—long before even the Egyptians began to mummify their dead—the Chinchorro culture developed a technique of its own to preserve bodies for eternity. They removed the extremities, skin, and soft organs, dried and strengthened the bodies with sticks and clay, and later reassembled them and painted them black (5000 B.C.–3000 B.C.) or red (2500 B.C.–2000 B.C.). The accomplishment is all the more remarkable considering the tribes were fishers and gatherers, living on the Pacific coast from Ilo in Peru down to Antofagasta 6000 B.C. to 2000 B.C. The museum, which previously had just four mummies on display, recently opened a new wing devoted to the Chinchorro culture, displaying dozens of mummies that were among 96 corpses discovered in 1983 just a few feet beneath the ground, by members of Arica's water company who were laying new pipes. Earlier examples date to the 20th century when German archaeologist Max Uhle became the first to understand that the preservation of these prehistoric remains involved a highly sophisticated form of mummification.

Camino Azapa, Km 12. ℂ **58/205555.** www.uta.cl/masma. Admission C$2,000 adults, C$1,000 children. Jan–Feb daily 10am–7pm; Mar–Dec daily 10am–6pm.

Where to Stay

The overwhelming majority of hotels in Arica are small downtown *residenciales*. Other options are limited, perhaps with the exception of backpackers' hostels.

EXPENSIVE

Hotel Arica ★★ ☺ This resort-style hotel has a great location at the foot of the Morro between the El Laucho and La Lisera beaches, ideally perched for Pacific Ocean sunsets. Despite renovations here and there, the rooms betray their 1970s utilitarian roots, but not in an overtly bad way. That said, the hotel rates are somewhat overpriced for the quality of the rooms; what you're paying for are the resort's amenities. Room sizes vary, but they're all decorated with cream-colored walls and appointed with bright orange and yellow bedspreads and drapes and chintzy furniture. Suites and junior suites come with outdoor terraces. The attractive cabins are darker, with funky crimson and white '70s tiles to help keep them cool. Service is friendly and professional, and the hotel offers loads of amenities and three outdoor pools, plus a dedicated staff to keep the kids entertained in summer, including the "Happy Club," a schedule of daily events including volleyball. The restaurant is one of the better options in town, but the gastronomic standards in Arica are quite low.

Av. San Martín 599, Arica. ☎ **58/254540.** Fax 58/231133. www.panamericanahoteles.cl. 114 units. $213 standard double; $247 superior double or *cabaña* for 2; $492 suite. AE, DC, MC, V. **Amenities:** Restaurant; bar; babysitting; exercise room; 3 outdoor pools; clay tennis courts. *In room:* A/C, TV, minibar, free Wi-Fi.

Hotel Diego de Almagro ★★ Despite the unimaginative, boxy exterior of this Chilean chain hotel, the Diego de Almagro is Arica's top lodging option, on the shore of the Chinchorro Beach, about a 5-minute taxi ride from downtown. The hotel is new, so the property is in excellent shape and will appeal to most tourists accustomed to a certain level of comfort and cleanliness; also, the price makes this hotel a value when comparing guest room quality to the Hotel Arica. Spacious rooms come with two double beds and a warm, rich decor with dark wood furniture and emerald-green carpets. Make sure you book a room with a sea view as the east side's parking lot/city views are drastically poorer, and they don't take in the evening sunset either. Corner doubles, dubbed VIP rooms by the staff, are the same price but are even roomier, come with a table and chairs, and have additional windows that look toward downtown as well as the beach; these rooms all end in 01 or 21.

Raul Pey 3105, Arica. ☎ **58/385800.** Fax 58/385900. www.dahoteles.com. 166 units. $149 standard double. AE, DC, MC, V. **Amenities:** Restaurant; bar; exercise room; Jacuzzi; outdoor pool; sauna. *In room:* A/C, LCD TV, hair dryer, minibar, free Wi-Fi.

MODERATE

Hostel Mirador El Buey ★ Travelers seeking an apartment-style lodging option in a good neighborhood should consider this new hostel, near El Laucho and La Lisera beaches, a 20-minute walk to town. Housed in a converted mock-Mediterranean condominium several streets up from the main thoroughfare and boasting sublime views, the hostel has three floors, each with its own fully loaded kitchen and living area. The caveat is that each floor has an average of four bedrooms, so you may need to share your common space with other travelers, many of whom are surfers keen on staying close to the area's prime waves, El Buey and El Gringo. On the other hand, this hostel is an excellent option for a group or family. The best rooms here are the suites, with sunset views and large outdoor terraces; also there is a rooftop terrace with a BBQ. Note that breakfast is not included and the only supermarkets are in town.

Punta del Este 605, Arica. © **58/325536.** www.miradorelbuey.com. 13 units. $32 per person double; $27 per person triples; $84 double suite. AE, DC, MC, V. **Amenities:** Kitchen for use; living area with LCD TV. *In room:* No phone, free Wi-Fi.

Hotel Savona ★ ☕ The Savona is a well located choice as it's within walking distance of all downtown sights. The prosaic two-story white building is set slightly away from the street, but the best rooms face the nearby Morro and attractive Mediterranean-style pool and terrace. The rooms themselves are compact in size and fusty in decoration, with heavy wooden furniture and dowdy bedspreads mildly relieved by walls painted in varying pastel shades from cream to green. Large rectangular windows flood the place with light. The amenities are of a higher standard than most hotels in this category, making it a good value, even at full price.

Yungay 380, Arica. © **58/231000.** Fax 58/256556. www.hotelsavona.cl. 31 units. $57 single; $75 double; $93 triple. AE, DC, MC, V. **Amenities:** Cafeteria; bikes; large outdoor pool; free Wi-Fi (in lobby). *In room:* TV, hair dryer.

INEXPENSIVE

Arica Surf House ★ 💼 As the name states, the Arica Surf House caters to surfers, but really this attractive, cheery hostel is a good bet for any traveler on a budget. Warm, luminous spaces abound as the hostel's hallways and common areas have open ceilings covered with billowy white canvas, including a voluminous back patio armed with an open-air public kitchen, a ping pong table, a surf video collection, and several old funky couches. Although the hostel is not located on the prettiest street in Arica (about 2 blocks from the 21 de Mayo pedestrian mall), it's a gem and the owners keep the premises squeaky clean. Rooms are tiny but comfortable and beds come with duvet comforters; rooms are also either en suite or come with a shared bathroom, and there is an 11-bed shared dormitory.

O'Higgins 661, Arica. © **58/312213.** www.aricasurfhouse.cl. 7 units. $12–$15; dorm room $10. No credit cards. **Amenities:** Bikes; kitchen use; free Internet kiosk. *In room:* TV, no phone; free Wi-Fi.

Where to Dine

Evenings start late in Arica, particularly on weekends, so seating shouldn't be difficult if you head off early. Despite its proximity to Peru, the food here is heavily Chilean, with some of the better restaurants dabbling in regional cuisine. For people-watching and casual dining, go to the downtown cafes on 21 de Mayo such as **Cafe del Mar,** 21 de Mayo 260 (© **58/231936**), which serves sandwiches, salads, burgers, and crepes. Another site for casual dining, especially during the afternoon to enjoy the sea breeze, are the cafes and restaurants on Raul Pey, a stone's throw from the Chinchorro beach; try **Dimango** at Raul Pey 2592 (© **58/211419**) with all-day service and a varied menu of hearty sandwiches, pastas, salads, and delicious gelato ice cream.

EXPENSIVE

Maracuyá ★ SEAFOOD The Azapa and Lluta valleys are Chile's tropical fruit orchards, and this restaurant makes ample use of its namesake, the passion fruit. For seafood, it's Arica's best choice, though the cuisine is certainly not gourmet and some dishes can be too salty. Many dishes are prepared with fruit flavored sweet-and-sour sauces: try the salmon in a piquant pineapple sauce or mango with crab, or the succulent sea bass with a light orange glaze. What is really special about Maracuyá is its location perched almost over the water on a rocky stretch of coastline near the Morro, one of the few restaurants, oddly, in Arica to take advantage of the coastal views. The terrace can be a little drafty, however—dress accordingly if you wish to sit outside, especially at night.

Av. San Martín 321. ℂ **58/227600.** www.restaurantmaracuya.cl. Reservations recommended for dinner and weekend lunch. Main courses C$6,000–C$11,000. AE, DC, MC, V. Daily 12:30am–3:30pm and 8pm–12:30am.

Terra Amata ★ INTERNATIONAL   One of Arica's better restaurants, the Terra Amata is housed in a semi-circular, white Mediterranean-style building that is light and airy and offers views of the historic square and the maritime government building. The menu is a blend of regional and Peruvian cuisine, with delicious pisco sours made with locally grown passion fruit, mango, and tumbo. A dozen steak dishes are on offer with sauces that range from pineapple with tamarind to carmenère, all served with a variety of quinoa or potato sides. Seafood dishes are simple but pack a lot of flavor and, according to availability, include local rockfish and shellfish, though sea bass, conger eel, and salmon are the mainstays (one dish serves all three on a bed of spinach). A la carte prices are more expensive than they should be; the real value at Terra Amata is the fixed-price lunch menu that includes an aperitif, appetizer, main course, dessert, and beverage for C$6,900.

Yungay 201. ℂ **58/259057.** reservasterramata@hotmail.com. Reservations recommended. Main courses C$6,500–C$12,900. AE, DC, MC, V. Mon–Sat noon–4pm and 8:30pm–2am; Sun noon–4:30pm.

MODERATE

Mojito ★ INTERNATIONAL   Arica locals pack this new sleek and chic beachfront restaurant every evening to see and be seen, as well as relax on the outdoor terrace and enjoy dining and drinking high-concept cocktails with the sea breeze. Mojito is located in the heart of Chinchorro Beach, but given that the restaurant offers the best beachfront dining in Arica, it's odd the restaurant isn't open for lunch outside of weekends; management may change the hours during the summer months, so call ahead. Sandwiches, thin-crust pizzas, sushi, and heartier main courses such as lasagna and steak and potatoes are all part of the varied menu. There is an outdoor wrap-around deck and a cavernous two-story dining area backed by a neon-lit bar, with a mood set by light electronic and bossa nova music. If you're looking for a late-night haunt, this is your place.

Raul Pey 2861, Arica. ℂ **9/213055.** Main courses: C$4,000–C$8,000. AE, MC, DC, V. Sun–Thurs 7pm–3am; Fri & Sat 7pm–5am; Sat–Sun noon–3pm.

INEXPENSIVE

Boulevard Vereda Bolognesi ★★ INTERNATIONAL   Arica's newest dining incarnation is a hip, tranquil haven tucked away on a bustling pedestrian walkway, and is seemingly out of place given the slightly scrappy look of Arica's downtown shopping area. In reality, Boulevard is not one restaurant but instead a small gallery of trendy boutiques that lead to a lovely, plant-filled courtyard with wooden tables, something like a high-end food court, that are serviced by four tiny restaurants that include **Nautilis Peruano, Schlettinni Italian Trattoria, Del Valle Salad Bar,** and **Otaku Sushi.** For a group or a couple who can't agree on what to eat, this is the ideal set-up, as diners can order from any restaurant even when sharing a table. All four restaurants serve excellent, high-quality cuisine and snack platters, and better still, prices are surprisingly economical. A daily two-for-one happy hour runs from 5 to 8pm.

Pedestrian Bolognesi between Sotomayor and Paseo 21 de Mayo, Arica. www.veredabolognesi.cl. ℂ **58/231273.** Main courses C$3,100–C$6,000. AC, DC, MC, V. Daily 10am–9:30pm.

Kong Chau ★★ CHINESE   Arica's best Chinese restaurant is also one of the best in Chile. Don't be fooled by the antiquated and lackluster ambience (fluorescent lights, metal tables, and faux flowers), the cuisine here is fresh, authentic, and delicious, and the price can't be beat. Chinese immigrants started this Cantonese-style restaurant more than 50 years ago, using recipes brought from China that have been passed down through the family, and whose grandchildren now run the business. Start with freshly prepared wontons and the fried chili *ají* stuffed with pork. The best dishes on the menu are the Mongolian beef made with filet mignon, the chicken in tamarind sauce, Peking duck, and sautéed tender crawfish in soy and ginger. Don Renato, the restaurant's stalwart waiter, has been here forever and manages the entire dining area deftly and with good humor.

General Lagos 659. ✆ **58/232275.** Main courses C$3,200–C$5,400. Mon–Thurs 7pm–1am; Fri–Sat 7pm–1:30am; Sun noon–4pm.

Mata Rangi ★ 🍴 SEAFOOD   This understated breezy fish restaurant inside the fishermen's harbor spot is a quirky, fun place for a seafood lunch. Upon entering, you'll feel as though you have just stepped into a family kitchen; the family-owned restaurant exudes a warm, relaxed, but bustling experience. The seafood is of very good quality and simply prepared—grilled or fried—but the vegetables tend to be of the canned variety. During lunch Monday to Friday, diners can order the *menu* for C$4,000, which includes a seafood soup followed by fried fish with tomato and onion salad. Don't come after dark, or you'll lose out on one of its top attractions: watching the sea lions coast through the green sea water, the pelicans fly by, or even the gigantic tires from mining trucks being recycled as shock absorbers lining the docks. The owner also offers boat tours to view penguins and sea lions.

Máximo Lira 501, inside the port area. ✆ **9/682-5005.** Main courses C$4,000–C$6,000. No credit cards. Daily 10am–4pm.

CHILE'S ALTIPLANO

Putre: 149km (61 miles) E of Arica; 2,202km (1,370 miles) N of Santiago

Rte. 11 will take you to the Andean highlands, first along the verdant Lluta Valley dotted by geoglyphs on its lower hills, later crossing a stretch of desert featuring pre-Columbian ruins 100km (62 miles) from Arica, including the *pukará* of **Copaquilla** and the *tambo* of **Zapahuira,** both visible from the highway. The Aymara influence is strongest here; this stretch of arid mountains is quite different from San Pedro and other places in the Atacama. Vast, centuries-old terracing surrounds tiny villages, and you can really feel that this area formed part of Peru until relatively recently. Higher up still, marvel at the spectacular landscape and unique flora and fauna along with one of the world's highest lakes and forests.

Note: It's better to get cash in Arica as there is only one ATM in Putre and it is closed on weekends.

Putre

Splendidly backed by the double summits of the 5,775m (19,000-ft.) Taapacá Volcano, this tranquil village of 1,200 people is the only real place to spend your first night upon arrival from the coast. Unfortunately, that first night likely won't be the most pleasant experience considering the jump in altitude: Putre is a vertiginous 3,500m (11,400 ft.) above sea level. Hikes in the vicinity of Putre are a good option

High-Altitude Health Warning

What's true for San Pedro is even truer in Putre and beyond: The altitude here will slow you down, and it's tougher to deal with because at 3,500m (11,500 ft.), Putre is .4km (¼ mile) higher up from San Pedro. It's even higher than Cuzco in Peru, and Lake Chungará is one of the world's highest bodies of water and much higher still at 4,500m (14,760 ft.). Take it easy; even the young and the fit have fallen gravely ill after overexerting themselves. Consult your doctor before heading here if you have a heart or lung condition, and only book tours that carry emergency oxygen equipment. (Putre only has a small clinic.) If traveling on your own with a rental vehicle, you might want to pick up a "medicinal oxygen" canister with a mouth piece sold at pharmacies and gas stations in Arica for about C$9,500. Headaches and nausea are common occurrences at first; drink plenty of water and have some coca tea to help you adjust. Yes, it's perfectly legal; and no, you won't become a drug addict.

to acclimatize, with ancient **cave paintings** at Incani and Wilaqawrani (unfortunately, these have been partially vandalized). Later, you can head to the rustic **Jurasi hot springs** to relax; it costs C$2,000 per person to enter, and tour agencies can offer transportation.

A picturesque mountain village, Putre was founded in 1580 and was once a center of Spanish settlement due to its healthier climate than that of then malaria-stricken Arica. Today the town has a charming central square and fine 17th- to 19th-century stone portals flanking many house doors. Some streets have central water runoffs reminiscent of pre-colonial Inca villages. The meek **San Ildefonso church** was restored in the late 19th century after suffering damage in an 1868 earthquake. The locals will tell you that the original church was a much more ostentatious affair, embellished with gold and silver.

Census data shows the Putre area lost a whopping third of its inhabitants between 1992 and 2002, many heading down to Arica, while the population of the villages farther to the north around Visviri has remained stable. Municipal and government offices are on the square, while most services are on Baquedano.

ESSENTIALS
Getting There
BY CAR   From Arica, head north for 9km (6 miles), then east on Rte. 11, the sole option. The road is good until about 35km (22 miles) from the Bolivian border, at which point it suffers major and frequent potholes. With care, the secondary roads can be managed by normal cars, but check ahead for conditions. Trips south from the Surire Salt Flat need major preparation. Fuel up in Arica and invest in some gas canisters (most car hire agencies rent canisters) if you're planning a multiday outing, as the only place to get fuel in the altiplano is the hardware store in Putre, and it charges 30% more than the going price in Arica. For rental locations, see the "Arica" section, earlier.

BY BUS   **La Paloma** (© **58/222710**) makes the daily trip from Arica to Putre, departing at 7am from Germán Riesco 2071 and returning from Putre at 2pm.

Visitor Information

In Putre, the municipality operates a **visitor center** on the main plaza, officially open Monday through Friday from 8:30am to noon and 3 to 6pm (☎ **58/252803**). You can also get information from the **tour agencies** on Baquedano, which are more likely to be staffed.

[FastFACTS] PUTRE

Currency Exchange There is a Banco Estado branch on the square that will exchange dollars. The bank has an ATM that is open only on weekdays until 6pm.

Hospital Putre's clinic is near the village entrance at Baquedano 261 (no phone).

Internet Access A handful of spots offer Internet access, including the **public library** on Carrera and **Quipon@t** on the square. The best is the phone and Internet center at Baquedano 501. Most of the hotels mentioned below offer free Wi-Fi.

Post Office Located on Carrera just off the plaza's south side, the post office is open Monday through Friday from 9am to 1pm and Saturday from 10am to 2pm.

WHAT TO SEE & DO

For tours of the Putre area, there are several operators on Baquedano—including **Cali Tours,** at no. 399 (☎ **8/518-0960**; www.calitours.cl); **Mayuru Tour,** at no. 411 (☎ **8/582-1493** and 8/844-6568 www.mayurutour.com); and **Tour Andino,** at no. 340 (☎ **9/011-0702**; www.tourandino.com)—that offer tours of the surrounding areas and farther afield, including to the Parque Nacional Lauca and Parque Nacional Volcán Isluga, to the colonial and Aymara villages of the area, and 2-day tours to the Salar de Surire. Tour Andino also offers climbs to the area's high summits. Another experienced outfit, **Alto Andino** (☎ **9/282-6195**; www.birdingaltoandino.com), run by U.S. naturalist Barbara Knapton, focuses on wildlife, with programs in the altiplano and also along the coast. She also offers accommodations for tour participants.

WHERE TO STAY

While a growing number of tour operators are touting Putre as "the next San Pedro," it's still fairly remote and there are fewer quality facilities for tourists. Even the more squalid accommodations offerings can often be booked solid. I therefore recommend you book a room ahead of your arrival regardless of the category of hotel you seek.

Moderate

Hotel Kukuli Just off Baquedano, Kukuli is a decent, clean place to stay. Rooms are a respectable size and airy, with high ceilings, comfortable beds, and new bedding. Rooms facing a dirt courtyard (a section of which is used as the parking lot) have little individual terraces. These make for nice spots to have your good-size breakfast (coca leaves for tea included), and gaze up toward the Taapacá summits. Some rooms have TVs but management doesn't seem too keen to make them operative as of yet. In fact, the only minor downside is that during the off season the staff is often absent and can be found manning the Kukuli's grocery store around the corner.

Baquedano 301, Putre. ☎ **9/161-4709.** www.hotelkukuli.com/hotel.php. 16 units. $53 double. No credit cards. **Amenities:** Bar. *In room:* No phone, free Wi-Fi.

Terrace Lodge ★ This is Putre's best lodging option, opened in early 2010 by two Italian travelers, Flavio and Patricia, who live on the premises. The five-room lodge is really an upscale hostel styled after the typical Putre architecture of straw and metal roofs and white stucco walls, with a small garden and gazebo looking out over fields of grazing cattle and sheep. The Terrace is well managed, comfortable, and the owners are very helpful with information, and they have a 4×4 vehicle for excursions (max. two guests, C$20,000 per person to Lago Chungará). Guest rooms are spanking clean and beds have crisp linens and duvets; my only qualm is that the windows are terribly tiny—larger ones would have provided beautiful views—which makes you not want to spend much time in your room other than to sleep.

Circunvalación 25, Putre. © **58/584275.** 5 units. $59 double. No credit cards. **Amenities:** Cafe. *In room:* Free Wi-Fi.

Inexpensive

Hostel Pachamama ★ Among the very few hostels in Putre, this is the top choice, located within a charming colonial-style house, with rustic, three- to four-bedrooms grouped around a pretty, shady courtyard decked out in wicker chairs. Two pet alpacas roam the courtyard and are curious and ridiculously cute. The clean bathrooms are shared, however there is a new cabaña for five people that has a private bathroom. The hostel has a dining area and a kitchen for guests' use, and they offer tour-planning services around the area. Try to get a room that doesn't face the entrance due to occasional noise. At press time, the Pachamama had planned to open a new restaurant serving local cuisine.

Lord Cochrane s/n, Putre. © **58/583328** or 9/304-5122. 6 units. $15 per person; cabaña $21 per person. No credit cards. **Amenities:** Cafeteria; kitchen. *In room:* No phone.

WHERE TO DINE

If you're here only for a brief stay, the altitude will likely stunt your appetite, which is perhaps as well since high altitude doesn't mean haute cuisine. The food is basic but authentically Andean. There are a handful of rustic restaurants in town; the godsend is **K'uchu Marka** on Baquedano, which caters mostly to tourists and has a cozy, rustic atmosphere. It has set meals for C$4,500 featuring typical ingredients such as alpaca meat and quinoa, rabbit stew, and a couple of standout vegetarian dishes. It also offers sandwiches at C$2,000 to C$3,000. **Flor de Rosamel** on the square is a bit cheaper, with set meals for around C$3,000, including simply prepared hearty stews and local meats, and regional dishes such as spicy chicken with *illaita* (a local algae) served with local *chuño* potatoes.

Aymara & Colonial Villages

Even little Putre dwarfs the tiny villages of the area, but these, too, deserve a visit. Much of this off-the-beaten-path area is still begging for proper archaeological study; pre-Columbian terracing abounds. However, in 2011 the nonprofit Fundación Altiplánico will enact a three-stage plan over the next decade to rebuild decaying buildings and churches in the Parinacota region in an attempt to prevent the further flight of locals to larger cities, and generate income through increased tourism, with the creation of new lodging options in the tiny, picturesque towns that dot the region.

Socoroma, 27km (17 miles) south of Putre and also just north of Rte. 11, is a tiny Aymara village clinging to a promontory at 3,060m (10,040 ft.). Its adobe **San Francisco** church was built in 1560 and reconstructed in 1873, but it suffered some damage in the mid-2005 earthquake. It has a spectacular view of the mountains, overlooking ancient terraces that are now used for growing oregano, infusing the entire town with its heady aroma. At the desert rest stop of Zapahuira, take the dirt road toward Belén. Past the small power plant and village at Chapiquiña, note the frequent

AYMARA indians

With a rich and complex history, the Aymara Indians are the second largest indigenous linguistic group in South America. They are believed to be the descendents of the ancient Tiahuanacan, the first great Andean empire that emerged in the Bolivian highlands around 600 B.C. and was centered around the southeastern side of Lake Titicaca.

Of the two million Aymara that remain, most communities or *ayllus* (traditional Aymara communes based on extended families living in single-room, gabled houses constructed of turf and thatched roofs) live in the altiplano regions of Peru, Bolivia, and Chile. Chile has the smallest number of Aymara people, around 45,000. Due to economic hardship and a propensity toward greater assimilation into typical Chilean life, many Aymara people have migrated from the altiplano to the coastal cities of Arica and Iquique and many small villages are now used only for ceremonial purposes.

Those who continue to carve out subsistence from the desolate altiplano utilize 2,000-year-old traditions and techniques based on animal husbandry—the herding of sheep and llama—and agriculture, namely the cultivation of quinoa, potatoes, and barley. Rather contentiously, the Aymara have cultivated coca plants for centuries, using its leaves in traditional medicines, a fact which has brought the Aymara into conflict with the government, especially in Peru and Bolivia, since coca contains cocaine alkaloids, the basis for cocaine.

Social organization varies from community to community and leadership, based on a complex system of social prestige, is achieved through community service, sponsorship of fiestas, and extending ties beyond each *ayllu*. Patriarchal kinship is based on extended families and premised upon economic cooperation. Daughters tend to marry and move in with their husbands, while sons seek to establish a separate household within the same community as their fathers.

The Aymara have a profound respect for their ancient traditions, ancestors, and religion, and their ritualistic culture reveals a passionate adherence to their belief in a multi-spiritual world in which shamans, diviners, and magicians take part. Festivals and rituals, which usually occur during harvest and to mark seminal life events such as baptism, marriage, and death, are ebullient community events involving frenzied dancing, singing, eating, drinking, and animal sacrifice. Each fiesta presents a compelling fusion of Catholic and supernatural indigenous religious rituals. At the apex of the Aymara's mystical devotion is the goddess Mother Earth, known as Pachamama.

The Aymara dress is adapted to the harsh conditions of the high-altitude altiplano. Men wear a *chullu* (a wool hat with ear-flaps) and striped ponchos over shirt and pants. Women wear bowler hats, ruffled blouses, brilliantly colored full skirts, sturdy boots, and an *aguayo* (a wool sling for carrying their baby on their backs). Chilean Aymaras typically wear a more modern version of this style than Bolivians.

stunted trees with flaking, twisted trunks. They're *queñua*, an endangered, slow-growing species and possibly the tree that grows at the highest altitude anywhere.

Continuing on, make the detour down to the village of **Pachama**, 68km (42 miles) from Putre, greener than most of the others. The short road is in so-so shape and the village almost abandoned, but its chalk-white late-17th-century church, **San Andrés ★★**, is a real gem of colonial architecture and painting. In typical Atacama style, the bell tower is separated from the church proper, surrounded by a wall with two arched entrances. If locked, make the effort to look for the person keeping the key—the very helpful, but not usually present, locals can point you in the right direction. The images of St. Andrew, the Virgin, and St. Peter above the door are unique—no other colonial church in the Atacama has exterior paintings. At the same time, they're just a hint of the fine polychrome 18th-century frescoes and painted altar you'll find inside. If you do venture inside, be sure to leave a tip.

A balmy climate and proximity to the route to Potosí led to the 1620 establishment of **Belén,** 77km (48 miles) from Putre and the only altiplano town founded by the Spanish, within proximity to an indigenous settlement. The smaller, older of the two churches here is on the higher ground of the main plaza; the more attractive is the 18th-century **Señora del Carmen ★**, most notable for its sculpted stone portal, featuring Solomonic columns in an otherwise adobe structure. The interior holds polychrome baroque sculptures.

Within walking distance, besides the obvious and ubiquitous terraces, are three pukarás, **Ancopachane** near the cemetery, and the adjacent **Chajpa** and **Huai-huarani,** the latter closest to a 5km (3-mile) stretch of the famous Camino del Inca (Inca road).

The drive out to these villages takes a few hours round-trip and all are best visited as a return trip to Arica, continuing past Belén through Tignamar and Codpa, with plenty of petroglyphs, pukarás, and colonial churches to see along the way. The detour to Guañacagua is worthwhile for its baroque church. This excursion can also be done as a day trip from Arica, if you have transportation of your own, though some tour agencies also offer the trip.

Parque Nacional Lauca ★★★

Stretching from Socoroma, Putre, and Belén eastward to the Bolivian border, Parque Nacional Lauca is one of the region's—and Chile's—unquestionable highlights. The park comprises some of the most spectacular landscapes in the entire Andes and one of the world's highest lakes, the stunning, blue-green Lago Chungará (at 4,500m/14,760 ft.), six peaks above 6,000m (19,700 ft.), volcanic calderas, and the famous altiplano village of **Parinacota.** Much of the 137,883-hectare (340,716-acre) park is accessible via the international highway and the secondary roads, though they're below the generally good standard of Chile's roads, affected as they are by heavy trucks and rain or snow in January and February during the "Bolivian Winter." Wildlife is abundant and easy to see, from cuddly vizcachas (see below) to lithe vicuñas—not to be confused with the larger, gray-faced guanacos you may see at lower altitudes—and over 130 species of birds, including the three species of flamingos that exist in Chile (the Andean, Chilean, and James's), along with rare hummingbirds.

Stop at **Las Cuevas,** which has a CONAF station (theoretically open daily 9am–12:30pm and 1–5:30pm), and take the path down toward the little hut that holds a rustic pool fed by a hot spring. On the way, and with a little luck, you'll pass through a warren of mountain vizcachas, long-tailed rodents with more than a passing resemblance to hares. They're easy to observe, and their slanted eyes and penchant to sit back on their haunches give them a positively relaxed expression.

A little farther along Rte. 11—past a ridiculous red, blue, and yellow pan-flute sculpture—you'll begin to approach the dramatic white cones of the 6,342m (20,807-ft.) **Parinacota Volcano** and the 6,282m (20,610-ft.) **Pomerape.** At **Parinacota,** stop to view the lovely 17th-century church; ask for Don Severino, who walks 3km

(1¾ miles) every day to open the church for visitors, so be sure to leave a tip in the box by the door before leaving. If you don't see him, ask the caretaker at the crafts stalls in the little square. Much like the church at Pachama, but with more somber motifs of hell and the crucifixion, the interior boasts splendid frescoes, along with religious paintings reminiscent of the Cuzco school. There is also a macabre selection of priests' skulls and a table that—in deference to the town's supernatural proclivities—has been chained down to keep it from moving around town on its own accord. The exterior is walled in, with the square tower on one corner, and simple red sculptures (some bearing faces) on top of the walls. At 4,400m (14,430 ft.) and 36km (22 miles) from Putre, the village also holds the CONAF's administrative center of the park, which can provide maps and information, and there's a small campground and a 3km (2-mile) trail head behind this administrative center.

A poor road heads north toward other villages outside the park, notably Visviri at the northern tip of Chile. An **obelisk** north of the village marks the spot where Chile, Bolivia, and Peru meet in the high-altitude desert. On Sundays, an Aymara market drawing participants from the three countries takes place there.

The **Cotacotani lagoons** east of Parinacota form a mesmerizing, surreal landscape of dark lava and cinder cones piercing the blue waters. A lookout point offers a good view from the highway, though it's spoiled a bit by power lines. If you have time and have acclimated, there's an easy but long 8km (5-mile) trail around them.

The view of **Lake Chungará**, finally, is the park's highlight. At daybreak, the summits are ablaze with orange, and when the wind is still, they reflect perfectly in its waters. Across the butterfly-shaped lake, you can see the 6,542m (21,460-ft.) Sajama, Bolivia's highest peak, among other mountains that almost encircle the lake. Some 150 species of birds inhabit the park, with many waterfowl species flocking to the lake, including native geese and duck species, giant coots, and of course flamingos. You will very likely also spot small herds of vicuñas that you can see from a short distance away, despite the proximity of the highway, as well as alpacas and llamas grazing in the *bofedal* high-altitude swamp. An unstaffed CONAF station near the lake is similar to the one at Las Cuevas and has a small refuge and the most basic of restrooms, along with a campsite. A short trail from the station's parking lot leads down to the lakeshore. A little farther on is the Chilean border station (note the visa reference in "Fast Facts: Arica," p. 233).

Vicuña Nature Preserve, Surire National Monument & Parque Nacional Volcán Isluga ★★

Because it's less accessible than Parque Nacional Lauca and has no public transport, your only option for exploring this remote area is to hire a 4WD or take an organized tour from Putre. However, this otherworldly altiplano landscape, dotted with the remains of ancient Aymara villages where graceful vicuñas roam beneath majestic snow-capped volcanoes, is nothing short of spectacular. This park has the largest concentration of the country's vicuña, some 20,000. In the 1980s, some were caught and exported to Ecuador to help reestablish a breeding population there. Vicuñas and guanacos—the wild form of the llama—almost never share a habitat, with the smaller, paler vicuña living at higher altitudes, because their unique wool provides protection against the nightly subzero temperatures. Poaching remains an issue, but the preserve boasts one of Chile's few environmental success stories: the recovery of the vicuña population hunted to the brink of extinction for their wool, the world's finest. Near Las Cuevas, a minor road—A-235—turns south off Rte. 11. Marked with a sign for Guallatiri, the road is manageable without too much difficulty south until Surire, though the trucks that run to the borax mine near there can be an annoyance en route (there is less traffic on weekends when truck drivers take a few days off). As an alternative to the road, consider heading back toward Putre via Itisa and Belén, which is also a long, bumpy ride of about 120km (75 miles).

At 83km (52 miles) from Putre, the pre-Hispanic village of **Guallatiri,** overshadowed by the active volcano of the same name, consists of some 50 houses and a white 17th-century Atacama church. The preserve also protects *queñua* (a small tree with a purplish trunk) along with the *llareta,* a very slow-growing shrub with leaves growing so tightly that, amazingly, it looks more like a rounded, moss-covered rock. Now rare and officially protected, it was previously burned for fuel in mining operations.

The far smaller Surire National Monument almost surrounds the salt lake of the same name, with beautiful views and relatively common rheas, ostrichlike birds called *suri* by the Aymara. It also has undeveloped hot springs at Polloquere. The borax plant at one side of the lake, however, is suspected of being responsible for a decline in flamingo hatchings; the company says it carries out periodic measurements with CONAF to make sure this isn't happening.

Even worse and lonelier is the road that continues to the 174,744-hectare (431,600-acre) **Parque Nacional Volcán Isluga.** I don't recommend traveling this route alone; this is a trip best done on a multiday tour. One can travel there roundabout heading south from Arica, but the nearest village with services, the border post of **Colchane,** sports only the most basic accommodations. Many of the villages marked on maps are virtually abandoned, with the houses locked and the original inhabitants returning only for religious festivities. This is the case at **Isluga,** 205km (127 miles) from Putre, a tiny, picture-perfect village similar to Parinacota, boasting a 17th-century Atacama church. The CONAF ranger station is at Enquelga, 10km (6 miles) inside the park; there are hot springs nearby at Aguas Calientes.

From Colchane, Arica is 401km (249 miles) away via the paved road, but you can also travel to the seaside city of **Iquique,** 220km (137 miles) away.

THE CHILEAN LAKE DISTRICT

S outh of the Bío-Bío River, Chile is transformed. The climate cools and becomes much more humid; dairy farms replace the vineyards; and lagoons, lakes, and emerald forests of ancient trees appear. The Andes lose altitude but more than make up for it in beauty, sprouting magnificent white-capped volcanoes. This is one of the most popular destinations in Chile, not only for its beauty, but also for the cultural and outdoor activities available, and its well-developed tourism infrastructure.

Only relatively recently did Chile manage to fully integrate the Lake District into the country. For some 350 years, the Mapuche Indians fiercely and successfully defended this land first against the Incas and later against the Spanish. Their influence spread into what is now Argentina, and only in the mid-1880s did Chile manage to subdue them. German-speaking settlers meanwhile had begun to clear land and fell timber for their characteristic shingled homes. Both ethnic groups have left their mark on the region through architecture, art, and food. In fact, German pastries have become so prevalent that the German word for cake, *küchen,* has largely replaced the Spanish word *pastel* in Chilean usage.

Its natural wonders continue to provide the basis for the region's economy, harboring tourism, farming, salmon production, and forestry—a mix tough to manage, to the detriment of its once nearly impenetrable forests. But the many national parks and preserves give visitors a chance to immerse themselves in virgin forest unique for its stands of umbrella-shaped araucaria and 1,000-year-old alerce trees (see "The Alerce & the Araucaria: Living National Monuments," on p. 255).

Exploring the Region

The Lake District stretches 350km (215 miles) south from the Bío-Bío to the Reloncaví Sound, where Chile's Central Valley sinks into the Pacific. The northern third around **Temuco** forms the Mapuche heartland; farther south, lakes, forests, and volcanoes combine into a fairy-tale landscape almost too perfect to be true. Resorts—above all **Pucón** and **Puerto Varas**—draw thousands of tourists in the summer months of January and February, but the area also has its charms in autumn when the leaves turn red, and in winter, you can soothe your limbs after a day of skiing with a soak in the area's numerous hot springs. The region's charm lies in its picturesque villages, boat rides, adventure sports, beaches, and kilometer after kilometer of bumpy dirt roads that make for lovely drives. An excellent alternative to the toll highway is the **Ruta**

Interlagos, a dirt road that interconnects the numerous protected areas and lakes from near **Victoria** down to Puerto Varas. Another great draw here is the proximity to the **Argentine Lake District,** where you'll find the gorgeously located towns of Bariloche and San Martín de los Andes. If you're planning on visiting both countries, it makes sense to cross the border in the Lake District, where Chile and Argentina are separated by a 1- to 2-day boat ride or several hours by road, year-round.

TEMUCO

677km (420 miles) S of Santiago; 112km (69 miles) NW of Pucón

Few cities in southern Chile are old, and Temuco isn't among them. Founded in 1881 as a military outpost in the very heart of Mapuche territory, its creation sealed the Mapuches' fate and set the foundations for modern-day development—which, so far, hasn't been pretty. Temuco is near a handful of beautiful national parks such as **Conguillío** and **Villarrica,** and is the gateway to the wildly popular **Pucón.** But unless you've got an early flight or you are driving a long distance down the Pan-American Highway and need a rest, I do not recommend an overnight stay here; there are plenty of excellent options around Parque Nacional Conguillío and even more in the Pucón area. You'll need to fly here and transfer to Pucón during the winter; there is direct service to Pucón during the summer.

Temuco grew like a boomtown as Spanish, German, French, Swiss, and English immigrants poured into the region within the first few years of its foundation. Only traces of their architectural influence remain as rampant development has converted Temuco into yet another hodgepodge Chilean city. It's still one of the country's fastest-growing cities, as evidenced by the thundering buses, bustling downtown crowds, and increasingly poor air quality that threaten to absorb whatever charm remains. Most Mapuche today live in reservations (*reducciones*), west of the city in rural areas approaching the coast, but Temuco, along with the suburb of Padre Las Casas, is the best place to approach the proud culture of Chile's main native people.

Essentials

GETTING THERE

BY PLANE **LANExpress** (✆ 600/526-2000 toll free, or 45/740375; www.lan. com) serves Temuco with an average of four daily flights from Santiago and one daily flight to Puerto Montt. **Sky Airline** (✆ 600/600-2828 toll free, or 45/747300; www.skyairline.cl) serves Temuco with two daily flights from Santiago and two weekly flights to and from Puerto Montt.

The **Maquehue Airport** (ZCO; ✆ 45/554801) is about 8km (5 miles) from the city center. To get to Temuco, take a cab—about C$5,000—or arrange transportation with **Transfer & Turismo de la Araucanía** (✆ 45/339900), a minivan service at the airport that charges C$3,000 for door-to-door service. This transfer service has service to Pucón for C$6,500 per person, but it might cost more if they are unable to arrange a group.

BY BUS To get to Temuco from Santiago by bus, **Tur Bus** (✆ 600/660-6600; www.turbus.com) leaves from the Terminal Alameda at Av. Bernardo O'Higgins 3786, or **Cruz del Sur** (✆ 2/779-0607) leaves from the Terminal Santiago at Av. Bernardo O'Higgins 3848. The trip takes 8 to 9 hours; a one-way economy ticket costs about C$12,500 and executive class costs C$21,000. Most buses arrive at Temuco's **Terminal**

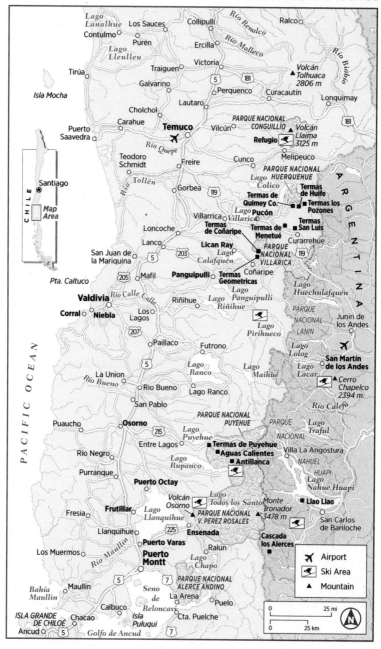

Airport
Ski Area
Mountain

Rodoviario at Vicente Pérez Rosales 01609 (① **45/225005**). From here, you can take a taxi to your hotel.

BY TRAIN   EFE (① **2/585-5000** in Santiago, or 45/233416 in Temuco; www. efe.cl) offers one of the few train services in Chile, with salon and sleeper coaches. Unfortunately, an ambitious expansion plan has gone very wrong, making train service terribly unreliable, and Santiago-Temuco service has once again been interrupted. Instead, Lake District trains now run from Victoria (north of Temuco) down to Puerto Montt; the daily trip costs C$6,000 for a long 8-hour ride. A connecting train does leave from Temuco three times a day (9:30am, and 4:10 and 8:30pm) to Victoria and vice versa; however, the time wasted during the transfer makes the bus much more attractive. It's safe to say that few take this route now and the Temuco station is languishing because of it. With things likely to continue in flux, check the website as you near your trip for updates (in Spanish only).

BY CAR   The Pan-American Highway (Rte. 5) takes motorists to Temuco. Tolls cost C$12,000 from Santiago to Temuco; fuel prices tend to be about average along the highway. If you're heading to the national parks east of Temuco, fill up in town or on the highway as fuel prices in the villages are much higher.

GETTING AROUND

Getting around Temuco is easy by foot. To get to outlying areas such as national parks, it's best to rent a car or go with a tour. To get to Pucón (see "Villarrica & Pucón," later in this chapter), try **Buses JAC,** at the corner of Balmaceda and Aldunate (① **45/231340**), which operates from its own terminal, leaving every half-hour on weekdays and every hour on weekends and holidays.

If you want to rent a car to see the outlying sights, Hertz, Avis, Budget, and Econorent all have kiosks at the airport. Outside of summer, it is possible for walk-ins to get a car easily. During the summer, it's important to reserve in advance. In downtown Temuco, **Hertz** can be found at Andrés Bello 792 (① **45/318585**), **Avis-Budget** at San Martín 755 (① **45/465-280** toll free, or 45/237575), or **Econorent Car Rental** at Patricio Lynch 471 (① **45/214911;** fax 45/214911).

VISITOR INFORMATION

Sernatur operates a well-stocked tourism office at the corner of Claro Solar and Bulnes streets at Plaza Aníbal Pinto (① **45/211969**). Hours from December to February are Monday through Saturday from 8:30am to 8:30pm, Sunday 10am to 2pm. The rest of the year, the office is open Monday through Friday from 9am to 2pm and 3 to 5pm.

[Fast FACTS]   TEMUCO

Currency Exchange   There are *casas de cambio* and banks with 24-hour ATMs along Calle Bulnes at the main plaza. Try **Intercam,** Casa de Cambios, Claro Solar 780, Local 5; **Global,** Bulnes 655, Local 1; or **Comex,** Prat 427.

Hospital   Temuco's highest-quality hospital is the **Clínica Alemana,** Senador Estébanez 645 (① **45/244244**).

Internet   Try the Internet cafe **Kafé.com,** Bulnes 314, Local 8 (Mon–Sat 9am–10pm; Sun 10am–8pm); or the **Entel** office, Prat 505 (Mon–Fri 10am–8pm; Sat 10am–2pm).

Laundry **Marva** Laundromat has two locations: 415 and 1099 Manuel Montt (*©* **45/952200**).

Travel Agency Try **Agencia de Viajes y Cambios Christopher,** Bulnes 667 (*©* **45/211680**).

What to See & Do

Within the manicured grounds of **Plaza Aníbal Pinto** in the city center, you'll find the sizable La Araucanía monument depicting the clash between the Mapuche and the Spanish. There's also a gallery here with temporary exhibits.

Walk up Calle Bulnes to Portales to enter one of Chile's best markets, the **Mercado Municipal** ★, open Monday through Saturday from 8am to 6pm (8pm in summer), Sunday and holidays from 8am to 3pm; April through September, the market closes at 5pm. Rows of stalls sell high-quality woven ponchos, knitwear, textiles, woodwork, hats, *maté* gourds, and assorted arts and crafts, but what's really special here is the abundance of silver Mapuche jewelry. Around the perimeter, fishermen and food stalls aggressively vie for business, while butchers in white aprons hawk their meats from behind dangling sausages and fluorescent-lit display cases. Another market, the **Feria Libre** ★, at Aníbal Pinto, offers a colorful chaos of fruit and vegetable stands as well; the highlight here is the traditional Mapuche Indian vendors who come in from *reducciones* to sell their goods. The market is open Monday through Sunday from 8:30am to 6pm; from March to December, it closes at 5pm. *Note:* Watch out for pickpockets.

The **Agrupación de Mujeres Artesanas "Wanglen Zomo,"** at Aldunate 585, is a rare Mapuche woman's craft cooperative that is worth checking out. It's open daily from 10am to 6pm.

For a sweeping view of Temuco, take a taxi or hike up the heavily forested **Cerro Ñielol,** which also features four trails and a restaurant near the summit. It's open daily from 8am to 10pm; admission is C$1,000 adults, C$500 children (*©* **45/298222**). At the site marked LA PATAGUA, you'll find a plaque commemorating the agreement signed in 1881 between the Mapuche and the Chilean Army for peaceful settlement of Temuco.

Temuco's **Museo Regional de La Araucanía,** Alemania 084 (*©* **45/730062**) is open Monday through Friday from 10am to 5:30pm, Saturday from 11am to 5pm, and Sunday from 11am to 2pm. The museum features exhibits charting Indian migration and history, along with displays of Mapuche jewelry and weapons; the Mapuche learned silver working from the Spanish, developing it into one of their most important forms of artistic expression. It also houses exhibits on immigration. Admission costs C$800.

Railway buffs will like the **Museo Nacional Ferroviario Pablo Neruda,** Barros Arana 565 (*©* **45/227613;** www.museoferroviariotemuco.cl), showcasing locomotives

---

Guided Tours in Temuco & Beyond

Multi Tour, Bulnes 307 (*©* 45/237913; www.chile-travel.com/multitour), offers a wide variety of bilingual excursions, including city tours, day trips to Parque Nacional Conguillío, and cultural trips to indigenous communities. These cultural trips include visits to a *ruca,* a typical Mapuche home, and the opportunity to visit with Mapuches.

from 1908 to 1962 and the 1923 Presidential Coach, along with a working antique train sometimes used in short trips. It's open Tuesday to Friday from 9am to 6pm and Saturday and Sunday from 10am to 5pm; admission is C$1,000.

Where to Stay

Holiday Inn Express ☺   Predictable in the way a Holiday Inn always is, this hotel is best used as an overnighter for those on their way out of Temuco. With clean rooms, comfortable beds, cable TV, and a location a half-block from an American-style shopping mall with the usual fast-food joints, you might feel like you're in the U.S. The principal drawback of this hotel is its distance from downtown; however, it is close to the highway. Kids under 18 can room with their parents for free, making this a good bet for families.

Ortega 1800, Temuco. ⒸⒸ **800/36666** or 45/223300. Fax 45/224100. www.holidayinn.cl. 62 units. $95 double. Children 17 and under stay free in parent's room. AE, DC, MC, V. **Amenities:** Exercise room; Jacuzzi; small outdoor pool. *In room:* A/C, TV.

Hotel Aitué   This family-owned and -operated hotel offers good value for the price, including a business center with an Internet connection and free airport pickup. Double rooms are average size; suites are substantially larger. Each well-lit room comes with mahogany furniture and fairly comfortable beds. The staff is knowledgeable and friendly, and strives to make guests feel at home. The hotel has a popular convention salon downstairs, and it also offers a small bar and lounge, as well as a fireside dining area serving breakfast and snacks.

Antonio Varas 1048, Temuco. Ⓒ **45/211917.** Fax 45/212608. www.hotelaitue.cl. 35 units. $94 double; $105 suite. AE, DC, MC, V. **Amenities:** Restaurant; bar; lounge; free airport transfer. *In room:* TV, minibar.

Panamericana Hotel Temuco ★★   This hotel, formerly called the Terraverde, is part of the Chilean Panamericana chain and is Temuco's top hotel, with excellent service geared primarily toward business travelers. At the foot of Cerro Ñielol but just 5 blocks from the main square, it's a modern, reddish, seven-story building amid pleasant green scenery, away from downtown's noise. It's not particularly exciting, but is very comfortable, from the outdoor pool to the very plushy tan carpeting in the rooms. Cream and brown colors—plus floral patterns on bedspreads and curtains—characterize the conservatively styled rooms. The larger, superior suites have views both of the Ñielol and of the Llaima volcano beyond. One floor is nonsmoking only. Wi-Fi is available in some rooms; check ahead of booking. As this is primarily a business hotel, it sometimes offers cheaper summer rates.

Av. Prat 220, Temuco. Ⓒ **45/239999.** Fax 45/233830. www.panamericanahoteles.cl. 74 units. $100 double; $130 suite. Rates include continental breakfast. AE, DC, MC, V. **Amenities:** Restaurant; bar; outdoor pool; sauna. *In room:* TV, minibar, free Wi-Fi.

Where to Dine

Head to the **Mercado Municipal,** open Monday through Saturday from 8am to 8pm and Sunday from 8:30am to 3pm, for a quick, inexpensive lunch at one of the market's dozen or so restaurants. To get there, enter at Portales at Bulnes or Aldunate streets. Waiters will harangue you until you're suckered into choosing their establishment, but the best bet is at **La Caleta** (Local 27). For sandwiches and other quick meals, try **Casa D'Empanada's** (no phone), at Mackenna 687.

Café Austral ★ INTERNATIONAL   This modern international restaurant/bar does a good job of closing itself off amid the hubbub of downtown foot traffic.

THE ALERCE & THE ARAUCARIA: living national monuments

The Lake District and its neighboring forests in Argentina are home to two of the oldest trees on the planet: the alerce and the araucaria, otherwise known as larch and monkey puzzle trees, respectively. The alerce is a sequoia-like giant that grows less than 1 millimeter each year and can live for more than 3,000 years, making it the world's second-oldest tree after the California bristlecone pine. They are best viewed in the Parque Nacional Alerce Andino and Pumalín Park.

The araucaria, called *pehuén* by the Mapuche, is unmistakable for its gangly branches and thick, thorny leaves that feel waxy to the touch. Mature trees can grow as high as 50m (164 ft.) and take on the appearance of an umbrella, which is why they're often called Los Paraguas (the Umbrellas). They do not reach reproductive maturity until they are about 200 years old, and they can live as long as 1,250 years. They are best seen in Tolhuaca, Villarrica, and Conguillío national parks, but they're virtually everywhere around the Lake District. The araucaria seed (*piñón*), an edible nut, was a principal source of food for the Mapuche; later the tree was coveted for its quality wood, and, as with the alerce, aggressive harvesting destroyed the majority of its forests. Today both the alerce and the araucaria have been declared protected national monuments.

Because it's split into two glitzy levels with large windows facing the street, there's ample people-watching while you munch on sandwiches, grilled meats, full breakfasts, and pastries. A lively bar—particularly for after-work drinks when they have two-for-one specials—makes up most of the lower level. The three-course executive lunch menus are the best deal in the house.

Bulnes 880. © **45/234880.** Main courses C$3,500–C$12,000. AE, DC, MC, V. Mon–Fri 9am–11pm and Sat 11am–4pm.

La Pampa ★ STEAK/ARGENTINE High-quality grilled meats, fresh salads, seafood, and an extensive wine list with export-only varieties make La Pampa a good place to dine. It was opened years ago by two Argentine transplants who came for a visit and never left. Try the trout with Roquefort sauce or one of the Argentine specialties such as *matambrito alla pizza*, thin meat rolled with spinach and egg. On weekends, there is an excellent *asado criollo*, thick ribs slowly grilled for 3 hours.

Caupolicán 0155. © **45/329999.** Main courses C$3,500–C$9,000. AE, DC, MC, V. Mon–Sat noon–4pm and 7:30pm–midnight; Sun noon–4pm.

Quick Biss ☺ 🍴 CAFE This modern cafeteria, with wooden booths and zebra-striped walls, is very popular with downtown workers for its reasonably priced meals. Diners fill their trays with items such as salads, hot dishes, sandwiches, soups, and desserts, or simple empanadas. Solo diners often sit at a large bar near the entrance where they watch the news or a soccer game while eating. The *autoservicio* (self-service) lunch runs from 12:30 to 4pm and dinner runs from 6 to 9pm, and there is also a simple menu offered all day.

Antonio Varas 755. © **45/211219.** Main courses C$2,000–C$6,000. AE, DC, MC, V. Daily 11am–11pm.

East of Temuco

The Río Bío-Bío is born out of Lake Gualletue east of Temuco. Much of the upper river valley is protected in a series of preserves from the Ralco hydroelectric power plant southward, featuring beautiful araucaria forests and plenty of places to stay, including several spas. Three volcanoes—Tolhuaca, Lonquimay, and Llaima—dominate the landscape.

PARQUE NACIONAL CONGUILLÍO ★★★

One of Chile's finest national parks, Parque Nacional Conguillío surrounds the spectacular smoking cone of **Volcán Llaima** and features a dense forest of spindly araucaria trees, which the park was created to protect. It's a lovely park and a great attraction year-round due to several splendid hiking trails, a ski resort, and an outstanding park information center. Volcán Llaima is one of the most active volcanoes on Earth and has registered 40 eruptions since 1640, most recently in April 2009. In the southern section of the park, it is also possible to witness the tremendous destruction lava has wreaked on the surrounding forest. Conguillío is divided into three separate sectors with as many access points. The western side of the park is commonly known as Los Paraguas (the Umbrellas); the eastern side is accessed from the north in Sector Laguna Captrén, and the south at Sector Truful-Truful. Visitors will find the park's administration center, campgrounds, and most hiking trails here in the eastern sector.

The eastern access point is at the village **Cherquenco;** from here a 21km (13-mile) rutted road ends at the **Centro de Esquí Las Araucarias** (© 45/274141; www.skiaraucarias.cl) in Los Paraguas. Las Araucarias is not well-known, and its four T-bars are tiresome, but if you are a ski buff and are in the area, this little resort is worth the visit for its surrounding forest of araucaria and simply breathtaking views. (The road here is in bad shape, so bring a vehicle with chains and high clearance.) The center also has a ski school, equipment rental, and a restaurant and bar. Ticket prices are C$15,000 Monday through Friday and C$16,500 on weekends. The center offers dormitory-style lodging in two single-sex rooms with about 10 to 15 bunk beds without bedding for $13 per person (and two dormitories for 10 to 11 people for $17 per person). Other lodging options are the **Apart Hotel Llaima** (five apartments with four beds each; $105 a night), **Refugio Pehuén** (three units; $21 per person), and the **Refugio Los Paraguas** ($17 dorm; $63 triple). Check www.skiaraucarias.cl for reservations.

An unpaved and poorly maintained road connects a CONAF (park service) **visitor center,** which is open daily from 9am to 1pm and 3 to 7pm (© 45/298213), with the towns **Curacautín** in the north and **Melipeuco** in the south. The information center has interpretive displays highlighting the park's flora, fauna, and physical geology, including an interesting section devoted to volcanism. During the summer, park rangers offer informative talks and walks and a host of educational activities, which they post in the visitor center. (English-language talks can sometimes be arranged; visit www.parqueconguillio.com, or check directly at the center.)

There's an easy, hour-long, self-guided trail that leaves from the CONAF center, but if you really want to get out and walk, you'll want to take the **Sierra Nevada trail.** This moderate 5-hour hike is the best in the park, taking visitors through thick forest and rising to two lookout points that offer sensational volcano and lake views before dropping back down to the Captrén Lagoon near the CONAF center. The trail head is on the western shore of Lake Conguillío, at the CONAF center. A second 5-hour hike along moderate terrain, **Los Carpinteros,** weaves its way through stands

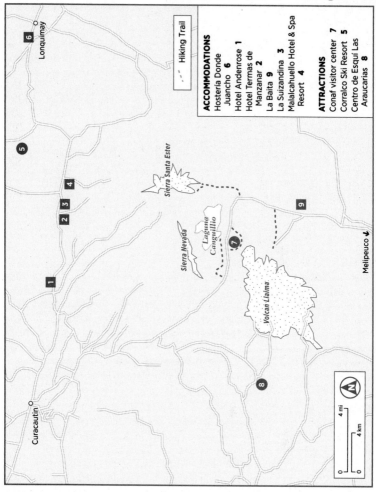

ACCOMMODATIONS
Hostería Donde
Juancho **6**
Hotel Andenrose **1**
Hotel Termas de
Manzanar **2**
La Baita **9**
La Suizandina **3**
Malalcahuello Hotel & Spa
Resort **4**

ATTRACTIONS
Conaf visitor center **7**
Corralco Ski Resort **5**
Centro de Esquí Las
Araucarias **8**

Hiking Trail

of araucaria trees that are several hundred—some more than 1,000—years old. This trail leaves from Laguna Captrén at the CONAF center.

GETTING THERE & BASICS   If you plan to rent a vehicle, try to get one with a high clearance—it's not essential, but it helps. Most tour companies in Temuco plan excursions to this park. Bus service from Temuco's main terminal is available only to Curaçautín and Melipeuco; from here you'll need to take a taxi or hitch a ride. The road is paved only to the park entrance, so during the winter, you'll usually need a 4×4 or tire chains to get to the ski center.

The park is officially open daily April through November from 8am to 11pm, and May through October 8:30am to 5pm—but you can really enter at any time of the day. In winter, the road through its eastern part isn't cleared, but it remains accessible—definitely take winter gear. The summer park entrance fee is C$3,000 for adults and C$1,000 for children (free for those under 12 years). There are a cafeteria and a store at CONAF's park information center in front of Lake Conguillío.

CORRALCO SKI RESORT ★

This small resort (with one chairlift and one T-bar) in the **Malalcahuello National Preserve** is a good option for beginners and more of a novelty for experts. The eight runs on Lonquimay Volcano's treeless slope are relatively short and none tougher than intermediate level, so you might well long for a lift extending higher up toward the summit. But there are some off-*piste* possibilities and a few steep drops for snowboarders. It also has great views of the Llaima Volcano and the Andes along the border with Argentina, beyond the araucaria forest. Line up early or pack a lunch as the cafeteria is easily overwhelmed even on normal days. Lift fees are C$20,000 per adult; C$16,000 for seniors and children 11 and under. The hotel, however, has six fine rooms paneled in light wood amid the araucarias. Doubles with half-board are C$69,000 per person Monday through Thursday and C$99,000 Friday through Sunday (⏍ 2/202-9326; www.corralco.com). To get there, turn left 4km (6 miles) after passing the village of Malalcahuello on Rte. 181, continuing for another 4km (6 miles), then turn left again on the forest road.

WHERE TO STAY & DINE

There are seven campsites along the shore of Lago Conguillío; backcountry camping is not permitted. Campsites cost about C$10,000. From October to April, the park has cabins that go for an average of C$30,000 per night; information about rentals can be found inside the store next to the visitor center in Sector Truful-Truful. A great alternative is at **La Baita** (⏍ 45/416410; www.labaitaconguillio.cl), from C$40,000 per night for one of the wooden cabins or C$40,000 per double in the lodge, located midway between CONAF and the town Melipeuco. Here you'll find a restaurant, a store, park information, and guided excursions such as hiking, alpine touring, and snowshoeing.

Expensive

Malalcahuello Hotel & Spa Resort ★★   The Conguillío area's top spa features a large, 1,300-sq.-m (14,000-sq.-ft.) glass-enclosed wellness area that belies its relatively small overall size of just 27 rooms on three floors. Grey stone, wood, and glass characterize the angular, modern hotel offering views of the Lonquimay volcano. In the large rooms, contemporary textile design meets more traditional wood furniture. Facilities are open to nonresidents, but the hotel imposes a limit on the number of people who can use it on a given day. Hence, it's a good idea to buy the passes ahead of your day of hiking or skiing. The staff is generally good, but can be a bit arrogant on an off day. The resort also has several five-person *cabañas* and six-person bungalows, each outfitted with Wi-Fi.

Rte. 181, Km 86, Malalcahuello. ⏍ 2/415-8109 or 45/281166. www.malalcahuello.cl. 27 units. $266 double; $317 suites; $430 bungalows. AE, MC, V. **Amenities:** Restaurant; lobby bar; spa w/large indoor pool; free Wi-Fi (in lobby). *In room:* TV/DVD player (by request).

Moderate

Hotel Termas de Manzanar   A half-century of operations to its credit makes this one of the most traditional hotels in the area. Built in traditional stone and wood in 1954, its pink rooms could stand an upgrade; the cheaper rooms in particular can be drafty. The more expensive rooms are supplied with thermal water. Its great draw is the garden's thermal pools, more rustic than at Malalcahuello and quite attractive under the trees and open sky. It also has basic cement "hot tubs." Nonguests may use the facilities for a fee, so I'd consider staying at the Andenrose (see below) or La Suizandina (see below) and stopping by for a soak.

Rte. 181, Km 83. ✆ **45/881200.** www.termasdemanzanar.cl. 32 units. $99 double; $133 suite with Jacuzzi. Half- and full-board available. AE, DC, MC, V. **Amenities:** Restaurant; bar; lounge w/TV. *In room:* TV, no phone.

Inexpensive

Hostería Donde Juancho ★★ 🎁   The little town of Lonquimay, surrounded by araucaria forest, sports this very charming little hotel, something between a bed-and-breakfast and a country inn, that has been open for almost 3 decades. Considering Lonquimay's remoteness, Donde Juancho's quality is a real surprise. The second-floor rooms are cozy, carpeted, and heated with slow-burning wood stoves. If I had to nitpick, I'd say they're a little small and dark, but its prices make it an excellent value. Its restaurant, featuring hearty, succulent Chilean cuisine (that is, meats), is also very good.

O'Higgins 1130, Lonquimay. ✆ **45/891140.** www.dondejuancho.cl. 5 units. $32 double. No credit cards. **Amenities:** Restaurant; free Wi-Fi. *In room:* TV, no phone; Wi-Fi (in some rooms).

Hotel Andenrose ★★ 😊 🎣   Irrepressible host and owner Hans Schöndorfer built this contemporary Bavarian hotel in the Araucanian Andes himself after finding a spot along the Cautín River with a little beach to drop a kayak. The spotless hotel has a central seating area alongside a massive ceramic oven, and the midsize rooms are very cozy, shielded from the nightly cool by thermopane windows. All rooms have their own bathroom; a few, however, are across the hallway. The hotel has one three-bed room and one four-bed room. Some of the best food in the valley—including copious breakfasts—is prepared in the Andenrose's kitchen.

Rte. 181 Km 68.5, E of Curacautín. ✆ **9/869-1700.** www.andenrose.com. 7 units. $33–$40 per person. AE, DC, MC, V. **Amenities:** Restaurant. *In room:* No phone.

La Suizandina ★★ 🎁   With the Swiss flag greeting you at this property's entrance, you might think you're in the Alps, unless one of the property's llamas ambles by. The two-building complex includes a rebuilt farmhouse with five rooms and a dorm-style guesthouse for up to 18 people. The midsize rooms feature hardwood floors with comfortable, duvet-clad wooden beds and the squeaky-clean bathrooms you'd expect from a Swiss family-run resort. The guesthouse, whose bunks continue in the same vein as those of the individual rooms, also has good-size kitchen facilities. It also runs a campsite, has a good restaurant, and offers horseback riding.

Rte. 181, Km 83. ✆ **45/891140.** www.suizandina.com. 8 units. Prices per person: $114 double; $27 per person dorms; $13 per person camping. Half-board available. AE, DC, MC, V. **Amenities:** Restaurant; bikes. *In room:* TV, no phone.

VILLARRICA & PUCÓN ★★

Villarrica: 25km (16 miles) W of Pucón, 764km (474 miles) S of Santiago; Pucón: 112km (69 miles) E of Temuco

Pucón is where the tourists head, but Villarrica is where the locals live. It's a quiet town that never really took off as a vacation resort, in spite of the fact that the view is so much better here, with the volcano rising majestically beyond the lake. There are a few good and inexpensive lodging options here, if you decide to leave the tourism hubbub of Pucón. But it's farther away from Villarrica and Huerquehue national parks and the ski resort.

Nationally and internationally known as the "Adventure Capital of Chile," Pucón offers a multitude of outdoor activities, including rafting, hiking, skiing, canyoning, kayaking, and fly-fishing. Yet what makes Pucón a great all-around destination is its flexibility. There's also an abundance of low-key activities, such as hot spring spas and scenic drives through gorgeous landscapes. Or you can just relax with a good book on the porch of a cabin or throw a towel on the beach and sun yourself, as hundreds do during the summer.

Villarrica

Villarrica is a more authentic Lake District pueblo, and some travelers find that aspect more appealing, especially in the summer. The center of town here hums with activity as regular townsfolk go about their daily business. The town is also closer to Temuco and attractions such as Lican Ray on Lake Calafquén, Panguipulli, and the Coñaripe hot springs.

ESSENTIALS
GETTING THERE Buses JAC (© **45/411447**) leaves Villarrica every half-hour for Pucón from its location at Bilbao 610, near Pedro de Valdivia. In Pucón, JAC's location is Uruguay 505, near the hospital. The fare is C$800. A taxi to or from Pucón costs about C$6,000. For more information on getting to the region, see "Getting There" for Pucón, later.

VISITOR INFORMATION A good **tourism office** can be found at Av. Pedro de Valdivia 1070 (© **45/206619**). It's open daily from 8:30am to 11pm December 15 through March 15, and daily from 8:30am to 6:30pm the rest of the year; it often closes on winter afternoons when the weather is rotten. You can also visit **www. villarrica.com** for more information.

WHAT TO SEE & DO
You might consider a 2-hour trip to Villarrica to stroll the streets, have lunch, and drop in to visit the **Museo Histórico y Arqueológico,** Pedro de Valdivia 1050 (no phone), with displays of Mapuche items and trademark silver pieces and jewelry. Outside, you'll find an authentically thatched *ruca,* a traditional Mapuche home. The museum is open Monday through Friday from 9am to 1pm and 3 to 7:30pm, and the entrance fee is C$500. The festival **Muestra Cultural Mapuche** takes place here in Villarrica from January to late February, with music, handicrafts, dancing, and other activities; for more information, call the visitor center at © **45/206618.**

HUIFQUENCO FUNDO ★★★ Whether you are staying in Villarrica or Pucón, a trip to the Huifquenco Farm, Camino Villarrica, Huifquenco at Km .5 (©/fax **45/ 415040;** www.fundohuifquenco.cl), is a must. Opened to visitors in 2002, this 862-hectare (2,129-acre) estate is the third largest in the region and boasts over 5,000 head of cattle, bulls, wild boar, llamas, and sheep, among other animals. Choose to tour the farm on your own horse or relax and enjoy the view in one of their antique carriages. A real-life *huaso* leads you along a magnificent tree-lined road, past lagoons, and along rolling meadows with fantastic volcano and lake views. Get a feel for farm life in the region; go fishing, cycling, or canoeing; or take in a rodeo show at the *media luna.* Finish off your tour with a Chilean-style barbecue. Full- and half-day tours are available, and special programs are available upon request. Contact the farm directly for transportation to Huifquenco and a bilingual guide.

WHERE TO STAY

Hostería de la Colina ★, Las Colinas 115 (℃/fax **45/411503;** www.hosteriadela colina.com), is owned and managed by an American couple, Glen and Beverly Aldrich, who have lived in Chile for 16 years. The inn is located on a hill with a panoramic view of the lake and volcanoes and offers seven comfortable rooms in the main house and two cottages located in the peaceful gardens, as well as a Jacuzzi. The owners will help you plan your stay, and they serve hearty Chilean meals in the pleasant dining room. Doubles run from $74 to $105 and cottages start at $158. Rates include full breakfast.

Patagon Andino Hotel ★, Matta 320 (℃ **45/419978;** www.patagonandino.cl), is in a charming little house just off the park and can arrange just about any activity in the area. Doubles run $82. **Hostería Kiel,** General Körner 153 (℃ **45/411631;** fax 45/410925), has comfortable rooms ($46–$69 double) and a direct view of Volcán and Lake Villarrica that you can enjoy from your very own porch. Or try **Cabañas Monte Negro,** at Pratt and Montt streets (℃ **45/411371**); it charges $147 for six people (no credit cards), and has eight cabins near the lake with direct views of the volcano. Private parking or ample street parking is available and free.

Villarrica Park Lake Hotel ★★   Luxurious and expansive, this property strives to be the best in southern Chile and its new affiliation with Luxury Collection should help push it in that direction. It has only 70 rooms, but it feels like a big corporate hotel, with its large lobby and aloof but polite staff. Extra-wide doors made of local wood lead into comfortable and spacious modern rooms, all with sliding French doors that open up onto a balcony with a view of the lake. The marble bathrooms come with a tub/shower combo and heated towel racks. The spa has an exquisite selection of facials and body-work offerings. This is an excellent base for travelers who prefer large, full-service hotels, although you'd be well advised to book way in advance, as it occasionally fills up with corporate retreat groups for days at a time. Always request promotional rates when making your reservations.

Camino Pucón–Villarrica, Km 13. ℃ **45/450000.** Fax 45/450202. www.vplh.cl. 70 units. $355 double; from $481 suite. AE, DC, MC, V. **Amenities:** Restaurant; bar; lounge; concierge; health club and spa; heated indoor pool; room service; limited watersports equipment. *In room:* TV, fax, minibar, hair dryer, free Wi-Fi.

WHERE TO DINE

For excellent seafood dishes, try **El Rey de Marisco,** on the coast at Valentín Letelier 1030 (℃ **45/412093**); or **Hostería Kiel,** General Körner 153 (℃ **45/411631**), for simple Chilean fare and a superb view of Volcán Villarrica. **The Travellers,** Valentín Letelier 753 (℃ **45/413617**), has an international traveler's hostel vibe, and a menu to match, with Chinese, Indian, Mexican, Thai, and Chilean dishes, plus the ever-popular happy hour from 6 to 9:30pm. Also try **Mamy Helga,** on the waterfront (℃ **45/415-085**), with a good view of the lake.

Pucón

Pucón is a picturesque little town almost entirely dependent on tourism but, thankfully, it has not embellished its streets with gaudy tourist traps. Instead, a creative use of timber sets the architectural tone. During the early 1900s, Pucón's economy centered on the timber industry, but the town's fate as a travel destination was sealed when the first hotel went up in 1923, attracting hordes of fishermen. Ten years later, the government built the stately Hotel Pucón, drawing hundreds more visitors each year, at that time traveling here by boat from Villarrica. Today there are many lodging options and even more adventure outfitters ready to fill your days.

It is important to note that the summer season, particularly from December 15 to the end of February, as well as Easter week, is jampacked with tourists. Hotel and business owners gleefully take advantage of this and jack up their prices, sometimes doubling their rates during that time.

ESSENTIALS
Getting There
BY PLANE Visitors normally fly into Temuco's **Maquehue Airport** (p. 250) and then arrange transportation for the 1- to 1½-hour ride into Villarrica or Pucón. Most hotels will arrange transportation for you, although it's usually at an additional cost. **Transfer & Turismo de la Araucanía** (℡ **45/339900**), a minivan service at the airport, will take a maximum of 10 guests (minimum 4) to Pucón for C$28,000. Pucón's airport is equipped to handle jets, but for the time being no airlines fly here.

BY CAR From the Pan-American Highway south of Temuco, follow the signs for Villarrica onto Rte. 199. The road is well marked and easy to follow. If coming from Valdivia, take Rte. 205 to the Carretera Panamericana Norte (Hwy. 5). Just past Loncoche, continue east, following signs for Villarrica and Pucón.

BY BUS Tur Bus (℡ **600/660-6600** toll free, or 2/270-7510; www.turbus.cl) offers service to Pucón from destinations such as Santiago, stopping first in Temuco and Villarrica. The trip is about 9 to 11 hours and generally a night journey; the cost is about C$12,000 for an economy seat and C$32,000 for an executive seat. **Buses JAC** (in Santiago, Av. Providencia 1072; ℡ **2/235-2484**) has service from Santiago to Pucón every half-hour from 6:30am to midnight from its Santiago terminal at Balmaceda and Aldunate (℡ **45/231330**).

Getting Around
There are dozens of tour companies providing transportation and tours to all points of interest around Pucón; they generally advertise everything in their front windows. However, this is another place where renting a car is a great option if you want to get out and see the sights in a leisurely manner. In Temuco, **Hertz** has an office at Andrés Bello 792 (℡ **45/318585**), and they operate a branch in Pucón at Ansorena 123—actually, an agency called **Enjoy Tour** (℡ **45/442303**). In Pucón, try **Pucón Rent A Car,** Colo Colo 340 (℡ **45/443052**); or **SPU Comercial Rent A Car,** 191 Ansorena (℡ **45/444485**). **Sierra Nevada,** at the corner of O'Higgins and Palguín (℡ **45/444210**), also rents cars and mountain bikes. Rates start at C$25,000 per day for a small car.

Visitor Information
The **Chamber of Tourism** (℡ **45/441671**) operates a helpful office at the corner of Brasil and Caupolicán streets; it's open daily from 9am to 8pm December through March, and from 10am to 6:30pm the rest of the year. However, the staff does not speak English very well. The city of Pucón has an excellent website at **www.pucon.com**.

WHAT TO SEE & DO
You'll find shops everywhere in Pucón, but the best independent boutiques are on Calle Fresia. Most sell some variation of adventure gear, wool sweaters and scarves,

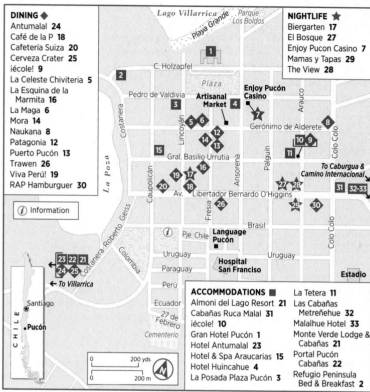

DINING ◆
Antumalal **24**
Café de la P **18**
Cafetería Suiza **20**
Cerveza Crater **25**
iécole! **9**
La Celeste Chiviteria **5**
La Esquina de la
  Marmita **16**
La Maga **6**
Mora **14**
Naukana **8**
Patagonia **12**
Puerto Pucón **13**
Trawen **26**
Viva Perú! **19**
RAP Hamburguer **30**

ⓘ Information

NIGHTLIFE ★
Biergarten **17**
El Bosque **27**
Enjoy Pucon Casino **7**
Mamas y Tapas **29**
The View **28**

ACCOMMODATIONS ■
Almoni del Lago Resort **21**
Cabañas Ruca Malal **31**
iécole! **10**
Gran Hotel Pucón **1**
Hotel Antumalal **23**
Hotel & Spa Araucarias **15**
Hotel Huincahue **4**
La Posada Plaza Pucón **3**
La Tetera **11**
Las Cabañas
  Metreñehue **32**
Malalhue Hotel **33**
Monte Verde Lodge &
  Cabañas **21**
Portal Pucón
  Cabañas **22**
Refugio Peninsula
  Bed & Breakfast **2**

carvings, or jewelry from boutique designers. There's also an excellent **Mercado Municipal,** at Ansorena 475, and a smaller **artisanal market,** at Alderete between Fresia and Ansorena (daily 10am–7pm). Both feature several dozen small independent shops selling handcrafted items like hand-carved wooden bowls and native birds—not the mass produced things you get in other Chilean shops—of surprisingly high quality. Brand names are not at all lost in Pucón, though: North Face, Lacoste, Jack Wolfskin, and Rockford all have shops here.

If you're staying in Pucón longer than a few days and you'd like to learn a little of the local lingo, try **Language Pucón,** Uruguay 306 (© **45/444967;** www.language pucon.com), which offers short but effective courses and home-stay opportunities. They also have a good book exchange in English and German.

For more things to see and do in this area, see "Hot Springs Outside Pucón" and "Natural Attractions Outside Pucón," later in this section.

Outdoor Activities

With so many outdoor adventures available here, it's no wonder there's a surplus of outfitters eager to meet the demand. Be very careful when selecting a tour operator in Pucón because few are 100% competent, and some are downright dangerous or simply don't have the years of experience in the area to provide responsible service. Ask about your guide's familiarity with the tour you are proposing to take (unbelievably, a few operators have periodically sent guides on trekking expeditions without having actually gotten to know the trail first) and what kind of experience and/or qualifications your guide has. Remember that you get what you pay for; be wary of seemingly fly-by-night operations. Most outfitters include insurance in the cost of a trip, but first verify what their policy covers.

Politur, O'Higgins 635 (© 45/441373; www.politur.com), is a well-respected tour company that offers fishing expeditions, Mapuche-themed tours, and sightseeing trips around the Seven Lakes area, in addition to volcano ascents. They're slightly more expensive than other agencies but are worth it. **Aguaventura,** Palguín 336 (© 45/444246; www.aguaventura.com), is run by a dynamic French group, and their main focus is snowboarding in the winter, with a shop that sells and rents boards, boots, and clothing; they also do volcano ascents with ski/snowboard descents, and rafting and kayaking, and they offer a half-day canyoneering and rappelling excursion. **Sol y Nieve,** Lincoyán 361 (© 45/444761; www.solynievepucon. com), has been on the scene for quite a while, offering rafting and volcano ascents as well as fishing, airport transfers, and excursions in other destinations around Chile; however, there have been some complaints recently of lackluster service. **Summit Chile,** Urrutia 585 (© 56/9277-4424; suziwortman@gmail.com), has a UIAGM certified, bilingual guide that leads almost any trip in Pucón: volcano ascents, rock climbing, rafting, horseback riding, and multi-day trips.

Trancura, O'Higgins 211-C (© 45/441189; www.trancura.com), sells cheap trips to the masses, and they are best known for their rafting excursions, which they've been doing forever. Beyond that, I do not recommend any other trips with this company because of their yearly roster of inexperienced guides hired on the cheap. They do have ski and bike rentals, however, with low prices.

BIKING   Several outfitters on the main street, O'Higgins, rent bicycles by the hour and provide trail information and guided tours. Bicycle rentals run an average of C$5,000 for a half-day. You can also just pedal around town, or take a pleasant, easy ride around the wooded peninsula. **Miropucón,** Fresia 415, Local 6 (© 45/444874; contacto@miropucon.cl), offers 3- and 4-hour medium-difficulty bike tours to the Ojos de Caburgua.

BIRDING   Chile's forests are full of avian life, though Lago Villarrica and the surrounding national parks are not normally thought of as a birding destination. Only one company offers guided birding excursions here, **Pucón Birding** (© 45/441011; www.puconbirding.cl). Four-day trips explore Parque Antumalal, the Saltos del Carileufu, Trailenco, and the Nevados. Prices depend on the season and amount of people in the group.

CLIMBING THE VOLCANO ★★★   An ascent of Volcán Villarrica is perhaps the most thrilling excursion available here—there's nothing like peering into this percolating, fuming crater—but you've got to be in decent shape to tackle it. The excursion begins early in the morning, and the long climb requires crampons and ice axes. Note that the descent has traditionally been a combination of walking and sliding on your behind in the snow, but so many have done this that the naturally formed "luge" run is now enormous, slippery, and fast, and people have been hurting themselves on it lately—so be cautious. Volcán Villarrica is perpetually on the verge of exploding, and sometimes trips are called off until the rumbling quiets down. Tour companies that offer this climb are **Politur** and **Sol y Nieve** (see earlier). The average cost is C$48,000, including transfers, entrance fee, insurance, equipment, and guides, but not lunch.

FISHING ★ You can pick up your fishing license at the visitor center at Caupolicán and Brasil. Guided fishing expeditions typically go to the Trancura or the Liucura rivers. See a list of outfitters above for information, or try **Off Limits,** O'Higgins 560 (© 45/441210 or 9/949-2481; www.offlimits.cl).

GOLFING ★ Pucón's private 18-hole **La Península de Pucón** golf course is open to the playing public. For information, call © 45/443965, ext 409. The cost is C$14,000 for 18 holes. This is really the only way to get onto the private—and exclusive—peninsula that juts into the lake, by the way.

HIKING ★★ The two national parks, Villarrica and Huerquehue, and the Cañi nature reserve offer hiking trails that run from easy to difficult. An average excursion with an outfitter to Huerquehue, including transportation and a guided hike, costs about C$14,000 per person. By far the best short-haul day hikes in the area are at Huerquehue and the Cañi nature reserve.

HORSEBACK RIDING ★ Half- and full-day horseback rides are offered throughout the area, including in the Parque Nacional Villarrica and the Liucura Valley. The **Centro de Turismo Huepilmalal** (© 9/643-2673; www.huepilmalal.cl) offers day and multiday horseback rides, including camping or a stay at the Termas de Huife, from a small ranch about a half-hour from Pucón (head east out of Pucón and then north toward Caburgua; take the eastern road toward Huife and keep your eyes open for the signs to Centro de Turismo Huepil). You'll need to make a reservation beforehand. All-inclusive multiday trips cost about C$60,000 per person, per day. A wonderful couple, Rodolfo and Carolina, run this outfit. Rodolfo is a superb equestrian professor who used to train the Spanish Olympic team. Beginning riders are given an introductory course in the corral before setting out. Contact a tour agency for day rides in Parque Nacional Villarrica, which go for about C$35,000 for a full day. Tour agencies will also organize rides that leave from the **Rancho de Caballos** (© 45/441575), near the Palguín thermal baths. If you're driving, the Rancho is at 30km (19 miles) on the Ruta International toward Argentina.

RAFTING & KAYAKING ★ Rafting season runs from September to April, although some areas might be safe to descend only from December to March. The two classic descents in the area are the 14km (8¾-mile) Trancura Alto, rated at Class III to IV, and the somewhat gentler Trancura Bajo, rated at Class II to III. Both trips are very popular and can get crowded in the summer. The 3-hour rafting trip on the Trancura Alto or Trancura Bajo costs an average of C$16,000. **Sol y Nieve** (see earlier) offers both trips. The rafting outfitter **Trancura** (see earlier) also offers an excursion rafting the more technical Maichin River, which includes a barbecue lunch. **Kayak Pucón** (© 45/716-2347; www.kayakpucon.net) runs 3- to 15-day trips around Pucón to as far away as the Futaleufú that begin at $380 per person and include all food, accommodations, equipment, and transportation.

SKIING The **Centro de Ski Pucón** (© 45/441901; www.skipucon.cl) gives skiers the opportunity to schuss down a smoking volcano—not something you can do every day. There's a sizable amount of terrain here, and it's all open-field skiing, but, regrettably, the owners (Gran Hotel Pucón; see review later) rarely open more than two of the five chairs, due to nothing else but laziness. You'll need to take a chairlift to the main lodge, which means that nonskiers, too, can enjoy the lovely views from the lodge's outdoor deck. There's a restaurant, child-care center, and store. The Centro has a ski school and ski equipment rental; slightly cheaper rentals are available from **Aguaventura, Sol y Nieve,** and **Trancura,** among other businesses along O'Higgins. Lift-tickets are C$22,000 for a full-day pass or C$1,800 for a half-day pass. Rates drop to C$16,000/$13,000 in the low season. Most tour companies offer transport to and from the resort, and a shuttle goes every hour on the hour from the Gran Hotel Pucón. For more information, contact one of the tour operators above.

SWIMMING   Pucón's **Lake Villarrica beach ★**, right in front of the Gran Hotel Pucón, is a hub of activity during the summer months and is the place for vacationers to see and be seen. Thousands of beach goers take up almost every inch of sand and the warm waters of Lago Villarrica are filled with windsurfers, kayakers, boats, and swimmers.

WHERE TO STAY

Pucón is chock-full of lodging options, nearly all of them good to excellent. If you're planning to spend more than several days in the region, you might consider renting one of the abundant *cabañas* here. Keep in mind that Pucón is very busy during the summer, and accommodations need to be reserved well in advance for visits between December 15 and the end of February. Prices listed below show the range from low to high season; high season is from November to February, but verify each hotel's specific dates. You might consider visiting during the off-season, when lodging prices drop almost 50%; November and March are especially good months to visit.

Expensive

Gran Hotel Pucón ☺   Gran Hotel is a landmark built by the government in 1936 when fishing tourism began to take off in Pucón. It is a good choice for families, but since it was purchased by casino chain Enjoy, it has gone downhill—sad because this was once one of the country's great hotels. The owners renovated the premises (and replaced a hideous peacock teal exterior with an insipid putty color), but one has the feeling they still have a long way to go, especially when it comes to service. The hotel's palatial hallways, stately dining areas, and lovely checkerboard patio give an aura of times gone by. Indeed, the old-world beauty of these common areas, with their marble and parquet floors, lofty ceilings, and flowing curtains, still looks scruffy. The rooms are not exactly noteworthy, but they are not bad, either: spacious, with comfortable beds and views of the volcano or the lake. The superior room has an alcove with one or two additional beds for kids; bathrooms are spacious and clean. The hotel is run somewhat like a cruise ship, with nightly dinner dances, stage shows, music, and comedy, as well as a team of activity directors who run a kids' "miniclub" and host classes for adults, such as cooking or tango. The hotel sits on the most popular beach in Pucón.

Clemente Holzapfel 190, Pucón. ℂ/fax **45/913300.** www.enjoy.cl. 133 units. $253 double. AE, DC, MC, V. **Amenities:** Restaurant; outdoor cafe; bar; lounge; children's programs; concierge; health club; large outdoor pool and small indoor pool; room service. *In room:* TV, fax, hair dryer, Internet access, minibar.

Hotel Antumalal ★★★ 🖻   This is simply one of the most lovely and unique hotels in Chile. It's 60 years old and still has not lost its original cozy, retro-chic essence or its quality. Low-slung and literally built into a rocky slope, the Antumalal was designed to blend with its natural environment; the property's electricity is completely generated by a stream on site. The friendly, personal attention provided by the staff heightens a sense of intimacy with one's surroundings. The rooms are all the same size, and they are very comfortable, with honeyed-wood walls; a private fireplace with a pile of wood; a big, comfortable bed; and large panoramic windows that look out onto the same gorgeous view. There's also a Royal Cottage for rent that comes with two bedrooms, a living room, and fireplace. It's perfect for families or as a romantic bungalow for two, as is another chic forest chalet suite.

The dining room not only serves up a spectacular view, but it also serves some of the best food in Pucón. Well-kept terraced gardens and an organic farm zigzag down the lakeshore, where guests have use of a private beach. Their spa was rebuilt in 2010 and the kidney-shape pool has been divided by a glass panel between the indoors and outdoors. The new facilities laden with rocks and waterfalls are as lovely, if not more so, than any of the thermal spas outside of town. It's all fit for a queen—indeed, Queen Elizabeth II graced the hotel with her presence several decades ago.

Camino Pucón–Villarrica, Km 2. © **45/441011.** Fax 45/441013. www.antumalal.com. 18 units. $308 double; $399; family suite; $641 Royal or Forest Chalet. Rates include full breakfast. Half-board available. AE, DC, MC, V. **Amenities:** Restaurant (p. 270); bar; lounge; pool; spa, tennis court. *In room:* TV, fax, hair dryer, Internet.

Hotel Huincahue ★ 📇 If you like to be in the center of town, steps from all the shops and restaurants, in a quiet and sophisticated setting, then this is your best bet. The hotel sits right on the main plaza and has an elegant, homey feel to it. From the cozy lobby lounge with a fireplace and adjoining library to the peaceful pool in the lovely garden, this place feels more like a private mansion than a hotel. Rooms have pleasant beige carpets and nice wrought-iron and wood furniture, and a few have spectacular views of the volcano (room no. 202 is best). Second-floor rooms have small balconies. The marble bathrooms are large and many have windows as well. The staff tries hard to accommodate, but their English is minimal, so be patient.

Pedro de Valdivia 375, Pucón. ©/fax **45/443540** or 45/442728. www.hotelhuincahue.com. 20 units. $200 double; $311 suite. Rates include continental breakfast. AE, MC, V. **Amenities:** Restaurant; bar; babysitting; outdoor pool; room service. *In room:* TV.

Moderate

Almoni del Lago Resort ★★ 📇 Location is everything at the Almoni, with its lush, gorgeous grounds leading down to the lapping shores of Lake Villarrica just a few meters from the deck of your cabin. Cabins for two, four, and eight guests are available; ask for specials for multiday stays. Cabins are fully equipped, very comfortable, and elegant; guests are given their own remote gate opener to help control access. A kiosk sells basic food items and other sundries. Most *cabañas* have their own deck right on the water; others have a deck farther up the hill. Either way, the cabins are fairly close together, so you might end up getting to know your neighbor. Prices drop 20% in the off-season.

Camino Villarrica a Pucón, Km 19. © **45/210676.** Fax 45/442304. www.almoni.cl. 8 *cabañas.* $84 *cabaña* for 2. MC, V. **Amenities:** Large outdoor pool; tennis courts. *In room:* TV, kitchen.

Hotel & Spa Araucarias The Hotel & Spa Araucarias is a good midrange option for its well-manicured grounds, indoor pool, outdoor deck, and extras such as an on-site gift shop. The size of the rooms is a little tight—not too much space to walk around in, but enough to open your suitcase. If you're looking for something a little more independent and spacious, try one of the four connected cabins in the back. The hotel has a "spa" room with a sauna and a heated indoor pool fitted with hydromassage lounges. Its name comes from the araucaria trees that flank the entrance;

there's also an araucaria sprouting from a grassy courtyard in the back. The hotel is within walking distance from the beach and is close to shops and restaurants.

Caupolicán 243, Pucón. ©/fax **45/441963**. www.araucarias.cl. 25 units. $148 double. Rates include continental breakfast. AE, DC, MC, V. **Amenities:** Restaurant; lounge; Jacuzzi; heated indoor pool; sauna. *In room:* TV.

La Posada Plaza Pucón ★

This traditional hotel is housed in a 78-year-old home built by German immigrants. Everything about this old-fashioned hotel, from its exterior to its dining area, to its backyard swimming pool, is very attractive—except the rooms, that is, which are plain and inexplicably do not keep up the charm of the hotel's common areas. These old buildings always seem to come with fun house floors that creak and slant in every direction. All in all, it's a comfortable enough place to hang your hat for the evening, and it is located on the plaza 2 blocks from the beach.

Av. Pedro de Valdivia 191, Pucón. © **45/441088**. Fax 45/441762. www.plazapucon.cl. 17 units. $103–$144 double. Rates include buffet breakfast. AE, DC, MC, V. **Amenities:** Restaurant; snack bar; lounge; large outdoor pool. *In room:* TV.

Las Cabañas Metreñehue ★ ☺

These pastoral *cabañas* are surrounded by dense forest and bordered by the thundering Trancura River, about a 10-minute drive from downtown Pucón, and are for those seeking a country ambience away from town. There are cabins built for seven guests; a few two-story cabins can fit eight. All are spacious and very comfortable, with wood-burning stoves, decks, and ample kitchens. Some come with bathtubs, and a few have giant picture windows; all have daily maid service. The two *cabañas* in the back have a great view of the volcano. Around the 10-hectare (24-acre) property are walking trails, a swimming pool, a volleyball court, a soccer field, and a river where guests can fish for trout. The cabins are popular with families in the summer, and sometimes large groups take advantage of the *quincho,* the poolside barbecue site. The German owners are gracious and multilingual, and live in the main house (and reception area), near the cabins.

Camino Pucón a Caburgua, Km 10. ©/fax **45/441322**. www.metrenehue.com. 7 units. $67 for 2; $147 for 6. AE, DC, MC, V. **Amenities:** Restaurant; bikes; large outdoor pool. *In room:* TV, kitchen.

Malalhue Hotel ★

This attractive, newer hotel is about a 15-minute walk from town, but it offers excellent value in handsome accommodations. It was designed to feel like a modern mountain lodge, made of volcanic rock and native wood, and is set on an open space in a residential area. The interiors are impeccably clean, and rooms are decorated with country furnishings. There's also a restaurant and a cozy lounge with a fireplace and couches. *Cabañas* have two bedrooms, a trundle bed in the living area, and a fully stocked kitchen. The location isn't ideal, but it is a good value nonetheless.

Camino Internacional 1615, Pucón. © **45/443130**. Fax 45/443132. www.malalhue.cl. 24 units, 3 *cabañas*. $183 double. Rates include buffet breakfast. AE, DC, MC, V. **Amenities:** Restaurant; bar; lounge; room service. *In room:* TV.

Monte Verde Lodge & Cabañas ★★

Built in 2003 and tastefully designed using nearly every kind of wood available in the area (including recycled alerce), this six-room hotel is about 6km (3¾ miles) from Villarrica, meaning you'll need a taxi or rental car to get here. The hotel and *cabañas* are perched on a hill to afford views of the volcano and the lake. All rooms are decorated differently; four have king-size beds and all but one have private balconies with lake views. The bathrooms are decorated with old-fashioned sinks and bathtubs obtained from a turn-of-the-20th-century hotel in Villarrica. Attentive service and a complimentary bottle of red wine upon arrival are welcoming touches. A cozy lounge boasts a wood-burning fireplace and board games; during the high season, there are kayaks and boats available for guest use at the beach below and an outdoor pool, whirlpool, and hot tub. Reservations are necessary for the *cabañas,* which can sleep two to seven guests.

Camino Villarrica–Pucón, Km 18. © **45/441351.** Fax 45/443132. www.monteverdepucon.cl. 6 units, 14 *cabañas.* $189 room; $179–$347 *cabaña.* Rates include buffet breakfast. AE, DC, MC, V. **Amenities:** Lounge; room service.

Inexpensive

Cabañas Ruca Malal ★ These custom-made, cozy wooden cabins are tucked away in a tiny forested lot at the bend where busy O'Higgins becomes the road to Caburgua. The grounds, however, are peaceful, and they burst with bamboo, beech, magnolias, and rhododendron. The design of each cabin features log stairwells, carved headboards, and walls made of slabs of evergreen beech trunks cut lengthwise. They are well lit and have full-size kitchens and daily maid service. A wood-burning stove keeps the rooms toasty warm on cold days. In the center of the property is a kidney-shape swimming pool; there are also a Jacuzzi and sauna, but, unfortunately, you'll have to pay extra to use them. As with most cabins, those designed for four people mean one bedroom with a double bed and a trundle bed in the living area; book a cabin for six if you prefer two bedrooms. Those with a sweet tooth will love the on-site chocolate shop.

O'Higgins 770, Pucón. ©/fax **45/442297.** www.rucamalal.cl. 10 units. $131 cabin for 4; $168 cabin for 6. MC, V. **Amenities:** Lounge; Jacuzzi; small outdoor pool; sauna; free Wi-Fi. *In room:* TV, free Internet, kitchen.

¡école! ★ 🖉 Nearly 40 environmental activist partners own this pleasant hostel, which offers small but clean and comfortable rooms with beds blanketed with goose-down comforters. ¡école! sees a predominantly international crowd, from backpackers to families traveling on a budget. It has a very good vibe throughout and a nice outdoor patio with picnic tables. The hostel provides great reading material in the small lounge, from travel guides to environment-oriented literature, to logging protest rosters. The hostel is equal parts restaurant/lodging/ecology center, offering day trips to various areas, but especially to the private sanctuary El Cañi, an araucaria reserve. It's very popular in the summer, when it's wise to book at least 1 or 2 weeks in advance. Note that some rooms are shared, meaning you may have to bunk with a stranger if the hostel fills up, although there are doubles located in the back for nonshared accommodations with a private bathroom.

General Urrutia 592, Pucón. ©/fax **45/441675.** www.ecole.cl. 16 units. $21 dorm; $63 double. Rates include continental breakfast. DC, MC, V. **Amenities:** Restaurant (p. 271).

La Tetera ★ Rooms at La Tetera are simple but meticulously clean, and shared bathrooms are not much of an issue, as they are just outside your door. It's all squeezed in pretty tight, but guests have use of a private, sunny common area with chairs and a picnic table, and a short walkway connects to an elevated wooden deck. A Swiss-Chilean couple own La Tetera; they offer a book exchange and good tourism information, and will arrange excursions and help with trip planning. La Tetera (the Tea Kettle) lives up to its name, with two menu pages of teas, along with sandwiches, daily specials, and pastries. A common area next to the cafe has the only TV in the place. The staff can arrange Spanish lessons, even if you're here for just a short time.

General Urrutia 580, Pucón. ©/fax **45/441462.** www.tetera.cl. 6 units. $32–$41 double. Rates include continental breakfast. No credit cards. **Amenities:** Restaurant; bar (for guests only).

Portal Pucón Cabañas ☺   Fourteen of these wooden cabins are spread out over a large, grassy lot overlooking Lake Villarrica, and the remaining five (built in 2003) are across the road that separates the cabins from the beach. They are comfortable and relatively inexpensive, and a good bet for families with kids, especially for the pool, play area, "kids' clubhouse," and babysitting service. All cabins have tiny kitchens, living areas, wood-burning stoves, small decks with a table and chairs, and sweeping views of the lake. However, five of the cabins (*cabañas chicas*) are large cabins split into two units, and are somewhat cramped. The cabins on the lakefront are the most spectacular for their views and have two bedrooms, one en suite, the other with bunk beds, and there is also a sofa bed in the living room. The spacious property features walking trails, and there's also a private beach and docking area a 5-minute walk down the hill and across the road. Portal Pucón is a 3-minute drive from downtown.

Camino Pucón–Villarrica, Km 4.5. ☏ **45/443322.** Fax 45/442498. www.portalpucon.cl. 19 units. $168 for 2; $232 for 4. AE, DC, MC, V. **Amenities:** Lounge; bar; large outdoor pool. *In room:* TV, kitchen.

Refugio Peninsula Bed & Breakfast ★   Of the inexpensive options mentioned here, this hostel has the best location, a half-block walk from the shore and just a 100m (328-ft.) walk from the main beach in Pucón. Tucked away on a quiet corner on the lush peninsula side of town, the hostel, which is associated with Hostelling International, offers shared accommodations, a few doubles, and a *cabaña* for five with a kitchenette, and all its furnishings and interiors are fresh and new. Like ¡école! this hostel has an outdoor patio; it also has a cozy, wood-hewn restaurant and bar for meals and drinks. Shared rooms (some with three beds, some with five) mean that you will bunk with a stranger on busy nights, but here each room has a private bathroom, unlike its competitors. There are also two double rooms for couples or a single seeking privacy. Service here is friendly.

Clemente Holzapfel 11, Pucón. ☏ **45/443398.** www.refugiopeninsula.cl. 8 units. $80 double; $157 *cabaña* for 5. Rates include continental breakfast (except *cabaña*). No credit cards. **Amenities:** Restaurant; bar (for guests only).

WHERE TO DINE

Pucón has a good selection of cafes that serve *onces,* the popular late-afternoon coffee-and-cakes snack, in addition to a lunch menu. **Café de la P,** Lincoyán 395 (☏ **45/442018;** www.cafedelap.com), has a menu with sandwiches, cakes, coffee drinks, and cocktails. It's a nice place to unwind with a drink in the evening and is open until 4am in the summer. **Cafetería Suiza,** O'Higgins 116 (☏ **45/441241**), has a menu with everything from milkshakes to full-fledged entrees, and does a booming business with the Santiago crowd in the summer.

  Patagonia ★★, Fresia 223 (☏ **45/443165**), holds the Cassis chocolate shop inside, and is a great place to get a tea and a piece of cake on a rainy day or a multi-flavored ice-cream cone in the heat of the summer. Their outside patio is a favorite spot for *onces,* not to mention people-watching, as is the laid-back patio at California-style health food cafe **Trawen** (O'Higgins 311; ☏ **45/442024**). For Chilean comfort food, try **Rap Hamburguer** (☏ **45/443336**), at O'Higgins 619, which serves up massive burgers stacked with eggs, avocado, or whatever else you have in mind.

Expensive

Antumalal ★★ 📷 INTERNATIONAL   The Hotel Antumalal's restaurant serves some of the most flavorful cuisine in Pucón, with creative dishes that are well prepared and seasoned with herbs from an extensive organic garden. In fact, most of the vegetables used here are local and organic; the milk comes from the family's own dairy farm. New chef Daniel Navarro has been trying to incorporate the original recipes of the resort, which utilize the hotel's organic farm and seasonal ingredients. Try a thinly sliced beef carpaccio followed by chicken stuffed with smoked salmon, grilled local trout, or any one of the pastas. There's a good selection of wine and an ultracool cocktail lounge for an after-dinner drink (but it's tiny and not a "happening" spot). It's worth a visit for the view of Lake Villarrica alone. This is my favorite dining experience in Pucón.

Camino Pucón-Villarrica, Km 2. ℂ **45/441011.** Fax 45/441013. Reservations recommended. Main courses C$6,000–C$9,500. AE, DC, MC, V. Daily noon–4pm and 8–10pm.

La Maga ★★ URUGUAYAN/PARRILLA Undoubtedly the best *parrilla* in town, this restaurant originated in the beach town of Punta del Este, Uruguay. The food is excellent, especially the meat, chicken, and fish grilled on the giant barbecue on the patio. Order a bottle of wine and a large fresh salad, and watch the people go by the large picture windows overlooking the street. Try the grilled salmon with capers, if you're in the mood for fish. But, really, the best cuts here are the beef filets, known as *lomos,* served with mushrooms, Roquefort, or pepper sauce. The *bife de chorizo* (sirloin) is thick and tender. For dessert, the flan here stands out.

Alderete 264. ℂ **45/444277.** Main courses C$4,000–C$10,000. AE, MC, V. Daily noon–4pm and 7pm–midnight.

Mora SUSHI/JAPANESE This new sushi restaurant in the old Naukana space is the sleekest kid in town. Bright pinks and oranges keep the lounge feeling lively. The menu gets mixed reactions because the dishes are often a bit more fusion and adventurous than necessary, though the sushi and sashimi are generally good. All-you-can-eat sushi specials are a reasonable deal.

Fresia 236. ℂ **45/444-857.** Main courses C$3,500–C$15,000. AE, MC, V. Daily noon–3pm and 7:30pm–midnight.

Puerto Pucón 🏠 SPANISH Puerto Pucón pays homage to its owner's Spanish heritage through its design and well-made classics such as paella. Seafood is the focus here, and it is served in a multitude of ways: Have your razor clams, shrimp, and calamari sautéed in garlic or wrapped in a crepe and smothered in crab sauce. The atmosphere is typical Spanish, with white stucco walls, bullfight posters, flamenco-dancer fans, and racks of wine bottles; the fireplace is especially nice, and there's also a small bar. The sangria is excellent, and during warmer months, there's seating on the front deck, which can get packed.

Fresia 246. ℂ **45/441592.** Main courses C$4,500–C$11,000. AE, MC, V. Daily 11am–3:30pm and 7–11:30pm (until 2am during summer).

Moderate

¡école! 🌿 VEGETARIAN This vegetarian restaurant, inside the hotel of the same name, includes one salmon dish among heaps of such creative dishes as calzones, quiche, pizza, burritos, chop suey, and more. Sandwiches come on homemade bread, and the breakfast is the best in town, featuring an American-style breakfast as well as Mexican- and Chilean-style. ¡école! uses locally and organically grown products and buys whole-wheat flour and honey from a local farm. There are also fresh salads here. The outdoor patio is a lovely place to dine under the grapevine in good weather. The service is very slow; they usually offer a shorter menu during the winter.

General Urrutia 592. ℂ/fax **45/441675.** Main courses C$3,000–C$8,000. MC, V. Daily 8am–11pm.

La Esquina de la Marmita ★ FONDUE   Cozy and candlelit, La Marmita specializes in warm crocks of fondue, as well as the other Swiss favorite, *raclette*. Both involve a diner's participation, which usually makes for an amusing dinner—but if you are a fondue fan, you won't be as impressed here as in Europe, for example (the right cheeses aren't always available). Fondue can be ordered a variety of ways, with standard bread cubes, squares of breaded meat, or vegetables. A *raclette* runs along the same lines; diners heat cheese to eat with cured meats and potatoes; it's not as fun as fondue, but enjoyable nevertheless. Unfortunately, this restaurant closes during the winter, which is the perfect season for this kind of food.

Fresia 300. ✆ **45/442431.** Fondue for 2 C$14,000. AE, DC, MC, V. Daily 7:30–11pm. Closed Apr–Nov.

Naukana ★ FUSION/ASIAN   A trendsetter since it opened in 2001, Naukana offers a menu that spans the Spice Route from Arabia to Japan. The plates are small and meant for sharing over drinks. Vietnamese spring rolls, pad Thai, kebabs, and tempura are a great way to start the night off, and their Tibetan salmon in a sauce of cilantro, coconut, and peanut is a fine entree. There are decent vegetarian offerings too. At last visit the restaurant had left its old space on Fresia and was in the process of moving into a much larger house on the edge of the center.

Colo Colo y Alderate. ✆ **45/444677.** www.naukana.cl. Reservations recommended. Main courses C$4,000–C$10,000. AE, DC, MC, V. Daily noon–4pm and 8–midnight.

Inexpensive

Viva Perú! ★★ ☺ PERUVIAN   This Peruvian restaurant is a favorite hangout for locals, offering warm, personalized service and tasty cuisine. For solo travelers, there is bar seating, and there is a patio with a volcano view. The restaurant specializes in *ceviche* and seafood *picoteos* (appetizer platters), which make an excellent accompaniment to a frosty pisco sour. Daily fixed-price lunch specials include a mixed salad, entree (steamed or grilled fish, pork loin, or chicken), and coffee for about C$3,325. The restaurant offers one of the few kids' menus in the area. Try the sugary-sweet *suspiro limeño*, a creamy Peruvian traditional dessert.

Lincoyán 372. ✆/fax **45/444025.** Main courses C$4,000–C$7,000. AE, MC, V. Daily noon–2am.

Cerveza Crater ★ GERMAN   This new brewpub on the road to Villarrica produces two beers right in the restaurant, a Golden Ale and a Porter, and you can see all the beer equipment through the inside windows. The menu is made up of a standard German fare, closer to what you might find farther south in Osorno or Puerto Montt: wurstchen (a type of thin frankfurter), goulash, and even pancakes in a beer syrup. They also have a series of large cabins that they rent out, just beyond the restaurant.

Ruta Villarrica-Pucón, Km 6.5. ✆/fax **45/450-427.** www.cervezacrater.cl. Main courses C$3,000–C$8,000. AE, MC, V. Daily noon–2am.

La Celeste Chiviteria ★ URUGUAYAN   Uruguayan sandwiches are the theme of this cool new shop run by the same team as La Maga, which sits right next door. The sandwiches are big and meaty and there are about a dozen variations that slap on toppings like avocado, egg, bacon, and special sauces. Pop open an artisanal beer as you wait at one of their patio tables or bar stools.

Alderate 266 B. ✆/fax **45/444-046.** Main courses C$3,500–C$5,000. AE, MC, V. Daily 1:30pm–midnight.

PUCÓN AFTER DARK

Pucón's casino, **Enjoy Pucón** (© 45/550000), can be found at Ansorena 121 and boasts three gaming rooms, the largest of which has slot machines. There's a good bar above their Aura restaurant here as well that appeals to all ages, and the place is open very late. For bars, **El Bosque,** O'Higgins 524 (©/fax **45/444025;** closed Mon), is a popular local hangout that is open from 6pm until around 3am, and has Internet access and a good fusion-cuisine menu. **Mamas & Tapas ★★**, O'Higgins 597 (©/fax **45/449002**), is a bar that serves food; it has long been one of the most popular bars in Pucón. It gets packed in the summer and has excellent music, including DJs during peak season. Also try the rooftop patio at **The View** (© 45/442032), at the corner of O'Higgins and Arauco, where on warm summer nights the people-watching in the street below is as good as it gets. A new bierhaus in the center called **Biergarten,** Lincoyán 361, which at last visit was under construction, sounded promising. Plans called for picnic-style tables like in a traditional German beer hall and German food and snacks to go with the brew.

Hot Springs Outside Pucón

All the volcanic activity in the region means there's plenty of *baños termales,* or hot springs, that range from rustic rock pools to full-service spas with massage and saunas. Nothing beats a soothing soak after a long day packed with adventure. Also, like the Cañi Reserve, the hot springs make for a good rainy-day excursion. Apart from those listed below, you might consider nearby **Termas de Quimey Co** (31km/19 miles from Pucón; www.termasquimeyco.com), which opened in 2008, and the more rustic **Termas Los Pozones ★** (Road to Huife, 34km/21 miles from Pucón; no phone), which is open 24 hours and is popular with the younger crowd that wants to keep the party going after a night in Pucón's discos.

Termas de Huife ★★ ☺ Termas de Huife, a relaxing escape for the body and mind, is popular with tourists and locals alike for its idyllic thermal baths and setting. Nestled in a narrow valley on the shore of the transparent River Liucura, Huife operates as a full-service health spa for day visitors and guests who opt to spend the night in one of their *cabañas* or suites. This is one of my favorite *termas,* for both its cozy accommodations and gorgeous landscaping, complete with narrow canals that wind through the property and river-rock hot springs flanked by bamboo and palm fronds. The complex features two large outdoor thermal pools kept at 96° to 98°F (36°–37°C) and a cold-water pool, as well as private thermal bathtubs, individual whirlpools, and massage salons arranged around an airy atrium. Recently, a hydrotherapeutic pool was added. The four-person *cabañas* and double suites are housed in shingled, rust-colored buildings along the river, about a 2-minute walk from the main building. All come with wood-burning stoves, and the *cabañas* have a living area. The bathrooms deserve special mention for their Japanese-style sunken showers and bathtubs that run thermal water. The only complaint I have about this place is that it can be busy, and lots of families means lots of kids.

Road to Huife, 33km (20 miles) E of Pucón. ©/fax **45/441222.** www.termashuife.cl. 10 units. $303–$324 double. Day-use fee C$8,000 adults, children 10 and under free. AE, DC, MC, V. Thermal baths daily 9am–8pm year-round. Take the road east out of Pucón toward Lago Caburgua until you see a sign for Huife, which turns off at the right onto an unnamed dirt road. Follow the road until you see the well-marked entrance for Termas de Huife. **Amenities:** Restaurant; cafeteria; 3 outdoor pools; exercise room; Jacuzzi; sauna. *In room:* TV, minibar.

Termas de Menetúe   In January 2008, Termas de Menetúe opened a dazzling indoor spa complex with two pools, a sauna, massage tubs, mud baths, and massage rooms that is now the focus of this resort. The reception area and restaurant look out onto a giant grass-encircled swimming pool, and a short path takes visitors around to a woodsier setting, with one average-size pool serenaded by a gurgling waterfall. It's a relaxing, bucolic place with giant ferns and a gently flowing stream. The pine cabins are for two to six people and sit a bit too far from the complex. They come with a fully stocked kitchen and wood-burning stove. Menetúe rents bicycles and can point out a few trails for walking. A restaurant serves decent Chilean cuisine, and there's a snack bar near the second pool.

Camino Internacional, Km 30. ℂ/fax **45/441877.** www.menetue.com. 6 *cabañas.* $316 *cabaña* for 2; full-board. Day-use fee C$11,000. No credit cards. Thermal baths Dec–Mar 9am–9pm; Apr–Nov 9am–6pm. **Amenities:** Restaurant; bar; 2 large outdoor pools; spa. *In room:* TV, kitchen.

Termas San Luis ★   Located high in the saddle of the Curarrehue Valley, the Termas San Luis is popular for its well-built thermal pools and view of Volcán Villarrica, but mostly for the rare paved access road that gets you there. The compact resort is centered on two swimming pools built with stone tiles, one outdoor and the other covered by a fiberglass shell much like a greenhouse; both are surrounded by plastic lounge chairs for reclining after a long soak. If you'd like to spend the night, San Luis has six wooden cabins perched on a slope overlooking, unfortunately, the parking lot, although a few are hidden behind trees. The cabins sleep four to six guests, meaning one double bed, three singles, and a living-room trundle bed. They are bright and very pleasant but can get very cold in the winter unless the wood-burning stove is continually stocked. The spa house features a tiny sauna and a massage salon at an additional cost. There is a restaurant here as well.

Ruta Internacional Pucón, Km 27. ℂ **45/412880.** www.termasdesanluis.cl. $168 double with half-board. Day-use fee C$7,000–C$5,000 children. No credit cards. Thermal baths daily 9am–11pm summer; daily 10am–7pm winter. **Amenities:** Restaurant; large outdoor pool and large indoor pool; spa; sauna; room service. *In room:* TV, kitchen.

Natural Attractions Outside Pucón

PARQUE NACIONAL HUERQUEHUE

Smaller than its rivals Conguillío and Villarrica, though no less attractive, Parque Nacional Huerquehue (www.parquehuerquehue.cl) boasts the best short-haul hike in the area, the **Sendero Los Lagos.** This 12,500-hectare (30,875-acre) park opens as a steeply walled amphitheater draped in matted greenery and crowned by a forest of lanky araucaria trees. There are a handful of lakes here; the first you come upon is Lago Tinquilco, which is hemmed in by steep forested slopes. At the shore, you'll find a tiny, ramshackle village with homes built by German colonists in the early 1900s. A few residents offer cheap accommodations, but the best place to spend the night is in a campground near the entrance or at the Refugio Tinquilco (see "Where to Stay," later).

There's a self-guided trail called **Ñirrico** that is a quick 400m (1,312-ft.) walk, but if you're up for a vigorous hike, don't miss the spectacular **Tres Lagos** trail that begins at the northern tip of Lake Tinquilco. The path first passes the **Salto Nido de Aguila** waterfall, then winds through a forest of towering beech, climbing to a lookout point with a beautiful view of Lago Tinquilco and the Villarrica volcano. From here, the trail begins zigzagging up and up through groves of billowy ferns and more tall trees until finally (2–3 hr. later) arriving at the beautiful, araucaria-ringed **Lago**

Chico, where you can take a cool dip. A relatively flat trail from here continues on to the nearby **Verde** and **Toro** lakes. Bring plenty of food and water, and come prepared with rain gear if the weather looks dubious.

On your way to or from the park, you can make a detour to the **Ojos de Caburgua,** where two aqua-colored waterfalls crash into the tiny Laguna Azul. There are a few picnic tables here, and you can take a dip if the weather's nice. The turn-off point is about 15km (9¼ miles) from Pucón.

GETTING THERE & BASICS The park is 35km (22 miles) from Pucón. **Buses JAC** (see p. 260) has daily service to the park (several times per day, depending on the season), and most tour companies offer minivan transportation and will arrange to pick you up later, should you decide to spend the night. If you're driving your own car, head out of Pucón on O'Higgins toward Lago Caburgua, until you see the sign for Huerquehue that branches off to the right. From here it's a rutted dirt road that can be difficult to manage when muddy. CONAF charges C$4,000 for adults and C$2,000 for kids to enter; camping is C$12,000; it's open daily from 8:30am to 6pm.

WHERE TO STAY CONAF has a campground near Lago Tinquilco and charges C$15,000 per site, for a maximum of six people. The best option for a roof over your head is the attractive, barn-shaped **Refugio Tinquilco** (© **9/539-2728;** www.tinquilco.cl), a spacious lodge with bunks for C$8,000 per person (you'll need your own sleeping bag), and regular rooms with bedding for C$32,000 per double. They also have a good restaurant and offer full pension for an additional C$6,000.

PARQUE NACIONAL VILLARRICA ★

This gem of a park is home to three volcanoes: the show-stealer Villarrica, Quetrupillán, and Lanín. It's quite a large park, stretching 61,000 hectares (150,670 acres) to the Argentine border and that country's Parque Nacional Lanín, and is blanketed with a thick virgin forest of araucaria, evergreen, and deciduous beech. A bounty of activities is available year-round, including skiing and climbing to the crater of the volcano (see "Outdoor Activities" under "Pucón," earlier in this chapter), hiking, horseback riding, bird-watching, and more.

The park has three sectors. Most visitors to the park head to **Sector Rucapillán** (the Mapuche's name for Volcán Villarrica, meaning House of the Devil). Volcán Villarrica is one of the most active volcanoes in the world, having erupted 59 times from the 16th century until now. There are two trails here, the 15km (9.25-mile) **Sendero Challupén** that winds through lava fields and araucaria, and the 5km (3-mile) **Sendero El Glaciar Pichillancahue,** which takes visitors through native forest to a glacier. The park ranger booth at the entrance can point out how to get to the trail heads. You'll also find the interesting **Cuevas Volcánicas** in this sector. Ancient, viscous lava that flowed from the volcano created underground tunnels, 400m (1,312 ft.) of which have been strung with lights and fitted with walkways that allow you to tour their dark, dripping interiors. Visitors are provided with a hard hat; the cave's humid, cold air requires that you bring warm clothing, regardless of the season. There are also exhibits describing volcanism and bilingual tours. It's open daily from 10am to 8:30pm during the summer, and from 10am to 6:30pm during the winter; admission is a steep C$3,000 for adults and C$1,000 for children (© **45/442002**). Camping costs C$12,000.

The second sector, **Quetrupillán,** is home to wilder, thicker vegetation and a multiple-day backpacking trail that wanders through virgin forest and past the **Termas de Palguín** (which is also accessible by road), a rustic hot springs. Here you'll also find several waterfalls, including the crashing **Salto el León.** There's a horse stable (see "Horseback Riding" under "Pucón," earlier in this chapter) that offers trips around the area. There is also an excellent day hike and the region's best thermal baths are here (see the Villarrica loop drive info below). Finally, the third sector, **Puesco,** is accessed by Rte. 119 south of Curarrehue. There's a CONAF (park service) post and several hikes through the park's wildest terrain, including pine forests, lakes, and rugged mountains.

SIETE LAGOS: PANGUIPULLI & LICAN RAY

Panguipulli: 54km (33 miles) S of Villarrica; Lican Ray: 31km (19 miles) S of Villarrica

Few day-long sightseeing drives surpass the beauty of the **Siete Lagos (Seven Lakes)** region south of Pucón, where you can follow a half-paved, half-dirt loop around Lago Calafquén, with stops in the picturesque resort towns Panguipulli and Lican Ray. As its name implies, the region is home to seven lakes, one of which is across the border in Argentina, and all are set among rugged, verdant mountains that offer photo opportunities at every turn. Because this area is also home to Chile's best hot springs, Termas Geométricas, it makes sense to make a detour here. This can be done by driving to Coñaripe and heading left toward Parque Nacional Villarrica (follow signs for the park or Pualafquén). For a more adventurous drive, and only if you have a rental car with high clearance (4×4 is necessary during inclement weather), drive the highly recommended loop through the national park from the other direction, as described below.

Driving the Siete Lagos Route & the Loop through Parque Nacional Villarrica

Renting a car is the best option here, but all tour companies can put this excursion together for you. Ideally, these drives are best when the sun is shining, for maximum views; however, visiting the various hot springs and driving through dense forest is also a good way to pass a rainy day.

For the Siete Lagos route, head south from Villarrica toward Lican Ray and then through Coñaripe, circling the lake until reaching Panguipulli. From here, you take the paved road toward Lanco (although signs might say LICAN RAY as well) until you see the sign for Lican Ray and Villarrica. This rough dirt road continues to Villarrica (there's a good lookout point along the way) or forks to the right to Lican Ray, where you can again catch the paved road to Villarrica. Take a good look at the map before making any decisions; note that none of these roads is numbered or has a name. Of course, the trip can be done in the reverse direction, which might be more desirable for an afternoon soak at the hot springs just south of Coñaripe.

It's a little more difficult (read: potholes, slippery mud, and short, steep pitches), but the loop through Parque Nacional Villarrica is more desirable for its views of virgin forest of towering evergreen beech and monkey puzzle (araucaria) trees, a good day hike, and a visit to the Termas Geométricas. This route is for high-clearance vehicles (4×4 in wet conditions) and should be undertaken from the north through the south only. Leaving Pucón, head east toward Curarrehue and drive for 20km (12 miles), turning right at the sign for Palguín (30km/19 miles from Pucón). These hot springs have a small hotel and several thermal pools; however, the service here is surly

A Note on Camping

The road between Lican Ray and Coñaripe is full of campsites, some of which have showers and barbecue pits. Try **Cabañas y Camping Los Arrayanes Del Foresta** (© 45/431480 or 9/817-1796; www.arrayanesforesta.cl), 2km (1¼ miles) from Lican Ray, which has well-built sites ($32) and comfortable cabins for 3 to 12 guests ($29–$178 winter; $51–$242 summer); check the website for exact prices at the time you'll be there.

and there are better hot springs in the area. Continue along the road until you reach the ranger station (37km/23 miles from Pucón; C$3,000 per-person entrance fee). There is a full-day hike here, the Los Nevados (16km/10 miles; about 10 hr. round-trip and moderate), but a preferred and shorter hike can be found about midway between the ranger station and Coñaripe, the Pichillancahue trail (7km/4 miles; about 4 hr. round-trip). This trail winds through dense virgin forest of the unusual, spindly monkey puzzle trees and has views of the surrounding volcanoes. The road from the ranger station to Coñaripe is about 27km (17 miles), with an obligatory stop at the most beautiful hot springs in the region, Termas Geométricas.

Termas de Coñaripe ★★ ☺ These *termas* (hot springs) boast a privileged location in a narrow valley hemmed in by lush, steep mountains and Lago Pellaifa. The full-service hot springs complex has lodging and a restaurant, whereas the Termas Geométricas (see later) is more remote and puts you in the middle of more natural surroundings (but with fewer services). Coñaripe is handsomely built, with touches of Japanese design. There are four outdoor pools, one with a slide, and one indoor pool with whirlpool lounges and a waterfall. A babbling creek meanders through the property. The thermal spa's on-site trout fishery is fun for kids, as they can feed the fish. Inside the lobby and the hallways, the floors are made of a mosaic of cypress trunks. Rooms are carpeted and spacious, and suites come with a queen-size bed. If you require quiet, you might not want a room near the busy pool. The *cabañas* come with two rooms with double beds and one with two twins.

Along with all this beauty and the deluxe amenities comes the inevitable crush during the summer months, and it's not unusual for these hot springs to see almost 1,000 visitors per day at peak high season from January 1 to February 15. During this time, there is a self-service cafeteria to alleviate the packed dining room at lunch; a restaurant serves Chilean food year-round. Off-season crowds drop dramatically, and during the winter you might have the place to yourself.

Camino Coñaripe to Liquiñe at Km 15. © **45/431407.** Fax 45/411111. www.termasconaripe.cl. 10 units, 3 *cabañas*, 1 apt. $265 double standard with full-board; $425 cabin with full-board for 4. Day-use fee C$8,000 adults, C$5,000 children. DC, MC, V. Thermal baths daily 9am–11pm year-round. **Amenities:** Restaurant; lounge; bikes; 4 outdoor pools and an indoor pool; room service; tennis courts. *In room:* TV.

Termas Geométricas ★★★ 📷 I can't stop raving about these hot springs, which were designed by famed Chilean architect Germán de Sol (architect of the explora hotels. If you have the time, try to plan a visit here because they are one of the best in Chile. More than a dozen pools, made of handsome gray slate tiles, descend an emerald, jungle-draped ravine, each one linked by a winding boardwalk. Each pool has a changing room and bathroom, with creative touches such as grass roofs and stream-fed sink taps, all very minimalist and decidedly Japanese in influence. It is so utterly relaxing here that you could float until your skin wrinkles like a prune. At the end of the gently sloping boardwalk, you will be taken aback by the sight of a tremendous, crashing waterfall that seems almost too perfect—it is such an ideal spot for a hot springs that it is hard to believe the area wasn't capitalized on earlier. There is a small restaurant that serves coffee, cakes, and cheese sandwiches; you might want to bring your own picnic lunch if you want something more filling. The hot springs are open at night, too, lit by tiny candles resting on the top of the pool walls. It's not cheap, but it's money well spent.

12km (7½ miles) from Coñaripe on the road to Palguín. © **2/214-1214** or 9/442-5420. Fax 2/214-1147. www.termasgeometricas.cl. C$14,000 adults, C$6,000 children 14 and under. Rate includes towel. No credit cards. Thermal baths daily Dec 21–Feb 28 10am–9pm summer, 11am–7pm rest of year. **Amenities:** Cafe.

Lican Ray

This tiny resort town hugs the shore of Lago Calafquén, offering toasty beaches made of black volcanic sand and a forested peninsula for a leisurely drive or stroll. The lake is warmer than others in the region and is, therefore, better suited for swimming; you can also rent a boat here. The name comes from Lican Rayén, a young Mapuche woman from the area who is said to have fallen in love with a Spanish soldier. The town was founded as a trading post, and today there are about 3,000 permanent residents, except for the period from December 15 to February 28, when the population doubles with the arrival of summer vacationers. The first weekend in January is the busiest time of year. There's also the **Noche Lacustre** the second week in February, when the bay fills with boats for a variety of contests and activities, followed by an evening fireworks display. Lican Ray is less crowded and less expensive than Pucón, and during the off-season you'll practically have the place to yourself.

There are a few places to stay here. South German–style **Hotel Becker,** Manquel 105 (© **45/431153**), has modest but comfortable rooms, a restaurant, and a deck from which you can enjoy the lakefront view, charging $36 for a double in the off season, $67 for a double in high season (includes breakfast). **Hostería Inaltulaf-quén,** Cacique Punulef 510 (© **45/431115;** fax 45/415813; jdf@universe.com), has good rooms and an even better dining area and deck, and it is ideally located across from the Playa Grande beach; it charges $46 per double. The *hostería* is run by two helpful Canadians, who also offer excursions. Another recommended hotel is the German-run **Hostal Hoffman,** Camino a Coñaripe 100 (© **45/431109**), a small B&B with five basic rooms for $32 for a double (there's also a restaurant; no credit cards accepted). For dining, try the restaurant at the *hostería* or **Ñaños,** General Urrutia 105 (© **45/431026**), with an extensive menu that offers everything from barbecue meats to clay oven–baked pizzas, and a daily fixed-price lunch for C$3,000. It also has outdoor seating during the summer but no lake view.

For **visitor information,** go to General Urrutia 310 (in front of the plaza). In January and February, the office is open daily 9am to 11pm; during the rest of the year, it's open Monday through Thursday from 9am to 1pm and 3 to 6pm, Friday from 9am to 1pm and 3 to 5pm.

Panguipulli

This little town with the impossible-to-pronounce name (try "Pan-gee-*poo*-yee") is spread across a cove on the shore of its eponymous lake. During the summer, Panguipulli's streets bloom a riot of colorful roses, which the town celebrates in February during the **Semana de las Rosas (Rose Week)** festival. During January and February, the town holds regular folkloric festivals, art exhibits, concerts, and more. Panguipulli was founded as a timber-shipping port and today has nearly 10,000 residents. The town's primary attraction is its charming church of **San Sebastián,** at Diego Portales and Bernardo O'Higgins (in front of the plaza). Mass is held from November to February from Thursday and Saturday at 8pm, Sunday and holidays 8:30am and 11am; the church is open all day (no phone). The Swiss priest who initiated the building of this church in 1947 modeled its design after churches from his native country, with two latticed towers painted in creamy beige and red and topped off with black-shingled steeples. For visitor information, go to O'Higgins and Padre Sigisfredo streets in front of the plaza (Jan–Feb daily 9am–9pm; rest of the year Mon–Fri 9am–6pm).

The town is better visited as a day trip, but there is a remote lodge here that is a wonderful place to hole up in the middle of a forest and take part in a variety of outdoor excursions. The lodge is the **Hotel Riñimapu** (©/fax **63/311388;** www.rinimapu.cl), located 27km (17 miles) south of Panguipulli and on the shore of Lago Riñihue. The Riñimapu draws guests from around the world for its fly-fishing, horseback riding, and hiking—but it is the tranquillity here that encourages guests to really lose themselves in the beauty of the surroundings. The woodsy lodge has 14 simple rooms and three suites, a restaurant, a bar, and a tennis court, and it charges $116 for a double. To get here, head south out of Panguipulli on the paved-then-dirt road toward Lago Riñihue, and continue for 20km (12 miles) until reaching the hotel; or contact the hotel for information about transfer shuttles from the Temuco or Pucón airports. If you want to stick to the town, try **Hotel & Restaurant Le Français** (© **63/312496;** www.hotelelfrances.cl) at Martínez de Rozas 880, with nine cozy doubles ($74 per night) and a decent French-Chilean restaurant.

Huilo Huilo

At the other, eastern end of Lake Panguipulli, the small Mocho-Choshuenco National Preserve protects the ecosystem of the volcanoes of the same name. A much larger, private preserve, Huilo Huilo stretches south from the narrow lake Pirihueico (the name means "water worm"). The 37m (121-ft.) Huilo Huilo waterfall dropping over a basalt lava deposit and the lower, wider Salto del Puma fall are the park's main features. The Choshuenco Volcano features the only snowboard park open year-round in Chile. Other local activities include horseback riding, zipline canopy riding at lofty, 70m (230 ft.) heights, rafting, and fishing. The private park also seeks to breed the highly endangered huemul, a deer similar to mule deer, and guanacos.

On the road leading to Puerto Fuy near Neltume sit several of Chile's most unique hotels. The aptly named **Montaña Mágica** ★ (© **63/197-2651;** www.huilohuilo.cl), or Magic Mountain, looks as if J. R. R. Tolkien himself designed it. A six-sided, cone-shaped little volcano of a stone building, water "erupts" from its summit, cascading down its sides. Each room is named for a different local species of bird and is on a different level as the interior spirals upwards. Each room is also slightly different, but they all have rustic, angular wood-paneled interiors in common. Beds are just a little on the soft side, and if you're tall, you should ask for a room farther down—it's a bit exaggerated to say the showers near the top are perfect for hobbits, but you get the picture. The restaurant has a similar, woodsy theme, featuring wild boar, and the hotel's service is quite good. Room prices range from $274 per double to $347 per suite. Set 35m (115 ft.) in the air amid the forest canopy, the bulb-shaped **Hotel**

Baobab ★ (© 63/197-2651; www.huilohuilo.cl) has a massive oak tree that runs right through its center and a waterfall that runs down its side. The hotel features 55 artfully decorated rooms that run $322 per double.

This is also one of the more remote spots to cross into Argentina in the Lake District. By taking the ferry that travels the length of Lake Pirihueico in 1½ hours from Puerto Fuy, you'll cross to tiny Puerto Pirihueico, 11km (18 miles) from the border. From there, the resort town of San Martín de los Andes is another 47km (76 miles) alongside Lake Lacar, another narrow lake, lying entirely in the Parque Nacional Lanín. It's a good alternative to the more southern Andes lake crossing, considering it's not nearly as overwhelmed by tourists. Note there's no fuel beyond Panguipulli or Lican Ray. You can also reach Puerto Pirihueico via a secondary road through the Huilo Huilo preserve.

VALDIVIA ★

839km (520 miles) S of Santiago; 145km (90 miles) SW of Pucón

Valdivia is a university town on the waterfront of a winding delta, and it often receives mixed reviews from visitors. If you are not planning to visit the coast near Santiago and you are in Pucón for several days, consider a quick visit here or an overnight stay. There are regal homes built by German immigrants and a vibrant market on the water's edge, but it is as though every building from every decade from every architectural style were thrown in a bag, shaken up, and randomly scattered about the city—like in every Chilean city except La Serena.

Valdivia does have more charm than Temuco and Puerto Montt, however, and there are many activities for kids here. The city is energetic, full of life, and very tenacious. Valdivia has suffered attacks, floods, fires, and the disastrous earthquake of 1960 that nearly drowned the city under 3m (9¾ ft.) of water (the strongest earthquake ever recorded). During World War II, Valdivia's German colonists were blacklisted, ruining the economy. So if Valdivia looks a little weary, well, it's understandable. There are tours here to visit the tiny towns and ancient forts at the mouth of the bay that protected the city from seafaring intruders. The market, where fishmongers peddle their catch of the day, and pelicans, cormorants, and fat sea lions wait for scraps, is a delight, and there are several good restaurants, opportunities to boat around the city's delta, and some of the best museums and galleries in Chile here, too.

Valdivia, with about 130,000 residents, is divided by a series of narrow rivers, notably the Río Valdivia and the Río Calle-Calle, that wrap around the city's downtown area. These rivers have produced some of the world's top rowing athletes, and many mornings you can see spidery figures plying the glassy water. Across the Río Valdivia is the Isla Teja, a residential area that's home to the Universidad Austral de Chile. It is common to see students pedaling around town.

Essentials

GETTING THERE

BY PLANE Valdivia's **Aeródromo Pichoy** (ZAL; © 63/272295) is about 32km (20 miles) northeast of the city. **LANExpress** (© 600/526-2000; www.lan.com) has two daily flights from Santiago, one daily flight to Concepción, two weekly flights to Temuco, and one weekly flight to Puerto Montt. A **taxi** to town costs about C$12,000, or you can catch a ride on one of **Transfer Valdivia's minibuses** for C$4,000 (© 63/225533).

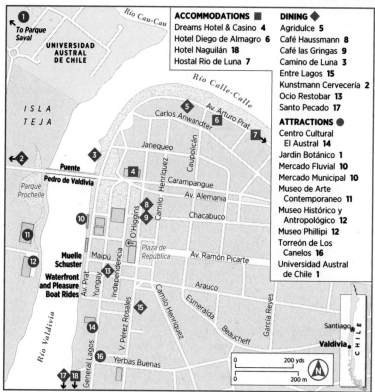

ACCOMMODATIONS ■
Dreams Hotel & Casino **4**
Hotel Diego de Almagro **6**
Hotel Naguilán **18**
Hostal Rio de Luna **7**

DINING ◆
Agridulce **5**
Café Haussmann **8**
Café las Gringas **9**
Camino de Luna **3**
Entre Lagos **15**
Kunstmann Cervecería **2**
Ocio Restobar **13**
Santo Pecado **17**

ATTRACTIONS ●
Centro Cultural
  El Austral **14**
Jardin Botánico **1**
Mercado Fluvial **10**
Mercado Municipal **10**
Museo de Arte
  Contemporaneo **11**
Museo Histórico y
  Antropológico **12**
Museo Phillipi **12**
Torreón de Los
  Canelos **16**
Universidad Austral
  de Chile **1**

BY BUS The bus terminal is at Anwandter and Muñoz (© **63/212212**), and nearly every bus company passes through here; there are multiple daily trips from Pucón and Santiago. The average cost for a ticket from Santiago to Valdivia is C$18,000; from Pucón to Valdivia, it is C$4,000.

BY CAR From the Pan-American Highway, take Rte. 205 and follow the signs for Valdivia. A car is not really necessary in Valdivia, as most attractions can be reached by boat, foot, or taxi. It's about a 2-hour drive from Pucón, 1½ hours from Temuco, and 4 hours from Puerto Montt.

VISITOR INFORMATION

Sernatur's helpful **Oficina de Turismo,** near Muelle Schuster at Arturo Prat 555 (© **63/215739**), has a well-stocked supply of brochures. The office hours from March to December are Monday through Thursday 8:30am to 5:30pm, and Friday from 8:30am to 4:30pm. January and February hours are Monday through Friday 8:30am to 7pm, Saturday and Sunday from 10am to 7pm. There's also an information kiosk at the bus terminal open daily from 8am to 9pm, and two websites with information at **www.valdiviachile.cl.**

SPECIAL EVENTS The city hosts a grand yearly event, the **Verano en Valdivia,** with several weeks of festivities that begin in January, culminating with the **Noche Valdiviana** on the third Saturday in February. On this evening, hundreds of floating candles and festively decorated boats fill the Río Valdivia; after dark, the city puts on a fireworks display. Note that Valdivia is crowded during this time, so hotel reservations are essential. For event info, check out www.munivaldivia.cl.

[FastFACTS] VALDIVIA

Car Rental **Assef y Méndez Rent A Car** can be found at General Lagos 1335 (ⓒ/fax **63/213205**), and **Hertz** at Ramón Picarte 640 (ⓒ/fax **63/218316**); both have airport kiosks.

Currency Exchange *Casas de cambio* can be found at **La Reconquista** at Carampangue 325 (ⓒ **63/213305**), but banks **Banco Santander-Santiago,** Pérez Rosales 585, and **Corpbanca,** Ramón Picarte 370, have ATMs in addition to money exchange. Redbanc ATMs are in grocery stores, gas stations, and all banks throughout the city.

Hospital The Clínica Alemana can be found at Beaucheff 765 (ⓒ **63/246200**).

Internet Several spots for Internet access are near the plaza; try **Entel,** Vicente Pérez Rosales 601, no. 2.

Laundry Self-service laundromats are **Lavamatic,** Walter Schmidt 305, no. 6 (ⓒ **63/211015**), and **Laverap,** Arauco 697, no. 2.

What to See & Do

The best tour is through Elisabeth Lajtonyi at **Outdoors Chile** (ⓒ **63/253377;** www.outdoors-chile.com). She can arrange your entire trip in Valdivia, from reserving hotels to airport transfers and personalized sightseeing tours.

BOAT TRIPS

A delightful way to explore the Valdivia region is with one of the many boat tours that depart from the pier Muelle Schuster at the waterfront, including yachts, catamarans, and an antique steamer. Tours are in full swing during the summer, and although there's limited service during the off-season, it's possible for a group to hire a launch for a private trip. The most interesting journeys sail through the **Carlos Anwandter Nature Sanctuary** to the **San Luis de Alba de Cruces Fort** and to **Isla Mancera** and **Corral** to visit other 17th-century historic forts; both tours run about 5 to 6 hours round-trip and usually include meals. The Nature Sanctuary was created after the 1960 earthquake sank the banks of the Río Cruces, thereby spawning aquatic flora that, with the surrounding evergreen forest, is now home to more than 80 species of birds, including black-neck swans, red-gartered coots, and buff-necked ibis. Boating here is an excellent attraction for kids.

  Embarcaciones Bahía (ⓒ **63/348727;** sergiosalgado60@yahoo.es) operates throughout the year with quick trips around Isla Teja (C$5,000 per person), and tours to Isla Mancera and Corral (see "Niebla, Corral & Isla Mancera," below) can be arranged during the off-season with a negotiated price or when there are enough passengers; children 9 and under ride free. Other trips to Isla Mancera and Corral are offered by **Orión III** (ⓒ/fax **63/247896;** hetours@telsur.cl), which also includes a stop at the Isla Huapi Natural Park (also a convention center; www.islahuapi.cl); the price is C$15,000 for adults, C$12,000 for children ages 3 to 12. Prices include the trip, lunch on Isla Huapi, and afternoon tea on board. By far the most luxurious is the

Catamarán Marqués de Mancera (© **63/249191**; www.marquesdemancera.cl), which offers Isla Mancera and Corral tours with lunch and snacks included, and evening dinner cruises (only specially organized for large groups); both cost from C$17,000 per person.

OTHER ATTRACTIONS

The bustling **Mercado Fluvial ★★**, at Muelle Schuster (Av. Prat at Maipú), is the principal attraction in Valdivia and is worth a visit for the dozens of fishermen who hawk fresh conger eel, hake, and spindly king crabs in front of colorful fruit and vegetable stands during the morning hours. Take a peek behind the fish stands to view the lanky pelicans and enormous sea lions barking for handouts. Across the street, the **Mercado Municipal** holds few attractions apart from a couple of souvenir shops and decent, inexpensive restaurants. Hours for the various shops here are erratic, but they are generally open Monday through Sunday from 9am to 7:30pm, closing at 9pm in summer, with some restaurants open later.

A block up from the waterfront, turn right on Yungay and head south until the street changes into **General Lagos** at San Carlos. A pleasant stroll for several blocks along General Lagos offers picturesque evidence of German immigration to the area through the stately, historic homes that dot the street. The houses, built between 1840 and 1930, belonged to affluent families, and many have been restored and maintained, despite the various earthquakes and other natural disasters that have beset them since construction.

Take a step back in time at the **Centro Cultural El Austral ★★**, Yungay 733 (© **63/213658**), commonly known as the Casa Hoffman for the Thater-Hoffman family, who occupied the home from 1870 until 1980. It's open Tuesday through Sunday from 10am to 1pm and 4 to 6pm; admission is free. The first floor of this handsome building has been furnished to re-create the interior as it would have looked during the 19th century, complete with period antiques, paintings, and a few very garish chandeliers. Upstairs, the center holds temporary art exhibitions and painting, literature, and history classes. At the junction of General Lagos and Yerbas Buenas is the **Torreón de Los Canelos,** a 1781 defensive tower built to protect the southern end of the city—but if you're strapped for time, forget it.

ISLA TEJA

Isla Teja is a tranquil residential area across the bridge from downtown that is also home to the Universidad Austral de Chile and a splendid history museum, the **Museo Histórico y Antropológico,** Maurice van de Maele **★★** (© **63/212872**; www.museosaustral.cl). It's open December 15 to March 15 Monday through Sunday from 10am to 8pm, and the rest of the year Tuesday through Sunday from 10am to 1pm and 2 to 6pm; admission is C$1,500 adults, C$400 children 12 and under. To get there, cross the Pedro de Valdivia Bridge, walk up a block, turn left, and continue for half a block. The museum is housed in the grand family home of Carl Anwandter, brewery owner and vociferous supporter and leader of German immigrants. Outside, two 19th-century carriages flank the entrance. Inside is a varied collection of antiques culled from local well-to-do families and notable figures such as Lord Cochrane (the noted admiral who helped secure independence for Chile, Peru, and Bolivia), including furniture (even a double piano), photos, letters, medals, and everyday objects. There are also a few conquest-era artifacts, such as a Spanish helmet, as well as an excellent display of Mapuche Indian silverwork, textiles, and tools. An interesting collection of sepia-toned photos depicts settlers' images of Mapuches.

The similarly themed **Museo Philippi** next door, inaugurated in January 2007 and housed in the transferred Schüler mansion, traces the history of German-born 19th-century explorer Rudolph Philippi and his descendents in unlocking Chile's natural secrets. You can view old watercolors, photographs, and letters, along with period furniture and scientific instruments; the museum is open during the same hours as the historical museum. Admission is C$1,500.

Also along the waterfront, and occupying the old Kunstmann brewery across the street that was nearly demolished after the 1960 earthquake, is one of Chile's best art museums, the **Museo de Arte Contemporaneo ★** (© 63/221968; www.macvaldivia.uach.cl), with excellent rotating displays of work by Chilean artists. It's open Tuesday to Sunday from 10am to 1pm and 3 to 6pm; admission is C$1,000.

Leaving the museum, turn right and continue north on Los Laureles until you reach the **Universidad Austral de Chile.** Once inside the campus, the road veers right; follow it and the signs to the **Jardín Botánico ★★**, a lovely botanical garden created in 1957 that features a labeled collection of native trees and vegetation from every region in Chile and around the world. It's open from October 15 to March 15 daily from 9am to 7:30pm, from March 16 to October 14 daily from 9am to 5pm. Cut west through the campus to Calle Los Lingues and turn right until you reach the gated entrance to **Parque Saval ★**, a sizable park with rodeo stands, a children's playground, a picnic area, and a small lagoon. Admission is C$400 for adults, C$200 for children, and it's open daily. From October to March, expositions, an arts-and-crafts fair, and agricultural demonstrations take place here.

NIEBLA, CORRAL & ISLA MANCERA

These three villages at the mouth of the bay were largely destroyed after the 1960 earthquake (on record as the strongest earthquake ever recorded). There's little left from that era, but what did survive were the relics of the 17th-century forts that once protected Valdivia from intruders, and a visit to these ancient relics, and the coastal views, makes for a very pleasant half-day trip—especially on a sunny day. If you are not planning to visit the coast near Santiago, do so here; there's enough to do and see to keep you occupied for at least a half-day, and Chile's only microbrewery is on the way back to town. Niebla lies 18km (11 miles) from Valdivia and is home to the **Castillo de la Pura y Limpia Concepción de Monfort de Lemus** (© 63/282084), a defensive fort founded in 1671 and renovated in 1767. It's open November through March daily from 10am to 7pm, and April through October from 10am to 5:30pm; it's closed Monday. Admission is C$600 for adults and C$200 for kids and seniors. The fort is carved partially out of rock and features details such as cannons and a powder room, as well as a small museum. The town itself is mostly a hodge-podge of seafood restaurants and tiny houses with the most privileged views anywhere in Chile. There's one great boutique hotel set right inside the curve in the center of town, **El Castillo** (© 63/282061; www.hotelycabanaselcastillo.com), with views of the water. Doubles run $76, including continental breakfast. To get there, take a private taxi for about C$5,000, or grab a *colectivo* taxi (or *micro* bus) for C$600 at the waterfront. In the summer, it is possible to take a tour boat to Niebla; in the off-season, you'll need to take the road. The trip takes about 15 minutes.

Across the bay sits **Corral** and the area's first and most powerful fort, the **Castillo San Sebastián de la Cruz** (© 63/471828), built in 1645 and reinforced in 1764. It's open from November through March daily 9am to 6pm and April through October from Tuesday to Sunday 10am to 5:30pm; admission is C$800. The city itself is a picturesque jumble of brightly painted wooden homes and fishing boats, an old German colony that never really recovered from the tidal wave that wiped out most of the town. To get to Corral, take a tour boat from Valdivia during high season, or take a ferry from the fishing dock just before entering Niebla (let your bus or taxi driver know you're getting off there). The mock battle that once was the highlight of this attraction has been put on hold due to overenthusiastic actors mishandling gunpowder and shooting themselves in the foot; it remains to be seen if the ritual will continue anytime soon.

Either on the way to Corral or on the way back, ask to be dropped off at idyllic **Isla Mancera** (and ask to be picked up again!) for an easy stroll and a visit to the fort **Castillo de San Pedro de Alcántara** (✆ 63/212872). Admission is C$600, and it's open from November 15 to March 15 daily from 10am to 6pm, and Tuesday through Sunday from 10am to 5pm the rest of the year. It was built in 1645 and restored in 1680 and again in 1762 to house the Military Government of Valdivia. Inside the grounds are the crumbling ruins of the San Francisco Convent and an underground supply room. It is possible to walk the circumference of the island in 20 to 30 minutes, and there is a site for picnics with great views.

Where to Stay

EXPENSIVE

Hotel Diego de Almagro   Opened in mid 2008 by a Chilean chain of the same name, the Diego de Almagro is in an attractive setting right where the river bends, giving ample water views from most rooms. Lost is the classic German feel, though this is the most modern of Valdivia's hotels by a mile and caters mostly to visiting execs. All rooms are spacious—about 30 square meters (322 sq. ft.)—and feature 25-inch LCD TVs that offset a rather run-of-the-mill contemporary decor.

Prat 433, Valdivia. ✆ **63/224744.** Fax 63/267000. www.dahoteles.com. 105 units. $148 double; includes breakfast buffet. AE, DC, MC, V. **Amenities:** Restaurant; bar; exercise room; pool; room service; sauna. *In room:* TV, minifridge, free Wi-Fi.

Hotel Naguilán ★★ 🔟   Although it sits about a 20-minute walk from the edge of downtown, the Hotel Naguilán boasts a pretty riverfront location and solid, attractive accommodations. The hotel is housed in an interesting structure (ca. 1890) that once held a shipbuilding business. All rooms face the Río Valdivia and the evening sunset; from here it's possible to watch waterfowl and colorful tugs and fishing skiffs motor by. Newer "Terrace" units sit directly on the riverbank and feature contemporary floral design in rich colors, classic furniture, ample bathrooms, and a terrace patio. The older wing is more economical and features a few dated items, such as 1960s lime-green carpeting, but the entire hotel is impeccably clean.

The staff offers professional and attentive service, and the hotel has a private dock from which guests board excursion boats. The Naguilán's restaurant, serving international cuisine, is one of the most attractive features of the property, with the river passing just outside the window.

General Lagos 1927, Valdivia. ✆ **63/212851.** Fax 63/219130. www.hotelnaguilan.com. 32 units. $105 standard double; $126 superior double. AE, DC, MC, V. **Amenities:** Restaurant; bar; concierge; pool; room service. *In room:* TV, minibar.

MODERATE

Dreams Hotel & Casino   This massive glass high-rise hotel and casino, which looks like something out of Dubai, opened downtown in early 2010 and has completely altered the Valdivia skyline. It's not that the rooms or the amenities are bad—they are actually quite nice—it's just it doesn't seem to fit in with the rest of town and several strip clubs have even sprung up around it. Unless you're a gambler or there is no other room in town, there are much better options in town with more character.

Carampangue 190, Valdivia. © **63/267-000.** www.mundodreams.com. 104 units. $95 double. AE, MC, V. **Amenities:** 2 restaurants; bar; casino; room service; spa. *In room:* TV, minibar, free Wi-Fi.

INEXPENSIVE

Hostal Rio de Luna ★ Amid several newer upscale hotels on the river and within walking distance from the bus station is this well-run inn that has been around for a few decades, but kept spotlessly clean and freshly painted. Rooms are utilitarian and lack polish, but are well put together with bluish-gray floors, sky-blue walls, and blue bedspreads. Room 11 on the top floor has the best views. While you eat your ham, cheese, toast and jam, and piece of pie for breakfast, you can watch the occasional row team advance by; it's a great way to start your day.

Prat 695, Valdivia. © **63/253333.** www.hostalriodeluna.cl. 11 units. $80 double. Rates include breakfast. AE, DC, MC, V. **Amenities:** Restaurant; bar; free Wi-Fi. *In room:* Fan, TV, CD player.

Where to Dine

For an inexpensive meal, try the **Municipal Market** near the waterfront at Yungay and Libertad, where you'll find several basic restaurants with fresh seafood and Chilean specialties. Microbreweries have sprung up on the fringe of town to refresh the German brewing tradition; among them are **Calle-Calle**, on Llanquihue s/n, 3km (2 miles) on the route to Osorno (© **63/226925**) and **Del Duende**, 8km (5 miles) on the route to Niebla (© **63/282780**). The most famous is Kunstmann (see review later).

EXPENSIVE

Agridulce ★ INTERNATIONAL This big restaurant boasts farmhouse-like details like horseshoes as decor and walls that can be opened up to catch the river breeze when the weather is nice. Agridulce won't wow you, it's just a great all around restaurant with a focus on protein: venison, beef, and salmon. There are also sandwiches and pastas, as well as a better than average wine selection, at least for Valdivia.

Pratt 327. © **63/433435.** Main courses C$4,000-C$11,500. AE, DC, MC, V. Mon-Sat noon-3pm and 8pm-midnight.

Café las Gringas ★ CAFE Just two doors down from Café Haussmann, this small corner cafe is best visited for its extensive microbrew list, which focuses on breweries in the region, many of them small and not found anywhere else. The cafe fare that accompanies the brew is light and fresh, such as sandwiches, crudos, tablas, steaks, salads, and *küchen*.

Pratt 327. © **63/433435.** Main courses C$4,000-C$11,500. AE, DC, MC, V. Mon-Sat noon-3pm and 8pm-midnight.

MODERATE

Camino de Luna SEAFOOD The Camino de Luna serves excellent seafood and other dishes aboard a floating restaurant moored at the waterfront. The menu includes delicious fare such as seafood crepes, abalone stew, and *congrio* steamed in wine, bacon, asparagus, and herbs, as well as Greek and chef salads and a long list of terrific appetizers. Inside, the well-appointed, candlelit tables are much nicer than the pea-green facade and red Coca-Cola neon outside would indicate. The restaurant does sway when vessels speed by, but not much.

Costanera at Arturo Prat. ℂ **63/213788.** Main courses C$4,000–C$8,500. AE, MC, V. Daily 12:30–11pm.

Entre Lagos ★ 🍴 CAFE   Entre Lagos is one of the best-known shops in the region for its mouthwatering chocolates and colorful marzipan, and its neighboring cafe is equally good. Nothing on the menu is short of delicious, from the juicy sandwiches and french fries down to the heavenly cakes and frothy cappuccinos. The restaurant serves a dozen varieties of crepes, such as ham and cheese, and abalone and shrimp in a creamy crab sauce. Entre Lagos is a great spot for lunch or to relax for an afternoon *once* or coffee. It also offers a set menu for C$2,850 that includes a main dish, dessert, and coffee.

Pérez Rosales 640. ℂ **63/212039.** www.entrelagos.cl. Main courses C$4,000–C$10,500. AE, DC, MC, V. Mon–Sat 9am–10pm; Sun 10am–10pm.

Kunstmann Cervecería ★★ GERMAN/PUB FARE   This is a nice place to stop on the way back from Niebla (see "Niebla, Corral & Isla Mancera," earlier); it's a 10-minute drive from town. The popular Kunstmann brewery serves four varieties of beer on tap (they'll let you sample before ordering) in a newer, microbrew-styled restaurant with wooden tables and soft, yellow light. The hearty fare includes appetizer platters of grilled meats and sausages, German-influenced dishes such as smoked pork loin with cabbage, and sandwiches, salads, and spaetzle. Kunstmann also has a small on-site brewery museum.

950 Rte. T-350. ℂ/fax **63/292969.** www.lacerveceria.cl. Main courses C$4,000–C$9,500. MC, V. Daily noon–midnight.

Santo Pecado ★★ 🍴 INTERNATIONAL   This hipster-heavy lounge and restaurant, with colorful walls adorned with pop art, is my favorite restaurant in Valdivia for its eclectic menu. Standard bistro dishes, such as steak frites, are excellently prepared, and they don't shy away from more creative dishes such as a *tortilla Ibérica* (a Spanish style omelet), crepes, chicken curry, and a mousse of pisco sour. *Tablas,* plates for sharing, pair well with a bottle of wine from their lengthy list.

Yungay 745. ℂ **63/239122.** www.santopecado.cl. Reservations recommended for dinner. Main courses C$4,000–C$7,500. AE, DC, MC, V. Mon–Sat noon–4pm and 8pm–midnight.

INEXPENSIVE

Café Haussmann ★★ 📷 CAFE   The Haussmann is known for its *crudos* (steak tartare and raw onion spread on thin bread), which it has served since opening its doors in 1959. This tiny, old-fashioned cafe has just four booths and a counter, and is frequently packed with downtown workers. There are no frills, but there are good sandwiches, local color, and their own brand of beer, as well as Kunstmann, on tap. It's *the* place for getting a feel for Valdivia's local flavor.

O'Higgins 394. ℂ **63/202219.** Sandwiches C$2,000–C$3,500. MC, V. Mon–Sat 8am–9pm (summer until midnight).

Ocio Restobar 🍴 FUSION   Plank wood floors and exposed pipes give an industrial feel to this stylish resto-bar and lounge, an "it" spot for the young, intellectual crowd for several years, that gets packed on weekend nights. The food is lighter than other restaurants in town and ranges from maki rolls to empanadas. Most of the menu items make for perfect snacking food to go with drinks. Video installations and a DJ spinning rock and house music will keep you entertained.

Arauco 102. © **63/239122.** Reservations recommended for dinner. Main courses C$4,000–C$6,500. AE, DC, MC, V. Tues–Thurs 7pm–midnight; Fri–Sat 8pm–2am.

PUYEHUE ★

Termas de Puyehue: 73km (45 miles) E of Osorno, 95km (59 miles) W of Antillanca, 93km (58 miles) W of the Argentine border

This region is home to the long-standing **Termas de Puyehue** spa, the **Antillanca** ski and summer resort at the base of the Casablanca Volcano, and one of Chile's underrated national parks, **Puyehue.** It is a remarkably beautiful area, with thick groves of junglelike forest, emerald lakes, picture-perfect volcano backdrops, waterfalls, and roads narrowed by overgrown, enormous ferns. You won't find a tourist-oriented town here, such as Pucón or Puerto Varas, but there are several good lodging options in the area. You'll also find a fair number of outdoor activities, scenic drives, and one of the best lookout points in Chile, which can be reached by car during the summer.

The Puyehue area is best suited as a diversion for travelers on their way to Argentina. I strongly recommend this journey; it is one of my favorite excursions in Chile, and visitors can even complete a "loop" through the lake districts of Argentina and Chile by booking a one-way ticket to Bariloche via the popular "lake crossing" (see "Parque Nacional Vicente Pérez Rosales & the Lake Crossing to Argentina," later in this chapter) and later returning to Chile via bus (or tour) to Puyehue, passing first through Villa la Angostura at the Argentina–Chile border and crossing at the international pass Cardenal Antonio Samoré, or vice versa. The scenery is breathtaking.

The road from Osorno to Puyehue is rather flat and banal, but the scenery viewed when crossing from Villa Angostura to Puyehue is stunning. Note that during the winter, chains might be required when crossing the border.

Getting There

BY PLANE LAN Airlines (© **600/526-2000;** www.lan.com) serves Osorno's **Aeródromo Cañal Bajo** (ZOS; © **64/247555**), with two daily flights from Santiago; one flight stops first in Temuco. Osorno is a 1-hour drive from Puyehue. LAN has more frequent flights from Santiago to Puerto Montt, a 2-hour drive from Puyehue.

BY BUS Bus service from Osorno is provided by **Buses Puyehue,** with almost hourly trips to and from Puyehue, departing from the Terminal de Buses Rurales at Errázuriz 1300 (© **64/201237**). From Bariloche, Argentina, **Andes Mar** and **Río de la Plata** buses head to Osorno and stop along the highway near Puyehue or directly at the Hotel Termas de Puyehue. If you're trying to get to Puyehue from Puerto Montt, you'll need to transfer at Osorno. From Santiago, the buses run by **Tas Choapa** (to Bariloche) depart Monday, Wednesday, and Friday, heading for Bariloche; they'll drop you off in Puyehue. From Puerto Varas, an excellent bilingual service, the Cruce TransAndino, offered by **LS Travel,** San José 130 (© **65/232424;** www.lstravel.cl), takes visitors to Bariloche, leaving at 9:30am, stopping for a swim at the Termas Puyehue, passing through Villa la Angostura and on to Bariloche. The tour agency has an office in Bariloche at Mitre 83 (© **02944/434111**). The cost is

PASSING THROUGH Osorno

Often missed by international tourists except as a transportation hub, Osorno, sometimes called the gateway to the lakes region, can be a useful stop for a day or two on your travels to Parque Nacional Puyehue or places further south. The city was founded in 1558, but was burned down after a Mapuche uprising in 1599 and wasn't reestablished until the Law of Selective Immigration in 1845 brought thousands of German settlers to Chile and pushed the Mapuche further into the mountains. Pioneer houses and buildings with distinct German architecture dominate parts of the city, like Calle Mackenna to the east of the plaza. Citizens are quite proud of their German heritage, much like in Frutillar and Puerto Octay, and several breweries and German restaurants can attest to this. If you want to stay overnight, try either the 106-room **Sonesta Hotel Osorno** (Ejercito 395; © **64/555-000;** www.sonesta.com; doubles $135), the city's newest property overlooking the Rahue river; or the more classic German guesthouse, **Hotel Villa Eduviges** (© **064/235-023;** Eduviges 856, www.hoteleduviges.cl; doubles $58). Visit Osorno's municipal website (www.osornochile.cl) for more information.

C$65,000 per person, with a minimum two guests (cheaper prices can be had for groups), and includes entrance fees and lunch.

BY CAR Termas de Puyehue is about 75km (47 miles) east from Osorno via Rte. 215. The border with Argentina, Control Fronterizo Cardenal Antonio Samoré, is open daily November through March from 8am to 9pm, and April through October from 8am to 7pm. The road is a bit curvy, and there are some potholes on the Chilean side, so drive slowly.

Exploring Parque Nacional Puyehue

Parque Nacional Puyehue (www.parquepuyehue.cl) is one of Chile's best-organized national parks, offering a variety of trails to suit all levels, well-placed park information centers, lodging, camping, restaurants, and hot springs. The 107,000-hectare (264,290-acre) park sits between the Caulle mountain range and the Puyehue Volcano, and is divided into three sectors: **Anticura, Aguas Calientes,** and **Antillanca.** Visitors head east toward Argentina to access Anticura, where they'll encounter a park ranger information station just before the border, as well as trail heads for day hikes and the 16km (10-mile) backpacker's trail up and around the Puyehue Volcano. There's also a self-guided, short hike to the Salto del Indio waterfall, where you'll see 800-year-old evergreen beech trees, known locally as *coigüe.*

To get to Antillanca, visitors pass first through the Aguas Calientes sector, where there are hot springs, 28 rustic cabins (five beds in each; all with kitchenettes) a restaurant, campgrounds, and a park information center (© **64/331710** or 64/331711). The most popular excursion in this region is the ascent to a spectacular lookout point atop the Raihuén crater, reached by foot or vehicle about 4km (2½ miles) past the Antillanca hotel and ski resort. This *mirador* can be reached only during temperate months (or during ski season via the center's ski lift) and is not worthwhile on a heavily overcast day. The view stretches into Argentina. The park ranger information stations are open daily from 9am to 1pm and 2 to 6pm, or you can contact CONAF for info (© **64/197-4573**). They sell an information packet about the region's flora and fauna, and issue fishing licenses. For information about day visits to the hot springs at Termas de Puyehue or Aguas Calientes, see "Where to Stay & Dine," later. To get here, you need to catch a bus in Osorno or book a tour with an operator out of Temuco, Puerto Montt, or Puerto Varas.

OTHER ATTRACTIONS

Along the road to Puyehue, at about Km 25 on Rte. 215, just before the ramshackle town of Entre Lagos, is Chile's first car museum, the well-designed **Auto Museum Moncopulli** (© **64/210744**; www.moncopulli.cl). Admission is C$2,000 adults, C$1,000 students, and C$500 kids; it's open from December through March 10am to 8pm, April through November 10am to 6pm. Owner Bernardo Eggers has assembled a collection of 42 Studebakers from the years 1928 to 1964, plus other vehicles, such as a 1928 Model A fire engine.

Where to Stay & Dine

Aguas Calientes Turismo y Cabañas   These A-frame cabins are a cheaper alternative to Termas de Puyehue and are owned by the same company. There's a hot spring/spa facility here, included in the price of the *cabañas,* and it can be used for the day for a fee. The *cabañas* sleep four to eight guests and are simple affairs with fully stocked, plain but decent kitchenettes (and *parrillas* for barbecues on the balcony). The drawback here is that the beds are really crammed into small spaces. Ask for a cabin with two floors; those come with separate living/eating areas. All cabins come with decks and a barbecue. There are also two nicely developed campgrounds here called Chanleufú and Los Derrumbes, with barbecue pits, free firewood, and a thermal spa. Prices for both are $32 for four campers, $6.30 each per extra camper.

The hot springs facility features indoor and outdoor pools (the outdoor pool is far nicer); there is also a picnic area. Day-use fees are C$20,000 for adults and C$15,000 for kids for the outdoor pool; for the indoor and outdoor pools, the cost is C$22,500 for adults, C$15,000 for kids. A private herbal bath costs C$32,000. Massages are C$75,000 an hour.

Camino a Antillanca, Km 4. ©/fax **64/236988** or 64/331700. www.termasaguascalientes.cl. 26 *cabañas.* $196 cabin for 4; $232 cabin for 4 superior. AE, DC, MC, V. **Amenities:** Jacuzzi; large outdoor pool and indoor pool; massage area. *In room:* TV, kitchen.

Antillanca Hotel and Tourism Center ★   Rooms at the Antillanca Hotel are nothing to write home about, but the lovely surroundings at the resort make this one of Chile's gems—if you can hit it on a good weather day. The hotel could really stand to renovate its rooms, especially considering the price. Couples would do well to view the options, as the only room that comes with a double bed also comes with two twins and is considered a quadruple. The rooms are fairly spacious, but many are nothing more than dormitory style, with four bunks to a room and early 1980s furniture. If you're looking for something cheaper, you might consider the *refugio,* the slightly shabby, older wing of the hotel, popular with students and young adults for its rooms costing about a third less. The split-level lobby/restaurant/bar/lounge area is a delight, however—it's cozy, with character derived from pillars made of tree trunks that still have branches, and a giant fireplace. There's also a deck for sunbathing and complimentary use of mountain bikes for registered guests.

Ski Resort: Lift tickets cost C$19,500 adults (C$16,500 half-day), C$16,500 students. Ski and snowboard equipment rental is available for C$29,000 for snowboards and boots or C$33,000 for skis and boots. If you're not skiing but want to ride a chairlift to the top, the cost is C$3,500.

Road to Antillanca, at about 12km (7½ miles) past Ñilque, or (in Osorno) O'Higgins 1073. ℰ/fax **64/ 235114.** www.skiantillanca.com. 73 units. $101 double *refugio*; $221 double hotel. AE, DC, MC, V. **Amenities:** Restaurant; bar; lounge; room service; sauna.

Termas Puyehue Wellness & Spa Resort ★ ☺✋

This large property features a view of Lake Puyehue and two attractively designed, enormous thermal pools, as well as massage rooms, mud baths, herbal baths, saunas, game rooms, and more. Though it was built between 1939 and 1942, the hotel has undergone substantial renovations and the addition of 55 roomy suites. Standard double rooms are disappointing, which is surprising for a hotel that esteems itself so highly. Perhaps the best lodging unit is their converted home on the shore of the lake.

This resort is a good option for skiers at Antillanca, or as a stop on the way to Argentina for a soak and lunch, because a night here as a "destination" is an overrated experience. The staff has no concept of customer service, and problems with plumbing have annoyed guests. But the activities and excursions offered, including horseback riding, trekking, mountain biking, windsurfing, fishing, tennis, and farm tours through organic gardens (all for an extra cost) might make a stay worthwhile. The spa facilities (which you can use even if you don't stay here) are more upscale than those at Aguas Calientes.

The cost charged to day visitors are C$30,000 adults and C$25,000 kids for the indoor pool, C$22,000 adults and C$15,000 kids for the outdoor pool. The indoor pool is open daily 8am to 9pm in summer, 8am to 8pm during the rest of the year; the spa is open 9am to 8pm year-round. Herbal, mud, sulfur, and marine salt baths cost C$8,000 to C$24,000; reflexology and herbal therapy cost C$8,000 to C$24,000.

Rte. 215, Km 76. ℰ **2/293-6000.** Fax 2/283-1010 or 64/23281 in Osorno. www.puyehue.cl. 137 units. $337 double with view of the forest; $364 double with view of the volcano. Rates are per person and all-inclusive. AE, DC, MC, V. **Amenities:** 3 restaurants; bar; lounge; bikes; exercise room; Jacuzzi; large outdoor pool and large indoor pool; room service; sauna; spa; tennis courts; limited watersports equipment rental; free Internet access. *In room:* TV, minibar.

AROUND LAGO LLANQUIHUE

Lago Llanquihue is the second-largest lake in Chile, a body of clear, shimmering water whose beauty is surpassed only by the 2,652m (8,699-ft.), perfectly conical, snowcapped **Volcán Osorno** (Osorno Volcano) that rises from its shore. The peaks of Calbuco, Tronador, and Puntiagudo add rugged beauty to the panorama, as do the rolling, lush hills that peek out from forested thickets along the perimeter of the lake. The jewel of this area is without a doubt the 231,000-hectare (570,570-acre) Parque Nacional Vicente Pérez Rosales, the oldest park in Chile and home to Volcán Osorno and the strangely hued emerald waters of Lago Todos los Santos.

This splendid countryside and the picturesque, German-influenced architecture of the homes and villages that ring Lago Llanquihue draw thousands of foreign visitors each year. Many adventure-seekers come to take part in the vast array of outdoor

A Health Warning

Every January, this region is beset by horrid biting flies called *tábanos*. Avoid wearing dark clothing and any shiny object, which seem to attract them; they are also more prevalent on sunny days.

sports and excursions to be had here, including fly-fishing, rafting, volcano ascents, trekking, and just sightseeing. Puerto Varas is similar to Pucón, in that it offers a solid tourism infrastructure, with quality lodging and restaurants, nightlife, and several reliable outfitters and tour operators. I urge visitors to lodge in Puerto Varas, Frutillar, or Ensenada instead of Puerto Montt, as these three towns are far more attractive and closer to natural attractions than Puerto Montt. Puerto Octay, about 46km (29 miles) from Puerto Montt, is the most remote lodging option, a sublime little village with one lovely lodge on the shore of the lake.

Frutillar & Puerto Octay ★

58km (36 miles) S of Osorno; 46km (29 miles) N of Puerto Montt

Frutillar and Puerto Octay offer a rich example of the lovely architecture popular with German immigrants to the Lago Llanquihue area, and both boast dynamite views of the Osorno and Calbuco volcanoes. The towns are smaller than Puerto Varas and less touristy. For a soft adventure, the towns make an excellent day trip, and the coastal dirt road that connects the two is especially beautiful, with clapboard homes dotting the green countryside—bring your camera. Apart from all this scenic beauty, there are a few museums documenting German immigration in the area. A helpful website on the area is **www.frutillar.com**.

Frutillar was founded in 1856 as an embarkation point with four piers. Later, the introduction of the railway created a spin-off town that sits high and back from the coast, effectively splitting the town in two: Frutillar Alto and Bajo, meaning "high" and "low," respectively. You'll drive straight through the ugly Alto section, a ratty collection of wooden homes and shops.

Puerto Octay was founded in the second half of the 19th century by German immigrants; folks in the region know it for its well-stocked general goods store—the only one in the region—run by Cristino Ochs. In fact, the name *Octay* comes from "donde Ochs hay," roughly translated as "you'll find it where Ochs is." Today there are only about 3,000 residents in this quaint little village, which can be reached by renting a car or with a tour (or bus if staying here).

ESSENTIALS

GETTING THERE   See the information under the "Puerto Varas" section, later.

VISITOR INFORMATION   The **Oficina de Información Turística** is along the coast at Costanera Philippi (✆ **65/421080**); it's open January through March daily from 8:30am to 1pm and 2 to 9pm. The **Oficina de Turismo Municipal** is open year-round and can be found at Av. Bernardo Philippi 753 (daily 8am–1pm and 2–5:30pm; ✆ **65/421685**).

WHAT TO SEE & DO

Excursions to **Parque Nacional Vicente Pérez Rosales** from Frutillar can be arranged by your hotel with a company such as **Alsur Expediciones** or **Aquamotion** out of Puerto Varas (see "Outdoor Activities" under "Puerto Varas," later). In

Frutillar, spend an afternoon strolling the streets and enjoying the town's striking architecture. The town really gets hopping during the last week of January and first of February when it hosts, for 10 days, the **Semanas Musicales,** when hundreds of Chilean and foreign musicians come to participate in various classical music concerts. Call the administration in Osorno (© **65/421290**); tickets are never hard to come by. The hulking building that juts out on a pier onto the lake in Frutillar southeast of the center, the **Teatro del Lago** (© **65/339-2293**), was finished in 2010 and is already one of Chile's premier classical-music venues. Performances are held throughout the year. Check the website www.teatrodellago.cl for listings.

The two most-visited attractions in town are the **Museo de la Colonización Alemana de Frutillar** and the **Reserva Forestal Edmundo Winkler.** The museum (© **65/421142**) is located where Arturo Prat dead-ends at Avenida Vicente Pérez Rosales. Admission is C$1,500 adults, C$1000 for kids 12 and under; it's open from April to November daily from 10am to 1pm and 2 to 6pm, and from December to March daily from 10am to 1pm and 2 to 8pm. It features a collection of 19th-century antiques, clothing, and artifacts gathered from various immigrant German families around the area.

The *reserva* (© **65/421291**) is run by the University of Chile and features a trail winding through native forest, giving visitors an idea of what the region looked like before immigrants went timber crazy and started chopping down trees. It's open year-round from 10am to 7pm; admission costs C$1,000 for adults and C$500 for kids. To get there, you'll have to walk a kilometer (a half-mile) up to the park from the entrance at Calle Caupolicán at the northern end of Avenida Philippi. You might also consider paying a visit to the town **cemetery,** which affords a panoramic view of the lake. To get there, continue farther north up Avenida Phillipi.

WHERE TO STAY

Hotel Ayacara ★★ 👔 The Ayacara is a top choice in Frutillar, housed in a superbly renovated 1910 antique home on the coast of Lago Llanquihue. The interior of the hotel is made of light wood, and this, coupled with large, plentiful windows, translates into bright accommodations. The rooms come with comfy beds, crisp linens, wood headboards, country furnishings, and antiques brought from Santiago and Chiloé. The Capitán room is the largest and has the best view. An attractive dining area serves dinner during the summer, and there's a small, ground-level outdoor deck and a TV/video lounge. The staff can arrange excursions around the area; fly-fishing excursions are their specialty.

Av. Philippi 1215, Frutillar. ©/fax **65/421550.** www.hotelayacara.cl. 8 units. $115 double; $147 Capitán double. Rates include breakfast. AE, DC, MC, V. **Amenities:** Restaurant; bar. *In room:* TV, free Wi-Fi.

Hotel & Cabañas Centinela ★★ 📷 At the tip of a peninsula, at the end of a lush tree-lined dirt road, 10 minutes from town and right on the lake, you'll find this hidden gem with its own private beach. Originally built in 1914 as a bordello, it has long since been turned into a homey lodge with 12 rooms and 18 *cabañas.* Rooms in the main building are quaint, with thick beige berber carpets, down comforters, and antique furnishings. The restaurant serves excellent Chilean cuisine cooked by a well-known chef, Juan Pablo Moscoso; there's a daily fixed-price three-course meal for C$8,000 for lunch and dinner. This place exudes charm, not luxury; there's no spa, but there's a rustic wood-fired hot tub. Six of the *cabañas* sit right on the water's edge; request nos. 21 to 26 when making your reservations, and you'll have the best views. The 12 A-frame *cabañas* that sit back from the water are pleasant for families and come with kitchenettes; all the *cabañas* have rather small bathrooms. The hotel's friendly staff can arrange for fishing trips, including fly-fishing expeditions.

Península de Centinela, Km 5, Puerto Octay. ℂ/fax **64/391326.** www.hotelcentinela.cl. 30 units. $178 double; from $181 *cabaña* for 4 people; $206 *cabaña* for 6 people. Rates include full breakfast. AE, DC, MC, V. **Amenities:** Restaurant; lounge; free airport transfers; Jacuzzi; limited watersports equipment rental. *In room:* Fridge (in *cabañas* only).

Hotel Elun ★★　This azure-colored hotel is a good bet for anyone seeking modern accommodations, a room with a view, and a quiet, forested location. The hotel, opened in 1999, is made almost entirely of light, polished wood and was designed to take full advantage of the views. The lounge, bar, and lobby sit under a slanted roof that ends with picture windows; there's also a deck, should you decide to lounge outside. Double standard rooms are decently sized and feature berber carpets and spick-and-span white bathrooms. The superiors are very large and come with a comfy easy chair and a table and chairs. Room no. 24 looks out over Frutillar. The hotel is attended by its owners, who will arrange excursions. A restaurant serves dinner during the summer, and breakfast can be ordered in your room.

200m (656 ft.) from start of Camino Punta Larga, at the southern end of Costanera Phillipi, Frutillar. ℂ/fax **65/420055.** www.hotelelun.cl. 14 units. $141 double. Rates include breakfast. DC, MC, V. **Amenities:** Restaurant (summer only); lounge; bikes; room service. *In room:* TV, free Wi-Fi.

Hotel Residenz am See ✦　This pleasant wooden hotel is a steal in the low season when you factor in the lakefront view and its clean, comfortable accommodations. Run by an elderly German couple, the Residenz has rooms that range in size, and a few of the doubles are large enough to fit an extra twin bed. The rooms that look out onto the lake are slightly more expensive than those facing the back, but the rooms in the back receive glorious afternoon sun. The owners have a shop selling arts and crafts, and have decorated the place with woven wall hangings that are for sale. Downstairs there's a tea salon where guests are served German breakfast; in the afternoon, folks drop by for tea and homemade *küchen*, bread, pâté, and marmalade. They also arrange excursions.

Av. Philippi 539, Frutillar. ℂ **65/421539.** Fax 65/421858. www.hotelamsee.cl. 6 units. $84 double; $126 suite. Rates include German breakfast. AE, DC, MC, V. **Amenities:** Restaurant. *In room:* TV.

Hotel Villa San Francisco ★　The Villa San Francisco sits high on a cliff and features a layout similar to the Hotel Elun (see earlier), with rooms that all face the lake, some with a view of the volcano. All of the rooms are identical, decorated with simple but attractive furnishings that include comfortable beds and wicker headboards. Some guests might find the rooms a little on the small side, but most come with a terrace and four have corner windows. The owners of this hotel have invested a great deal in gardens that surround the property. There's also a great barbecue area that sits on a grassy perch looking straight out toward the volcano, as does a pleasant glass-enclosed dining area. The staff will arrange excursions around the area for guests.

Av. Philippi 1503, Frutillar. ℂ/fax **65/421531.** iberchile@telsur.cl. 15 units. $124 double. AE, MC, V. **Amenities:** Restaurant; bar. *In room:* TV.

Salzburg Hotel & Spa ★　This large hillside spread with sweeping views of Lago Llanquihue is one of the most tranquil places in an already tranquil town. Designed in a traditional black-forest architectural style, the bungalows each feature three rooms and can sleep up to eight people. Rooms in the main lodge are simple and classic, nothing flashy, but they're clean and comfortable. They have recently added a new full service spa and a pool that looks out onto the lake. They also make their own beer, which they serve at the bar. Rates include a German breakfast.

Camino Playa Maqui s/n, Frutillar. ℂ 65/421589. www.salzburg.cl. 31 units. $109 double; $301 bungalows. Rates include German breakfast. AE, DC, MC, V. **Amenities:** Restaurant; bar; pool; tennis courts. *In room:* TV.

WHERE TO DINE

Apart from the restaurants listed below, near the Teatro del Lago in Frutillar Bajo there are a cluster of new modern cafes, bars, and restaurants, including a decent steakhouse, **Tierra del Fuego,** Phillipi 1065 (ℂ **65/421155**).

Club Alemán GERMAN/CHILEAN   Nearly every city in the Lake District has a Club Alemán, and Frutillar is no exception. You'll find a few German dishes here, such as pork chops with sauerkraut, but the menu leans heavily toward traditional Chilean fare. Periodically, game specials such as duck and goose are on the menu, and there are set lunch menus for C$4,000 on weekdays and C$8,000 on Sunday that include a choice of fish or meat. The atmosphere here is congenial, and the service is very good.

Philippi 47. ℂ **65/421249.** Main courses C$3,500–C$7,000. AE, DC, MC, V. Daily noon–4pm and 8pm–midnight.

Guten Appetit GERMAN   Beside the church, this rustic and popular eatery on the lakefront is not as touristy as some of the others nearby with similar menus. It's a good choice for reliable *onces* with *küchen* or strudel, as well as grilled trout and simple lunch plates. This restaurant also serves up a few German dishes and on some weekend nights hosts live music.

Balmaceda 98. ℂ **65/421145.** Main courses C$2,500–C$5,000. AE, MC, V. Daily noon–4pm and 8pm–midnight.

Puerto Varas ★★

20km (12 miles) N of Puerto Montt; 996km (618 miles) S of Santiago

Puerto Varas is one of Chile's most charming villages, located on the shore of Lago Llanquihue. Like Pucón, it is an adventure travel hub, and it is also the gateway to the **Parque Nacional Vicente Pérez Rosales** (see "Parque Nacional Vicente Pérez Rosales & the Lake Crossing to Argentina," later in this section). Unlike its neighbor Puerto Montt, 20 minutes away, it is a spruce little town, with wood-shingled homes, a rose-encircled plaza, a handsomely designed casino, and an excellent tourism infrastructure that provides all the necessary services for visitors without seeming touristy. It can get crowded during the summer months, but not as busy as Pucón, seemingly because of its distance from Santiago. The city was built by the sweat and tenacity of German immigrants, and later it became a port for goods being shipped from the Lago Llanquihue area to Puerto Montt (mostly timber). Today most of the area's middle- and upper-middle-class residents call Puerto Varas home and commute to Puerto Montt and other surrounding places for work.

ESSENTIALS
Getting There
BY PLANE El Tepual airport (PMC; ℂ **65/294161**) is almost equidistant from Puerto Montt and Puerto Varas; it's about 25km (16 miles) from the airport to Puerto Varas. A taxi from the airport costs between C$20,000 and C$26,000, or you can

arrange a transfer with **ETM,** by either calling ahead or approaching their booth at the airport (☏ 32/294294; www.busesetm.cl). They charge C$5,000 per person. Because there are fewer flights here, there normally are a few people waiting for a transfer, so the price can drop if there are others. **LANExpress** serves the El Tepual airport with nine daily flights from Santiago. **Sky Airline** (☏ 600/600-2828; www.skyairline.cl) also has three daily flights to El Tepual airport. Ask your hotel about a transfer shuttle, as many include one in their price.

BY BUS   The following buses offer service to and from major cities in southern Chile, including Santiago: **Buses Cruz del Sur,** San Francisco 1317 and Walker Martínez 239 (☏ 65/236969 or 65/231925; www.cruzdelsur.com.pe); and **Buses Tas Choapa,** Walker Martínez 320 (☏ 65/233831). Buses **Tas Choapa** and the Argentine company **Andesmar,** Walker Martinez 320 (☏ 65/233831; www.andesmar.com.ar), have service to Bariloche, Argentina (Tas Choapa Thurs–Sun; Andesmar on Mon, Wed, and Fri). **Bus Norte,** Walker Martínez 239, has daily service to Bariloche (☏ 65/236969).

BY CAR   Puerto Varas is just 20km (12 miles) north of Puerto Montt and 88km (55 miles) south of Osorno via the Panamericana. There are two exits leading to Puerto Varas, and both deposit you downtown. To get to Frutillar, you need to get back on the Panamericana, go north, and take the exit for that town. There is a C$500 toll to enter the off-ramp, and another C$1,000 toll to enter Puerto Montt.

Getting Around

BY BUS   **Buses Cruz del Sur** offers transportation to Chiloé and nearly 20 daily trips to Puerto Montt, leaving from an office in Puerto Varas, at Walker Martínez 239 (☏ 65/236969 or 65/231925; www.cruzdelsur.com.pe). There are also cheap minibuses that leave frequently from the corner of Del Salvador and San Pedro across from the pet shop, leaving you at the bus terminal in Puerto Montt. You'll find minibuses at San Bernardo and Walker Martínez that go to Ensenada, Petrohué, and Lago Todos los Santos every day at 9:15, 11am, 2, and 4pm. **Andina del Sud,** Del Salvador 72 (☏ 65/232811; fax 65/232511; www.andinadelsud.com), has daily trips to this area as well.

BY CAR   Renting a car is perhaps the most enjoyable way (but also the most expensive) to see the surrounding area. In town, try **Adriazola Turismo Expediciones,** Santa Rosa 340 (☏ 65/233477; www.adriazolaflyfishing.cl) or **Hunter Rent a Car,** San José 130 (☏ 9/920-6888; www.lstravel.com); though prices are lower at the airport.

Visitor Information

The **Casa del Turista** tourism office can be found at the pier on the shore (☏ 65/237956; www.puertovaras.org) and is open daily from December to March from 9am to 10pm, and the rest of the year daily from 9am to 1:30pm and 3 to 7pm.

   Travel Sur exchanges dollars at its office on San José 261 (☏ 65/236000).

WHAT TO SEE & DO

Puerto Varas is compact enough to explore by foot, which is the best way to view the wooden colonial homes built by German immigrants from 1910 until the 1940s. Eight of these homes have been declared national monuments, yet there are at least a dozen more constructed during the period of expansion that began with the installation of the railroad connecting Puerto Varas with Puerto Montt.

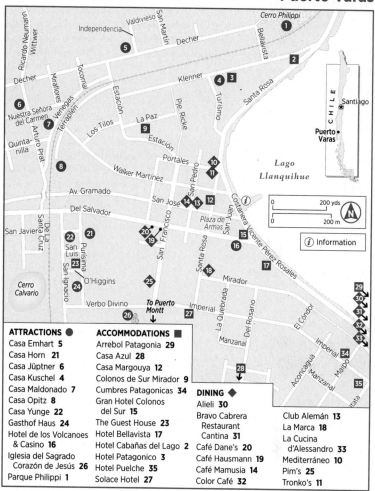

ATTRACTIONS ●
Casa Emhart 5
Casa Horn 21
Casa Jüptner 6
Casa Kuschel 4
Casa Maldonado 7
Casa Opitz 8
Casa Yunge 22
Gasthof Haus 24
Hotel de los Volcanoes & Casino 16
Iglesia del Sagrado Corazón de Jesús 26
Parque Philippi 1

ACCOMMODATIONS ■
Arrebol Patagonia 29
Casa Azul 28
Casa Margouya 12
Colonos de Sur Mirador 9
Cumbres Patagonicas 34
Gran Hotel Colonos del Sur 15
The Guest House 23
Hotel Bellavista 17
Hotel Cabañas del Lago 2
Hotel Patagonico 3
Hotel Puelche 35
Solace Hotel 27

DINING ◆
Alieli 30
Bravo Cabrera Restaurant Cantina 31
Café Dane's 20
Café Hausmann 19
Café Mamusia 14
Color Café 32
Club Alemán 13
La Marca 18
La Cucina d'Alessandro 33
Mediterráneo 10
Pim's 25
Tronko's 11

Walk up San Francisco from Del Salvador until you reach María Brunn, where you turn right to view the stately **Iglesia del Sagrado Corazón de Jesús,** built between 1915 and 1918. The neo-Romantic design of the church, made entirely of oak, was modeled after the Marienkirche in the Black Forest. Continue along María Brunn and turn right on Purísima, where you'll encounter the first group of colonial homes. The first is **Gasthof Haus** (1930), now run as a hotel; then **Casa Yunge** (1932), just past San Luis on the left; and on the right, **Casa Horn** (1925), where you turn left. If you'd like to see more, walk to Calle Dr. Giesseler and turn right, following the train tracks for several blocks, passing the **Casa Opitz** on the right (1913, and now a hotel) until you see **Casa Maldonado** (1915) on the left.

Turn left on Nuestra Señora del Carmen to view the five homes left and right, including the **Casa Jüptner** (1910). Double back and continue along Dr. Giesseler, turn left on Estación, and then right on Decher, passing the **Casa Emhart** (1920) and several other homes on the left. Continue through the forested road that winds up the hill to reach **Parque Philippi** (home to the giant cross, which is lit up at night and can be seen from downtown Puerto Varas), where you'll find an excellent lookout point. Double back, and turn left on Bellavista, right on Klenner, and left on Turismo; at the corner sits the eclectic **Casa Kuschel** (1910), with its Bavarian baroque tower. At the end of Turismo is the Avenida Costanera; turn right and stroll down the boardwalk.

Outdoor Activities

Tour companies and outfitters have changed ownership over the past few years, but, thankfully, many have matured and I can now recommend several with a clear conscience. **Tranco Expediciones,** San Pedro 422 (©/fax **65/311311**), and **CTS Turismo**, San Francisco 333 (© **65/237-330**; www.ctsturismo.cl) both offer ascents of Volcano Osorno, for about $180 for two, which includes gear, lunch, and transportation.

For city tours and sightseeing tours around the Lake District, including trips to Frutillar, Puyehue, and Chiloé, try **Andina del Sud,** Del Salvador 72 (© **65/232811;** fax 65/232511; www.andinadelsud.com). Andina del Sud is the company that provides boat excursions on Lago Todos los Santos and the Chilean leg of the lake crossing to Argentina (for information, see "Parque Nacional Vicente Pérez Rosales & the Lake Crossing to Argentina," later in this section).

For sightseeing trips to Bariloche via road, contact **LS Travel,** San José 130, Puerto Varas (© **65/232424;** www.lstravel.com).

BOATING   During the summer, it is possible to rent kayaks and canoes at the pier, located near the main plaza. For a sailing cruise around Lago Llanquihue, try **Moto-velero Capitán Haase** (© **65/235120;** fax 65/235166; www.teambuilding.cl). The amicable owner and captain offers one daily cruise aboard his "antique" yacht (built in 1998 to resemble a turn-of-the-20th-century boat using antique designs). You can't miss it moored in the bay. "Sunset with the Captain," from 6:30 to 9:30pm, is a quiet, romantic trip using sails and no motor; the cost is C$12,000 per person, which includes an open bar. Inquire about charters if you have a large group.

FISHING   This region is very popular for fly-fishing, principally along the shores of Río Puelo, Río Maullín, and Río Petrohué—but there's fish in the lake, too. The best and most exclusive fishing expeditions are offered to guests at the Yan Kee Way Lodge (p. 306). There's also **Gray's Fly-Fishing Supplies,** which has two shops, at San José 192 and San Francisco 447 (© **65/310734;** www.grayfly.com). Gray's is a central hub for information, gear, and fishing licenses, and they can arrange day trips for river and lake fishing. Another good option for day trips is **Adriazola Fly Fishing,** Santa Rosa 340 (© **65/233477;** www.adriazolaflyfishing.cl). The owner, Adrian, will custom-arrange any fly-fishing and trolling day tour with a bilingual guide. Both outfitters charge around $140 for a half-day and $300 for a full day (for two guests, including transportation, boat, lunch, wine, and fishing guides).

The exclusive, full-service **Río Puelo Lodge** (© **2/229-8533** in Santiago; fax 2/201-8042; www.posadapuelo.cl) caters to fly-fishermen and hunters, but also offers horseback riding, boat rides, water-skiing, and more. The stately wood-and-stone lodge is tucked well into the backcountry on the shore of Lago Tagua Tagua, and it caters mainly to groups of guys who come to have fun in the backcountry. Packages average around $350 per person per day, including meals, an open bar, guide, boats, horseback riding, trekking, and use of a heated pool. Ask about discounts for groups.

HORSEBACK RIDING **Campo Aventura,** San Bernardo 318, Puerto Varas (©/fax **65/232910;** www.campo-aventura.com), offers horseback riding year-round, leaving from their well-designed camp in Valle Cochamó, south of the national park. Both day and multiday trips can be planned with the outfitters, with lodging in rustic shelters they have set up along the trail. Gear and bilingual guides are provided, and multiday trips are all-inclusive. Horseback riding through a forested area is a good option for a rainy day—just throw on a waterproof jacket and pants, and let the horse walk through the mud for you.

KAYAKING **Ko'Kayak,** a small outfit run by French kayak enthusiasts, is the best choice for kayaking both for the day and for multiday kayak/camping trips. They have a base in Ensenada at Km 40, but make a reservation at their main office at Casilla 898 (© **65/511648** or 9/310-5272; www.kokayak.com).

RAFTING Few rivers in the world provide rafters with such stunning scenery as the Río Petrohué, with frothy green waters that begin at Lago Todos los Santos and end at the Reloncaví Estuary. Rafters are treated to towering views of the volcanoes Osorno and Puntiagudo. The river is Class III and suitable for nearly everyone, but there are a few rapids to negotiate with sudden bursts of heavy paddling, so timid travelers might consult with their tour agency before signing up. For rafting, go to **Alsur Expediciones,** Del Salvador 100 (© **65/232300;** www.alsurexpeditions.com).

Shopping

There is an **arts and crafts fair** on the Del Salvador street side of the plaza. For high-end arts, clothing, and jewelry, head to **Primitiva,** Santa Rosa 302, or **Vicki Johnson,** Santa Rosa 318. The little wagons at the shore in front of the pier offer arts and crafts, but hours are erratic and most are open during the summer only. There are dozens of large international designer chains surrounding the casino, though for something completely different, try **Artesanias de Chile,** Salvador 109 (© **65/346332**). They offer an excellent collection of fine woolen blankets, home decorations, baskets, pottery, and jewelry that are created by independent producers from the region.

WHERE TO STAY

You'll find hotels and hostels in the town center area. Along the coast (both the Puerto Chico coast and all the way to Ensenada), it's mostly *cabañas* (cabins for two to eight people with living spaces and kitchenettes). The following are the best hotels available in the area, plus a couple of *cabañas* along the coast for those who want quiet accommodations in more bucolic settings. Ask where the *cabaña* is located on the complex when booking because many are filed in a row from the shore, meaning only the first two *cabañas* have a view. Also, some *cabañas* consider a fold-out couch bedding for two.

Expensive

Arrebol Patagonia ★★★ 🖼 Anyone with an eye for design and style won't find a more appealing hotel in the entire Lake District of Chile. The woodwork alone is truly stunning, from an ancient and giant tree root that serves as the reception desk to recycled alerce-wood closets. In fact, all the wood is recycled and the inn also has geothermic heating. Contrasting with the wood are white walls, sheets, and ceilings, and touches of color. It's sophisticated and simple at once. The design was highly influenced by the Hotel Antumalal in Pucón (p. 266). Rooms, for example, have no TVs, but all have a terrace and Scandinavian-styled baths. Downstairs is one of the hippest bistros in the area, with an excellent wine bar. The owners, a local family, were also the designers and builders, and provide guests excellent service. The range of unique excursions the hotel offers are superior to any other operator in town. They'll make anything happen—from a gourmet lunch with champagne under a remote waterfall or heliskiing on untouched powder.

Camino Ensenada Km 2, Ruta 225. © **65/564900.** www.arrebolpatagonia.com. 22 units. $240 double; $280 suite. AE, DC, MC, V. Rates include breakfast. **Amenities:** Restaurant; bar; spa.

Colonos de Sur Mirador   Sister hotel to the Gran Colonos de Sur, the Mirador is less centrally located but has better panoramic views, cheery interiors, and an outdoor pool, along with lower prices. You can't miss the Mirador: It's a red-and-white building perched high on the hills just above downtown, with the giant sign HOTEL affixed to the roof. The corner rooms offer the best views, so try to get one of those.

Estación 505, Puerto Varas. © **65/235555.** www.colonosdelsur.cl. $120 double. AE, DC, MC, V. **Amenities:** Restaurant; bar; outdoor pool. *In room:* Cable TV, fridge, hair dryer, minibar, free Wi-Fi.

Cumbres Patagónicas ★★   The newest mainstream hotel in Puerto Varas blends the notable characteristics of the area (the incredible view and lots of local wood) with great service and extremely comfortable rooms. The hotel has a gorgeous lobby with a towering fireplace, giant leather sofas, and cathedral windows overlooking the lake. The rooms are equally plush, among the largest in Southern Chile, with small terraces, gentle wool blankets set atop crisp white duvets, a small seating area, and separate bathrooms. There's a small rooftop spa and indoor pool. The excellent buffet breakfast has homemade pastries, granolas, and local jellies. Service is certainly above standard.

Imperial 561, Puerto Varas. © **65/494000.** www.cumbrespatagonicas.cl. 92 units. $245 double; $345 suite. AE, DC, MC, V. Rates include excellent buffet breakfast. **Amenities:** Restaurant; bar; lounge; spa. *In room:* A/C, hair dryer, minibar, free Wi-Fi.

Gran Hotel Colonos del Sur & Hotel Colonos de Sur ★   Boasting a waterfront location next door to the casino and charming German colonial architecture, the Gran Colonos del Sur used to be a standard favorite among travelers to Puerto Varas but began to lag behind newer properties. A total reconstruction of the hotel that involved many of the top designers in the country came to an end in 2009. It still doesn't compare to the Arrebol or Cumbres Patagónicas, though the modern decor and amenities are definitely a step up.

Gran Hotel: Del Salvador 24, Puerto Varas. © **65/233369** or for reservations 65/233039. www.colonos delsur.cl. 98 units. $322 double. **Amenities:** Restaurant; bar; pool; spa. *In room:* Cable TV, minibar, fridge, hair dryer, free Wi-Fi.

Hotel Cabañas del Lago ★★ ☺   Sweeping views of Puerto Varas and Volcán Osorno make Hotel Cabañas del Lago the highest-quality lodging available in town. The lakeview and park suites are luxuriously appointed and colossal in size; one could get lost in the bathroom alone. A junior suite is a slightly larger double and might be worth booking for the larger windows and better decorations. Doubles are not overly spacious and have cramped bathrooms, but curtains and bedding have been updated. Doubles with a lake view are the same price as rooms that overlook the *cabañas*.

The hotel takes advantage of its location, with lots of glass in its attractive lounge and restaurant, which, like all the rooms, sports a country decor. The common areas have the feel of a mountain lodge, complete with deer-antler chandeliers. There's also a large sun deck. The small two- to five-person *cabañas* are not as pleasant as the hotel rooms but are a bargain for a family of four, if you're willing to be a bit cramped. The excellent restaurant **El Mirador** serves wild game and other daily specials from an extensive menu. The hotel is a 2-block walk up from town.

Klenner 195, Puerto Varas. ✆ **65/232291.** Fax 65/232707. www.cabanasdellago.cl. 130 units, 13 *cabañas*. $158 double; $227 junior suite; $179 *cabañas* for up to 4 people. *Cabaña* rates do not include buffet breakfast. AE, DC, MC, V. **Amenities:** Restaurant; bar; lounge; babysitting; indoor heated pool; room service; sauna. *In room:* Cable TV, hair dryer.

Hotel Patagónico This hotel isn't technically located in Patagonia, so don't let the name fool you. It is set above the city of Puerto Varas, with premium views—in some of the rooms at least—of Lake Llanquihue and the Osorno Volcano. The decor throughout is tasteful and little touches, such as furs and Neruda's poetry adorning the walls, add to the mystique. Rooms are spacious, have personal Wi-Fi routers, and every amenity you could ask for, though many look out onto the parking lot. Service leaves something to be desired. You can occasionally find deals at the hotel when booking online that are 10% to 25% less than those listed. The hotel was originally managed by Spanish chain Melia when it opened in 2007 and was never well regarded. Unfortunately, only the name has changed since the new management took over.

Klenner 349, Puerto Varas. ✆ **65/201000.** Fax 65/201001. www.hotelpatagonico.cl. 91 units. $200 double; $360 suite. AE, DC, MC, V. **Amenities:** Restaurant; bar; children's program; exercise room; pool; spa w/sauna. *In room:* TV, minibar, hair dryer, free Wi-Fi.

Hotel Puelche ★ Puerto Varas's first real boutique hotel has the look and feel of an upscale mountain lodge, albeit a smaller one. It lacks its own character, but does a decent job of imitating pricier accommodations with lots of space, quality bedding and bath accessories, big windows, and modern-day decor that isn't too over the top. Rooms vary considerably as a few have lake views, porches, and/or skylights. Puelche is in a quiet area on a hill southeast of the center, a longer walk than most, so having a car helps.

Imperial 695, Puerto Varas. ✆ **65/233600.** www.hotelpuelche.com. 21 units. $175 double standard; $215 junior suite. AE, DC, MC, V. **Amenities:** Restaurant; bar; spa. *In room:* TV, minifridge, hair dryer.

Moderate

The Guest House ★★ 🎒 Owned and operated by Vicki Johnson, an American who owns the crafts and foods store downtown (see "Shopping," earlier), this bed-and-breakfast is a more intimate hotel, located in a quiet residential area about a 4-block walk from the plaza. The hotel is housed in a 1926 renovated mansion, and, like most bed-and-breakfasts, the lodging experience here is a little like staying in one of your friends' homes, with a comfy living area decorated with art that has been collected, not store bought, and a collection of reading material; a dining area with one long, family-style table; and a big kitchen where you are given the opportunity to help out with the cooking, if you so wish. What's also special about the location of this B&B is that nearly all the homes that surround it are the lovely shingled style popular at the time of this home's inception. The rooms have high ceilings, comfortable beds, and a simple, clean decor.

O'Higgins 608, Puerto Varas. ℂ **65/231521.** Fax 65/232240. www.vicki-johnson.com/guesthouse. 10 units. $95 double standard. Rates include continental breakfast. AE, MC, V. **Amenities:** Room service.

Hotel Bellavista ★★ 🔥 Another waterfront hotel with gorgeous views, the Bellavista renovated all of its guest rooms a few years ago, giving it the edge on its competitors, Colonos and Cabañas del Lago. The hardwood floors here aren't as cozy as the carpeted rooms found in other hotels; however, the fresh linens and handsome earth-toned decor are quite sophisticated, and their restaurant and bar is an inviting place to while away an hour with a coffee and admire the view of the volcano. There is also a cozy fireside lounge. There are four larger guest rooms that face a forested cliff for those seeking quieter accommodations, and, best of all, the duplex apartments for five to six people are the best in town: duplexes with two-storied, panoramic windows—good deals for a group of friends or families with kids. The Bellavista's restaurant has a good range of international dishes.

Av. Vicente Pérez Rosales 60, Puerto Varas. ℂ **65/232011.** Fax 65/232013. www.hotelbellavista.cl. 50 units. $177 double; from $274 suite. Rates include buffet breakfast. AE, DC, MC, V. **Amenities:** Restaurant; bar; lounge; sauna. In room: TV, minibar, hair dryer.

Solace Hotel ★ 🔥 The Solace opened in May 2008 just 5 minutes from the center and has the feel, at least on the inside, of a smaller version of the Hotel Patagónico, with a friendlier staff and better service. Most of the rooms get decent views of the lake, and you'll find the same level of high-tech amenities as the Melia, plus the same cozy beds and a similar decor, but for a third less of the price. Like most of the new constructions in Puerto Varas, this one lacks personality, however.

Imperial 211, Puerto Varas. ℂ **65/364100.** www.solacehotel.cl. 62 units. $170 double. Rates include buffet breakfast. AE, DC, MC, V. **Amenities:** Restaurant; bar. In room: TV, minibar, hair dryer, free Wi-Fi.

Inexpensive

Casa Azul This German-Chilean budget/backpacker's hostel in a large, blue-and-red shingled house sits in a large garden a 10-minute walk from the center and 5 minutes to the lakefront. Rooms are entirely in wood from the floor to the walls to the ceiling, and feature comfortable, modern beds—you get a bit of a contemporary farmhouse feeling here. Casa Azul has a four-bed dorm, singles and doubles with shared bathrooms, and doubles with private bathrooms. Its buffet breakfast is an additional C$2,375. Reservations aren't guaranteed for stays of less than 2 nights.

Manzanal 66 and Rosario, Puerto Varas. ℂ **65/232904.** www.casaazul.net. 9 units. $40 double with shared bathroom; $32 double with private bathroom; $9 per person in dormitory. No credit cards. **Amenities:** Kitchen. In room: No phone, free Wi-Fi.

Casa Margouya This hostel is in a well-situated area on Santa Rosa, close to everything and across the park from the beach. It's on the second floor, and there's a central living area with large tables and couches, and a kitchen that is open for guest use. It's a comfortable place and the service is friendly. There are five rooms, two of which have one double bed; the rest are shared accommodations that range in price according to the number of beds in the room. Bathrooms are clean but communal. This is a good place to meet other travelers. Breakfast is not included.

Santa Rosa 318, Puerto Varas. ℂ **65/237640.** www.margouya.com. 5 units. $57 double; $17 per person for shared rooms. No credit cards. **Amenities:** Kitchen. In room: No phone.

WHERE TO DINE

Puerto Varas has many good to excellent restaurants, but the service in this area tends to be slow, so have patience. In addition to the restaurants below, there is **Pim's,** San

Francisco 712 (☏ **65/233998**), a country-western–style pub with burgers, sandwiches, and such American-style appetizers as buffalo wings and salads. It is popular with locals, and the nighttime ambience is very lively. If you didn't get the chance to visit the landmark **Café Haussmann** in Valdivia (p. 287), you can try their famous *crudos* at their branch at San Francisco 644.

Expensive

Alieli ★★ 🍴 CHILEAN   This romantic restaurant that looks out over the nighttime lights of the city and the lake at the Arrebol hotel is one of the great foodie finds in the city. The restaurant isn't promoted to the public, though it is certainly open to walk-ins for dinner. The chef specializes in modern interpretations of traditional regional dishes, especially that of Chiloé. Try a wildflower salad with duck satay or grilled conger with a murta (a local berry) sauce. Finish with a beautiful lucuma crème brûlée. Their wine cellar is superb.

Camino Ensenada Km 2, Ruta 225. ☏ **65/564900.** www.arrebolpatagonia.com. AE, DC, MC, V. Main courses C$6,000–C$16,000. Daily 8:30pm–midnight.

La Marca ★★ STEAKHOUSE   La Marca has quickly become *the* steakhouse in Puerto Varas. As it is owned by a butcher, Carnes El Maitén, the restaurant gets the very best cuts of meat in town and they know what to do with it. Lamb is roasted over open fires outside and *bife de chorizo* comes to the table in a tender red mass with a perfectly seasoned crust. The wine list is quite good and reasonably priced. If you don't like meat, you're still going to walk out smelling like it.

Santa Rosa 539. ☏ **65/232031.** www.restaurantlamarca.cl. AE, DC, MC, V. Main courses C$6,000–C$18,000. Mon–Sat 7–11pm and Sun 1–4pm.

Tronko's ★ INTERNATIONAL   This newish brewpub is one of the better options in town for brew and a bite. The service is excellent and the atmosphere of hand carved wooden tables and chairs has its charm. Some dishes, such as rolled chicken with *aji amarillo* (yellow chile) and *lomo saltado* (a beef stir-fry over french fries and rice), have a Peruvian slant, and others, such as the lamb risotto or *merluza* (white fish), have a more eclectic feel.

Santa Rosa 218. ☏ **65/233080.** AE, DC, MC, V. Main courses C$6,000–C$14,000. Apr–Nov Tues–Sat 6pm–1am; Dec–Mar 11am–1am.

Moderate

Bravo Cabrera Restaurant Cantina ★★ PIZZA   With about 50 beers on hand, mostly craft beers from around Chile, the perennially packed "BC" has become my go-to spot in Puerto Varas. The decor consists of wood: the ceiling, the floor, the walls—all of different types of trees and patterns. The specialty are wood-fired pizzas, which are so cheap and way bigger than you expect; you can almost split a personal. There's also a small selection of *tablas*, salads, steaks, seafood, and sandwiches. The bar fills up on weekend nights when the music gets turned up. Occasionally a DJ is on hand to add a soundtrack.

Rosales 1071. ☏ **65/233-441.** AE, DC, MC, V. Main courses C$10,000–C$15,000. Daily noon–3:30pm and 7:30–11pm.

Club Alemán GERMAN/CHILEAN   This Club Alemán seems to offer more German specialties than most, with goose, duck, and bratwurst served with onions, potatoes, and applesauce; pork chops with caramelized onions and sauerkraut; goulash with spaetzle; steak tartare; and other dishes, in addition to Chilean favorites. Sandwiches are much cheaper than main dishes ($3–$6) and are substantial. There are also appetizing desserts, such as crepes *diplomático*, with bananas, ice cream, and chocolate sauce.

San José 415. ☎ **65/338291.** Main courses C$4,000–C$7,000. DC, MC, V. Daily 11am–midnight.

Color Café ★ INTERNATIONAL   The Color Café calls itself a wine restaurant, for it has more than 100 top wines on offer, plus a diverse menu. Clean, crisp interiors offset by contemporary oil paintings, a long bar, and a blazing, wood-burning stove set the ambience here. It's a bit of a walk from the town center (about 15–20 min.). The periodically changing menu features good bistro-style cuisine, including Caesar salads, soups, quiches, pastas, and main courses such as venison in a berry sauce and salmon *tataki*. This is a good place for a cocktail and an appetizer of regional smoked salmon.

Los Colonos 1005. ☎ **65/234311.** Main courses C$4,000–C$7,500. AE, DC, MC, V. Dec–Mar daily noon–2am; Apr–Nov daily 8pm–midnight.

Mediterráneo ★ ⬛ INTERNATIONAL   Boasting an excellent location right on the Costanera, this restaurant has a glass-enclosed terrace with water views. The cheerful orange tablecloths add to its brightness, as does the pleasant waitstaff. Mediterráneo is known for its imaginative dishes (think Chilean-Mediterranean fusion) that change weekly. The owners use mostly local produce, including spices bought from the Mapuche natives. Here, you'll find big, fresh salads mixing such ingredients as endives, Swiss cheese, anchovies, olives, and local mushrooms. For the main course, the venison here is excellent, served with a yummy zucchini gratin. Other standouts are the fresh sea bass with a caper white-wine sauce, and a delicious lamb cooked in a rosemary wine reduction and served with roasted potatoes. For dessert, try one of the fruit sorbets.

Santa Rosa 068, corner of Portales. ☎ **65/237268.** AE, DC, MC, V. Main courses C$6,000–C$15,000. Apr–Nov daily noon–3:30pm and 7:30–11pm; Dec–Mar daily 10am–2am.

Inexpensive

Café Dane's ★ 🍴 CHILEAN/CAFE   It's often hard to get a table during the lunch hour in this extremely popular restaurant. Dane's serves inexpensive, hearty food in good-size portions, plus mouthwatering desserts. The interior is simple and unassuming, and much of the food is standard Chilean fare, all of it good or very good. The fried empanadas, especially shellfish, deserve special mention. Dane's serves a daily set menu for C$2,850 Monday through Saturday and C$4,275 on Sunday, as well as a special dish, or *plato del día*, for C$16,625. It's less busy before 1pm or after 3pm. You can also buy food to go from the front counter.

Del Salvador 441. ☎ **65/232371.** Main courses C$1,500–C$6,000; sandwiches C$2,000–C$4,000. No credit cards. Daily 7:45am–1am.

Café Mamusia 🍴 CHILEAN/BAKERY   The Mamusia is locally renowned for its delicious chocolates and pastries. The atmosphere is somewhat like a tearoom or ice-cream parlor, but there are delicious sandwiches, served on homemade bread, and full meals throughout the day as well, including typical Chilean favorites such as *pastel de choclo* and *escalopas*, as well as lasagna, pizza, and grilled meats and fish. Café Mamusia is also a good place for breakfast and serves a continental version for C$2,375.

San José 316. ☎ **65/233343.** Main courses C$2,000–C$4,500; sandwiches C$3,000. MC, V. Summer daily 8:30am–2am; winter Mon–Fri 9am–10:30pm, Sat–Sun 10am–11pm.

La Cucina d' Alessandro ★ PIZZA/ITALIAN   The authentic, fresh pastas and thin-crust pizzas at this restaurant are excellent because they are made by an Italian family who emigrated to Puerto Varas only a few years ago, bringing with them real Italian gastronomic know-how. The pizzas really shine here, and their special two-for-one pizza offer from 4 to 8pm every day makes this restaurant a good value. The restaurant has a cozy atmosphere and is housed in a typical shingled home across from the beach. There are a few wooden tables that are large enough for groups of six to eight diners. It's a 15-minute walk from downtown. Apart from pasta and pizza, La Cucina has good seafood dishes, and it is open all day. It's a tiny restaurant, so make reservations for dinner and come early for lunch.

Av. Vicente Perez Rosales 1290. ✆ **65/310583.** Main courses C$2,500–C$7,500. No credit cards. Daily noon–midnight.

PUERTO VARAS AFTER DARK

At night, the stately **Hotel de los Volcanoes & Casino,** Del Salvador 021 (✆ **65/492000;** www.enjoy.cl), gives visitors a chance to depart with their travel money (or hopefully win enough for a hotel upgrade) via slot machines and gaming tables offering blackjack, baccarat, roulette, and more. The gaming salon is open daily from noon to 7am, the slot machine floor from noon to 5am, and every Monday the minimum bet drops to C$713, and roulette to C$14,250. The casino's bar and restaurants are open from noon to 4am, if you're looking for a midnight snack. It's an exciting place to be on weekends, and the decor is quite stylish.

Two good spots for a drink at night are **Garage** (no phone; located on San José next to the Copec gas station), a two-story place with wood tables and electronic music that is popular with 20- and 30-somethings; and **Bruno Cabrera's** (see above). **Urbano** (✆ **65/233081**), at San Pedro 516, is a trendier pub with bar food and is occasionally home to DJs and acoustic music. Bars and pubs are also clustered near the old yacht club, which becomes lively during summer weekends.

A SIDE TRIP FROM PUERTO VARAS TO ENSENADA

Ensenada is a tiny settlement at the base of Volcán Osorno. Its proximity to Petrohué and Lago Todos los Santos makes it a convenient point for lodging if you plan to spend a lot of time around Parque Nacional Vicente Pérez Rosales. There is no town to speak of here, just a few vacation rentals, hotels, and a couple of shops. About 4km (2½ miles) outside Puerto Varas on the way to Ensenada is a Chilean rodeo *medialuna* (half-moon), where events are held during February and on Independence days, September 18 and 19. Check with the visitor's office if you are here during this not-to-miss event, which provides an in-depth look into Chilean rural culture.

GETTING THERE   If you have your own vehicle, take the coastal road east out of Puerto Varas and continue for 46km (29 miles) until you reach Ensenada. In Puerto Varas, you'll find minibuses at the intersection of San Bernardo and Martínez that go to Ensenada, Petrohué, and Lago Todos los Santos every day at 9:15 and 11am, and 2 and 4pm. **Andina del Sud,** Del Salvador 72 (✆ **65/232811;** www.andinadelsud.com), has daily trips to this area as well.

Where to Stay

There are many *cabañas* on the shore; the **Cabañas Bahía Celeste** (✆ **9/873-6568;** www.bahiaceleste.cl) stand out. These self-service units have lake views, living areas, and kitchens for travelers seeking a little more freedom (although there are a few restaurants here if you would like to dine out at night). The *cabañas* are attractive stone-and-wood units on the lakeshore for two, four, or six guests. There is also maid service, and each *cabaña* comes with a wooden deck. Prices are $139 for a two-person cabin, $179 for a four-person cabin, and $232 for a six-person cabin.

As is true with the majority of hotels in rural settings (ecolodges, for example), the hotels in this area do not have TVs, though many have added Wi-Fi.

Hotel Ensenada ★ 🖋 The Hotel Ensenada is a veritable museum, with a lobby jam-packed with colonial German antiques. The hotel itself is a living antique, built more than 100 years ago. Although it offers an acceptable level of comfort, the rooms do reflect the hotel's age. It's such a fun place, though, that most visitors, many of them foreigners, don't seem to mind. All rooms on the second floor have private bathrooms, and, for the most part, the rest share with just one other room. Rooms are sparsely decorated. If they're not too full, ask to see several rooms, as each one is differently sized. The hotel is situated on a 500-hectare (1,235-acre) private forest that's perfect for taking a stroll or riding a bike—which comes free with the room— and there's a tennis court, canoes, and motorboats. The old-fashioned kitchen serves simple Chilean cuisine with vegetables straight from the garden.

Ruta Internacional 225, Km 45. ℂ **65/212017.** Fax 65/212028. www.hotelensenada.cl. 23 units. $100 double; $150 double with volcano view. AE, DC, MC, V. Closed Mar–Sept. **Amenities:** Restaurant; lounge; bikes.

Yan Kee Way Lodge ★★★ 📷 The name "Yan Kee Way" is a play on words, a gringo's pronunciation of Llanquihue, and it is owned and managed by an American. The owner could not have chosen a more picture-perfect site for this luxurious property: nestled in a thick forest of cinnamon-colored *arrayán* trees on the shore of Lago Llanquihue, and facing the astounding view of Osorno Volcano directly in front of the lodge.

The Yan Kee Way Lodge takes just eight fishermen on outings per day (the lodge capacity is higher, however) via inflatable boats, horseback, or walk-and-wade fishing. The best fishing season is from November to early May, yet fishermen have done well year-round—in fact, this lodge offers the best fly-fishing opportunities in the area because they can get to areas that are inaccessible to others. The hotel complex has independent units in standard rooms, two-story bungalows, and apartments; the latter are very spacious and good for a family or group of friends. Blending with the surroundings, each elegant building here is painted in tones of terra cotta and forest green, with contemporary decor such as ebony leather couches and furniture, and art imported from Mexico and Argentina. Service is attentive and very friendly, and the owner strives to provide the very best, including an extensive wine cellar and the region's finest restaurant, Latitude 42 (see later). Yan Kee Way is not just a fly-fishing lodge, however, and they offer adventure all-inclusive packages, including rafting, mountain biking, hiking, and horseback riding. At the end of the day, many guests unwind in the spa or in the two wood-fired hot tubs that face the lake and the volcano.

Road to Ensenada E of Puerto Varas, Km 42. ℂ **65/212030.** Fax 65/212031. www.southernchilexp.com. 18 units. $280 double; $360 per person per day all-inclusive sport adventure package, which includes all meals and house wines with dinner and 20 activities from which to choose. AE, DC, MC, V. **Amenities:** Restaurant; bar; lounge; Jacuzzi; room service; sauna; spa; watersports equipment. *In room:* Fridge, hair dryer, Wi-Fi (free).

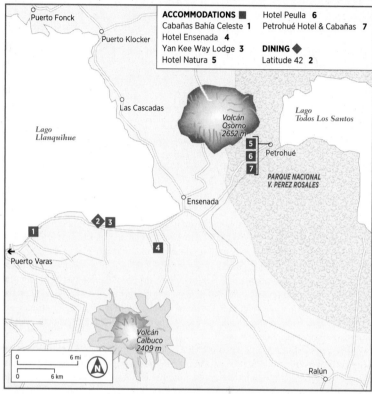

ACCOMMODATIONS ■

Cabañas Bahía Celeste **1**
Hotel Ensenada **4**
Yan Kee Way Lodge **3**
Hotel Natura **5**

Hotel Peulla **6**
Petrohué Hotel & Cabañas **7**

DINING ◆

Latitude 42 **2**

Puerto Fonck

Puerto Klocker

Las Cascadas

Lago Llanquihue

Volcán Osorno 2652 m

Lago Todos Los Santos

5
6 Petrohué
7

PARQUE NACIONAL V. PEREZ ROSALES

Ensenada

2 3

1

← Puerto Varas

4

Volcán Calbuco 2409 m

0   6 mi
0   6 km

Ralún

Where to Dine

Latitude 42 ★★★ ☑ INTERNATIONAL   This is one of the finest restaurants in southern Chile, located right on the lake overlooking the volcano. The elegant decor features marble and brass chandeliers, fireplaces made of volcanic rock, orangey leather chairs, picture windows overlooking the water, a basement "cave" for wine tasting, and a cigar bar that sells Havanas. Service is superb. The chef uses only the highest-quality produce, mostly local and organic, to create the most tantalizing dishes. The salmon is smoked in-house using apple cider, and the meat is aged on the premises. Fish is brought daily from Puerto Varas and Puerto Montt, usually sea bass, salmon, and con-ger eel. Specials change daily and the entire menu changes occasionally throughout the year. The cellar houses outstanding wines, an impressive collection from over 40 vine-yards. Pastries and desserts are also terrific; even the heavenly chestnut ice cream is homemade. The menu is surprisingly economical for the high quality of this restaurant. It is a good idea to make a reservation if you are not staying in the lodge.

In the Yan Kee Way Lodge, on the road to Ensenada, E of Puerto Varas, Km 42. ℭ **65/212030.** Reservations recommended. Main courses C$5,000–C$14,000. AE, DC, MC, V. Daily noon–3pm and 7–10pm.

Parque Nacional Vicente Perez Rosales & The Lake Crossing To Argentina

About 65km (40 miles) from Puerto Varas sits Chile's oldest national park, Vicente Pérez Rosales, founded in 1926. It covers an area of 251,000 hectares (619,970 acres), incorporating the park's centerpiece, **Lago Todos los Santos, Saltos de Petrohué,** and three commanding **volcanoes:** Osorno, Tronador, and Puntiagudo. The park is open daily from December to February 8:30am to 8pm, March to November 8:30am to 6:30pm; admission to Saltos de Petrohué is C$1,200 adults, C$1,000 kids. A new speedboat service runs 20-minute trips on the river to the base of the lower falls (C$15,000 per person). CONAF's **information center (© 65/486115)** can be found toward the end of the road.

By far the most popular excursions here are boat rides across the crème de men-the–colored waters of **Lago Todos los Santos,** and there are several options. **Turismo Peulla (© 65/236150;** www.turismopeulla.cl) offers trips departing from Puerto Montt or Puerto Varas to Peulla on the far side of the lake.

From Petrohué, you can book a day trip to Margarita island in the middle of the lake or cross to Peulla, a 1¾-hour crossing that departs daily at 10:30am October through April and in July; the rest of the year, the ship doesn't cross on Sundays.

Travelers may then return or continue on to Bariloche with the Argentine company **Cruce de Lagos (© 65/236150;** www.crucedelagos.cl). **Andina del Sud** (the owner of Turismo Peulla) has a ticket office at the pier and an office in Puerto Varas, at Del Salvador 72 (© **65/232811;** $160–$190). This is a very popular and very touristy journey; though the trip to Bariloche offers rugged, panoramic views, the trip is not worth the money on stormy days. And too much of the cattle herd mentality exists here as tourist-weary guides shuttle passengers—over 50,000 per season—in and out quickly. The ferry portions of this journey are broken up by short bus rides from one body of water to the other.

There are relatively few hiking trails in this national park. The shortest and most popular trail leads to the **Saltos de Petrohué,** located just before the lake (admission C$1,200). Here you'll find a wooden walkway that has been built above the start of the Río Petrohué; from here it is possible to watch the inky-green waters crash through lava channels formed after the 1850 eruption of Volcán Osorno. Apart from the one perfect photo opportunity of the crashing emerald water with the volcano in the background, there isn't really much to see here. If you're serious about backpacking, pick up a copy of the map *Ruta de los Jesuitas* for a description of longer trails in the park, one of which takes you as far as Lago Rupanco and Puerto Rico (the town, not the Caribbean island), where you can catch a bus to Osorno. Day hikes take

---

 Get on the Road

I have found that a better way than boat to travel from Puerto Varas to Bariloche is via the international highway (which is dirt is some areas), pausing for a stop at Termas de Puyehue, driving through the high Andes, dropping in through the picturesque village of Villa la Angostura, and finally circumnavigating the lake to arrive at Bariloche. Your car-rental agency can arrange the paperwork for you, or try a service such as LS Travel (© 65/232424; www.lstravel.com).

visitors around the back of Volcán Osorno. One of my favorite treks here is a 1-night/2-day trek to the **Termas del Callao** thermal baths, the trail head of which is accessible only by boat. You can hire one of the boats at the dock (six-person maximum, C$23,750), or arrange a trip with **Expediciones Petrohué,** which will get you a guide and take care of gear and meals for the overnight stay. There is a rustic cabin at the hot springs; check with Expediciones before leaving for this trip to see if it is already booked. They also have rafting, 4×4 photo safaris, climbing, trekking, fly-fishing, and canyoneering opportunities. Expediciones organizes excursions for guests of the hotel and also for day visitors (Petrohué s/n, Rte. 225, Km 64, Parque Nacional; ✆ 65/212045; www.petrohue.com), plus they have bike rentals.

Volcán Osorno Ski Resort ★ (✆ 65/233445; www.volcanosorno.com) on the western slope of the volcano, with two basic chairlifts and a T-bar, is a small resort on the volcano of the same name. It has just 600 hectares (1,482 acres) of terrain, but there are sweeping views and runs appropriate for every level. This is not a ski resort that travelers head to Chile specifically for, such as Valle Nevado or Portillo; it's more of a novelty for those in the area during the mid-June to early October season. The snow can be armor piercing, as this side of the lake receives a lot of wind, and all the terrain is above tree level. Lift prices run C$18,500 for a full day, C$15,000 for a half-day, and C$15,000 for students.

WHERE TO STAY

Hotel Natura ★★ 🏨 Built in 2005 on the fringe of the forest and the floodplain near Peulla, this property is less of a lodge than its name suggests; in fact, the main building has the sort of traditional grand wood-and-stone style you see in much older hotels. Don't let that deter you. Rooms are chic and large; the matrimonial suit features a king-size bed, chimney, flatscreen TV, and a Jacuzzi, along with a balcony. The hotel also has a two-room family apartment, and 23 doubles with king-size beds. Irrespective of its traditional looks, it offers plenty of modern outdoor activities: canopying 15m (49 ft.) in the air over an 800m (half-mile) span, horseback riding, and fly-fishing. You can zoom down nearby rivers such as the Río Negro on a jet boat, and wind down with one of the 85 wines on the restaurant's list.

Lago Todos los Santos. ✆ **65/560483.** www.hotelnatura.cl. 45 units. $277 double; $343 triple. AE, MC, DC, V. **Amenities:** Restaurant; bar; gym; sauna; watersports equipment. In room: TV, hair dryer, free Wi-Fi.

Hotel Peulla ★ 🏨 Passengers on the 2-day journey to Bariloche stop for the night at this giant lodge, which sits on the shore of Lago Todos los Santos inside Parque Nacional Vicente Pérez Rosales. It's possible to spend several days here if you'd like, to take part in trekking (limited), fishing, kayaking, and horseback riding in the area. The lodge's remoteness is perhaps its biggest draw, surrounded as it is by thick forest and not much else. Built in 1896, the Peulla is a mountain lodge, with enormous dining rooms, roaring fireplaces, and lots of wood. It's an agreeable place, with a large patio and sprawling lawn, though it is older and not as exclusive as it once was. Guest rooms haven't really changed since the hotel was built; they are simple and slightly dark, with hardwood floors. Try reserving rooms at a lower rate through a travel agency.

Lago Todos los Santos. ✆ **65/232145** in Santiago. www.hotelpeulla.cl. 76 units. $162 double. AE, MC, V. **Amenities:** Restaurant; bar; exercise room; watersports equipment. In room: TV, free Wi-Fi.

Petrohué Hotel & Cabañas ★★ The Hotel Petrohué (built to replace the previous lodge, which burned to the ground in 2002) puts travelers right where the outdoor action is, without having to commute from Puerto Varas—and the hotel has an outfitter with a range of daily activities. It sits perched above the shore of Todos los Santos Lake, within the confines of the national park, meaning it gets busy when the lake-crossing boat pulls in (but this doesn't last very long, as they're bused out quickly). The forested location is gorgeous, even on a rainy day. The hotel itself is a tad austere, given its absence of homey touches such as artwork or plants, but the contemporary design of its interiors (stone, heavy wood beams, fresh white couches) is attractive, and the rooms are very comfortable, with crisp linens and panoramic windows. What's an even better idea is bunking up in one of their four cozy *cabañas* a little closer to the shore, all of which come with kitchenettes.

Petrohué s/n Rte. 225, Km 64, Parque Nacional. © **65/212025.** www.hotelpetrohue.cl. 13 units, 4 cabins. $220 double; $250 double with half-board; $200 cabin for 4; $290 cabin for 8. AE, MC, V. **Amenities:** Restaurant; bar; lounge; outdoor pool; room service. *In room:* Kitchenette in *cabañas*.

PUERTO MONTT

20km (12 miles) S of Puerto Varas; 1,016km (630 miles) S of Santiago

This port town of roughly 155,000 residents is the central hub for travelers headed to Lagos Llanquihue and Todos los Santos, Chiloé, and the parks Alerce Andino and Pumalín. It is also a major docking zone for dozens of large cruise companies circumnavigating the southern cone of South America and several ferry companies with southern destinations to Laguna San Rafael and Puerto Natales in Patagonia.

Puerto Montt was founded in 1853 by German immigrants and their stalwart promoter Vicente Pérez Rosales, who named the town after another promoter of immigration, President Manuel Montt. The waterfront here was rebuilt after the devastating earthquake of 1960, which destroyed the city's port, church, and neighborhood of Angelmó. Today it is the capital of Chile's southern Lake District, a thriving city that invests heavily in salmon farming, shipping, and tourism. There isn't much to see or do here, and most visitors head straight out of town upon arrival, but Puerto Montt's small downtown offers a quick, pleasant stroll on a sunny day, and there is an extensive outdoor market that sells Chilean handicrafts.

Essentials

GETTING THERE

BY PLANE Puerto Montt's **El Tepual** airport (PMC; © 65/294159) is currently served by airlines **LANExpress** (© 600/526-2000; www.lan.com) and **Sky** (© 600/600-2828; www.skyairline.cl), with multiple daily flights to Santiago, Punta Arenas, Balmaceda (Coyhaique), and Temuco. An **ETM bus** from the airport to the city's downtown bus terminal costs C$1,500; a taxi costs C$7,500. Agree on the fare before getting into the cab. There are several **car-rental agencies** at the airport, including Hertz, Alamo, and Avis.

BY BUS Puerto Montt's main terminal is at the waterfront (Diego Portales s/n), a 10- to 15-minute walk from downtown, or there are taxis to transport you. Regular bus service to and from most major cities, including Santiago, is provided by **Cruz del Sur** (© 65/254731), **Tur Bus** (© 65/253329), **Tas Choapa** (© 65/254828), and **Bus Norte** (© 65/252783).

BY CAR The Pan-American Highway nearly ends at Puerto Montt, before continuing on to the ferry port to Chiloé.

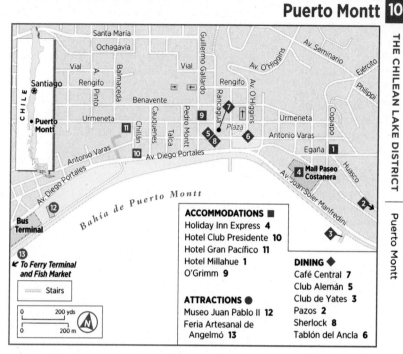

ACCOMMODATIONS ■
Holiday Inn Express **4**
Hotel Club Presidente **10**
Hotel Gran Pacífico **11**
Hotel Millahue **1**
O'Grimm **9**

ATTRACTIONS ●
Museo Juan Pablo II **12**
Feria Artesanal de
    Angelmó **13**

DINING ◆
Café Central **7**
Club Alemán **5**
Club de Yates **3**
Pazos **2**
Sherlock **8**
Tablón del Ancla **6**

GETTING AROUND

Puerto Montt is divided into *poblaciones,* or neighborhoods, scattered around the city's hilltops. From the city center to the east is the **Pelluco** district, where many of the city's good restaurants can be found, and to the west is the district **Angelmó,** with the city's fish market, port departures, and Feria Artesanal with great shopping; the two districts are connected by the coastal road Diego Portales. The city center is laid out on a grid system that abuts a steep cliff.

BY FOOT   The city center is small enough to be seen on foot. The crafts market and fish market in Angelmó are a 20-minute walk from the center, but you can take a cab. You'll need a taxi to reach the Pelluco district.

BY BUS   **Buses Cruz del Sur** (ⓒ **65/254731**) leaves for Puerto Varas 19 times daily from the bus terminal, and so do the independent white shuttle buses to the left of the coaches; look for the sign in the window that says PUERTO VARAS. Cruz del Sur also serves Chiloé, including Castro and Ancud, with 25 trips per day. **TransChiloé** (ⓒ **65/254934**) goes to Chiloé seven times per day from the terminal.

BY CAR   This is one of those places where renting a car can come in handy, given the ample sightseeing opportunities and pleasant drives in the area. Local car-rental agencies in Puerto Montt include **Hertz,** Calle de Servicio 1031 (ⓒ **65/313445;** www.hertz.com); **Avis,** Benavente 670 (ⓒ/fax **65/258199;** www.avischile.cl); and **Econo Rent,** Guillermo Gallardo 450 (ⓒ **65/254888;** econorent@telsur.cl). Hertz and Avis rent cars to travelers who wish to drive south along the Carretera Austral (see the "Driving the Carretera Austral" section in chapter 12, beginning on p. 338), and they can arrange to have the vehicle dropped off in Coyhaique. Some companies insist that you rent a 4×4 for the Carretera Austral (the importance of this during the summer is debatable if you stick to the main road; during the winter it could help if the road turns muddy). Calling the local office of each company is usually the best way to get bargain rates; but, in general, the rental drop-off fee is C$237,500, in addition to the daily cost.

VISITOR INFORMATION

The municipality has a small **tourist office** in the plaza at the corner of Antonio Varas and San Martín (☎ **65/261823**); it's open December through March daily from 9am to 9pm, and April through November Monday through Friday from 9am to 1pm and 2:30 to 7pm, Saturday and Sunday from 9am to 1pm. There is a largely unhelpful tourism kiosk in the main plaza (☎ **65/261808;** www.puertomonttchile.cl).

SPECIAL EVENTS   During the second week of February, the city holds its annual **Semana Puertomontina** (www.puertomonttchile.cl), with weeklong festivities that culminate in a fireworks display over the bay celebrating Puerto Montt's anniversary. Throughout the summer, arts and crafts exhibits are held in public plazas.

[FastFACTS]   PUERTO MONTT

Currency Exchange   You can exchange currency at **Trans AFEX,** Av. Diego Portales 516; **Cambios Inter,** Paseo Talca 84, Oficina 7 (☎ **64/253745**); **La Moneda de Oro,** in the bus terminal, Oficina 37; and **Eureka Tour,** Antonio Varas 445. Exchange houses are generally open Monday through Friday from 9am to 1pm and 2 to 6pm, Saturday from 9am to 2pm. For **ATMs,** look for banks at Urmeneta and Guillermo Gallardo downtown. Banks are open Monday through Friday from 9am to 2pm.

Hospital   Try either **Hospital Base,** Seminario, s/n (☎ **65/261100**), or **Hospital de la Seguridad,** Panamericana 400 (☎ **65/257333**).

Internet Cafe   Internet cafes come and go quickly, so it's best to walk to Urmeneta street and look for a sign, or simply ask at your hotel. Try **Arroba Cibercafé,** Guillermo Gallardo 218-A, or **New Ciber,** San Martín 230. Internet service costs C$500 per hour, but most hotels now have Wi-Fi access for guests.

Laundry   **Anny,** San Martín 167 (☎ **65/255397**); **Lavaseco Arcoiris,** San Martín 230; and **Lavatodo,** O'Higgins 231, are all spots to do your wash.

What to See & Do

The **Museo Juan Pablo II,** Av. Portales 991 (☎ **65/344457**), contains a medley of artifacts culled from this region. There's an interesting interpretive exhibit here of the Monte Verde archaeological dig that found bones estimated to be 12,000 years old. There's also an open-air railway exhibit next to the museum, but truthfully, the museum is worth a visit only if you have time to kill. It's open Monday through Friday from 9am to 7pm, Saturday and Sunday from 10am to 6pm. Admission is C$1,000.

TOUR OPERATORS & TRAVEL AGENCIES   **Ace Lagos Andinos,** Antonio Varas 445 (☎ **65/257686** or 9/707-9445), offers just about everything you could want, including tours to Parque Nacional Vicente Pérez, Termas de Puyehue, and Chiloé; sightseeing tours around the circumference of Lago Llanquihue; 2-night treks around Volcán Osorno with an overnight in a family home; and more.

Andina del Sud, Antonio Varas 437 (☏ **65/257797;** www.andinadelsud.cl), is the tour agency with the monopoly on Lago Todos los Santos for the lake crossing to Bariloche; they also offer city tours and sightseeing journeys, and transportation service to attractions. **Darwin's Trails,** Angelmo 2456, 2nd Floor (☏ **65/262099;** www.darwinstrails.com), is somewhat like a one-stop travel shop, with information and booking arrangements with nearly every outfitter, hotel, and program around Chile. Their location is far from the city center, though it is close to the arts and crafts market Feria Artesanal de Angelmó. They have a book exchange here, too.

SHOPPING   Puerto Montt is a great place to pick up souvenirs. On Avenida Angelmó, from the bus terminal to the fish market, is the **Feria Artesanal de Angelmó ★** (daily 9am–7pm, until 9pm in the summer), with dozens of stalls and specialty shops that peddle knitwear, ponchos, handicrafts, jewelry, regional foods, and more from areas around the Lake District, including Chiloé. It's about a 20-minute walk from the plaza, or you can take a taxi. There is also a large, tacky shopping mall south of the main plaza, with national and international chains.

Where to Stay

While most visitors will prefer to stay in Puerto Varas, there are numerous inexpensive small hostels and *residenciales* in Puerto Montt that might be convenient if you're planning an early morning departure via plane, bus, or ferry. Among them, **House Rocco** at Pudeto 233 (☏ **65/272897;** www.hospedajerocco.cl) and **Casa Perla** at Trigal 312 (☏ **65/262104;** www.casaperla.com) cater to international visitors.

EXPENSIVE

Hotel Club Presidente   This rather faded, somewhat overpriced hotel's classic, nautical-themed design appeals equally to executives and tourists, and handy kitchenettes give guests a little extra freedom. Located on the waterfront, in a central location close to shops, the Presidente is on busy Avenida Portales, but double-paned windows keep noise to a minimum. All rooms have either queen-size or king-size beds. The doubles are spacious, but the superiors are much larger and worth the extra $5; they also have ocean views. Most come with a small loveseat and a table and chairs. The rooms are decorated with creams and terra cotta, striped curtains, and nubby bedspreads. A breakfast buffet is served daily in the comfortable restaurant/bar on the eighth floor.

Av. Diego Portales 664, Puerto Montt. ☏ **65/251666.** Fax 65/251669. www.presidente.cl. 50 units. $163 double. Rates include buffet breakfast. AE, DC, MC, V. **Amenities:** Restaurant; bar; small heated pool; sauna. *In room:* TV, kitchenette.

MODERATE

Holiday Inn Express ★   Yes, it's a Holiday Inn, but the location is excellent, the views outstanding, there are all the amenities you need, and this is the best hotel for business travelers in town. It opened in 2006 over the Paseo Costanera shopping center right on the waterfront. Big windows, about half of which look out onto the harbor, are the highlight of the otherwise average rooms, which feature standard Holiday Inn unadventurous beige walls, carpet, and bedding.

Av. Costanera s/n, Puerto Montt. ☏ **65/566000.** www.hiexpress.com. 105 units. $117 double. Rates include buffet breakfast. AE, DC, MC, V. **Amenities:** Restaurant; bar; exercise room; room service. *In room:* TV, hair dryer, free Wi-Fi.

Hotel Gran Pacífico ★   Opened in late 2001, the Gran Pacífico is the city's only luxurious hotel, and its imposing 10-story structure towers over the waterfront. The imitation Art Deco lobby is sleek and modern, with lots of wood and marble. The rooms follow the same motif and are spacious, modern, and very bright. They have wood headboards for the beds, off-yellow wallpaper, and large-screen TVs. Those overlooking the water have breathtaking views (request an upper-level oceanview floor when you check in). The marble bathrooms are a tad small, but the size of the room makes up for it. For such a high-caliber hotel, the staff is not too efficient, nor do they speak much English, so be patient.

Urmeneta 719, Puerto Montt. *ℂ* **65/482100.** Fax 65/292979. www.hotelgranpacifico.cl. 48 units. $162 double; $255 suite. AE, DC, MC, V. **Amenities:** Restaurant; bar; lounge; exercise room; room service; sauna. *In room:* TV, minibar.

O'Grimm   One of the city's most established hotels, the O'Grimm is run by a friendly English-speaking staff and is adjacent to the popular O'Grimm Pub. Rooms are of varying sizes and each comes with sleek black and gray furniture and dark satinlike bedspreads. There's no view to mention, really, and the rooms are not as inviting as the price may suggest. Bathrooms are small and aging, but clean. The restaurant, pub, and bustling atmosphere downstairs are pleasant, and there's live music most nights.

Guillermo Gallardo 211, Puerto Montt. *ℂ* **65/252845.** Fax 65/258600. www.ogrimm.com. 26 units. $110 double; from $120 suite. AE, DC, MC, V. **Amenities:** Restaurant; bar; free Internet in business center. *In room:* TV, minibar, Wi-Fi (in some rooms).

INEXPENSIVE

Hotel Millahue   This older hotel is not particularly fancy, but it does offer clean, large double rooms and friendly service. All double rooms are sized differently but priced the same, and rooms on the fourth and fifth floors are the nicest, especially those whose numbers end in 06 and 07. There's a dining area for breakfast and hearty, set-menu Chilean meals, should you decide to eat in. Beds are average but offer standard comfort. The hotel is run by its owner, a friendly woman who strives to make guests feel at home.

Copiapó 64, Puerto Montt. *ℂ* **65/253829.** Fax 65/256317. www.hotelmillahue.cl. 25 units. $65 double. Rates include breakfast. MC, V. **Amenities:** Restaurant.

A HOTEL OUTSIDE OF PUERTO MONTT

The Cliffs Preserve ★★★ 📷   The Cliffs Preserve is set in as magical a setting as you will find in Chile. Their massive 3,200-hectare (8,000-acre) property, in a suburb about an hour from Puerto Montt, is covered in primary coastal rainforest, and a number of active excursions are arranged by top guides and naturalists. Horseback riding, hiking, boat trips to see penguins, sea lions, otters, and whales—the world's largest blue whale nursery is not far off shore—and even heliskiing are offered. The resort is also actively involved with the local community of Los Muermos; it funds an orphanage there and the hotel property includes a home for the families of fishermen.

The huge and well-designed two- to four-suite villas, each with their own wood-fired hot tub, are isolated from each other and overlook a breathtaking sheltered beach. You can rent an entire villa, just a suite, or a suite with the use of a common area that includes a kitchen and living room. The cuisine and wine on offer at the restaurant are as good as any resort in Chile; produce comes from an organic farm on the property.

1 hr. W of Puerto Montt. *ℂ* **888/780-3011.** Fax 65/256317. www.cliffspreserve.cl. 16 units. $2,700 4 nights/5 days per person Dec–Mar; $3,900 4 nights/5 days per person Apr–Nov. Rates based on double occupancy; all-inclusive with meals, wine, excursions, spa treatment, laundry service, and transport. MC, V. **Amenities:** Restaurant; bar; Jacuzzi; pool; sauna; spa. *In room:* A/C, free Wi-Fi.

Where to Dine

Puerto Montt is Chile's seafood capital. If you're feeling adventurous, try a Chilean favorite, such as abalone, sea urchin, or the regional barnacle. And where better to see, smell, and taste these fruits of the sea than the **Fish Market of Angelmó ★★★**, located at the end of Avenida Angelmó, where the artisan market terminates? It's open Monday through Sunday from 10am to 8pm during the summer, until 6pm during the winter. Like most fish markets, it's a little grungy, but it's a colorful stop nevertheless and there are several restaurant stalls offering the freshest local specialties around. *Be aware:* There have been reports that a few food stalls like to overcharge tourists, so double-check your bill with the menu.

Apart from the restaurants below, there are a handful of inexpensive cafes in Puerto Montt, including **Café Central,** Rancagua 117 (*©* **65/482888**). You'll find German pastries and beer from microbreweries at **Café Haussmann,** San Martín 185 (*©* **65/293380**), or **Club Alemán,** Varas 264 (*©* **65/252551**). If you're short on carbohydrates, try the pub **Tablón del Ancla,** Varas 350 (*©* **65/367554**), which serves greasy platters of sandwiches, *a lo pobres* (meat with french fries, onions, and a fried egg), *pichangas* (various meats, cheeses, olives, and salami drizzled with vinegar), and even pork knuckle. It's especially popular in the evenings or when a game is on, as it has some of the cheapest draft beer in town.

Club de Yates ★ SEAFOOD   The light-blue Club de Yates looks like a traditional seafood restaurant that sits out over the water like a pier. Inside, though, the atmosphere is white tablecloths, candlesticks, and sharp waiters in bow ties; it's one of the more elegant dining areas in town. This is a good place to come if you're looking for typical Chilean seafood dishes, such as razor clams broiled with Parmesan or sea bass *margarita* (sea bass in a creamy shellfish sauce). It has a great waterfront view and is about 1km (½ mile) from the plaza toward Pelluco.

Av. Juan Soler Manfredini 200. *©* **65/282810.** Main courses C$10,000–C$15,000. AE, DC, MC, V. Daily noon–4pm and 7:30pm–midnight.

Pazos CHILEAN   This is the place to come if you're interested in sampling *curanto* but don't have time to make it to Chiloé. *Curanto* is that island's specialty, a mixture of mussels, clams, sausage, chicken, pork, beef, and a gooey pancake steamed in a large pot and served with a cup of broth. Pazos also serves a variety of other seafood items, such as sea urchin omelets and the shellfish cornucopia, *sopa marina.* The restaurant is on the waterfront in Pelluco, in a 90-year-old home. It's very popular with summer visitors to Puerto Montt.

Av. General Juan Soler Manfredini s/n, Balneario Pelluco. *©* **65/252552.** Main courses C$3,500–C$8,000. AE, DC, MC, V. Daily 12:15–3pm and 8:15–10pm.

Sherlock ★ 🏛 CHILEAN/PUB FARE   The most happening place in Puerto Montt is this centrally located pub, cafe, and restaurant all rolled into one. There's lots of charm, a nice bar, and wood furniture, and it fills with locals at all hours of the day. This is a good place to get some local color, and they serve excellent homemade Chilean cuisine and delicious sandwiches. Try the albacore steak with a Chilean tomato-and-onion salad or the Sherlock sandwich with beef strips, tomato, corn, cheese, bacon, and grilled onion.

Antonio Varas 542. *©* **65/288888.** Main courses C$3,500–C$6,000; sandwiches C$1,500–C$4,000. MC, V. Daily 9am–2am.

10 FERRY CROSSINGS TO THE CARRETERA AUSTRAL & CRUISES TO PATAGONIA

Few fjordlands in the world can match the elegant beauty of Chile's southern region. Its entire coast is composed of thousands of little-explored islands, canals, and sounds. A few companies offer trips through these remote channels south to Puerto Chacabuco in the Aysén region, principally **Naviera Austral. Navimag** offers a popular trip through the southern fjords as far as Puerto Natales in Southern Patagonia, and to the Laguna San Rafael Glacier, as does the luxury liner *Skorpios*. (Please note that the itineraries can vary, and you need to reserve a berth well in advance of your trip.)

FERRY SERVICES Puerto Montt is the hub for ferries heading south. If you are planning a trip down the Carretera Austral, you'll need to travel to or from Puerto Montt or Chiloé by ferry (unless you enter through Argentina). During the summer, passengers and autos can cross to Pumalín Park and Caleta Gonzalo by ferry. This route is preferred but available only from December to March. For information about ferry crossings to Caleta Gonzalo as well as between La Arena and Puelche at the start of the Carretera Austral, see "Pumalín Park," in chapter 11.

To reach Chiloé, you need to head to Pargua west of Puerto Montt, see "Getting to the Island," in chapter 12. **Naviera Austral,** at Angelmó 2187 (in the ferry terminal or Terminal de Transbordadores), in Puerto Montt (© **65/270400;** www.naviera ustral.cl), offers ferry crossings to Chaitén on the Carretera Austral, the quickest and, in the end, the cheapest way to get a vehicle to the famed highway. Tickets cost C$18,000 per passenger and C$70,000 per car.

Navimag Ferries ★ 🛥 Navimag offers 24-hour trips to Puerto Chacabuco in Aysén and 70-hour journeys to Puerto Natales, memorable for the sublime, pristine landscape, tiny outposts of civilization, and the camaraderie that grows between travelers. While you'll mostly travel through forested, sheltered channels dotted with cascades, it can get rough across the Golfo de Penas, where some passengers may suffer seasickness. The ships are passenger and freight ferries with a variety of cabins, from basic shared accommodations to higher-end cabins and low-end bunks separated only by curtains. Check the website for schedules and fares.

Offices in Puerto Montt, at Av. Angelmó 1735, in the Terminal de Transbordadores. © **2/442-3114.** www.navimag.com (online tickets). Prices vary but average $370–$1,800 per person for the 4-night round-trip journey to Puerto Natales, and $80–$306 per person for the 2-night round-trip journey to Puerto Chacabuco.

Nomads of the Seas ★★★ 📷 This is one of the world's great small-scale luxury cruise-ship operators. The ship *Atmosphere,* which departs and returns from Puerto Montt, doesn't visit better-known sites, such as Laguna San Rafael, in an effort to journey to places with absolutely no other ships or tourists. Although the price tag is outrageous, it's a small price to pay to visit the farthest reaches of a wild and unruly Patagonia filled with glaciers, mountain lakes, snow-covered volcanoes, hot springs, and fjords that few others have ever laid eyes on. To accomplish this feat, the 159-ft. *Atmosphere* fuses nature and technology like few cruise ships have ever done. It carries an army of machinery including a Bell 407 helicopter, six custom-built jet boats, a Hurricane 920 RIB zodiac, four Helitour Mission zodiacs, various rescue boats, and top fly-fishing gear.

Even though it frequently charters rough seas, it's nothing but smooth sailing on this ship. Each of the 14 windowed cabins comes with such perks as soft beds with high thread-count sheets. The main deck combines a sleek circular bar, living space with plush designer couches and chairs, a small library, and elegant dining room. A "wet room" for gear and a spa area with hot tubs and Jacuzzis fill different levels on the back end of the ship. The eco-friendliness of this operation leaves something to be desired, however; this is one instance where being green might not be possible with the use of such high powered, gas-guzzling machines.

Nomads also offers 3-day gastronomic cruises near Puerto Montt and Chiloé during the shoulder season.

Del Inca 4446, Piso 4, Las Condes, Santiago. ⓒ **2/414-4600** in Santiago, 866/790-4560 from U.S. and Canada. www.nomadsoftheseas.com. 14 units. $17,850 per person fly-fishing tour, $12,138 per person ecotourism tour Dec 27–Mar 14. $14,875 per person fly-fishing tour; $10,115 per person ecotourism tour Oct–Dec 27 and Mar 14–May; $4,200 per person tasting Chile tour. Rates include food and alcohol; excursions include use of helicopter and jet boats, plus transfers. **Amenities:** Restaurant; bar; Jacuzzi. *In room:* Hair dryer.

11 CHILOÉ

The "Great Island of Chiloé" is a land of myths and magic—of emerald, rolling hills shrouded in mist, and tiny, picturesque coves that harbor a colorful palette of wooden fishing skiffs. This is Chile's second-largest island, located south of Puerto Montt with an eastern coast that faces the Gulf of Ancud and a western, wet Pacific shore. With the exception of a few small towns, the landscape here by and large is pastoral, with a deference to development that tends to make travelers feel as if they have been transported back a century. Across the island, wooden churches modeled after a Bavarian, neoclassic style appear like a beacon in every bay; they are so lovely and architecturally unique that UNESCO deemed them World Heritage sites.

Visually appealing as it is, Chiloé is truly defined by its people, the hardy, character-rich Chilotes, who can still be seen plowing their fields with oxen or pulling in their catch of the day the same way they have for centuries. Spanish conquistadors occupied Chiloé as early as 1567, followed by Jesuit missionaries and Spanish refugees pushed off the mainland by Mapuche Indian attacks. For 3 centuries, Chiloé was the only Spanish stronghold south of the Río Bío-Bío, and its isolation produced a singular culture among its residents, who, after so much time, are now a *mestizo* blend of Indian and Spanish blood. The Chilotes' rapid and closed speech, local slang, mythical folklore, and style of food, tools, and architecture were and still are uniquely different from their counterparts on the mainland. The downside of Chiloé's limited contact with the outside world is a dire poverty that has affected (and continues to affect) many of the island's residents. Most families eke out a living by relying on their own garden patch and livestock, animals that can be seen pecking and grazing along the side of the road. Off the main highway, it is as common to see residents traveling on horseback or by fishing boat as it is by vehicle.

I recommend a day or overnight trip to Chiloé rather than spending time in the grimy environs of Puerto Montt, but with one caveat: Rent a car. While the principal cities **Ancud** and **Castro** can easily be reached by bus, the true pleasure of visiting Chiloé is losing yourself on backcountry roads and discovering picturesque little bays and lookout points that are otherwise inaccessible by bus, and stopping at roadside stands for local cheese, fresh fish, and other delicacies. This chapter covers the highlights here, but the island is easy to navigate with a road map. (See "Driving to & Around Chiloé," later). Chiloé also boasts the **Parque Nacional Chiloé,** where visitors can indulge themselves with a walk through primordial old-growth rainforest that once blanketed the island. The island's tourism infrastructure is improving, but visitors should still

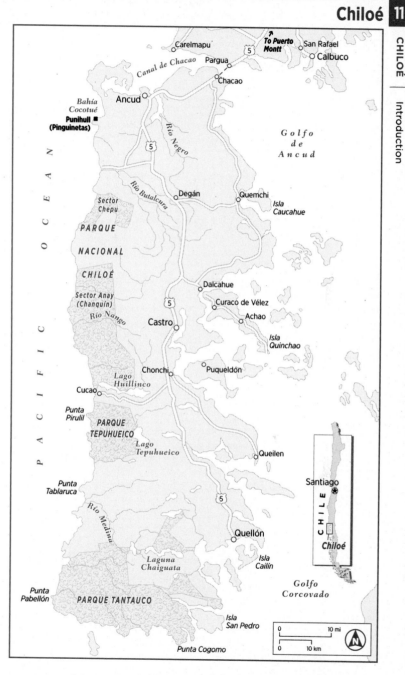

To Puerto Montt

Carelmapu

San Rafael
Calbuco

Canal de Chacao   Pargua
Chacao

Ancud

Bahía
Cocotué
Punihuil ■
(Pinguinetas)

Río Negro

Golfo
de
Ancud

Sector
Chepu

PARQUE

NACIONAL

CHILOÉ

Sector Anay
(Chanquín)

Río Nango

Río Butalcura   Degán

Quemchi

Isla
Caucahue

Dalcahue
Curaco de Vélez
Achao

Castro

Isla
Quinchao

Chonchi   Puqueldón

Lago
Huillinco

Cucao

Punta
Pirulil

PARQUE
TEPUHUEICO

Lago
Tepuhueico

Queilen

Punta
Tablaruca

Río Medina

Punta
Pabellón   PARQUE TANTAUCO

Laguna
Chaiguata

Quellón

Isla
Cailín

Isla
San Pedro

Punta Cogomo

Santiago ✪

CHILE

Chiloé

Golfo
Corcovado

PACIFIC   OCEAN

0   10 mi
0   10 km

expect modest accommodations. The tedious rain that falls more than half the year here makes for soggy shoes and limited views; nevertheless, Chiloé rates as one of Chile's top attractions for its cultural value and natural beauty. Useful websites for information about Chiloé are **www.chiloe.cl** and **www.interpatagonia.cl**.

EXPLORING THE ISLAND

Most visitors use Castro as a central base for exploring the island. I wouldn't really recommend a stay in Ancud unless you are short on time. Quellón is considered primarily a ferry departure point for Chaitén on the Carretera Austral (see chapter 12), but it may well emerge as a site for embarking on whale-watching in the coming years. On a clear day—not very often—one can see Volcán Osorno and the towering, snowcapped Andes in the distance.

You'll need a day or two to explore Castro, Dalcahue, Achao, and Chonchi; a day to see the national park (more if you wish to do a long hike or camp out); and about a half-day to see Ancud (with a stop in Chacao). Also consider visiting Parque Tantauco at the island's southern tip, for which you should plan 2 days due to its difficult access.

Getting To the Island

BY BOAT   Fortunately, the plan to build a giant bridge between the mainland and Chiloé—a surefire white elephant—has been scrapped. Meanwhile, two ferry companies operate continuously between Pargua (on the mainland) and Chacao (on the island), shuttling passengers and vehicles. If you are taking a bus to Chiloé, you won't need to worry about paying the fare because it's included in the price of the bus ticket; but if you've rented a car, the cost is C$9,000 one-way. The ride lasts 30 to 40 minutes. (And, yes, there are toilets on board the ferry.) In compensation for the end of the plan to build the bridge, Santiago has promised to invest heavily in infrastructure on the

---

 DRIVING TO & AROUND chiloé

Chiloé is a sightseer's paradise and, therefore, it is highly recommended that visitors rent a vehicle. You will be able to cover more ground and take full advantage of seemingly endless photoworthy vista points, historic churches, and charming little villages. Hopping from island to island in a vehicle is a snap, and visitors can pack a lot of action into just 1 day. In years past, you would need to rent a car in Puerto Montt or Puerto Varas, where the rates are still the cheapest, though you would need to pay the C$9,000 one-way ferry fee. Recently rental service became available in Castro at **Salfa** (Mistral 499; ✆ **65/630422**).

Local bus service from town to town is frequent and inexpensive. More information about bus service can be found in the sections for each specific town later. If you're driving your own rental car onto the ferry, don't line up behind the trucks and buses, but go to the front of the line and park to the left—that will make you visible to the ferry attendants, and they'll squeeze you onto the next available ferry.

Gas stations are sporadic. Fill up in Puerto Montt or Puerto Varas, and again in Ancud. If visiting the national park, fill up in Castro or Conchi.

CHILOÉ's world heritage churches

Some 70 of Chiloé's churches, without a doubt, are the island's most singular attractions, and together with some in Germany, Norway, and the U.S., unique in having been built entirely of wood and without any nails. The humble yet striking churches represent a rare form of architecture, the Chiloé "school" of religious architecture brought about by the fusion of European and indigenous cultural traditions, namely those of the Jesuit missionaries of the 17th and 18th centuries and the island's early inhabitants, the Chonos and Huilliches.

Jesuit missionaries first arrived on the island in 1608, conducting circular missions wherein they traveled the archipelago throughout the year, stopping for several days at a mission site and spreading their brand of religion. But unlike other missionary groups, the Jesuits attempted to learn the languages and the cultural traditions of those they were hoping to convert. Thus, it was both their respect for traditional building methods and the Jesuits' absence for much of the year that afforded the indigenous peoples of the island the opportunity to lay such a heavy influence on the construction of each church.

The styles and layouts of the churches can be traced back to Europe: **Chonchi's** represents neoclassicism; the church in **Nercón** is neo-Renaissance;

and in **Achao,** you'll find baroque, inspired by the first Bavarian Jesuits. However, the interiors and the locations chosen for each church reflect the inspiration of their local indigenous builders. A close look inside each church offers numerous examples of techniques that were borrowed from shipbuilding, such as the use of wooden pegs and joints instead of nails. The center of the roof, if imagined inverted, often resembles the hull of a boat, with three naves to a church. Moreover, nearly all the chapels in Chiloé face the water, with central towers that functioned as beacons for sailors. The influence of the island's early maritime inhabitants continues to be a point of pride for those who call it home.

Although each church shares the same facade of semicircular arches, each church varies greatly in color and size, the latter representing what type of festivals were to be held at the church. The church at Achao is the oldest and at Quinchao the largest, but the church at Tenaún, with its royal blue exterior and white facade—upon which are painted two large white stars—is probably the most impressive. Sixteen have been declared UNESCO World Heritage sites, but there are many more. Visit **www.rutadelasiglesias.cl** for more information.

---

island, so expect construction work for the next several years. Long distance ferries also run from Quellón to Chaitén and Puerto Chacabuco. For information, call **Naviera Austral** (✆ **65/682207;** www.navieraustral.cl). Offices are located in Quellón.

BY BUS   Several companies provide service to Ancud, Castro, and Quellón from Puerto Montt, and even Santiago and Punta Arenas. In Puerto Montt, daily departures for Ancud and Castro leave from the bus terminal. **Cruz del Sur** (✆ **65/254731;** www.busescruzdelsur.cl) has 18 trips per day, **Transchiloé** (✆ **65/254934**) has 7 trips per day, and **Queilén Bus** (✆ **65/253468**) has 8 trips per day. From Puerto Varas, try **Cruz del Sur,** at San Francisco 1317, with five trips per day (✆ **65/236969**). **Cruz del Sur** (✆ **2/779-0607**) also offers three services per day from Santiago to Chiloé; the trip takes about 15 hours. Buses ride over on the ferry; you can remain in your seat or step out and walk around.

11 ANCUD

95km (59 miles) SE of Puerto Montt; 146km (91 miles) N of Castro

Ancud, home to 27,000 residents, was founded in 1767 as a fort to monitor passing sea traffic to and from Cape Horn. It was, for many years, the capital of Chiloé until the provincial government pulled up stakes and moved to Castro in 1982. Ancud is a bustling, rambling port town with much to see, but Castro is a more convenient base if you want to reach the island's outlying areas. This was the last Spanish outpost in Chile, and visitors can view the fort ruins here; there's also a good museum depicting Chilote history and culture and another introducing the island's world heritage churches.

Essentials

GETTING THERE

BY BUS For regular bus service from Puerto Montt to Ancud, see "Getting to the Island," earlier. Ancud has a central bus station, the **Terminal Municipal,** at the intersection of Avenida Aníbal Pinto and Marcos Vera; from here, you'll need to take a taxi to the center of town, or a local bus headed toward the plaza. Frequent buses leave from this station for destinations such as Castro, Dalcahue, and Quellón; try **Cruz del Sur/Transchiloé** (© 65/622265) or **Queilén Bus** (© 65/621140).

BY CAR Rte. 5 (the Pan-American Hwy.) is a well-paved road that links Ancud with nearly every city on the island. The paved highway ends just south of Quellón.

ORIENTATION

Ancud is spread across a minor peninsula, with the Canal de Chacao to the east and the Golfo de Quetalmahue to the west; it is 27km (17 miles) from the Chacao ferry dock. The city is not laid out on a regular grid pattern, and its crooked streets might easily confuse anyone driving into the city. Avenida Aníbal Pinto is the main entrance road that funnels drivers into the center of town. Most attractions are located within several blocks of the plaza.

VISITOR INFORMATION

Sernatur's office is on the plaza, at Libertad 655 (© **65/622800;** fax 65/622665). It's open daily from 8:30am to 7pm during January and February; the rest of the year it's open Monday through Thursday from 8:30am to 5:30pm, Friday from 8:30am to 4:30pm, and closed on weekends.

SPECIAL EVENTS From the second week in January to the last week of February, the city hosts the "Different and Magical Summer of Ancud." The event kicks off with classical music concerts and a 3-day food and folklore festival at the Arena Gruesa (third week in January), a shore-fishing contest (second week of February), and culminates with a fireworks display, again in Arena Gruesa (third week of February). For more information, call © **65/628163** (municipal tourism information) or Sernatur (© **65/622800**).

[FastFACTS] ANCUD

Currency Exchange There are no places to exchange money here, but there are a couple of ATMs on Ramírez, near the plaza.

Hospital The hospital is at Almirante Latorre 301 (© **65/622356**).

Internet Access   Internet access can be found at **Entel,** on Pudeto 219 (on the Plaza, near Correos de Chile).

Laundry   Laundry services are available at the **Clean Center,** Pudeto 45, half a block from the plaza.

What to See & Do

Fuerte San Antonio   Built in 1770 and fortified with cannons aimed at the port entrance, Fort San Antonio was Spain's last stronghold in Chile after the War of Independence. The Spanish flag last flew here on January 19, 1826, and just 6 days later, Peru's El Callao surrendered, ending Spanish rule in South America forever. Okay, it's not much, but the site affords a sweeping ocean view, and the Hostería Ancud is next to the site if you're looking for a place for lunch.

San Antonio and Cochrane (below Hostería Ancud). No phone. Free admission. Daily 24 hrs.

Iglesias de Chiloé Centro de Visitantes   While Ancud doesn't have a particularly important church of its own, this new museum is the best introduction to exploring the island's world heritage churches. Old doors and walls hang artfully in the middle of the room amid the glow of the stained glass windows. Scale models that peel back some of the layers of wood are rather astonishing. For a nice view of Ancud, you can climb up into the church tower.

Errázuriz 227. ✆ **65/621046.** www.iglesiasdechiloe.cl. Free admission. Daily 10am-12:30pm and 2:30-5:30pm.

Museo Regional de Ancud Audelio Bórquez Canobra ★ ☺   This handsome, well-designed museum features a wide variety of exhibits related to the history and culture of Chiloé. The museum includes a large courtyard with sculptures depicting the mythological characters that form part of Chilote folklore. Inside you'll find interactive displays designed for kids and a variety of archaeological items, such as Indian arrowheads and nautical pieces, as well as displays explaining the farming and wool-production techniques used by Chilotes. A permanent exhibit covers the entire span of Chiloé's history, from the pre-Columbian era to the 20th century. Temporary exhibits display photography, sculpture, and contemporary art.

Libertad 370. ✆ **65/622413.** Admission C$1,000 adults, C$500 children. Jan-Feb Mon-Sun 10:30am-7pm; Mar-Dec Mon-Fri 10:30am-12:30pm and 2:30-5:30pm, Sat-Sun 10am-2pm.

Pingüineras Puñihuil   One of the only places in the world where Humboldt and Magellanic penguins habitats overlap is at this large colony 28km (18 miles) outside of Ancud. It's also an important habitat for seabirds and marine otters. All wildlife can be found on a set of three small islets, just 5 minutes from a beautiful beach, which can be seen on 35-minute boat tours that leave every 20 minutes throughout the day. Joint efforts among tour operators have ensured shorter wait times, a limited number of boats per day, and a stronger conservation effort. The national monument is now watched over by CONAF, the national park service, and conditions have improved drastically.

Reservations are essential, especially during the summer, as there are a limited number of spots available. An office should be open in Ancud sometime in 2011. There are a few small restaurants and cabins on and near the beach, which are worth sticking around in as the setting is rather stunning. The road from Ancud tends to be bumpy, though there are plans to have it paved in the near future. If you do not have your own transportation, it's best to visit the Pingüineras on a tour with Austral Adventures

(☏ 065/625-977; www.austral-adventures.com; C$30,875 per person) or to hitch-hike, as public transportation (buses from Ancud stop 2km/1.5 miles away) is sporadic. Taxis from Ancud average about C$20,000 roundtrip, including a wait while you take a tour. Ecoturismo Puñihuil also accepts volunteers to become guides and will provide lodging and some food, though they require a 1- to 2-month commitment.

Puñihuil. ☏ **8/317-4302.** www.pinguineraschiloe.cl. C$5,000 per person. Daily 10am-7pm (Aug-March).

SHOPPING

For a selection of regional handicrafts, including knitwear, baskets, local foodstuffs, and carved wooden utensils and crafts, try the **Fería Rural y Artesanal,** between Prat and Dieciocho streets (no phone; Mon–Sat 8am–9:30pm, Sun and holidays 8:30am–7:30pm). For mouthwatering smoked salmon and other local foodstuffs, stop on your way in or out of Chiloé at **Die Raucherkate,** a German-owned smokery located about 2km (1¼ miles) before the Chacao ferry dock (☏ **9/444-5912**). There is a SMOKED SALMON sign that can be easy to miss, so keep your eyes peeled.

Where to Stay

MODERATE

Caulín Lodge ★★ ☺ 🎒   The Caulín Lodge is not a woodsy hotel, but rather consists of eight cabins fronting an isolated beach and backed by a forest called the Fundo Los Cisnes, a private ecological reserve. These features make Caulín the best choice for visitors who seek quiet, undeveloped surroundings. The cabins at Caulín are more suitable for visitors with a private vehicle because the hamlet of Caulín is about 25km (16 miles) from Ancud, although taxi service is available for a moderate C$5,000. All wooden cabins face a splendid estuary that's home to flamingos and black-necked swans; the cabins are rustic but comfortable and clean, and have kitchens. Cabins have two or three bedrooms, one with a full-size bed and the other(s) with a twin and a bunk bed. The spacious living area has wood floors and is warmed by a *cancahua*, a ceramic fireplace typical of the region. There is a cozy rough-hewn wood pub/restaurant, although a few minutes' walk down the beach sits the popular Ostras Caulín (see "Where to Dine," later).

Road to Caulín, 9km (5½ miles) from port of Chacao. ☏ **9/330-1220.** www.caulinlodge.cl. 8 cabins. $80-$140 cabin. AE, DC, MC, V. **Amenities:** Restaurant; outdoor pool; sauna; tennis court. *In room:* Kitchen.

Hostería Ancud ★   Part of the Panamericana Hoteles chain, the Hostería Ancud is as upscale as it gets in Ancud, and it is the logical choice for travelers who are not comfortable sleeping in a hostel or a funky little hotel. It fronts the Gulf of Quetalmahue and is next to the ruins of the old Fort San Antonio. All rooms come with a partial view of the ocean, as does the airy, split-level lounge and restaurant and the large outdoor deck. Rooms are tight and somewhat worn but offer all the necessary comforts. The interior bedroom walls are made of polished alerce logs, and the lobby is adorned with woodcarvings from the region. The *hostería* also has one of the better restaurants in town (see "Where to Dine," later), as well as a cozy bar with a giant fireplace.

San Antonio 30. ☏ **65/622340.** Fax 65/622350. www.panamericanahoteles.cl. 24 units. $91 double. AE, DC, MC, V. **Amenities:** Restaurant; bar; lounge. *In room:* TV, free Wi-Fi.

Hotel Galeón Azul ★   Like the Hostería Ancud, this hotel's strength is its location—perched high on a cliff above the sea—and although the rooms are not nearly as nice, some travelers prefer the character of this bed-and-breakfast to that of the

"see food" EVERYWHERE: WHAT TO EAT ON CHILOÉ

One of the best experiences in Chiloé is sampling the local specialties of fish and shellfish dishes the Chilotes have invented over time. You'll commonly see dried and smoked mussels hanging in markets, but I haven't had the courage to try them yet. Another common sight (though widespread throughout Chile) is the **cochayuyo,** dried seaweed tied in bundles that Chileans use for stew. Chile's plentiful salmon farms are across the sound in the Andean fjords, and Chiloé has several oyster farms along its coast, so you'll see both items frequently on the menu.

Cancato   Salmon stuffed with sausage, tomatoes, and cheese, and steamed in tinfoil.

Carapacho   A rich crab "casserole" with a breaded crust.

Curanto   Perhaps the most famous dish here in Chiloé, traditionally prepared in a hole in the ground (similar to a New England clambake). First, hot rocks are placed in the hole and then layered with mussels, clams, beef, pork, chicken, sausage, and potatoes, and topped off with tasteless, chewy pancakes called **milcaos.** Most restaurants cook this dish in a pot and often call it **pulmay;** it is then served with a cup of broth. You are supposed to take a bite and then sip the broth; I recommend you just pour the broth over the meat and fish for a tastier meal.

Ancud. With porthole windows, a nautical motif, and curved walls, the big, sunflower-yellow hotel feels somewhat like a ship—an aging ship, that is, since rooms are rather drab and lifeless. Upstairs an intriguing, narrow hallway has a high ceiling that peaks into skylights. The hotel is next to the regional museum; large windows look out onto the museum's sculpture garden. The most attractive part of the hotel is its sunny restaurant, with glass walls that look out onto the ocean.

Av. Libertad 751. ℂ **65/622567.** Fax 65/622543. www.hotelgaleonazul.cl. 15 units. $125 double. No credit cards. **Amenities:** Restaurant. *In room:* TV, free Wi-Fi.

INEXPENSIVE

Mundo Nuevo ★ 🛏   This is a hostel? You might ask yourself this question while standing in front of the fine, three-story wooden building right on the waterfront overlooking the Ancud Bay. On a sunny day, you'll be tempted to look over the sea from the terrace alongside the entrance. The spotless, pastel yellow rooms are bright and airy except for one spectacular top-floor double featuring a wooden floor polished to a mirror finish and a boat-shaped double bed, under an angled, unpainted wooden ceiling. Prices include breakfast.

Costanera (Salvador Allende) 748. ℂ **65/628383.** www.newworld.cl. 12 units. Dorm $20 per person; double $26 with shared bathroom; double $38 with private bathroom. Rates include breakfast. No credit cards. **Amenities:** Restaurant; kitchen; bikes; Internet (in lobby); TV room. *In room:* No phone, free Wi-Fi.

Where to Dine

For good, inexpensive seafood meals, including Chilote dishes such as *curanto, carapacho,* and *cancato,* try **La Pincoya,** Av. Prat 61 (ℂ **65/622613**), which also offers views of fishermen at the pier engaging in hectic business from their colorful fishing skiffs. One restaurant popular with tourists and locals alike is **Sacho** (© **65/622260**), which can be found inside the somewhat grungy market (Local 7). Across from the market is **El Cangrejo,** Dieciocho 155 (© **65/623091**), which serves dishes such as crab *carapacho* in a kitschy ambience. Reservations at these establishments are neither necessary nor accepted. Also try **El Mundo de la Papa,** Cochrane 412 (© **65/621-618**), a small cafe and bistro serving native potato dishes.

EXPENSIVE

Casa Mar ★ INTERNATIONAL   This upscale two-level pub and restaurant, a block from Mundo Azul hostel on the waterfront, has the most international menu on the island. Chilean and Chilote staples, such as *lomo a la pobre* (steak topped with a fried egg) and *caldillo de congrio* (conger eel stew), are served along with farther-afield dishes such as turkey curry, spaghetti, and sushi.

Costanera and Errázuriz. © **65/624481.** Main courses C$4,500–C$7,500. AE, DC, MC, V. Mon–Fri noon–late; Sat noon–7pm.

Hostería Ancud ★★ INTERNATIONAL/CHILEAN   The expansive dining area here commands a superb view of the ocean, and there are good offerings from the menu that mix Chilean specialties with international dishes. Seafood such as oysters on the half-shell and king crab are offered as appetizers, as well as king crab casserole and conger eel with sea urchin sauce for entrees. Meat dishes include pork loin with mustard sauce and risotto. There's also a bar for a quiet evening drink. If weather permits, you can watch the sunset from the deck.

San Antonio 30. © **65/622340.** Main courses C$4,500–C$8,500. AE, DC, MC, V. Daily noon–11pm.

MODERATE

Galeón Azul ★ CHILEAN   The Galeón's yellow-painted dining area has sweeping ocean views, so be sure to get a table that sits up against the front windows. The menu here features several Chilote specials, such as *curanto,* as well as standard Chilean fish and meat grilled and served with a choice of sauces. Try the salmon stuffed with ham and mushrooms or the garlicky *locos* (abalone).

Av. Libertad 751. © **65/622567.** Main courses C$4,500–C$6,500. No credit cards. Daily 11am–3pm and 7–11pm.

Kurantón ★★ CHILEAN   As the name implies, this restaurant specializes in *curanto.* Other standards include *paila marina* (a fish stew), but what really stands out is their luscious, creamy *carapacho* that is speckled with crabmeat. The walls of Kurantón are covered with old photos and antiques, making for an amusing place to split a bottle of wine and sample local specialties.

Prat 94. © **65/623090.** Main courses C$4,000–C$6,000. MC, V. Daily noon–11pm.

Ostras Caulín ★★ 🎁 CHILEAN/SEAFOOD   Oyster lovers won't want to miss this tiny restaurant on the shore of Caulín, about 9km (5½ miles) from Chacao and 25km (16 miles) from Ancud (from the ferry, follow the signs and turn right onto a gravel road). The restaurant, with its hardwood floors and cheery red tablecloths, sits on an estuary where they farm their own oysters, and they offer three sizes: *especial, extra,* and *exportación,* all on the half-shell and all exceptionally fresh. The menu is really just oysters served fried, stewed, and cocktailed, but there is salmon and beef stew, too. Afternoon tea is served with cakes and sandwiches daily from 3 to 7pm. An adjacent six-person cabin (C$40,000) is available to rent, and the owners run bird-watching tours.

On the shore in Caulín. ℰ/fax **9/643-7005.** www.ostrascaulin.cl. Main courses C$4,500–C$15,000. AE, DC, MC, V. Daily 8am–10pm (until midnight Jan–Feb).

INEXPENSIVE

Pastelería Pedersen ★ ▮ CAFE/BAKERY   This is the place to blow your diet. There are plenty of cakes and numerous tarts to choose from, but it's the raspberry-topped cheesecake, a perennial favorite, that often sells out. They serve a rare cup of decent Joe, too. The pastry house is located in an old home with plenty of windows from which to watch a storm come in over the sea.

Cochrane 470. ℰ **65/622642.** Desserts C$1,500. No credit cards. Daily noon–7pm.

CASTRO

146km (91 miles) S of Ancud; 99km (61 miles) N of Quellón

Castro is spread across a promontory on the eastern shore of Chiloé, midway between Ancud and Quellón. It is the capital of Chiloé, and Chile's third-oldest city, with about 29,000 inhabitants. Visitors to the island often choose Castro as a base for its central proximity to many attractions. While not the most architecturally charming of towns, Castro's shores are nonetheless interesting for their rickety homes on stilts, known as *palafitos,* and the main church, which is painted as colorfully as an Easter egg.

Essentials

GETTING THERE & AROUND

BY BUS   You'll find the bus terminal at the corner of Esmeralda and Sotomayor. For buses to Dalcahue and Isla Quinchao, take **Buses Arriagada,** San Martín 681; for Dalcahue and Chonchi, take **Colectivos** from the Terminal Municipal; for Isla Lemuy, take **Buses Gallardo** from its office at San Martín 681; and for transportation to the national park, take **Buses Arroyo** or **Buses Ojeda** from the Terminal Municipal. The majority of these bus companies are independently owned and operated, so it's difficult to obtain reliable information about schedules and fares in advance. I recommend showing up at the terminal or checking at the tourist information kiosk (see "Visitor Information," below) to ask questions or book a tour.

BY CAR   To get to Castro from Ancud, head south on the island's only highway for 146km (91 miles), and from Quellón, north on the highway for 99km (61 miles). The cheapest car rentals anywhere in Chiloé can be found at **Salfa** (Mistral 499; ℰ **65/630422**). Reserve well in advance, especially in the summer.

Chiloé is expanding its small airstrip with the hopes of turning it into a commercial airport in the near future, though scheduled flights were a long ways away at press-time.

VISITOR INFORMATION

A municipal **tourism kiosk** (no phone; daily 9am–6pm) on the main plaza offers a decent selection of brochures and tourist information, and the staff is fairly good at answering any questions on travel in Chiloé. There are also scale models of a handful of the area's UNESCO churches, which are an interesting diversion.

SPECIAL EVENTS   A weeklong gastronomic celebration takes place the third week in February, known as the **Festival Costumbrista Chilote.** If you like to eat, this enormous feast could very well be the highlight of your trip to Chiloé. The festival centers on traditional food and Chilote culture and mythological folklore, with men roasting meat over open fires and *curanto* simmering in grand cauldrons. Come hungry. For more information, call ☎ **65/633760.**

[FastFACTS] CASTRO

Currency Exchange   **Julio Barrientos,** Chacabuco 286 (☎ **65/635079**), is open Monday through Friday from 9am to 1pm and 3 to 7pm, and Saturday from 9am to 1pm; from December to March, it does not close for lunch. There are several ATMs in the downtown area.

Hospital   Castro's hospital is **Augusta Rifat,** Freire 852 (☎ **65/632444**).

Internet Access   Almost every hotel in Castro offers Internet access for its guests free of charge, though you can also try **Café la Brújula,** O'Higgins 308 (☎ **65/633229**), open daily from 9am to 2am, or even better, the **Entel** office at Bernardo O'Higgins 480 (☎ **65/620271**), open daily from 10am to 6pm.

Laundry   **Clean Center** is located at Balmaceda 230 (☎ **65/633132**).

Travel Agency   LAN Airline's representative is **Turismo Pehuén,** Blanco 299 (☎ **65/635254;** www.turismopehuen.cl), open Monday through Friday from 9am to 1:30pm and 3 to 7pm, and Saturday from 10am to 1pm; it's closed Sunday.

What to See & Do

You might begin a tour of Castro at the plaza and the neo-Gothic **Iglesia de San Francisco ★★**, painted in lilac and peachy-pink for Pope John Paul II's visit in 1987. Impossible to miss, the 1912 national monument glows on a dreary, gray Chiloé day (which is pretty much three-quarters of the year). A 2-year renovation ended in 2010, though the facade of the church looks more tired than ever.

From there, head down Esmeralda toward the waterfront and drop by the town's small **Museo Municipal de Castro ★**, half a block from the plaza (☎ **65/635967**). It's open from January to February Monday through Saturday from 9:30am to 7pm, and Sunday from 10:30am to 1pm; from March to December Monday through Friday from 9:30am to 1pm and 3 to 6:30pm, Saturday from 9:30am to 1pm, and is closed on Sunday. Admission is free, although a donation is encouraged. This earnest, small museum features displays of Chilote farming and household wooden implements that take visitors back in time to days when day-to-day living could be an arduous chore. There are also Indian artifacts such as arrowheads, bones, *boleadoras* (hunting tools); scale models; and a dramatic photographic exhibit of the damage done to Castro after the 1960 earthquake and flood.

Castro's curious ***palafitos,*** ramshackle houses built near the shore but atop stilts over water, are a colorful attraction and a tourism favorite, in spite of the fact that locals consider *palafitos* a somewhat unsanitary mess. There are four main spots to view these architectural oddities. The first two sites are at the town entrance, the third site is on the coast at the end of San Martín, and the fourth is at the cove of the Castro Fjord, on the way out of town on Rte. 5.

A short taxi ride will take you to the **Parque Municipal,** home to the Costumbrista Festival in February and the **Museo de Arte Moderno** (MAM; ☎ **65/635454**). Admission is free, and it's open daily January and February from 10am to 6pm and November, December, and March from 11am to 2pm. Opening hours can randomly change. If the museum is closed, call to arrange a private viewing. If the weather is clear, visitors to the park are treated to extended views of Castro and the Andes. MAM, housed in several renovated shingled barns, is one of the few contemporary

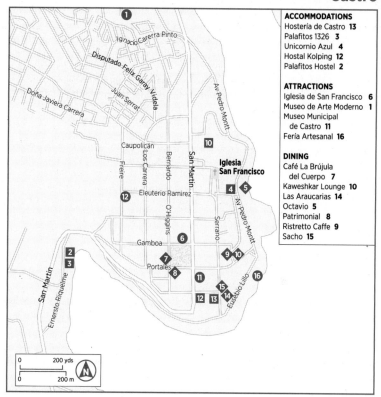

ACCOMMODATIONS
Hostería de Castro **13**
Palafitos 1326 **3**
Unicornio Azul **4**
Hostal Kolping **12**
Palafitos Hostel **2**

ATTRACTIONS
Iglesia de San Francisco **6**
Museo de Arte Moderno **1**
Museo Municipal
   de Castro **11**
Fería Artesanal **16**

DINING
Café La Brújula
   del Cuerpo **7**
Kaweshkar Lounge **10**
Las Araucarias **14**
Octavio **5**
Patrimonial **8**
Ristretto Caffe **9**
Sacho **15**

art museums in the country, and it often hosts exhibitions by some of Chile's most prominent artists. A cultural museum was also built here—it's the odd, grey-shingled, boat-shaped building on the harbor—but never opened due to bad construction. There are rumors of the city reinvesting to get things straightened out, but at last check it was still languishing.

SHOPPING

The **Fería Artesanal,** on Lillo at the port, brings together dozens of artisans who offer a superb selection of hand-knitted woolen goods, artisanal liquors and marmalades, and handicrafts. Here you'll find the island's typical tightly woven ponchos; the raw wool used makes them water resistant. Vendors open their booths independently, and hours are roughly from 10am to 5pm April through November, and from 10am to 9pm December through March.

Where to Stay
MODERATE

Hostería de Castro ★★ This *hostería* is about as upscale as hotels get in Castro. Built in 1970, the Hostería Castro is solidly comfortable and clean, and underwent a major overhaul in 2008. They added a new wing with 20 spacious suites, all with floor-to-ceiling windows offering ocean views (rooms on the western side have a leafy view), and a small spa with an indoor pool. The older rooms have been updated slightly and offer all the standard amenities of a midrange hotel; however, the rooms are still a little cramped. Ask to see several rooms, if you can, because a few are larger. Probably the best feature of the hotel is its cast-iron fireplace in the bar for cozying up with a pisco sour, and the decent bar/disco downstairs. The white-tiled bathrooms are ample. The A-frame, shingled roof has a lengthy skylight that brightens the interior hallways. Service is friendly, and the bar is popular with traveling Europeans, as is Las Araucarias restaurant (see "Where to Dine," later).

Chacabuco 202. ✆ **65/632301.** Fax 65/635688. www.hosteriadecastro.cl. 49 units. $84 double, $129 suite. AE, DC, MC, V. **Amenities:** Restaurant; bar; room service. *In room:* TV, free Wi-Fi.

Palafitos 1326 ★★★　This boutique property has proven just how much potential Castro's *palafitos* hold. Architect Edward Rojas Vega, who led the original fight in the 1970s and 80s to preserve Chiloé's stilted houses, transformed this building with a contemporary reinterpretation. Black-and-white tile floors and cool modish carvings and artwork are striking against the bare polished light wood walls, recycled doors, and many windows. Rooms vary in size (singles-triples) and view (sea or street), though the hip hand-woven wool and fiber textiles and cozy white comforters are uniform in each room. Sea-view rooms come with a small balcony. Facilities are limited to a small breakfast nook, a roof deck where you can watch the fishing boats pass with the ebb and flow of the tide, and a small library.

Riquelme 1326. ✆ **65/530-053.** www.palafito1326.cl. 12 units. $93-$116 double. MC, V. **Amenities:** Breakfast nook; free Wi-Fi.

Unicornio Azul ★　Many people say this is the best place to stay in Castro. It's a fun place to stay, but don't expect regal comfort. Certainly, the hotel has character; it's housed in a pretty, large Victorian on the waterfront, with funky interiors decorated with framed prints of unicorns. The best rooms sit high above the main building facing out toward the water, and they come with tiny balconies and wooden floors. But they're unremarkable, and you have to hike up a long flight of stairs to get to them. Downstairs rooms are darker but newly carpeted, and a few come with bathtubs, unlike the rooms upstairs, which have showers only. The exterior is painted as pink as a Mary Kay Cadillac, and many of the wooden beams and floor-runner carpets are sugary shades of pink, too. Ongoing renovations have improved many of the mediocre rooms. The hotel has the same owners as Ancud's Hotel Galeón Azul (p. 324).

Pedro Montt 228. ✆ **65/632359.** Fax 65/632808. www.hotelunicornioazul.cl. 17 units. $85-$120 double. No credit cards. **Amenities:** Restaurant; bar. *In room:* TV, no phone (in some units), free Wi-Fi.

INEXPENSIVE

Hostal Kolping 🗝　This hostel is a great value for the price, and really the best place to stay if you're looking for inexpensive lodging. The rooms are sunny and immaculately clean, and they come with beds with thick foam mattresses that are adequately comfortable. The rooms are all rather nondescript, but they are reasonably spacious and so are the bathrooms. A cheery dining area brightens gloomy days.

Chacabuco 217. ✆/fax **65/633273.** kolpingcastro@surnet.cl. 11 units. $35-$45 double. No credit cards. **Amenities:** Lounge. *In room:* TV.

Palafitos Hostel ★ 🎒　There's no better way to see Castro's signature architectural monuments than by staying in one. I waited years for someone to open a hotel in a stilted house, and this B&B was the first to do so in the famous Gamboa district. The construction is wood from the floor to the ceiling and lots of windows let in ample light. The rooms are quite plain, with little more than a nightstand and lamp, though all have private bathrooms. Contemporary art adorns the walls throughout the building, plus there's a small lounge area with a wood-burning stove and an outdoor patio right over the water.

Riquelme 1210, Gamboa. ℂ **65/531008.** www.palafitohostel.com. 9 units. $63–$84 double. Rates include breakfast. No credit cards. **Amenities:** Kitchen. *In room:* Free Wi-Fi.

Where to Dine

Several *palafitos* on the south side of downtown offer hearty local cuisine and a good way to view one from the inside. They're readily identifiable when they're serving meals. For a quick snack, on the corner across from the Cruz del Sur bus station, there is a small stand with a handful of women selling empanadas and *milcaos* (potato pancakes).

MODERATE

Kaweshkar Lounge VEGETARIAN/INTERNATIONAL   This is one of several trendy pubs and lounges to have sprung up in Castro aimed at mostly backpackers and vacationing Chileans. The small, funky dining space serves mostly vegetarian and organic food, though they do offer some seafood dishes, sandwiches, and crepes. DJs spin on weekends, and they occasionally host live music in the basement.

Encalada 31. ℂ **56/8516-0475.** Main courses C$4,000–C$6,500. No credit cards. Daily noon–4pm and 8pm–midnight.

Las Araucarias ★ INTERNATIONAL/CHILEAN   Las Araucarias is Hostería Castro's restaurant, and it is one of the top places to dine in town. The atmosphere is better during lunchtime, with the view and the airy interiors brought on by the two-story-high ceilings and a wall of windows; at night the dining room's airiness seems to encourage echoes, but it is comfortable nevertheless. The menu is steak and seafood, featuring Chilean classics and Chilote specialties such as *carapacho* and *curanto*. There's also a wide selection of meat dishes, such as filet mignon wrapped in bacon and served with sautéed vegetables. You might want to call ahead; the hotel often has a buffet special that is usually themed (German or Thai food, for example), and although it is quite good, it might not be what you're in the mood for.

Chacabuco 202. ℂ **65/632301.** Fax 65/635688. Main courses C$4,000–C$10,000. AE, DC, MC, V. Mon–Sat noon–midnight.

Octavio ★★ CHILEAN   Octavio has the best atmosphere in Castro, with a wood-shingled, airy dining area that sits directly over the water, and a panorama of windows showcasing the view. The restaurant specializes in Chilote specials—it's known around town for its *curanto*. It also serves seafood specials such as *mariscal,* a shellfish stew made with onion and cilantro, and other typical Chilean dishes, such as breaded cutlets and filet mignon. Fish is delivered daily. This place has a simple menu and simple food, but it is all very good, including a few sandwiches and soups if you don't want a full meal. Octavio is typically more popular with visitors to Castro, while Sacho (see below) is more popular with locals, most likely because it is cheaper.

Pedro Montt 261. ℂ **65/632855.** Main courses C$3,500–C$8,500. No credit cards. Daily 10am–midnight.

Patrimonial ★ INTERNATIONAL 🍴 This new hipster drinking den hidden on the second level of a wood building on the corner of the square has taken over as

Castro's it spot since longtime hangout Años Luz closed in 2009. Cheap lunch specials (*ceviche*, grilled salmon, and a dessert) attract a small lunch crowd off the street, though at night the meals are lighter: seafood or meat *tablas* (trays of seafood or charcuterie), grilled lamb and tomato sandwiches, or mussels. The idea is to pair the food with their small but carefully chosen wine list, large microbrew selection, or original cocktails using homemade syrups.

Balmaceda 291. ℂ **65/534-990.** Main courses C$2,500–C$6,000. No credit cards. Daily noon–4pm and 8pm–midnight.

Sacho ★ ⬥ SEAFOOD/CHILEAN It doesn't have the most eye-catching ambience, but Sacho serves some of the best cuisine in Castro, a fact clearly evident by the throngs of locals who patronize the restaurant daily. The upstairs dining room has large windows and a view of the water. The specialty here is seafood, and they serve the cheapest abalone *locos* I've seen anywhere in Chile. Try starting off with a plate of raw, steamed, or broiled clams, served with onion, lemon, whiskey, and Parmesan; then follow it up with a *cancato*. Typically the only fish served here is *congrio* (conger eel) and salmon, but they do have hake and sea bass from December to March.

Thompson 213. ℂ **65/632079.** Main courses C$2,000–C$5,500; C$7,000 buffet first Sun of each month. No credit cards. Mar–Dec daily noon–4pm and 8pm–midnight; Jan–Feb daily noon–midnight.

INEXPENSIVE

Café La Brújula del Cuerpo CAFE This sizable cafe on the plaza (the name translates as "the Body's Compass") is the social center for residents of Castro. It's perennially active thanks to its friendly service and extensive menu offering sandwiches, salads, main dishes, ice cream, desserts, espresso, and delicious fresh juices. The cafe/restaurant is open all day, and you'll often find travelers writing out postcards here. There's also one computer for Internet use.

O'Higgins 308. ℂ **65/633229.** Main courses C$3,000–C$5,000; sandwiches C$2,000–C$3,000. MC, V. Daily 11am–midnight.

Ristretto Caffe CAFE This new coffee bar and cafe serves proper espresso, cappuccinos, and macchiatos, as well as English and Chinese teas, infusions, and cakes made with *murta* (a local berry) or figs and pistachios. It's a clean and elegant spot for a pick-me-up snack.

Blanco 264. ℂ **65/532-769.** Main courses C$2,500–C$6,000. MC, V. Daily 8am–9pm.

EXCURSIONS BEYOND CASTRO

Few Chilean towns surpass the entrancing beauty of **Dalcahue, Achao,** and **Curaco de Vélez,** the latter two located on the **Isla Quinchao.** The towns and the countryside separating them are Chiloé highlights, offering lush scenery and a glimpse into the Chilote's culture and day-to-day life.

Just off Rte. 5, the island's only major highway, **Dalcahue** is a little town whose prosperity is best illustrated by the hustle and bustle of salmon industry workers at the pier, unloading and loading crates of fish byproducts to be processed. Dalcahue's other thriving industry (although on a smaller scale) is its **Fería Artesanal ★★**, located at the waterfront about 2 blocks southwest of the plaza. Every Thursday and Sunday, artisans drive or paddle in to Dalcahue from the surrounding area to hawk their knitwear, baskets, hand-carved wood items, clothing, and more. In a boat-shaped wooden building beside the restaurant, several relatively slick countertop restaurants have been installed serving Chilote cuisine. All are decent.

At the plaza sits one of the larger Chiloé churches, with scalloped porticos. Across the plaza, on the corner, you'll find the tiny **Museo Histórico Etnográfico ★**, Pedro Montt 105 (*C* **65/642375**), which houses a cluttered array of stuffed birds and Indian and colonial-era artifacts. It's open daily from 9am to 5pm and admission is free. For directions to Dalcahue, see "Essentials" under Castro, earlier. All transportation stops in Dalcahue first before crossing over to Quinchao.

Several blocks away at Dalcahue's pier is the ferry to **Isla Quinchao.** The ferry makes the 5-minute ride almost continuously from 7am to 10:30pm every day (C$4,000 for cars round-trip). This is one of Chiloé's most populated islands, a magical landscape of plump, rolling hills, where smoke slowly wafts from clapboard homes and Chilote farmers can be seen tilling their land with oxen and a plow. The island also affords visitors with spectacular views of the Gulf of Ancud and the scattered, pint-size islands that sit between the Isla Quinchao and the mainland.

The first town you'll encounter upon exiting the ferry is **Curaco de Vélez,** a historic village whose former prosperity brought about by wool production and whaling can be witnessed through the grand, weather-beaten homes that line the streets. If you are hungry and are feeling adventuresome, follow the yellow OSTRAS street signs to an open-air restaurant, **Ostras El Trunco,** across the street from the water. Here you can slurp three different kinds of oysters, shucked right in front of you, for a quarter of the price you would pay back home.

Continue southeast along the island's single, unnamed main road to **Achao,** a former Jesuit colony founded in 1743 and home to the oldest church in Chiloé. Made entirely of cypress, alerce, and mañío, this church is as plain as a brown paper bag from the outside, but take one step inside and all impressions change due to its multicolored interiors and whimsical decorations. Take a walk along the waterfront for people-watching, and bring your camera for a photo op along the shore, where red, yellow, and sky-blue fishing boats bob and dance in the bay. Throughout the island of Quinchao, you'll find wooden gazebos atop well-designed lookout points along the road. Here's hoping the weather allows you to take full advantage of them. The homes in Achao are characterized by the region's penchant for adapting shingles into a variety of geometrical patterns, from concave to convex, circular to triangular, all nailed tightly together to keep the rain out.

At the pier you can hire boatmen (just be prepared to negotiate) to take you to some more remote islands such as **Mechuque,** a rustic fishing village where most of the houses are *palafitos.* The island is a common stop for kayaking expeditions. There is nowhere to stay on Mechuque, so be sure to arrange your return with your boatman. If you have time before or after your trip, take a seat at **Mar y Velas,** in the building overlooking the harbor just steps away. It's known as one of the best traditional Chilote restaurants anywhere on the archipelago and serves some of the freshest mussels and clams around.

I recommend that you make the aforementioned destinations a priority, but if you still have enough time, try to make it to **Chonchi.** About 32km (20 miles) south of Castro, on the main highway, this pleasant town is home to the best-preserved 18th-century buildings on the island. The early prosperity brought on by the timber export industry (mostly cypress) at that time is reflected in the handsome wooden houses and buildings around town. Made from fermented cow's milk, *Licor de Oro* is as much a cultural experience as it is an intoxicating elixir. Chonchi has created a cottage industry out of this liqueur's production, and drinking it here is the norm. Made with fruits, herbs, or, in some cases, sugar and egg (think eggnog), the liqueur isn't as bad as you might think. You'll find it at Chonchi's *fería* (market), located on the corner of Irarrázaval (along the coast) and Canessa streets.

Chonchi has one decent lodging option if you want to stay overnight, **Esmeralda by the Sea** (© 65/671328; www.esmeraldabythesea.cl), which charges $42 to $63 for a double. Not far from town on the road to Queilén in Aituy, don't miss eating at **Espejo de Luna ★★** (© 56/7431-3090; www.espejodeluna.cl), where the architecture resembles an overturned ship. The gourmet menu sources from local farmers and fishermen and turns the ingredients into contemporary plates that can be paired with a good wine list or microbrews. It's hard to not stick around in their collection of stunning **cabins ★★★**, perhaps the finest on the island, which are surrounded by forested trails and have ocean views to die for; rates start at $34.

Quellón, at the southern end of the Pan-American Highway, is another 72km (45 miles) south. It's not particularly attractive, but it's the departure (or arrival) port for ferries to Chaitén on the Carretera Austral or for the ferries that ply the fjords southwest to Puerto Chacabuco, a fantastic, 37-hour alternative to the more common trip directly from Puerto Montt. The latter is served by Aysén Express (© 65/680047 in Quellón, or 67/240956, Coyhaique head office), and Naviera Austral, Pedro Montt 457 (© 65/682207; www.navieraustral.cl); reserve well in advance for either of the two. Quellón is also the departure point for boat trips to Inio in the Tantauco private preserve that takes up much of the island south of the town (see later). One of the most modern hotel options on the entire island is **Patagonia Insular** (Ladrilleros 1737; © 65/681610; www.hotelpatagoniainsular.cl; $103 double) a Wi-Fi–enabled 30-room hotel on a hill with a nice water vista.

Parque Nacional de Chiloé

Parque Nacional de Chiloé, on the western coast of Chiloé, covers 43,000 hectares (106,000 acres) and is divided into three sectors: **Chanquin, Middle,** and **North.** This park's strong suit is its **short hikes** that allow you to savor the best the park has to offer; in fact, the 19km (12-mile) backpacker's hike is disappointing. Lodging at the park is a super deal, too, with attractive cabins for about $46 a night. The Chanquin sector is connected by a dirt road that branches off Rte. 5, about 35km (22 miles) south of Castro; this is where you'll find the CONAF ranger station and a visitor center. This is the only truly suitable part of the park for visiting, due to its easy access and good trail conditions (unlike the North, or "Chepu," sector). The Middle section (also referred to as "Metalqui") is a protected island with a large sea lion colony, but visitors are not allowed there.

For transportation to the national park, take **Buses Arroyo** or **Buses Ojeda** (no phone) from the Terminal Municipal. Buses depart once daily in low season and twice daily in high season, though schedules vary. The park is wild and wet—very, very wet—but it is one of the few places to see old-growth, thick rainforest bordering the coast. Many backpackers come in the summer to hike through the park's forest and along vast stretches of sandy beach that often peak into sand dunes.

Visitors first arrive at the tiny village of **Cucao,** the gateway to the national park, which was devastated by a 1960 tidal wave; today it is a collection of rickety homes. This is where you'll find the four **Cabañas CONAF,** each for six guests, and they have kitchenettes, so come prepared (© 65/532502; pnchiloe@conaf.cl). After the suspension bridge, visitors will find the park interpretation center run by CONAF (Chile's national park service), which has environmental displays and information about hiking trails. From here hikers have an option of three trails. The short, though very informative (English-language signs are here) 770m (2,926-ft.) **Sendero El Tepual** winds through thick, humid tepú forest. The **Sendero Dunas de Cucao** is about 1.5km (a little less than 1 mile), and it passes alternately through dense vegetation and open stretches of sand dunes blanketed in golden grass.

Vast and desolate, this stretch of coastline is one of the most beautiful in Chile. If you are lucky and arrive at low tide, a handful of locals might be here digging *machas*, or razor clams, out of the sand, which they sell to buyers all the way to Puerto Montt. There is a 20km (12-mile) backpacker's trek via a long trail on the coast, which weaves in and out of evergreen forest and sandy beach until arriving at CONAF's backcountry refuge, **Cole-Cole.** In truth, the hike is overrated, but backpackers will enjoy camping out in this lovely environment. From here it's another 2 hours to CONAF's other refuge, **Anay.** The refuges are in bad condition, and it is recommended that you bring a tent. Parque Nacional Chiloé has a variety of campsites, and it is open every day from 9am to 7:30pm; admission is C$2,000 for adults and free for children.

South of the national park, a private preserve 30km (19 miles) southwest of Chonchi has recently been established. Called **Tepuhueico,** it features a lake and a fine eco-lodge of the same name, built in gray cypress wood in a style that reminds me of Le Corbusier (📞 **65/633958**). The lodge has seven doubles with en-suite bathrooms, along with two *cabañas*. Electrical light runs from 9pm to midnight. It has a hot tub in the garden and plenty of possibilities for hiking and fishing.

Another much larger but very remote private preserve, **Tantauco ★★** opened here in 2005. Bought by billionaire entrepreneur and now president Sebastián Piñera, the park comprises some 100,000 hectares (250,000 acres), uninhabited except for the 30-family fishing hamlet of Inio on its southern coast. At press time, facilities were limited. One very rough road leads through a northern sliver to the Chaiguata and Chaiguaco lagoons, with one campground with 20 sites charging $15; at Inio, there's a campground with 15 sites, and a modern barbecue grill, for the same fee. A dozen hiking trails have been established in the park. One weekly boat heads to Inio from Quellón for C$12,000. Information for the park is at Av. La Paz 68 in Quellón (📞 **65/680066;** www.parquetantauco.cl), which is open daily from 9am to 6pm. In Santiago, contact **Fundación Futuro,** Av. Apoquindo 3000, 19th floor (📞 **2/422-7322;** www.fundacionfuturo.cl/parque_chiloe.php).

Sports, Guided Tours & Other Activities

Turismo Pehuén, Blanco 299 in Castro (📞/fax **65/635254;** www.turismopehuen. cl), is the most reliable, respected agency in Chiloé, offering a variety of tours in the area that include hiking in the national park and guided visits to Dalcahue and Achao; during the summer only, horseback riding, boat tours, and overflight tours are offered that give passengers an aerial view of the island. It's really the most complete tour agency; however, **Queilén Bus,** Villa Llau Llau s/n (📞 **65/632594;** fax 65/635600; queilenbus@surnet.cl), also offers guided tours around the area.

The calm, fairy-tale bays and coves of Chiloé and the emerald Andean fjords across the sound render this the best region in Chile for **sea kayaking** and **boating.** I strongly recommend that visitors interested in these sports consider the following two excellent tour operators that offer trips for several days or longer. These operators can customize trips according to your experience and stamina; in many cases, you don't need kayak experience at all, just a willingness to learn.

Altué Expeditions is Chile's foremost tour operator for trekking, horseback riding, and kayaking, and their kayak center on the shore of Dalcahue, one of the prettiest areas of Chiloé, is the ideal base for practicing the sport. The center has a Chiloé-style shingled and very attractive lodge for overnight stays, and they plan longer journeys that include the Andean fjords and hot spring visits, using a Chilote boat as a support vessel (camping at night). There's a hot tub at the lodge, and they treat guests to a typical *curanto* meal while visiting. The superb crew is not only knowledgeable, but friendly, too. Trips around Chiloé archipelago last 4 days and 3 nights; trips including the Andean fjords last 9 days and 8 nights. Call or e-mail for pricing information, as group size is a factor in cost (© **2/233-2964** in Santiago, or 65/641110 in Chiloé; www.seakayakchile.com).

For kayaking, and especially sailing and soft-adventure nature and cultural tours, try the top-notch operation **Austral Adventures** (© **65/625977** or 9/642-8936; www.austral-adventures.com). The U.S./Chilean outfit specializes in luxury excursions around Chiloé and the Andean fjords, offering a 3-day/2-night round-trip "Island Kayak Adventure" tour ($450 per person) and a 6-day/5-night "Patagonian Fjords & the Wonders of the Chiloé Archipelago" tour ($1,775 per person). Their tours include a bilingual guide, private transport from Ancud, and lodging and meals. For those short on time, Austral Adventures also offers some day options for C$21,850 per person from Ancud, including a coastal hike and visit to a penguin colony (minimum four people), and sea kayaking the Ancud bay (minimum three people). In April and May, **Nomads of the Seas** (© **56/414-4600;** www.nomads oftheseas.com) offers 3-day/2-night ultra luxurious gastronomic cruises with well-known Chilean chefs on board the *Atmosphere* cruise ship, which departs Puerto Montt and stops in Chiloé. Call or e-mail for pricing and schedules.

For boat trips that will take you to view **blue whales** in the December-to-February season, contact Carlos Villalobos at **Agencia Tic-Toc** (carlosv@surnet.cl) in Quellón. The cost is C$57,000 per person, with a minimum of four passengers, for a full day excursion.

THE CARRETERA AUSTRAL

S
outh of Puerto Montt, the population thins, the mountains squeeze up against the coast, and the vegetation thickens. This is the region of northwest Patagonia commonly called the "Carretera Austral," named for the rugged route that runs south to tiny Villa O'Higgins between 48° and 49° latitude. It's a 1,240km (769-mile) dirt-and-gravel road that bends and twists through thick virgin rainforest, past glacial-fed rivers and aquamarine lakes; jagged, white-capped peaks that rise above open valleys; and precipitous cliffs with cascading ribbons of waterfalls at every turn. If you like your scenery remote and rugged, this is the place for you. Though much less traveled than the famous national park Torres del Paine, in many ways, a journey down this "highway" is the quintessential Patagonian road trip, and many of its natural attractions are as stunning as any you'll find farther south. There are some of the country's best fly-fishing lodges, one of the world's top rivers for rafting, hot springs, and a sailing journey to one of Chile's most awe-inspiring glaciers. It is also home to fjords that are ideal for kayaking, as well as the rainforest jungle of Pumalín Park and the village of Chaitén, which were both severely affected by the May 2008 eruption of Volcán Chaitén.

The Carretera Austral runs from Puerto Montt in the north to **Villa O'Higgins** in the south, and passes through two extensive regions: the southern portion of the **Región de Los Lagos** and the vast **Región de Aysén,** whose capital, **Coyhaique,** holds almost half the sparse population of the region, home to less than one person per square kilometer. This is the least-populated region of Chile; a 2008 census counted 102,600 residents in nearly 110,000 square kilometers. Aysén is also considered the "youngest" region in Chile since it was the last of Chile's 15 regions to join the nation.

This area largely straddles the Andes, unlike most of Chile, where the range's summits form the eastern border. A first few roads appeared in the 1930s, but before the mid-1970s, much of the area could only be reached by ferry or plane, and trucks servicing its tiny villages and fishing hamlets mostly had to enter from Argentina. Worried about a very real threat of war with Argentina in the 1970s, then-dictator Augusto Pinochet sought to fortify Chile's presence in this isolated region by connecting the existing roads with the rest of the country. More than 30 years later and at a staggering cost above $300 million (and counting) and the lives of more than two dozen men, work continues on paving and extending the highway.

DRIVING THE CARRETERA AUSTRAL ★★

Although it is possible to reach most destinations in this region by ferry, bus, or plane, road improvements and an expansion of services mean an increasing number of travelers are choosing to drive the Carretera Austral. It's not as enormous an undertaking as it sounds, but it can be costly, especially when you factor in the cost of ferry rides, rental car drop-off fees (about $500), and gas. Don't underestimate, though, how difficult it is to organize the logistics of driving a vehicle here, especially if you hope to start in Puerto Montt—ferry service is always subject to change. Also, the remoteness and increasing popularity of the region among travelers makes it one of Chile's more expensive destinations.

Several agencies in Puerto Montt (at the airport) and Coyhaique offer one-way car rentals, and some allow you to cross into Argentina or leave the car as far away as Punta Arenas, Chile. (See "Essentials" under "Puerto Montt," in chapter 10.) The online agency **Visit Chile** (℗ **800/560-2340** in North America: www.visitchile. com) has an 8-day package that includes a 4×4 rental car, ferry reservation, lodging, and various meals, starting at $2,200 for two people. Alternatively, you could rent a car in Coyhaique and drive north, stopping in Puyuhuapi before heading on to Futaleufú. Although you'd have to backtrack to Coyhaique to return the car, this is a less expensive option, even if you pay the extra insurance necessary to return via Argentina. (See "Coyhaique," later in this chapter, for information.)

The most troublesome considerations are changes in ferry service, flat tires, slippery roads, and foul weather, any of which can strike at any time. Renting an extra spare tire is a wise add-on.

Essentials

FERRY CROSSINGS If possible, make reservations for ferry services well in advance, as they tend to fill up, even during the low season. Service is most reliable in January and February. The trip from Puerto Montt to Chaitén requires a ferry crossing (ferries are in operation all year, though the frequency is less than in previous years and service seems to shift week to week). Contact **Naviera Austral** (℗ **65/270430;** www.navieraustral.cl) for information and give yourself a few days of flexibility if the departure dates suddenly change.

GAS Service stations can be found at reasonable intervals, and some smaller towns such as Futaleufú or Villa O'Higgins sell gas in jugs from stores or private residences, but some travelers feel safer carrying a backup canister of fuel. Canisters can be purchased from any service station or rented from any car rental agency. Fill up every chance that you get.

CROSSING INTO ARGENTINA Drivers who head into Argentina must prove that they are the owner of their car, or have their rental agency set up the proper paperwork, which must be completed by the agency 48 hours in advance, to show you are driving a rental car. Extra insurance usually has to be purchased; check with the rental agency. The department store **Falabella's Obligatory Mercosur Insurance**

(**℡ 600/390-1000;** www.segurosfalabella.com) offers a 10-day plan for around C$22,325 and a 30-day plan for around C$34,675, depending on the vehicle. Drivers must fill out a detailed form and are then given a copy to carry with them until crossing back into Chile.

ROAD CONDITIONS The Carretera Austral is made largely of dirt and gravel, which can get slippery during storms. A 4×4 vehicle is necessary if going beyond any town center, especially if snow is in the forecast. Some rental agencies insist that you rent a truck with high clearance. Depending on the weather and season, giant potholes are the exception, not the norm, but they can cause a car to spin out or even flip if driving too fast. For this reason, drivers are cautioned to keep their speed between 40kmph (25 mph) and 60kmph (37 mph). When it's wet or the road curves, you need to slow down even more.

HITCHHIKERS Road courtesy dictates that you might have to pick up a hitchhiker or two along the way. Most hitchhikers are humble local folk who simply do not have the means to get from place to place (during the summer many foreign backpackers try to get a lift, too). Use your own judgment. You should always lend a hand to anyone whose car has broken down.

MONEY Once you journey outside any major town here, cash is king. Be sure to keep your wallet supplied with an adequate supply of Chilean pesos.

Getting Around by Bus

There is inexpensive, frequent summer service and intermittent winter service to and from destinations along the Carretera Austral for those who choose not to drive. It takes longer, and you won't have the opportunity to stop at points of interest along the way, but every town has a tour operator that can usually get you to outlying sites for day trips. Also, the breathtaking scenery never fails to dazzle, even if you can't get off the bus.

The 5-hour journey from Puerto Montt to Hornopirén (which hooks up for the summer-only ferry to Caleta Gonzalo) runs sporadically depending on ash conditions caused by the Chaitén volcano. Call **Buses Fierro** (**℡ 65/421522**) for updated information. Buses from Chaitén previously left for Futaleufú an average of five to six times per week during the summer, and about three times per week during the winter, though again, service has been significantly affected here; you should check on the present conditions before making any plans.

Buses from Chaitén to Coyhaique, stopping first in Puyuhuapi, used to leave up to four times per week year-round, though timetables will continue to be affected by the eruption. For information about buses from Chaitén, see "Getting There," under "Chaitén," later. Note that bus schedules are subject to change without notice. Farther south, the main bus hub is Coyhaique, from where buses depart daily to Cochrane, and then most days of the week journey to Caleta Tortel and Villa O'Higgins.

PARQUE NACIONAL ALERCE ANDINO ★★

46km (29 miles) SE of Puerto Montt

The Carretera Austral is also known as Rte. 7, and it begins just outside the city limits of Puerto Montt, following the coast of Reloncaví Sound until it reaches **Parque Nacional Alerce Andino,** a place to indulge in quiet walks or canoe rides through dense forest. This 39,255-hectare (96,960-acre) park is home to the alerce tree, which is often compared to the sequoia for its thick diameter and height. These venerable giants can live more than 3,000 years, making them the second-oldest tree, after the American bristlecone pine. Heavy fines are levied against anyone caught harming or cutting one down, though a flourishing black market in the wood still threatens the trees even in some protected areas. Other species in the park include evergreen beech, mañío, canelo, ulmo, and thick crops of ferns. It can get pretty wet here year-round, so bring rain gear just in case.

Getting from here to the next section of the Carretera Austral requires advanced planning; if you have a vehicle, you are 100% dependent on the ferry linking Hornopirén and Caleta Gonzalo; ferry service is only a sure-thing in January and February.

The park itself is serviced by a rough dirt road that leads to a **CONAF guard station** in what's known as the **Chaica sector,** where there is a campground and the trail head for the half-hour round-trip walk to a waterfall and a fenced-off 3,000-year-old alerce tree. The walk to Laguna Chaiquenes is about 5.5km (3.5 miles), and to Lago Triángulo about 10km (6.25 miles) from the campground. Roads, trails, and campgrounds are often washed out or impeded by falling trees. Be sure to check for road conditions before heading out. For more information, contact the CONAF office in Puerto Montt, at Ochagavía 464 (© **65/254882;** www.conaf.cl).

The park's second sector, **Laguna Sargazo,** is at Lago Chapo, and it also has campgrounds and two muddy trails for day hikes through the park's rainforest, a section of which has a thick stand of alerce trees. This sector sees fewer visitors as it is more difficult to get to if you do not have your own vehicle; buses go only as far as Correntoso, a 2-hour walk from the park entrance (although it is possible to arrange a tour; see "Getting There," below). At the park ranger station here, you can rent canoes for a paddle across Lago Chapo.

Getting There

If driving, head south on Rte. 7, winding past tiny villages on the gravel road until you reach Chaica, about 35km (22 miles) from Puerto Montt, where a sign indicates the road to the park entrance at the left. The park ranger station is open from 9am to 5pm, so leave your car outside the gate if you plan to return later than 5pm. Travelers without a vehicle can take **Buses Fierro** (© **65/289024** or 65/253022) headed in the direction of Hornopirén from the main terminal in Puerto Montt (ask to be dropped off at Chaica); however, the bus (six daily services), which costs C$2,019, leaves visitors at an entrance road 4km (2½ miles) from the park ranger station. You might consider hiring a tour operator to take a day trip or possibly to organize an advance pickup date if you plan to camp. To get to the Lago Chapo sector, head south on Rte. 7 for about 9km (5½ miles) to Chamiza; just before the bridge, take a left toward the town Correntoso and drive 19km (12 miles) to the park entrance. **Buses Fierro** (© **65/289024** or 65/253022) has two daily trips to Correntoso, costing C$1,500, that leave from the main terminal in Puerto Montt; from here, it's a 2-hour walk to the park entrance. The Puerto Varas–based adventure travel company **Miralejos** (© **65/234892;** www.miralejos.com) has an overnight tour that includes hiking and ocean kayaking, and a night at a campground.

Where to Stay

Alerce Mountain Lodge ★★ 🛏 This quiet, remote lodge sits on the shore of a small lake—which must be crossed by a hand-drawn ferry—at the edge of the national park and is surrounded by dense stands of stately 1,000-year-old alerce trees. This is where you go to get away from crowds. The lodge is built almost entirely of handcrafted alerce logs, with giant trunks acting as pillars in the spacious, two-story lobby. The woodsy effect continues in the cozy rooms, which are decorated with local crafts and feature forest views. The cabins have a view of the lake and come with a living room and two bedrooms, and accommodate a maximum of six guests. One of the highlights at this lodge is that the surrounding trails are not open to the general public, so you'll have them to yourself. Bilingual guides lead horseback rides and day hikes that can last as long as 7 hours or as little as a half-hour. Packages include transfers, all meals, and excursions.

Carretera Austral, Km 36. ℰ/fax **65/286969.** www.mountainlodge.cl. 11 units, 3 *cabañas*. All-inclusive packages run per person, double occupancy: 2 nights/3 days $690; 3 nights/4 days $1,035. Inquire about other packages and off-season discounts. AE, DC, MC, V. **Amenities:** Restaurant; bar; Jacuzzi; sauna.

PARQUE PUMALÍN ★★

The Pumalín Park Project, the world's largest private nature reserve, spans roughly 300,000 hectares (742,000 acres) and incorporates temperate rainforest, glaciers, fjords, thundering waterfalls and rivers, and stands of ancient alerce trees. It's a marvelous place, a park that exists thanks to U.S. millionaire and philanthropist Douglas Tompkins, who bought his first chunk of land here in 1991.

The project has generated considerable controversy and will continue to do so for the foreseeable future. At its narrowest point, just 15km (9 miles) separate the Pacific Ocean from the Argentine border here in Pumalín, effectively cutting the country in half, and Chile has no shortage of politicians on all sides of the political spectrum to openly worry about a foreign citizen owning strategic lands. Many also question the idea of protecting an area on this scale rather than exploiting its resources in what is still a developing country.

Over 20 years since Tompkins started accumulating the properties, he continues in the spotlight. Major energy companies Endesa Chile and Colbún seek to develop the Aysén region's vast hydrology resources (including the Baker River, which runs next to his wife's project, a similar nature reserve at Estancia Chacabuco) to supply power to central Chile, and the power lines would run through the park. The government, meanwhile, wants to complete the Carretera Austral by slicing through the park, an idea Tompkins criticizes as expensive and unnecessarily destructive, arguing for a road along the coast. He and his wife meanwhile have continued to buy land on both sides of Patagonia (see "The Future Patagonia National Park," later in this chapter).

At the same time, Parque Pumalín has largely won acceptance, and was officially declared a nature sanctuary in 2005, run by Tompkins's foundation, the Conservation Land Trust. In May 2008, however, problems came from a new angle. The eruption of the Chaitén volcano almost completely destroyed the infrastructure of the entire southern end of the park around Caleta Gonzalo, which was the main entrance and had some of the finest facilities in all of Chile. The park reopened in December 2010 but getting here remains a complicated option.

It is imperative that you get up-to-date information before visiting Parque Pumalín. The main road is slated to be in good shape by early 2011. An alternative is to visit the region's fjords and the Cahuelmó hot springs in the northern sector of the park, which can be done by rented boat, kayak, or tour only (see "Organized Tours," later).

Visitor Information

For advance information about Parque Pumalín, contact their U.S. office (© **415/229-9339;** www.parquepumalin.cl). Travelers coming from the north should stop at Pumalín's office in Puerto Varas at Klenner 299 (© **65/250079**).

Getting There

Hornopirén can be reached by private vehicle; take Rte. 7 south from Puerto Montt for 45km (28 miles) until reaching La Arena, from which there is a 30-minute-long ferry that leaves nine times per day, year-round, to Puelche. South from La Arena, the ferry runs from 8am to 8pm; north from Puelche, it operates from 7:15am to 7:15pm (run by Transmarchilay's **Naviera Puelche;** © **65/270000** in Puerto Montt). From here it is 55km (34 miles) to Hornopirén. Bus service to Hornopirén is offered from the Puerto Montt bus station by **Buses Fierro** (© **65/253022**), leaving three times per day (twice on Sun).

The southern entrance to the park at Caleta Gonzalo was severely affected during the May 2008 eruption but reopened in December of 2010. You can get to Caleta Gonzalo and the southern section of the park from either Chaitén, 20km (12 miles) to the south (see "Chaitén," later), or by a 6-hour ferry ride from Hornopirén. (In years past, during Jan and Feb, the ferry left daily at 3pm from Hornopirén and 9am from Caleta Gonzalo; the ride takes 5 hours and costs C$66,500 per private vehicle with four passengers. Outside of January and February, visitors will need to go first to Chaitén to visit Pumalín. Reservations are necessary for vehicles; contact **Naviera Austral**, Av. Angelmó 1673 in Puerto Montt or at Av. Corcovado 266 in Chaitén (© **65/270431;** www.navieraustral.cl).

What to See & Do

Once you have successfully navigated your way to Pumalín, you will discover a magic kingdom that you have practically all to yourself. The fjords that plunge into the sea rival Norway's and are simply magnificent, and the remote, natural hot springs make for a divine way to end the day, especially if you've been kayaking. Thick forests cover the slopes in every direction. Of course, it rains profusely at times, and that can test your patience, especially when setting up camp. If you cannot stand the mud and watching your fingers turn to prunes, consider a boat trip with interior sleeping arrangements.

HIKING   The park has a dozen trails, ranging from lengthy, multiday ones to easy, short walks. At Caleta Gonzalo, trails include the 3-hour round-trip **Sendero Cascadas,** which meanders along a footpath and elevated walkways through dense vegetation before terminating at a crashing waterfall. The **Sendero Tronador,** 12km (7½ miles) south of Caleta Gonzalo, takes visitors across a suspension bridge and up, up, up a steep path and wooden stepladder to a lookout point, with views of Volcán Michinmahuida, then down to a lake with a campground, taking, round-trip, about 3½ hours. The **Sendero Los Alerces** is an easy 40-minute walk through old stands of alerce.

ORGANIZED TOURS   The northern section's hot springs and fjords are accessible only by boat. Tours can include kayaking, camping or on-ship lodging, and hiking. The park's "official" tour operator is **Alsur Expeditions,** in Puerto Varas at Del Salvador 100 (©/fax **65/232300;** www.alsurexpeditions.com), which has horseback riding and trekking tours, specializing in sailing aboard their small yacht (Puerto

Montt–Chiloé–Pumalín) or kayaking, using a Chiloé-style support boat. But the best sea kayaking is with **Altue Sea Kayaking,** based out of Santiago, at Encomenderos 83, Las Condes (© **09/419-6809** [cell]; www.seakayakchile.com), with outstanding kayak trips around Pumalín, which they normally combine with a kayak tour of Chiloé (where they own a coastal lodge). Altue also has a motorized support vehicle. **Austral Adventures,** Ave. Costanera 904, Ancud (© **65/625977**; www.austral adventures.com), an American-owned operation based out of Chiloé, specializes in sailing, bird-watching, and fly-fishing journeys from Puerto Montt to Pumalín, including Chiloé, aboard their newer Chiloé-style boat. Lastly, the company **Yak Expeditions** focuses on kayaking and getting from one place to another by kayak and without a support boat. It is a quieter, more activity-oriented journey, with camping where there are no lodges (© **09/8332-0574** [cell]; www.yakexpediciones.cl).

OTHER ACTIVITIES Pumalín offers **horse pack trips** and trips to the remote **Cahuelmó Hot Springs,** all with advance reservation only. You can also tour an **organic farm;** sign up for **boat trips** around the fjord and to the sea lion rookery; or take flights over the park. Contact the official outdoor operator for the park, **Alsur Expeditions** (see below). It offers daily transportation to the hot springs for C$35,000, which includes camping and bathing.

Where to Stay & Dine

Cabañas Caleta Gonzalo ★★★ These stylish yet rustic cabins are built for two to five guests and feature details like nubby bedspreads, gingham curtains, and carved wood cabinets (but no kitchenettes). The cabins are small but very cozy, with a double bed and twin on the bottom floor and two twins above in a loft; all are bright. They've been refurbished following the eruption of Chaitén.

The sites at **Camping Pumalín,** on the beautiful Fiordo Reñihué, are well-kept with a fire pit (firewood costs extra), a sheltered area for cooking, bathrooms with cold-water showers, and an area for washing clothing; the cost is $10 per person. About 14km (8¾ miles) south of Caleta Gonzalo is the **Cascadas Escondidas Campground,** with sheltered tent platforms, picnic tables, cold-water showers, bathrooms, and the trail head to three waterfalls. The cost to camp here is $10 per campsite. There are more than 20 campsites throughout the park, many of them accessible by boat or by backpacking trail; consult the park for more information.

Caleta Gonzalo s/n. © **65/250079,** or 415/229-9339 in the U.S. reservas@parquepumalin.cl. 7 units. $158 for double; $200 triple; $284 five people. AE, DC, MC, V. **Amenities:** Restaurant.

CHAITÉN

420km (260 miles) N of Coyhaique

Chaitén was once the main jumping-off point for exploring Pumalín, Futaleufú, and the Carretera Austral; however, the May 5, 2008 eruption of the Chaitén volcano changed the face of this charming port village forever. When the first rumbles began, most residents thought **Volcán Michinmahuida** was erupting, but they eventually realized the "extinct" **Volcán Chaitén,** which had been inactive for 10,000 years, was erupting. The town, a few days after being evacuated, was nearly wiped out when the water from a melting glacier mixed with significant ash deposits and a deluge ran right through the center of town. At press time, Chaitén was slowly emerging from the rubble and attempting to reestablish its infrastructure. Since the government gave residents a cash payout, the majority have resettled elsewhere, however.

If you visit the town now, you will find a modern day Humberstone, Chile's UNESCO World Heritage ghost town in the north near Antofagasta. Some parts of the town survived under a coating of a few inches of ash, but those toward the river were more or less demolished. In a brief walk through town, you will see houses with missing walls and broken windows and some that have been moved completely off their hinges and torn apart. The beach, which used to sit right off the edge of town, has been extended for hundreds of meters into the bay. It is a sorrowing, eerie sight that reveals just a glimpse of the awesome power of Mother Nature.

As of December 2010, about 200 people were living in the village, with just a couple of small shops open and all restaurants still closed. Several hotels, such as Hotel Schilling and Cabañas Pudú, welcome guests, though there were still no phones, little electricity, and no running water. There is no telling when, or if, the town will fully rebuild. Before heading to Chaitén, it is important to get up-to-date information before showing up.

Getting There

BY BOAT **Naviera Austral,** at Angelmó 2187 in Puerto Montt (© **65/270000;** www.navieraustral.cl), runs four weekly trips from Puerto Montt (10 hr.; one-way tickets from C$16,500 to C$22,000) and three weekly trips from Castro, Chiloé (7 hr.; C$16,000). At press time, Naviera Austral could not confirm if vehicles were to be allowed onboard; the service remains passenger-only. From Quellón, south of Castro, ferries cross to Chaitén twice a week; Naviera Austral's offices in Quellón are at Pedro Montt 457 (© **65/682207**).

BY PLANE For charter flights from Puerto Montt to Chaitén, contact **Cielo Mar Austral,** Quillota 245 local 1, Puerto Montt (© **65/264-010;** cielomaraustral@ surnet.cl); or **Aerotaxis del Sur** (© **65/330726;** www.aerotaxisdelsur.cl).

BY BUS Bus schedules in this region are always subject to change. Both **Chaitur** (©/fax **65/731429;** www.chaitur.com) and **B&V Tours** (© **65/731390**) have information about service to destinations such as Futaleufú, Puyuhuapi, and Coyhaique. Buses to all destinations used to leave daily, from December to March; from April to November, buses to Futaleufú and Coyhaique leave several times weekly, with a stop at Puyuhuapi. Check with park officials for updated information on the route.

SOUTH FROM CHAITÉN: FUTALEUFÚ ★

155km (96 miles) SE of Chaitén

The road south between Chaitén and Villa Santa Lucía, where drivers turn for Futaleufú, passes through mountain scenery that affords direct views of Volcán Michinmahuida rising high above the wilderness, Yelcho Glacier, and Lago Yelcho. At 25km (16 miles), you'll arrive at Amarillo, a tiny village and the turnoff point for the 5km (3-mile) drive to Termas de Río Amarillo.

TERMAS DE RIO AMARILLO These hot springs have a large temperate pool along with several outdoor and private indoor pools (C$3,500; daily 9am–dusk). Check out Pumalín's website (www.parquepumalin.cl) for updated information about their trail to the Amarillo Valley that, in 2 hours, will take you to one of the best campgrounds in the area, with extensive alpine and glacier views. Or lodge at the modest, family-run **Cabañas y Hospedaje Los Mañíos,** about 100m (328 ft.) from the hot springs, for C$32,000 for a cabin for four, C$39,500 for a cabin for six (**℡ 65/731210**).

Lago Yelcho

Farther south, the road curves past the northern shore of Lago Yelcho and the Yelcho en la Patagonia Lodge (see below), and at 60km (37 miles) crosses the Puente Ventisquero, which bridges a milky green river; this is where you'll find the trail head to **Yelcho Glacier.** To get there, take the short road before the bridge and then walk right at the almost imperceptible sign indicating the trail. A muddy 1½-hour hike takes you through dense forest to Yelcho Glacier. The 50km (31-mile) lake itself is a hub for fly-fishing (see the lodges listed below).

At Villa Santa Lucía, the Carretera Austral continues south to Puyuhuapi, but visitors should not miss a stay, or at the very least, a detour, to Futaleufú, an idyllic mountain town with adventure activities and one of the most challenging rivers to raft in the world. The road to Futaleufú is worth the trip itself for its majestic views at every turn, first winding around the southern end of Lago Yelcho before passing the Futaleufú River and lakes Lonconao and Espolón, and on to the emerald valley surrounding the town of Futaleufú. Views of the river's massive Class IV+ rapids can't be had from the road; you'll have to sign up for a commercial rafting trip to see them.

AN ADVENTURE LODGE

Yelcho en la Patagonia Lodge ★★ 🎒   The Yelcho Lodge is a remote tourism complex on the shore of the Lake Yelcho, a beautiful emerald lake bordered by tall peaks crowned with glaciers. It is the region's only complete resort, with woodsy, attractive accommodations and a full range of excursions, especially fly-fishing. Yelcho offers three options: rooms in the lodge, cabins for four to six guests, and 15 well-equipped campsites complete with barbecues. The white, shingled cabins come with spacious kitchenettes, but there's also a restaurant that serves gourmet cuisine as well as barbecue roasts. The cabins have a deck and barbecue and a view of the lake seen through a stand of *arrayán* trees; note that cabins for six mean two sleep in the living area. The lodge and the indoor accommodations have handsome two-tone floors made of mañío and alerce. The lodge offers excursions with bilingual guides for fly-fishing the Yelcho River and Lago Yelcho, locally renowned for its plentiful salmon and trout. Apart from fly-fishing (which costs $3,000 per person for a 7-day/6-night package), the lodge also has treks to Yelcho Glacier, mountain biking, horseback riding, and visits to the El Amarillo hot springs, Futaleufú, Chaitén, and Pumalín. The lodge will pick you up from nearly any nearby location.

Lago Yelcho, Km 54, Carretera Austral, Región X. ℡ **65/576-005.** www.yelcho.cl. 8 units, 6 cabins, 15 campsites. $132 double; $170 cabins for 4; $60 camping for 4. Rates include full breakfast (except cabins). AE, DC, MC, V. **Amenities:** Restaurant.

Futaleufú ★★★

155km (96 miles) SE of Chaitén; 196km (122 miles) NE of Puyuhuapi

Futaleufú is one of the prettiest villages in Chile, a town of 1,200 residents who live in colorful clapboard homes nestled high up in an awe-inspiring amphitheater of rugged, snowcapped mountains. Futaleufú sits at the junction of two rivers, the turquoise Río Espolón and its world-renowned cousin, the Río Futaleufú, whose white-water rapids are considered some of the most challenging on the globe. Every

November to April, this quaint little town becomes the base for hundreds of rafters and kayakers who come to test their mettle on the "Fu," as it's colloquially known, although just as many come to fish, hike, mountain-bike, paddle a canoe, or raft the gentler Río Espolón. Futaleufú is just kilometers from the Argentine border; it's possible to get here by road from Puerto Montt by crossing into Argentina, a route sometimes preferred for its paved roads.

There's now an ATM at the Banco Estado bank in town, but it has been known to run out of cash. There are no gas stations here in Futaleufú. However, residents do sell gas out of wine jugs and other unwieldy containers; just look for signs advertising BENCINA. Note that ash did blanket the town and surrounding area during the eruption of the Chaitén volcano in May 2008, though the minor damages have been dealt with and tourist operations are back to normal.

GETTING THERE

BY PLANE Air service into Futaleufú via the airport at Palena, about 2 hours south, is possible through a private charter plane from **Aerotaxis del Sur** (© 65/ 330726 in Puerto Montt, or cell 95/838374; www.aerotaxisdelsur.cl) from Puerto Montt, weather permitting. There is also a small landing strip just outside town. It's entirely feasible to fly into Esquel in Argentina from Buenos Aires and then travel by road 65km (40 miles) to Futaleufú; just be sure to factor in a possible delay at the border crossing and plenty of time to make the 2-hour journey.

BY BUS The fastest way to get to Futaleufú from Puerto Montt is through Argentina on a bus that stops in Osorno, Bariloche, and Esquel. **Turismo Futaleufú** (© 65/721215) has a Tuesday trip for C$19,950, returning Thursdays. **Trans Austral** (© 65/721360) operates weekly (dates change depending on the season) connecting to Esquel, from where many companies, including **Don Otto** (© 54/2945-453012 in Argentina; www.donotto.com.ar), depart for Bariloche and Puerto Montt. During the summer, bus service with **Chaitur** (© 65/731429; www.chaitur.com) sells tickets on the six weekly buses from Chaitén to Futaleufú, a 4-hour journey (C$20,000); however, timetables have been affected by the eruption and you should definitely check ahead for updated information.

BY CAR From Chaitén, take Rte. 7 south and go left to Rte. 235 at Villa Santa Lucía. The road winds around the shore of Lago Yelcho until Puerto Ramírez, where you head northeast on Rte. 231 until you reach Futaleufú. From Esquel, Argentina, it's 56km (35 miles) to the border, which is open during daylight hours only, and then another 9km (5.5 miles) to town.

WHAT TO SEE & DO

Futaleufú was put on the map by travelers with one goal in mind: to raft or kayak the internationally famous Class V waters of the village's namesake river, although just as many come to enjoy the opportunities to fly-fish, horseback ride, or just hang out amid the pristine alpine setting here. The Futaleufú is one of the most challenging rivers in the world. You've got to be good—or at least be experienced—to tackle frothing white-water so wild that certain sections have been dubbed "Hell" and "The Terminator." But rafting and kayaking companies will accommodate more prudent guests with shorter sections of the river, and the nearby Río Espolón offers a gentler ride. A paddling trip in this region is undoubtedly one of the best far-flung adventures a traveler can have in Chile.

RAFTING ON THE río futaleufú

The Futaleufú River is known as one of the best white-water rivers in the world, and an adventure down the rapids here rates as one of the highlights of a Chilean holiday. Tour operators can organize hard-adventure rafting expeditions, or shorter rafting on more mellow sections of the Futaleufú. There is also the Espolón River closer to town, which is suitable for light day rafting and kayaking trips (the **Hostería Río Grande,** see below, has sit-on-top kayak day rentals for the Espolón). The following three outfitters are the best around, and they offer weeklong all-inclusive packages that cost between $3,100 and $3,500.

The rafting and kayaking company with the most experience and local knowledge is **Expediciones Chile,** run by former American Olympic kayaker Chris Spelius. This outfit has a large selection of options to experience the Futaleufú, including multi-sport trips based out of their three-story townhouse **Adventure Lodge,** and get-away-from-it-all cabins and campsites at **CondorNest Ranch at Tres Monjas.** Both are serviced by a staff that leaves every evening to ensure absolute privacy, and there are wood-fired saunas, organic food, and massage service on the premises. Depending on

your desire, Expediciones Chile can organize a week that can include rafting, kayaking, horseback riding, hiking, and fly-fishing. Contact them ahead of time for day trips if you are short on time.

Another outstanding foreign-run pick is the all-inclusive rafting outfit **Earth River Expeditions** (✆ 800/643-2784; www.earthriver.com), with a 400-hectare (1,000-acre) private ranch outside of Futaleufú fitted with camp-style lodging in lofty tree houses and "cliff dwellings" with tent platforms and sweeping views. They've been around for more than 15 years, and, like Expediciones Chile, they boast superb guides whose local knowledge is as keen as their concern for safety. They also have outdoor hot tubs and massage services.

Lastly, try the rafting pros **Bío Bío Expeditions** (✆ 800/246-7238 in the U.S.; www.bbxrafting.com), another U.S.-based company with a passion for the Futaleufú. Like the other two outfits mentioned above, Bío Bío utilizes river-front lodging in the form of camping (on forest-canopied tent platforms) and cabins, and they combine a full-day horseback ride to a glacier to raft the river that runs from it. They also have a sauna and yoga classes.

For **fishing licenses,** go to the municipal building at O'Higgins 596 (✆ 65/721241); it's open April to November Monday through Friday from 8am to 1:30pm and 2:30 to 5pm, December to March Monday through Friday 9am to 7pm (outside the Municipalidad). For more information on fishing, see the "Fly-Fishing Lodges on the Carretera Austral" section later.

WHERE TO STAY

Most visitors to this area join one of the organized trips mentioned in the "Rafting on the Río Futaleufú" box, above. Those with a rental vehicle will find a few local cabins or basic *hospedajes* during the summer in town, although for hotels it is slim if increasing pickings here, and you'll be charged a lot for what you get. In town, decent budget accommodations include **Posada Ely** (✆ 65/721205; fax 65/721308).

Hostal Antigua Casona   At over 60 years old, this three-story building right in front of the town's main square is one of the oldest in town, but has been restored and modernized. The ground floor houses its cafe, offering full meals by reservation only. It also sells local crafts. Rooms are on the top two floors, and typically furnished in wood, with wool rugs and bedspreads.

Manuel Rodríguez 215, Futaleufú. ©/fax **65/721311.** www.antiguacasona.cl. 4 units. $84 double; $100 triple, includes breakfast. AE, DC, MC, V. **Amenities:** Restaurant; bar. *In room:* No phone.

Hostería Río Grande This wooden, two-story *hostería* is popular with foreign tourists for its outdoorsy design and especially its restaurant and pub. While simple, and no longer the new place in town, it's one of the better inns. It has lost a lot of its energy of late, and it could really stand to be upgraded, as the rooms seem expensive for their dull, standard furnishings and office-building carpets. But the atmosphere is relaxed and guests can expect a standard level of comfort. There's also an apartment (but no kitchen) for six guests. The Río Grande's restaurant is the unofficial hangout spot in town, and it has a nice atmosphere for relaxing with a beer. There's seafood throughout the week, but try to make it on Wednesday or Saturday, when the restaurant receives its fresh fish delivery by air.

O'Higgins 397, Futaleufú. ©/fax **65/721320.** www.pachile.com. 10 units, 1 apt for 6. $116 double; $156 triple; $189 apt for 6. AE, DC, MC, V. Closed June–Oct. **Amenities:** Restaurant; bar; bikes; extensive watersports equipment rental. *In room:* No phone.

Hotel El Barranco ★ This large, green-roofed, ranch-style building is probably the best place in town, with prices to match. Its rustic rooms are certainly the most attractive in Futaleufú, particularly the bathrooms, featuring wash basins placed on objects like a tree stump or on an antique sewing machine. Rooms have ash-colored carpeting and stark white linens; apart from that they're entirely in wood, with beams on the ceiling and wooden window panels. It has all the same outdoor tours and activities of every place in town. Best of all, there's a pool and a chilled-out courtyard.

O'Higgins 172, Futaleufú. ©/fax **65/721314.** www.elbarrancochile.cl. 10 units. $208 double. Half- and full-board available. Rates include breakfast and bicycle use. AE, DC, MC, V. **Amenities:** Restaurant; bar; bikes; pool. *In room:* Wi-Fi.

WHERE TO DINE

Hotel El Barranco and the **Hostería Río Grande** are the better places to eat in town (see earlier), but you might also check out **Restoran Skorpion's,** Gabriela Mistral 225 (© **65/721228**), which offers about four choices per day of simple meat and seafood dishes (no credit cards accepted; daily 6pm–2am). **Restaurante Futaleufú,** O'Higgins 393 (© **65/721295**), has a short menu with 10 or so simple dishes that all cost the same (C$6,000; no credit cards accepted). Sample items include homemade spaghetti, salmon, and chicken stewed with peas (daily 8am–midnight).

Parque Nacional Corcovado

The Yelcho Glacier is largely inside the 209,623-hectare (517,990-acre) **Parque Nacional Corcovado,** established in 2005, but at press time services and trails weren't available beyond the glacier access point. The park stretches almost from the Yelcho River south to the Río Rodríguez, skirted by the Carretera Austral along its eastern fringe. It features two volcanoes, the Corcovado with its angled summit and the Nevado, and is being developed for whale-watching—most famously in the amusingly named Tic Toc Bay—similarly to the Tantauco project on Chiloé across the Corcovado Gulf.

The nearest village to the bay is miniscule **Puerto Raúl Marín Balmaceda,** where the Palena River meets the ocean at the end of the road from La Junta. The road, however, doesn't quite reach it yet; there's a spot upstream on the Palena River where boats depart for the 40-minute trip to the village.

Visits to a few hot springs along the Palena are also available from Puerto Raúl Marín Balmaceda.

La Junta

At the spot where the Palena and Rosselot rivers meet, this is the first main settlement south of Chaitén, and you'll see the first of many impressive orange bridges that characterize the Carretera Austral. La Junta is generally considered the midway point between Chaitén and Coyhaique. Stop for a homemade bite to eat at **Mi Casita de Te,** Carretera Austral s/n (© **67/314206**). There's a friendly full-service mountain lodge right across from town, **Espacio y Tiempo ★★** (© **067/314141;** www. espacioytiempo.cl), which makes a great base for exploring the Palena watershed nearby.

Fly-Fishing Lodges on the Carretera Austral

Anglers around the world consider Patagonia to be one of the last great regions for fly-fishing, especially now that fishing clubs, lodges, and private individuals have bought up stretches of some the best rivers in the U.S., strictly limiting access to some of the sweetest spots for casting a line. Some of the highest trout-yielding rivers in Patagonia see only a few dozen or so fly-fishermen per year, and, therefore, angling fanatics, some of Hollywood's biggest stars, and many international bigwigs (such as ex-president George H. W. Bush, Michael Douglas, Robert Redford, and Harrison Ford) pay a visit here to escape the crowds and be at one with nature. Options range from the Lakes District to Tierra del Fuego, on both sides of the border, and competition between lodges is fierce. Some of the lodges listed later on in this chapter are fishing-focused as well, but offer good options for other types of sports and excursions (see Cinco Rios Lodge and Hacienda Tres Lagos below).

Due to the recent recession, many lodges are now closed, and some are unsure of their services year-to-year. The ones that are open are offering significant discounts, often retaining rates from 2009. They aren't cheap, though; most run from $550 to $800 per night per person, all-inclusive (nonfishing spouses sometimes pay less, and some offer "father-son" deals, so ask before booking). Typically, they cater to few guests—around 12 at most—though larger hotels also tend to offer non-fishing excursions. All of the following rate three Frommer's stars (our highest ranking) for their one-of-a-kind location, direct access to prize streams and lakes, service, and friendliness.

El Patagon Lodge ★★★   Owned and operated by the landmark Yan Kee Way Lodge (p. 306) near Puerto Varas, El Patagon is nestled in the temperate rainforest south of Futaleufú and Palena, and it is a remote, rustic version of the aforementioned lodge. The area's trout-filled streams and lakes draw other fly-fishing guides with clients who must drive hours to reach the region, making this lodge's immediate access a bonus for longer fishing days. In fact, the American owners of this lodge purchased the land from a float pilot and fly-fishing enthusiast who sold his map of "secret" fishing spots along with the property. The property houses four rough-hewn wood cabins for a total of eight fly-fishing guests, plus an Oregon yurt dining room, and a sauna and hot tub perched high above the Figueroa River. There are also multiday fishing journeys outside the property, with horseback rides to remote fishing streams, and stays that combine local Chilean accommodations.

Región XI. ✆ **65/212030.** www.southernchilexp.com. 7-night all-inclusive packages cost, per person, $3,000 Nov–Dec, $5,000 Jan–Mar. AE, DC, MC, V. **Amenities:** Restaurant; bar; lounge; sauna; Jacuzzi. *In room:* No phone.

La Posada de los Farios ★★★   Founded by a North American who came to Chile nearly 20 years ago as a guide and never left, this very small lodge specializes in *farios*, or brown trout. The lodge is north of Coyhaique, in a refashioned country home on a private, tranquil ranch, and it caters predominately to foreigners. Nevertheless, the lodge keeps its roots firmly planted in the local culture, serving hearty Chilean cuisine and giving guests close access to rural folk whose traditional way of life has long disappeared in other parts of the world. Los Farios has a capacity of just six guests at a time, who not only can take advantage of fishing rivers and lakes that are the secret of the guides, but also can navigate the fjords of Parque Nacional Queulat for saltwater fishing, if they are so interested. The lovely American/Chilean couple who run this lodge provide very friendly, personal attention, and they arrange activities such as horseback riding, bird-watching, and more for nonfishing guests. The lodge is open from November to April.

Casilla 104, Coyhaique. ✆ **800/628-1447** in the U.S., or 67/236402. www.chilepatagonia.com. 5-night all-inclusive packages $3,040, per person, double occupancy. AE, DC, MC, V. **Amenities:** Restaurant. *In room:* No phone.

Patagonia Baker Lodge ★★★   This is one place really focused on fly-fishing enthusiasts' needs, from McKenzie drift boats to zodiacs to a tie-table in an upstairs lounge with a glacier view to sit down and prepare to outsmart the fish. The lodge rests right on the waterfront at the headwaters of the Baker River, the most powerful in the country. At this point, the crystal-clear river is relatively wide, and the lodge takes in the marvelous view of the forest, topped off by Andean glaciers. It has roughly 1,000 sq. m (10,764 sq. ft.) of floor space but just six double rooms, all with a river view. The white-shingle, green metal–roofed building is one-storied except for the double-story lounge, decorated with Gothic wall tapestries and featuring a terrace overlooking the river. The carpeted rooms are conservative in style, with comfortable beds, tan- and cream-colored walls, and wood-burning stoves. Fishing season runs from late October to late April. The lodge can receive up to 24 guests. Payments must be made in advance, by wire transfer to the lodge's Chilean bank account.

Carretera Austral, 2km (1¼ miles) S of Puerto Bertrand. ✆/fax **02/201-5503** in Santiago, or 67/411903. www.pbl.cl. 6 units. All-inclusive $3,000 for 4 nights, $4,000 for 6 nights and $4,650 for 7 nights per person per night based on double occupancy No credit cards. **Amenities:** Restaurant; bar; free Wi-Fi (in main lodge only).

PUYUHUAPI ★

198km (123 miles) S of Chaitén; 222km (138 miles) N of Coyhaique

Chile's Región X ends just south of Villa Santa Lucía. The view in Región XI or Aysén (often spelled Aisén) begins to pick up farther along, until the scenery goes wild as the valley narrows and thick green rainforest rises steeply from the sides of the road, just outside the entrance of Parque Nacional Queulat. Glacier and snowpack above drop into steep waterfalls, which turn into raging rivers making their way to the coast. When the valley opens, the Seno Ventisquero (Glacier Sound) unfolds dramatically, revealing the charming town of Puerto Puyuhuapi on its shore, which was founded by four young German immigrant brothers and their families who set up camp here in 1935. They ran a surprisingly successful carpet factory, **Alfombras de Puyuhuapi,** whose humble, shingled building you can still visit Monday through Friday from 8:30am to noon and 3 to 7pm, Saturday and Sunday 9am to noon. Admission is free (✆ **67/325131;** www.puyuhuapi.com). It really is worth a visit.

The most popular attractions in this region are **Parque Nacional Queulat** and the **Puyuhuapi Lodge & Spa** (see "Outside Puerto Puyuhuapi," later), just south and on the other side of the sound, a 5-minute boat ride away. If the Puyuhuapi Lodge's prices are beyond your limit, you might opt to stay at a more economical hotel in Puerto Puyuhuapi or, during the off-season, at El Pangue *cabañas,* and take a soak in the hot springs for the day; or visit the less luxurious but still charming springs right beside the main road at **Termas Ventisquero de Puyuhuapi** (✆ **67/325228;** www.termasventisqueropuyuhuapi.cl; C$15,000 per person; daily 9am–11pm), 6km (3¾ miles) south of Puyuhuapi. You can then spend the following day at Parque Nacional Queulat.

Parque Nacional Queulat

Parque Nacional Queulat is one of Chile's least-explored national parks, due to its dense concentration of virgin rainforest—in fact, some areas of this park remain practically unexplored. Yet you can drive through the heart of it, and there are several lookout points reached by car or in brief to moderate walks. Be sure to keep your eyes open for the *pudú,* a miniature Chilean deer that is timid but, with luck, can be seen poking its head out of the forest near the road.

The 154,093-hectare (380,610-acre) park has several access points but few paths and no backpacking trails. If entering from the north, you first pass a turnoff that heads to the shore of **Lago Risopatrón,** which is within the park, and a very attractive camping spot at **Angostura** that charges C$4,500 per site (C$750 for firewood and C$2,000 for a short boat ride). There's a 5.8km (3.5-mile) round-trip trail here that leads trekkers through rainforest and past Lago Los Pumas (a 4-hr. hike). Continuing south of Puerto Puyuhuapi, visitors arrive at the park's star attraction, the **Ventisquero Colgante,** a tremendous U-shape river of ice suspended hundreds of feet above a sheer granite wall. From the glacier, two powerful cascades fall into Laguna Témpanos below. Visitors can drive straight to a short trail that takes them to the glacier's lookout point at no charge. To get closer, cross the hanging bridge and take the **Sendero Mirador Ventisquero Colgante,** a moderate 3- to 4-hour hike (3.5 km/2.25 miles) that takes you to the lake below the glacier. The park service CONAF offers boat rides in this lake for about C$2,500 per person; the park station is open daily November through March from 8:30am to 9pm, and April through October from 8:30am to 5:30pm. To camp in this area, the park charges C$4,500 per site. For more information, contact CONAF's offices in Coyhaique at ✆ **67/212225** or 65/212142, or check the website at www.conaf.cl.

Farther south, the scenery becomes more rugged as the road takes visitors up the steep and narrow Cuesta de Queulat and to views of glacier-capped peaks, and then down again where the road passes the trail head to the **Sendero Río Cascada.** Even if you don't feel like walking the entire 1.7km (1-mile) trail, at least stop for a quick stroll through the enchanting forest. The trail leads to a granite amphitheater draped with braided waterfalls that fall into an ice-capped lake. Check with CONAF at the Ventisquero Colgante entrance for the status of a trail, or factor obstacles into your trip time. The station is open daily November through March from 8:30am to 9pm, and April through October from 8:30am to 5:30pm (✆ **67/212225** or 65/212142).

Where to Stay & Dine

IN PUERTO PUYUHUAPI

Try **Café Restaurant Rossbach,** Aysén s/n, next to the carpet factory (© 67/325203), if you're looking for something to eat; cakes are the specialty here. **El Pangue** has a restaurant, but it's 18km (11 miles) away. Call beforehand to see if you can get a table (see "Outside Puerto Puyuhuapi," later).

Casa Ludwig ★★   One of the few *residenciales* open most of the year (mid-Sept to Mar), Casa Ludwig can be found on the homestead of one of the original founders of the Puyuhuapi. It dates back more than 50 years, and was constructed entirely out of native woods. The rooms and furniture are on the older side, but well kept. Some rooms have bathrooms and some don't.

Av. Otto Uebel 850, Puerto Puyuhuapi. © **67/325220.** www.casaludwig.cl. 10 units. C$27,500 double with private bathroom; C$21,000 double with shared bathroom. Rates include breakfast. No credit cards. **Amenities:** Lounge. *In room:* No phone.

Hostería Alemana 🎁   This is the best option in town, although it still lacks in fundamentals like good heating and a decent restaurant. Delicious breakfasts include sliced meats and *küchen*. The hotel is in a well-maintained, flower-bordered antique home with colorful character. Only one room comes with a private bathroom, and one triple comes with a wood-burning stove. All rooms are spacious and scrubbed.

Av. Otto Uebel 450, Puerto Puyuhuapi. © **67/325118.** www.hosteriaalemana.cl. 6 units. C$26,500 double; C$33,500 triple. Rates include full breakfast and dinner. No credit cards. **Amenities:** Lounge. *In room:* No phone.

OUTSIDE PUERTO PUYUHUAPI

Fiordo Queulat Ecolodge ★   This lodge that butts up against a fjord smack in the heart of the lush coastal rainforests of Parque Nacional Queulat features four fine cabins with hardwood floors and wood-burning stoves and one main, newer eco-chic clubhouse with a living and dining area. Bird-watching, fly-fishing, treks to the Moraine Hanging Glacier, kayaking through the fjords, visits to hot springs, and treks through the park are all offered separately, though package deals tend to be a better value.

212 Km North of Coyhaique, Parque Nacional Queulat. © **67/233-302.** www.queulatlodge.com. 6 units. $230 double, $375 quadruple. Rates include lunch and dinner. AE, DC, MC, V. **Amenities:** Restaurant; bar; airport transfers for a fee.

Hotel y Cabañas El Pangue ★★ ☺ 🎁   El Pangue is just kilometers from the edge of Parque Nacional Queulat, 30m (98 ft.) from Lago Risopatrón, and 18km (11 miles) north from Puerto Puyuhuapi. Dense rainforest encircles the complex; a winding stream provides a fairy-tale spot for a quiet walk or a quick dip. Tremendous *nalca* plants abound on the property, some so large they'd serve as an umbrella. It's a jungle-like temperate rainforest. The staff is friendly and facilities are of good quality, and although the lodge focuses heavily on fly-fishing from November to May, other excursions include mountain biking, hiking, canoeing, and boat rides.

Lodging consists of cozy, attractive wood-paneled rooms that fit two to three guests. There is also one "house" with a kitchen for seven guests, which is good for families; all cabins have kitchens. The open-room, split-level cabins have a small table and chairs and an extra bed/couch; bathrooms have sunken tubs. The main building houses an excellent restaurant, game room, and lounge; outside is a *quincho* where there are frequent lamb barbecues. As on a ranch, there are ducks, geese, pheasants, and chickens squawking from a fenced-in area. Off-season rates drop dramatically.

Carretera Austral Norte, Km 240, Región XI. ℂ/fax **67/325128.** www.elpangue.cl. 12 units. $209 *cabañas* for 5; $129 exterior room double. Rates include buffet breakfast (*cabañas* excluded). 4 day/3-night all-inclusive packages from $1,625 per person in double occupancy. AE, DC, MC, V (only during high season). **Amenities:** Restaurant; bar; lounge; bikes; Jacuzzi; outdoor heated pool; room service; sauna; limited watersports equipment; free Wi-Fi (in lobby).

Puyuhuapi Lodge & Spa ★★ 📷 This is one of the best hotel/thermal spa complexes in Chile and draws visitors from around the globe for its remote, magnificent location, elegant design, thermal pools, and full-service spa. The hotel is nestled in thick rainforest on the shore of the Seno Ventisquero; to get here, guests must cross the sound via a 10-minute motorboat ride.

The baths were just a handful of ramshackle cabins until German immigrant Eberhard Kossmann bought the property and built this handsome complex of shingles and glass. There are, however, a few signs of wear and tear, and staff members are generally aloof and impersonal. The food has improved of late, though. The nine large suites on the lakefront come with a deck that hangs out over the water during high tide. There are six newer nonsmoking suites that come with a similarly stylish decor (especially the "Captain's Suite"). Other options include budget-friendly duplexes, but they do not come with a kitchen stove or a view.

Indoor facilities include a large pool, steam baths, whirlpools, and massage services—but who wants to be inside? Three outdoor thermal pools are accessible 24 hours a day, the smallest surrounded by ferns. Two paths run through the rainforest, and there's a pier where you can drop a kayak in the sound. But the big outdoor attraction here is the connection with *Patagonia Express,* a boat that takes visitors to Laguna San Rafael Glacier, an excellent option (see p. 355). It's sold as a package. Guests typically fly into Balmaceda (Coyhaique) and transfer to the lodge by boat. If you're not staying at the hotel but want to use the facilities, there's an average charge of C$22,000 for adults and C$10,000 for children for day use of the spa. For the outdoor pools, adults pay C$12,000 and the price for kids is C$6,000.

Bahía Dorita s/n, Puerto Puyuhuapi, Región XI. ℂ/fax **2/225-6489** in Santiago, or 67/325103 in Puyuhuapi. www.patagonia-connection.com. 33 units. $270 double; 3-night packages, including the cruise to Laguna San Rafael, $1,760 per person high season, $1,540 low season; half-price for kids. Lunch and dinner $30 adults, $11 children. AE, DC, MC, V. **Amenities:** Restaurant; bar; lounge; Jacuzzi; large indoor pool and 3 outdoor pools; sauna; spa.

COYHAIQUE

222km (138 miles) S of Puyuhuapi; 774km (480 miles) N of Cochrane

Aysén includes natural preserves whose rivers and lakes draw thousands every year for superb fly-fishing opportunities. Visitors who are not traveling the length of the Carretera Austral can fly into Coyhaique from Santiago or Puerto Montt; travel to southern Patagonia from here requires that you fly again to Punta Arenas, unless you have your own car and plan to take the long and gravelly road through flat Argentine steppe, enter via sea at Puerto Chacabuco, or hike in through remote Villa O'Higgins.

South out of Queulat, the scenery provokes oohs and ahhs at every turn. The pinnacle of Cerro Picacho comes into view before you enter Villa Amengual, a service village for farmers.

ACCOMMODATIONS ■
Cabañas Don Joaquín **5**
Cabañas Lodge La Pasarela **16**
Cabañas Los Pinos **1**
Cinco Rios Lodge **4**
Hostal Glady's **13**
Hotel El Reloj **14**
Raices B&B **15**
Residencial Mónica **8**

i Information

16

Ejército

Av. General Baquedano

José de Moraleda

Santiago

CHILE

Coyhaique

Tapera
Presidente
Puyuhuapi
Portales
21 de
Mayo
Riquelme
José M.
Carrera

Dr. Jorge Ibar
Manuel
Ibáñez
Rodríguez

Balmaceda

13 14

15

Río

General Balmaceda

Parra

9 10

Bulnes

i

Condell

Pradena

Coyhaique

Dussen

Plaza de
Armas

M. Montt

11

Eusebio
Lillo

■ Museo Regional
de la Patagonia

Cementerio
Municipal

Avenida Norte Sur

Gabriela
Mistral

Magallanes

6

3

Horn

7

S. Tte.
Cruz

Francisco Bilbao

12

Av. General Baquedano

21 de Mayo

Río Simpson

18 de Septiembre

12 de Octubre

Arturo Prat

Ramón Freire

Simón Bolívar

Almirante Barroso

Sargento Aldea

2

Lautaro

Lord Cochrane

Presidente Errázuriz

Ignacio Serrano

Cristóbal Colón

Pedro Aguirre Cerda

Héctor Monreal

■ Piedra
El Indio

Av. Almirante Simpson

Eusebio Lillo

Av. Ogana

Los Coigües

1

Camino Piedra el Indio

8

| 0 | 200 yds |
| 0 | 200 m |

N

4/5

DINING ◆
Café Confluencia **11**
Café Oriente **10**
Casino
 de Bomberos **9**
Dalí **2**
La Casona **3**

Restaurante
 Histórico Ricer **7**

NIGHTLIFE ★
Bajo Cero **12**
Bar West **6**

The road passes through a few rinky-dink towns before arriving at a paved road that appears like a heaven-sent miracle after hundreds of kilometers of jarring washboard. At a junction south of Villa Mañihuales, drivers can head to Puerto Aysén and Puerto Chacabuco, the departure point for boat trips to Laguna San Rafael and Puerto Montt, or southeast toward Coyhaique, passing first through the Reserva Nacional Río Simpson.

Founded in 1929, **Coyhaique** is a town that doesn't quite do justice to its stunning location beneath a towering basalt cliff called Cerro Mackay, surrounded by green rolling hills and pastures. This region of Patagonia takes a back seat to its southern counterpart around Torres del Paine, yet outside Coyhaique, new expeditions to unexplored areas start up every year; because of this, it's easy to get away from the crowds. The city is home to about 44,000 residents, almost half the population of the whole of Aysén. It's the only place in the region you'll find a full range of services and a sweet small-town feel. It also sits at the confluence of the Simpson and Coyhaique rivers, both renowned for trout and salmon fishing and a reason so many fly-fishing enthusiasts flock to this area. The other prime attraction relatively close to here is the **Laguna San Rafael Glacier,** a colossal ice field that can be visited on a modest ship or a luxury liner from Puerto Chacabuco; there are also flyovers that provide unforgettable memories. Beyond fishing, visitors can choose from a wealth of activities within a short drive of the city.

Essentials

GETTING THERE & AROUND

BY PLANE Coyhaique's **Aeropuerto de Balmaceda** (BBA; no phone) is a gorgeous 1-hour drive from downtown and is the landing and departure point for larger jets. **LAN Airlines** has two to three daily flights from Santiago, with a stop in either Puerto Montt or Temuco (there are no nonstops from Santiago); there's also one to two daily flights from Punta Arenas. The LAN office is at General Parra 402 (© **600/526-2000** toll-free; www.lan.com). **Sky Airline** has one or two daily flights depending on the season, with a stop in Puerto Montt and several flights per week to Punta Arenas, which originate in Puerto Montt (Prat 203; © **67/240827** in Coyhaique, or 600/600-2828 toll-free; www.skyairline.cl). Note that this airport doesn't have an ATM.

Charter flights (all small propeller planes) to closer destinations, such as Villa O'Higgins, Chile Chico, and Cochrane, leave from the **Aeródromo Teniente Vidal** (no phone), 7km (4¼ miles) outside town. Two charter-flight companies offer tourist overland flights, even over the Laguna San Rafael Glacier. Both are the same in terms of price and quality (about C$475,000 for 3 hr. for one to five people): **Aerotaxis del Sur** (© **67/252-253;** www.aerotaxisdelsur.cl) and **Empresas Don Carlos,** Baquedano 315 (© **67/231981;** www.doncarlos.cl). The latter also flies to Cochrane and Villa O'Higgins.

BY BOAT Some travelers arrive at Puerto Chacabuco by boat from Puerto Montt or Quellón on Chiloé and then transfer to Coyhaique. It is 67km (42 miles) to Coyhaique. For schedule information, see "Puerto Aysén, Puerto Chacabuco & Laguna San Rafael National Park," later in this chapter. In Coyhaique, **Navimag** is at Ibáñez 347 (© **67/233306;** www.navimag.cl).

BY BUS Coyhaique has a bus terminal at Laurato and Magallanes streets and companies are gradually moving their offices there. For buses with a final destination in Chaitén, try **Buses Becker,** Presidente Ibáñez 358 (© **67/232167;** busesbecker@123.cl), which leaves on Monday, Thursday, and Saturday at 8am. For Puyuhuapi and La Junta, try **Buses Terraustral** at the terminal (© **67/254335**), with buses daily at 6am, or **Buses Queulat** at Parra 329 (© **67/242626**), which connects with Futaleufú-bound buses on Wednesday, Friday, and Sunday departing at 8am. For Cochrane, take **Buses Don Carlos,** Arturo Prat 334 (© **67/522150;** www.doncarlos.cl), which leaves on Tuesday, Thursday, and Saturday at 9am. For Puerto Aysén and Chacabuco, take **Suray,** with 20 trips per day, at Prat 265 (© **67/238387**); or **Interlagos** at the Terminal (similarly frequent departures; © **67/240840**). For Puerto Ibáñez, try **Minibus Don Tito,** Pasaje Curicó 619 (© **67/250280**).

BY CAR Heading south on Rte. 7 from Puyuhuapi, the highway comes to a fork—one paved road and one dirt. The choice here is clear, especially if you've been driving on gravel all day. The well-signed, paved route heads first toward Puerto Aysén–Puerto Chacabuco and then heads southeast for a beautiful drive through the Río Simpson National Reserve before hitting town. At the city entrance, a sign points left for the center of town.

Car Rental for Local Trips & the Carretera Austral

Car rental is very expensive here, but there are plenty of offers; even the odd cafe has a pickup truck it will rent. Fortunately, the popularity of this trip has made competition fierce and prices have dropped considerably. Most require that you rent a truck if heading anywhere off paved roads (about C$50,000–C$60,000, or C$200,000 for a 4×4). **Hertz** (Para 280 and at Balmaceda airport; © 67/272178; www. hertz.cl) or **Budget** (Errázuriz 454 and at the Balmaceda airport; © 67/255171; www.budget.cl) are here. For local rental, try: **AGS Rent a Car,** Av. Ogana 1298, and at the airport (©/fax 67/231511; agsrentacar@entelchile.net); **International,** General Parra 97, and at the airport (© 67/214770); **Traeger,** Av. Baquedano 457 (©/fax 67/231648; www.traeger.cl); **Turismo Prado,** Av. 21 de Mayo 417 (© 67/231271; ventas@ turismoprado.cl); or **Automundo AVR,** Francisco Bilbao 510 (© 67/231621; wfritsch@patagoniachile.cl). If you can't find what you want with these companies, request a list from Sernatur.

ORIENTATION

Coyhaique has a pentagon-shape plaza—which happens to also be a Wi-Fi hotspot—in the northwest corner of town and many one-way streets that can easily confuse a visitor with a rental car. Most services and hotels are near the plaza, and you'll find it convenient to stick to walking downtown. The rest of the city is on a regular grid pattern.

VISITOR INFORMATION

A helpful English-speaking staff can be found at the **Sernatur** office at Bulnes 35 (© 67/270290; www.sernatur.cl); it's open January and February Monday through Friday from 8:30am to 8:30pm, Saturday and Sunday from 11am to 6pm; and March through December Monday through Friday from 8:30am to 5:30pm. Sernatur produces a glossy magazine packed with information about the region and full listings of services, and provides a brochure on fishing. Don't skip the **Oficina de Turismo Rural,** 2 blocks away on Ogana 1060 (© 67/214031; www.rutatranspatagonia.cl), which is very helpful, offering contact information and a good brochure for even the remotest lodgings well beyond the end of the Carretera Austral. For information about the natural parks and preserves, you can try **CONAF's** office at Los Coigües s/n (© 67/212225; www.conaf.cl).

[FastFACTS] COYHAIQUE

Currency Exchange Options include **Turismo Prado,** Av. 21 de Mayo 417 (© 67/231271), and **Emperador,** Freire 171 (© 67/233727). Both are open Monday through Friday 9am to 1:30pm and 3 to 7pm, and Saturday 9am to 2pm.

Fishing Licenses Get your fishing license from the office of SernaPesca online year-round at www.sernapesca.cl. Or try the Sernatur office in town (Bulnes 35; © 67/270290), which is open during summers only.

Hospital The city's Regional Hospital is at Jorge Ibar 0168 (© 67/219100). For emergencies, dial © 131, as in every city in Chile.

Internet Access   **Entel** has Internet access and a calling center at Prat 340. **Camello Patagón,** at Condell 149, is smoker-friendly, and has the best coffee to accompany your surfing. The cafe **Confluencia** (see later) has Wi-Fi.

Laundry   Try **Lavaseco All Clean,** General Parra 55, no. 2 (✆ **67/219635**), or **QL,** Francisco Bilbao 160 (✆ **67/232266**).

Outdoor & Fishing Gear   Go to **Suraypesca,** Prat 267 (✆ **67/234088**), for outdoor and fishing gear. **Condor Explorer,** Condell 87 (✆ **67/573634**), has mountaineering equipment.

Post Office   Correos de Chile is at Cochrane 226 (✆ **67/231787**).

What to See & Do

IN COYHAIQUE

Museo del Maté   This tiny museum on the road to the airport in the town of El Blanco is dedicated to the strong herbal tea called yerba maté, which is a far more popular drink in neighboring Argentina and Uruguay, especially among the gaucho community. The one-room museum features old photos of the area, a variety of *guampa* gourds (drinking vessels made from a cow's horn), and *bombillas* (metal straws used to drink maté). It's worth a quick look; vendors across the street sell maté for purchase.

Airport road, El Blanco. ✆ **67/213175.** Admission C$1,800. Tues–Fri 11am–1pm and 3–6pm; Sat–Sun 11am–1pm and 3–7pm.

Museo Regional de la Patagonia ★   This small museum was closed in 2010 for a major renovation. When reopened in mid-2011, it will offer information about regional flora and fauna, with stuffed birds, armadillos, and turtles; rock and petrified wood samples; and an ethnographic exhibit featuring photographs, colonial machinery, and other antique items. There is also a photo exhibit of workmen building the Carretera Austral.

Av. Lillo 23, corner of Baquedano. ✆ **67/213175.** Admission C$1,800 adults, free for kids. Mid-Dec to Feb daily 8:30am–8pm; Mar to mid-Dec Mon–Fri 8:30am–1:30pm and 2:15–5:30pm.

Reserva Nacional Coyhaique ★   You don't need to go far in Coyhaique to surround yourself in wilderness. This little preserve (2,670 hectares/6,595 acres) is just under 5km (3 miles) from town on the road to Puerto Aysén and is a good place to go for a light walk through native forest, have a picnic, or pitch a tent. A ranger station at the entrance has complete trail information. From here, a short trail leads to a campground and then continues to Laguna Verde, with picnic and camping areas. There is a longer trail called the Sendero Las Piedras, which rewards hikers with wide-open views of the surrounding area and city below. The reserve's proximity to the city means it's entirely feasible to walk there. ✆ **67/212225.** www.conaf.cl. Admission C$1,500 adults, C$500 children; camping C$4,500 for up to six people. Nov–Mar daily 8:30am–9pm; Apr–Oct daily 8:30am–5:30pm.

Reserva Nacional Río Simpson   The only way to really see this reserve is by car—which you'll do anyway if you drive from Coyhaique to Puerto Aysén. The road winds along the shore of the Río Simpson, passing through impressive scenery and offering two crashing waterfalls, the Bridal Veil and the Virgin, which are signposted. There's also a museum here without anything of much interest and an information center. Unfortunately, trails in this reserve are not regularly maintained and are, therefore, tough to hike; inquire at the information center as to their status.

Road to Puerto Aysén, Km 37. ℂ **67/212225.** www.conaf.cl. Admission C$600; camping C$4,500. Nov–Mar daily 8:30am–9pm; Apr–Oct daily 8:30am–5:30pm. Information center daily 8:30am–1:30pm and 2:15–6:30pm.

OUTDOOR ACTIVITIES IN THE AREA

Tour operators plan day trips, multiday trips, and full expeditions to areas as far as the Southern Ice Field. **Adventure Expeditions Patagonia,** Riquelme 372 (ℂ **67/ 219894;** www.adventurepatagonia.com), can put together unforgettable expeditions to areas rarely seen by travelers, including a hut-to-hut hiking expedition along the Aysén Glacier, a 14-day horseback-riding trip along the Pioneer Trail, and an "Ice to Ocean" 11-day horseback, hiking, and rafting adventure; they are highly recommended and they have an excellent staff of guides.

Andes Patagónicos, Horn 48, no. 11 (ℂ **67/216711;** www.ap.cl), has tours around Coyhaique, such as trips to the Lake Carrera and the Capillas de Mármol; 5-day journeys to Caleta Tortel with stops at archaeological sites, immigrant posts, glaciers, and rivers; 1-day and multiday fly-fishing tours; trips to the Laguna San Rafael and Termas de Puyuhuapi; and more.

Condor Explorer, Condell 87 (ℂ **67/573634;** www.condorexplorer.com), specializes in mountaineering excursions, including the tough ones to the Northern Ice Field and San Lorenzo, and offers logistical support for overseas expeditions. It's one of few tour operators that are active year-round, offering ski treks/randonee (alpine touring), hiking, trekking, and horseback riding. Their agency has the sole mountaineering store in Coyhaique.

For a private fly-fishing guide, try **Expediciones Coyhaique,** Portales 195 (ℂ/fax **67/231783;** www.coyhaiqueflyfishing.com). For sightseeing trips along the Carretera Austral and to Puerto Aysén, and trips to view Tehuelche Indian rock, try **Turismo Prado,** 21 de Mayo 417 (ℂ/fax **67/231271;** www.turismoprado.cl).

NOLS Patagonia, 11km (7 miles) south of Coyhaique (ℂ **800/710-NOLS** [710-6657]; www.nols.edu), is the Chilean branch of the U.S.-based National Outdoor Leadership School. Set on a 200 hectare (500-acre) working organic farm, intensive training courses here range from 14- to 34-day kayaking and mountaineering trips ($3,470–$6,155) to semester-long wilderness courses that include studies in mountaineering, first aid, survival, and other outdoor activities.

FISHING Since their introduction in the late 1800s, trout and salmon have thrived in the crystalline waters in southern Chile, but nowhere in the country has fly-fishing taken off as it has here in the Aysén region. The burgeoning number of guides alone bears testament to the truth of this region's claim as one of the premier fishing destinations on the globe, drawing thousands of anglers from around the world to reel in 3-, 5-, and even 10-pounders. Even if you've never fished before, this might be your opportunity to try. Each tour operator has a list of its own fly-fishing guides in the Aysén region, some of whom work independently. If you're coming here mainly to fish, there are several full-service luxury lodges in the region. All have on-site guides, both Chilean and foreign, many from the U.S. Most offer activities for nonangling spouses and friends (see the "Fly-Fishing Lodges on the Carretera Austral" section on p. 350).

Tour operators organize day, multiday, and weeklong excursions to fly-fishing spots such as the Simpson, Baker, and Nirehuao rivers, and Bertrand and General Carrera lakes. Some combine excursions with other activities, such as horseback riding or hiking.

HORSEBACK RIDING Trips often head to the Coyhaique Reserve and Lago Margaritas, but tour companies offer a variety of destinations. Some arrange all-inclusive, multiday trips; for this, try **Andes Patagónicos** (see earlier).

SKIING It's not a world-class ski resort (two T-bars are the lift service), but it can be fun to visit if you're here between June and September. The **Centro de Esquí El Fraile** (☎ 67/198-3007) is 29km (18 miles) from Coyhaique, offering five ski runs serviced by two T-bars. It's a tiny resort but can make for a fun day in the snow, and it's one of the few resorts in Chile that has tree skiing. There are also cross-country skiing opportunities here. Tickets cost about C$14,500 per day, and it's possible to rent equipment for an average of C$8,500. **Andes Patagónicos** and **Condor Explorer** can get you there (see earlier).

Where to Stay

There are many clean *residenciales* in Coyhaique that are inexpensive but pretty basic, and rooms are small and noisy; also, most have shared bathrooms and you must bring your own towel. **Residencial Mónica**, at Lillo 664, has a very attractive dark violet, shingled facade (☎ 67/234302) and private bathrooms, while **Hostal Gladys,** at Parra 65 (☎ 67/245288; patagoniagladys@hotmail.com), is both clean and friendly. Both hotels are a good notch above the rest, so book ahead. The backpacking crowd will like Spanish-owned lodge **Albergue Las Salamandras** (☎ 67/211865; www. salamandras.cl), in the woods across the Simpson River, a 20-minute walk from town.

EXPENSIVE

Cabañas Lodge La Pasarela ★ 🖻 These attached rooms and cabins nestled on the shore of Río Simpson (on the fork with Río Coyhaique) are good for those who like more rural surroundings. The complex is on the other side of the river, away from the main road, and to get there guests must first cross a wooden suspension bridge. Cabañas La Pasarela is geared toward fly-fishermen, with private guides from Chile and the U.S. But guests also like this lodge because you can fish right at the bank of the Río Simpson outside your door. All of the structures are made of cypress logs and have black, shingled roofs. With a dated style and a bit too much clutter for some tastes, it's certainly not an elegant or upscale place. Riverside lodge rooms are large, have queen-size beds, and extras like a minibar. A pebbled walkway goes up to four A-frame *cabañas*. They arrange bilingual fly-fishing tours: C$160,000 a day for two people, including transportation, fishing licenses, and lunch. It's open October through May only.

Km 2, road to Puerto Aysén, Coyhaique. ☎ **67/9818-7390** cell. www.lapasarela.cl. 15 units. $152 double; $181 cabin for 5. Rates include buffet breakfast (except *cabaña*). No credit cards. **Amenities:** Restaurant; bar; lounge; limited Wi-Fi (in lobby). *In room:* TV.

Cinco Rios Lodge ★★ This fine lodge opened in 2006 and is just a few kilometers outside of town on the road to the airport. It's close enough for quick drives into the city, but far enough away that you'll still soak in dramatic views and feel the vastness that is Patagonia. The six spacious contemporary cabins with floor-to-ceiling windows overlooking the Río Simpson are the best rooms in town. Each room has two king beds, a rarity in these parts. Their gourmet restaurant is worth a visit in its own right. Fly-fishing is the focus of the lodge, and they have special arrangements with *estancias* as far south as the Río Baker to use their properties for excursions. They also have a small fly-fishing lodge on the Argentine border, Estancia El Zorro.

Km 5 on the road to Balmaceda, Coyhaique. ☏ **67/244917**. www.cincorios.cl. 6 units. $525 per person per night including meals and excursions; 6 days/7 nights $3,675 per person. Rates include all meals plus wine, transportation, tours/fishing. AE, DC, MC, V. Closed June–Oct. **Amenities:** Restaurant; bar; lounge; free Wi-Fi (in lobby). *In room:* TV.

MODERATE

Cabañas Don Joaquín ★ ✦ This group of modern two-story *cabañas*, nestled among the pine trees above the Simpson River, are fully equipped, including maid service, making them an upscale alternative to the nearby Las Salamandras. Polished tree-trunk–framed beds make the woodsy atmosphere even more rustic, as do the wood-burning furnaces. Some people like it so much they rent it for long periods of time, according to the Argentine administrator. The cabins are suitable for up to six people. Don Joaquín also has a good restaurant on the premises. For a group or family, this is a great value.

Camino Aeródromo Teniente. Vidal, Km 2, Coyhaique. ☏ **67/214553**. www.coyhaique.com. 9 units. $95 for double; $105 triple; $179 cabin for up to seven people. No credit cards. **Amenities:** Restaurant. *In room:* TV, kitchenette.

Cabañas Los Pinos ★ 📷 These handcrafted log cabins are nestled in a pine for-est on the shore of Río Simpson, about a 5-minute drive from downtown. There are cabins for three, four, or six people, each with a wood-burning stove; the cabin for six has one bedroom with a full-size bed and one with two bunks. All have shared bath-rooms. The cabins for four are a little tight, but the charm of the place makes up for it. The cabin for six comes with a kitchen; the other two cabins share a separate eating area, which guests usually don't mind, considering the eating area is an idyllic little cabin with a beautiful view, great cooking facilities, and two tables for four. The couple who owns and runs the property is very friendly, and they have a vehicle for excursions.

Camino Teniente Vidal, Km 1.5, Parcela 5, Coyhaique. ☏ **67/234898**. www.lospinos-chile.com. 5 units. $53 cabin for 2; $80 cabin for 4; $95 cabin for 6. No credit cards. **Amenities:** Restaurant. *In room:* TV, kitchenette, no phone.

Hotel El Reloj ★ This bed-and-breakfast-style hotel is housed in a forest-green-and-lemon old home flanked by two *lenga* trees. The hotel is surrounded by an abundance of greenery, which is pleasant, but it shades the windows, so the rooms are fairly dark. The rooms are a little on the small side and are pretty basic, but they do have character in their sloped ceilings and old wood floors. It's a cozy enough place and very clean. There's a common living area and a small restaurant serving local fare, such as wild hare, sheep cheese, and fresh salmon. The restaurant is open to the public, but limited seating keeps the numbers low. It's located close to the plaza.

Av. Baquedano 828. ☏/fax **67/231108**. www.elrelojhotel.cl. 20 units. $150 double. Rates include buffet breakfast. No credit cards. **Amenities:** Restaurant; lounge; bar; room service; free Wi-Fi. *In room:* TV.

Raices Bed and Breakfast ★★ 📷 It seems there's better taste in this new inn than in most of the town of Coyhaique put together. The common room faces out on the green space overlooking the river below. Guest rooms face the street, but are actually quite quiet. They're simply decorated with white walls and linens, and spots of natural-hued woolen accents. The breakfast is relatively gourmet for these parts. The owner, Cecilia, also has a lovely store on the main plaza selling high-quality knit-ted wear from vicuña wool.

Av. Baquedano 444. ☏ **67/210490**. www.raicesbedandbreakfast.com. $116 standard double, $137 superior double. Rates include buffet breakfast. No credit cards. **Amenities:** Common room. *In room:* No TV.

Where to Dine

There are several cafes downtown that are good for a quick bite, such as **Café Confluencia** (📞 67/245080), 21 de Mayo 544, with healthy food and Wi-Fi; and **Café Oriente** (📞 67/231622), Condell 201, with pizzas and sandwiches. In the evening, drop by **Bar West** (📞 67/210007), Bilbao 110, for a pint.

EXPENSIVE

Bajo Cero ★★ 🍴 INTERNATIONAL   This relatively new restaurant has something Coyhaique sorely needed: good food at decent prices, with a Patagonian grill for meats, seafood such as conger eel in chardonnay, or pie-like *chupe* of king crab and crabmeat. It departs from the log-cabin decor that's standard in these parts in favor of a more generous, traditional restaurant layout, mixing modern touches like curved, polished walls and a flattened wood-paneled ceiling with aboriginal wall decorations. Its *capillas de mármol* gin cocktail is interesting; it's a little sweet but its color spectacularly mimics the crystal waters of its namesake landmark.

21 de Mayo 655. 📞 **67/233243.** Main courses C$4,000–C$7,500. AE, DC, MC, V. Daily noon–3pm and 7–10:30pm.

Dalí ★ SPANISH/INTERNATIONAL   The trendiest, most modern place in town is a 16-seat bistro run by chef Cristián Balboa, who lives upstairs. The sizeable wine list pairs well with their luscious rack of lamb, salmon, and chorizo plate, and whatever else that's in season in Patagonia. The restaurant is hidden away in a residential area 5 blocks from the plaza. Just look for the oversized mural of Salvador Dalí.

Laurato 82. 📞 **67/245422.** Reservations required. Main courses C$8,000–C$13,000. AE, DC, MC, V. Daily 7:30–11pm.

MODERATE

La Casona 🍴 CHILEAN   Locals generally agree that this is the best place to eat in town. Clean and austere, with a traditional menu and reasonable prices, you can sample the best of the area here, from oysters and salmon to king crab and lamb. Don't miss the seafood empanadas as a starter. There's no wine list; diners help themselves to whatever is open at the bar. It's definitely a local's kind of place.

Obispo Vielmo 77. 📞 **67/238894.** C$4,000–C$6,200. MC, V. Tues–Sun noon–3pm and 7–10:30pm.

Restaurant Histórico Ricer ★ ☺ CHILEAN/INTERNATIONAL   This restaurant is a favorite with traveling gringos, and just about everyone else in town who can afford it, too. It's located right in the center of the action, overlooking the main plaza and pedestrian street. The large, crowded, pub-style restaurant is fashioned of logs, and a handcrafted wood staircase leads to a mellower, slightly more formal dining area upstairs. All in all, the food is decent, although terribly overpriced, and the service is absent-minded: Waitresses tend to group at the cash register and gossip rather than wait on tables. There is food available any time of the day.

Horn 48. 📞 **67/232920.** www.ap.cl/restaurante.htm. Main courses C$4,000–C$8,000. AE, DC, MC, V. Daily 8:30am–2am (to 3am in summer).

INEXPENSIVE

Casino de Bomberos 🍴 CHILEAN   Chile's volunteer firemen need some way to make a buck, and here's their solution: Open a cafe in the fire station. The atmosphere is plain but fun, and the menu features such classic dishes as roasted chicken and calamari with tomato sauce. The food is tasty and the fixed-price lunch is cheap at C$2,850, including a salad, soup, main dish, and dessert. On Sunday, there are baked and fried fresh empanadas.

General Parra 365. © **67/231437.** Main courses C$2,500–C$3,500. No credit cards. Daily noon–4pm and 7pm–midnight.

PUERTO AYSÉN, PUERTO CHACABUCO & PARQUE NACIONAL LAGUNA SAN RAFAEL ★★★

Puerto Aysén: 68km (42 miles) W of Coyhaique

Puerto Aysén was a vigorous port town until the 1960s, when silt filled the harbor and ships were forced to move 16km (10 miles) away to Puerto Chacabuco. While it's in the midst of gorgeous landscape, it offers few attractions to the visitor. The same could be said for Puerto Chacabuco; however, the majority of visitors to this region pass through here at some point to catch a ship or ferry to Laguna San Rafael Glacier or to Puerto Montt. Most travelers arriving by ferry from Puerto Montt head straight to Coyhaique, and vice versa, but the full-day ferry ride to Laguna San Rafael leaves early and returns late, so many travelers find it convenient to spend a night here in Puerto Chacabuco.

It's recommended that you at least take a day trip to Puerto Aysén and Puerto Chacabuco, more than anything for the beautiful drive through the Reserva Nacional Río Simpson and the equally beautiful view of Aysén Sound at the journey's end. That said, both towns are a little scrappy. **Restaurant Isla Verde** (Tte. Merino s/n; © **67/332551**) in Puerto Aysén is the best spot for lunch before heading back to Coyhaique. If you don't have your own transportation, you can try **Buses Suray,** Eusebio Ibar 630 (© **67/336222**), which connects in Puerto Aysén for Coyhaique. The best bet is to call **Patagonia Austral,** Condell 149, no. 2 (©/fax **67/239696;** www.australpatagonia.cl), which offers day trips around this area, especially bird-watching tours. The tours operate from November 15 to March 15 only, but the agency will arrange trips any time of the year for small groups. **Turismo Rucaray,** in Puerto Aysén, at Tte. Merino 660 (© **67/332862;** rucaray@entelchile.net), offers other excursions around the area and sells ferry tickets.

Parque Nacional Laguna San Rafael ★★★

If you're not planning a trip to the parks in southern Patagonia, Parque Nacional Laguna San Rafael is a must-see. It's the foremost attraction in the Aysén region, drawing thousands of visitors each year to be dazzled by the tremendous vertical walls of blue ice that flow 45km (28 miles) from the Northern Ice Field and stretch 4km (2½ miles) across the Laguna San Rafael. It's the closest sea-level ice field to the Equator. Around these walls, thousands of aquamarine icebergs float in soupy water, forming jagged sculptures.

The glacier is actually receding, and quite quickly; it may well stop dropping ice into the lagoon within only a few years, but in the meantime, you will likely see numerous, heavy chunks of ice plunging into the deep water. The first explorers here in 1800 described the glacier as having filled three-quarters of the lagoon; when you're here, you can appreciate how much has disappeared, and the speed at which it is shrinking is unsettling.

Parque Nacional Laguna San Rafael is a staggering 1.75 million hectares (4.3 million acres). Most of the park is inaccessible except by ship, on which visitors slowly cruise through narrow canals choked with thick vegetation. Like Torres del Paine, Laguna San Rafael is a UNESCO World Biosphere Reserve. Visitors set sail in Puerto Chacabuco or Puerto Montt aboard an all-inclusive luxury liner or modest ferry for day and multiple-day trips. The ship anchors near the glacier and passengers board zodiacs (inflatable motorized boats) for a closer look at the icebergs and the glacier, which in some places rises as high as 70m (230 ft.), causing the zodiacs to rock when the ice hits the water. A smaller fraction of visitors book an overflight excursion for a bird's-eye view of the glacier's entirety, which includes a touchdown at the park's center, near the glacier, for an hour-long visit.

Your best bet for clear skies is from November to March. Even on foul-weather days, the glacier is usually visible, as the clouds tend to hover just above it. Bring protective rain gear just in case, or inquire when booking a ticket, as many companies provide guests with impermeable jackets and pants.

CONAF administers the park and charges a C$12,000 admission fee (ferry passengers do not pay; only those landing in planes do, but please donate something at the park ranger station anyway, as every bit of funding helps). CONAF offers several services at the park, including a boat ride near the glacier for C$35,000 per person, and five sites for camping (C$2,500 per tent).

FERRY JOURNEYS THROUGH THE FJORDS TO LAGUNA SAN RAFAEL ★★★

This extraordinary journey is about a 200km (124-mile) sail from Puerto Chacabuco, but many visitors leave from Puerto Montt for a round-trip journey or to disembark in Puerto Chacabuco. Some visitors plan a multiday journey to Laguna San Rafael as the focal point of a trip to Chile that also includes a stopover at the Puyuhuapi Lodge and hot springs (see above). When booking a trip, consider the journey's length and whether you will be traveling at night and, therefore, missing any portions of scenery. In addition to the companies below, **Navimag Ferries** (p. 316) offers 5-day round-trip cruises directly from Castro on the island of Chiloé, with prices ranging from C$390,000 to C$600,000, and from Puerto Chacabuco from C$340,000 to C$550,000 per person.

Catamaranes del Sur ★ This catamaran service to Laguna San Rafael also owns the hotel at the port in Puerto Chacabuco, the Hostería Loberías del Sur, and they offer packages ranging from 3 to 6 days. Catamaranes has its own private park, Aikén del Sur, which it visits for a half-day tour included in the 2- to 3-night packages. Also included in the packages is a typical Patagonian lamb barbecue. The company has a fleet of ships that are smaller and, therefore, offer a more personalized experience than the large Navimag ships, making this a good choice for day trips to the Laguna (the price is slightly higher than with Navimag). Trips include all meals, an open bar, onboard entertainment, and inflatable zodiac boat rides near the glacier.

In Santiago, Pedro de Valdivia 0210. © **2/231-1902.** Fax 2/231-1993. www.catamaranesdelsur.cl. AE, DC, MC, V. 2-night packages $864 per person based on double occupancy. Includes all meals, open bar, and excursions.

Patagonia Connection ★★★ Patagonia Connection works in conjunction with the Puyuhuapi Lodge & Spa (p. 354), leaving from Puerto Chacabuco and including

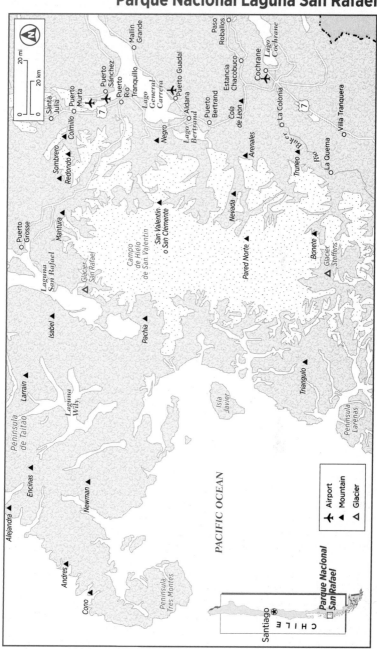

a 2-night stay at the hotel and 1 night in Puerto Chacabuco. This is another premium excursion with sharp service and wonderful accommodations, but unlike Skorpios, you do not spend the night onboard the ship. It departs Tuesday and Saturday from September to April. During the entire long trip, the ship is kept amazingly spotless.

In Santiago, Fidel Oteiza 1921, no. 1006. ✆ **2/225-6489** or 800/898-7334 in North America. Fax 2/274-8111. www.patagonia-connection.com. AE, DC, MC, V. Prices average $1,550 per person for the 3-night package, including 1 night in Puerto Chacabuco and 2 nights at the Puyuhuapi Lodge & Spa; half-price for kids 15 and under. Includes all meals and excursions.

Skorpios ★★★ Skorpios is the upscale cruise service to Laguna San Rafael, offering deluxe onboard accommodations, great food, and all-around high quality. The rough-hewn wood cabins come with berths or full-size beds (or both, for families), in standard rooms or suites. The *Skorpios II* boards 130 people, although the trips are not usually heavily booked. Skorpios offers 7-day cruises along the eastern coast of Chiloé near Castro, then down to the glacier. On the return trip, the ship detours up the Fjord Quitralco to visit the remote hot springs there. Heading back to Puerto Montt, the ship cruises along the southern coast of Chiloé, stopping in Castro for an afternoon excursion. Skorpios offers service from September to May.

In Santiago, Augusto Leguía Norte 118, Las Condes. ✆ **2/477-1900.** Fax 2/232-2269. www.skorpios.cl. AE, DC, MC, V. Cost for the 7-day/6-night journey is $1,350–$1,700 per person. Prices include all meals, drinks, and excursions, and vary from high season to low season. Half-price for kids 11 and under in parent's room.

OVERFLIGHT TRIPS TO THE LAGUNA SAN RAFAEL

A handful of companies arrange 2-hour overflight trips to the Laguna San Rafael, including disembarking near the glacier. It is a spectacular experience to view the glacier in its entirety (which means you won't want to do this trip on a cloudy day). These are charter flights, so you'll have to get a group together or fork over the entire price, but in a group, the price is competitive when you compare it with the cruises. Companies offering the service include **Don Carlos,** Subteniente Cruz 63 (✆ **67/231981;** www.doncarlos.cl); and **Transportes San Rafael,** 18 de Septiembre 469 (✆ **67/232048**). CONAF charges passengers C$12,000 for admission to the park.

Where to Stay & Dine

Hotel Loberías del Sur This landmark keeps relatively full due to the fact that it has a good view, and a supreme location right above the docks. Still, rooms are dated and standard; service is only so-so, and the restaurant is sub par. In fact, it's far more of a business hotel than a Patagonian lodge. This is where most travelers with ferry connections spend the night when they don't want to make the early morning journey from Coyhaique.

Carrera 50, Puerto Chacabuco, Región XI. ✆ **67/351115.** Fax 67/351188. www.catamaranesdelsur.cl. 60 units. $180 double. Rates include buffet breakfast. DC, MC, V. **Amenities:** Restaurant; bar; lounge; exercise room; room service; sauna. *In room:* TV, hair dryer.

South From Coyhaique

A SIGHTSEEING EXCURSION AROUND LAGO ELIZALDE

The Seis Lagunas (Six Lagoons) and Lago Elizalde region just south of Coyhaique offers a sightseeing loop that passes through fertile, rolling farmland and forest, and past several picturesque lakes, all of which are known for outstanding fly-fishing. Because few people visit, this is a great place to escape the crowds. If you're tempted to stay and fish for a few days here, there are lodges that cater to this sport, described in "Fly-Fishing Lodges on the Carretera Austral" on p. 350. If you rent your own car, pick up a good map because many of these roads have no signs.

Leaving Coyhaique via the bridge near the Piedra del Indio (a rock outcrop that resembles the profile of an Indian), head first to Lago Atravesado, about 20km (12 miles) outside town. The road continues around the shore and across a bridge, and enters the Valle Laguna. From here, you'll want to turn back and drive the way you came until you spy a road to the right that heads through country fields, eventually passing the "six lagoons." Take the next right turn toward Lago Elizalde. This pretty, narrow lake set amid a thick forest of deciduous and evergreen beech is a great spot for picnicking and fishing. There is often a boat-rental concession here in the summer. There's also a lodge, but it's open only occasionally, usually when it books a large group. From here you'll need to turn back to return to Coyhaique; follow the sign for Villa Frei, which will lead you onto the paved road to Coyhaique instead of backtracking the entire route. Keep an eye open for El Salto, a crashing waterfall that freezes solid in the winter.

RESERVA NACIONAL CERRO CASTILLO & LAGO GENERAL CARRERA ★★★

At a moderate 57km (35 miles) south of Coyhaique, this nature preserve protects beautiful Andean scenery almost rivaling that of Torres del Paine. On a sunny day, you'll marvel at the 2,318m (7,603-ft.) **Cerro Castillo** or Castle Peak, named for the many granite needles that crown the summit, reminiscent of a medieval European fortress. The 179,550-hectare (443,490-acre) park holds glaciers, lagoons, and wildlife, including the rare huemul deer, along with several hiking trails. The Carretera Austral crosses the park, and tour operators from Coyhaique and around Lake General Carrera offer excursions. A great place to stop for a bite is **La Cocina de Sole,** where a young lady named Soledad whips up good sandwiches and simple lunches in a bus-turned-diner along the highway as it passes Villa Cerro Castillo. Don't miss the nearby **Manos de Cerro Castillo** national monument (admission C$4,000; daily 10am–6pm), about 5km (8 miles) from town. Under a rocky ledge in view of the summit, it preserves some of the oldest artistic remains yet discovered in the Americas—some 10,000 years old. Here, Tehuelche tribespeople, including children, left red, black, and brown positive and negative handprints on the walls. It's a touching spot.

Another 30km (19 miles) south by the most direct route, Chile shares its largest lake, the huge **Lago General Carrera,** with Argentina (where it is called Lago Buenos Aires). The landscape once again is gorgeous, with the water mostly a robin's-egg blue, surrounded by snow-capped mountains. Under mushroom-shaped islands, the lake features a series of marble caves polished and sculpted by centuries of wind and water, known as the marble "cathedrals" or "chapels." Their gray, yellow, or black-and-white swirls are a magnificent contrast to the blue water below. The best known is the **Capillas de Mármol ★★**, which is best visited by hiring a boatman in Puerto Río Tranquilo. There is a trailer just across from the gas station that sets up 1½-hour tours (C$25,000 per boat; up to eight people), though they are highly dependent on the weather. Also consider visiting the less popular but larger islands from Puerto Sánchez; to get there, take the dirt road past Bahía Murta.

If the trip to the San Rafael glacier will bust your budget, head for the spectacular **Glaciar Leones**—like the former, part of the San Valentín Ice Field—which juts into the lake and river of the same name west of Puerto Río Tranquilo. Hire a guide, since the trail to the Leones lakeshore is poorly marked, as well as a small boat to take you close to the glacier's face. It's a marvelous excursion, but it can be frigid in inclement weather. Other excursions include the **Exploradores Glacier,** easy to walk on, up Río Tranquilo. Those with a rental car might consider returning to Coyhaique by rounding the lake to **Chile Chico** on the Argentine border. From here, travelers must put their vehicle on a ferry, which crosses the lake and lands in Puerto Ibañez, from where drivers continue north to Coyhaique (reservations for cars are a good idea; contact **Motonave Pilchero** at Ⓒ **67/233466;** C$2,500 for passengers, C$18,000 for vehicles; one round-trip service Mon–Wed and Fri only from Puerto Ibáñez). This journey is for independent travelers with a fair amount of time.

Where to Stay

While good food other than hearty Patagonian barbecue is an issue in Aysén, quite a number of places to stay have sprung up recently in this area, from lakeshore *cabañas* to basic residences and some real gems. In Puerto Ibañez on the north shore, you can stay at the **Cabañas Shehen Aike** (Ⓒ 67/423284; www.aike.cl). In Puerto Río Tranquilo (www.riotranquiloaysen.cl), two lakefront *hosterías* form bookends to the village. The first (from the north), **Hostería Costanera** (Ⓒ 67/411121), has better rooms with private bathrooms and lake views, but also a rudimentary gas station; the friendlier **Carretera Austral** (Ⓒ 67/419500) has better shared rooms with cleaner baths and a fine *cabaña*. On the south shore of the lake, on the road toward Chile Chico, consider the upscale **Mallín Colorado Lodge** (Ⓒ/fax 2/274-1807; www.mallincolorado.cl). In Chile Chico on the south shore, try the charming **Hostería de la Patagonia** (Ⓒ 67/411337), just outside town on the Camino Internacional; there are cheap, basic *residenciales* in the village.

To the south, on the shore of the lake of the same name, Puerto Bertrand holds several *residenciales* and the high-quality **Cabañas Campo Baker** (Ⓒ 67/411447; campobakerchile@123.cl), with fine views of the lake from most of the two-story bungalows, and owned and run by the charming Italian Orlando Scarito; full-board and multiday programs are available. The similarly simple but slightly more rustic **Green Baker Lodge** (Ⓒ 9/179116; www.greenlodgebaker.cl), a few kilometers away on the shore of the Baker River, is a slice of fly-fishing heaven, "next door" to the **Patagonia Baker Lodge** (Ⓒ 67/411903; www.pbl.cl) and **Cabañas Rapidos del Rio Baker** (Ⓒ 67/441-550; www.rapidosdelriobaker.com).

El Puesto ★★★ 🏠 One of Patagonia's top places to stay is this three-room boutique hotel in tiny Puerto Río Tranquilo, on Lake General Carrera. The boxy, contemporary building was built with native woods, with furniture upholstered in white, helping to create a cozy, light atmosphere reminiscent of Scandinavian design. Rooms are similar, with one offering a terrace and another with one bunk bed that's best for a party of friends; you might find the triple just a tad on the small side. While not directly on the lakeshore, family-run El Puesto is the perfect place to relax after a day of wilderness activities, including hiking on glaciers, visits to the beautiful Capillas de Mármol, rock and ice climbing to fossil pits in Puerto Guadal, and soaring through forest canopies. El Puesto organizes 2- to 10-day tours, as well as dinners for groups.

Pedro Lagos 258, Puerto Río Tranquilo. Ⓒ **02/196-4555.** www.elpuesto.cl. 3 units. C$55,000 double. No credit cards. **Amenities:** Restaurant. *In room:* Free Wi-Fi; no phone.

Hacienda Tres Lagos ★★★ ☺ Nestled near the southwest corner of spectacular Lake General Carrera, this *estancia*-style luxury resort has a lake—and beach—of its own. Accommodations vary from hotel suites in the main lodge to family-oriented,

The Future Patagonia National Park: Wilderness Philanthropy in Action

With the purchase of the sprawling **Estancia Valle Chacabuco** north of Cochrane in 2004, American eco-philanthropist Kristine Tompkins (wife of Douglas Tompkins, see Parque Pumalín, p. 342) instigated what will eventually be a massive national park in one of the most ecologically diverse corners of Patagonia. With the help of international donors and volunteers, the project is reclaiming and restoring over-grazed lands, removing sheep and cattle, and returning this truly picturesque valley to its pre-colonial ways. Local species like endangered huemul deer, guanacos, and pumas are already enjoying the results. Visitors are welcome, especially if they are able to pitch-in. There's a beautiful exclusive lodge now open, with six tastefully deluxe rooms, and campgrounds in the works. The valley is part of the headwaters for the emblematic Baker River, which is the site of a polemic debate over a proposed massive hydro-electric project. See www.conservacionpatagonica.com for more information.

independent *cabañas* to romantic luxury apartments, but all share the lakefront view of Lago Negro and the Patagonian Andes beyond, have balconies or terraces with rattan furniture, and are finely decorated with great attention to detail—guests are even loaned hotel iPods with speakers and music to suit the ambience.

The main complex has its own telescope for stargazing, a game room with pool table, darts, and Ping-Pong, plus a stone fireplace where they do *asados* (traditional Patagonian barbecues). As befits its location, it offers plenty of outdoor activities on foot, horseback, and boat, or farther afield to the Tamango National Reserve to try to glimpse the endangered huemul deer. And, while not a fly-fishing lodge per se, it also offers several fly-fishing and trawling excursions in the area and a 6-day/5-night tour. They have a new fishing-only lodge in the works as well.

Carretera Austral Sur, Km 274, Cruce El Maitén, near Puerto Guadal. ⓒ **02/333-4122.** www.hacienda treslagos.com. 20 units. $156–$186 double. Rates include breakfast and afternoon tea. Lunch and dinner $30 per person. AE, DC, MC, V. **Amenities:** Restaurant; bar; bikes; sauna; free Wi-Fi (in main lodge). *In room:* Minibar, iPod dock.

The Terra Luna Lodge ★ ☺ This remote adventure lodge is owned by the French-Chilean outfitter company Azimut, which offers every kind of excursion throughout Chile. The lodge sits on a grassy slope above Lake General Carrera. Because the owners are renowned mountaineers and outdoors lovers, they can arrange serious adventure trips scaling regional peaks, long treks to glaciers, or rafting trips to the white-water rapids of Río Baker. The lodging options consist of a spacious pine lodge with doubles and triples, a bungalow for four with a kitchenette, another for two with a whirlpool, a "family" house for two to eight guests seeking total independence, a low-cost cabin with bunks for two, and a beautiful brand new "tree house" that sleeps two. There are also huts available for low-budget travelers, a step up from camping.

Km 1.5, Camino Puerto Guadal–Chile Chico. ⓒ **67/431263** or 2/235-1519. www.terra-luna.cl. 8 rooms and 2 bungalows. $130 double (apt room); $170 for four people; all-inclusive packages run an average of 4 days/3 nights at $1,590 per person. All rates include breakfast. AE, MC, V. **Amenities:** Restaurant; theater; bikes; Jacuzzi; sauna; watersports equipment; free Wi-Fi (in main lodge).

Cochrane

It gets even more remote the farther south you travel. That may change over the next decade as a result of the giant hydroelectric projects planned along the Baker River, which has enough power to light up all of Belgium, tempting companies seeking to feed Chile's energy-guzzling economy. The number of residents could double temporarily for construction, worrying environmentalists. (See "Parque Pumalín," earlier in this chapter.) In the meantime, **Cochrane** is the last place where you can reliably buy gas and get cash from an ATM; Banco Estado has an outlet on the main square. There are a few hotels and basic restaurants, but Cochrane is a rather gloomy, windswept place. The Esso station near the town's entrance has some information and brochures for travelers. Cochrane is the closest place from which to visit the **Estancia Valle Chacabuco,** a huemul and guanaco haven alongside the **Tamango** and **Jeinimeni** preserves, which the Conservación Patagónica Foundation, associated with Douglas Tompkins, bought in 2004 and seeks to transform into **Patagonia National Park** (see above).

There are a number of decent places to stay here including the popular **Hostería Lago Esmeralda** (San Valentín 141; © 67/522621; C$10,000 double) and larger, and more modern **Hotel Ultimo Paradiso** (Lago Brown 455; © 67/522361; C$35,0000 double). The best place to eat is **Restaurante Adas** (Tte. Merino 510; © 67/995-889), which serves Chilean standards and is pretty much the place to see and be seen. For supplies, head to Casa Melero at Las Golondrinas 148, the last place until Punta Arenas for fishing equipment, camping gear, most basic food stuffs, and wine.

Cochrane is the transportation "hub" for the limited southbound bus services: **Turismo Interlagos** (© 67/522606; daily to Coyhaique at 9am), and **Don Carlos** at Prat 281 (© 67/522150; Wed, Fri, and Sun to Coyhaique at 9:15am). **Los Ñadis** (© 67/211460) heads to Villa O'Higgins Mondays and Thursdays and returns on Tuesdays and Fridays. **Buses Acuario 13,** Rio Baker 349 (© 67/522143), runs to Caleta Tortel (3 hr.) Tuesday to Friday and Sunday at 9:15am. The frequency of buses drops significantly outside of the summer.

Caleta Tortel

Continuing onward, the road narrows, but the scenery stays spectacular, passing through the Andes along multicolored peat bogs, finally descending into deep temperate rainforest. The road branches off to the remarkable little logging town of **Caleta Tortel ★★★**, an unreal, S-shaped place suspended somewhere between the steep slopes of a cypress rainforest and the pistachio green waters at the mouth of the Baker River, resembling a Patagonian Venice of sorts. Wood-shingled houses in bright or natural colors cling precariously to the hillside; cypress wood walkways and boats are the only ways to get around. Cars are banished to a lot at the end of the Carretera Austral—even the fire engine is a boat, just like in Venice. The scent of the planks and wood-burning stoves adds spice to the fresh mountain, forest, and sea air. There's little to do beyond exploring the boardwalk maze, though this can be as magical an experience as a walk through Torres del Paine. Hiking trails and fishermen's boats can take you to even more remote spots, including the **Montt** and **Steffens glaciers** and the **Isla de los Muertos;** check at the helpful tourist information by the parking lot (see above for detailed information on how to get there). A lovely new inn, **Entre Hielos Lodge ★★★** (© 2/196-0271; www.entrehielos.cl), has without doubt the most interesting, tasteful accommodations in town, with cozy rooms, naturally inspired decor, and superb food; doubles with breakfast are $120. Besides Entre Hielos, other options for dining are **El Mirador** (no phone; above the Plaza de Armas), the town's most formal restaurant with the best menu, though it tends to be pricey; and **Sabores Locales,** up a narrow staircase (no phone; look for a sign on the waterfront), with cheaper meals, though the menu is simpler—comprising basically whatever they have fresh that day. There is an Entel office for phone calls on the plaza, and the library has free Internet service available in 30-minute increments.

Villa O'Higgins

A ferry, **Padre Antonio Ronchi,** takes vehicles across the Bravo River from the hamlet of Puerto Yungay (summer hours: 10am, noon, and 6pm, returning at 11am, 1, and 7pm) for travelers heading on to the end of the road at **Villa O'Higgins,** an unattractive frontier outpost in a broad valley. It's like a mini-Cochrane with fewer services. The deep azure, multi-fingered lake by the same name is fed by the Southern Ice Field, the world's biggest non-polar mass of ice. Again, the landscape is marvelous, and hikers with plenty of time can cross into Argentina without too much trouble via lovely Laguna del Desierto, eventually ending up in El Chaltén (see chapter 13). Tour outfitter **Hielo Sur/Villa O'Higgins** (© 67/431821; www.villaohiggins.com) offers boat trips to see glaciers and Mount Fitz Roy from the lake, and 1-day to 1-week hiking and horseback tours, including the crossing to El Chaltén.

The area's next big attraction is a **Cruce del Lagos** cruise from Villa O'Higgins to El Chaltén that avoids the cattle herd feel of the one from Puerto Montt to Bariloche—few realize that it even exists. It includes two ferries and an interior road that won't be able to receive 4×4 vehicles for another few years. Currently, you can hike or bike the crossing. The website www.villaohiggins.com has plenty of solid information (in Spanish), while the public library has free Internet service. The village has about a dozen basic places to stay. Check with the **Oficina de Turismo Rural** in Coyhaique (Ogana 1060; © 67/214031; www.rutatranspatagonia.cl) for even more remote lodgings.

SOUTHERN PATAGONIA

13

F ew places in the world have captivated the imagination of explorers and travelers like Patagonia has. Almost 500 years ago, the first Europeans sailed through on four ships captained by Ferdinand Magellan. But this vast region was one of the last on the planet to be settled and remains pristine and sparsely populated, protected by the harsh, cold climate. Sailors from around the world continue to test their luck and courage in the harrowing Strait of Magellan. Mountaineers stage elaborate excursions through rugged territories, only to be beaten back, like their predecessors, by unrelenting storms. What seduces so many people to Patagonia is the idea of the "remote"—indeed, the very notion of traveling to the End of the World. It is a seduction, but also an illusion. People do live here—very few people, but those who do are hardy survivors.

A harsh, wind-whipped climate and Patagonia's geological curiosities have produced some of the most beautiful natural attractions in the world: the granite towers of Torres del Paine and Mount Fitzroy; the Northern and Southern Patagonian Ice Fields with their colossal glaciers (the greatest masses of ice and fresh water reserves outside the polar caps); the flat steppe broken by multicolored sedimentary bluffs; and the emerald fjords and lakes that glow an impossible sea-foam blue. In the end, this is what compels most travelers to plan a trip down here. Beyond landscapes, the region's cowboys (called *gauchos* in Argentina and *baqueanos* in Chile) lend a certain air of romanticism. Top the natural allure with an excellent array of new lodges and guiding services, and it's more appealing, and easier that ever, to journey to the "end of the world."

Exploring the Region

Despite its remoteness, Patagonia is surprisingly easy to travel. Once you get here, that is—airfare can be expensive, and flights are at least 4 hours from the major hubs of Santiago, Chile, or Buenos Aires, Argentina. Flying between Argentina and Chile is virtually impossible without returning via the national capitals. But, making use of increasingly excellent roads and traveling by local bus or car, it's entirely feasible to plan a circuit that loops through, for example, Punta Arenas, Torres del Paine, and then on to El Calafate and El Chaltén across the border in Argentina. There's so much to see and do here, you'll really want to include a visit to this region in your trip to Chile, if possible.

Southern Patagonia

PACIFIC OCEAN

Puerto Edén
Lago del Desierto
Lago O'Higgins
ISLA WELLINGTON
Parque Nacional Bernardo O'Higgins
Fitz Roy
El Chaltén
Lago San Martín
Lago Cardiel
Gobernador Gregores
Parque Nacional Los Glaciares
Lago Viedma
Glaciar Perito Moreno
Lago Argentino
El Calafate
Santa Cruz
Puerto Santa Cruz
Parque Nacional Torres del Paine
Cueva del Milodón
ARGENTINA
Bahía Grande
Reserva Nacional Alacalufes
Puerto Natales
Coig
CHILE
9
Gallegos
Río Gallegos
Parque Nacional Pali Aike
Punta Delgada
Estrecho de Magallanes
Reserva Nacional Magallanes
Penguin colony
Isla Magdalena
Magallanes
ATLANTIC OCEAN
Seno Otway
Punta Arenas
Porvenir
Reserva Nacional Laguna Parrillar
Fuerte Bulnes
Camerón
ISLA GRANDE DE TIERRA DEL FUEGO
Río Grande
Parque Nacional Alberto de Agostini
Parque Nacional Tierra del Fuego
ARGENTINA
Lago Fagnano
Tolhuin
Ushuaia
Beagle Channel
Puerto Williams
Mar Chileno
Parque Nacional Cabo de Hornos
Cabo de Hornos

50 mi
50 km

✈ Airport
▲ Mountain

Santiago
Buenos Aires
CHILE
ARGENTINA
Map Area

Calling Between Chile & Argentina

One would think that two neighboring countries would offer low telephone rates for calls made from one to the other, but not so with Chile and Argentina. Visitors can expect to pay the same or higher rates as a call to the U.S., often around C$950 per minute. When calling from Argentina to Chile, first dial **00-56**, then the area code and number. The prefix for Chilean cellphones is **09**, but callers from Argentina have to drop the 0; so to call a Chilean cellphone from Argentina, dial **00-56-9**, then the number.

When calling from Chile to Argentina, you must first call whichever carrier you're using (ask your host, your hotel, or at a calling center for the carrier prefix, usually **123, 181, or 188**), followed by **0-54**, then the area code and number. Argentine area codes always begin with a 0 prefix, which you'll drop when dialing from Chile. For example, if dialing from Punta Arenas, Chile, to Ushuaia, Argentina, you'll dial 123 (or whichever carrier you're using), then 0-54-2901 and the number. When dialing Argentine cellphone numbers (which begin with 15), drop the 15 and replace it with the region's area code.

How much time you plan on spending in Patagonia is entirely up to you. If you're planning a backpacking trip in Torres del Paine, for example, you'll want to spend between 5 and 10 days there; but those with plans for a few light walks and sightseeing drives in that national park might find that 2 to 3 days are enough. A quick trip to Patagonia might include 2 days in El Calafate, 3 in Torres del Paine, and a full day in Punta Arenas. A longer journey could begin with several days in El Chaltén, 2 in El Calafate, 5 in Torres del Paine, 1 in Puerto Natales, 1 in Punta Arenas, and a flight or cruise to Ushuaia for 3 to 4 days. Remember, you need a day to get here from Santiago—it's a 4-hour flight to Punta Arenas alone.

Prices jump and crowds swell from early November to late March, and some businesses open during this time frame only. The busiest months are January and February, but these summer months are not necessarily the best months to visit Patagonia, as calmer weather usually prevails in October and from mid-March to late April. And winter travel is growing in popularity.

Note: Unless stated otherwise, hotel rates listed in this chapter are for high season (Oct–Mar) and include breakfast.

PUNTA ARENAS

254km (158 miles) SE of Puerto Natales; 3,090km (1,916 miles) S of Santiago

Punta Arenas, with a population of 150,000, is the capital of the Magellanic and Antarctic Región XII, and it is Patagonia's most important city, founded where the forest meets the steppe and the southern coast. The streets hum with activity, and its airport and seaports bustle with traffic. The town has made a living from coal mines, wool production, oil and natural gas, and fishing, and as a service center for cargo ships and the Chilean navy.

Punta Arenas' post-colonial wealth (it was a true cornerstone of global trade before the opening of the Panama Canal) is reflected in the grand stone mansions that encircle the main plaza, which were built with earnings from the sheep *estancias*

ACCOMMODATIONS ■
Chalet Chapital **11**
Hostal del Sur **14**
Hotel Cabo de Hornos **8**
Hotel Carpa Manzano **21**
Hotel Dreams del Estrecho **2**
Hotel Ilaia **13**
Hotel José Noguiera **10**
Hotel Rey Don Felipe **12**

DINING ◆
Damiana Elena **20**
El Mercado **17**
La Luna **7**
La Marmite **18**
O Sole Mio **6**
Pub 1900 **16**
Puerto Viejo **4**
Santino **15**
Sotitos Bar **3**

ATTRACTIONS ●
City Cemetery **22**
Insituto de la Patagonia/
   Museo del Recuerdo **23**
Main Dock **1**
Museo Naval y Marítimo **5**
Museo Regional de
   Magallanes **9**
Museo Salesiano
   Maggiorino Borgatello **19**
Palacio Braun Menendez **8**

13

SOUTHERN PATAGONIA | Punta Arenas

(ranches) of the late 1800s. Gold fever followed, and subsequently, hundreds of immigrants from Europe poured into the region from Britain, Germany, Yugoslavia, Russia, Spain, and Italy. Today Punta Arenas' streets are lined with residential homes with colorful, corrugated rooftops; business offices and hotels downtown; and an industrial port where cruise ships dock. The main waterfront area is undergoing a massive redevelopment project. The Magallanes region considers itself somewhat of an independent republic due to its isolation from the rest of Chile—you'll see its attractive blue and yellow flag often—and this, in turn, has affected the personality of its people, an indefatigable bunch who brace themselves every summer against the gales that blow through this town like a hurricane. The wind, in fact, is so fierce at times that the city has fastened ropes around the plaza for people to hold on to. If that weren't enough, residents here also have to contend with a paper-thin ozone layer, which nearly dissipates for the summer around November.

Although for most travelers, Punta Arenas is simply an arrival and departure spot, the history of this region and the extremity of Punta Arenas' location on the famous Magellan Strait make for a fascinating place to explore. The most appealing reason to stop here is to visit one of the nearby penguin colonies (possible roughly from Oct–Mar).

But if you have a few hours to kill, you'll find the human history on display in the mansions and museums also very intriguing and, in their own way, exotic.

Essentials

GETTING THERE & AWAY

BY PLANE Punta Arenas' **Aeropuerto Presidente Ibáñez** (PUQ; ✆ **61/218131**) is 20km (12 miles) north of town, and, depending on the season, it's serviced with up to 10 flights per day from Santiago. **LAN,** Lautaro Navarro 999 (✆ **600/526-2000** or 61/241100; www.lan.com), has the most flights per day to both Santiago and Puerto Montt. They tend to be more expensive, but have been experimenting with rock-bottom prices for flights arriving or leaving in the wee hours of the morning. **Sky Airline,** Roca 935 (✆ **600/600-2828;** www.skyairline.cl), has one flight per day that is a bit of a milk-run, stopping twice en route. There is an ATM on the airport's ground floor.

The regional **Aerovías DAP,** O'Higgins 891 (✆ **61/223340;** www.aeroviasdap. cl), has three flights a day from Monday through Friday, and one on Saturday, to Porvenir, and six flights a week to Puerto Williams as well. They also have charter flights to such places as Ushuaia and Antarctica, and charter sightseeing flights to Cape Horn and Torres del Paine.

To get to Punta Arenas from the airport, hire a taxi for about C$5,500 or take one of the transfer services there (which can also arrange to take you back to the airport; their booths are at the baggage claim area). **Buses Transfer Austral** (✆ **61/229673;** www.transferaustral.com) has door-to-door service for C$3,500 per person.

BY BUS From and to Puerto Natales: **Bus Sur,** José Menéndez 552 (✆ **61/614224;** www.bus-sur.cl), has four daily trips; **Buses Fernández,** Armando Sanhueza 745 (✆ **61/221812;** www.busesfernandez.com), has seven daily trips; and **Buses Pacheco,** Av. Colón 900 (✆ **61/242174;** www.busespacheco.com), has five daily trips. The cost is about C$4,000, and the trip takes about 3 hours.

To and from Ushuaia, Argentina: **Buses Tecni Austral,** Lautaro Navarro 975 (✆ **61/222078**), leaves Punta Arenas Tuesday, Thursday, and Saturday, and returns from Ushuaia on Monday, Wednesday, and Saturday; the cost for either is C$24,700. **Buses Pacheco,** Av. Colón 900 (✆ **61/242174**), has direct service to Ushuaia on Tuesday, Thursday, and Sunday, and returns on Monday, Wednesday, and Friday, via Rio Grande. The direct trip to Ushuaia takes about 12 hours and costs C$34,000.

BY CAR Rte. 9 is a paved road between Punta Arenas and Puerto Natales. Strong winds—and fog and ice in winter—often require that you exercise extreme caution when driving this route. To get to Tierra del Fuego, there are two options: Cross by ferry from Punta Arenas to Porvenir, or drive east on Rte. 255 to Rte. 277 and Punta Delgada for the ferry crossing there (for more information, see "Isla Navarino: Puerto Williams," later in this chapter). I recommend crossing Punta Delgada at least in one direction; the trip is shorter, more frequent, and will allow a detour to Parque Nacional Pali Aike and Estancia Lolita.

CAR RENTAL **International Rental Car,** Waldo Seguel 443 (✆ **61/228323;** www.international-rac.com), is a helpful and locally owned agency with an office at the airport. You can drop your car off in Puerto Natales or Coyhaique for an extra fee. Another option is **Southland Rent a car,** Chiloé 957 (✆ **61/241143;** www.southland rentacar.com).

cruising FROM PUNTA ARENAS TO USHU

Cruceros Australis runs an unforgettable journey between Punta Arenas and Ushuaia aboard its ships, the MV *Mare Australis* and the MV *Via Australis*. This cruise takes passengers to remote coves and narrow channels and fjords in Tierra del Fuego, and then heads into the Beagle Channel, ending at Ushuaia, Argentina. There's also a stop at the absolute end of the world, Cape Horn, although the chances that you will be able to get off the boat and touch *tierra firma* there aren't likely due to notorious winds. The trip can be done as a 4-night one-way from Punta Arenas or a 3-night one-way journey from Ushuaia. I recommend that you take just the one-way journey, ideally departing Punta Arenas, leaving you to explore a new city and then travel by air or land from there. It's a fantastic way to link both countries and turn your Patagonian itinerary into a loop.

What is unique about this cruise is the intimacy of a smaller ship and its solitary route that takes passengers to places in Tierra del Fuego that few have a chance to see. Passengers are shuttled to shore via zodiacs (motoriz able boats) for two daily excu can include visits to glaciers or guin colony, or walks to view elaborate beaver dams and lookouts. There are several excellent bilingual guides who give daily talks about the region's flora, fauna, history, and geology. Service is stiff but professional, and the food is quite good. The accommodations are comfortable, ranging from suites to simple cabins. All-inclusive, per-person prices (excluding cocktails) range from $1,770 to $3,450 one-way from Punta Arenas and $1,050 to $2,566 one-way from Ushuaia. It's not really worth it to pay extra for an upper deck; second-floor berths at the front of the ship are the most stable, quiet, and comfortable. This cruise operates from early October to late April. For reservations or information, contact their U.S. offices in Miami, at 4014 Chase Ave., Ste. 215 (© **305/695-9615** or 877/678-3772; fax 305/534-9276), or in Santiago, at Av. El Bosque Norte 0440 (© **2/442-3115;** fax 2/203-5173); or visit www.australis.com.

GETTING AROUND

Downtown Punta Arenas is compact enough to explore on foot, but taxis are plentiful and you can hail one off the street—you'll find many around the Plaza de Armas. Travel anywhere within the city limits will not cost more than C$5,500; always confirm the fare with your driver before getting in the car. Cheap buses are also abundant and run either north–south on calles Bulnes and Nogueira or east–west along Independencia.

Note: Road blockades imposed in January 2011 to protest decreases in the Magallanes District's natural gas subsidies caused havoc for travelers and locals alike. For more than a week, all roads in and out of Punta Arenas (including those to the area's most important airport) were closed. The government negotiated an agreement with local protesters, but the area's reliance on subsidized utilities, and the importance of transportation to the tourism industry, are more obvious than ever.

VISITOR INFORMATION

There's an excellent **Oficina de Turismo** (© **61/200610**) inside a glass gazebo in the Plaza de Armas. The staff is helpful, and they sell a wide range of historical and

pological literature and postcards. The office is open from December to March
ᴉonday through Friday from 8am to 5:30pm, Saturdays and Sundays from 9am to
2pm. From March through November, it's open weekdays only. **Sernatur's** office at
Lautaro Navarro 999 (📞 **61/225385;** www.sernatur.cl), on the other hand, is also
helpful; it's open Monday through Friday from 8:30am to 6pm.

Currency Exchange
Banks and currency exchange houses are mainly located on the 1000-block of Lautaro Navarro. Exchange money at **La Hermandad,** Lautaro Navarro 1099 (📞 **61/710710**); **Sur Cambio de Moneda,** Lautaro Navarro 1001 (📞 **61/225083**); or **Cambios de Moneda Opitz,** Lautaro Navarro 1070 (📞 **61/246216**). *Casas de cambio* are open Monday through Friday from 9am to 1pm and 3 to 7pm, and Saturday from 9am to 1pm.

For banks with 24-hour ATMs, go to **Banco Santander,** Magallanes 997 (📞 **61/201020**); **Banco de Chile,** Roca 864 (📞 **61/735433**); or **Banco de A. Edwards,** Plaza Muñoz Gamero 1055

(📞 **61/241175**). Banks are open Monday through Friday from 9am to 2pm.

Hospitals The local hospitals are **Hospital de las FF. AA. Cirujano Guzmán,** Avenida Manuel Bulnes and Guillermos (📞 **61/207500**); and **Clínica Magallanes,** Av. Manuel Bulnes 1448 (📞 **61/211527**).

Internet Access Try **E-Green Internet,** Jose Nogueira 1179 (📞 **61/617010**), which is open Monday through Friday from 9am to midnight and Saturday and Sunday from 10am to midnight, or **Tele-fónica,** Bories 798 (📞 **61/248230**), open Monday through Friday from 9:30am to 5pm. There are also plenty of small Internet cafes, and Wi-Fi is widely

available, including at the **Cyrano Café,** Bulnes 999 (📞 **61/242749**), and **Café Montt,** Pres. P Montt 976 (📞 **61/220381**).

Laundry Try **Lavandería Antártica,** Jorge Montt 664; **Autoservicio Lavasol,** O'Higgins 969; or **Lavandería Lavasuper,** José Nogueira 1595.

Pharmacy Go to **Farmacia Ahumada,** Bories 950 (📞 **61/220423**); **Farmacia Cruz Verde,** Bories 858 (📞 **61/246572**); or **Farmacia Salcobrand,** Bories 971 (📞 **61/240973**).

Post Office The central post office is at José Menéndez and Bories (📞 **61/222210**); hours are Monday through Friday from 9am to 6pm, and Saturday from 9am to 1pm.

What to See & Do

There are a surprising number of activities and sights to fill your day(s) while in Punta Arenas. When the wind is not overwhelming, it's a lovely town to stroll about. Begin your tour of Punta Arenas in the central **Plaza Muñoz Gamero,** where you'll find a bronze **sculpture** of Ferdinand Magellan donated by the region's long-ago wool czar José Menendez. Magellan is surrounded by lounging natives, one of whom has a shiny toe polished by the hundreds of visitors who kiss the nub each year; local lore says that if you kiss the toe, you'll be lucky enough to visit Patagonia once again. The tranquil little plaza, delineated by cypress and other regional trees, has the visitor center gazebo, and several vendors here display crafts and souvenirs for sale. Around the plaza are old Punta Arenas' principal **mansions and edifices** from its boom times, which have, fortunately, been well kept over the decades.

From the plaza on Av. 21 de Mayo, head north toward Avenida Colón for a look at the **Teatro Municipal,** designed by the French architect Numa Mayer and modeled after the Teatro Colón in Buenos Aires. Head down to the waterfront and turn south toward the pier, where you'll find a 1913 clock imported from Germany that has complete meteorological instrumentation and hands showing the moon's phases and a zodiac calendar. The entire port area is currently being redeveloped. There's a lovely, new wide walkway and boulevard along the coast as well as a giant new resort with a casino (see p. 383), but further work is ongoing to expand dock space for cruise ships.

City Cemetery ★★   They say you can't really understand a culture until you see where they bury their dead, and in the case of the cemetery of Punta Arenas, this edict certainly rings true. The City Cemetery was opened by the Governor Señoret in 1894 and is fronted by a giant stone portico donated by Sara Braun (see the review of Palacio Sara Braun below) in 1919. Inside this necropolis lies a veritable miniature city, with avenues that connect the magnificent tombs of the region's founding families, immigrant colonies, and civic workers, and a rather solemn tomb where lie the remains of the last Selk'nam Indians of Tierra del Fuego. It's a melancholy place, with lovely sculpted European cypress trees adding a gentle tone. The cemetery is about a 20-minute walk from the plaza, or a quick cab ride.

Av. Manuel Bulnes and Angamos. No phone. Free admission. Oct–Mar daily 7:30am–8pm; Apr–Sept daily 8am–6:30pm.

Instituto de la Patagonia/Museo del Recuerdo ★   The Instituto de Patagonia is run by the University of Magallanes and directed by the region's chief historian, Mateo Martinic. Here you'll find an engaging exhibit of colonial artifacts called the Museum of Memories. Antique machinery and horse-drawn carts are displayed around the lawn and encircled by several colonial buildings that have been lifted and transported here from ranches around the area. One cabin shows visitors what home life was like for a ranch hand, another has been set up to resemble a typical dry goods store, another is a garage with a 1908 Peugeot, and another is a carpenter's workshop. There's a library on the premises with a collection of books and maps on display and for sale. The museum is about 4km (2½ miles) out of town, so you'll need to take a taxi.

Av. Manuel Bulnes 01890. (✆ **61/217173.** Admission C$1,500. Mon–Fri 8:30am–noon and 2:30–6pm; Sat 8:30am–noon; erratic hours and closing policies on Sun, so call ahead.

Museo Naval y Marítimo   Punta Arenas' tribute to its seafaring history is this Naval and Maritime Museum. Here you'll find photos depicting the various ships and port activity over the past century, as well as small ship replicas and other artifacts. Although it has an interesting display on Sir Ernest Shackleton, this museum is really recommended only for those with a strong interest in nautical-related items.

Pedro Montt 981. No phone. Admission C$500. Tues–Sat 9:30am–12:30pm and 3–6pm.

Museo Salesiano Maggiorino Borgatello ★★ ☺   This mesmerizing museum offers an insight into the Magellanic region's history, anthropology, ecology, and industrial history. That said, the lobby-level floor is packed with a fusty collection of stuffed and mounted birds and mammals that at turns feels almost macabre, considering that many have lost their shape; nevertheless, it allows you to fully appreciate the tremendous size of the condor and the puma. Several rooms in the museum display Indian hunting tools, ritual garments, jewelry, and colonial and ranching implements, as well as the inevitable religious artifacts from the Catholic missionaries who played such a large role in the deterioration of native Indians' culture. Perhaps some of the most intriguing items on view here are the black-and-white photos of the early missionary Alberto d'Agostini.

Av. Manuel Bulnes and Maipú. (✆ **61/221001.** Admission C$1,500. Tues–Sun 10am–12:30pm and 3–6pm.

Palacio Sara Braun & Museo Regional de Magallanes ★★ 📷 These two attractions are testament to the staggering wealth produced by the region's vast 19th-century sheep and cattle *estancias*. The museums are the former residences of several members of the families Braun, Nogueira, and Menéndez, who believed that any far-flung, isolated locale could be tolerated if one were to "live splendidly and remain in constant contact with the outside world." And live splendidly they did in these veritable palaces, until the falling price of wool and the nationalization of *estancias* during the early 1970s forced the families to lose a large percentage of their holdings, and their descendants to relocate to places such as Buenos Aires.

The Palacio Sara Braun is now partially occupied by the Hotel José Nogueira and the Club de la Unión, a meeting area for the city's commercial and political leaders. The homes are national monuments, and both have been preserved in their original state, which allows visitors to appreciate the finest European craftsmanship available at the end of the 19th century. French architects planned the neoclassical exteriors, and craftsmen were brought from Europe to sculpt marble fireplaces and hand-paint walls to resemble marble and leather. The interior fixtures and furniture were also imported from Europe. For some visitors, the knowledge that these families to a large extent exterminated native Indians and suppressed labor movements in the region because of their quest for wealth may temper the appreciation for the grandeur of these palaces. If one wants European grandeur, one normally goes to Europe, not to Patagonia. Still, both museums are impressive.

Palacio Sara Braun: Plaza Muñoz Gamero 716. 📞 **61/248840.** Admission C$1,000 adults, free for those 15 and under. Mon-Sat 10:30–5pm; Sun 10:30am–2pm. Museo Regional de Magallanes: Magallanes 949. 📞 **61/244216.** Admission C$1,000 adults, C$250 children 15 and under. Nov-Apr Mon-Fri 10:30am–5:30pm; May-Oct daily 10:30am–2pm.

Shopping

Punta Arenas is home to a duty-free shopping center called the **Zona Franca,** with several blocks of shops hawking supposedly cheaper electronics, home appliances, imported foodstuffs, sporting goods, perfumes, clothing, toys, booze, and cigarettes. It's a massive shopping mall, with big-box stores a la North America. The savings here are very negligible, except for on alcohol, although there certainly is a lot on offer, including a few supermarkets. This does make it a fair place to stock up on supplies if you're planning a backpacking trip to Torres del Paine—otherwise, forget it. The Zona Franca is on Avenida Manuel Bulnes on the northern outskirts. It's open Monday through Saturday from 10am to 12:30pm and 3 to 8pm, and closed on holidays.

For regional crafts in town, try **Chile Típico,** Carrera Pinto 1015 (📞 **61/225827**), which has knitwear, carved-wood items, lapis lazuli, and more. For high-end, artsy-craftsy household items, such as picture frames, candles, throws, curtains, and the like, try **Almacén Antaño,** Colón 100 (📞 **61/227283**). Most afternoons see a collection of local artisans selling handicrafts in the city's main square, the Plaza de Armas. Look for wool sweaters and wooden toys there.

Excursions near Punta Arenas

Many tour operators run conventional city tours and trips to the penguin colonies, as well as short visits and multiday, all-inclusive trekking excursions to Parque Nacional Torres del Paine; but for excursions within the park I recommend that you stick with one of the outfitters listed under tour operators in the Puerto Natales section. The city tours provide useful historical information on this region and undoubtedly enrich a visitor's understanding of the hardship the immigrants and native aboriginals faced during the past century.

Turismo Yamana, Errázuriz 932 (© **61/710567;** www.yamana.cl), offers full-day city tours (C$31,850 per person), penguin tours (C$39,000 per person), and tours to Parque Nacional Pali Aike (C$130,000 per person), as well as multiday kayaking and whale-watching expeditions and an exhausting 14-hour "Torres del Paine in a day" tour (C$189,000 per person). Prices drop significantly for groups of four or more. The company also offers multiday trips to Lago Blanco in Tierra del Fuego for trekking, horseback riding, and fishing.

Turismo Comapa, Magallanes 990 (© **61/200200;** www.comapa.com), is the leader in town for conventional tours such as city tours and visits to the penguin colonies. **Turis Otway,** Mejicana 122 (© **61/224454;** www.turisotway.cl), also goes to the Seno Otway penguin colony for the bargain price of C$20,000.

Turismo Viento Sur, 585 Fagnano (© **61/613845;** www.vientosur.com), is another respected company offering more outdoorsy excursions in and around Punta Arenas, including hiking to the San Isidro lighthouse, horseback riding, kayaking, fly-fishing, and bird-watching.

Fantástico Sur ★, José Menéndez 858 (© **61/615794;** www.fantasticosur.com), has naturalist tours including a day-long bird-watching tour where you can spot condors, penguins, waders, and passerines. They also have multiday naturalist tours of Patagonia, and their guides are passionate, professional, and superb.

Whale Sound, Lautaro Navarro 1163, 2nd floor (© **61/710511;** www.whale sound.com), offers multiday whale-watching tours in the distant waters off Carlos III Island, a breeding ground of the humpback whale. They also have a day-long helicopter whale-watching trip to the Parque Marino Francisco Coloane, appealing if you have the time and, perhaps more importantly, the money. A 3-day, 2-night trip starts at C$480,000 per person.

FUERTE BULNES

In 1843, Captain Juan Williams, the naturalist Bernardo Philippi, 16 sailors and soldiers, and two women set sail from Ancud in Chiloé to the Strait of Magellan to plant the Chilean flag in this region before other powers could beat Chile to it. They chose a rocky promontory that dominated the strait and named it **Fuerte Bulnes.** Although this promontory was strategically appropriate for monitoring seafaring traffic, the location proved undesirable, and they pulled up stakes and moved 25km (16 miles) north, founding what is today Punta Arenas. In recognition of the historical value of Fuerte Bulnes, the Chilean government reconstructed the site in 1943, its centenary anniversary, and made it a national monument. At the gorgeous location, you'll find reconstructions of the log cabins that housed the settlers, a chapel, and several cannons. It is approximately 60km (37 miles) south of Punta Arenas on Rte. 9, the Panamericana. There are no set hours, and admission is free.

Just before Fuerte Bulnes is a short road leading to **Puerto Hambre.** The site was founded as Rey Felipe by Pedro Sarmiento de Gamboa in 1584, and settled by 103 colonists who were tragically stranded after tremendous storms prevented their ships from returning to shore. The name Puerto Hambre (Port Hunger) was given by the British captain Thomas Cavendish, who found only one survivor when he docked here in 1587 (the rest had died of starvation and exposure). In 1993, the Chilean ambassador José Miguel Barros found the plan for Rey Felipe in the library of the Institute of France in Paris, and it is the oldest known document of urban history in

Chile. The only things you'll find here are a plaque and the remains of a chapel, but imagining yourself in the place of these settlers on this forsaken plot is worth the short detour from Fuerte Bulnes. Admission for both sites is free, with unspecified hours. To get here, sign up for a tour with Comapa or Viento Sur (see earlier).

PENGUIN COLONIES & ESTANCIA LOLITA

If you have a day or a half-day to kill in Punta Arenas, from October through March, the most appealing activity is a visit to one of the penguin colonies at Seno Otway or Isla Magdalena. Both colonies allow visitors to get surprisingly close to the amusing Magellanic penguins (also called jackass penguins, for their characteristic bray) at their nesting sites. November through February provides the best viewing. Isla Magdalena is by far the best place to view the penguins, but the trip here involves a ferry ride and will take up more of your time.

Penguins form lifelong partnerships and divide their chores equally: Every morning around 10am and in the afternoon around 5pm, the penguin couples change shifts—one heads out to fish, the other returns from fishing to take care of their young. When this changing of the guard begins, the penguins politely line up and waddle to and from the sea.

Seno Otway is accessible by road about 65km (40 miles) from Punta Arenas. A volunteer study group has developed the site with roped walkways and lookout posts, including a peek-a-boo wall where you can watch the penguins diving into the ocean. Tours are offered in four languages, and there is a tiny café here, too. It's open October 15 to March 31 daily from 8am to 8pm. The best time to visit is between 9 and 10am and 5 and 7pm, when the majority of activity takes place (the crowds of visitors are thinner during the morning shift); give yourself 3 hours. Most tour companies in town (see earlier) will provide transportation with daily departures in the afternoons, but if you have a rental car you can go on your own. The cost of a tour here ranges from C$10,000 to C$15,000, plus a C$7,000 entrance fee (free for kids; © 61/224454; www.turisotway.cl). Take Rte. 9 toward Puerto Natales, then turn left on the dirt road that branches out near the police checkpoint. Keep your eyes open for the ostrichlike rhea on the ride here.

Isla Magdalena ★ is much larger than Seno Otway, with an estimated 150,000 penguins sharing nesting space with cormorants, compared to 3,000 penguins at Seno Otway. These penguins are more timid than those at Seno Otway, but the sight of so many of these birds bustling to and fro is decidedly more impressive. To get here, you need to take a roughly 2-hour ferry ride to the island, where you can get out and walk amongst the penguins for an hour, and then board the ferry again, making for a pleasant 5-hour afternoon excursion. **Turismo Comapa,** Av. Magallanes 990 (© 61/200200; www.comapa.com), puts this tour together. Its boat, the *Barcaza Melinka,* departs from the pier at 4pm and returns at 9pm on Tuesday, Thursday, and Saturday, from late October to the end of March (C$25,000 for adults; C$12,000 for children under 12).

Estancia Lolita ★★ (© 61/8-233-0008 cell; www.faunapatagonica.com; adults C$3,000, children C$1,500) is a wildlife refuge and zoo for Patagonian fauna and the best place to view rarely seen species; it's 42km (16 miles) north of Punta Arenas. Josefina, a tame, rambunctious culpeo fox who loves to play with visitors, is one of the most charming living souls you'll meet in Patagonia. Guanacos, pumas (who seem happy enough, though their pens are on the small side) and other wild cats, and parrots and other endemic birds are among the denizens of the *estancia,* which has over 30 species in all. If you don't have a rental car, ask a local travel agency in Punta Arenas to organize transfers.

PARQUE NACIONAL PALI AIKE ★★

You may not be the only who finds the Patagonian steppe bleak and forlorn: In the language of the Aonikenk, or Tehuelches, the original inhabitants, the name Pali Aike means "Desolate Place." Though windswept and strewn with volcanic craters, the starkly beautiful area was inhabited thousands of years ago, with cracks in the lava forming caves that served as shelters and were excavated in the 1930s. The Cueva Fell has Stone Age cave paintings 9,000 years old. Fauna in the 5,000-hectare (12,350-acre) park include guanaco, fox, puma, armadillo, and waterfowl; Pali Aike also has several easy hikes, though the Cueva Pali Aike–Laguna Ana is a long 9km (5.5 miles). It's a fine side trip en route to or from Tierra del Fuego or Río Gallegos, but unless you have your own transportation, you'll need to book a tour in Punta Arenas, and you'll hardly see a thing on a foggy day. Note the minefields not far from the park entrance; the rustiness of the warning signs will chill your spine.

Where to Stay

In general, lodging in Punta Arenas is expensive for the caliber of accommodations available. For hostels not mentioned below, however, check with the Tourism Office for recommendations. Note that many hotels are willing to negotiate a price.

EXPENSIVE

Hotel Cabo de Hornos ★★   For decades, this has been Punta Arenas' top hotel, conveniently located on the northeast corner of the plaza. It's comfortable and professionally run. The Cabo de Hornos sports an impressive, elegant, gray stone–clad reception and lounge area, very nicely decorated in a mixture of modern and rustic. A separate room, with a massive fireplace, is where stylish locals meet for a cocktail, coffee, or business lunch. Most rooms don't quite match the wow factor of the ground floor, being just a little on the small size. Top floor rooms have slanted ceilings and the best views.

Plaza Muñoz Gamero 1039, Punta Arenas. ⓒ **61/715000.** www.hoteles-australis.com. 110 units. $210 double; $290 triple. AE, DC, MC, V. **Amenities:** Restaurant; lounge exercise room; free Internet (in business center); room service. *In room:* TV, hair dryer, free Wi-Fi.

Hotel Dreams del Estrecho   Chile's top five-star resort chain opened this splashy new hotel on the waterfront in Punta Arenas in 2009. It's a full-service hotel, with everything from a spa to a casino, making it heads and tails above any other place in town in terms of modern facilities. It's designed more for business travelers than adventurers. Rooms are sunny and bright, with open bathrooms, efficient work stations, and flatscreen TVs. If you're a non-smoker, be sure to request a non-smoking room. The spa here is the best in town, by a long shot.

O'Higgins 1235, Punta Arenas. ⓒ **61-204500.** www.mundodreams.com. 88 units. $152–$190 double; $183–$228 suite. AE, DC, MC, V. **Amenities:** Restaurant; lounge; bar; casino; exercise room; pool; sauna; full-service spa. *In room:* TV, hair dryer, Wi-Fi (free for 1 hour/day, then C$1,425 per hour).

Hotel José Nogueira   This classic hotel is in the partially converted neoclassical mansion once owned by the widow of one of Punta Arenas' wealthiest entrepreneurs; half of the building is still run as a museum (p. 380). The mansion was built between 1894 and 1905 on a prominent corner across from the plaza, with materials imported entirely from Europe. The José Nogueira is appealing for its historical value but also offers old-world, if dated, ambience. The rooms here are not as large as you would expect, but high ceilings accented by floor-to-ceiling curtains compensate for that. All are decorated with oriental rugs and lithographs of local fauna; the marble bathrooms are sparkling. The Nogueira's singles are unusually spacious. The suites have ample bathrooms with Jacuzzi tubs and a living area in the open bedroom. Keeping with the old-fashioned theme, the maids here dress in long smocks. I find the hotel dark and stuffy, but it is more intimate than its neighbor, the Hotel Cabo de Hornos. The mansion's old "winter garden" is now a restaurant, La Pérgola, housed under the Nogueira's glass-enclosed terrace.

Bories 959, Punta Arenas. © **61/711000.** Fax 61/711011. www.hotelnogueira.com. 22 units. $190 double; $270 suite. AE, DC, MC, V. **Amenities:** Restaurant; bar; room service. *In room:* TV, minibar.

MODERATE

Chalet Chapital 🏅   A classic Punta Arenas mansion that was transformed into a simple, pleasant little inn, the best part of this hotel is the loving, friendly staff. Breakfasts, for example, are typically simple Chilean offerings. Rooms have comfortable beds, private bathrooms with hydro-massage showers, and nothing else fancy. There's a TV room downstairs. Like most small inns in town, it can be noisy when other guests get up early for excursions. This is a great midrange choice if you're not up for a hostel and your budget's not up for one of the hotels above.

Armando Sanhueza 974, Punta Arenas. © **61/730100.** www.hotelchaletchapital.cl. 11 units. $95 double, $105 triple. AE, DC, MC, V. **Amenities:** TV lounge. *In room:* Hair dryer, Wi-Fi.

Hotel Carpa Manzano   With a recently remodeled exterior, this clean and comfortable small hotel has improved. Simple colorful rooms are spacious and have lots of light—they're a step up for backpackers. Superior rooms have new LCD TVs. The breakfast is standard Chilean (Nescafe, toast, ham, and cheese), and it's a 10- to 15-minute walk into town.

Lautaro Navarro 336, Punta Arenas. © **61/613386.** www.hotelcarpamanzano.com. 21 units. $95 double standard, $115 superior. AE, DC, MC, V. **Amenities:** Concierge. *In room:* TV, free Wi-Fi.

Hotel Ilaia ★   This new option outside downtown is full of heart. Cozy and very friendly, Ilaia is part inn and part yoga–new age center—its modern exterior is pretty groundbreaking stuff in a conservative city like Punta Arenas. Rooms are light, with white-washed walls and smart lighting; most have panoramic views. There's a nice garden and a top-floor common room that has views of the city. The breakfast consists of fusion treats like chapatti bread and a Chilean version of guacamole. It's a fun place if you're looking to mingle and chill out. They even throw in a free yoga class.

Ignacio Carrera Pinto 351, Punta Arenas. © **61/223592.** www.ilaia.cl. 9 units. $105 double. AE, MC, V. **Amenities:** Lounge. *In room:* Hair dryer, free Wi-Fi.

Hotel Rey don Felipe ★ 🎒   Little known, off the beaten-track, comfortable, and very quiet, this new hotel is cozy and private. There is an element of natural luxury here that stands out in Punta Arenas' hotel offerings. The spacious lobby has a giant fireplace and comfortable couches. Rooms are modern and plush, with neutral colored carpets, and small details such as old maps decorate the walls. All have deep bathtubs and wooden bathroom counters. Service is a bit stiff, but that may be due to the fact that there's hardly ever anybody at this hotel. Rooms vary in size; if you want to ensure a big room, be sure to ask. Located 3 blocks up the hill from the Plaza de Armas, it's farther from the water, so it's protected from the stormy weather.

Armando Sanhueza 965, Punta Arenas. ☏ **61/617500.** www.hotelreydonfelipe.cl. 43 units. $120 double; $158 suite. AE, DC, MC, V. **Amenities:** Restaurant; bar; exercise room. *In room:* TV, minibar, free Wi-Fi.

INEXPENSIVE

Hostal del Sur 🕯 This little hostel is tucked away on a residential street among a grove of pine trees, and it has been popularized by word of mouth. It is more of a family-style hostel, with exceptionally pleasant service and a friendly tan Labrador that welcomes you at the door. Simple yet clean rooms and private bathrooms in every room make it a good value.

Mejicana 151, Punta Arenas. ☏ **61/227249.** Fax 61/222282. www.hostaldelsur.net. 7 units. $53 double. No credit cards. **Amenities:** Lounge. *In room:* TV, free Wi-Fi.

Where to Dine

There are plenty of decent restaurants in Punta Arenas, most of which serve local fare such as lamb, king crab, and shellfish. The best strip of tourist-friendly restaurants is along O'Higgins. For a quick bite, head to a local favorite, the slightly overpriced diner-style **El Mercado,** Mejicana 617 (☏ **61/247415**). For pastas at a good price, try **O Sole Mio,** O'Higgins 974 (☏ **61/242026**). With a big menu and a lively bar, **La Luna,** O'Higgins 1017 (☏ **61/228555**), is laid-back and friendly. The liveliest cafe for drinks or sandwiches is the **Pub 1900,** at the corner of Bories and Colón (☏ **61/242759**); it is the social center for townsfolk here and it has giant windows for people-watching. The best casual spot for dinner and a pint of beer is **Santino,** Colón 657 (☏ **61/710882**), a spacious pub/restaurant that is the happening spot at night; they have sandwiches and simple Chilean dishes such as *lomo a lo pobre,* that heart-attack-on-a-plate dish of steak, fries, and a fried egg.

Damiana Elena ★★ 🍴 CONTEMPORARY CHILEAN With a menu that changes so frequently it's not even printed, and a packed house most nights, this may be the best restaurant in Punta Arenas. There are eight daily specials, usually including a seafood, meat, and pasta option. The chef's recommendation will be something like king crab cannelloni with artichokes and fine herbs. Vegetarian lasagna is usually on offer. It's set in a refurbished old house in a residential area, far from the touristy-strip on O'Higgins. The service (mostly bilingual!) is more youthful, relaxed, and friendly than in the other traditional restaurants in town. Upstairs is the nonsmoking section. There is also a large wine list, and a funky bar on the main floor.

Magallanes 341. ☏ **61/222818.** Reservations highly recommended. Main courses C$6,500–C$9,000. AE, DC, MC, V. Mon–Sat 8pm–12:30am.

La Marmite ★★ REGIONAL CHILEAN/VEGETARIAN Focusing on unpretentious and fresh Chilean classics such as *curanto* (a traditional meal of fish and meat steamed over hot rocks in the ground), conger eel with quinoa, or the classic stew *charquicán* (made of beans, corn, potatoes and meat, and topped with a fried egg), La Marmite is funky and friendly. Buns are warmed, and coffee is brewed on a giant wood-burning stove in the middle of the tables; great lunch specials are usually on offer. Located in a colorful heritage building, the restaurant's decor is slightly tongue-in-cheek, with random bits of ironic art displayed. In a sea of conservatism, La Marmite is a happy and fun oasis. And they have real espresso, a novelty in Chile.

Plaza Sampaio 678. ☏ **61/222056.** Reservations recommended on weekends. Main courses C$3,500–C$9,500. AE, DC, MC, V. Mon–Sat 12:30–3pm and 6:30–11:30pm, Sun 6:30–11:30pm.

Puerto Viejo ★ SEAFOOD/GRILL   The slickest, coolest restaurant in town is right across from the new Hotel Dreams del Estrecho and Casino (p. 383). Remodeled with a marine inspiration, the focus here is on food from the sea. Specialties include king crab, eel's cheeks in mustard sauce, and hake with cider and swordfish. At the back, Patagonian lamb roasts on a spit. There are also classic cuts of beef, and an excellent wine list heavy with Chilean cabernets sauvignon and sauvignon blanc.

O'Higgins 1166. ☎ **66/225-103.** Reservations recommended. Main courses C$7,500–C$11,000. AE, DC, MC, V. Daily 8pm–12:30am.

Sotito's Bar ★ CHILEAN   Don't be fooled by the plain green front and weathered sign: Sotito's has handsome semiformal interiors with brick walls and white linen tablecloths. A favorite for upper-class locals, Sotito's offers more menu items than most Chilean restaurants, including steak and seafood, local baked lamb, Valencia shellfish rice (which must be ordered ahead of time), pastas, and fresh salads. The key is that everything is of high quality, regardless of how simple the dish. The fish is very fresh. The service here, however, is only so-so. On Friday, Saturday, and Sunday, the restaurant fires up its *parrilla* (grill) for barbecued meats. There's a nonsmoking section up front, which is usually empty.

O'Higgins 1138. ☎ **61/221061.** www.chileaustral.com/sotitos. Reservations recommended. Main courses C$6,000–C$10,500. AE, DC, MC, V. Mon–Sat 11:30am–3pm and 7–11:45pm.

Punta Arenas After Dark

The city has a handful of good bars and pubs, plus a few discos, which I recommend only if you like to hang out with teenagers and listen to bad techno music. One of the most popular places to get a drink is **Sotito's Bar** (see "Where to Dine," above), and it is especially suitable for large groups. Other popular spots are **Pub 1900** (see "Where to Dine," above) and **El Galeón**, Av. 21 de Mayo 1243, below the Hotel Isla Rey Jorge (☎ **61/222681**). The **Cabo de Hornos Hotel** (☎ **61/242134**), on the plaza, has a chic bar with a more somber atmosphere.

The **Cine Estrella**, Mejicana 777 (☎ **61/225630**), is the only cinema in town. Call or check newspaper listings to see what's playing.

PUERTO NATALES

254km (158 miles) NW of Punta Arenas; 115km (71 miles) S of Torres del Paine

Puerto Natales is a rambling town of 19,000, spread along the sloping coast of the Señoret Canal between the Ultima Esperanza Sound and the Almirante Montt Gulf. This is the jumping-off point for trips to Torres del Paine, and many visitors to the park will find themselves spending at least a night here. The town itself is a small center with rows and rows of weather-beaten tin and wooden houses. Within the ramshackle buildings are some truly cozy and delightful inns, cafes, and bistros. Puerto Natales has a frontier-town appeal and boasts a stunning location with grand views out onto a grassy peninsula and glacier-capped peaks in the distance. From May to September, the town virtually goes into hibernation, but come October, the town's streets are crowded with international tourists decked out in parkas and hiking boots on their way to or back from the park.

Puerto Natales was founded in 1911 as a port for the export of lamb's meat and wool. Tourism has now replaced wool and coal to dominate the economy, evident by the plethora of hostels, restaurants, and tour companies found here, though it appears the period of rapid growth is leveling off.

Essentials

GETTING THERE

BY PLANE   There is a tiny airport in Puerto Natales that operates sporadically. Tickets are often sold late in the season by **Sky Airline** (© **2/352-5600;** www. skyairline.cl), but flights are often cancelled or re-routed to Punta Arenas due to wind. The closest alternate airports are in El Calafate, Argentina (4–5 hr.; p. 405) and Punta Arenas (3–4 hr.; p. 376).

BY BUS   Puerto Natales is the hub for bus service to Parque Nacional Torres del Paine and El Calafate, Argentina. For information about bus service to and from Torres del Paine, see "Parque Nacional Torres del Paine," later in this chapter. There are frequent daily trips between Punta Arenas and Puerto Natales. In Puerto Natales, each bus company leaves from its own office.

TO AND FROM PUNTA ARENAS   **Buses Fernández,** at Ramirez and Esmeralda streets (© **61/411111**), has seven daily trips; **Bus Sur,** Baquedano 668 (© **61/ 411859**), has two daily trips; **Buses Pacheco,** Baquedano 500 (© **61/414513**), has four daily trips (and the most comfortable buses); and **Transfer Austral,** Baquedano 414 (© **61/412616**), has two daily trips. The trip takes about 3 hours and the cost is about C$3,500 to C$4,000 one-way. Reserve early during the busy season, as tickets sell out fast. Round-trip fares to Punta Arenas are a little cheaper. There is no central bus terminal in Puerto Natales; each bus company has a different office, although most are along Baquedano Street.

TO EL CALAFATE, ARGENTINA   Options include **Buses Zaahj,** Arturo Prat 236 (© **61/412260;** www.turismozaahj.co.cl), departing at 8am Tuesdays, Thursdays, and Saturdays; and **Cootra,** Baquedano 456 (© **61/412785**), which leaves at 7:30am daily. The cost is C$16,500 one-way. The trip takes 4 to 5 hours, depending on the traffic at the border crossing.

BY CAR   Rte. 9 is a paved road that heads north from Punta Arenas. The drive is 254km (158 miles) and takes about 3 hours. If you're heading in from El Calafate, Argentina, you have your choice of two international borders: Cerro Castillo (otherwise known as Control Fronterizo Río Don Guillermo) or Río Turbio (otherwise known as Controles Fronterizos Dorotea y Laurita Casas Viejas). Both are the same in terms of road quality, but Río Turbio is busier, with Chileans heading to Argentina for cheaper goods and most of the bus traffic. Both are open 24 hours from September to May, and daily from 8am to 11pm the rest of the year. Gas is much cheaper in Argentina, so fill up there.

BY BOAT   **Navimag** runs a popular 3-night ferry trip between Puerto Natales and Puerto Montt, cruising through the southern fjords of Chile. This journey passes through breathtaking (though repetitive) scenery, and it makes for an interesting way to leave from or head to Chile's Lake District. Navimag leaves Puerto Montt every Friday afternoon. Rates for a private berth start at $530. Its offices in Puerto Natales are at Pedro Montt 308 (© **61/411642;** www.navimag.com).

GETTING AROUND

Puerto Natales is built on a grid pattern, and you'll spend most of your time within a 5-block radius, from the coast up to the main plaza, Plaza de Armas, along which runs Calle Eberhard, the street where you'll find the post office and the town's yellow cathedral. Calle Eberhard dead-ends a block away at Blanco Encalada; this street, Avenida Manuel Bulnes (1 block to the right), and Baquedano (1 block up from

Blanco Encalada) are the principal streets, with most of the supermarkets, banks, and tourism-oriented businesses. Along the shore of Puerto Natales runs Pedro Montt, also called the Costanera, which is an excellent place for a stroll.

All taxis charge a flat rate of C$1,000 for trips within the town limits. They can be hailed off the street, or else found around the main plaza. Car rentals in Puerto Natales are offered by **International Rental Car** (𝄽 **61/228323;** www.international-rac. com), and **Amazing Patagonia,** Baquedano 558 (𝄽 **61/414949;** www.amazing patagonia.com), among others. You don't need a car to get around the town, but a rental car can come in handy for longer-distance trips, including those into Parque Nacional Torres del Paine.

VISITOR INFORMATION

Sernatur operates a well-stocked office on the Costanera at Pedro Montt and Philippi (𝄽 **61/412125;** www.sernatur.cl); it's open October through March Monday through Friday from 8:30am to 8pm, Saturday and Sunday from 10:30am to 1pm and 2:30 to 6pm. April through September, it's open Monday through Friday from 8:30am to 1pm and 3 to 6pm; it's closed on holidays. Better yet is the **Municipal Tourism office,** tucked in a corner of the historical museum at Bulnes 285 (𝄽 **61/414808**), with a wealth of information on lodgings, restaurants, and day trips; the staff here is far more helpful than at Sernatur. It's open Monday to Friday from 9am to 12:30pm and 2:30 to 6pm, and Saturdays from 3 to 6pm. **CONAF** has its park headquarters at Baquedano 847 (𝄽 **61/411411;** www.conaf.cl), but you'll get better park information from a tour operator (see "Tour Operators & Adventure Travel Outfitters," later).

[FastFACTS] PUERTO NATALES

Camping Equipment If you don't feel like lugging your own camping gear down here, there are several agencies that rent equipment. Typical daily rental prices are two-person tents for C$3,000 to C$4,000, sleeping bags for C$2000, stoves for C$1,000, sleeping mats for C$500, and backpacks of various sizes for C$2,000. During the high season, it's best to reserve these items ahead of time. **La Madera Outdoor,** Arturo Prat 297 (𝄽 **61/413318;** www.lamadderaoutdoors. com), is recommended for its high-quality equipment; or try **Glaciares en Patagonia**, Pueblo Artesano local 7 (𝄽 **61/415960**).

Currency Exchange There are several exchange houses on Blanco Encalada; try **Mily,** Blanco Encalada 266 (𝄽 **61/411262;** Mon– Sat 10am–8pm). ATMs can be found at **Banco Santiago,** at the corner of Blanco Encalada and Bulnes, and **Banco Chile,** at Bulnes 544.

Hospitals The town's hospital, at the corner of Pinto and O'Higgins (𝄽 **61/ 411583**), only attends to serious emergencies. For any other medical issues, visit the clinic **CEFAM,** Javiera Carrera 1300 (𝄽 **61/411000**).

Internet Access There are tons of cafes offering free Wi-Fi in Puerto Natales. And most hotels have a

computer you can use. Also, try **Internet Melissa,** Blanco Encalada 258, and **Chilnet,** 343 Manuel Bulnes. Note that connections in Puerto Natales can be painfully slow.

Laundry The multilingual team at **ServiLaundry,** Prat 357 (𝄽 **61/412869**), gets your clothes back clean within 2 hours, and offers tourist information.

Pharmacy Farmacia Puerto Natales is at Esmeralda 701 (𝄽 **61/411306**).

Post Office The post office is on the Plaza de Armas, next to the cathedral (𝄽 **61/410202**); it's open Monday through Friday from 9am to 6pm, Saturday from 9am to 1pm.

What to See & Do

TOUR OPERATORS & ADVENTURE TRAVEL OUTFITTERS

The many tour operators in Puerto Natales can be divided into two groups: conventional sightseeing day tours to Torres del Paine, Perito Moreno Glacier in Argentina's Parque Nacional Los Glaciares, the Cueva del Milodón, the Nordenskjöld Trail hike, and the icebergs at Lago Grey; and adventure travel outfitters that arrange multiday, all-inclusive excursions, including trekking the W or the Circuit (see "Exploring Torres del Paine," later in this chapter) and climbing in Torres del Paine, kayaking the Río Serrano in Parque Nacional Bernardo O'Higgins, and taking horseback trips. Keep in mind that it's quite easy to arrange your own trekking journey in Torres del Paine; the bonus with these outfitters is that they carry the tents (which they'll set up) and food (which they'll cook). They also will pick you up from the airport and provide guided information about the flora and fauna of the park.

CONVENTIONAL DAY TOURS   These tours are for people with a limited amount of time in the area. Tours typically leave at 7:30am, return around 7:30pm, and cost about C$35,000 per person, not including lunch or park entrance fees. For day tours, try **Turismo Comapa,** Eberhard 555 (© 61/414300). Probably the most interesting way to see the Cueva del Milodón is with **Estancia Travel** (© 61/412221; www.estanciatravel.com), which offers a horseback-riding trip there for C$43,000 to C$54,000, including transfers, equipment, a bilingual guide, snacks, and a well-trained horse.

ADVENTURE TRAVEL   Dozens of international adventure travel companies run trips to Torres del Paine, and most work with a local operator. You can save money by going directly to the operator. Most of the following ones offer custom packages. **Indómita,** Bories 206 (© 61/414525; www.indomitapatagonia.com), is one of the most respected local outfitters for climbing, mountaineering, and kayaking. One of their most popular trips is a 3-day kayak descent of the River Serrano, with a paddle around Serrano Glacier. Partner **Antares,** Barros Arana 111 (© 61/414611; www.antarespatagonia.com), focuses on the "softer" (meaning less strenuous and/or technical) side of adventure travel, with a variety of multiday trekking journeys through the park that can include horseback riding, kayaking, and sailing; they have an office in the U.S. (© 800/267-6129). **Chile Nativo Expeditions,** Eberhard 230 (© 61/411835 or toll-free from North America 800/649-8776; www.chilenativo.com), offers high-end trekking, bird-watching, and horseback-riding adventures outside of the more "touristy" areas. **Fantástico Sur,** Esmeralda 661 (© 61/614184; www.fantasticosur.com), has wildlife-viewing tours, including a puma-watching tour that has a 70% guarantee of catching a glimpse of the elusive cat. **Onas** (©/fax 61/09-8739-3205 cell; www.onaspatagonia.com) has a half-day zodiac trip down the Río Serrano; see "Getting There & Away," later in this chapter. For fly-fishing outings, contact www.puertonatalesflyfishing.com.

Excursions Near Puerto Natales

CUEVA DE MILODON

In 1896, explorer Hermann Eberhard found a scrap of hairy skin and a few bones in a large cave near his property north of Puerto Natales that were later determined to be from a *Mylodon,* a prehistoric, giant ground sloth. The story of the *Mylodon* was popularized by Bruce Chatwin's travelogue *In Patagonia.* Although the *Mylodon* is depicted in a full-size replica at the cave's entrance, most of the *Mylodon*'s remains were shipped off to London, which means the real attraction is the 30m (98-ft.) high, 200m (656-ft.) deep cave itself, which has a weird, shaggy roof and is surrounded by interesting conglomerate rock formations. There's an interpretative center with a few *Mylodon* bones and a display showing the geological formation of the cave, as well as a historical display of the Indians who inhabited this and nearby caves as far back as 12,000 years ago. Its modern restaurant was designed to reflect the shape of the cave. While not too touristy, this attraction is recommended only if it's on your route, if you are interested in paleo-fauna, or if you've run out of things to do in Puerto Natales.

The cave is 24km (15 miles) north of Puerto Natales, so you'll need your own car or a tour to get here. To get here, take the road to Torres del Paine; at 20km (12 miles), turn left, and then drive for 4km (2½ miles) to the cave's turnoff. The site is managed by CONAF and is open daily from 10am to 7pm; admission is C$3,000 (© 61/411411 in Puerto Natales).

SAILING TO PARQUE NACIONAL BERNARDO O'HIGGINS

This national park, tremendous in its size, is largely unreachable except for boat tours to the glaciers Balmaceda and Serrano, tours that involve kayaking (for kayaking trips, see Indómita under "Tour Operators & Adventure Travel Outfitters," earlier), and the Skorpios journey to the grand Pío XI glacier (see later). A low-key, traditional day trip takes travelers to the Serrano and Balmaceda glaciers, with a stop at the Monte Balmaceda Hostel and a short walk along the glacier and its iceberg-studded bay. The ride kicks off with a trip past the old mutton-canning factory, an *estancia*, and a cormorant nesting site, among other sites of interest. The return trip is a straight shot back to Natales—which can be repetitive, so bring a book in the event of boredom or bad weather. The trip is dull except for the glacier visits, and visitors are prone to being herded about.

Punta Alta (© 61/410115; www.puntaalta.cl) has a handful of boats that have regular departures during the high season including a half-day trip to the fjords surrounding Puerto Natales, and to the Balmaceda and Serrano glaciers.

Turismo 21 de Mayo, Eberhard 560 (© 61/614420; www.turismo21demayo. cl), has two cutters and a yacht, and leaves daily (weather permitting) November through March and every Sunday from April to October (other days dependent on demand). The trip leaves at 8am, arriving at Serrano Glacier at 11:30am, where it stays for 1½ hours, returning at 5:30pm. They also offer custom-made charter rides for groups. The luxury cruise company **Skorpios,** Augusto Leguía Norte 118 (© 2/477-1900 or 305/484-5357 in North America; www.skorpios.cl), has an all-inclusive 6-day journey from Puerto Natales to Pío XI Glacier, the largest and only "advancing" (some scientists call it "stable") glacier in the Southern Hemisphere. This glacier measures an astounding 6km (3¾ miles) in length and peaks in height at 75m (246 ft.); it is also the least-visited glacier, and this alone makes a visit all the more special. The size of the Pío XI simply dwarfs other glaciers, such as Glacier Grey in Torres del Paine. I recommend this journey for travelers who are not very physically active and who don't want to miss a visit to Torres del Paine but wish to add on a special journey to an out-of-the-way destination. Active travelers might get bored on a 6-day tour.

Where to Stay

Puerto Natales must have the most interesting hotel scene in Patagonia, with stunning high-end design-forward hotels as well as sweet hosterías. It's one of the most expensive places to stay in South America, though. The newest, and perhaps mᴏ ambitious, is a 57-room waterfront five-star hotel set amidst the historic Puerto Bories meat packing district; **The Singular Patagonia** (www.thesingular.com) is slated to open in November of 2011. The high season in Puerto Natales is longer than in any other city in Chile—it's generally considered to run from October to April— and the price ranges shown below reflect this.

VERY EXPENSIVE

Indigo ★★★ ◫ The Indigo is a world-class design-forward boutique hotel. Conveniently located both on the waterfront and in town, it also sports the finest views of the glaciers across the sound. Rooms are in the multistory, red-and-black shipping container–inspired cube that overshadows the shingled former hostel, now with a funky lounge on the ground floor and a good restaurant on the top floor.

The hotel's divine top-level spa features three outdoor hot tubs. Even the sauna and massage areas offer views of the landscape. The airy, midsize rooms have fine views as well, separated bathrooms (most with open showers), and beds that feature crisp linens and wool blankets. The corner rooms are slightly larger, but are still outdone by the suite, which features a large, freestanding white bathtub. Many efforts have been made to keep the hotel eco-friendly, including through natural heat management, organic composting, an efficient waste water treatment system, and recycling. For location, views, and amenities, Indigo just slightly edges out Remota as the best place in town, and will be preferred by more independent travelers.

Ladrilleros 105, Puerto Natales. ✆ **61/413609.** www.indigopatagonia.com/hotel. 29 units. $289 double; $378 suite. AE, DC, MC, V. **Amenities:** Restaurant; bar; Jacuzzi; sauna; spa. *In room:* Hair dryer, free Wi-Fi.

Remota ★★★ ◫ You will either love or hate this hotel. The architecture alone is provocative, alternately uncomfortable and brilliant. Built by a renowned Chilean architect (the same who designed the explora) it's a unique mix of a bunker with a greenhouse, inspired by the *estancias* of Patagonia. Black and a bit forbidding from the outside, it's the complete opposite inside, featuring huge floor-to-ceiling windows that flood the white walls and columns with light amid a generous lounge and dining areas. Huge fireplaces add to the coziness, while a collection of archaeological finds from around the country draw your eye. Rooms feature native woods—wallboards even show off shreds of bark—along with washed cement floors and white ceilings. With natural grass on the roofs and energy-efficient lighting, Remota's design will please those looking to leave a small eco-footprint. Bathrooms have rainshower heads and deep tubs. Their all-inclusive packages (all meals, transfers, and excursions) tend to focus on lesser-traveled areas, and now include twice-weekly transfers from El Calafate, Argentina. They have packages ranging from 2 to 14 nights.

Ruta 9, Km 1.5, Puerto Natales. ✆ **61/414040.** www.remota.cl. 72 units. All inclusive 3-night package $1,548 per person double. Rates include excursions. AE, DC, MC, V. **Amenities:** Dining area; bar; bikes; indoor pool; spa. *In room:* Hair dryer, free Wi-Fi.

EXPENSIVE

Altiplánico Sur ★★★ ◫ Leaning heavily on contemporary style, the Altiplánico Sur is the southern brother of San Pedro's Altiplánico (p. 227), but sports completely different architecture. From the outside, it appears a bit reminiscent of a two-story brick school, but on approach, you'll see much of the property is in fact hidden underground with grass-covered roofs, and the exterior walls are made of a dark, unpainted adobe-type material. It shares a nearby stretch of waterfront property just north of

the Remota (see above). Spacious on the inside, the ambience relies heav-
ily on style concrete, trimmed by zigzagging wood and some metal decor. Views offer, across the road, are lovely. Rooms, down the corridor, are good-size, airy, and feature such warm touches as plush sheepskins and bright cushions that offset other eye-catching but cooler materials. Bathrooms are similar—modern, functional, and elegant. Because they don't offer the all-inclusive packages that are so popular elsewhere, this is a good bet for independent travelers looking for a low-profile hotel.

Huerto Familiar 282, Puerto Natales. (© **61/412525.** www.altiplanico.cl. 22 units. $220 double. AE, DC, MC, V. **Amenities:** Restaurant; bar; lounge w/TV; Jacuzzi; room service; Wi-Fi (in main lobby).

Hotel CostAustralis   This hotel is certainly traditional, but compared to the other options in the area, it's conservative and dull. The lobby, lounge, and main floor feel large and empty, although they boast lovely views of the sunset. Spacious doubles come with a sea view or a somewhat depressing view of the buildings in the back; the 28 rooms on the fourth floor, though priced the same, are newer, with marble bathrooms and plenty of closet space, so ask for one. The price is fairly high, even by North American and European standards, and therefore might not be appealing to anyone who plans to arrive late and leave early. For its size, it best suits tour groups.

Pedro Montt 262, Puerto Natales. (© **61/412000.** Fax 61/411881. www.australis.com. 110 units. $248–$300 double. AE, DC, MC, V. **Amenities:** 2 restaurants; bar; room service. *In room:* TV.

Hotel IF Patagonia   This modern new hotel is clean and bright—bright enough, in fact, that the hotel essentially heats itself via solar energy. The rooms are very simple, with plenty of white everywhere. Bathrooms are modern and functional but quite small. Walls are adorned with unique woven art, creating a visually warm, friendly atmosphere. A giant atrium leads up to a fourth floor terrace for fabulous views and there's a small bar for lounging. The owners run a fly-fishing outfitter. This is the best new mid-range option in town, a step down from Indigo (see above).

Magallanes 73, Puerto Natales. (© **61/410312.** www.hotelifpatagonia.com. 15 units. $170 standard double, $210 superior double, including breakfast. AE, DC, MC, V. **Amenities:** Dining area; lounge. *In room:* Hair dryer, free Wi-Fi.

MODERATE

Amerindia Hostel ★   If you are looking for a laid-back and friendly place to lay your head, this is a great choice. It's also a great option for more upscale backpackers. Rooms are all doubles, most with private baths. Some are tucked along a hallway at the back of a typical local home while there are seven new rooms in a refurbished heritage building next door. The style is simple and warm, and the breakfasts are a superb value. Some bathrooms have showers and some have tubs. Room 5 has a view of the water. The best part of Amerindia is the caring, utterly unpretentious staff, who will welcome you as if you were a member of their family.

Barros Arana 135, Puerto Natales. (© **61/411945.** www.hostelamerindia.com. 15 units. $60 double with shared bathroom; $80 double with private bathroom. No credit cards. **Amenities:** Breakfast room; Internet (in lobby). *In room:* Free Wi-Fi.

INEXPENSIVE

Casa Cecilia ✍   Casa Cecilia is a budget favorite in Puerto Natales, consistently garnering rave reviews from guests for its full range of services, pleasant rooms, and delicious breakfasts. The front lobby acts as a travel agency of sorts, providing information, arranging excursions, and renting camping equipment; beyond that is a

common area and a kitchen that guests can use—and they ⟨...⟩
two floors and encircle an atrium; some come with private bath⟨...⟩
and they are a good value for the price. Light flows into the rooms ⟨...⟩
interior atrium. The Swiss-Chilean couple (she's Cecilia) speaks seve⟨...⟩
and both are very friendly. This hostel is popular with a wide range of ages a⟨...⟩

Tomás Roger 60, Puerto Natales. ©/fax **61/613560**. www.casaceciliahostal.com. 15 units. $51 do⟨...⟩
with shared bathroom; $74 double with private bathroom. AE, DC, MC, V. **Amenities:** Kitchen. *In room⟨...⟩*
Free Wi-Fi.

Where to Dine

Along with the following restaurants, there are several that serve inexpensive fare. **La Mesita,** Arturo Prat 196 (© **61/411571**), is a popular place for pizzas, salads, and hanging out. For an early morning (they're open from 6am) or afternoon coffee with great views, try **Cerritos Coffee & Café,** Miguel Sánchez 11 (© **61/412989**). **Mocho's,** Ladrilleros 328 (© **61/415854**) is open all day and has sandwiches and typical Chilean hot dogs loaded with extras.

MODERATE

Afrigonia ★★ FUSION   One of the most interesting dining experiences in all of Chile is this tiny, unassuming spot that surprisingly blends Chilean cuisine with an East African influence. The curries and tandooris made here use real spices, and the *ceviche* in coconut milk with mango may be the best you'll have in Chile. It's small and very popular, so reserve ahead.

Eberhard 343. © **61/412232**. Reservations recommended. Main courses C$5,500–C$9,500. AE, MC, DC, V. Daily 1–3pm and 7–11pm.

Angelica's MEDITERANEAN   The menu here is long, and the service wonderfully friendly. Specialties include sea bass, hake, and the classic and warm Chilean seafood stew called *paila marina*. I loved the king crab cannelloni. There are also lots of fresh salads. This place tends toward the upscale, at least by Puerto Natales standards.

Bulnes 501. © **61/410007**. www.angelicas.cl. Main courses C$6,000–C$10,500. AE, MC, V. Daily noon–3:30pm and 6pm–12:30am.

Cormorán de Las Rocas 📷 SEAFOOD   This is Puerto Natales' best seafood restaurant, and the top local choice for upscale dining. In a top-floor dining room designed to feel like a ship, the views are superb and the seafood-heavy menu large. Specialties include a king crab tart with four cheeses, rosemary octopus with a green apple salad, and salmon or hake in coconut and saffron sauce. For dessert, try the cheesecake with calafate sauce. Service is very professional. The bar offers lighter tapas, and is open late.

Miguel Sanchez 72. © **61/413723**. Main courses C$6,500–C$9,000. AE, MC, V. Daily 12:30–3pm and 7:30–11pm.

Restaurant Ultima Esperanza ★ 🍴 SEAFOOD   This may not in fact be your last hope for a good meal, as the name implies. But it may well be the best in Chilean Patagonia, and it offers good food at competitive prices. Its location in a simple, half-timbered building near the square and its basic if conservative decor might not look like much, but it's what your taste buds say that counts. Above all, it prepares some of the best abalone, king crab, and *curanto* in the whole country. Try the poached conger eel in shellfish or king crab sauce. Magellanic lamb is also on the menu.

...ntultimaesperanza@hotmail.com. Main courses C$4,500–
...pm and 6:30pm–midnight.

...ETARIAN   If you're looking for a friendly, comfort-
...nd the evening, then look no further. At El Living, run
...who have lived in the area for more than a decade, you
... sofa with a pisco sour or have an excellent vegetarian
...dmade wooden dining tables. The menu is simple and
...delicious. The Sweet and Sour Red Salad is a perfect mix
of bee... ...idney beans, and onion; the veggie burger is delicious and
served on a whol...   baguette. This is one of the only places in Chile that serves
a peanut-butter-and-jelly sandwich. There's also French toast with fried bananas, and
a variety of cakes baked daily. A full bar and wine list round out this excellent place.
Arturo Prat 156. ✆ **61/411140.** Main courses C$4,500–C$7,000. No credit cards. Daily 11am–midnight.

Puerto Natales After Dark

Little more than a few years ago, the only nightspot in Puerto Natales was a brothel.
Now there are several bars where the party doesn't wind down until about 5am.
There's a nice new brewpub, **Cervecería Baguales,** at Barros Arana 146 (✆ **61/
613648**) that's owned by an American and two Chileans. **Toore Bar,** Eberhard 169
(no phone), is a hip new spot to sample a pisco sour. **The Pub El Bar de Ruperto,**
Bulnes 310 (no phone), has pool tables and loud music. The bar and lounge at **Indigo,**
Ladrilleros 105 (✆ **61/413609**), are good for a drink and view of the sunset.

PARQUE NACIONAL TORRES DEL PAINE ★★★

113km (70 miles) N of Puerto Natales; 360km (223 miles) NW of Punta Arenas

This is Chile's prized jewel, a national park so magnificent that few in the world can
claim a rank in its class. Granite peaks and towers soar from sea level to upward of
2,800m (9,184 ft.). Golden pampas and the rolling steppes are home to llamalike
guanacos and more than 100 species of colorful birds, such as parakeets, flamingos,
and ostrichlike rheas. During the spring, Chilean firebush blooms a riotous red, and
during the autumn, the park's beech trees change to crimson, sunflower, and orange.
A fierce wind screams through this region during the spring and summer, and yet
flora such as the delicate porcelain orchids and ladyslippers somehow weather the
inhospitable terrain. Electric-blue icebergs cleave from Glacier Grey. Resident
baqueanos ride atop sheepskin saddles. Condors float effortlessly even on the windiest day. This park is not someplace you just visit; it is something you experience.

Although it sits next to the Andes, the Torres del Paine is a separate geologic formation created roughly 3 million years ago when bubbling magma began growing and
pushing its way up, taking a thick sedimentary layer with it. Glaciation and severe
climate weathered away the softer rock, leaving the spectacular Paine Massif whose
prominent features are the *Cuernos* (which means "horns") and the one-of-a-kind
Torres—three salmon-colored, spherical granite towers. The black sedimentary rock
is visible on the upper reaches of the elegant Cuernos, named for the two spires that
rise from the outer sides of its amphitheater. *Paine* is the Tehuelche Indian word for
"blue," and it brings to mind the varying shades found in the lakes that surround this

massif—among them the milky, turquoise waters of Lagos Nordenskjöld and Pehoé. Backing the Paine Massif are several glaciers that descend from the Southern Ice Field.

Torres del Paine was once a collection of *estancias* and small-time ranches; they were forced out with the creation of the park in 1959. The park has since grown to its present size of 242,242 hectares (598,338 acres), and in 1978 was declared a World Biosphere Reserve by UNESCO for its singular beauty and ecology. This park is a backpacker's dream, but just as many visitors find pleasure staying in lodges here and taking day hikes and horseback rides—even those with a short amount of time here are blown away by a 1-day visit. There are options for everyone, part of the reason the number of visitors to this park is growing by nearly 10,000 per year.

Essentials

WHEN TO COME & WHAT TO BRING

This is not the easiest of national parks to visit. The climate in the park can be abominable, with wind speeds that can peak at 161kmph (100 mph) and rain and snow even in the middle of summer. On average, the windiest days happen between mid-November and mid-March, but the only predictable thing about the weather here is its unpredictability. **Note:** Come with your expectations in check—it's not uncommon to spend a week here and not see the towers even once due to bad weather.

Spring is a beautiful time for budding flowers and birds; during the fall, the beech forests turn colors, which can be especially striking on walks up to the Towers and to the glacier. The winter is surprisingly temperate, with relatively few snowstorms and no wind—but short days. You'll need to stay in a hotel during the winter, but you'll practically have the park to yourself. Summer is, ironically, the worst time to come, especially from late December to mid-February, when the wind blows at full fury and crowds descend upon the park. When the wind blows, it can make even a short walk a rather scary experience or just drive you nuts—just try to go with it, not fight it, and revel in the excitement of the extreme environment that makes Patagonia what it is.

I can't stress enough the importance of bringing the right gear, especially waterproof hiking boots (if you plan to do any trekking), weatherproof outerwear, and warm layers, even in the summer. The ozone problem is acute here, so you'll need sunscreen, sunglasses, and a hat as well.

VISITOR & PARK ENTRANCE INFORMATION

Your visit to Torres del Paine will require logistical planning, unless you've left it up to an all-inclusive tour or hotel. Begin your research at **www.torresdelpaine.cl**, an English-language overview of the park and its surroundings, including maps, activities information, events, photos, hotel overviews and links, and more. The park service, CONAF, has a relatively unhelpful Spanish-only website at **www.conaf.cl**.

The park's administration and visitor center can be reached at © **61/691931;** it's located at the southern end of the park. The park is open year-round from 8:30am to 10:30pm. The entry fee is C$15,200 for adults; during the winter, the cost is C$7,600 for adults. If you're staying outside the park, get your ticket stamped for multiple visits.

GETTING THERE & AROUND

Many travelers are unaware of the enormous amount of time it takes to get to Torres del Paine. There are no direct transportation services from the airport in Punta Arenas to the park, except with package tours and hotels that have their own vehicles, or by chartering an auto or van (try **Vía Terra;** ✆ **61/410775;** www.viaterra.cl). The earliest flight from Santiago to Punta Arenas arrives at around noon; from there it's a 3-hour drive to Puerto Natales. The last bus to the park leaves at 2:30pm for the 2-hour journey to the east side of the park. Thanks to a relatively new road, the west side (where such lodgings as explora, Patagonia Camp, and Hostería Lago Grey are) is now only 1 hour from Puerto Natales. If you're relying on bus transportation (and if you are not staying at an all-inclusive hotel), you will likely need to spend the night in Puerto Natales. If you've arranged a package tour or hotel stay that picks you up at the airport, remember that the 3- to 5-hour trip from here can be very tiring if you've just taken a 4-hour flight from Santiago.

BY BUS Several companies offer daily service from October to April. During the low season, only Bus Sur offers service to the park. Buses to Torres del Paine enter through the Laguna Amarga ranger station, stop at the Pudeto catamaran dock, and terminate at the park administration center. If you're going directly to the Torres trail head at Hostería Las Torres, there are minivan transfers waiting at the Laguna Amarga station that charge C$2,500 one-way. The return times given below are when the bus leaves from the park administration center; the bus will pass through the Laguna Amarga station about 45 minutes later.

Trans Via Paine, Bulnes 516 (✆ **61/413672**), leaves daily at 7:30am via Laguna Amarga. **Gomez,** Arturo Prat 234 (✆ **61/411971**), also leaves at 7:30am, returning from the administration building at 1pm. **Buses JB,** Arturo Prat 258 (✆ **61/410242**), also departs at 7:30am, returning at 1pm. The cost is C$8,000 one-way and C$15,000 round-trip.

BY TOUR VAN If you don't have much time to spend in the park or would like to get there at your own pace, check into the minivan tour services that plan stops at the Salto Grande waterfall and carry on to Lago Grey for a walk along the beach to view giant icebergs (see "Tour Operators & Adventure Travel Outfitters," earlier in this chapter).

BY CAR Heading north on Pedro Montt out of town, follow the dirt road for 51km (32 miles) until you reach Cerro Castillo. From here the road turns left and heads 47km (29 miles) toward the park (keep your eyes open for another left turn that is signposted TORRES DEL PAINE). You'll come to a fork in the road; one road leads to the Lago Sarmiento CONAF station, another to the Laguna Amarga station. If you are planning to head to the Torres trail head and Hostería Las Torres hotel complex on your way out, then take the Lago Sarmiento entrance; it's faster, and you'll get to view the striking blue waters of Lago Sarmiento. You can park your car at the Hostería Las Torres, the park administration center, the Pudeto catamaran dock, or the Lago Grey ranger station. To get to the western side of the park (to such places as Lago Grey and Lago Pehoé, and to hotels such as explora and Patagonia Camp), take a left just north of town toward the Cueva de Milodón cave, and continue north to the CONAF Station. Check with the park service at www.conaf.cl or ask your rental-car agency for updated road information.

CROSSING LAGO PEHOE BY CATAMARAN Day hikes to the Glacier Grey trail and backpackers taking the W or Circuit trails will need to cross Lake Pehoé at some point aboard a catamaran, about a 45-minute ride. The cost is C$11,000 one-way or C$19,000 round-trip. Buses from Puerto Natales are timed to drop off and pick up passengers in conjunction with the catamaran (Nov 15–Mar 15 leaving Pudeto at 9:30am, noon, and 6pm, and from Pehoé at 10am, 12:30, and 6:30pm; Oct

1–30 and April from Pudeto at noon, and from Pehoé at 12:30pm; Nov 1–15 and Mar 16–31 from Pudeto at noon and 6pm, and Pehoé at 12:30 and 6pm; closed May–Sept). Hikers walking the entire round-trip Glacier Grey trail can do so only taking the 9:30am boat and returning at 6:30pm from mid-November to March 15. For more information, contact (✆ **61/411380** or visit www.hielospatagonicos.cl.

GETTING TO THE PARK BY BOAT   Zodiac-catamaran combinations that take visitors from Puerto Natales through the Ultima Esperanza Sound and up the Río Serrano, or vice versa, are available. This is an interesting alternative to getting to the park via bus or van, but it's an all-day affair. Also, you'll need to arrange transportation with your hotel to or from the administration office. Along the winding turquoise river, visitors are taken through territory that rivals Alaska, past the Tyndall and Geike glaciers, and eventually to Serrano Glacier. Here they disembark for a walk up to the ice, then board another boat for a 3½-hour ride to Puerto Natales. The one-way ride costs C$69,000 per person, depending on the season. You can also do a round-trip journey leaving from and returning to the park for about C$87,500. See "Tour Operators & Adventure Travel Outfitters," earlier in this chapter, for more information. **Onas's** zodiac is an adventure, and their guides are fun (✆/fax **61/614300;** www.onaspatagonia.com).

Active travelers will be interested in following the same Río Serrano route but by **kayak,** about a 3-day journey. This trip is suitable for travelers on their way back to Puerto Natales, to take advantage of the river's downward current; at night, travelers camp out on shore. Check with **Indómita** (✆ **61/413247;** www.indomitapatagonia. com), on Bories 206, in Puerto Natales.

Exploring Torres del Paine
TRAILS
Torres del Paine has something for everyone, from easy, well-trammeled trails to remote walks through relatively people-free wilderness. Which path you choose depends on how much time you have and what kind of walking you're up for. If you have only a few days, I suggest you stick to the major highlights. If you have a week or more, consider a horseback-riding trip to the base of Mount Donoso, a bird-watching trip through the Pingo Valley, or a walk to the Valle de Silencio beyond the Towers. The best way to plan a multiday hike is to begin at Hostería Las Torres, reached from the Laguna Amarga ranger station, although it is just as feasible to start at Lago Pehoé by catamaran and begin the trip up to the glacier or French Valley. In addition to checking out the map on p. 401, you may want to pick up one of **JLM's Torres del Paine maps** (sold at most bookstores and at the park entrance), or download a map from **www.torresdelpaine.com** to begin planning your itinerary. Walking times shown below are average. The minimum number of days shown assumes walking 4 to 8 hours a day; plan for extra days if you want to take it easy, and factor 1 or 2 days for bad weather.

Long-Haul Overnight Hikes
The Circuit ★★★   The Circuit is a spectacular, long-haul backpacking trip that takes hikers around the entire Paine Massif. It can be done in two ways: with or without the W included. Including the W, you'll need 8 to 11 days; without it, from 4 to 7 days. The Circuit is less traveled than the W because it's longer and requires that you camp out at least twice. I don't recommend doing this trail if you have only 4 or 5 days. This trail is for serious backpackers only because it involves several difficult hikes up

and down steep, rough terrain and over fallen tree trunks. You'll be rewarded for your effort with dazzling views of terrain that varies from grassy meadows and winding rivers to thick virgin beech forest, snowcapped peaks, and, best of all, the awe-inspiring view of Glacier Grey seen from atop the John Garner Pass. Always do this trail counter-clockwise for easier ascents and with the scenery before you.

If you're here during the high season and want to get away from crowds, you might contemplate walking the first portion of this trail, beginning at Laguna Azul. This is the old trail, and it more or less parallels the Circuit, but on the other side of the river, passing the *baqueano* post La Victorina, the only remaining building of an old *estancia*. At Refugio Dickson, you'll have to cross the river in the *refugio's* dinghy for C$2,500. To get to Laguna Azul, you'll need to hitchhike or arrange private transportation. Do not underestimate the isolation of most of this hike—snowstorms, injuries, not having enough food—a lot can go wrong on this trek, so be fully prepared.

Approx. 60km (37 miles) total. Beginning at Laguna Amarga or Hostería Las Torres. Terrain ranges from easy–difficult.

The W ★★   This segment of the Paine Massif is so called because hikers are taken along a trail that forms a W, up three valleys. This trail leads to the park's major geological features—the Torres, the Cuernos, and Glacier Grey—and it's the preferred multiday hike for its relatively short hauls and a time frame that requires 4 to 5 days. In addition, those who prefer not to camp or carry more gear than a sleeping bag, food, and their personal goods can stay in the various *refugios* along the way. Most hikers begin at Hostería Las Torres and start with a day-walk up to the Torres. From here, hikers head to the Los Cuernos *refugio* and spend the night, or continue on to the Italiano campsite near the base of the valley; then they walk up to French Valley. The next stop is Pehoé *refugio*, where most spend the night before hiking up to Glacier Grey. It's best to spend a night at Refugio Grey and return to the Pehoé *refugio* the next day. From here, take the catamaran across Lago Pehoé to an awaiting bus back to Puerto Natales.

Approx. 56km (35 miles) total. Beginning at Hostería Las Torres or Refugio Pehoé. Terrain ranges from easy–difficult.

Day Hikes

These hikes run from easy to difficult, either within the W or from various trail heads throughout the park. Again, the times given are estimates for the average walker.

Glacier Grey   Hike here for an up-close look at the face of Glacier Grey, though warm summers of late have sent the glacier retreating. There aren't as many steep climbs as the trail to Las Torres, but it takes longer to get there (about 3½ hr.). I recommend that hikers in the summer walk this lovely trail to the glacier lookout point, then take the boat back to Hostería Grey (see "Excursions around Glacier Grey," later). The walk takes hikers through thick forest and stunning views of the Southern Ice Field and the icebergs slowly making their way down Lago Grey. A turnoff just before the lookout point takes you to Refugio Grey.

3½ hr. one-way. Difficult.

Lago Grey 🛉   Not only is this the easiest walk in the park, but it also is one of the most dramatic for the gigantic blue icebergs that rest along the shore of Lago Grey. A flat walk across the sandy shore of the lake takes visitors to a peninsula for a short hike to a lookout point with Glacier Grey in the far distance. This walk begins near the Hostería Lago Grey; they also offer a recommended boat ride that weaves past icebergs and then takes passengers to the face of the glacier (see "Excursions around Glacier Grey," below).

1–2 hr. Easy.

Lago Pingo 🎒   Lago Pingo consistently sees fewer hikers and is an excellent spot for bird-watching for the variety of species that flock to this part of the park. The trail begins as an easy walk through a pleasant valley, past an old *baqueano* post. From here the trail heads through forest and undulating terrain, and past the Pingo Cascade until it eventually reaches another old *baqueano* post, the run-down but picturesque Zapata *refugio*. You can make this trail as long or as short as you'd like; the return is back along the same trail. The trail leaves from the same parking lot as the Lago Grey trail.

1–4 hr. one-way. Easy–moderate.

Las Torres (The Towers) ★★   The trail to view the soaring granite Towers is a classic hike in the park but certainly not the easiest. Those who are in decent shape will not want to miss this exhilarating trek. The trail leaves from the Hostería Las Torres and begins with a steep 45-minute ascent, followed by up-and-down terrain for 1½ hours to another 45-minute steep ascent up a slippery granite moraine. Midway is the Refugio Chileno, where you can stop for a coffee or spend the night. Don't give up—the Torres do not come into full view until the very end.

3 hr. one-way. Difficult.

Mirador Nordenskjöld   The trail head for this walk begins near the Pudeto catamaran dock. This trail begins with an up-close visit to the crashing Salto Grande waterfall. Then it winds through Antarctic beech and thorny bush to a lookout point with dramatic views into the French Valley and the Cuernos, looking over Lago Nordenskjöld. This trail is a good place to see wildflowers in the spring, but it can get really windy in late summer. Most day tours of the park include this hike.

1 hr. one-way. Easy.

Valle Francés (French Valley)   There are several ways to hike this trail. From Refugio Pehoé, you'll pass by the blue waters of Lake Skottsberg and through groves of Chilean firebush and open views of the granite spires behind Los Cuernos. From Refugio Los Cuernos, you won't see French Valley until you're in it. A short walk through the campground leads hikers to direct views of the hanging glacier that descends from Paine Grande, and enthusiastic hikers can continue the steep climb up into the valley itself for a view of French Valley's enormous granite amphitheater.

2½–4½ hr. one-way. Moderate–difficult.

OTHER OUTDOOR ACTIVITIES IN THE PARK

A **horseback ride** in Torres del Paine can be one of the most enjoyable ways to see the park. Both Hotel Las Torres and explora have their own stables, but only the hotel has daily horseback rides, even to the Refugios Chileno and Los Cuernos (©/fax **61/363636;** www.lastorres.com). The full-day trips cost C$75,000 per person, and they leave from the hotel. Your hotel can reserve a horseback ride leaving from the concession-run stable near the administration center, too. For multiday horseback-riding trips, contact **Chile Nativo Expeditions,** Eberhart 230 (© **61/411835** in Chile or 800/649-8776 in the U.S.; www.chilenativo.com). Chile Nativo can plan custom-made journeys within the park and to little-known areas, some of which include an introduction to the *baqueano* and *estancia* (ranching) way of life. Most trips require prior experience.

Excursions Around Glacier Grey

A surprisingly accessible and electrifying excursion in the park is taking a crampon-shoed **walk across the quickly disappearing Glacier Grey.** Trips begin from the Refugio Grey with a 15-minute zodiac boat ride to the starting point on the western arm of the glacier. The excursion is a full-day trip, so the only way to participate is to lodge at the *refugio.* Guests are provided with full equipment, including crampons, ice axes, ropes, and harnesses, and are given basic ice-climbing instructions. Visitors who have taken this hike have consistently given it rave reviews for the chance to peer into deep blue crevasses and explore the glacier's otherworldly contours up close.

Now that the glacier has receded, the best way to view it up close is to ride **Hostería Grey's half-day boat ride,** which takes passengers past floating icebergs and directly to the face of the glacier. Passengers ride round-trip from the shore at Lake Grey; hikers can take the Pehoé ferry, walk approximately 4 hours to the Grey *refugio,* and then ride back on the Hostería Grey boat (C$32,000 one-way), and transfer to the administration center and wait for a bus to drop them back at their hotel (though most hotels will arrange pickup for this excursion). The price is C$40,000 round-trip and C$28,000 one-way, and there are three trips leaving daily, at 8:30am, noon, and 3:30pm. Best of all, the journey runs year-round. Reservations are imperative, as are transfer reservations from the administration center; contact the *hostería* at ✆ **61/410220** or www.turismolagogrey.com. Travelers who are not lodging at the Refugio Grey may take the early boat from the Hostería Grey, participate in the glacier walk (see above), and head back with the late boat.

Where to Stay & Dine

Beyond the hotels listed in greater detail here, there are several rural hotels between Puerto Natales, Cerro Castillo, and the park itself. For travelers with a vehicle at their disposal, these lodgings are more moderately priced and hence a good option if you don't mind a fair amount of driving, since park entrance fees are valid for multiple entries. Among them, consider the half-timbered **Hotel Posada Tres Pasos** ★, between Natales and Cerro Castillo (✆ **61/245494** or 2/196-9630; www.hotel3pasos.cl), built in 1904 and visited by Nobel Prize Laureate Gabriela Mistral. At the development outside the far southwest limits of the park is the sprawling **Hotel Río Serrano** ★ (✆ **61/240528;** www.hotelrioserrano.cl), a giant complex with a whopping 105 rooms and nice views of the Paine Massif. Another option is the *estancia* lodging operated by Baqueano Zamora, Baquedano 534 in Puerto Natales (✆ **61/613521;** www.baqueanozamora.com), including **Tercera Barranca** 20km (12 miles) from Laguna Amarga.

HOTELS & HOSTERÍAS

Estancia Cerro Guido ★★★ 🖾 This luxurious lodge may be a fair distance from the park proper, but it's the only top hotel with a view of the distinctive Torres, from its perspective due west across the plains. It also has a marvelous view of the vast steppe, and of Sierra Baquedano to the east, and is one of the only properties by the park to offer an authentic *estancia* experience. While the sheep ranch covers a vast 99,000 hectares (247,000 acres) between the park and Argentine border and includes the entire village of Cerro Guido, the facilities themselves include two *estancia* buildings formerly occupied by the administrators and owners, a dining area, and a few service areas such as a horse stable. The finest view of the Torres is from the excellent restaurant, which has barbecue facilities indoors and out. Rooms, with fine

Parque Nacional Torres del ...

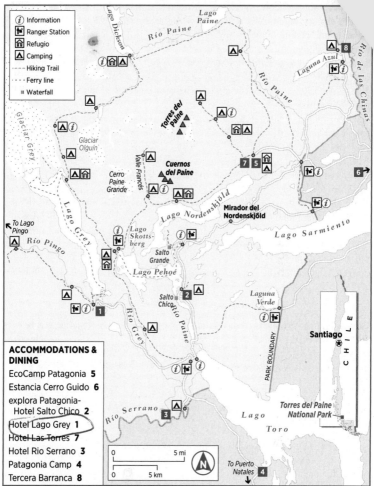

Legend:
- (i) Information
- Ranger Station
- Refugio
- Camping
- ---- Hiking Trail
- ---- Ferry line
- ₪ Waterfall

Map labels: Lago Dickson, Lago Paine, Río Paine, Laguna Azul, Río de las Chinas, Torres del Paine, Glaciar Olguín, Glaciar Grey, Cerro Paine Grande, Valle Francés, Cuernos del Paine, Lago Nordenskjöld, Mirador del Nordenskjöld, Lago Sarmiento, Lago Grey, Lago Skottsberg, Salto Grande, Lago Pehoé, Salto Chico, Laguna Verde, To Lago Pingo, Río Pingo, Río Grey, Río Paine, Río Serrano, Lago Toro, Santiago, CHILE, Torres del Paine National Park, PARK BOUNDARY, To Puerto Natales

ACCOMMODATIONS & DINING

EcoCamp Patagonia **5**
Estancia Cerro Guido **6**
explora Patagonia-
  Hotel Salto Chico **2**
Hotel Lago Grey **1**
Hotel Las Torres **7**
Hotel Rio Serrano **3**
Patagonia Camp **4**
Tercera Barranca **8**

0   5 mi
0   5 km

polished hardwood floors, are furnished largely according to the lodge's original, country English–style, early-20th-century decor, with the nicest being the superior rooms in the former administrator's mansion; at a 10% higher price, they're larger and have fireplaces along with central heating. It's the perfect place for a genuine dive into Patagonia's rural traditions, and Cerro Guido now offers 2- to 4-day all-inclusive packages that allow guests to take sheep-shearing tours and personal guided horseback and hiking excursions to the park, as well as to a nearby aboriginal gravesite with a spectacular view.

Cerro Guido. ℡ **61/411818.** www.cerroguido.cl. 15 units. $210 standard double, $262 superior double; 4-day all-inclusive package including excursions and meals for $2,090 per person. AE, DC, MC, V. **Amenities:** Restaurant; bar; lounge; Wi-Fi (in lobby). *In room:* Hair dryer.

401

a—**Hotel Salto Chico ★★★** 📷   explora in Patagonia has
than any other hotel in Chile, and deservedly so. It's a one-stop
ble experience. Few hotels in the world offer as stunning a view
ed above the milky, turquoise waters of Lago Pehoé and facing
nphitheater of the Paine massif. It is terribly expensive, but
can afford it. explora's style is comfortable elegance, and its
belie the contemporary exterior: softly curving blond-wood walls
entirely from native deciduous beech, a band of picture windows wrapping
around the full front of the building, and large windows in each room. The furniture
was handcrafted using local wood, and the crisp guest rooms are accented with Spanish checkered linens, handsome slate-tiled bathrooms, and warming racks for drying
gear. Upgrades in 2011 include a new wine bar, steam bath, and renovations of the
pool area.

The hotel has begun completing certification with the LEED (Leadership in
Energy and Environmental Design) body to recognize its many efforts to promote
sustainability. All-inclusive prices cover airport transfers, meals, open bar, and excursions, on regular 4-day rotations. Excursions range from easy half-day walks to photo
safaris. The set menu is limited to two choices, generally a meat and vegetarian dish,
and it must be said that the food quality has at times been uneven—but never bad,
and the food is remarkably fresh given the extreme distances from any decent market.
Guests will want to consider explora's "Travesías," add-on journeys to Chaltén and the
Parque Nacional Fitzroy and El Calafate, both in Argentina.

In Santiago, Américo Vespucio Sur 80, 5th floor. ✆ **866/750-6699** in the U.S., or 2/206-6060 in Santiago. Fax 2/228-4655. www.explora.com. 50 units. Package rates are per person, double occupancy: 4
nights from $2,780; 6 nights from $4,410. Rates include all meals, excursions, transportation, gear, and
guides. AE, DC, MC, V. **Amenities:** Restaurant; bar; lounge; outdoor Jacuzzi; large indoor pool; sauna; spa.

Hotel Lago Grey ★   This spruce and traditional white hotel is tucked within a
beech forest, looking out onto the beach at Lago Grey and the astounding blue icebergs that drift to its shore. It's well on the other side of the park, but the view is
better here than at the Hostería Las Torres (below), and they have a transfer van and
guides for excursions to all reaches of the park, for an extra cost. There's a new wing
with 30 "superior" rooms, effectively doubling the size of the hotel and leaving the
common areas crowded during high season. The price suggests more luxurious
rooms, but the walls are a tad thin and have little decoration. Also, when the wind
whips up, this side of the park is colder. Another problem is that nothing is included
except for breakfast; expect to rack up quite a bill on expensive "extras," such as
transfers and other meals. On the plus side, there are plenty of trails that branch out
from here, including the stroll along the beach out to the Pingo Valley and the
strenuous hike up to Mirador Ferrier.

Office in Punta Arenas, Lautaro Navarro 1077. ✆ **61/712143.** www.turismolagogrey.com. 60 units. $308
double standard, $368 double superior. AE, DC, MC, V. **Amenities:** Restaurant; lounge.

Hotel Las Torres ★★ ☺   This used to be an original working cattle *estancia*, sitting at the trail head to the Torres. But it's now a full-blown hotel, with the traffic to
match. The complex includes a low-slung, ranch-style hotel, a two-story hotel wing
next door, a large campground, and a hostel. In the afternoon, horses and the odd cow
graze just outside your hotel room door, making this a fun place for kids. This is an
ideal lodge for horseback-riding enthusiasts due to their on-site stables, and its access
to the Towers is convenient; however, it is a long drive to the other side of the park,

Due to the soaring popularity of Torres del Paine, it is recommended that travelers book well in advance if planning on visiting the park between late November and late March. Nearly every business now has a website or, at the very least, an e-mail address, so trip planning is easier than ever. Hotels can be booked directly, and often they offer their own transportation from the airport or, at the very least, can recommend a service to call or e-mail. One-stop agencies such as **Fantástico** Sur (Esmeralda 661, in Puerto Natales; (*C*) 61/614185; www.fantasticosur.com) and **Chile Native** (Eberhard 230, in Puerto Natales; (*C*) 61/411835, or toll-free from North America 800/649-8776; www.chilenativo.com), are good places for *refugio* reservations, horseback-riding trips, or camping equipment rentals, and they can sometimes offer lower hotel rates at *hosterías* in the park. They can also solve tricky transfer problems.

and rooms have no views. Las Torres also has a small spa, with mud therapy and massage treatments, as well as a sauna. The buffet-style restaurant is above par, but pricey at C$15,675 per person for dinner.

The hotel offers expensive packages that include guided tours, meals, and transportation, much like explora, and excellent off-season trips to little-explored areas. Packages run from 3 to 7 nights, or you can pay separately for day trips. Try spending 2 nights here and 2 at Hostería Lago Grey, thereby avoiding the steep price of an excursion there.

Office in Punta Arenas, Sarmiento 846. (*C*)/fax **61/617450.** www.lastorres.com. 84 units. $270 double standard, $305 double superior. Rates include buffet breakfast. 4-night packages per person, double occupancy, are from $1,674. AE, DC, MC, V. **Amenities:** Restaurant; lounge; room service; spa.

Patagonia Camp ★★ ☺ ▣   This is a camp for grownups. With a mountaineer's heart and a luxury bent, it is not a hotel, it's an experience in nature. Set on a slope above Lago del Toro, with stunning views of the Paine massif, it feels similar to safari camps found in the African savannah. There are 18 wood-framed *yurts* (Mongolian-inspired wood-framed tents) situated along wooden walkways tucked inside a beech forest. Incredibly bright, cozy, and plush, the yurts have such high-end touches as woven blankets, central heating, deep tubs, and copper showerheads. If the night's clear, you'll have delightful stargazing from your bed; if you have trouble sleeping, you may curse the way the tents flap loudly during strong storms. Still, the atmosphere is incredibly natural, secluded, and romantic. In the main lodge, meals (and pisco sours) are served. Their all-inclusive packages, again, mirror those of explora, but Patagonia Camp is much more quiet and intimate. Your outing will need to accommodate wishes of other guests since groups are so small; be prepared to negotiate for your first-choice excursion.

Hernando de Aguirre 414, Santiago. (*C*) **2/335-6898.** www.patagoniacamp.com. 18 units. $440 double with breakfast and open bar. 3-night programs $2,320 single, $1,550 double. Rates include all meals, excursions, transfers in/out, guides. AE, DC, MC, V. **Amenities:** Restaurant.

REFUGIOS & HOSTELS

Five cabinlike lodging units and one hostel, all with shared accommodations, are distributed along the park's Circuit and W trails, and they are moderately priced sleeping options for backpackers who are not interested in pitching a tent. Although most have bedding or sleeping bags for an expensive rental price, your best bet is to bring your own. The price, at $63 on average per night (about $66 for room and full board), may seem steep for a simple dorm bed; still, it is a far cry cheaper than many shared accommodations in national parks in the U.S. All come with hot showers, a simple cafe, and a common area for hiding out from bad weather. Meals served here are simply prepared but hearty, or alternatively, guests can bring their own food and cook. Each *refugio* has rooms with two to six bunks, which you'll have to share with strangers when they're full. During the high season, consider booking weeks in advance, although many visitors have reported luck when calling just a few days beforehand (due to cancellations). All agencies in Puerto Natales and Punta Arenas book reservations and issue vouchers, but the best bet is to call or e-mail (see info below). There is a scrappy *refugio* near the park administration center, with two rows of sleeping berths that I do not recommend except in an emergency situation. This *refugio* is on a first-come, first-served basis.

The first three *refugios* are owned and operated by **Fantástico Sur.** Rates are $37 for a bed, plus C$4,750 for breakfast and C$9,025 for dinner. They can be booked by contacting ℂ/fax **61/614185;** www.fslodges.com:

o **Refugio El Chileno.** This is the least-frequented *refugio* because it is located halfway up to the Towers (most do the trail as a day hike). Hikers will find it more convenient to stow their stuff in the campground at the *hostería,* but, then again, this *refugio* puts you away from the hubbub below, and is the best place to stay if you want to see the sun rise on the Torres.

o **Refugio Los Cuernos.** This may be the park's loveliest *refugio,* located at the base of the Cuernos. The wood structure (which miraculously holds up to some of the strongest winds in the park) has two walls of windows that look out onto Lago Nordenskjöld.

o **Refugio Torres.** This *albergue* (lodge) is the largest and most full-service *refugio* in the park; it sits near the Hostería Las Torres. This is also the trail head for the W-circuit and the Full Circuit. You may dine in the hotel or eat simple fare in the *refugio* itself. Horseback rides can be taken from here.

All three of the following *refugios* can be reserved at ℂ **61/412742** or online at www.verticepatagonia.cl. Rates are $53 to $63.

o **Lodge Paine Grande.** This hostel-like "lodge" replaces the old *refugio* Pehoé, at the busiest intersection in the park. It is the hub for several of the trail heads to the park administration center, Glacier Grey, and French Valley, as well as the docking site for the catamaran. Utilitarian in style, the hostel has 60 beds, two lounges, and a cafeteria that can serve 120 people. Day walks to Glacier Grey and French Valley can be taken from here.

o **Refugio Dickson.** This is one of the park's loneliest *refugios,* due to its location well on the other side of the park (part of the Circuit trail). There are a lot of mosquitoes in the summer, but you can't beat the rugged location on a grassy glacial moraine, facing Dickson Glacier.

o **Refugio Grey.** Tucked in a forest on the shore of Lago Grey, this log-cabin *refugio* is a 10-minute walk to the lookout point for the glacier. It's a cold but refreshing setting, and it has a cozy fireside seating area. This is a good base for taking a walking tour on the glacier (see "Excursions around Glacier Grey," above).

Dome, Sweet Dome: Patagonia's ecoCamp

Somewhere between a lodge and a tent, the accommodations at **EcoCamp Patagonia** (✆ **800/901-6987** in the U.S., or 2/232-9878 in Chile; www. ecocamp.travel), across from Hotel Las Torres, are a series of permanent domes that offer refuge for budget-minded, eco-friendly travelers. You'll get a real bed under a real roof, but no electricity and shared outhouse-style toilets. The "Suite domes" have running water. Each dome sleeps two, and all have composting toilets. Meals are held in the "dining dome," and there's a cozy "living dome" for chilling out. All lodging is based on all-inclusive packages, starting at $1,055 per person for 4 days.

CAMPING

Torres del Paine has a well-designed campground system with free and concession-run sites. **Camping Pehoé** (www.campingpehoe.com) is a roadside campground with great facilities, including electricity, phones, gear rental, a small supermarket, firewood, fresh water, hot showers, and a restaurant. All *refugios* have a campground, too, and these and other concession sites charge C$4,000 to C$5,000 per person, which includes hot showers, clean bathrooms, and an indoor dining area to escape bad weather and eat under a roof. The site at Las Torres provides barbecues and firewood. Free campgrounds are run by CONAF, and they can get a little dingy, with deplorable outhouses. Mice are sometimes a problem for campers, so always leave food well stored or hanging from a tree branch. The JLM hiking map (available at every bookstore, airport, kiosk, and travel agency, and at the park entrance) denotes which campgrounds are free and which charge a fee.

EL CALAFATE, ARGENTINA

222km (138 miles) S of El Chaltén; 2,727km (1,691 miles) SW of Buenos Aires

On to Argentina

If you're planning on spending a lot of time touring around Argentine Patagonia, be sure to pick up a copy of *Frommer's Argentina.*

El Calafate was born a small center for nearby *estancias* but today is a tourist-oriented town hugging the shore of turquoise Lago Argentino, a location that, combined with the town's leafy streets, gives it the feel of an oasis in the desert pampa of this region. The town depends almost entirely on its neighboring natural wonder, Perito Moreno Glacier, for tourism.

Essentials

GETTING THERE

BY PLANE   From late October through March, El Calafate's **Aeropuerto Lago Argentino** (FTE; ✆ **2902/491220**) is a busy spot. Service is from Argentine destinations only: **Aerolíneas Argentinas/Austral** (✆ **0810/222-86527**; www.aerolineas. com.ar) has up to six daily flights from Buenos Aires, as well as a daily flight from Bariloche, Trelew, and Ushuaia. There are flights arriving directly from Ezeiza International Airport in Buenos Aires during the high season (before, most flights left from downtown Aeroparque); be sure to specify which airport you'd like to fly from. **LAN**

(© 0810/999-9526) flies from Buenos Aires daily, with two flights on Saturdays and Sundays. Four of the weekly flights continue on to Ushuaia.

Aerovías Dap, Av. del Libertador 1329 in El Calafate (© 61/223340; www. aeroviasdap.cl), has charter-only flights from Punta Arenas.

From the airport, **Ves Patagonia** (© 02902/494355) operates a bus to all the hotels in town for $8; they can also pick you up for your return trip if you call 24 hours ahead. A taxi into town should cost no more than $28 for up to four people.

BY BUS El Calafate has a bus terminal on Julio A. Roca, reached by taking the stairs up from the main street, Avenida del Libertador. To and from Puerto Natales, Chile: **Buses Sur** (© 02902/491631) and **Turismo Zaahj** (© 02902/491631; www.turismozaahj.co.cl) have a daily bus departing Puerto Natales at 8am and 2pm, returning also at 8am ($30 per leg); **Cootra** (© 02902/491444) also has daily buses departing Puerto Natales at 8:30am. The trip takes 5 to 6 hours, depending on how long you get held up at the border.

BY CAR In summer only, from just outside Parque Nacional Torres del Paine, you can cross through the border at Cerro Castillo, which will lead you to the famous Rte. Nacional 40 and up to the paved portion of Rte. 11. During the rest of the year, take the border crossing at Rio Turbio, which leads from Rte. 9 straight to Puerto Natales. The drive from Puerto Natales is roughly 4 to 5 hours, not including time spent at the border checkpoint.

VISITOR INFORMATION

The city's **visitor information kiosk** can be found inside the bus terminal. It offers an ample amount of printed material and staff can assist in planning a trip to Perito Moreno Glacier. It's open October through April daily from 8am to 11pm, and May through September daily from 8am to 8pm (© 02902/491090).

What to See & Do

El Calafate serves mostly as a service town for visitors on their way to visit the glaciers (see "Parque Nacional Los Glaciares," later in this section), but it does present a pleasant main avenue for a stroll, and as expected, there are lots of souvenirs, bookstores, and crafts shops to keep you occupied.

NEAR EL CALAFATE

For information about visiting the glaciers and the national park, see "Parque Nacional Los Glaciares," later in this section.

HORSEBACK RIDING **Cabalgata en Patagonia,** Av. Del Libertador 4315 (© 2902/493278; cabalgataenpatagonia.com), offers two horseback-riding options: a 2-hour ride to Bahía Redonda for a panoramic view of El Calafate ($70), and a fullday trip bordering Lago Argentino, with an optional stop at the Walicho Caves, where one can supposedly view Indian "paintings," which are billed as real but are really reproductions as the originals have been badly damaged. This tour costs $133 per person and includes lunch and transfer to the hotel. Book directly or with a travel agency.

VISITING AN ESTANCIA As the world's wool market declines, many of the *estancias* (ranches) in Patagonia have opened their doors to tourists, including some very close to El Calafate. Most offer lodging as well. Within walking distance of town, **Estancia 25 de Mayo** ★★ (© 2902/491059; www.estancia25demayo.com.ar) has a late afternoon program that includes a tour, a show, and a barbecue dinner. The

El Galpón del Glaciar (20km/12½ miles from El Calafate; ℂ **2902/491793**; www.elgalpondelglaciar.com.ar) has day tours. **Estancia Alta Vista ★★** (35km/22 miles from El Calafate; ℂ **2902/491247**; www.hosteriaaltavista.com.ar) is part of the Estancia Anita, which has more than 75,000 hectares in the surroundings of El Calafate and has long been the most influential *estancia* in the area. **Estancia Nibepo Aike** (56km/35 miles from El Calafate; ℂ **2902/422626**; www.nibepoaike. com.ar) is quite rustic but gets you on a still-working *estancia* dedicated to cattle and sheep raising.

Where to Stay & Dine

The Relais & Chateaux luxury lodge **Eolo ★★** (Rte. 11, Km 23, El Calafate; ℂ **02902/492042** or ℂ 11/4700-0075 for reservations in Buenos Aires; www.eolo. com.ar) has a sublimely beautiful setting and refined services. It's a good 20-minute drive from town. For the ultimate Patagonian experience, combining history, adventure, isolation, and comfortable lodging, spend a night or two at **Estancia Cristina ★★★** (Av. Del Libertador 1033, El Calafate; ℂ **02902/491133** for reservations or ℂ 2902/ 491133; www.estanciacristina.com). It's a 30-minute drive and then a 2-hour boat ride to get there. Closer to town on a historic *estancia* is **Kau Yatun** (Estancia 25 de Mayo, El Calafate; ℂ **02902/491059** or in Buenos Aires 11/4523-5894; www.kauyatun. com). On the outskirts of town overlooking the lake is **Hotel Edenia** (Punta Soberana, Manzana 642, El Calafate; ℂ **02902/497021**; www.edeniahoteles.com.ar). It's got a style similar to what you'd find in a standard business hotel, with very large rooms and modern bathrooms.

The best restaurant in town remains **Casimiro Biguá** (Av. del Libertador 963; ℂ **02902/492590**). The best grillhouse—and the competition is fierce—is at **Don Pichon** (Puerto Deseado s/n; ℂ **0202/492577**). For something lighter, try **Viva La Pepa** (Emilio Amado 833; ℂ **02902/491880**) or **Pura Vida** (Av. del Libertador 1876; ℂ **02902/493356**).

Parque Nacional Los Glaciares ★★★

The Parque Nacional Los Glaciares covers 600,000 hectares (1.5 million acres) of rugged land that stretches vertically along the crest of the Andes and spills east into flat pampa. Most of Los Glaciares is inaccessible to visitors except for the park's two dramatic highlights: the granite needles, such as Fitzroy near El Chaltén (covered in "El Chaltén & Mt. Fitzroy, Argentina," later), and this region's magnificent Perito Moreno Glacier. The park is also home to thundering rivers, blue lakes, and thick beech forest. Parque Nacional Los Glaciares was formed in 1937 and declared a World Heritage region by UNESCO in 1981.

Named after famed Argentine scientist Francisco "Perito" Moreno ("perito" is the title given to someone considered an expert in his or her field), the famous glacier Perito Moreno is a must-see, as important to Argentine culture and tourism as Iguazú Falls or the Casa Rosada. Few natural wonders in South America are as spectacular or as easily accessed as this glacier, and unlike the hundreds of glaciers that drain from the Southern Patagonian Ice Field, Perito Moreno is one of the few that are not receding. Scientists like to say it is "stable," and it generally cycles through growing toward the Península Magallanes, touching land, and forming a dam in Lago Argentino, then receding with a majestic "dam break." Perito Moreno is usually reliable for sending a few huge chunks hurling into the channel throughout the day, especially around sunset, when movements lead to plenty of snapping, cracking, and splashing ice.

What impresses visitors most is the sheer size of Perito Moreno Glacier, a wall of jagged blue ice measuring 4,500m (14,760 ft.) across and soaring 60m (197 ft.) above the channel. To give you some perspective of its length: You could fit the entire city of Buenos Aires on it. From the parking lot on the Península Magallanes, a series of boardwalks descend, which take visitors directly to the glacier's face. It's truly an unforgettable, spellbinding experience, particularly at dusk, when the sun colors the ice red and shadows turn it deep blue. There are opportunities to join an organized group for a walk on the glacier, as well as boat journeys that leave from Puerto Banderas for visits to the neighboring glaciers Upsala and Spegazzini. From El Chaltén, you can visit the nearby Viedma glacier.

ESSENTIALS

At Km 49 (30 miles) from El Calafate, you'll pass through the park's entrance, where there's an information booth with erratic hours (© **02902/491005**). The entrance fee is $19 per person. If you're looking for information about the park and the glacier, pick up an interpretive guide or book from one of the bookstores or tourist shops along Avenida del Libertador in El Calafate. There is a restaurant near the principal lookout platform near the glacier and a good, though expensive, restaurant inside the Los Notros hotel (see "Where to Stay Near the Glacier," later).

Getting There

BY CAR   Following Avenida del Libertador west out of town, the route turns into a mostly paved road. From here it's 80km (50 miles) to the glacier.

BY TAXI OR REMISE   If you want to see the glacier at your own pace, hire a taxi or *remise* (a radio taxi). The cost averages $70 for two, $75 for three, and $100 for four, although many taxi companies will negotiate a price. Be sure to agree on an estimated amount of time spent at the glacier, and remember that the park entrance fee is not included.

BY ORGANIZED TOUR   Several companies offer transportation to and from the glacier, such as **Infinito Sud,** Pasaje los Cerezos 74 (© **02902/493032;** www.infinitosud.com); **Caltur,** Av. del Libertador 1177 (© **02902/491368;** www.caltur.com.ar); and **Los Glaciares Turismo,** Av. Almirante Brown 1188 (©**02902/491159**). These minivan and bus services provide bilingual guides and leave around 9am and again at around 2:30pm, spending an average of 4 hours at the peninsula; the cost is C$16,625 to C$26,125 per person, not including lunch. For a more personalized tour—a private car with driver and a bilingual, licensed guide—contact **SurTurismo,** Av. Del Libertador 1226 (© **02902/491266;** suring@cotecal.com.ar); they can arrange for a half-day trip costing $78 to $130 for two people (prices vary with the seasons).

OUTDOOR ACTIVITIES

There are several exciting activities in this region. **"Minitrekking"** (although there is nothing "mini" about it) takes guests of all ages and abilities for a walk upon the glacier. The trip begins with a 20-minute boat ride across the Brazo Rico, followed by a 30-minute walk to the glacier. From here guests are outfitted with crampons and other safety gear, and then they spend approximately 1½ hours atop the ice, complete with a stop for a whiskey on the thousand-year-old "rocks." This great trip gives visitors the chance to peer into the electric-blue crevasses of the glacier and fully appreciate its size. More experienced, fit, and adventurous visitors can opt for the **Big Ice** ★★

option, which has a more technical approach and gives you much more time (upwards of 4 hr.) to walk on the glacier. Both Big Ice and Minitrekking are organized exclusively by **Hielo y Aventura,** which has its main office at Av. del Libertador 935 (© **02902/ 492205;** www.hieloyaventura.com). Big Ice costs $180, including the transfer from El Calafate. Minitrekking will run you $12 with a transfer. Remember, you have to bring your own lunch from town, pay the park entrance fee yourself, and don't forget sunscreen.

Fernandez Campbell, Av. Del Libertador 867 (© **02902/491155;** www.fernandez campbell.com), runs hour-long cruises along the Brazo Norte to the face of Perito Moreno for $12.50, departing hourly from 10:30am to 3:30pm from the Muelle Moreno port next to the glacier's visitor center. Their 7-hour **Todo Glaciares ★★** trip departs from Puerto Punta Bandera and visits the glaciers Spegazzini (the tallest glacier in the park), Upsala (the largest), and Onelli glaciers for $85 plus the park entrance fees.

WHERE TO STAY NEAR THE GLACIER

Los Notros ★★★ 📷 Few hotels in Argentina (or in the world) boast as spectacular a view as Los Notros—but it doesn't come cheap, and it's not quite up to the standards of explora on the Chilean side. This luxury lodge sits high on a slope looking out at Perito Moreno Glacier, with expansive views capitalized on from every window of the hotel. Rooms, especially those in the Cascada Wing out back, are small and lacking in sophistication. Upstairs premium rooms are more quiet and tasteful. Keep your stay to no more than 2 nights.

Main office in Buenos Aires: Santa Fe 1461, 3rd floor. © **11/5277-8200.** www.losnotros.com. 32 units. $1,029 per person for 2-night package Cascada wing; $1,401 per person for 2-night package in double superior; $1,642 per person for 2-night package in double premium. Rates include all meals, park entrance, excursions, and transfers. Room-only rates available by request only. AE, DC, MC, V. **Amenities:** Restaurant; bar; lounge w/TV; room service. *In room:* Minibar, Jacuzzi (in Premium rooms).

EL CHALTÉN & MT. FITZROY, ARGENTINA ★★

222km (138 miles) N of El Calafate

El Chaltén is a rugged village of about 800 residents whose lifeblood, like El Calafate's, depends entirely on the throng of visitors who come each summer. This is the second-most-visited region of Argentina's Parque Nacional Los Glaciares and quite possibly its most exquisite, for the singular nature of the granite spires that shoot up, torpedolike, above massive tongues of ice that descend from the Southern Patagonian Ice Field. In the world of mountaineering, these sheer and ice-encrusted peaks are considered some of the most formidable challenges on the planet, and they draw hundreds of climbers here every year. The valleys beneath them provide absolutely world-class trekking trails that any hiker can enjoy.

Just 10 years ago, El Chaltén counted just a dozen houses and a hostel or two, but the Fitzroy massif's rugged beauty and great hiking opportunities have created somewhat of a boomtown. The town sits nestled in a circular rock outcrop at the base of the Fitzroy and is fronted by the vast, dry steppe. Visitors use El Chaltén either as a base from which to take day hikes or as an overnight stop before setting off for a multiday backpacking trip.

Essentials

GETTING THERE

BY PLANE   All transportation to El Chaltén originates from El Calafate, which has daily plane service from Ushuaia and Buenos Aires. From El Calafate, you need to take a bus or rent a car; the trip takes from 2½ to 3 hours.

BY CAR   From El Calafate, take Rte. Nacional 11 west for 30km (19 miles) and turn left on Rte. Nacional 40 north. Turn again, heading northwest, on Rte. 23 to El Chaltén. The road is almost completely paved.

BY BUS   Buses from El Calafate leave from the bus terminal, and all cost about $50 round-trip. A giant new bus terminal has opened in El Chaltén at the entrance to town, but buses continue to use their normal drop-off/pickup locations listed here. **Chaltén Travel,** with offices in El Chaltén, at Avenida Güemes and Lago del Desierto (℃ **02962/493092;** www.chaltentravel.com), leaves El Calafate daily at 8am and 6:30pm year-round, and at 1pm during January and February only, and El Chaltén at 7:30am and 6pm daily year-round, and at 1pm in January and February only, departing from the Rancho Grande hostel, Av. San Martín 724. **Caltur,** which leaves from El Chaltén's Hostería Fitz Roy at Av. San Martín 520 (℃ **02962/493062;** www.caltur.com.ar), leaves El Calafate daily at 7:30am and 6:30pm, and leaves El Chaltén at 3pm.

VISITOR INFORMATION

El Chaltén has a decent visitor center at the town's entrance—the **Comisión de Fomento,** Perito Moreno and Avenida Güemes (℃ **02962/493011**), open daily from 8am to 8pm. Here you'll find maps, pamphlets, and brief interpretive displays about the region's flora and fauna. In El Calafate, the **APN Intendencia** (park service) has its offices at Av. del Libertador 1302, with a visitor center that is open daily from 9am to 3pm (℃ **02902/491005**).

Note: There is currently no ATM in El Chaltén and many places won't accept credit cards. Be sure to stop at a bank in El Calafate before making the trip here.

Outdoor Activities

TOUR OPERATORS   **Fitz Roy Expediciones ★★**, Av. San Martin 56 (℃/fax **02962/493017;** www.fitzroyexpediciones.com.ar), offers heaps of excursions, including a full-day excursion trekking through Valle de Río Fitzroy combined with ice climbing at Glacier Torre. No experience is necessary, but they do ask that you be in fit condition. **Mountaineering Patagonia,** Av. San Martin 16 (℃ **2962/493194;** www.mountaineeringpatagonia.com), also offers guided treks and mountaineering trips in the area. **Patagonia Aventura,** Av. San Martin 56 (℃ **2962/493110;** www.patagonia-aventura.com), currently runs the outstanding ice-treks on nearby Viedma Glacier.

HIKING & CAMPING   If you're planning on doing any hiking in the park, you'll want to pick up a copy of Zagier & Urruty's trekking map, *Monte Fitz Roy & Cerro Torre,* available at most bookstores and tourist shops in El Calafate and El Chaltén. You'll also need to register at the park service office at the entrance to El Chaltén. Day hiking is superb here; you won't find a well-defined overnight circuit as you will in Torres del Paine, but there is a loop of sorts, and all stretches of this 3- to 4-day loop can be done one leg at a time on day hikes. Trails run from easy to difficult and take anywhere from 4 to 10 hours to complete.

One of the most spectacular day hikes, which can also be done as an overnight, 2-day hike, is the 19km (12-mile) trail to the **Mirador Maestri** above Laguna Torre. It offers exhilarating views of the spire Cerro Torre needlelike granite peak. The hike takes 6 to 7½ hours to complete and is classified as challenging, although the first 3 hours could be considered easy. It's possible to camp nearby at the D'Agostini campground (formerly Bridwell). Another demanding, though beautiful, trail heads to several campsites and eventually the **Laguna de los Tres,** where there is a lookout point for views of Mount Fitzroy. If you're in decent shape, you can do the round-trip hike to Laguna de los Tres in a day. Campgrounds inside the park's boundaries are free but do not have services; paid campgrounds (outside the park) have water, and some have showers. I also recommend a trip to the lovely tree-lined Laguna del Desierto, the scene of several border skirmishes between Chile and Argentina; border crossings on foot to Villa O'Higgins and the Carretera Austral in Chile are possible beyond the lake (see chapter 12).

WHERE TO STAY & DINE

The premium place to stay is **Los Cerros del Chaltén** (El Chaltén s/n; ✆ **11/5277-8200** or 02962/493182; www.loscerrosdelchalten.com), which towers above town with an air of exclusivity. It has generous-sized rooms and excellent cuisine. Right in front of the bus station is the lovely mountain lodge **Senderos Hostería ★★** (Perito Moreno s/n, El Chaltén; ✆ **2962/493336;** www.senderoshosteria.com.ar). Trekkers will like the location of **Hostería El Pilar** (RP 23; ✆ **2962/493002;** www.hosteria elpilar.com.ar), 17km (10miles) from town at the trailhead to the Río Eléctrico. The explora hotel chain (www.explora.com) also has a new hotel in the works just north of El Chaltén.

El Chaltén has some excellent dining options, too. For good food and ambience try the climber's hangout **Patagonicus,** M.M de Güemes 140 (✆ **02966/493025**), which serves mostly pizza and enormous salads in a woodsy dining area; no credit cards are accepted. **Fuegia ★**, San Martín 342 (✆ **2962/493243**), has an eclectic, global menu including coconut chicken with cashews and good vegetarian options. In a ramshackle old house loaded with character, **Ruca Mahuida,** at Lionel Terray 55 (✆ **2962/493018**), has the feel of an old alpine hut. The food is pure Patagonian, with stews, trout, and hearty pastas to fill you up after a day on the trail. Diners gather around a handful of tables, making this a great spot to make new friends. Reservations are recommended. For a funky scene with cool music and creative food, head to **La Estepa,** at the corner of Cerro Solo and Antonio Rojo (✆ **2962/493069**). The lamb in soft mint sauce, pizzas, and pumpkin *sorrentinos* (raviolis) are superb.

CHILEAN TIERRA DEL FUEGO ★

"Where there's smoke, there's fire," thought Magellan in 1520 when he named Tierra del Fuego for the smoke rising from the native Selk'nams' campsites. And more fire came: Settlement in the 19th century meant death for the four native groups on the island, bordering on genocide despite the brave efforts of Anglican and Catholic missionaries to protect them.

The border between Chile and Argentina slices the main island in half, with far more people living on the Argentine side in Río Grande, Ushuaia, and little Tolhuin. The southern tip of the Americas peters out into a series of archipelagos besides the main island, ending at Cape Horn. There's plenty of hiking and fly-fishing available, along with winter sports near Ushuaia.

Foggy, windy, and wet, the Chilean side of Tierra del Fuego is a remote and lonely place. Long gravel roads connect tiny settlements and distant estancias, many of which are now turning to tourism (primarily as fly-fishing lodges) as they cling to a way of life that's fading. In between are thick forests and few people—there are only 7,000 people living on the entire Chilean side of the island, with 5,000 in Porvenir. For all of them, regular trips by plane or ferry to Punta Arenas are the only connection to civilization.

The Chilean government has been working away at the completion of a road connecting Porvenir with the Beagle Channel. At a rate of 5km (3 miles) per year, they're closing in on opening a new connection between Punta Arenas and Puerto Williams. Give it another 3 to 5 years, though.

Porvenir

316km (196 miles) SE of Punta Arenas; 3,406km (2,116 miles) S of Santiago

Porvenir is the largest town on Chilean Tierra del Fuego, at roughly 6,000 inhabitants. It's a collection of picturesque clapboard Victorian houses, including Tierra del Fuego's first cinema, which opened in 1900. Settled by Croatian pioneers during a gold rush in the 1880s, the colorful houses nestled amidst the harsh climate give Porvenir a timeless appeal.

GETTING THERE

BY PLANE   Aerovías DAP, O'Higgins 891 (© **61/223340** in Punta Arenas; www. aeroviasdap.cl), flies three times a day (weather permitting) Monday through Friday and twice on Saturdays, for C$23,750 one way. Flights last 15 minutes and book up fast, so be sure to reserve.

BY BOAT   The **Transbordadora Austral Brown** ferry (Bulnes 5075 in Punta Arenas, © **061/218100** in Punta Arenas and 061/580-089 in Porvenir; www.tabsa.cl) departs daily from a small port called Tres Puentes, 5km (3 miles) north of Punta Arenas, at 9:30am, returning at 5pm, making it possible to come to Porvenir as a day trip. The ferry takes around 140 minutes (which can seem excruciatingly long if the weather's bad) and costs C$5,100 for passengers and C$32,300 for vehicles.

WHAT TO SEE & DO   Half a day is plenty to stroll to the old wharf, watch for gulls and cormorants, then head up Avenida Señoret past Victorian heritage homes and buildings to the main square. You can visit the **Casa de Miguel Radonich,** the home of a pioneering filmmaker who operated a cinema here up until 1945 (on the corner of Av. Señoret and Calle Silva, no phone). A small museum, the **Museo Fernando Cordero Rusque,** Valdivieso 402 (© **61/581800**), has archaeological displays and photographs of the island's natives, and details the history of the region's gold rush and *estancias*. The main plaza, formerly Parque Yugoslavia, now Parque Croata, is dominated by the stark, stone-walled **Iglesia San Francisco de Sales,** at Chiloé s/n (© **61/580106**). It's the village's original church and a large restoration project, started in 2009, is still underway here. There's a tourism information center at the corner of Zavattaro and Jorge Schythe.

WHERE TO STAY & DINE   There are seven rooms with private baths at **Hostería Yendegaia** (Croacia 702; © **61/581665**), which is inside a sunny yellow heritage home on the plaza. The best food in town is at the **Club Croata** (Señoret 542; © **61/580053**), which also serves as the town's meeting place. The food is

---

Fishing Lodges in Tierra del Fuego

As on the Argentine side of the island, times are tough for the traditional *estancias* of Chilean Tierra del Fuego. What's bad for the sheep business is good for the fly-fisher, as more and more exclusive fishing lodges are opening up. Some of the best are **Tierra del Fuego Lodge** (© 02/196-0624; www.tierradelfuegolodge.cl), **Hostería Las Lengas** (© 02/196-4842; www.hosteria laslengas.com) and the **Estancia Cameron Lodge** (© 61/215029; www.estanciacameronlodge.com); the latter sits amidst a 100,000 hectare ranch.

13

simple and the portions are generous. Their specialty is a *triologia austral*—shellfish, oysters, and king crab crepes.

ISLA NAVARINO: PUERTO WILLIAMS

287km (178 miles) SE of Punta Arenas; 3,240km (2,013 miles) S of Santiago

Puerto Williams is the southernmost town in the world, though it functions primarily as a naval base with a population of less than 2,500 residents. The town occupies the northern shore of Isla Navarino in the Beagle Channel, an altogether enchanting location framed by towering granite needles called the "Teeth of Navarino." These peaks are being called the "next Torres del Paine." It's much more wild, remote, and "undiscovered" here than it is across the channel in Argentina's Ushuaia, and Puerto Williams has little tourism infrastructure. It's hard to get here, but it can be even harder to leave. Storms and wind often cancel any boat or air service.

Apart from a few hiking trails and a museum, there's not a lot to do here, but adventurers setting out for or returning from sailing and kayaking trips around Cape Horn use the town as a base. And really, there is a certain cachet to setting foot in this isolated village and knowing you're at the end of the world. The best way to visit Puerto Williams is via ship, ranging from a zodiac that whizzes across the Beagle Channel (in good weather only) to regular service cargo ships. The culture of the Yamana Indians, who so perplexed the first Europeans with their ability to withstand the harsh environment with little clothing, is long gone, but visitors may still view the last vestiges of their settlements and a well-designed anthropological museum in town. Plans are in the works to expand the airport, start a ferry service from Ushuaia, and to finally bring Wi-Fi and cellphone reception to the town. A new regular ferry service from Ushuaia (see below) is certainly accelerating development.

Getting There

BY PLANE **Aerovías DAP,** O'Higgins 891 (© **61/223340** in Punta Arenas, 61/621051 in Puerto Williams; www.aeroviasdap.cl), runs a handful of flights each week from Punta Arenas. Contact DAP for information about occasional flights from Ushuaia to Puerto Williams. DAP also has charter flights, and overland flights to Cape Horn from Punta Arenas.

BY BOAT There are possibilities to get here crossing the Beagle Channel from Ushuaia. **Ushuaia Boating,** Gob. Godoy 190, Ushuaia (© **2901/436193;** www.ushuaiaboating.com.ar), runs a small, speedy zodiac service to and from Puerto

Williams, whenever they have enough people to fill the boat (a minimum of three is needed)—and whenever weather permits, for $130 one-way and $240 round-trip. The passenger and cargo ferry **Transbordadora Austral Broom** offers cheaper passage to Puerto Williams with a 34-hour journey from Punta Arenas (Av. Bulnes 05075; ✆ **61/218100;** www.tabsa.cl). During the summer, the ferry leaves Punta Arenas four times a month on Wednesday and returns on Saturday; sleeping arrangements consist of reclining seats ($175 adult one-way) and bunks ($210 adult one-way). Kids receive a 50% discount.

Victory Adventure Expeditions, based out of Puerto Williams at Teniente Munoz 118, no. 70 (✆ **61/621010;** www.victory-cruises.com), specializes in sailing journeys around the Beagle Channel and Cape Horn, and as far away as Antarctica. The schooner-style ships are not luxurious, but they are warm and comfortable, and their small size allows for a more intimate, hands-on journey than the *Australis* cruises. A 7-day trip starts at $3,100 per person. **Sea & Ice & Mountains,** in Puerto Williams (in the Coiron Guesthouse; ✆ **61/621150;** www.simltd.com), is a German-run agency with a 6-passenger and 12-passenger yacht that takes visitors on 5- to 12-day journeys around Cape Horn and past the Darwin mountain range; contact the agency for prices. For general travel agency needs, including city tours, airline tickets, and hotel reservations, contact **Turismo Akainij,** Uspashum 156 (✆ **61/21327;** www.turismoakainij.cl).

What to See & Do

The **Museo Martín Gusinde,** Aragay 01 (✆ **61/621043**), features a good collection of Yaghan and Yamana Indian artifacts, ethnographic exhibits, and stuffed birds and animals. The museum's docent is an anthropologist, naturalist, and all-around expert in the region; he is usually on hand to provide tours in the area. The museum is open Monday through Thursday and Saturday from 10am to 1pm and 3 to 6pm.

About 3km (1¾ miles) southeast of Puerto Williams on the main road, at the La Virgen cascade, is a medium-level **hiking trail** with an exhilarating, sweeping panorama of the Beagle Channel, the Dientes de Navarino mountain range, and Puerto Williams. The hike takes 3 hours round-trip. One of Chile's best backpacking trails, the **Dientes de Navarino Circuit ★★**, is also here, thanks to an Australian who blazed the trail in 1991. The circuit is 53km (33 miles) in length and takes 4 days minimum to walk, with a difficulty level of medium to high, and the mountains are very remote. The trail is open only from late November to April; otherwise, snow makes this walk dangerous and disorienting. The best map to refer to is JLM's *Tierra del Fuego* map, sold in most local shops and bookstores.

The last descendents of the Yamana Indians live at Villa Ukika to the west of town. Attempts are underway to rescue what can be salvaged of their culture, including their language. They sell crafts in the **Centro de Artesanía Yamana Kipa-Akar.** A little farther west are the **Omora botanical gardens** (no phone; www.cabodehornos.org), a project to study and protect the world's southernmost forests.

Where to Stay & Dine

Dining and accommodations pickings here are slim but reasonably priced; you won't find luxury hotels in Puerto Williams except for the 24-room **Hotel Lakutaia** at Seno Lauta s/n (✆ **61/621733;** www.lakutaia.cl), with all-inclusive multiday programs starting at $1,970 for 5 days/4 nights. Basic, clean accommodations can be found at the **Hostería Camblor,** Calle Patricio Capdeville (✆ **61/621033;**

hosteriacamblor@hotmail.com), which has six rooms for $38 to $58 per person; some rooms come with a kitchenette. The Camblor also has a restaurant that occasionally serves as the local disco on Friday and Saturday nights, so noise could be a problem.

For dining, try the convivial **Club de Yates Micalvi** (✆ 61/621042), housed in an old supply ship that is docked at the pier, which serves as the meeting spot for an international crowd of adventurers sailing around Cape Horn. Or try the Hostería Camblor's restaurant (see earlier); **Los Dientes de Navarino** (✆ 61/621074), on the plaza; or **Restaurant Cabo de Hornos,** Ricardo Maragaño 146 (on the second floor; ✆ 61/621067), for Chilean specialties.

ARGENTINE TIERRA DEL FUEGO: USHUAIA

Encircled by a range of rugged peaks and fronted by the Beagle Channel, Ushuaia is the southernmost city in the world (although the naval base and small town of Puerto Williams is farther south across the channel—so as Puerto Williams expands, Ushuaia may lose that status). The view across the channel to Chile's Navarino Island is spellbinding; the mountains on that side are reminiscent of Torres del Paine. To the west of Ushuaia, the Darwin Range offers more gorgeous mountains.

Founded in the late 1800s, Ushuaia was a penal colony until 1947. The region grew as a result of immigration from Britain, Croatia, Italy, and Spain, and migration from the Argentine mainland, with government incentives such as tax-free duty on many goods being part of the draw. Today the city has about 70,000 residents. Ushuaia is a great destination with plenty of activities, and many use the city as a jumping-off point for trips to Antarctica or sailing trips around Cape Horn.

Essentials

GETTING THERE

BY PLANE   The **International Airport Malvinas Argentinas** is 5km (3 miles) from the city (USH; ✆ 02901/431232). There is no bus service to town, but cab fares are only about $7. Always ask for a quote before accepting a ride. **Aerolíneas Argentinas** (✆ 0800/222-86527 or 2901/437265; www.aerolineas.com.ar) operates four or five daily flights to Buenos Aires, one of which leaves from Ezeiza and stops in El Calafate. The average round-trip fare is $65. Frequency increases from November to March, when there's also a daily flight from Río Gallegos and twiceweekly flights from Trelew. **LAN** (✆ 0810/999-9526 or 2901/424244) flies from Buenos Aires daily via El Calafate. **Aerovías DAP,** Deloqui 575 (✆ 2901/431110; www.aeroviasdap.cl), runs charter flights from Punta Arenas and over Cape Horn. It costs around $3,000 for a group of seven people (round-trip), leaving whenever you want.

BY BUS   There is no bus station in the city. Buses usually stop at the port (Maipú and Fadul). The service from Punta Arenas, Chile, costs $33 to $45 and takes about 12 hours. **Tecni Austral** (✆ 2901/431408 in Ushuaia, or 61/613423 in Punta Arenas) leaves Punta Arenas, via Rio Grande and Rio Gallegos, on Tuesday, Thursday, and Saturday at 8:30am; tickets are sold in Ushuaia, from the Tolkar office at Roca 157, and in Punta Arenas, at Lautaro Navarro 975. **Pacheco,** San Martín 1267 (✆ 2901/437727;

www.busespacheco.com), has trips to Punta Arenas via Río Grande, leaving on Tuesday, Thursday, and Sunday at 9am; the trip costs $56.

GETTING AROUND

BY CAR   Everything in and around Ushuaia is easily accessible via bus or taxi or by using an inexpensive shuttle or tour service, so renting a car is not necessary. However, with more and more of the top hotels being built on the far outskirts of town, having a car will help you explore these more rural areas. **Hertz,** San Martín 245 (☎ **2901/437529;** www.hertz.com), has an office in town right next to the Cruceros Australis office and another at the airport.

VISITOR INFORMATION

The **Subsecretaría de Turismo** has a helpful, well-stocked office at San Martín 674 (☎ **02901/432001;** fax 02901/434550; www.e-ushuaia.com). They also have a counter at the airport that is open to assist passengers on all arriving flights and a booth at the main pier. The offices are open Monday through Friday from 8am to 10pm, Saturdays and Sundays from 9am to 8pm. The national park administration office can be found at San Martín 1395 (☎ **02901/421315;** Mon–Fri 9am–3pm).

What to See & Do

IN & AROUND USHUAIA

Museo del Fin de Mundo ★   The main room of this museum has an assortment of Indian hunting tools and colonial maritime instruments. There's also a natural history display of stuffed birds and a "grandfather's room" set up to resemble an old general store, packed with antique products. But the strength of this museum is its 60 history and nature videos available for viewing and its reference library with more than 3,650 volumes, including a fascinating birth record. Its store has an excellent range of books about Patagonia for sale.

Maipú 173. ☎ **02901/421863.** www.museodelfindelmundo.org.ar. Admission $8 adults, $2 students, free for children 13 and under. Daily Oct–April 9am–8pm; May–Sept Mon–Sat noon–7pm. Guided tours daily at 10:30am, 2 and 5pm.

Museo Marítimo y Presidio de Ushuaia ★★ 📷   Ushuaia was founded primarily thanks to the penal colony set up here in the late 1800s for hundreds of Argentina's most dangerous criminals. The rehabilitation system consisted of forced labor to build piers and buildings, and creative workshops for teaching carpentry, music, tailoring, and other trades—all of which, coincidentally, fueled the local economy. The museum offers a fascinating look into prisoners' and prison workers' lives through interpretive displays and artifacts. A newly renovated wing houses modern art exhibits next to former jail cell doors; the art mainly focuses on marine themes. The restaurant features "prison" meals and other themed items. It all adds up to a really outstanding museum experience.

Yaganes and Gobernador Paz. ☎ **02901/437481.** www.museomaritimo.com. Admission $13 adults, free for children 11 and under. Daily 9am–8pm. Guided tours at 11:30am and 6pm.

OUTDOOR ACTIVITIES

BOATING   The best way to explore the Beagle Channel is by boat. Numerous companies offer a variety of trips, usually in modern catamarans with excellent guides. Many of them run kiosks near the pier; you'll see a cluster of them by the water. The most popular excursion is a half-day cruise of the Beagle Channel to view sea lions, penguins, and more. **Catamaranes Canoero** (☎ **2901/433893;**

EXCURSIONS NEAR ushuaia

One of the most intriguing destinations around Ushuaia is the **Estancia Harberton** (www.estanciaharberton.com), the first ranch founded in Tierra del Fuego. It is now run as a museum. The ranch is located on the shore of the Beagle Channel and can be reached by road or boat. The entrance fee is $9 for adults, free for children 13 and under. It's open daily from 10am to 7pm. Transportation to the *estancia,* 90km (56 miles) from Ushuaia, is provided by most travel agencies in town, for an average cost of $65 per person plus the entrance fee, provided you are in a group of four or more. Roughly from October to April, several tour companies offer a catamaran ride to the *estancia,* a 6-hour excursion for $85 per person; try **All Patagonia,** Juana Fadul 60 ((C) **02901/ 433622**). Tour groups will also arrange a boat excursion to a **penguin colony** from the *estancia,* an add-on excursion that costs about $67 per person.

www.catamaranescanoero.com.ar) has a variety of options ranging from 3 hours to 9 hours, on four different boats. **Motonave Barracuda** ((C) **2901/437066**) leaves every afternoon for its 3-hour trip around the channel for $35 per person, stopping at Isla de Lobos, Isla de Pájaros, and a lighthouse.

From November through February, most companies visit the teeming penguin colony and pull the boats up to the shore where travelers can close in tight to watch these marvelous animals. It costs roughly $75 per person. **Piratour,** B. Yaganes Casa 127 ((C) **2901/435557;** www.piratour.com.ar), offers walking tours onto the colony with controlled groups. **Motovelero Patagonia Explorer** ((C) **2901/1546-5842**) has an 18-passenger maximum and leaves daily; it visits the sea lion colony and includes a walk on the Isla Bridges for $46. This company also works with the Aventuras Isla Verde in the park for a full-day sail; inquire at their kiosk.

FISHING For a fishing license and information, go to the **Club de Pesca y Caza,** Av. Maipú 822 (no phone). The cost is about $15 for foreigners per day. Tierra del Fuego's northern area, around the Río Grande, has some of the absolute finest fly-fishing in the entire world, and is known mainly for its monster sea brown trout. For information on high-end, all-inclusive fishing packages at some of the area's outstanding lodges, contact **The Fly Shop, Inc.,** 4140 Churn Creek Rd., Redding, CA 96002 ((C) **800/669-3474** or 530/222-3555; www.theflyshop.com), or **Nervous Waters,** Figueroa Alcorta 3351, Buenos Aires, Argentina ((C) **877/637-8420** in the U.S. or 54-11/4801-1008; www.nervouswaters.com).

PARQUE NACIONAL TIERRA DEL FUEGO

Parque Nacional Tierra del Fuego was created in 1960 to protect a 63,000-hectare (155,610-acre) chunk of Patagonian wilderness that includes mighty peaks, crystalline rivers, black-water swamps, forests of lenga, and deciduous beech along the border with Chile, where private parks are being developed.

Views of the Beagle Channel and the Darwin Range on both sides of the border are the park's main attractions, and it offers easy and medium day hikes to get out and stretch your legs, breathe some fresh air, take a boat ride, or bird-watch. The park service issues maps at the park entrance showing the walking trails here, ranging from 300m (984 ft.) to 8km (5 miles); admission into the park is $9. Parque Nacional Tierra del Fuego is 11km (6¾ miles) west of Ushuaia on Rte. Nacional 3. Camping

JOURNEYING TO antarctica

It may be the coldest spot on the planet, but it's a hot destination for travelers seeking the next great adventure. Antarctica is its own continent, but the hook of the Antarctic Peninsula is closest to the tip of South America, and, therefore, the majority of people depart for Antarctica from Ushuaia.

Its remoteness alone is enough to compel many people to travel here. Like the early explorers who first visited this faraway continent in the 1800s, travelers today revel in the chance to venture to a pristine region where relatively few humans have stepped foot before. But this comes at a price: No matter how you get here, it's expensive, and the traveling time is tediously long (unless you take a brief and expensive plane trip). Almost all travelers come via ship, rented by various tour operators. Trips range from 8 to 21 days, mainly departing from Ushuaia, and making stops at the Antarctic Peninsula, the South Shetland Islands, and the Weddell Sea.

Prices range from $4,500 to $15,000, so do your research.

Top tour operators include **Abercrombie & Kent** (© **800/544-7016** or 630/954-2944; www.abercrombiekent.com); **Lindblad Expeditions** (© **800/397-3348** or 212/765-7740; www.expeditions.com); and **Quark Expeditions** (© **800/892-0334** or 203/803-2888; www.quarkexpeditions.com). See the "Active Vacation Planner" chapter for more options.

For a quick trip, your only option is a fly-over. Flights either access man-made airstrips on certain islands close to the Antarctic Peninsula, or land on natural snow and ice runways. The logistics for flights are complicated and can be delayed by days or even weeks due to weather conditions. The two main companies running flights are **Adventure Network International** (© **801/266-4876;** www.adventure-network.com) and **Aerovías DAP** (© **61/223340;** www.aeroviasdap.cl).

in the park is free; there are no services, but potable water is available. At the end of the road to Lago Roca, there is a snack bar/restaurant. At Bahía Ensenada, you'll find boats that take visitors to Isla Redonda, where there are several walking trails. The cost is about $10 or $16 with a guide. All tour companies offer guided trips to the park, but if you just need transportation there, call shuttle bus company **Pasarela** (© **02901/433712**).

Where to Stay & Dine

Accommodations are not cheap in Ushuaia, and quality is often not on par with price. The best full-service hotel in town is **Los Cauquenes Resort** (Calle Reinamora 3462, Ushuaia; © **2901/41300;** www.loscauquenes.com), located right on the Beagle Channel outside town. For a smaller inn, try **Tierra de Leyendas** (Calle Tierra de Vientos 2448, Ushuaia; © **2901/443565;** www.tierradeleyendas.com.ar). The best restaurant in town remains **Chez Manu** (Av. Fernando Luis Martial 2135; © **02970/432253**), run by a French chef who specializes in using seasonal and local ingredients. It's high above town with a breathtaking view—you'll need to take a taxi to get here. For a lighter meal or a coffee and to soak up some historical ambience, don't miss the **Almacén de Ramos Generales** (Maipú 749; © **02901/424317;** www.ramosgeneralesushuaia.com), across from the port.

EASTER ISLAND

E aster Island is the most isolated inhabited island in the world. Called "Rapa Nui" by the local population and "Isla de Pascua" by Chileans, the island's name comes from its discovery by Dutch explorers on Easter Sunday in 1722. At 3,540km (2,200 miles) west of continental Chile, and 2,075km (1,290 miles) east of the closest body of land, Pitcairn Island, it is difficult to fathom the remoteness of this island, which is no larger than the District of Columbia. A visit to this ethereal land will exceed every expectation you've held—and then some. The island is a veritable living museum that will fascinate and enrapture you, and make you wish you'd planned a few more days to soak up the indelible magic that makes this one of Chile's most special destinations.

Of course, the island's famous moai sculptures that stand like mute sentinels are the first thing that you'll think of when you picture Easter Island, but really there is so much more here: 20,000 archaeological sites, a rich culture of truly beautiful people, dramatic views of volcanic craters, scuba diving in crystalline waters, white-sand beaches, and that unmistakable hang-loose island vibe that makes you want to throw your agenda away after day one.

The Rapa Nui are Polynesian descendents who, according to the most recent studies, arrived at the island some time around the 8th century. Legend has it that it was King Hotu Matu'a who first arrived here on a double-hulled canoe with his extended family; researchers believe they most likely came from the Marquesas, Cook, or Pitcairn islands. The population flourished and created a society characterized by a written language and megalithic art, including moai and petroglyphs. But it all went horribly wrong when the Rapa Nui deforested the island and its population exploded, bringing about war and starvation. The first Europeans here found a culture in decline. Many were carted off to work on the guano islands in Peru in the 19th century or died in epidemics. Catholic missionaries came next and destroyed much of their cultural art, including their *rongorongo* written tablets; and experts have been unable to decipher the few that remain. Nevertheless, the Rapa Nui are experiencing a cultural renaissance, and they take great pride in their culture and native language, which they habitually speak among themselves, in addition to Spanish.

The climate here is marine subtropical, with temperatures between lows of 60°F (16°C) and highs of 74°F (22°C) during the winter (June–Aug), and an average of 82°F (28°C) during the rest of the year. The island has a persistent breeze that can make it feel cooler, especially if it's raining, so bring a sweater or light jacket. Downpours can occur at any time, but generally May is considered the wettest month. High season is December through March. It is recommended that you spend at least 4 days here given the travel distance and the wealth of things to see and do.

ESSENTIALS

Getting There

Easter Island's **Mataveri International Airport** in Hanga Roa, about 2km (1.5 miles) from the center, is served by **LAN Airlines** only (IPC; © **866/435-9526** in the U.S., or 600/526-2000 in Chile; www.lan.com), with daily flights to/from Santiago (except Mon and Thurs) and two flights on Wednesday and Sunday. This flight carries on to Papeete, Tahiti, twice a week on Wednesday and Sunday. LAN also recently added two flights per week between Lima, Peru and Easter Island, on Wednesdays and Sundays, which shave off about 3 hours of flying time for North American travelers. On arrival, most hotels pick you up at the airport and greet you with a garland of flowers.

Visitor Information

The **Sernatur** office is at Avenida Policarpo Toro at Tu'u Maheke (© **32/210-0255**); it's open weekdays from 8:30am to 1:30pm and 2:30 to 5:30pm. They also have an information desk at the airport that is open daily when flights arrive. You'll find information galore here, plus maps.

SPECIAL EVENTS   Tapatai, held since 1975 for 2 weeks in late January and early February, is the largest cultural gathering and celebration of Rapa Nui culture. Craft expositions, horse races, fishing and swimming competitions, and dance and theater performances make up this festival. A few of the more unusual and interesting events are the Tau'a, a totora reed raft race held inside the Rano Raraku volcano, and the Haka Pei, where contestants slide down a mountain on a banana tree trunk and try to stay on the longest. The festival culminates in the crowning of a queen.

Orientation

Easter Island measures just 168 sq. km (65 sq. miles), and there is only one village, **Hanga Roa.** The island is roughly triangular in shape, with each point dominated by an extinct volcano: Maunga Terevaka at the northern point, Maunga Pu A Katiki on the eastern edge at the Poike Peninsula, and Rano Kau, a vast crater on the southern edge next to Hanga Roa. The island is principally composed of a wide, grassy expanse and about 70 smaller volcanic craters and cones, as well as lava beds peppered with so many volcanic chunks of rock that it is said that certain areas "bloom" stones. Most of the island's roads are paved, with the exception of the western coast and the road to Ahu Akivi. Given the island's relative lack of significant coral reef, the pounding ocean has created towering, sheer sea cliffs in some areas. The island's two beaches, Anakena and Ovahe, are located on the northeast coast.

Getting Around

BY FOOT   Hanga Roa is small enough to be seen on foot. Throughout the island, there are walking trails (not very well marked, however) that can be found principally in flatter areas, providing easy to moderate treks. Some tour guides, including those used at explora (p. 424), traverse between archaeological sites on the west coast or

Easter Island & Hanga Roa

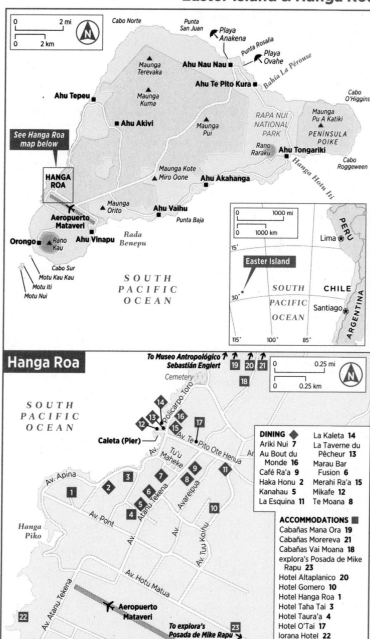

Easter Island & Hanga Roa map

0 — 2 mi
0 — 2 km

Cabo Norte
Punta San Juan
Playa Anakena
Punta Rosalia
Playa Ovahe
Bahía La Pérouse
Maunga Terevaka
Ahu Nau Nau ■
Ahu Te Pito Kura ■
Cabo O'Higgins
Ahu Tepeu ■
Maunga Kuma
Maunga Pu A Katiki
RAPA NUI NATIONAL PARK
Ahu Akivi ■
Maunga Pui ▲
PENÍNSULA POIKE
See Hanga Roa map below
Rano Raraku
Ahu Tongariki ■
Cabo Roggeween
HANGA ROA
Maunga Kote ▲ Miro Oone
Ahu Akahanga ■
Hanga Hotu Iti
Aeropuerto Mataveri
Maunga Orito ▲
Ahu Vaihu ■
Punta Baja
Orongo ■
Rano Kau
Ahu Vinapu ■
Rada Benepu
Cabo Sur
Motu Kau Kau
Motu Iti
Motu Nui
SOUTH PACIFIC OCEAN

0 — 1000 mi
0 — 1000 km

PERU
Lima ✪
15°
Easter Island
SOUTH PACIFIC OCEAN
30°
CHILE
Santiago ✪
ARGENTINA
115° 100° 85°

Hanga Roa

To Museo Antropológico Sebastián Englert
Cemetery
SOUTH PACIFIC OCEAN
0 — 0.25 mi
0 — 0.25 km
Caleta (Pier)
Policarpo Toro
Av. Te Pito Ote Henua
Av. Tu'u Maheke
Av. Apina
Av. Pont
Av. Atanu Tekena
Avareipua
Av. Tuu Koihu
Av. Hotu Matua
Av. Atanu Tekena
Hanga Piko
✈ Aeropuerto Mataveri
To explora's Posada de Mike Rapu ↘

DINING ◆
Ariki Nui **7**
Au Bout du Monde **16**
Café Ra'a **9**
Haka Honu **2**
Kanahau **5**
La Esquina **11**
La Kaleta **14**
La Taverne du Pêcheur **13**
Marau Bar Fusion **6**
Merahi Ra'a **15**
Mikafe **12**
Te Moana **8**

ACCOMMODATIONS ■
Cabañas Mana Ora **19**
Cabañas Morereva **21**
Cabañas Vai Moana **18**
explora's Posada de Mike Rapu **23**
Hotel Altaplanico **20**
Hotel Gomero **10**
Hotel Hanga Roa **1**
Hotel Taha Tai **3**
Hotel Taura'a **4**
Hotel O'Tai **17**
Iorana Hotel **22**

the Rano Kau volcano. None of the hikes are that intense, and if you have the time there is not a more beautiful way to see the island.

BY CAR OR SCOOTER Renting a vehicle is a great way to get out and explore the island at your own pace and prices tend to be less than you'll pay to explore the island by tour group (though cars don't come with a guide). Rental agencies ask that you keep your speed down to 30kmph (19 mph) outside of Hanga Roa, which is a smart idea considering that animals are often found on or near the island's roads. Also, rental agencies do not offer insurance.

The following car rental agencies can deliver a vehicle to the airport for your arrival or hotel, or you can pick up a rental in town: **Rent a Car Insular** (✆ **32/210-0480;** www.rentainsular.com) and **Oceanic Rent a Car** (✆ **32/210-0985;** www.oceanic rapanui.cl), which also rents scooters, motorcycles, and ATVs. Book a reservation in advance or race to rent a vehicle upon arrival, as they do sell out.

BY TAXI Taxis charge about C$2,000 for destinations within Hanga Roa. Call **Radiotaxi Avareipua** (✆ **32/210-0700** or 32/221-0398).

[Fast FACTS] EASTER ISLAND

Banks A Banco Santander was constructed near the harbor in mid-2009 and has a 24-hour Visa/Plus ATM, as well as another ATM at the airport. This is the island's best bank. There is also a 24-hour ATM at Banco Estado across the street from Sernatur on Tu'u Maheke (✆ **32/276-5500**). However, the machine only accepts Cirrus network cards (like MasterCard); Visa/Plus cardholders need to have a bank representative run their card through the bank system in order to receive cash, which can also be done at Honu Vaikava on Atamu Tekena (✆ **32/255-1950**). Bank hours are Monday through Friday from 8am to 1pm.

Emergencies For a **police** emergency, call ✆ **133**. For **fire,** call ✆ **132**. To call an **ambulance,** dial ✆ **131.**

Hospital The **Hospital Hanga Roa** (✆ **32/210-0183**) has basic medical services, but more serious cases need to be treated back on the mainland.

Internet Access Most hotels have an Internet station and even Wi-Fi. Or try **Omotohi Cibercafé** at Te Pito o Te Henua, open daily from 8:30am to 10pm. **Rapu Call** (✆ **32/255-1600**) has a call center and Internet services.

Laundry Most hotels will do your washing for you at a fairly reasonable price. Or try **Lavandería Tea Nui,** at Avenida Atamu Tekena s/n, Monday through Saturday from 10am to 1:30pm and 4 to 8pm.

Pharmacies **Farmacia Cruz Verde** (✆ **32/255-1540**) is at Atamu Tekena s/n and open Monday through Saturday from 9am to 1pm and 4:30 to 8pm.

Post Office The post office is on Avenida Te Pito o Te Henua s/n (across from the Hotel O'tai) and is open weekdays from 9am to 1pm and 2:30 to 6pm.

Telephone The country code for Chile is 56, and the city code for Hanga Roa is 32. Note that all phone numbers are now prefixed with a 2 for a seven-digit phone number, but many published numbers still do not reflect this (for example, 32/005555 is now 32/200-5555).

HANGA ROA

Hanga Roa is the only town on Easter Island, and virtually all of the island's 3,800 residents live here. In spite of LAN Airlines bringing in more tourists by increasing its Santiago flights and adding direct flights to Lima, Hanga Roa still holds on to its quintessentially laid-back ambience. Many of the town's roads outside of the main commercial area are unpaved, and laws prohibiting ownership by non-islanders means the town has grown organically and has thus far avoided encroachment by high-rise resorts and chain stores. It's not a terribly sophisticated place, but then that is part of its appeal. Nearly all of Hanga Roa's residents earn a living from tourism, and the "downtown" area is replete with simple hotels and guesthouses, shops, tour companies, and restaurants. You don't need a car to see Hanga Roa, just your feet, and part of the enjoyment of visiting is simply strolling around and taking in the town's mellow charm.

While here, you'll want to visit the **Museo Antropológico P. Sebastián Englert** in the Tahai Sector (© **32/255-1020;** www.museorapanui.cl; Tues–Fri 9:30am–12:30pm and 2–5:30pm, Sat–Sun 9:30am–12:30pm; admission C\$1,000), and the **Biblioteca William Mulloy** (Tues–Sat 9:30am–12:30pm). The museum focuses more on ethnology than archaeology, but there is a tiny display of artifact replicas. The museum's bookstore and the excellent Mulloy library are stocked with diverse literature and photo books about Easter Island. They occasionally hold free lectures in both English and Spanish on recent archaeological research and theories. Also worth visiting, especially during Mass on Sundays (in both Rapu Nui and Spanish) is the **Iglesia Hanga Roa,** located at Te Pito o Te Henua and Tu'u Koihu streets. Inside are intricate wood carvings that illustrate the adaptation of Rapa Nui culture to Catholicism, while outside to the right are the tombs dating back to the mid-1800s of several important Catholic priests who lived on the island.

The best displays of moai lie scattered around the island, but there are two broken moai at **Ahu Tautira** overlooking the Caleta Hanga Roa harbor, where there are several of the best cafes and restaurants and both dive shops. If you look around under the dive boats, you can usually spot a green sea turtle floundering about.

For a better archaeological excursion near town, visit one of the island's best reconstructions of an ahu (ceremonial altar) at **Ahu Tahai,** past the island's colorful cemetery and near the museum. There are actually three ahu here: The first is **Ahu Vai Uri,** with five reconstructed moai, followed by the solitary Tahai moai, and the **Ahu Ko Te Riko,** with its topknot and coral and obsidian eyes. The moai front a grassy expanse with stone walls and a canoe ramp; here you'll also see the oval foundations of a *hare paenga*, or "boathouse," so-called for the traditional home's resemblance to a capsized boat. There is no better place to watch a sunset than at Tahai, so bring your camera and join your tourist brethren for a superb photo session.

There are fine beaches at Anakena and Ovahe, but **Playa Pea** near the harbor has a rock pool for swimming.

Where to Stay

Lodging on Easter Island is overpriced for what you get, and no hotel other than explora's Posada de Mike Rapu can be considered higher than a middle-range hotel. Every hotel is about the same: a moderately comfortable bed, nightstand, maybe a

THE mysterious MOAI

Where moai came from and how they were made and moved to their final resting ground is clear, but *why* still ranks as one of the world's great mysteries. The Rapa Nui carved moai from compressed volcanic ash found on the slopes of the Rano Raraku crater; today there are more than 850 moai spread around the island, either erected atop an ahu, left lying in transit to an ahu, or half-finished in the Rano quarry. Moai average 4m (13 ft.) in size and weigh an average of 10,890kg (12 tons); the largest moai, Te Tokanga, reached 21m (71 ft.), but was never finished and remains in the Rano quarry. It is generally believed that the statues were commemorative images of family or clan leaders, even though the moai are not portraits of individuals but instead abstract designs with angular faces and long bodies. Why they chose this design and what their obsession with the moai was are unclear, but what is known is that the transportation of the moai atop tree trunks is a principal factor in the widespread deforestation of the island that stressed the environment and the community and led to eventual war and the destruction and toppling over of the moai. The moai you see erected today are thanks to the restoration efforts of archaeologists.

television and desk, ceramic floors, and cheap linens. Even the most basic hotels charge at least $60 a night, and anything less than that can be pretty grim. All hotels on the island are located in Hanga Roa, but some are a 10- to 15-minute walk to restaurants and services. All lodging options include breakfast in the price, and most can organize tours and set up rental vehicles. As a last resort, you can usually find locals selling rooms in small *residenciales* and family homes awaiting arriving flights.

VERY EXPENSIVE

explora's Posada de Mike Rapu ★★★ 📷 The combination of breathtaking nearby archaeology, spaceship-like architecture, and fine food and drinks leaves most visitors to this hotel, a replacement of the island's smaller explora hotel, in awe. Many of their treks, led by native Rapa Nui guides and capped at a maximum of eight people, are rarely done by other operators and they even have exclusive access to several trails. Excursions are so superbly timed that you rarely encounter the hordes of bus tours that plague most sites. While the price to stay here is high, it includes all excursions (two a day) plus contemporary Pacific Rim meals and fine wines, not to mention the best rooms on the entire island. The high-ceilinged guest rooms are set six to a building and utilize lots of wood, volcanic stone, and glass, offering distant ocean views over the pastoral setting just a 15-minute ride from town; they offer free shuttle transfers in the afternoons to Anakena Beach or to town. Each room also features ambient lighting, linen bedspreads draped over ultra comfortable beds, and lavish bathrooms. Little extras such as the amuse-bouche and pisco sours that are passed out after excursions are the ahu topping on one fine moai. The hotel was also the first in Latin America to garner LEED certification from the U.S. Green Building Council.

6km from Hanga Roa; Te Miro Oone Sector, s/n. ✆ **866/750-6699** in the U.S., 2/206-6060 in Santiago. Fax 2/228-4655. www.explora.com. 30 units. 3 nights $2,280–$3,030 per person; 4 nights $3,040–$4,040 per person; 5 nights $3,710–$4,915 per person; 7 nights $4,949–$6,440 per person. AE, DC, MC, V. Rates based on double occupancy. **Amenities:** Restaurant; bar; transfers; Jacuzzis; pool; spa. *In room:* Hair dryer, free Wi-Fi.

Hotel Hanga Roa At the end of 2008, after being purchased by the same family as Termas de Puyehue (p. 291), this once classic hotel shut its doors to undergo a complete overhaul that will add a theater, museum, pool, plus dozens of new guest rooms and cabañas. The expectation is that the hotel will become the center of tourist activity on the island, as well as a luxury alternative to explora. While the hotel was expected to open at the start of 2011, a land dispute with a local clan led to an occupation of the hotel for several months that has delayed the final phase of construction of the property. Chances are the hotel will be operating by the summer of 2011, and may change names; check the website or call for rates.

Av. Pont s/n. ⓒ **32/210-0299.** Fax 2/210-0695. www.hotelhangaroa.cl. 75 units. **Amenities:** Restaurant; bar; theater; transfers; pool; spa. *In room:* Hair dryer, free Wi-Fi.

EXPENSIVE

Hotel Altiplanico ★★ Opened in 2009 by a small Chilean chain with three other hotels around the county, the Altiplanico quickly carved out a niche in its price range. The 11 large, nearly identical round cabanas with native designs are spread out on a hillside facing the Pacific a few kilometers north of town in the Hinere sector, which is a bit too far to walk to from Hanga Roa. All rooms feature open-air showers and sliding glass doors that open up to a small patio that faces the ocean. They lack TVs and A/C, but that's part of the charm, and a gentle sea breeze and inviting pool help combat the bright sun. The cozy main building is the property's main hangout and the bar, restaurant, lobby, lounge, and small pool are all here.

Lot E, sector Hinere. ⓒ **56/2-212-3021.** www.altiplanico.cl. 11 units. $350 double, includes breakfast. AE, DC, MC, V. **Amenities:** Restaurant; bar; transfers; pool. *In room:* Free Wi-Fi.

Hotel O'Tai ★ The O'Tai's central location and palm-fringed swimming pool are definite perks and make it one of the better of the hotels right in town. The guest rooms are nothing to write home about, but they are spacious, and there is an overall cleanliness to the establishment and a staff that provides cheery service. Guest rooms are set back from the street motel-like and surrounded by lush gardens. Most doubles come with a sliding glass door and a sitting area terrace, and there are rooms designed for groups in which five guest rooms center around a common seating area.

Te Pito o Te Henua s/n. ⓒ **32/210-0250.** www.hotelotai.com. 40 units. $138 standard double; $170 superior double. AE, DC, MC, V. **Amenities:** Restaurant; bar; outdoor pool. *In room:* A/C (superior rooms only).

Iorana Hotel The rooms need a serious makeover—the property looks like it hasn't been touched since they opened over 2 decades ago—general character is severely lacking, service tends to be mediocre, and the property is a long way from town, but the view from Iorana is spectacular enough to make up for these faults. This large hotel is wedged between the airport and the Rano Kau crater on a dramatic bluff overlooking an inspiring stretch of Pacific coast. The standard rooms are a bit dingy and lack A/C, and though the superior rooms and suites are more spacious, they're still unspectacular.

Av. Ana Magaro s/n. ⓒ **32/2100-608.** www.ioranahotel.cl. 52 units. $145 standard; $180 superior; $190 suite. AE, MC, V. **Amenities:** Restaurant; bar; free airport transfers; 2 pools; tennis court. *In room:* A/C (in superior and suites), TV, Jacuzzi (in suites).

Taura'a Hotel ★★ This is the kind of hotel you could recommend again and again and feel good about it, considering its consistent service, sparkling clean guest rooms, and neatly manicured grounds. The Taura'a isn't even really a hotel; it's a small

B&B in a converted home with extra units added on, tucked away off the main street. Guest rooms have fresh linens, quality beds, wicker furniture, and a small terrace. For the price, rooms are basic by North American standards, but they are tastefully decorated enough to put them a step above other rooms in Hanga Roa. What's really worth mentioning is the attentive service provided by the good-natured and helpful owners, Aussie Bill and his Rapa Nui wife Edith, not to mention their tail-wagging, friendly dogs.

Atamu Tekena s/n. ℂ **32/210-0463.** www.tauraahotel.cl. 31 units. $140 double. AE, DC, MC, V. **Amenities:** Restaurant; bar; pool. *In room:* A/C, minibar, free Wi-Fi.

MODERATE

Cabañas Mana Ora ★   A cabin at Mana Ora is ideal for DIY travelers with their own rental car; it comes with fully stocked kitchenettes, a deck that faces the distant ocean and the afternoon sunset, and it's located in a more rural setting about 10 minutes outside of town. The cabins here are simple, made of wood and artistically decorated with local art and colorful cushions. There is one bedroom and a sofa bed. Stock up on food in town, or better yet, bring cheaper supplies with you from Santiago.

Sector Hinere. ℂ **32/210-0769.** www.manaora.cl. 3 units. $168 for 2 people. No credit cards. **Amenities:** Free airport transfers. *In room:* Kitchenette, no phone.

Cabañas Morerava ★★ 🏠   These four large wood *cabañas* sleep four to six people (one king bed, two twins, and a fold-out couch) and are by far the best of about a dozen DIY rental options on the island. The eco-friendly design reduces the need for energy use and their solar heated water actually stays steamy hot all day long. There are two patios, one of which has a hammock and the other cool wicker chairs. The main sitting area is adjoined to the full kitchen and features an LCD TV (even though there are just two channels on the island). There's no front desk, just a friendly caretaker who will help you arrange tours, rent a car, or pick you up from the airport. It's a bit far from town, though they have a fleet of bikes you can use to get back and forth.

Colonia Agricola. ℂ **32/335-8978.** www.morerava.com. 4 units. $250 per night plus $80 cleaning service on check out. No credit cards. **Amenities:** Airport transfers; bikes. *In room:* TV, full kitchen, no phone, free Wi-Fi.

Cabañas Vai Moana ★   Set behind a rock wall and nestled in a sylvan garden near the ocean, these *cabañas* are an utterly delightful place to stay, though high demand has caused them to jack up their prices significantly. While the staff offers a gracious welcome, the owner is grumpy and his negativity can put a damper on your experience if you're unlucky enough to be here when he's on duty. Both standard and superior rooms are simple units without much flair, but the premises are kept clean, and they are grouped together in detached units of two rooms each and spaced throughout the well-manicured property. Most units have sunny terraces that are ideal for relaxing and feeling the ocean breeze. The Vai Moana is located next to the Museo Antropológico Sebastián Englert and is a good 15-minute walk to the main street.

Atamu Tekena s/n. ℂ **32/210-0626.** www.vai-moana.cl. 18 units. $102 standard double; $147 superior double. Rates include breakfast. AE, DC, MC, V. **Amenities:** Restaurant. *In room:* Minibar, no phone.

Hotel Gomero   Just 2 blocks from the main street lies this little gem of a moderate hotel, known for its bright, spacious rooms and trim grounds that wrap around a nice swimming pool. Given the preponderance of frilly bedspreads and curtains, it's nothing fancy in terms of style, but the owners have added touches of local Rapa Nui art throughout the property. Prices are considerably lower from January to August; high season prices are a poor value in comparison.

Av. Tu'u Koihu s/n. ⓒ **32/210-0313.** www.hotelgomero.com. 13 units. $156 double; $196 superior. Rates include breakfast. AE, MC, V. **Amenities:** Restaurant; bar; airport transfers; pool. *In room:* A/C (superior), minibar.

Hotel Taha Tai ★   One of the largest, full-service hotel complexes on the island, the glossy Taha Tai is well run by a friendly staff and kept spotlessly clean. Rooms 17 to 26 have views of the ocean for no additional cost, so try to nab one. The cabins are smallish and not much of a value. The restaurant has excellent views of the sea, and there are many soothing common spaces for just hanging out. The hotel recently underwent a light renovation that has improved the atmosphere considerably.

Av. Policarpo Toro. ⓒ/fax **32/255-1192.** www.hotel-tahatai.cl. 40 units. $160 double. AE, DC, MC, V. **Amenities:** Restaurant; bar; outdoor pool. *In room:* TV.

Where to Dine

Easter Island is the place to savor Pacific fish—you simply ask what's fresh and order it. Easter Island's native fish types include kahi (big-eye tuna), kana kana (a white fish similar to turbot), konzo, and toreno (yellowtail tuna). A popular side dish is *camote,* which is similar to a sweet potato, and taro, a starchy root.

In-and-out cheap meals can be found at the three converted trailers on Policarpo Toro Street next to the school playing field, which offer fresh *ceviche,* sandwiches, empanadas, tuna *chorrillanas* (grilled tuna with French fries, onions, and a fried egg), *completos* (a hot dog topped with mustard, mayo, and sauerkraut), burgers, and *lomo a la pobre* (beef topped with onions and a fried egg). The best of the stand options is **Ahi-Ahi.** Lastly, **Empanadas Tía Berta** serves fabulous fried empanadas made of tuna, seafood, cheese, and meat, and salads and simple dishes. Look for the sign on the main street Atamu Tekena on your left-hand side almost before reaching the gas station.

EXPENSIVE

Ariki Nui PACIFIC RIM/CHILEAN   This restaurant is where you go for exotic meat dishes such as grilled wild boar or ostrich stroganoff. Like many restaurants on the island, much more thought was put into the concept of this restaurant than in the actual execution of its cuisine, but nevertheless the food is better than at other restaurants, and the Kon-Tiki ambience of bamboo, low-slung ceilings, and glass walls backed by green tree fronds is cool and relaxing. A good bet for a group is their Ariki Nui platter with mixed seafood such as tempura, *ceviche,* and carpaccio, and they have fresh salads and some pasta dishes.

Oho Vehi s/n. ⓒ **32/255-2017.** Main courses C$7,000-C$12,000. No credit cards. Daily 11:30am-3:30pm and 6:30-11:30pm.

Au Bout du Monde ★★ PACIFIC RIM/BELGIAN   Opened in 2009, this restaurant quickly became one of the top spots in town. The Belgian chef's menu is the most technically advanced in town: foie gras with onion marmalade, prawns in a ginger coconut sauce, and a trilogy of native fish wrapped in banana leaves with coconut milk. Their kana kana or tuna in Tahitian vanilla sauce with *camote* (sweet potato) puree might be one of the best fish dishes on the island. The two-level restaurant is split between one intimate downstairs dining room and a large upstairs terrace where the folkloric group Matato'a performs several nights each week.

Av Policarpo Toro s/n. ⓒ **32/255-2060.** www.restaurantauboutdumonde.com. Main courses C$8,000-C$20,000. MC, V. Tues-Sun 1-2:30pm and 7-10:30pm.

Haka Honu ★★ CONTEMPORARY PACIFIC RIM   Haka Honu was called El Jardin de Mau before being taken over by new owners in 2008 and given a fresh contemporary feel. The ambience of this cafe is so enjoyable, it is almost worth visiting for this aspect alone. It is bright and airy, with an artsy decor and an outdoor patio that offers a view of the ocean crashing against the shore. The cafe serves melt-in-your-mouth tuna sashimi, along with heaping plates of coconut milk *ceviche,* grilled fish, steaks, and pasta. This is also a good spot for an afternoon coffee or glass of wine, and the service is friendly. Note that the patio can be windy on some days.

Ave. Policarpo Toro s/n. ✆ **32/255-1677.** Reservations not accepted. Main courses C$5,000–C$8,000. AE, DC, MC, V. Daily 10:30am–10pm.

La Kaleta ★★ 🍴 PACIFIC RIM   This new restaurant that sits near the pier, hidden behind the dive shops, is one of the best additions to the island's dining scene in years. The food is comparable to all of the best restaurants, though it's their incredible patio seating that extends directly over the turquoise Pacific water that puts La Kaleta in a league of its own. Their fish dishes (*ceviche,* carpaccio, grilled plates) can be served as either the white flesh kana kana or darker tuna. There are also fine stews from the mainland like *chupe de mariscos* (thick shellfish stew) and *caldillo de pescado* (fish soup). It's a great place to come for lunch or to enjoy the sunset with a bottle of Mahina, Easter Island's own microbrew.

Caleta Hanga Roa. ✆ **32/255-2244.** Main courses C$4,000–C$8,000. MC, V. Daily 12:30–3:30pm and 7:30–11:00pm.

La Taverne du Pêcheur ★ FRENCH/PACIFIC RIM   Yearning to splurge? This is Easter Island's most expensive restaurant, serving meals prepared with the freshest, highest quality ingredients available. Owned and operated by a grouchy French chef who married a local woman, the specialty here is seafood such as *rape rape* (local lobster, costing C$19,000–C$35,625 depending on size), sea urchin, dorado, and seafood platters, with all this plus mussels and shrimp. La Taverne also imports its meat from Argentina, and serves dishes such as entrecote with pepper or Roquefort sauce. Every dish is lavishly presented on giant platters and served with a variety of accompaniments like taro, potato, and vegetables—truthfully, the portions are almost too big, apart from the steaks. The wine list is excellent but outrageously expensive. In spite of the prices, La Taverne's atmosphere leans more toward rusticity, with rough-hewn wood interiors, lots of plants, and softly lit, boothlike seating. With chocolate marble cake, sorbets, and crepes on offer, you'll want to save room for dessert. The restaurant sits at the harbor beside the dive shops.

Av. Te Pito o Te Henua s/n. ✆ **32/210-0619.** Reservations recommended for dinner. Main courses C$7,000–C$12,000. AE, DC, MC, V. Mon–Sat noon–3pm and 6–11pm. Closed May–June.

Te Moana CONTEMPORARY PACIFIC RIM   The Te Moana is one of the coziest spots for a meal. The ambience is stylishly rustic, built of wood, bamboo, and volcanic rock, and there is a tiny patio for watching street life parade by. Te Moana is known for its coconut milk *ceviche.* On the whole the food is good, not great, with standouts such as Thai fish soup, fish in green curry with rice noodles and veggies, shrimp tempura, and a surf-and-turf platter with a T-bone or entrecote steak and seafood. Te Moana occasionally hosts live music during the evenings.

Av. Atamu Tekena s/n. ✆ **32/255-1578.** Reservations not accepted. Main courses C$6,000–C$15,000. MC, V. Mon–Sat 6:30pm–1:30am.

MODERATE

Kanahau ★ PACIFIC RIM　Though it's more stylish than any other option around town, Kanahau manages to keep its prices rather reasonable. Their Japanese-lantern lit patio is hidden from the street by a row of shrubs and is the best place to sit. There's also an indoor dining room that's a bit loungey with a few low couches to kick your feet back. They specialize in Pacific Rim seafood dishes and native recipes, such as *heke* (octopus with wheat tabbouleh), fried calamari with oyster sauce and camote chips, plus the same grilled fish, steaks, and *ceviches* as every other restaurant in Hanga Roa.

Av. Atamu Tekena s/n. ℂ **32/255-1923.** Main courses C$6,000–C$14,000. MC, V. Thurs–Tues midnight-noon.

Marau Bar Fusion ★★ FUSION/SUSHI　On the main drag, this sushi restaurant has become one of the liveliest evening spots in Hanga Roa. There are just a handful of handmade wooden tables on a small patio and a simple dining room that holds the bar. Sushi and sashimi are the specialty here and there are a dozen specialty rolls like the Ika Rapa Nui (tuna, avocado, banana, and coconut tempura). There are also gyozas, a teriyaki sandwich, steaks, and grilled fish dishes. Marau's cocktail menu list includes several different pisco sours (guayaba, ginger, strawberry), while their beer selection includes Hinano, a Tahitian beer, as well as the local Mahina and quite a few imports.

Av. Atamu Tekena s/n. No phone. Main courses C$6,500–C$11,000. MC, V. Thurs–Tues 7–11pm.

INEXPENSIVE

Café Ra'a ★ CAFE　One of the most popular cafes in town, the small patio of the Café Ra'a is almost always packed with visitors and locals soaking in the vibe and gossiping. Most come for the best breakfast on the island, with everything from pancakes and *küchen* to eggs to real coffee. The reasonably priced dinner and lunch menus feature fettuccine, tuna carpaccio, seafood soups, and sandwiches.

Av. Atamu Tekena s/n. ℂ **32/551-1530.** Reservations not accepted. Main courses C$4,000–C$8,000. MC, V. Daily 8am–8pm.

La Esquina PIZZA　Rapa Nui's first real pizzeria, just across the road from the church, dishes out several dozen types of specialty pies that are fired in a wood-burning oven. Try the spicy pil-pil, tuna, or several variations of Hawaiian pizzas. Personal pies are rather big and not too expensive.

Te Pito o Te Henua s/n. ℂ **8/892-5551.** Main courses C$4,000–C$7,000. MC, V. Daily 10:30am–11:30pm.

Merahi Ra'a ★ 🍴 PACIFIC RIM/CHILEAN　As a *picada* (Spanish for a dive), there isn't much ambience here, but this little eatery is an excellent spot for lunch for its reasonable prices and ultrafresh fish served in a variety of ways, including scallop and tuna carpaccio. I love their tuna *ceviche*, as it has just the right tanginess and comes with a green salad and *camote* (sweet potato). Meals here are nearly abundant enough for two diners. The restaurant has outdoor and indoor seating and is located by the harbor.

Av. Te Pito o Te Henua s/n. ℂ **32/255-1125.** Reservations not accepted. Main courses C$4,000–C$7,000. No credit cards. Fri–Wed noon–10pm.

Mikafé ★ CAFE/DESSERT　This island patio hangout sits beside Mike Rapu's dive shop and looks out over the "hustle and bustle" of the harbor. Their artisanal ice creams in flavors such as banana, passion fruit, *camote* (sweet potato), and taro are the main objective here, particularly on hot days. They also offer a decent tea menu, brewed coffees, *küchen* (cake), hot cakes, and sandwiches.

Caleta Hanga Roa. ⓒ **32/255-1055.** Reservations not accepted. Main courses C$2,500–C$6,000. No credit cards. Mon–Sat 9am–1:30pm and 4:30–9pm.

PARQUE NACIONAL RAPA NUI

Nearly all of Easter Island is within the confines of Parque Nacional Rapa Nui, in an effort to protect the island's moai, petroglyphs, beaches, and 20,000 archaeological sites. **CONAF** (ⓒ **32/210-0236;** www.conaf.cl) administers the park and charges a C$30,000 entrance fee at their office in Orongo that is good for all sites during the length of your stay. The best way to tour archaeological sites is with a knowledgeable guide, but plenty of travelers go it alone and at their own pace with a rental car. Either way, if it's high season, reconsider taking a tour with a large group as it seems to spoil the mysterious ambience of the island. *Important note:* It is imperative that travelers understand that all archaeological sites and the moai statues and their ahu platforms are considered sacred and should not be walked upon or altered in any way.

The best tour guides in the area are bilingual Ramon Edmunds and Josie Nahoe Mulloy, who form **Haumaka Archaeological Tours** (ⓒ **32/210-0274;** haumaka@entelchile.net); unfortunately they can be quite busy during high season, so contact them well in advance. **Aku Aku Turismo** (ⓒ **32/210-0770;** www.akuakuturismo.cl) is a competent tour operator with bilingual guides and large group half-day tours around the island, including boat tours and horseback riding.

Exploring the Island
THE SOUTH COAST

Begin your tour of the island by heading early to the **Rano Raraku** crater ★★★, the quarry and birthplace of the island's moai, and undeniably Easter Island's most extraordinary site. Before reaching Rano Raraku, you'll pass two ahu, **Ahu Vaihu** and **Ahu Akahanga,** with their toppled-over moai; scattered along the road to Rano Raraku there are dozens of prone moai abandoned midway to their final resting place. To say that the approach to Rano Raraku is an emotive experience is an understatement—the most common reaction is an expletive! Scattered about the crater's slope are upright, half-buried moai, and even more half-finished moai attached to the matrix rock—in all, nearly 400 moai of all shapes and sizes can be viewed here in varying states of completion. There is a ranger's station here and picnic tables under eucalyptus trees. Follow the path along the slope to "El Gigante," the largest moai on the island at 21m (71 ft.). A short but steep path leads up to the crater's edge and into its interior, where you can view more moai and the crater's freshwater lake, and grasp your first view of the famous **Ahu Tongariki** moai site ★★★. Located at the shoreline east of Rano Raraku's sheer volcanic walls, Ahu Tongariki is the largest collection of erect moai on the island, 15 statues in all, the tallest reaching 6.6m (22 ft.). Tongariki is a captivating place—together with Rano Raraku you'll want to spend your entire day exploring both.

At the eastern tip of Easter Island is the **Poike Peninsula** ★, a high plateau formed by the extinct volcano **Maunga Pu A Katiki.** There is no road access here and few travelers take the time to visit the peninsula, except to hike or horseback ride.

SOUTH OF HANGA ROA

The **Rano Kau volcano** ★★★ and its crater is the island's most impressive natural attraction—prepare to be left breathless as you stand before it. The crater measures 1.6km (1 mile) in diameter and has steep slopes that descend to a reed-choked lake (which you can walk to if you're in shape). It is possible to follow a path around the crater, but it will take the better part of a day. To get here, drive or walk (about an hour). Clinging to the crater's edge and fronting the steep coastal escarpment is **Orongo,** the ceremonial and ritual site dedicated to the Birdman cult. This annual ritual was a brutal competition whereby men battled to obtain the first egg laid by the sooty tern, which nested on the islet **Motu Nui.** The men would descend the rocky cliff, swim through shark-infested waters, and wait for days or weeks until the first egg was found. The winner, or his "sponsor," would swim back with the egg in a head strap, and spend the following year in seclusion while his family was granted special status to dominate others. The reconstructed, stone slab structures at Orongo demonstrate clearly how ritual participants lived during the ceremony. Also here are basalt rocks with beautifully carved petroglyphs depicting half-human, half-bird figures.

Closer to Hanga Roa, about a half-hour walk south from town, is **Ana Kai Tangata** ★, a sea-cliff cave used as a refuge during days of social conflict. Inside the cave is what remains of rather remarkable prehistoric paintings of birds.

Southeast of Hanga Roa, following the road at the end of the airstrip, is the island's most curious ahu, **Vinapu** ★. The perfectly symmetrical stones used to build the ahu platform gave rise to the theory that the people of Easter Island came from South America, due to the platform's similarity to stonework seen in Peru.

NORTH OF HANGA ROA

Following the rough coastal route north out of Hanga Roa will take you to the **Caverna Dos Ventanas** ★★, or the "Cave of Two Windows." Unfortunately, it's difficult to find. Drive a little less than 3km (2 miles) until you are parallel to two offshore islets; there's usually a rock cairn here indicating the turnoff, or maybe another car or van will guide you as to where the cave's entrance lies. The cave entrance is a small hole in the ground, but it leads to two fantastic cliff openings (bring a flashlight) where you can watch the crashing sea. Farther north lies **Ahu Tepeu** ★, a well-built ahu whose moai lies fallen over. Scattered around this area are the foundations of the *hare paenga* boat houses, and reconstructions of chicken coops and walled gardens.

More cave dwellings lie at **Ana Te Pahu** ★. Follow the poorly marked road from Ahu Tepeu until you see lots of greenery, which is a garden planted with typical root vegetables and bananas, and the cave's entrance. These caves provided refuge for people escaping island battles, and are made from lava tubes. Note that it is common for travelers to hike or bike to Ahu Tepeu and the Dos Ventanas caves.

Farther inland, seven finely reconstructed moai can be viewed at **Ahu Akivi** ★★. These are the only moai that face out to sea, oriented toward the summer solstice. From here, a rutted road leads up to **Maunga Terevaka** ★★, the highest point on the island. From this point it is possible to see the island in its entirety. The road's closed to traffic, although some locals still sneak up in a 4×4. Hiking here takes about 1 to 1½ hours, depending if you walk the road from Akivi or from the other entrance near Vaitea. Heading south on the road from Ahu Akivi, you'll see a turnoff to **Puna Pau** ★, the quarry for the *pukao,* or topknot, that some moai sport. There are two dozen half-finished topknots here, and a splendid view of Hanga Roa and the coastline.

THE NORTHEAST COAST

Come here to relax. The island's two beaches, **Anakena ★★★** and **Ovahe ★★★**, can be found here, and they are dreamy, with cerulean sea lapping at white sand. Anakena is the larger beach, and legend holds that this is where King Hotu Matu'a landed when he arrived at Easter Island. You'll find a few shacks selling grilled meats, snacks, beverages, and beer here. Overlooking the beach are **Ahu Ature Huki,** with one moai, and **Ahu Nau Nau ★★**, with seven moai etched with petroglyphs, four of which have topknots. Ovahe has pinkish sand and is backed by a cliff and is usually less crowded than Anakena, but it is best before the sun hides behind the cliff.

Worth exploring is **Ahu Te Pito Kura ★★**, named for a perfectly rounded and magnetic boulder here that local lore says was brought over by King Hotu Matu'a, as there is no other rock like it on the island. The name means the "navel of the earth," and it was the name of the island before it was called Rapa Nui. The ahu here once supported the largest moai to have been transported to an ahu, measuring 10m (33 ft.) and lying face down, with his topknot knocked off. Following the coast east on foot will take you past a rich assortment of boathouse foundations, chicken coops, and even an ancient observatory.

Other Activities

OUTDOOR FUN

BIKING   You can rent a bike from one of the many shops on the main street Atamu Tekena (around C$6,000–C$10,000 per day).

CANOPY TOURS & EXTREME SPORTS   Islander Nicolas Yurkovitch, who works as an explora guide and with local environmental groups, has established **Ma'ari Canopy** (✆ **9/507-2540** or 7/897-3102), a zipline course in a eucalyptus grove, 100m (328 ft.) from the NASA station, 10 minutes from town on the road to Anakena. The five tracks stretch for a total of 500m (1640 ft.) and use top-of-the-line, secure equipment. The company has ambitious plans to build another course near the Rano Kau volcano, pending approval of the local development commission. The course costs C$14,250 per person and includes a pickup from town if needed. It's important to call ahead for reservations. Ma'ari also runs extreme tours around the island like surfing, rock climbing, fishing, spelunking, and kayaking.

HORSEBACK RIDING   Riding horseback is one of the most enjoyable ways to see Easter Island. Although you can hire a horse for an hour or so and limit the ride to sites around town, a more thrilling, full-day journey is up to the top of the volcano Terevaka, the highest point of the island. **Uri Tahai** (✆ **32/255-1499** or 9/492-8291), with seven routes available, is the place to call for a tour.

KAYAKING, SURFING & OTHER WATERSPORTS   Rent boards and kayaks at Orca Diving Center's **Hare Orca** shop (✆ **32/255-0375;** www.seemorca.cl), and pick up information about the best spots to do both. Surfboards rent for C$10,000 a day and single ocean kayaks and bodyboards for C$7,000 a day. A shack beside the food carts next to the soccer pitch also rents boards.

SCUBA DIVING & SNORKELING   The waters off Easter Island are some of the bluest—and clearest—in the world, providing scuba divers with up to 60m (200 ft.) of visibility. Diving here is in open-sea conditions, with limited coral reef. You won't see the throngs of sea life found at other South Pacific destinations, but you will see wild volcanic landscapes such as sheer cliffs, ledges, arches, caves, and possibly the moai that Mike Rapu sunk 25m (82 ft.) below sea level in honor of his ancestors. Water temperatures that average 65° to 80°F (18°–27°C) oblige divers to wear a wetsuit. Absolute beginners can join in, too, with a guide-assisted Discovery Dive, or an easygoing snorkeling trip (Mike Rapu's trips even include a Rapa Nui lunch). If you're up for it, don't miss this fascinating underwater opportunity. You'll find two companies at the harbor; both are reputable operations with high-quality dive masters, and both offer PADI scuba classes. **Mike Rapu Diving Center** (© **32/255-1055;** www.mikerapu.cl) is owned by "Mike," a Rapa Nui co-owner of explora's Casas Rapa Nui and the South American breath-holding champion; **Orca Diving Center** (© **32/255-0375;** www.seemorca.cl) is owned by a French diver who arrived here in 1978 with Jacques Cousteau and stayed.

Shopping

Souvenir shops line the streets Atamu Tekena and Te Pito o Henua. There are two large markets—the **Feria Municipal** at the corner of Atamu Tekena and Tu'u Maheke, and the **Mercado Artesanal** at Roa Rakei and Tu'u Koihu. Both are open Monday through Saturday in the morning and afternoon. There's also a small **market at the airport** that opens and closes according to the flow of passengers.

The internationally recognized carver **Luis Hey** sells his pricey yet high quality crafts in shops around town, though you can contact him directly at his website (www.rapanuicrafts.3m.com). Nearly every shop in town sells a near identical collection of carvings, T-shirts, books, and jewelry. The biggest selection is at **Hotu Matu'a's Favorite Shop** on Av. Atamu Tekena. **Rapa Nui Natural Products** at Atamu Tekena, near the small plaza, stocks a decent selection of locally produced teas, spices, guayaba marmalade, and artisanal chocolates; **Mana Gallery** at Petero Atamu s/n, towards Tahai, is the first true art gallery in Hanga Roa and features a rotating mix of emerging local artists.

Hanga Roa After Dark

Hanga Roa's three funky nightclubs are a riot, and really ignite on weekends—just don't show up before midnight or you might be sipping your rum and Coke alone. **Toroko,** on Avenida Policarpo Toro, has music, dancing, and a mellow atmosphere and is one of the older hangouts in town. The current "it" spot is **Topatangi** ★ on Avenida Atamu Tekena (© **32/255-1554**), with a huge dance floor that gets packed late nights with young Rapa Nui girls and guys, along with a smattering of gringos, there to dance to a mix of live music, performed by local folkloric groups using electric instruments and sometimes joined by native dancers, and recorded hits. It's open Thursday to Saturday from 10pm until the early morning. Admission is C$3,000 and includes a free drink. **Piriti,** across from the airport, was under renovation at last visit and should be open by mid 2011.

The dance troupe **Kari Kari** puts on a thoroughly entertaining Rapa Nui folkloric show 3 nights a week (Tues, Thurs, and Sat) at 9pm, showcasing native dance, elaborate costumes, and music. They used to perform at the Hotel Hanga Roa, but since it closed for renovations, they have moved to a new theater on Atamu Tekena. Check with your hotel to make reservations or call directly (© **32/210-0767** or 32/7881-9114). The show costs C$12,000. On Au Bout du Monde's second level stage, the group **Matato'a** (© **32/255-2060**) performs on Wednesday and Friday to Sunday at 9pm. The price is C$10,000.

FAST FACTS: CHILE

Area Codes   See "Staying Connected" in chapter 3.

ATM Networks/Cashpoints   See "Money & Costs," p. 36.

Business Hours   Banks are open Monday through Friday from 9am to 2pm, and are closed on Saturday and Sunday. Many commercial offices close for lunch hour, which can vary from business to business. Generally, hours are Monday through Friday from 10am to 7pm, closing for lunch around 1 or 1:30pm and reopening at 2:30 or 3pm.

Car Rentals   See "By Car," in chapter 3.

Cellphones (Mobile Phones)   See "Staying Connected," p. 45.

Drinking Laws   The legal age for purchase and consumption of alcoholic beverages is 18; alcohol is sold every day of the year, with the exception of general elections.

Driving Rules   See "Getting There & Around," p. 32.

Electricity   Chile's electricity standard is 220 volts/50Hz. Electrical sockets have two openings for tubular pins, not flat prongs; adapters are available from most travel stores. Always bring a **connection kit** of the right power and phone adapters. The majority of hotels and even hostels now have Wi-Fi in public spaces and increasingly in guestrooms, but you'll want to bring a spare Ethernet network cable if you plan to do a lot of computer work and are unsure if your hotel offers wireless.

Embassies & Consulates   The only U.S. representative in Chile is the **U.S. Embassy** in Santiago, located at Av. Andrés Bello 2800 (© **2/330-3000;** http://chile.usembassy.gov). The **Canadian Embassy** is at Nuevo Tajamar 481, 12th floor (© **2/652-3800;** www.canadainternational.gc.ca/chile-chili). The **British Embassy** can be found at El Bosque Norte 0125 (© **2/370-4100;** www.britemb.cl). The **Australian Embassy** is at Isidora Goyenechea 3621, 13th floor (© **2/550-3500;** www.chile.embassy.gov.au). The **New Zealand Embassy** is at Isidora Goyenechea 3000, 12th floor (© **2/616-3000;** www.nzembassy.com/chile).

Emergencies   You'll want to contact the staff if something happens to you in your hotel. Otherwise, for a police emergency, call © **133.** For fire, call © **132.** To call an ambulance, dial © **131.**

Gasoline (Petrol)   At press time, in Chile, the cost of gasoline was C$680 per liter. Taxes are already included in the printed price. One U.S. gallon equals 3.8 liters or .85 imperial gallons.

Holidays   See "When to Go" in chapter 3.

Insurance   Travel insurance is a must for U.S. travelers. U.S. insurance companies require travelers to pay up front and be reimbursed later, and major medical emergencies can be very expensive and therefore difficult to pay even on a credit card. European, Australian, and New Zealand medical insurance companies normally pay medical emergency costs directly to a Chilean hospital, but check your policy beforehand to see if this is the case. For more information on traveler's insurance, trip cancellation insurance, and medical insurance while traveling, please visit www.frommers.com/tips.

Internet Access   See "Staying Connected" on p. 45.

Language   Spanish is the official language of Chile. Many Chileans in the tourism industry and in major cities speak basic English, but don't count on it. Try to learn even a dozen basic Spanish phrases before arriving; *Frommer's Spanish PhraseFinder & Dictionary* will facilitate your trip tremendously. See also Chapter 16, "Glossary of Spanish Terms & Phrases."

Legal Aid   If you are "pulled over" for a minor infraction (such as speeding), never attempt to pay the fine directly to a police officer; this could be construed as attempted bribery, a much more serious crime. Pay fines by mail or directly into the hands of the clerk of the court. If accused of a more serious offense, say and do nothing before consulting a lawyer. Here the burden is on the state to prove a person's guilt beyond a reasonable doubt, and everyone has the right to remain silent, whether he or she is suspected of a crime or actually arrested. Once arrested, a person can make one telephone call to a party of his or her choice. International visitors should call their embassy or consulate.

Lost & Found   Be sure to tell all of your credit card companies the minute you discover your wallet has been lost or stolen, and file a report at the nearest police precinct. Your credit card company or insurer may require a police report number or record of the loss. Most credit card companies have an emergency toll-free number to call if your card is lost or stolen; they may be able to wire you a cash advance immediately or deliver an emergency credit card in a day or two.

If you need emergency cash over the weekend when all banks and American Express offices are closed, you can have money wired to you via **Western Union** (© **800/325-6000;** www.westernunion.com).

Mail   The postal service, called **Correos de Chile** (© **800/267736** or 2/956-0200; www. correosdechile.cl), is very reliable and offers regular and certified mail. Prices for a letter under 20 grams (¾ ounces) are C$370 for North America, C$420 for Europe, and C$1,180 for New Zealand and Australia. For express mail services, try **FedEx** (www.fedex.cl) or **DHL** (www.dhl.cl), both of which have several locations in Santiago and around Chile.

Newspapers & Magazines   The country's major dailies are the conservative *El Mercurio* and the more moderate *La Tercera. La Segunda* is an afternoon paper with scant news and screaming headlines; *La Cuarta* is a sensationalistic rag but a lot of fun to read if you know anything about Chilean politics or celebrities. Another fun read is *The Clinic,* a satirical weekly named for the London hospital where Pinochet was arrested. You'll find 2-day-old editions of the *New York Times* and North American and European magazines at one of two kiosks in downtown Santiago. Both are located on the pedestrian walkway Ahumada (Metro: Univ. de Chile) on the right-hand side when heading up from Avenida Alameda; one is a half-block from Avenida Alameda, and the other is at Húerfanos. The underground kiosk at the Plaza Peru parking lot in El Golf has a range of very expensive English-language magazines; otherwise the only other place to find English-language magazines is at the airport.

Passports   The websites listed below provide downloadable passport applications as well as the current fees for processing applications. For an up-to-date, country-by-country listing of passport requirements around the world, go to the "International Travel" tab of the U.S. Department of State at **http://travel.state.gov**.

For Residents of Australia   You can pick up an application from your local post office or any branch of Passports Australia, but you must schedule an interview at the passport office to present your application materials. Call the **Australian Passport Information Service** at © **131-232,** or visit the government website at www.passports.gov.au.

For Residents of Canada Passport applications are available at travel agencies throughout Canada or from the central **Passport Office,** Dept. of Foreign Affairs and International Trade, Ottawa, ON K1A 0G3 (☎ **800/567-6868;** www.ppt.gc.ca).

For Residents of Ireland You can apply for a 10-year passport at the **Passport Office,** Setanta Centre, Molesworth Street, Dublin 2 (☎ **01/671-1633;** www.irlgov.ie/iveagh). Those under age 18 and over 65 must apply for a 3-year passport. You can also apply at 1A South Mall, Cork (☎ **21/494-4700**) or at most main post offices.

For Residents of New Zealand You can pick up a passport application at any New Zealand Passports Office or download it from the website. Contact the **Passports Office** at ☎ **0800/225-050** in New Zealand or 04/474-8100, or log on to www.passports.govt.nz.

For Residents of the United Kingdom To pick up an application for a standard 10-year passport (5-yr. passport for children under 16), visit your nearest passport office, major post office, or travel agency; or contact the **United Kingdom Passport Service** at ☎ **0300/222 0000** or search its website at www.ukpa.gov.uk.

For Residents of the United States Whether you're applying in person or by mail, you can download passport applications from the U.S. Department of State website at **http://travel.state.gov**. To find your regional passport office, either check the U.S. Department of State website or call the **National Passport Information Center** toll-free number (☎ **877/487-2778**) for automated information.

Police See "Emergencies" above.

Smoking In 2006, Chile introduced new laws requiring restaurants to provide designated nonsmoking areas, or allow smoking but prohibit minors 18 and younger from entering a smoking establishment (which is mostly now nightspots and bars). There is also a prohibition of cigarette sales within 90m (300 ft.) of schools. Most hotels no longer allow smoking.

Taxes Chile levies a steep 19% VAT tax, called IVA *(Impuesto al Valor Agregado)* on all goods and services. Foreigners are exempt from the IVA tax when paying in dollars for hotel rooms and vacation packages.

Time Chile is 4 hours behind Greenwich Mean Time (GMT) from the first Sunday in October until the second Sunday in March; the country is 6 hours behind during the rest of the year. An easy way to remember the time zone switch is that from mid-March to mid-October, Chile is in the same time zone as the eastern U.S. or 5 hours behind Greenwich Mean Time; from mid-October to mid-March, Chile is 2 hours ahead of the eastern seaboard of the U.S.

Tipping The customary tip in restaurants is 10%. Taxi drivers do not receive tips, nor do hair stylists. Bellhops should be tipped C$1,000 to C$2,000. Gas stations are full-serve, and attendants are tipped C$200 to C$500, depending on any extra services provided such as checking oil and water levels, cleaning the windshield, and the like.

Toilets Public bathrooms *(baños)* in bus stations, gas stations, or markets may cost a nominal fee, around C$100. In rural areas and places with a local septic system, paper and other items cannot be deposited into toilets and should be deposited into the trash.

Visas See "Entry Requirements" in chapter 3.

Visitor Information Every city has a municipal tourism office, and the national tourism board **Sernatur** has offices in major cities. Sernatur rarely has useful printed information in its offices, however. Research travel and background information about Chile and upcoming events at Sernatur's new website, **www.chile.travel**, or check out news, events, and other information at Image Chile's site **www.thisischile.cl**. You'll also find trip-planning ideas with maps and good photos at **www.turismochile.travel**. Turismo Chile is a private-public association that promotes Chile as a tourism destination in international markets.

Some regional sites also provide thorough content, but may not be updated frequently. See **www.sanpedroatacama.com**, **www.sanpedrochile.com**, and **www.torres delpaine.com**. Also see the "Useful Websites" box in chapter 3.

Water   See "Staying Healthy" in chapter 3.

Wi-Fi   See "Staying Connected," p. 45.

AIRLINE WEBSITES

MAJOR U.S. AIRLINES

American Airlines
www.aa.com

Continental Airlines
www.continental.com

United Airlines
www.united.com

US Airways
www.usairways.com

MAJOR INTERNATIONAL AIRLINES

Aeroméxico
www.aeromexico.com

Air New Zealand
www.airnewzealand.com

British Airways
www.british-airways.com

LAN Airlines
www.lan.com

Qantas Airways
www.qantas.com

South African Airways
www.flysaa.com

MAJOR DOMESTIC AIRLINES

LAN
℗ 866/I-FLY-LAN [435-9526] (in the U.S.)
℗ 600/526-2000 (in Chile)
www.lan.com

Sky Airline
℗ 600/600/2828 (toll-free in Chile)
℗ 2/352-5600
www.skyairline.cl

GLOSSARY OF SPANISH TERMS & PHRASES

T he official language of Chile is Spanish, and few Chileans outside of the tourism industry speak more than rudimentary English—so bone up on a few handy phrases before arriving. Chileans appreciate the effort, and really, part of the fun of traveling is learning the local lingo.

That said, even Spanish speakers have a difficult time understanding singsong, high-pitched Chilean Spanish, which has grown to be known as *chilensis* for its rapid-fire delivery and heavy use of local phrases and slang. The most notable peculiarity about Chilean Spanish is the merge of the formal *vosotros* with the casual *tu* verb forms, which over the centuries has created a verb tense unique to this country. Chileans use *"tu estas,"* or *"tu comes,"* but it's very common to hear instead *"tu estai"* or *"tu comai."* This *-ai* ending is used in very informal settings; most popular is the greeting, *"¿Como estai?"* Another oddity in Chilean Spanish is *"pues,"* which puts emphasis on a word, and is more commonly shortened to *"poh,"* as in *"Sí, poh,"* meaning "Well, yes!" Words that end in *-ado* or *-ido* typically drop the "d," so that *pelado* becomes *"pelao."* Chileans also drop the "s" in words, so that *más* becomes *"ma."*

While some Latin countries such as Argentina have virtually dropped the *usted* verb form except in the most formal of occasions, Chileans use the *usted* form habitually. Waiters, doormen, strangers, and any new business associate should be greeted with *usted* until you become better acquainted.

BASIC WORDS & PHRASES

GREETINGS & FORMALITIES

English	Spanish	Pronunciation
Hello	**Buenos días**	*bweh*-nohss *dee*-ahss
How are you?	**¿Cómo está usted?**	*koh*-moh ehss-*tah* oo-*stehd*
Very well	**Muy bien**	mwee byehn
Thank you	**Gracias**	*grah*-syahss
Good-bye	**Adiós**	ad-*dyohss*
Please	**Por favor**	pohr fah-*vohr*
Yes	**Sí**	see
No	**No**	noh
My name is . . .	**Me llamo . . .**	meh *yah*-mo
And yours?	**¿Y usted?**	ee oo-*stehd*
It's a pleasure to meet you.	**Es un placer conocerle.**	ehs oon plah-sehr koh-noh-*sehr*-leh
No problem.	**No hay problema.**	noh aye proh-*bleh*-mah

LANGUAGE DIFFICULTIES

English	Spanish	Pronunciation
Excuse me (to get by someone).	**Perdóneme.**	pehr-*doh*-neh-meh
Excuse me (to begin a question)	**Disculpe**	dees-*kool*-peh
Do you speak English?	**¿Habla usted inglés?**	ah-blah oo-stehd een-glehss
I don't understand Spanish very well.	**No (lo) entiendo muy bien el Español.**	noh (loh) ehn-*tyehn*-do mwee byehn el ehss-pah-*nyohl*
Would you spell that?	**¿Puede deletrear eso?**	pweh-deh deh-leh-treh-ahr eh-so
Would you please repeat that?	**¿Puede repetir, por favor?**	*pweh*-deh rreh-peh-*teer* pohr fah-*vohr*
What does ___ mean?	**¿Que significa ___?**	Keh seeg-*nee*-fee-ka
Would you speak slower please?	**¿Puede hablar un poco más lento?**	*pweh*-deh ah-*blahr* oon *poh*-koh mahs *lehn*-to

DIRECTIONS & TRAVEL

English	Spanish	Pronunciation
Where is . . . ?	**¿Dónde está . . . ?**	*dohn*-deh ehss-*tah*
the station	**la estación**	la ehss-*tah*-syohn
the bus stop	**la parada**	la pah-*rah*-dah
a hotel	**un hotel**	oon oh-*tehl*
a restaurant	**un restaurante**	oon res-tow-*rahn*-teh
the toilet	**el baño**	el *bah*-nyo
To the right	**A la derecha**	ah lah deh-*reh*-chah

English	Spanish	Pronunciation
To the left	**A la izquierda**	ah lah ees-*kyehr*-dah
Straight ahead	**Adelante**	ah-deh-*lahn*-teh
How do I get to . . . ?	**¿Cómo llego a . . . ?**	*koh*-mo *ye*-go a . . .
Is it far?	**¿Está lejos?**	es-*ta le*-hos
What time does?	**¿A qué hora?**	ah keh *o*-ra
leave/arrive	**sale/llega**	*sa*-le/*ye*-ga
the flight	**el vuelo**	el *vweh*-loh
the train	**el tren**	el tren

KEY QUESTIONS

English	Spanish	Pronunciation
Who?	**¿Quién? ¿Quiénes?**	*kyehn? kyeh*-nehs?
What?	**¿Qué?**	keh
When?	**¿Cuándo?**	*kwahn*-doh
Where?	**¿Dónde?**	*dohn*-deh
Why?	**¿Por qué?**	pohr-*keh*
How?	**¿Como?**	*koh*-moh
Which?	**¿Cuál?**	*kwahl*
How many?/How much?	**¿Cuánto?/¿Cuántos?**	*kwahn*-toh/*kwahn*-tohs

SHOPPING & DINING

English	Spanish	Pronunciation
I would like	**Quiero**	*kyeh*-roh
to eat	**comer**	ko-*mehr*
a room	**una habitación**	*oo*-nah ah-bee-tah-*syohn*
the check	**la cuenta**	la *kwen*-tah
the Laundromat	**la lavanderia**	la-ven-da-*re*-ah
the pharmacy	**la farmacia**	la far-ma-*cee*-ah
the ATM	**cajero automático**	el ka-*heh*-roh ow-to-*mah*-tee-ko
I'm looking for a size . . .	**Busco una talla . . .**	*boos*-koh *oo*-nah *tah*-yah
small	**pequeño**	peh-*keh*-nyoh
medium	**mediano**	meh-*dyah*-noh
large	**grande**	*grahn*-deh
How much is it?	**¿Cuánto cuesta?**	*kwahn*-toh *kwe*-sta
Can I see it?	**¿Puedo verlo/a?**	*pweh*-doh *ver*-lo
I'll take it	**Lo llevo**	lo *ye*-voh
Breakfast	**Desayuno**	deh-sah-*yoo*-noh
Lunch	**Comida**	coh-*mee*-dah
Dinner	**Cena**	seh-nah

English	Spanish	Pronunciation
A menu please?	¿Una carta por favor?	oo-nah kahr-ta pohr fah-vohr
What do you recommend?	¿Qué recomienda usted?	keh reh-koh-myehn-dah oos-tehd

WHO

English	Spanish	Pronunciation
I	yo	yoh
you	usted/tú	oo-stehd/too
him	él	ehl
her	ella	eh-yah
us	nosotros	noh-soh-trohs
them	ellos/ellas	eh-yohs, eh-yahs

WHEN

English	Spanish	Pronunciation
now	ahora	ah-oh-rah
later	después	dehs-pwehs
in a minute	en un minuto	ehn oon mee-noo-toh
today	hoy	oy
tomorrow	mañana	mah-nyah-nah
yesterday	ayer	ah-yehr
in a week	en una semana	ehn oo-nah seh-mah-nah
at	a las	ah lahs

NUMBERS

English	Spanish	Pronunciation
0	cero	(seh-roh)
1	uno	(oo-noh)
2	dos	(dohss)
3	tres	(trehss)
4	cuatro	(kwah-troh)
5	cinco	(seen-koh)
6	seis	(sayss)
7	siete	(syeh-teh)
8	ocho	(oh-choh)
9	nueve	(nweh-beh)
10	diez	(dyehss)
11	once	(ohn-seh)
12	doce	(doh-seh)
13	trece	(treh-seh)

English	Spanish	Pronunciation
14	catorce	(kah-*tohr*-seh)
15	quince	(*keen*-seh)
16	dieciséis	(dyeh-see-*seh*-ees)
17	diecisiete	(dyeh-see-*syeh*-teh)
18	dieciocho	(dyeh-*syoh*-choh)
19	diecinueve	(dyeh-see-*nweh*-veh)
20	veinte	(*beh*-een-teh)
21	veintiuno	(beh-een-*tyoo*-noh)
30	treinta	(*treh*-een-tah)
40	cuarenta	(kwah-*ren*-tah)
50	cincuenta	(seen-*kwehn*-tah)
60	sesenta	(seh-*sehn*-tah)
70	setenta	(seh-*tehn*-tah)
80	ochenta	(o-*chehn*-tah)
90	noventa	(noh-*behn*-tah)
100	cien	(syehn)
200	doscientos	(doh-*syehn*-tohs)
500	quinientos	(ken-ee-*en*-tos)
1,000	mil	(meel)
5,000	cinco mil	(*seen*-koh meel)

DAYS OF THE WEEK

English	Spanish	Pronunciation
Monday	**Lunes**	*loo*-nehss
Tuesday	**Martes**	*mahr*-tehss
Wednesday	**Miércoles**	*myehr*-koh-lehs
Thursday	**Jueves**	*wheh*-behss
Friday	**Viernes**	*byehr*-nehss
Saturday	**Sábado**	*sah*-bah-doh
Sunday	**Domingo**	doh-*meen*-goh

CHILEAN MENU GLOSSARY

GENERAL TERMS

Lomo Beef/steak
Pan Bread
Pollo Chicken
Postre Dessert
Huevos Eggs
Pescado Fish

Fruta Fruit
Cordero Lamb
Carne Meat
Cerdo/puerco Pork
Papas Potatoes
Papas fritas French fries
Arroz Rice

Asado Roast
Ensalada Salad
Mariscos Seafood
Sopa (chupe) Soup
Camote Sweet potato
Verduras Vegetables

MEAT

Adobo   Meat dish in a spicy chili sauce
Alpaca   Alpaca steak
Anticuchos   Shish kebab
Cabrito   Goat
Carne de res   Beef
Chicharrones   Fried pork skins
Conejo   Rabbit
Cordero   Lamb

Empanada   Pastry turnover filled usually with meat, cheese, or shellfish
Estofado   Stew
Lomo asado   Roast beef
Parrillada   Grilled meats
Pato   Duck
Pollo a la brasa   Spit-roasted chicken
Venado   Venison

SEAFOOD

Camarones   Shrimp
Centolla   King crab
Corvina   Sea bass
Congrio   Conger eel
Jaiva   Crab
Lenguado   Sole

Machas   Razor clams
Merluza   Hake
Mero   Grouper
Ostiones   Scallops
Ostras   Oysters

BEVERAGES

Cerveza   Beer
Jugo   Juice
Leche   Milk
Bebida   Soft drink

Agua   Water
con gas   carbonated
sin gas   still
Vino   Wine
Cóctel/trago   Cocktail

SOME TYPICAL CHILEAN WORDS & PHRASES

Altiro   Right away
¿Cachai?   You know? Do you get it?
Choro   Good, as in "Cool!"
Cuico/a   Wealthy elite, snob
Curado/a   Drunk
Ene   A lot
Fome   Boring
Guagua   Baby
Harto   Many, a lot
Huevón/ona   Idiot, stupid person; can be used as an insult but is peppered innocuously in all Chilean speech, somewhat like "dude"
La Caña   Hangover
Lucas   1,000; used like "bucks" for money
¡Oye!   "Listen!"; used to get someone's attention
Paco   Cop
Pega   Work, job
Pesado   Boring, stick in the mud, or an annoying person
Polera   T-shirt
Pololo/a   Boyfriend/girlfriend
Por si acaso   Just in case
Rasca   Tacky, low class (other common words for this are *ordinario* or *roto*)
¿Te fijas?   Do you see? Do you get it?

CHILEAN FLORA & FAUNA

What Chile lacks in quantity of flora and fauna, it makes up for in its high rate of endemic species found either solely in Chile, or unique to the Andes and found in both Chile and Argentina. The information below is meant to be a selective introduction to plants and animals that you might encounter while exploring Chile. In many instances, the prime viewing recommendations should be understood within the reality of actual wildlife viewing. Most casual visitors and even many dedicated naturalists will never see a puma, but anyone working with a good guide should be able to see a broad selection of Chile's impressive flora and fauna.

There are several good field guides out there; two of the best general guides are *A Wildlife Guide to Chile,* by Sharon Chester, and *Trees in Patagonia,* by Bernardo Gut. A comprehensive guide to the birds of Chile is **Birds of Chile,** by Alvaro Jaramillo and illustrated by Peter Burke and David Beadle. See "The Lay of the Land," in chapter 2 for tips on viewing wildlife.

FAUNA

Chile is not teeming with animals, but what the country does have are crowd-pleasing mammals such as the four camelids (llamas, alpacas, guanacos, and vicuñas); the rabbitlike viscacha; and Magellanic and Humboldt penguins. More elusive are the country's pumas and the miniature deer, the pudú. Colossal condors can often be seen soaring near the Andes Mountains, and three of the world's five species of flamingos can be spotted in the high-altitude lakes of the northern desert and in lakes across Patagonia. Chile's waters harbor a rich variety of marine species and waterfowl including seals, sea lions, gargantuan sea elephants, dolphins, and nearly 50 percent of the planet's whale species, including humpback and blue whales. What is noticeably absent are a large amount of reptiles, invertebrates, and creepy crawlies; in fact, no poisonous animals are found here other than several kinds of spiders.

Mammals

Guanaco (*Lama guanicoe*)   One of the four camelids in existence in Chile, the guanaco can be seen from the far northern reaches of the country to Tierra del Fuego. Guanacos, which are not dimorphic (two-humped), are cinnamon-colored with white chests and doe-like, dark eyes, and can be seen from November to December with their newborn *chulengos*. Guanacos typically live in all-female groups led by an alpha male, or in large groups of bachelor males. **Prime Viewing:** Parque Nacional Torres del Paine is the easiest place to see guanacos, as well as higher elevations in the Atacama Desert and near Parque Nacional Lauca.

Guanaco

Huemul (*Hippocamelus bisulcus*)   A short, stocky deer found in isolated groups in Patagonia, the huemul is, along with the condor, Chile's national animal—its likeness can be seen on the national park service shield. The huemul is teetering on the edge of extinction, with an estimated 1,200 to 1,500 left, and surprisingly little is known about the animal. Nonprofit conservation efforts such as the Estancia Chacabuco Project (www.conservacionpatagonica.com) are crucial to studying the deer's habitat and finding ways to protect it from further extinction. **Prime Viewing:** During the fall or winter, when huemuls head from high altitudes to lower forested valleys.

Huemul

Pudú (*Pudu mephistophiles*)   The world's smallest deer places high on the cute factor. Standing at just over a foot tall, the pudú weighs only 15 to 30 pounds and can be found throughout dense temperate rainforests. Pudús have dark brown fur with some white spotting on females, and males sport

Pudú

tiny 7½ to 10cm (3- to 4-inch) antlers that are shed every year. Pudús are notoriously independent and like to hide in foliage and escape with nimble feet up steep rocks, and are therefore not easily spotted. **Prime Viewing:** Southern Chile along the Carretera Austral (Southern Highway) and in Chiloé.

Puma (*Puma concolor*)   Pumas live in the Chilean Andes but can be found throughout the Americas; it's the mammal with the largest range in the Western Hemisphere. Measuring 1½- to 2¾m (5–9 ft.) long from nose to tail, the puma is a solitary creature

Puma

that slinks among the underbrush and in forests, and therefore is very difficult to view unless, by chance, you come across a puma with a fresh kill. The puma is sleek and agile, feeding mostly on wild hares and young camelids, and often sheep, and is prey to illegal hunting by sheep farmers in spite of its protected status. **Prime Viewing:** It's not the same as seeing the animal in the flesh, but during the winter in southern Chile it's common to catch sight of puma tracks in snow. Otherwise, Torres del Paine is your best shot.

Vicuña (*Vicugna vicugna*) Along with the guanaco, the vicuña is one of the two wild camelids found in Chile. The vicuña is similar in appearance to the guanaco, but smaller and with softer, more delicate features. In spite of this, the vicuña lives at altitudes higher than 3,658m (12,000 ft.) and is specially adapted to the rigors of the Andes. The vicuña's fur is considered the finest in the world, and it works to trap air and keep the animals warm in frigid temperatures; however, this has made it especially vulnerable to hunters, and the population has only recently made a comeback after threatening population declines. **Prime Viewing:** High altitudes throughout the northern region of Chile.

Vicuña

Viscacha (*Lagidium viscacia*) This rabbitlike animal is from the chinchilla family, and can often be seen sunning itself on rocks in a frozen position that makes it easy to miss— its yellow-brown and gray coloring often blends into the background. Like the vicuña, the viscacha lives at high altitudes up to 4,267m (14,000 ft.), but can be found along the length of Chile. The viscacha prefers dry areas and likes to hide in rock cracks and caves, or in underground tunnels as a

Viscacha

means of evading predators. **Prime Viewing:** The Atacama's Tatio Geysers and other high regions of the Atacama Desert, and Parque Nacional Lauca.

Birds

Chile has more than 440 identified species of resident and migrant birds, certainly not as high as Latin America's Caribbean and Amazon regions, yet many species are highly prized by birdwatchers, and include larger species such as condors and albatrosses.

Andean Condor (*Vultur gryphus*) Revered by indigenous groups throughout the Andes of South America and considered the national symbol of many Andean countries, the condor can be seen floating on thermals with hardly a flap of the wings or perched on sheer cliffs throughout Chile. Though regal and graceful while sailing slowly through the sky, the condor is quite gruesome up close, with a featherless head set off by a fluffy white feather collar, and males have a mottled, rubbery crest. Condors

Andean Condor

sport the largest wingspan of any land bird on the planet at 2¾ to 3m (9–10 ft.), and are scavengers who will fly over more than a 61km (100-mile) area in search of an animal carcass to feed on. **Prime Viewing:** With a sharp eye, you should be able to catch a glimpse of a condor flying in Chile's Andes; it's rarer to encounter a condor up close—your odds are best if you happen upon a freshly killed animal.

Black-faced Ibis *(Theristicus melanopis)* The black-faced ibis is common throughout Patagonia and the Lake District, but its relative, the buff-necked ibis, is widespread but harder to spot in northern Chile. This large bird has a distinctive long, crescent-shaped beak it uses to poke around grassy plains and marshy undergrowth for seeds, insects, and even frogs. The ibis' coloring is quite beautiful, and as the name suggests the bird has a black face, with a cinnamon-shaded head

Black-faced Ibis

and a beige-colored chest. The bird is perhaps best known for its characteristic and loud metallic honk. **Prime Viewing:** The ibis is commonly seen in groups on plains and wet marshes, and is not difficult to spot in the Lake District and Patagonia.

Chilean flamingo *(Phoenicopterus chilensis)* In spite of its name, the Chilean flamingo can be found across South America, and is one of the largest of the flamingo species. The bird's plumage ranges from salmon to light pink, and is most distinguishable by its gray legs and pink knees. The Chilean flamingo can often be seen grazing for tiny shrimp and other

Chilean flamingo

mollusks near its relative the Puna (or James) flamingo *(Phoenicopterus jamesi)*; this flamingo has black wing tips and a yellowish beak. **Prime Viewing:** Across Chile, especially at Los Flamingos National Reserve in the Atacama Desert, at the Salar de Surire, and at low-lying lakes in Patagonia.

Magellanic Woodpecker *(Campephilus magellanicus)* The largest South American woodpecker, the Magellanic woodpecker lives in dense beech forest, feeding on insects and nesting in tree trunks. Both females and males have a curled crest, although the male draws more attention with its ruby-red head. It's surprisingly large—measuring around 36 to 38cm (14–15 inches) in length. The Magellanic woodpecker is phantomlike but not impossible to spot; the bird is best glimpsed by birdwatchers who hike quietly and listen intently for the bird's telltale "toc-toc" on wood. **Prime**

Magellanic Woodpecker

Viewing: From the Bío-Bío region to southern Patagonia, in forests and often far from human activity.

Rhea *(Rhea pennata)*   The ostrichlike rhea is the grand bird of the Patagonian steppe and the northern Altiplano, reaching heights of 1½m (3.5 ft.). The rhea is adept at running at high speeds and uses its large wings to quickly change direction, often in a zigzag fashion, and has prehistoric-looking feet with sharp claws. During mating season, the male builds a huge basketlike nest for several females to lay eggs that he incubates and raises alone, often in groups of 10 to 15 chicks. Southern Chile is home to the lesser rhea or Darwin's rhea, named for the famed biologist, which is slightly smaller than the northern rhea, the *Rhea tarapacensis*. **Prime Viewing:** Across the grassy plains of Patagonia and in northern Chile, in higher altiplanic regions.

Rhea

Upland Goose *(Chloephaga picta)*   Upland geese are a common sight in Patagonia and are somewhat of a symbol of the region given their ubiquity. Commonly seen in pairs, the upland goose is monogamous and very territorial, especially during mating season. It's easy to identify the sex of upland geese, since males have white heads and chests and females are ruddy and have yellow feet. **Prime Viewing:** Upland geese can be seen in groups in grassy fields and in lakes and wetlands throughout Patagonia and Tierra del Fuego.

Upland Goose

Wandering Albatross *(Diomedea exulans)*   Chile is home to several varieties of albatross, however the wandering albatross is a favorite with visitors because it is the largest sea bird and has the longest wingspan of any living bird in the world, reaching up to an astonishing 3½m (12 ft.) in length. The bird's powerful wings combat the difficulties posed by the southern and Antarctic region's merciless gales and storms; the wandering albatross's powerful wings, in fact, allow the bird to soar for hours without so much as a flap. For many centuries, sailors have found the albatross to provide uplifting companionship during insufferable bouts of solitude, and are considered a sign of

Wandering Albatross

good luck. **Prime Viewing:** The albatross is typically viewed when at sea in the southernmost regions of Chile and en route to Antarctica, and on remote islands such as South Georgia Island.

Penguins

What's not to love about penguins, with their comical waddle, their clockwork routines, and curiosity and engagement with humans? Chile's coastline and islands are home to several species of penguins, but by far the most common and easily seen are the **Humboldt penguin** (*Spheniscus humboldti*) and the **Magellanic penguin** (*Spheniscus magellanicus*). The name of the Humboldt penguin comes from the frigid Humboldt current that runs the length of Chile and provides penguins with a rich source of krill and fish. The Humboldt penguin's habitat stretches from Peru to the island Chiloé in Chile's Lake District, and the Magellanic penguin from Chiloé to Tierra del Fuego. Where the penguin habitats overlap it is difficult to differentiate between the two, but visitors will notice the Magellanic penguin has two upper chest bands and the Humboldt just one. Both measure anywhere from 46 to 69cm (18–27 inches) in height, and their "tuxedo" suit provides camouflage: the white chest allows the birds to blend in while on land and the dark cloak allows them to hide while racing underwater.

Humboldt penguin

Both penguins come ashore to nest between September and March at established colonies; the Humboldt penguin will nest in rocky caves and in guano, while the Magellanic penguin will either dig an underground burrow or reclaim a past burrow, and reconnect with its partner with an individu-

Magellanic penguin

alistic bray. The male and female take turns hunting and caring for their chicks. The Magellanic penguin is best viewed at around 10am and 5pm, when dozens line up to waddle down to the ocean shore. **Prime Viewing:** The two easiest Magellanic penguin colonies to visit are **Isla Magdalena** in the Strait of Magellan, reached by a boat ride, and **Seno Otway,** about 65km (40 miles) north of Punta Arenas by road. There is also a protected penguin colony at **Puñihuil** in northeastern Chiloé, with predominately Magellanic and occasionally Humboldt penguins. Humboldt penguin national reserves are at **Isla Chañaral** and **Isla Choros y Damas** north of La Serena. You can also see Humboldt penguins at the **Isla Cachagua National Reserva,** just off the coast at Cachagua; you can't set foot on this island, but can view the penguins up close on a boat tour.

Sea Life

With slightly less than 6,440km (4,000 miles) of shoreline and an enormous labyrinth of fjords and waterways, Chile boasts a rich diversity of marine life. Yet given that scuba diving is uncommon here except for at the Juan Fernandez Archipelago and at

Easter Island, it is difficult to see marine life other than marine mammals or what is served in restaurants. A fish market is a good place to view the bounty of seafood available, and you might catch fishermen pulling up crates of king crab near Punta Arenas, or diving for razor clam *machas* along the western coast of Chiloé. Chile has recently established its waters as a whale sanctuary, and in addition to the blue whale listed below, is seeing increasing numbers of migrating humpback whales, sperm whales, sei whales, minke whales, and southern right whales.

Blue Whale *(Balaenoptera musculus)*   Blue whales are the largest animals on the planet (and the loudest, too), reaching lengths of 20 to 30m (65–100 ft.) long. They migrate to Antarctic waters during the summer and return north to breed. During the early 2000s, scientists discovered a blue whale nursery in the Gulf of Corcovado, a thrilling discovery given that blue whale populations are highly endangered. The blue whale can swim up to 48km (30 miles) per hour. **Prime Viewing:** Near Melinka, in the Gulf of Corcovado, and off the coast of Chiloé.

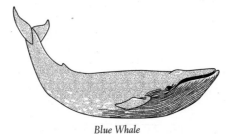

Blue Whale

Chilean dolphin *(Cephalorhynchus eutropia)*   Relatively little is known about this common dolphin, occasionally seen swimming and jumping at a fast clip in a ship's wake in the country's cold southern waters. This dolphin has a blunt-shaped head and a white chest, with paddle-like flippers. **Prime Viewing:** Most common in the channels from Cape Horn to Chiloé and open bays and river mouths north of Chiloé.

Chilean dolphin

Sea Elephant *(Mirounga leonina)*   This sluglike mammal gets its name from its enormous size (from 2.5 to 5 tons in weight for males) and the male's engorged proboscis, used to snort and wail during the mating season. The sea elephant can spend weeks on land while mating, more so than any other seal, and group in harems led by an alpha male who must fight violently with other males to establish his hold on his territory. **Prime Viewing:** Seen during mating season during the spring and summer on Tierra del Fuego and other southern Patagonian islands.

Sea Elephant

FLORA

The dry Atacama Desert is an inhospitable landscape with regions that are virtually devoid of vegetation. Here it is common to see *chañar* and *algarrobo* trees along rivers and in irrigated valleys and plains, but the higher altitudes are barren save a handful of species of cacti and tufts of *coiron* grass. In the central regions, seasonal rainfall and a more humid environment produce shrubbery and trees with leaves known as *sclerophyllous* (leaves that facilitate a greater absorption of water). Predominant tree species include the *guayacan, litre, lun,* and *peumo*. The central valley is also characterized by hard *espinos*, a species of cactus, as well as the endangered Chilean palm, which can be seen in abundance at **Parque Nacional La Campana** (p. 150).

Desert brush lands sweep the *altiplano* (a high Andean plateau comprised of intermontane basins), which yield to more verdant grasslands on the lower slopes of the Andes. In the region south of the Bío-Bío River, temperate rainforests with high precipitation have yielded over 45 species of endemic trees. Magnolias, laurels, oaks, conifers, and beeches thrive in the dense forests here. The most striking and emblematic tree found in this region is undoubtedly the *araucaria* or monkey puzzle tree, a spindly, prehistoric looking tree that grows as high as 30m (100 ft.). The *copihue* (*Lapageria rosea*) yields Chile's national flower, the scarlet Chilean bellflower. The *alerce* tree is the second oldest tree in the world with a life span of up to 3,500 years.

The frigid temperatures and violent winds of Patagonia preclude a rich diversity of forestation. The *coigüe, lenga,* and *ñirre* beech trees are the three principal endemic tree species of Patagonian forests. Most of the Patagonia region is steppe covered with *coiron* grass.

Trees

Alerce (*Fitzroya cupressoides*) Often referred to as the "South American Sequoia," the alerce, like the llareta, can live beyond 3,000 years and is the second-oldest tree on the planet after the bristlecone pine. Reaching heights of more than 45m (150 ft.), the alerce is protected as a national monument following mass destruction by loggers and poachers who value the hardwood and its waterproof qualities. **Prime Viewing:** Southern Lake District and northern Patagonia, especially the Parque Nacional Los Alerces and Parque Pumalín.

Alerce

Antarctic beech (*Nothofagus antarctica*)   Commonly described as a "natural" bonsai tree for its stunted growth pattern and twisted trunk, the Antarctic beech, or ñirre, is special for its smell: grab a handful of leaves and breathe in a wonderfully fragrant cinnamon scent. The local name comes from the Mapuche tribe and means fox, because that animal likes to build a den under the beech's branches. During the fall, the Antarctic beech turns bright yellow, orange, or crimson red. **Prime Viewing:** Easily viewed in Patagonia forests and steppe.

Antarctic beech

Araucaria (*Araucaria araucana*)   Nicknamed the monkey puzzle tree (so-named when a surprised Englishman stated "it would puzzle a monkey to climb that"), the Araucaria takes its moniker from the Mapuche tribe in southern Chile, the Araucanos, who depended heavily on the tree's nuts for subsistence. It is an evergreen and is exceptionally hardy, and looks almost reptilian, with symmetrical and tough leaves, gangly branches, and a pyramid silhouette that can give the tree the appearance of an umbrella, or *paraguas*. **Prime Viewing:** The Araucaria likes high elevations and crisp, wet weather.

Araucaria

Chilean Wine Palm (*Jubaea chilensis*)   The only member of the Jubaea palm family, the Chilean palm is the southernmost palm in the world and features a characteristic gray, smooth, and thick trunk that bulges slightly in its middle. The palm favors Mediterranean climates and does not like tropical weather, and can grow up to 24m (80 ft.) in height. At the time of the Spanish conquest, there were literally millions of Chilean Wine Palms blanketing the Central Valley, but palm populations have been decimated by excessive harvesting of the palm's sap, used to make a sweet syrup or palm wine. Early settlers considered the Chilean palm an ugly cousin to the African palm, but today's tastes have changed and the palm's beauty is undeniable. **Prime Viewing:** Parque Nacional La Campana is the prime viewing area, however Chilean palms can be seen on the road to Valparaíso and across the Central Valley.

Chilean Wine Palm

Flowers, Shrubs & Other Plants

Calafate (*Berberis darwinii*)   This well-known and ubiquitous plant in Patagonia is part of the region's folklore (they say once you eat a Calafate berry, you'll always return to Patagonia). The Calafate is a spiny, dark green shrub that flowers in spring with dark yellow, bell-shaped petals. Later, the shrub produces a dark purple berry that is

Calafate

widely used in jams and other confections. **Prime Viewing:** Easily seen on the grassy plains and *steppe* of Patagonia.

Chilean firebush or Notro (*Embothrium coccineum*) Firebush is an appropriate moniker for this bush, which explodes with fiery red flowers during the early springtime throughout the Lake District and Patagonia. It can grow to appear as a shrub or as a small tree. The wood of the notro is often used in ornamental woodcarving, and the plant is grown by garden enthusiasts in the U.S. and Europe as an ornamental plant. **Prime Viewing:** It's easy to see this plant in the French Valley of Torres del Paine, but it can also be spotted throughout Patagonia (more as a shrub) and the Lake District (as a small tree).

Chilean firebush

Copihue (*Lapageria rosea*) The copihue, or Chilean bellflower (sometimes referred to as the Chilean glory flower), is the country's national flower. The flower has waxy petals that range from ruby-red to pink to white, although red is more commonly seen than white. The flower is a climbing plant that twines counterclockwise around the branch of a tree or shrub, reaching more than 9m (30 ft.) high, and is normally seen during the late summer and fall. **Prime Viewing:** In shady, humid areas from the southern central valley to the Lake District.

Copihue

Llareta (*Azorella compacta*) One of the oldest living plants in the world, sometimes reaching 3,000 years old, the llareta is a pin cushion plant that grows a scant .4 to 1¼cm (¹⁄₁₆–½ inches) a year on rocks in northern Chile's high altitude desert. The waxy green and immensely dense plant looks almost brainlike, growing in rounded humps, and is so strong it could take the weight of a human sitting down upon it. Dried llareta makes an outstanding source of peat-like fuel. Overharvesting of the plant for such use has led to its decimation and the llareta has now been declared protected by the Chilean government. **Prime Viewing:** Above 3,000m (10,000 ft.) in Chile's *altiplano,* such as Parque Nacional Lauca.

Llareta

Nalca (*Gunnera tinctoria*) A giant rhubarb with enormous leaves that can reach 2.4m (8 feet) in diameter, the Nalca plant is edible and frequently used in jams or eaten raw with a bit of salt. The Nalca is common throughout the Valdivian forest of southern Chile, and the plant grows in clusters off a cone-shaped stem. Many comment that the Nalca would work well as a makeshift umbrella. **Prime Viewing:** Along the Carretera Austral and the southern reaches of the Lake District.

Nalca

Index